MISUNDERSTANDING CULT SEARCHING FOR OBJECTIVITY IN A CONTROVERSIAL FIELD

Edited by Benjamin Zablocki and Thomas Robbins

Misunderstanding Cults provides a uniquely balanced contribution to what has become a highly polarized area of study. Working towards a moderate 'third path' in the heated debate over new religious movements (NRMs) or cults, this collection includes contributions both from scholars who have been characterized as 'anticult' and from those characterized as 'cult apologists.' The study incorporates diverse viewpoints as well as a variety of theoretical and methodological orientations, with the stated goal of depolarizing the discussion over alternative religious movements. A large portion of the book focuses explicitly on the issue of scholarly objectivity and the danger of partisanship in the study of cults.

The collection also includes contributions on the controversial and much misunderstood topic of brainwashing, as well as discussions of cult violence, child rearing within unconventional religious movements, and the conflicts between NRMs and their critics. Thorough and wide-ranging, this is the first study of new religious movements to address the main points of controversy within the field while attempting to find a middle ground between opposing camps of scholarship.

BENJAMIN ZABLOCKI is a professor in the Department of Sociology at Rutgers University.

THOMAS ROBBINS is an independent scholar and lives in Rochester, Minnesota.

Misunderstanding Cults

Searching for Objectivity in a Controversial Field

Edited by Benjamin Zablocki *and* Thomas Robbins

UNIVERSITY OF TORONTO PRESS
Toronto Buffalo London

© University of Toronto Press Incorporated 2001
   Toronto Buffalo London
   Printed in Canada

   ISBN 0-8020-4373-9 (cloth)
   ISBN 0-8020-8188-6 (paper)

Printed on acid-free paper

National Library of Canada Cataloguing in Publication Data

Main entry under title:
   Misunderstanding cults : searching for objectivity in a
   controversial field

   ISBN 0-8020-4373-9 (bound)   ISBN 0-8020-8188-6 (pbk.)

   1. Cults.   I. Zablocki, Benjamin David, 1941–   II. Robbins,
   Thomas, 1943–

   BP603.M58 2001   291.9   C2001-900830-9

The University of Toronto Press acknowledges the financial assistance to its
publishing program of the Canada Council for the Arts and the Ontario Arts
Council.

University of Toronto Press acknowledges the financial support for its
publishing activities of the Government of Canada through the Book
Publishing Industry Development Program (BPIDP).

This book is dedicated to Lisa Zablocki with love and appreciation, and to the memory of Tom's beloved cat, Blueboy (1990–2001)

Contents

Preface   ix

Caveat   xiii

Introduction: Finding a Middle Ground in a Polarized
Scholarly Arena   3
Benjamin Zablocki and Thomas Robbins

PART ONE: HOW OBJECTIVE ARE THE SCHOLARS?

1 'O Truant Muse': Collaborationism and Research
   Integrity   35
   Benjamin Beit-Hallahmi

2 Balance and Fairness in the Study of Alternative
   Religions   71
   Thomas Robbins

3 Caught Up in the Cult Wars: Confessions of a Canadian
   Researcher   99
   Susan J. Palmer

4 Pitfalls in the Sociological Study of Cults   123
   Janja Lalich

PART TWO: HOW CONSTRAINED ARE THE PARTICIPANTS?

5 Towards a Demystified and Disinterested Scientific Theory of
   Brainwashing   159
   Benjamin Zablocki

6 Tactical Ambiguity and Brainwashing Formulations: Science or
   Pseudo Science   215
   Dick Anthony

7 A Tale of Two Theories: Brainwashing and Conversion as
   Competing Political Narratives   318
   David Bromley

8 Brainwashing Programs in The Family/Children of God and
   Scientology   349
   Stephen A. Kent

9 Raising Lazarus: A Methodological Critique of Stephen Kent's
   Revival of the Brainwashing Model   379
   Lorne L. Dawson

10 Compelling Evidence: A Rejoinder to Lorne Dawson's
    Chapter   401
    Stephen A. Kent

PART THREE: HOW CONCERNED SHOULD SOCIETY BE?

11 Child-Rearing Issues in Totalist Groups   415
    Amy Siskind

12 Contested Narratives: A Case Study of the Conflict Between a
    New Religious Movement and Its Critics   452
    Julius H. Rubin

13 The Roots of Religious Violence in America   478
    Jeffrey Kaplan

Appendix   515

Contributors   521

Preface

We deliberately gave this book an odd title. *Misunderstanding Cults* is not, of course, a guidebook on how to misunderstand cults. Rather it is a book about what makes cults (or 'new religious movements' as they are sometimes called) so hard to understand. Its purpose is to better comprehend why these groups are so often comically or tragically misunderstood by 'experts' as well as by the general public. Specifically, we have focused on the problem of academic misunderstanding and its correlative polarization of academic experts into opposing camps holding mutually hostile points of view. Our hope is to make a contribution towards overcoming this polarization and introducing a greater degree of cooperation and humility into the study of a subject matter that would be difficult to comprehend even under more collegial investigatory conditions.

Polarization in the study of cults has fostered a toxic level of suspicion among scholars working in this field. This polarization, for the most part, is between those focusing on 'macro-meso' issues and those focusing on 'meso-micro' issues. Social scientists tend to distinguish three levels of social analysis. The macro level is concerned with the largest social aggregates: governments, societies, social classes, and so on. The micro level is concerned with the smallest social units: individuals and very small groups such as nuclear families. The meso level is concerned with intermediate-sized social groupings such as neighbourhoods, cities, business firms, denominations, sects, and cults. Unfortunately, it is rare for social scientific theories to span all three of these levels simultaneously, although just such breadth is what is called for by the puzzle of cults. Between the macro-meso specialists, whose chief concern has been the problem of repressive over-regulation of cults by government and society, and the meso-micro specialists, whose chief concern has been the problem of cultic exploitation of individual devotees, there has been little trust and little mutual respect. The historic reasons for this tension will become clear to anyone reading this book.

There is a need to shake people out of comfortable oversimplifications. Squabbles at the level of 'Cults are evil!' 'No! Cults are OK,' do nothing to further our understanding of these complex sociocultural phenomena. Cults are a genuine expression of religious freedom deserving toleration. At the same time, they are opportunities for unchecked exploitation of followers by leaders deserving civic scrutiny. As fragile new belief systems, they need the protective cover of benign neglect by the state. But as religious movements, it is always possible that a few of them may turn into potential incubators of terrorism or other forms of crime and abuse.

This situation has made it a challenge to us, as editors, to assemble a dozen authors to write chapters for the book from a wide range of viewpoints. We recognize that many of these authors have had to endure criticism from some of their colleagues for 'sleeping with the enemy,' as it were. A few scholars who originally intended to write chapters for this volume actually dropped out of the project because of its controversial nature. We therefore want to gratefully acknowledge the courage of our authors in enduring this criticism in pursuit of higher goals of cooperation and collegiality as well as answers to the intriguing puzzles caused by the cult phenomenon.

In the early 1990s, Thomas Robbins was loosely affiliated with the macro-meso scholars and shared their concerns about the dangers of statist religious repression. Benjamin Zablocki was loosely affiliated with the meso-micro scholars and shared their concerns about the dangers of economic, physical, and psychological abuse of cult members by cult leaders. But the two of us found that we shared a worry about the unusually high degree of polarization that plagued our field. Through many long discussions and exchanges of letters and 'position papers,' the two of us were gradually able to move to a more tolerant understanding of each other's concerns. This book grew directly out of our enthusiasm about the positive effects of our private dialogue, and out of a desire to take this dialogue 'wholesale' by promoting the value of a moderate and inclusive perspective with our colleagues and with the interested general public.

This book itself cannot entirely overcome the polarization that has long blighted our field of study. Although most of our authors have tried to modulate their perspectives, we are painfully aware that almost every reader will find a chapter that will offend. At most we have made a beginning: to paraphrase Joni Mitchell, 'We've looked at cults from both sides now, from up and down, but still, somehow, it's mostly cult's illusions that we're stuck with.' Further progress in understanding this subject matter will require both patience and a great deal of additional collaboration. It will also require receptive listening to the viewpoints of others with whom we may initially disagree.

We would like to acknowledge the help of several colleagues with whom we discussed our project. These include William Bainbridge, Rob Balch, Eileen Barker, Michael Barkun, Jayne Docherty, Mimi Goldman, Massimo Introvigne, Michael Langone, Anna Looney, Phillip Lucas, John Levi Martin, James Richardson, Jean Rosenfeld, Ramon Sender, Thomas Smith, and Lisa Zablocki. We don't mean to imply that all of these people completely endorsed this project. Some were highly critical and some made suggestions that were ignored. So it is more than a matter of 'preface boilerplate' to state that none of them is in any way responsible for the points of view expressed in these pages. But all of them did help us approach the task of editing this volume with a richer and more inclusive perspective.

We also wish to acknowledge the assistance of a number of people who helped us in various ways. Jean Peterson provided valuable clerical and computing assistance to Thomas Robbins during this project. Melissa Edmond, Lauren O'Callaghan, and Maria Chen provided diligent editorial assistance to Benjamin Zablocki. Virgil Duff, our editor at the University of Toronto Press, has been supportive and helpful from the beginning. Two anonymous readers have offered constructive suggestions many of which we have attempted to incorporate into our revisions, and which we believe have strengthened the organization of the volume.

Caveat

Of necessity, given its aims, this is a controversial book. Be warned that almost every reader will take issue with at least one of the essays we have included. The principal aim of the book is to restore a moderate perspective to the social scientific study of cults. Our strategy for achieving this goal has been to invite essays from as wide a range of scholarly points of view as possible, not only from moderates but from the polarized extremes as well. We believe that only by giving public voice to controversy can some degree of consensus and compromise begin to emerge. Hopefully, therefore, it will be understood that the opinions expressed in these chapters are those of each author, and do not necessarily reflect the views of the editors.

An additional issue of fairness arises in those chapters in which scholars take aim, not at other scholars but at various specific cults or anticult organizations. Two points need to be made about such criticisms. The first point is that all the data reported in this book are historical, and therefore none of the criticisms of specific organizations should be taken to apply necessarily to any of these organizations at the present time. The second point is that, even so, a fair-minded reader may very well wish to learn the point of view of the organization being criticized before evaluating the plausibility of the criticism. We, the editors, strongly urge readers to take the trouble to do so. One point upon which we both wholeheartedly agree is that, ultimately, nothing but good can come from exposure to the widest variety of intellectual perspectives. As an aid to the reader in gaining access to these points of view, we have included an appendix listing of publications and websites written by or maintained by the various cults and anticult organizations discussed in this book.

Finally, we wish to emphasize a point we repeat at greater length in the introduction. The word *cult* in this volume is not meant to be evaluative. The word existed as an analytic category in the social sciences long before it was vulgarized in the mass media as an epithet. In our opinion, simply describing an organization as a cult does not, in itself, imply that we believe that the organization is good or bad or that its ideology is authentic or inauthentic. Indeed we consider these sorts of judgments outside the analytic realm of competence of the social scientist.

Benjamin Zablocki
Thomas Robbins

MISUNDERSTANDING CULTS:
SEARCHING FOR OBJECTIVITY IN A CONTROVERSIAL FIELD

Introduction: Finding a Middle Ground in a Polarized Scholarly Arena

Benjamin Zablocki and Thomas Robbins

Every once in a while, cults make news in a big way.[1] Jonestown, Waco, Aum Shinrikyo, and Heaven's Gate are only some of the keywords that remind us of the capacity of religious and other ideological movements to act in ways that leave much of the public thunderstruck. When bewildering events happen, there is a natural tendency to turn to 'experts' to explain what at first seems inexplicable. This is a well-established role of the academic expert in our society. But the striking thing about cult events is that the experts rarely agree. This is a field with little or no convergence. The more channels you turn to on your TV set, the more different contradictory opinions you run into. Eventually, the public loses interest and goes away, either with pre-existing prejudices reinforced or with the conclusion that some things are just beyond explanation and cults are one of them. This book is an attempt to discern what it is about religious cults that make them so intractable to expert analysis and interpretation. What is it about cults that makes it so easy for even the experts to misunderstand them?

This book has developed out of a series of conversations between its editors. Both of us have long deplored the divisive polarization, which, at least until recently, has plagued the academic study of religious movements.[2] This polarization, into a clique of academic 'cult bashers' on the one hand and a clique of academic 'cult apologists' on the other, has impeded learning and has added confusion rather than clarity to a class of phenomena already beset with more than its share of confusion and misunderstanding. It is the goal of the editors of this book to encourage and facilitate the carving out of a moderate middle ground for scholars who wish to see charismatic religious movements in shades of grey rather than as either black or white. To aid in this effort, we have deliberately recruited contributors to this book from both extremes,[3] as well as from scholars whose work is already considered more moderate.

Most books about cults, whether monographs or collections of essays, represent a single point of view or a narrow band on the viewpoint spectrum. Even when a contrarian voice is solicited, the context is clearly one of tokenism. One divergent point of view helps to set off and define the points of view of all the rest. This book is very different in two ways: (1) we have invited essays from scholars representing all of the various viewpoints within the social sciences; (2) we have urged all of our contributing essayists to eschew polemics and treat perspectives other than their own with respect and seriousness. Although this book by itself cannot overcome the residual polarization that still lingers in the study of cults, it may accomplish two important prerequisites. First, we hope it will get scholars talking to one another who in the past have always avoided reading each other's work. Second, we hope it will enable the informed public to understand that the reason we misunderstand cults is not that they are intrinsically beyond comprehension, but rather that they pose challenges that have thus far divided scholars but which careful research may help to overcome.

Academic Polarization

We have made an assertion that perhaps will not seem immediately evident to many: that the academic study of new religious movements has been sharply divided into two opposed camps in a way that is highly detrimental to intellectual progress in the field. Probably, we need to document this assertion before attempting to draw certain conclusions from it. There is a cluster of scholars who have tended to be labelled (by their opponents) as 'cult apologists' who have generally taken a tolerant attitude of qualified support towards these groups. There is another cluster of scholars who have been labelled (again by their opponents) as 'cult bashers' who have generally taken a negative and critical attitude towards these same groups.

Until a few years ago, there was little alternative but to be a part of one or the other of these groupings. In recent years, however, a moderate interdisciplinary position has slowly and painfully begun to develop. Examples of this can be seen in the recent work of Robert

Balch and John Hall in sociology, Michael Barkun in political science, and Marc Galanter in psychiatry, among others. So it should be emphasized that we use the terms 'cult apologist' and 'cult basher' in this book mainly in a historical sense;[4] thus, the use of these terms is not indicative of our validation of the stigma embodied in them. Nevertheless, because the present situation cannot be understood without understanding the roots of this historical polarization, we will continue to use these terms in referring to these two intellectual clusters.

Evidence for the existence of these clusters can be seen in the very terms 'cult' and 'new religious movement.' The use of either of these terms is a kind of shibboleth by which one has been able to know, with some degree of accuracy, how to classify a scholar in this field. In the past, it was only the 'apologists' who tended to use the latter term; the bashers preferred the former term. The difference of opinion is not just a matter of linguistic style. The term cult is an insult to those who are positively disposed towards these groups or who feel that it is important to actively support their right to exist even while perhaps deploring some of their practices. The term new religious movement is a misleading euphemism to those who are negatively disposed. It is also thought to be misleading in that it ignores political and psychotherapeutic cults, implying, as it does, that all such groups are religious in nature.

We will try to display our own moderate colours by referring to these groups sometimes as cults and sometimes as new religious movements (NRMs). In neither case is it our intention to be judgmental. Historically the word cult has been used in sociology to refer to any religion held together more by devotion to a living charismatic leader who actively participates in the group's decision-making than by adherence to a body of doctrine or prescribed set of rituals. By such a definition, many religions would be accurately described as cults during certain phases of their history, and as sects, denominations, or churches at other times. The mass media sometimes make a distinction between 'genuine religions' and cults, implying that there is something non-genuine about the latter by definition. We do not share the implicit bias that seems to be embedded in this usage. Nor, by calling a group an NRM, do we necessarily imply that the group must be benign.

Polarizing issues in this field are not limited to the cult versus NRM controversy. Attitudes towards the concept of 'brainwashing' and towards the methodological device of making use of ex-member (apostate) accounts as data are two of many other issues that divide scholars into these two camps. Beliefs about the advisability of scholars accepting financial support from NRMs is still another issue upon which opinions are sharply divided.

The historical reasons for the development of this polarization are too complex to be reviewed here, especially as they have been discussed extensively elsewhere by ourselves and others (Anthony and Robbins 1995; Zablocki 1997). Much of it has to do with a quarter-century of involvement by scholars from both camps in high-stakes litigation involving these religious groups. The law courts, with their need for absolutes and their contempt for scholarly ambivalence, helped to push both those who started with mildly positive dispositions towards cults into the extreme posture of the 'cult apologist,' and those who started with mildly negative dispositions towards these same NRMs into the extreme posture of the 'basher.'[5]

If these events had merely produced a tendency towards a bipolar distribution of attitudes in this scholarly subdiscipline the results would have been bad enough. But even worse was the crystallization of these two loosely affiliated clusters of scholars into what Fleck has called 'thought communities' (Fleck 1979). Through one group's involvement with the organized anticult movement and the other's attempt to establish or sustain hegemony in key scholarly organizations of social and behavioral scientists, these clusters gradually crystallized into mutually reinforcing, self-perpetuating scholarly communities. Rather than combining perspectives to get closer to the truth, these communities came to define themselves, increasingly, in terms of words that could or could not be uttered and ideas that could or could not be thought about. Hardened positions on such issues as brainwashing or apostasy, for example, exemplify Fleck's notion of the 'fact' as 'a signal of resistance (by a thought community) opposing free arbitrary thinking' (101). Dialogue practically ceased between the two camps for awhile, as each preferred to talk mainly to those who shared the same perspective.

In the manner of insular thought communities throughout history, these sought to reinforce solidarity not only by mutual intellectual congratulation of comrades in the same camp but by vilification of those in the other camp. In this way, the rivalry came to take on a bitter emotional dimension that served to energize and exacerbate the initial cognitive disagreements (Allen 1998).

Each side has had its poster child depicting the horrors that the other side was able somehow to callously condone. For the 'apologists,' it was the image of the sincere religious seeker kidnapped by unscrupulous deprogrammers and thrust into a dark basement of an anticult-movement safe house to be inquisitorially pressured to renounce her faith. The fact that the most notorious of the early coercive deprogrammers happened to be a husky African-American male and the archetypical religious kidnappee was generally depicted as a frail, sincere, but very frightened white female helped to assure that the revulsion caused by this portrait was never overly tepid, although this, of course, was never mentioned out loud. For the 'bashers,' the poster image was just as heart-rending; a little girl looking trustingly up at her hopelessly brainwashed daddy while he feeds her poisoned Kool-Aid at the behest of his ranting paranoid prophet, or a little boy being beaten half to death by the community elders for his inability to memorize the weekly portion of the Bible.

We don't mean to be dismissive of these emotional concerns. Overblown as the symbols have become, each has its roots in instances of very real suffering and injustice. The problem for the academic discipline is to be found not in the emotional sympathy of its practitioners, which is commendable, but in the curious fact that these two emotional stimuli have come to be seen as mutually exclusive. Caring about one required that you be callous about the other. In fact, our own personal litmus test in our quest for scholars who could be called 'moderates' is precisely the capacity to be moved to sympathy by the poster children of each of the two thought communities, i.e., to engage in what Robbins, in his chapter in this volume, calls 'pluralistic compassion.' Gradually, a critical mass of such moderate scholars has begun to emerge.

Through twenty-five years of wrangling, both in journals and in courtrooms, the two thought communities we have been discussing have worked out internally consistent theoretical and methodological positions on a wide variety of issues regarding cult research. Although a number of scholars have come forth professing to be moderates (Bromley 1998, 250), it is not yet nearly as clear how such a moderate stance will eventually come to be defined in this field.

Fortunately, we have a good role model to help us get started. The field of new religious movements has not been the only area in the social sciences that has ever been plagued by such divisions. In fact the larger and more general subdiscipline known as 'social movements' gives us some clues concerning the repairs we must make. Almost a decade ago, sociologist John Lofland published a paper taking his colleagues in the Social Movements field to task for counterproductive tendencies similar to the ones we have been discussing here (Lofland 1993). The situation he describes is not identical, of course. The role of litigation was much less of a factor in his field, for example. Nevertheless, the suggestions he makes can be helpful to us.

Lofland distinguishes two alternative mind-sets for studying social movements. He calls one of them the 'theory bashing' mind-set and the other the 'answer-improving' mind-set. The theory bashing mind-set is defined as: 'a set of contending 'theories' whose respective merits must be assessed; a set of constructs that must be pitted against one another; [and] a field of contenders in which one professes allegiance to one, has alliances with others, and zealously pursues campaigns to discredit and banish yet others' (Lofland 1993: 37). In contrast, the answer-improving mind-set is defined as one in which the study of social movements is constructed as 'a set of questions for which we are trying to provide ever-improved answers through processes of successive revision in order to delete erroneous aspects of answers and to incorporate more accurate elements into answers. Rather than aiming to discredit or vindicate a 'theory,' one aims to construct a more comprehensive, accurate, and powerful answer to a question' (37–8).

A Moderate Agenda

Our argument is that just such a shift in mind-set is precisely what is needed to create and sustain a moderate third path for scholars studying new religious movements. Although easy to envision, such a shift will be tricky to implement. However, the effort is worth it for two reasons. First, the study of religion is a very difficult business and none of us has all the answers. We will make more progress once we recognize that none of our paradigms comes even close to being able to claim to be the master paradigm. We work within a multi-paradigmatic discipline precisely because every single one of our research paradigms is severely limited. Second, as David Bromley (1998) has pointed out, the study of new religious movements has been marginalized by the rest of sociology precisely because of our lack of consensus on so many key issues. Establishing a moderate alternative is essential if we expect our area of research to be taken seriously by colleagues outside the field.

It seems to us that five steps are involved in such a process. The first is a move in the direction of paradigmatic toleration, including a recognition that no one paradigmatic approach can hope to capture the full complexity of religious movements. The second is a move in the direction of greater consensus and precision in conceptual vocabulary. The third is a move towards agreement on a set of principles regarding respect for scholar privacy and demand for scholar accountability in the research process. The fourth is a move towards agreement on a set of principles regarding respect for the privacy of the religious movements we study, and the legitimacy of the demand for their accountability. The fifth, and perhaps most controversial, is a move towards disestablishing the primacy that policy issues have assumed over intellectual issues in our field. That is not to say that policy issues and policy advocacy should be declared illegitimate, but rather that they should be relegated to their traditional position as secondary to our primary academic function which is to observe and to record.

Paradigmatic Toleration
Of the five steps that we mentioned, the most important is the move towards paradigmatic toleration. It is generally well established that there is no master paradigm that effectively organizes theoretical inquiry in sociology. Rather, sociology is acknowledged to be a multi-paradigmatic discipline at this point in its evolution (Effrat 1972; Friedrichs 1970). In most areas of sociology it has been argued that these multiple paradigms are at least, nevertheless, unified by what Charles Lemert (1979:13) has called homocentrism, 'the ... idea which holds that man is the measure of all things.' But the sociology of religion is perhaps the only redoubt within the discipline of nonhomocentric paradigms as well, making the multiplicity that we have to deal with even richer and more bewildering.

How does one cope with working within a multiparadigmatic discipline? Does one treat it as a burden or an opportunity? Is the idea to strive for hegemony for one's own paradigm or an atmosphere of mutual toleration or even of cooperation? It was Robert Merton's contention that there need not be contention among our various paradigms. He argued that they are 'opposed to one another in about the same sense as ham is opposed to eggs: they are perceptively different but mutually enriching' (Merton 1975: 30). This is a notion upon which we hope that a moderate position in our field can crystallize. Since none of us has made all that impressive progress in understanding NRMs from within our own paradigms, maybe coming at them with multiple cognitive approaches will allow us to do better.

The specific paradigms that do battle within the sociology of cults are too numerous and the various alliances too complex to be dealt with here comprehensively. We will have to make do with just one example. No doubt the most egregious example of the paradigmatic intolerance and conflict that has plagued the study of religion is that between the positivists and the phenomenologists. (The former perspective is sometimes embodied in controversial 'rational choice' models of religious behaviour.) Each has a reputation for being a pretty arrogant bunch. However, think for a minute what it means to be studying religion, to be trying to understand the actions of people who are motivated by their relation to the sacred, to be attempting to participant-observe the ineffable, or at least the consequences of the ineffable, and then to report on it. Such undertakings ought to make us humble. They ought to make us understand that it is highly unlikely that either a pure positivist approach or a pure phenomenological approach will come away with all the answers. Such undertakings seem to us to cry out for all that the right brain can tell the left brain, and vice versa. Under these circumstances, it is not unreasonable for each of us to consider giving up our own allegiance to paradigmatic chauvinism.

Conceptual Precision and Consensus
A symptom of the extreme polarization of this field is that certain words have become emotionally charged to an abnormally high degree. Although scholars in all fields tend to argue about conceptual definitions of terms, the extent to which vocabulary choice determines status in the NRM field would delight an expectation-states theorist. To paraphrase Henry Higgins, 'The moment that a cult scholar begins to speak he makes some other cult scholar despise him.' Why do people get so worked up over the question of whether to call certain groups cults or NRMs, or certain processes brainwashing or resocialization, or certain people apostates or ex-members?

Choices among these words are extremely important to some people. Their use is often taken as the external sign of membership in one or another rigid thought community. Therefore, it follows that a moderate thought community needs its own identifying vocabulary. We would have hoped that Stark and Bainbridge (1996) might have at least partially satisfied that need with the dozens of painstaking definitions they offered in their comprehensive theory of religion. But a shared vocabulary is of no value unless people agree to use it, and this has not yet happened.

We speculate that the structural resistance to the adaptation of a consensually accepted moderate vocabulary is to be found in large part in the cosiness of using the vocabulary of one of the two polarized thought communities. When Zablocki speaks of brainwashing he immediately has a hundred allies in the anticult movement, all of whom are inclined to speak favorably of his work even if they have never read it (and even though some of them might be horrified if they ever actually did read it). When Robbins calls a group a NRM instead of a cult he is thereby assured that he is recognized as a member in good standing of that valiant confraternity that has pledged itself to the defense of religious liberty. Such warm fuzzies are difficult to relinquish merely for the sake of increased intellectual vitality.

It might just be possible to adopt a 'bureaucratic' solution to this problem. We would be happy to abide by a set of rational standards governing conceptual vocabulary, and we imagine that many of our colleagues would as well. Many of our colleagues have told us that convening a committee to propose a set of standards on the use of conceptual terms in the study of NRMs is not practical. We don't see why. If we restrict ourselves for the moment to those writing in English, there are probably not many more than a couple of hundred scholars actively studying cults at the present time. And probably fewer than fifty of these have any serious interest in actively creating the kind of moderate thought community that we are proposing. It seems to us that these numbers are small enough to allow us to hope that a working committee of four or five representatives might be able to speak for them.

Respect for Scholarly Privacy and Demand for Scholarly Accountability

One of the most painful consequences of the polarization of the NRM field is the lack of trust that has developed among scholars in opposing camps. Generally this is expressed in the form of questioning the motivations of specific writings or specific research projects. In extreme cases, the charge of selling out for money may also be levelled.

Honest differences of opinion regarding professional norms tend to become amplified in their stridency because the arguments tend to be expressed as ad hominem attacks, and they therefore evoke strong emotional responses. It's hard for two scholars to even talk to each other if one feels accused of something as crass as selling out for money. On the other hand, it is hard to discuss objectively the possible distortive effects of large amounts of money coming into the field with-out some people feeling personally attacked.

A closely related issue has to do with affiliations of scholars with government agencies that regulate religious activities or non-govern-ment organizations that have a role in controversies regarding cults. All sorts of rumors abound concerning the power, wealth, influence, and backing of organizations on both 'sides,' such as INFORM (In-formation of Religious Movements, AWARE (Association of World Academics for Religious Education), CESNUR (Center for Studies on New Religions), CAN (Cult Awareness Network), and AFF (American Family Foundation). Scholars who have worked hard for these organi-zations may come to identify with them and to consider an attack on one's organization as an attack on one's self.

It seems clear to us that a moderate position on these issues has to be based on two complementary principles: the *freedom to choose*, which needs to be respected, and the *responsibility to disclose*, which needs to be demanded. It is very unlikely that even a small, moderate group of scholars will ever be able to reach consensus on the issue of from whom and for what one should accept fees. The same is true for the organizations that a scholar chooses to work with. At the same time, in a highly polarized field like this, disclosure is particularly important. If we want to write a book on Scientology, we are the only ones in a posi-tion to decide if we feel we can (or wish to) remain objective in this task if we take financial help for this project from Scientology itself, or from the 'anticult' AFF. On the other hand, our colleagues have a right to know if we have received support from either of these agencies (or oth-ers) so that each of them can decide how to assess possible impacts on our objectivity.

If a cohort of moderate scholars begins the practice of voluntarily adhering to a norm requiring frank disclosure of sources of financial support and organizational affiliations, this will put a lot of pressure on others to do likewise.

Respect for NRM Privacy and Demand for NRM Accountability

In some ways, the greatest gulf between the 'cult apologists' and the 'cult bashers' is to be found in the question of where to draw the line between the privacy rights and the accountability duties of religious groups. There is consensus only on the rather obvious norm that reli-gious groups must obey the laws of the land and that religious convic-tion cannot be used as an excuse for criminal behavior.

Once we move beyond this, however, the issues quickly get murkier. Are religious movements more like large extended families with the presumption of comprehensive privacy rights that by custom adhere to kin groups? Or are they more like business corporations or government bureaucracies with the presumption that a wide variety of investigatory probes and regulatory fact-finding demands are simply part of the cost of doing business? The problem is that neither model fits very well. In some respects, cults are like families, and, as long as they mind their own business and keep their lawns mowed, they are entitled to conduct their business in as much privacy as they care to have. To the extent, however, that cults proselytize for new members, solicit funds, or manage business based upon government-approved, tax-exempt status, or raise young children in households where the lines of authority are extra-parental, it may be argued that there needs to be some degree of secular accountability.

It is not, of course, the responsibility of the academic community to draw these lines, nor are we competent to do so. Even so local an issue as private versus public schooling raises problems of enormous complexity such as can only be worked out gradually, mostly by trial and error, between the cult and the society (Keim 1975).

But, as scholars, we do have a responsibility first of all to recognize that religious movements are not all identical in this respect and to learn to distinguish those that fall closer to the private end of the continuum from those that fall closer to the public end. We need further to discuss and work out at least a rough code of ethics regarding the limits of scholarly intrusiveness for religions at various points on this continuum.

As editors of this book, we do not claim to have the answers to these questions. We are simply suggesting that the emerging thought community of moderate cult scholars discuss these issues and consider if it might be feasible to work out some rough guidelines. For what it's worth, our thoughts on a few of these matters are as follows. First, we rather incline to the view that scholarly infiltration is not justified for private or public religion. A scholar should always be up-front and candid about her research intentions from the time of very first contact.[6] Second, fair use of religious documents should be interpreted broadly in the direction of full disclosure for public religions. This remains true even if these documents are regarded as restricted by the movement itself. Stealing documents is of course wrong. But, if as usually happens in cases like these, an apostate or dissident decides to break her vow of secrecy and share esoteric documents with a scholar, then the scholar is not obligated to refuse to receive them. Third, public religions are still religions and are thus inherently more fragile than business corporations or government agencies. The scholar needs to understand that the general public can very easily misunderstand many benign religious practices and lash out defensively against them if they are presented out of context, especially to the media.

De-emphasis on Policy Issues

It was initially an overemphasis on policy issues that polarized this field, and only de-emphasis of these issues will allow it to become depolarized. By this we do not mean that scholars should cease to be interested in the policy outcomes that relate to NRMs, only that their research programs and their writing should not be dominated by policy considerations. As Weber pointed out, scholarship and politics are closely related pursuits, and, for this very reason, they must be kept separate from each other (Weber 1946a, 1946b).[7] Those scholars who are moved to work actively in defense of freedom of religious expression need to avoid having this work prevent them as scholars from delving into exploitative, intolerant, and manipulative aspects of the groups they study. Those who are moved to work actively to alert society to cultic excesses need to avoid having this work prevent them as scholars from delving into more attractive aspects of the groups they study and the rewarding and/or volitional dimension of devotees' involvement.

We do not believe that all of the policy issues dividing scholars in this field are amenable to mediation. The best one can hope for is that some people will come to recognize the validity of the concerns of others even if they think their own are more important. But severe policy disagreements in the NRM area will be slow to disappear. And, inevitably, such policy disputes will spill over into debates over purely academic questions.

It is for this reason that we are arguing that the moderate camp has got to be composed primarily of scholars whose desire to find out the answers to academic questions is significantly greater than their desire to win policy battles. Ironically, such a coalition, by giving up the opportunity to influence cult policy in the short run, may be in the best position to help shape a wise enduring policy towards these groups in the long run by actually improving our understanding of what makes cults tick.

Many older scholars have had their perspectives so decisively shaped by ideological issues that it is doubtful they will ever be willing to have collegial relations with those whose ideologies are on the other side. But as younger people whose attitudes were not shaped during the cult wars of the last twenty-five years enter this field, it is vital that they confront three rather than two options for collegial affiliation. We think it important that a group, however small at first, of scholars whose interests are guided primarily by the answer-improving mind set that we discussed earlier, be available as an alternative to the two warring factions.

Significance of Cult Controversies

Before discussing the specific plan of our book we want to briefly present our view that the issues raised by controversies over cults possess a fundamental sociocultural significance, which would remain salient even if the particular movements to which these issues currently pertain were to decline. James Beckford, an English sociologist of religion, wrote in 1985 that contemporary sociological conflicts over new religious movements raise questions which 'are probably more significant for the future of Western societies than the NRMs themselves. Even if the movements were suddenly to disappear, the consequences of some of their practices would still be left for years to come' (1985: 11).

Beckford's comments are reminiscent of some ideas which were expressed earlier by Roland Robertson (1979: 306–7), who noted that authoritarian sects contravene the 'Weberian principle of consistency' in that they demand autonomy from the state while arguably denying substantial autonomy to their individual participants. 'It is in part because of "inconsistency" ... [that such groups] ... apparently create the necessity for those who claim to act on behalf of *society* to formulate principles of *consistent societal participation*' [emphasis in original]. Authoritarian new religious movements, notes Beckford, represent an extreme situation, which, precisely because it is extreme, throws into sharp relief many of the assumptions hidden behind legal, political, and cultural structures.' The controversial practices of some NRMs have in effect 'forced society to show its hand and declare itself' (Beckford 1985: 11).

What Beckford, Robertson, and others (Robbins and Beckford 1993) appear to be putting forward is sort of a Durkheimian argument to the effect that controversial authoritarian and 'totalistic' cults and the reactions they are eliciting are serving to pose in sharper relief and possibly to shift the moral boundaries of the contemporary Western societies. Controversies over cults and what to do about them may thus produce a situation in which normative expectations which are generally merely implicit and half-submerged may come to be explicitly articulated and extrapolated, and may be transformed in the process. Cults and their critics may articulate and extrapolate differing versions of implicit moral boundaries (Beckford 1985).

One example of a way in which cult controversies help to highlight such implicit moral boundaries is to be found in the assumptions that cults often challenge about the complex three-way relationships that exist among individuals, communities, and the state (Robertson 1979). A generally unstated value of western culture is that individual persons ought to be able to manifest autonomous inner selves which transcend their confusing multiple social roles (Beckford 1985). Contemporary 'greedy organizations' (Coser 1974), including many cults, are perceived by many as contravening modern norms of individualism and personal autonomy. In extreme instances, the devotee of a tight-knit sectarian enclave may appear to the public at large as enslaved, and dehumanized, and as something less than a culturally legitimate person. Such a devotee may be deemed incapable of rational self-evaluation or autonomous decision-making (Delgado 1977, 1980, 1984). Defenders of high-demand religious movements argue to the contrary that people can find real freedom through surrender to a transcendent religious goal, and that it is really the overbearing 'therapeutic state' that threatens true individual choice by discouraging people from choosing religious abnegation of self (Robbins 1979; Shapiro 1983; Shepard 1985).

Another way of looking at the impact of cult controversies on moral boundaries and on the linchpin issue of personal autonomy is in terms of a conflict between the *covenantal* ethos of traditional close-knit religious sects and early churches, which entails broad and diffuse obligations between individuals and groups, and the modern *contractual* ethos, which implies more limited, conditional, and functionally specific commitments to groups (Bromley and Busching 1988). Some scholars have argued that much of the recent litigation and legislative initiatives bearing upon 'cults' has entailed attempts to impose a modern contractual model on close-knit and high-demand religious groups' relations with their members (Delgado 1982; Heins 1981; Richardson 1986).

The involvement of scholars in cult-related litigation has been one of the principal sources of polarization in the field (Pfiefer and Ogloff

1992; Richardson 1991; Robbins and Beckford 1993; Van Hoey 1991). The present volume, however, does not deal specifically with legal issues and developments except to the extent that the litigiousness of some cults is able to intimidate some scholars from freely publishing their results. But the essays in this volume do touch on a range of substantive, ethical, and methodological issues arising from the practices of high-demand religious, political, and therapeutic movements. Such issues include, but are not limited to, the following: sexual exploitation of female devotees (Boyle 1998), child rearing and child abuse in totalist milieux (Boyle 1999; Palmer and Hardman 1999), compensation sought for induced emotional trauma, fraud, and psychological imprisonment in totalist groups (Anthony and Robbins 1992, 1995; Delgado 1982), child custody disputes pitting members against former members and non-members (Greene 1989), violence erupting in or allegedly perpetuated by totalist millennialist sects (Robbins and Palmer 1997), and attempts to 'rescue' adult devotees through coercive methods (Shepard 1985).

The problem for objectivity is that scholars have gotten involved as expert witnesses (on both sides) in court cases in which such issues have been raised. It has been very difficult for these scholars to then turn around and look at brainwashing (or any of these other issues) from a disinterested scientific perspective apart from the confrontational needs of pending litigation. Disagreements among scholars in this area have been sharp and acrimonious, perhaps irrationally and dysfunctionally so (Allen 1998). As editors of this volume we believe that the explosion of litigation in these areas, however justified in terms of either combating cultist abuses or defending religious freedom, has thus had a net deleterious effect on scholarship and has led to an extreme polarization which has undermined both objectivity and collegiality. Far too much research and theorizing has been done by scholars while experiencing the pressure of participation in pending litigation. Scholarship in other areas is often permeated with disputes, polarization, and recrimination. But polemical excess in this realm has been egregious. To the extent that the litigational perspective continues to dominate, it threatens to make a mockery of the enterprise of scholarship in this field.

The Structure of This Book

In designing this book, we first identified what seem to us the three major sources of confusion and misunderstanding surrounding charismatic religious movements.

The first of these is the role confusion of scholars and helping professionals studying cults. How can they (and should they even try to) investigate groups that specialize in the construction and maintenance of alternate views of reality without being influenced by those views of reality? Can they ever really hope to understand groups with beliefs and practices so fundamentally different from their own?

The second is a type of confusion sometimes found among those participating in religious movements. Are they doing so solely out of their own prior motives or are they being manipulatively influenced by the charismatic organizations themselves? And if the latter, is this influence of the same order (even if perhaps of greater intensity) as that practised routinely in school classrooms and television advertising, and in the preaching of conventional religion? Or is it sufficiently more intense to warrant being called brainwashing or thought reform? Do movements employing manipulative methods of indoctrination and commitment-building represent a significant contemporary social problem and menace?

It should be noted that the controversy over the existence of cultic brainwashing has been the issue which has most sharply divided many of the polarized commentators in this field. They have exhibited little consensus, among themselves, even about what they are fighting over (the existence of a social process or the existence of a social outcome). The one thing they all seem to agree on is that the resolution of this question – Does brainwashing really happen in cults or is it a paranoid and bogus invention of the 'anticultists'? – is critical for our understanding of cults and their role in our society. For this reason we have devoted by far the greatest amount of space in this volume to a discussion of this subject.

The third is confusion among the public as to what, if anything, *to do about* these charismatic religious groups. Do they deserve constitutional protection on the same basis as all mainstream religions in the Western world? Or do they require special kinds of surveillance and 'consumer protection' in order to protect innocent seekers and innocent bystanders?

This book is organized around groupings of essays devoted to each of these three topic areas. Although all of these issues have been addressed in other books, this volume is unique in two respects. First, it is the only book which brings together these three interrelated sources of confusion within one volume. This is important because the cloud of misunderstanding surrounding these religious movements can best be understood in terms of the interplay of all three of these types of confusion. Second, most other collections of essays have been distinctly inclined towards one or the other of the two divisive academic poles mentioned above. At most there has been a token representation of a scholar from 'the other side,' and often not even that. This book, by way of contrast, has deliberately solicited contributions entailing a wide range of scholarly perspectives.

The contributors to this volume are mainly drawn from the ranks of senior scholars, with a few promising younger scholars included for generational balance. On the whole the authors on the list have published a cumulative total of over thirty books. They have been actively involved for years in research on controversial movements. They include one scholar who is a member of an esoteric (but not particularly controversial or authoritarian) group, one who is an ex-member of a cult and one who grew up in a cult.

We, the editors, are delighted that a group of scholars with such divergent views were willing to come together within the covers of a single volume. However, we quickly recognized that if we allowed continuing rejoinders and counter-rejoinders until all were in agreement, this book would never have been published. Therefore, we adopted a strict rule that each author's text would have to stand on its own merits and that no comments by authors on other chapters would be included. Of course, it follows from this that each author in the book is responsible only for his or her own chapter, and that no endorsement of the views of other authors is implied by the mutual willingness of each to be published in the same volume. One set of unique circumstances did require that we relax our 'no rejoinders' rule in one instance, which is explained below.

The first section of our volume deals with issues of scholarly objectivity, methodology, and professional norms. Allegations of partisanship, bias, and the shallow quality of fieldwork have recently been debated in a number of published articles (Allen 1998; Balch and Langdon 1998; Introvigne 1998; Kent and Krebs 1998, 1999; Zablocki 1997).[8] The section is divided into two sets of paired essays. The first pair (chapters 1 and 2) concern the perspectives, motivations, and objectivity of scholars investigating cults. Benjamin Beit-Hallahmi, an Israeli psychologist of religion, presents a hard-hitting critique of the irresponsibility of scholars of religion who appear to have been frequently overly solicitous towards the controversial movements they have dealt with, and to have too often been animated by an imperative of defending and vindicating putatively persecuted cults. These issues are also discussed by a sociologist, Thomas Robbins, who relates the intensity of recent conflict among 'experts' on cults to the earlier hot controversy over physically coercive 'deprogramming' and to the role of experts in an adversarial system of law and policy-making. Employing a multi-faceted analogy between contemporary 'cult wars' and agitation in previous decades against domestic communist subversion, the author maintains that rigid orientations of apologetic defensiveness as well as crusading 'countersubversive' perspectives tend ultimately to sacrifice objectivity.

The second pair of essays in our first section (chapters 3 and 4) deal with the actual process of field research in the context of somewhat manipulative, close-knit, and often authoritarian and secretive groups. First, Susan Palmer, a researcher of esoteric movements, is frank and humorous in her discussion of the manipulative ploys of some esoteric sects and their desire to co-opt or domesticate the researcher. Seemingly aware of the many pitfalls, Palmer defends the ultimate necessity of first-hand observation of esoteric groups and interviews with current participants. In the second essay the pitfalls related to persuasive impression management on the part of a manipulative group are strongly emphasized by Janja Lalich, a recent PhD and a former member of an authoritarian and regimented Marxist cult. The author draws upon her own past experiences in arranging for the misleading of outside observers and constructing facades for their bemusement. She warns observers what to watch out for.

The second section of our volume is concerned with brainwashing. The literature on cultic 'brainwashing' is lengthy, acrimonious, and polarized (Anthony 1996; Anthony and Robbins 1994; Barker 1984; Bromley and Richardson 1983; Introvigne 1998; Katchen 1997; Lifton 1991; Martin et al. 1998; Melton forthcoming; Ofshe 1992; Ofshe and Singer 1986; Richardson 1998; Zablocki 1998; Zimbardo and Anderson 1993). The basic conceptual and evidentiary issues are discussed from three different perspectives by Benjamin Zablocki, Dick Anthony, and David Bromley

In chapter 5, Zablocki returns to the original mid-century definition in developing a concept of brainwashing that is less polarized, less partisan, less 'mystical' and more scientific than those that became popular during the cult wars of the 1980s. Zablocki's chapter seeks to demonstrate the epistemological validity of the concept and the empirical evidence for its existence in cult settings. He sees brainwashing as an objectively defined social influence mechanism, useful for understanding the dynamics of religious movements, not for making value judgments about them. He argues that brainwashing is not about free will versus determinism, but rather about how socialization places constraints on the willingness of individuals to make choices without regard for the consequences of social disapproval. In this context, he sees brainwashing as nothing more than a highly intense form of ideological socialization.

In chapter 6, Dick Anthony sharply criticizes this approach, as embodied in earlier books and papers by Zablocki. He develops a concept, which he refers to as 'tactical ambiguity,' to explain how brainwashing theorists have attempted to avoid empirical tests of their arguments by continually shifting the grounds of their key assumptions. Using this concept he argues that, disguised behind a veneer of pseudo-scientific jargon, Zablocki has essentially resurrected the old thoroughly discredited United States Central Intelligence Agency model of brainwashing from the 1950s. This CIA model argued that it was possible to perfect a formula that would rapidly and reliably allow the agency to remold ideologically any targeted subject against his or her will, in order to become an effective secret agent of the United States government. Anthony further argues that part of Zablocki's theory can be dismissed as double-talk, and that the rest is unscientific dogma (disguising Zablocki's personal scepticism about the authenticity of innovative religion) because it is based on the intrinsically untestable notion that any subject's free will can be overwhelmed by irresistible external psychological forces. Anthony argues that the term brainwashing has such sensationalist connotations that its use prejudices any scientific discussion of patterns of commitment in religious movements.

In chapter 7, David Bromley argues that the whole controversy over cultic brainwashing is essentially ideological and political – not scientific. From Bromley's perspective, competing 'narratives' in this area are not really susceptible to a definitive empirical resolution. Bromley aims at neutrality between conflicting 'ideological' perspectives. His relativistic approach is not directly critical of either Zablocki's or Anthony's position. However, it undercuts the position of the more absolutist crusaders against the utility of using the brainwashing concept as a tool for understanding cults, as well as the position of those who see brainwashing as the single key for understanding these movements.

22   Benjamin Zablocki and Thomas Robbins

Section 2 has a second subsection which revolves around evidence advanced by sociologist Stephen Kent that the Church of Scientology in the recent past, and the Children of God (now called The Family) in the 1970s, employed rigorous programs for resocializing deviant members, which, he argues, not only qualify as brainwashing but contain as well an element of physical coercion or captivity (chapter 8). Kent's notion of brainwashing is convergent with Zablocki's treatment in terms of seeing brainwashing not so much as a way of initially converting or recruiting devotees but as an intensive (and costly) method of sustaining commitment and orthodoxy among existing high-level converts in danger of straying into heterodoxy, dissent, or defection.

Kent's argument is subjected here to a methodological critique by sociologist Lorne Dawson (chapter 9). Dawson argues that Kent's analysis is one-sided, since it uses ex-member accounts as a source of data but does not attempt to balance their perspective by obtaining countervailing accounts from the cults themselves. Dawson maintains that Kent fails to demonstrate that his explanation of the data is more convincing than a number of other explanations that can be found in the literature on new religious movements.

The Kent-Dawson dialogue departs from our rule that authors would not be given additional space in the book to reply to other authors with whom they might disagree. We made an exception here, allowing Kent to write a brief rejoinder to Dawson's critique (chapter 10). The reason for this exception is that, at the time we commissioned Kent's chapter, we were not aware that Dawson had written a critique of Kent's paper that he wished to publish in our book. By the time we received Dawson's critique, Kent had already submitted his chapter, unaware that it might be followed by a critique. In courtesy to Kent, therefore, we asked his permission to include the Dawson critique, and Kent agreed providing that he be allowed to append a brief rejoinder. Since both authors were happy with this arrangement, we agreed to make an exception in this one case.

The final section of our volume is structured somewhat differently from the preceding two sections. Instead of sets of paired or clearly interrelated essays, section 3 consists of three papers, each of which explores a separate topic relevant to questions of public policy with regard to cults. Since it was not possible, in a volume of this size, to cover all the relevant public policy issues, we devote a chapter to each of three such issues: the problems of children growing up in cults, cultic pressures on scholars to suppress evidence, and problems raised when new religious movements become violent in their relations with society.

The treatment and experiences of children brought up in cults has attracted significant critical attention and is now producing increasing scholarly research (Boyle 1999; Palmer and Hardman 1999). Sociologist Amy Siskind (1994) grew up in a radical, communal therapeutic movement. Her present contribution (chapter 11) seeks to conceptualize totalistic child-rearing systems and to describe and compare five communal groups in this area. Each group featured an 'inspired' charismatic leader/theoretician. In each group parents were to some degree displaced as caretakers and disciplinarians of their children by movement leaders. In two of the groups, patterns of child rearing clearly shifted significantly over time and were influenced by several key variables. Siskind argues that children growing up in regimented totalistic groups may be susceptible to certain psychological or developmental problems and will probably face difficult problems of adjustment if they later leave the group. She affirms that child rearing in totalist groups should be investigated objectively without preconceptions.

Sociologist Julius Rubin has studied and developed a critical perspective on the communal Bruderhof sect. His views and expressions are strongly resented by the movement, which, in Rubin's view, does not tolerate criticism. The group's retaliatory tactics appear to Rubin to embody the ability of some manipulative cults to use the law courts to intimidate or punish 'enemies' and thus endeavor to suppress criticism and to encourage what seems to him arguably a form of implicit censorship. As Rubin reports (chapter 12), what is particularly dangerous about this practice is the ability and willingness of some of the wealthier cults to litigate against critical scholars even in cases they cannot win, knowing that this tactic may very well intimidate both authors and academic publishing houses without deep pockets.

During the period of the millennium, increasing scholarly focus is being directed to catastrophic outbreaks of collective homicide/suicide associated with totalist cults such as the People's Temple, the Branch Davidians, The Solar Temple, Aum Shinrikyo, and Heaven's Gate. There is concern over the volatility of various millennialist movements as well as their persecution (Bromley and Melton forthcoming; Maaga 1999; Robbins and Palmer 1997; Wessinger 2000; Wright 1995, 1999; Young 1990). Much of this growing literature revolves around a duality in which intrinsic or endogenous sources of group volatility such as apocalyptic worldviews, charismatic leadership, totalism, and 'mind control' are played off against extrinsic or exogenous sources related to external opposition, persecution, and the rash and blundering provocations of hostile officials.

Jeffrey Kaplan's earlier study of Christian identity, 'Nordic' neopaganism, and other militant millennialist movements, *Radical Religion in America* (Kaplan 1997) inclined somewhat towards the relational or extrinsic perspective and emphasized the dynamic whereby negative stereotypes of controversial movements, which are disseminated by hostile watchdog groups, tend to eventually become self-fulfilling prophecies. In his present contribution (chapter 13), Kaplan presents an overview of millenarian violence in American history with a particular focus on Christian identity paramilitarists, extreme antiabortion militants, nineteenth-century violence employed by and against the early Mormons, violence arising within a youthful Satanism subculture, and the violence of cults such as the Branch Davidians led by David Koresh and UFO movements such as Heaven's Gate. With regard to cult-related violence, Kaplan rejects the extreme popular scenario of members 'going unquestioning to their deaths for a charismatic leader,' as well as the apologetic 'counter-scenario ... that if only the group had been left entirely to its own devices, all would have been well.' Simplistic, polarized stereotypes of lethal cult episodes are misleading, in part because, as Kaplan notes, there are salient differences among several recent situations in which cults have been implicated in large-scale violence. Extreme violence erupts in only a small percentage of millenarian groups; moreover, sensational cult episodes such as Jonestown, Waco, or Heaven's Gate account for only a fraction of the violence related to some form of millenarianism. Yet our understanding of such episodes 'remains at best incomplete.'

Conclusions

We are under no illusion that the chapters in this book will serve to completely dispel misunderstanding of cults. Nor do we seek to disguise the many serious and acrimonious disagreements that still sharply divide scholars working in this field. After decades of polarization, it is an important first step that these authors have been willing to appear side by side in the same book. In the future we would encourage them to continue to debate these ideas in other media.

We are optimistic that the dialogue begun in these pages will have the kind of momentum that will weaken the rigid 'thought communities' that have polarized this field of study in the past. Somewhat more cautiously, we are hopeful that this weakening of the two extreme positions will lead to the growth and vitality of a flexible and open-minded, moderate scholarly cluster.

Notes

1 For purposes of this introductory essay we, the editors, will use the term 'cult' to denote a controversial or esoteric social movement which is likely in most cases to elicit a label such as 'alternative religion,' or 'new religious movement.' Such groups generally tend to be small, at least in comparison with large churches, and are often aberrant in beliefs or practices. They are sometimes very close-knit and regimented ('totalist') and manifest authoritarian, charismatic leadership. They may be strongly stigmatized. Although the term cult has become somewhat politicized and has taken on definite negative connotations, we do not intend to employ this term in a manner which settles contested issues by definition (i.e., we do not consider violence, 'brainwashing,' or criminality to be automatic or necessary attributes of cults). We also do not imply that all cults will appear to all observers to be specifically 'religious.' The term has sometimes been applied to groups which do not claim religious status, such as Transcendental Meditation, or which have a contested religious status, such as the Church of Scientology. Some commentators have referred to 'therapy cults' or 'political cults.' However, most well-known, controversial cults such as the Unification Church (Moonies), Hare Krishna, The Family (formerly The Children of God), the Branch Davidians, or Heaven's Gate tend to be distinctly religious or at least supernaturalist. Our neutral use of the term cult precludes the view that cults, being pernicious, cannot be authentic religions.

2 As co-editors of this volume, we have not been and are not now entirely neutral or non-partisan in conflicted discourse over cults. Professor Zablocki is sympathetic to organizations concerned with abuses perpetuated by authoritarian groups employing manipulative indoctrination. Robbins has long been associated with avowed defenders of religious liberty and the rights of religious minorities. We thus remain divided over a number of crucial issues. But we are united in deploring the partisan excesses of past discourse, and in our desire to encourage depolarization and the development of a 'moderate' agenda among scholars concerned with controversial religious movements.

3 Although we speak of two extremes, we are mindful that the misunder-

standing of cults is made even more convoluted by the fact that voices in the debate also include representives of institutionalized religions. These are also polarized, but in terms of very different issues and with quite different agendas. Matters of doctrine (and possible heresy) are important to some of those within what is known as the 'counter-cult' movement, to distinguish it from the more secular 'anticult' movement. But other representatives of organized religion are energized by the felt need to defend even the most offensive of the new religions out of concern with the domino effect, once religions come to be suppressed. This book deals only tangentially with the very different set of issues raised about cults by organized religions. But their influence is impossible to ignore, even by secular scholars, if only because of the alliances to these groups that influence public stands on cult policy.

4 The term 'cult apologist' is in fact frequently employed by critics of cults to devalue scholars who are deemed to be too sympathetic towards or tolerant of objectionable groups. However, the term 'cult basher' is somewhat less ubiquitous. Scholars who disdain the views of strong critics of cults are usually more likely to refer to 'anticultists' or the 'anticult movement.' Deceptively mild, these terms can actually convey a significant stigma in an academic context. There is a clear implication that anticultists are movement activists, crusaders, and moral entrepreneurs first, and only secondly, if at all, are they scholars and social analysts; this is in contrast to putatively objective scholars who labor to dispel the myths and stereotypes disseminated by anticultists. However, since the term cult basher has an appealing surface equivalence to the more ubiquitous cult apologist, we will continue to use cult basher to denote one pole of the controversial discourse on cults.

5 Robbins's chapter in this volume discusses the way in which growing litigation in this area and the interaction of the 'cult of expertise,' with the underlying adversarial system for resolving questions of law and policy in the United States operates to polarize conflicts involving cults.

6 This is a difficult issue, and we will pause before adopting an absolutist position. Some kinds of information may be accessible only to an observer who is trusted as an 'insider' (i.e., full participant). This may be the case not only with respect to 'secret' arrangements and practices, but also with regard to the thought patterns, verbal styles, and demeanor of devotees, which may vary according to whether they believe they are relating to insiders or outsiders (Balch 1980). What does seem objectionable is when an observer has used deception to gain access to a group, but with the hidden purpose of hurting or embarrassing the group, i.e., what might be termed the 'Linda Tripp mode of participant observation.' But must 'undercover' researchers

always be obliged subsequently to be supportive of the (sometimes seriously flawed or objectionable) groups they have investigated?

7 We do not wish to appear unduly naive or as ivory tower isolationists. We realize that policy concerns often drive social research. The study of particular 'social problems' has often been constituted by social movements which have addressed or even constructed social issues. Thus a current boom in research on aspects of memory has responded in part to controversies over recovered memory syndrome and false memory syndrome. But this example may also illustrate the pitfalls of researchers becoming too partisan and committed to policy orientations. A prominent participant in recovered (vs. implanted) memory controversies has recently warned against researchers becoming too beholden to a priori commitments and thus tending to surrender the residual operational neutrality which sustains the authenticity of the research process and the credibility of emergent findings (Loftus and Ketcham 1994).

8 Some of these issues were raised earlier in the 1983 symposium, Scholarship and Sponsorship. The centerpiece of the symposium was a somewhat accusatory essay by the eminent sociologist Irving Horowitz (1983) who called for 'neutral,' non-religious funding in the sociology of religion, particularly with respect to controversial movements. The divisive impact of Horowitz's critique may have been muted because Horowitz was neither a scholar specializing in religion, a member of an 'anticult' organization, or a supporter of conceptualization of commitment-building within cults in terms of 'brainwashing.' The issue of partisanship and objectivity is closely related to the substantive scholarly conflict over brainwashing because allegations of 'procult' and apologetic bias are employed to explain why brainwashing notions are so intensely resisted by professional students of religion (Allen 1998; Zablocki 1997, 1998).

References

Allen, Charlotte. 1998. 'Brainwashed: Scholars of Religion Accuse Each Other of Bad Faith.' *Lingua Franca* (December/January): 26–37.

Anthony, Dick. 1996. 'Brainwashing and Totalitarian Influence: An Exploration of Admissibility Criteria For Testimony in Brainwashing Trials.' PhD diss. Graduate Theological Union, Berkeley, Calif.

Anthony, Dick, and Thomas Robbins. 1992. 'Law, Social Science, and the "Brainwashing" Exception to the First Amendment.' *Behavioral Sciences and the Law* 10: 5–29.

28   Benjamin Zablocki and Thomas Robbins

- 1994. 'Brainwashing and Totalitarian Influence.' In *Encyclopedia of Human Behavior*. New York: Academic Press.
- 1995. 'Negligence, Coercion, and the Protection of Religious Belief.' *Journal of Church and State* 37: 509–36.
Balch, Robert W. 1980. 'Looking Behind the Scenes in a Religious Cult: Implications for the Study of Conversion.' *Sociological Analysis* 41: 137–43.
Balch, Robert W., and Stephan Langdon. 1998. 'How the Problem of Malfeasance Gets Overlooked in the Study of New Religious Movements. In *Wolves Among the Fold*, edited by A. Shupe. New Brunswick, N.J.: Rutgers University Press.
Barker, Eileen. 1984. *The Making of a Moonie: Choice or Brainwashing?* Oxford: Basil Blackwell.
Beckford, James A. 1985. *Cult Controversies: The Societal Response to the New Religious Movements*. London: Tavistock.
Boyle, Robin. 1998. 'Women, the Law, and Cults.' *Cultic Studies Journal* 15: 1–32.
- 1999. 'How Children in Cults May Use Emancipation Laws to Free Themselves.' *Cultic Studies Journal* 16: 1–32.
Bromley, David. 1998. 'Listing (in Black and White) Some Observations on (Sociological) Thought Reform.' *Nova Religio* 1: 250–66.
Bromley, David, and Bruce Busching. 1988. 'Understanding the Structure of Convents.' *Sociological Analysis* 49: 15–32.
Bromley, David, and J. Gordon Melton. Forthcoming. *New Religious Cults and Violence in Contemporary Society*. Cambridge: Cambridge University Press.
Bromley, David G., and James T. Richardson. 1983. *The Brainwashing/Deprogramming Controversy: Sociological, Psychological, Legal and Historical Perspectives*. New York: Edwin Mellen.
Coser, Lewis A. 1974. *Greedy Institutions: Patterns of Undivided Commitment*. New York: Free Press.
Davis, Derek. 1998. 'Religious Persecution in Today's Germany.' *Journal of Church and State* 40: 741–56.
Delgado, Richard. 1977. 'Religious Totalism: Gentle and Ungentle Persuasion under the First Amendment.' *Southern California Law Review* 51.
- 1980. 'Religious Totalism as Slavery.' *Review of Law and Social Change* 4: 51–68.
- 1982. 'Cults and Conversion.' *Georgia Law Review* 16: 533–74.
- 1984. 'When Religous Exercise Is Not Free.' *Vanderbilt Law Review* 37: 22–9.
Effrat, Andrew. 1972. 'Power to the Paradigms.' *Sociological Inquiry* 42: 3–33.
Fleck, Ludwik. 1979. *Genesis and Development of a Scientific Fact*. Chicago: University of Chicago Press.
Friedrichs, Robert. 1970. *A Sociology of Sociology*. New York: Free Press.

Greene, Ford. 1989. 'Litigating Child Custody with Religious Cults.' *Cultic Studies Journal* 6: 69–75.

Heins, Marjorie. 1981. 'Other Peoples' Faith: The Scientology Litigation and the Justiciability of Religious Fraud.' *Hastings Constitutional Law Quarterly* 4: 241–57.

Hexham, Irving, and Karla Powe. 1999. 'Verfassungsfeindlich: Church, State, and New Religions in Germany.' *Nova Religio* 2: 208–27.

Horowitz, Irving. 1983. 'Universal Standards Not Uniform Beliefs: Further Reflections on Scientific Method and Religious Sponsors.' *Sociological Analysis* 44: 179–82.

Introvigne, Massimo. 1998. 'Blacklisting or Greenlisting? A European Perspective on the New Cult Wars.' *Nova Religio* 2: 16–23.

Kaplan, Jeffrey. 1997. *Radical Religion in America*. Syracuse: Syracuse University Press.

Katchen, Martin H. 1997. The Rate of Dissociation and Dissociative Disorders in Former Members of High Demand Religious Movements. PhD diss., Department of Sociology, Sydney University, Sydney, Australia.

Keim, Albert N. 1975. *Compulsory Education and the Amish: The Right Not to Be Modern*. Boston: Beacon.

Kent, Stephen A., and Theresa Krebs. 1998. 'Academic Compromise in the Social Scientific Study of Alternative Religions.' *Nova Religio* 2: 44–54.

– 1999. 'When Scholars Know Sin: Alternative Religions and Their Academic Supporters.' *Skeptic* 6: 36–43.

Lemert, Charles. 1979. *Sociology and the Twilight of Man: Homocentrism and Discourse in Sociological Theory*. Carbondale: Southern Illinois University Press.

Lifton, Robert Jay. 1991. 'Cult Formation.' *The Harvard Mental Health Letter*, 7 February (8): 1–2.

Lofland, John. 1993. 'Theory-bashing and Answer-improving in the Study of Social Movements.' *The American Sociologist* 24: 37–57.

Loftus, Elizabeth, and Katherine Ketcham. 1994. *The Myth of Repressed Memory: False Memories and Allegations of Sexual Abuse*. New York: St Martin's.

Maaga, Mary. 1999. *Hearing the Voices of Jonestown*. Syracuse: Syracuse University Press.

Martin, Paul, Lawrence Pile, Ron Burks, and Stephen Martin. 1998. 'Overcoming Bondage and Revictimization: A Rational/Empirical Defense of Thought Reform.' *Cultic Studies Journal* 15: 151–91.

Melton, J. Gordon. Forthcoming. *The Brainwashing Controversy: An Anthology of Essential Documents*. Stanford, Calif.: Center For Academic Publication.

Merton, Robert K. 1975. 'Structural Analysis in Sociology.' In *Approaches to the Study of Social Structure*, edited by P. Blau. New York: Free Press.

Ofshe, Richard. 1992. 'Coercive Persuasion and Attitude Change.' In *The Encyclopedia of Sociology*, edited by E. Borgatta and M. Borgatta. New York: Macmillan.

Ofshe, Richard, and Margaret Singer. 1986. 'Attacks on Peripheral versus Central Elements of Self and the Impact of Thought Reform Techniques.' *Cultic Studies* 3(1): 3–24.

Palmer, Susan, and Charlotte Hardman. 1999. *Children in New Religions*. New Brunswick: Rutgers University Press.

Pfiefer, Jeffrey, and James Ogloff. 1992. 'Cults and the Law.' *Behavioral Sciences and the Law* 10.

Richardson, James. 1986. 'Consumer Protection and Deviant Religion.' *Review of Religious Research* 28: 168–79.

– 1991. Cult/Brainwashing Cases and Freedom of Religion. *Journal of Church and State* 33: 55–74.

– 1998. The Accidental Expert. *Nova Religio* 2: 31–43.

Robbins, Thomas. 1979. Cults and the Therapeutic State. *Social Policy* 5: 42–6.

Robbins, Thomas, and James Beckford. 1993. Religious Movements and Church-State Issues. *Religion and the Social Order* 3B: 199–218.

Robbins, Thomas, and Susan Palmer. 1997. *Millennium, Messiahs, and Mayhem*. New York: Routledge.

Robertson, Roland. 1979. 'Religious Movements and Modern Societies.' *Sociological Analysis* 40: 297–314.

Shapiro, Robert. 1983. 'Of Robots, Persons, and the Protection of Religious Beliefs.' *Southern California Law Review* 56: 1277–1318.

Shepard, William. 1985. *To Secure the Blessings of Liberty: American Constitutional Law and the New Religious Movements*. Chico, Calif.: Scholars' Press.

Siskind, Amy. 1994. The Sullivan Institute/Fourth Wall Community. *Religion and the Social Order* 4: 51–78.

Stark, Rodney, and William Sims Bainbridge. 1996. *A Theory of Religion*. New Brunswick, N.J.: Rutgers University Press.

Van Hoey, Sara. 1991. 'Cults in Court.' *Cultic Studies Journal* 8: 61–79.

Weber, Max. 1946a. 'Politics as a Vocation.' In *From Max Weber: Essays in Sociology*, edited by H. Gerth and C.W. Mills. New York: Oxford University Press.

– 1946b. 'Science as a Vocation.' In *From Max Weber: Essays in Sociology*, edited by H. Gerth and C.W. Mills. New York: Oxford University Press.

Wessinger, Catherine. 2000. *How the Millennium Comes Violently*. Chappaqua, N.Y.: Seven Bridges Press.

Wright, Stuart. 1995. *Armageddon in Waco*. Chicago: University of Chicago Press.

– 1999. 'Anatomy of a Government Massacre.' *Terrorism and Political Violence* 11: 39–68.

Young, Thomas. 1990. 'Cult Violence and the Christian Identity Movement.' *Cultic Studies Journal* 7: 150–57.

Zablocki, Benjamin D. 1997. 'The Blacklisting of a Concept: The Strange History of the Brainwashing Conjecture in the Sociology of Religion.' *Nova Religio* 1: 96–121.

– 1998. 'Exit Cost Analysis: A New Approach to the Scientific Study of Brainwashing.' *Nova Religio* 1: 216–49.

Zimbardo, Philip, and Susan Anderson. 1993. 'Understanding Mind Control: Exotic and Mundane Mental Manipulations.' In *Recovery from Cults: Help for Victims of Psychological and Spiritual Abuse*, edited by M.D. Langone. New York: Norton.

Part One

HOW OBJECTIVE ARE THE SCHOLARS?

1. 'O Truant Muse': Collaborationism and Research Integrity

Benjamin Beit-Hallahmi

In early May 1995, as Japanese law-enforcement authorities were collecting evidence linking the Aum Shinrikyo NRM to the 20 March poison gas attack which killed twelve commuters on the Tokyo subway, and preparing what they thought was a strong case, they discovered to their utter surprise that they were under attack from an unexpected direction. Four Americans arrived in Tokyo to defend Aum Shinrikyo against charges of mass terrorism. Two of them were scholars whose names are well known in the NRM research community, thanks to their many scholarly activities. But on this trip they were acting as both super-sleuths and as defenders of religious freedom. They stated that Aum Shinrikyo could not have produced the sarin gas used in the attack, and called on Japanese police not to 'crush a religion and deny freedom.' These statements, made at two news conferences, were met with open disbelief in the Japanese media. The fact that all travel expenses for the U.S. experts were covered by Aum Shinrikyo did not help (Reader 1995; Reid 1995). Later, one of the U.S. visitors published an account of the 1995 gas attack, which claimed that the North Korean secret services were behind it. Aum Shinrikyo was notorious in Japan long before the 1995 events. Its belief system made it likely to attract less than friendly attention. Thus, children in its schools are taught to regard Adolf Hitler as a living hero, and its official publications have carried stories of the Jewish plan to exterminate most of humanity (Kowner 1997). Still, all of us would agree that unusual beliefs, however distasteful to some, should be no justification for state action against religious groups. As students of religion, we deal with a huge variety of unusual beliefs. Was Aum Shinrikyo a victim of majority prejudice against NRMs?

Reliable reports since 1995 have indicated that Japanese authorities were actually not just overly cautious, but negligent and deferential if not protective regarding criminal activities by Aum, because of its status as an NRM. 'Some observers wonder what took the Japanese authorities so long to take decisive action. It seems apparent that enough serious concerns had been raised about various Aum activities to warrant a more serious police inquiry prior to the subway gas attack' (Mullins 1997: 321). The group can only be described as extremely and consistently violent and murderous. 'Thirty-three Aum followers are believed to have been killed between ... 1988 and ... 1995 ... Another twenty-one followers have been reported missing' (320). Among non-members, there have been twenty-four murder victims. There were at least nine germ-warfare attacks by Aum Shinrikyo in the early 1990s, most of which had no effect (Reuters 1998). One triple murder case in 1989 and another poison gas attack in 1994 which killed seven have been committed by the group, as well as less serious crimes which the police was not too eager to investigate (Beit-Hallahmi 1998; Haworth 1995; Mullins 1997). So it is safe to conclude that religious freedom was not the issue in this case. Nor is it likely, as some Aum apologists among NRM scholars have claimed, that this lethal record (77 deaths on numerous occasions over 7 years) and other non-lethal criminal activities were the deeds of a few rogue leaders. Numerous individuals must have been involved in, and numerous others aware of, these activities. The Japanese authorities, as of May 1998, have charged 192 Aum Shinrikyo members with criminal activities (Reuters 1998).

Another claim by the Aum apologists is that the trip to Japan was initiated and financed by Aum 'dissidents,' shocked by the acts of their leaders. The reality is that the trip was initiated by the NRM scholars involved, who contacted Aum to offer their help, and that there are no Aum dissidents. As of 1999, Aum Shinrikio is alive and well, one and indivisible, its members united in their loyalty to Shoko Asahara, and this includes the alleged dissidents who hosted our colleagues in 1995. Let me make clear at the outset that no one in his right mind should even hint that NRM scholars were knowingly defending the Aum murderers. They were assuming Aum Shinrikio was another NRM worthy of defence. That is why they were ready to take Aum Shinrikio's money. They did not think they were taking unreasonable risks.

They were acting out of a certain mind-set, which to them was not just reasonable but commendable. The Aum episode was symptomatic of an ideology that sees our world as a place in which NRMs are maliciously attacked by forces of the state, and are always presumed to be innocent.

Are we stunned by this grotesque and surrealistic episode? Do we look away? Do we raise our eyebrows? Do we shrug our shoulders? Are we shocked by the involvement of NRM researchers in this tragic story? Some NRM scholars have suggested that the trip to Japan, as reported in the media, caused the field an image problem (Reader 1995). Let me make clear right away that my concern here is not with images, but with the reality of scholarship. I am afraid that in this case, as in many others, the reality may be actually worse than the image. Is it just an isolated case of bad judgment? After all, only two NRM scholars were involved, and they were both independent scholars. Given the climate and culture of the NRM research community, and earlier demonstrations of support for NRMs in trouble, the Aum case is not some statistical outlier.

Something like a party line has developed among NRM scholars, and much of the discourse in NRM research over the past twenty years has been characterized by a happy consensus on the question of the relations between NRMs and their social environment, especially in situations of overt conflict. This consensus is responsible for a new conformity which must put strict limits on researchers' curiosity. The level of conformity to the reigning consensus has been remarkable. This is not problematic in itself, and does occur in various fields, but it has also led to advocacy – as in the cases of Aum Shinrikyo and David Koresh – which is a public expression of support for an NRM and its vested interests, in any conflict with its social environment. NRM researchers engaged in advocacy are expressing a feeling and a reality of partnership and collaboration with NRMs in a common cultural struggle. If there had been only some isolated incidents, the only need to discuss them would have been as rare exceptions to the prevailing norms, but what we have observed is a clear pattern expressed in a total mobilization for the cause. The problem with the party line is not just that it has undermined scholarly credibility, but that it has crippled our main effort, which should be to understand and explain, rather than defend, the phenomenon under study. Discussions on the ethics of research with human subjects have to do with protecting those defined as research subjects (or objects) from abuse by researchers.

Quite correctly, it is assumed that in the encounter between humans and those who study human behavior, the former have to be defended from the latter, who are seen as quite powerful (Weisstub 1998).

What should be the proper and desirable relationship between scholars and the groups they study? Naturally, this relationship must be problematic, marked by tension on both sides. No one likes to be under scrutiny of any kind, and we are all sensitive to the self-serving ways in which humans, scholars included, present themselves to others. The outsider, or even the insider, who chooses to report behind-the-scenes realities in any organization or culture is likely to produce an embarrassing expose (Alper 1997). All academic research threatens all religions, and in particular new and weak NRMs. The minute we claim the role of the researcher in human groups, we adopt a peculiar position, which is judgmental, uninvolved, and alienated from raw experience and from true believers. The basic position is voyeuristic and reductionist; otherwise all I do is share the experience. A critical attitude and an interpretive bent are the marks of the scholar, who is unlikely to take messages from the subjects of his study at face value. Even as voyeurs we are quite peculiar, and this is exploited in a fictional satire on sociologists observing a failure of prophecy, which proves how little is really known about social science and its real dilemmas (Lurie 1967/1991). Things are a lot more serious and more complicated than the novelist Lurie ever imagined.

Credibility must be negotiated and earned by both informants and scholars, and what is at issue here is the credibility of NRM research. The official ideology of an academic field, i.e., its claims of being autonomous, expert-oriented, and accountable only to its own authorities – is a way of preventing attacks on its basic theoretical conception. Looking at the question of integrity and credibility in NRM scholarship must lead into a broader critical discussion of the field, because ideology clearly dictates research directions and questions. It is not just a problem of integrity, but of basic knowledge. This is an occasion for stocktaking, or, to borrow a religious term, soul-searching. The role of ideology in research is not a startling, novel issue – not only because of the impact of the sociology of knowledge, and not only because of Spengler's (1926) radical theory of the historical nature of science. Awareness of the primacy of ideology in social science has been commonplace throughout this century (Beit-Hallahmi 1974a, 1974b, 1975, 1976, 1977a, 1977b, 1981, 1987, 1989, 1991, 1992b, 1995), and the suggestion that all inquiry about the social world is value laden is universally accepted (Keita 1998). The classical study by Pastore (1949) on the nature-nurture debate in psychology showed ideology clearly precedes action in academic work. What we have here is a case study of a peculiar ideological bias affecting academic work and non-academic advocacy.

We, as students of religion and members of the academic community, are all biased (Robbins 1983). Our differing ideological commitments do not prevent us from communicating and collaborating as colleagues. Scholars are expected to be sophisticated consumers of their colleagues' work. They detect errors, bias, and oversights, and separate valuable gold nuggets from slag. In the study of religion, bias and religious commitments should not necessarily undermine scholarship; they may only set its limits. There have been religion scholars with strong religious commitments who were still great scholars (Beit-Hallahmi 1989, 1991, 1996b). Our conflicting biases should naturally lead to debates and controversy. It is indeed baffling when we observe in a particular research network the strange silence of conformity. Scholars in perfect agreement are like the dog that didn't bark. They should make us curious, if not suspicious. I must say that until fairly recently I had what was a 'naive faith in the professional impartiality of one's colleagues' (Lurie 1967/1991: 185). Having to deal with this issue and blow the whistle on my colleagues made me uncomfortable, and then I realized that I myself had gone through many years of denying what was literally staring me in the face. I should also mention that I have shared earlier versions of this chapter with colleagues in psychology, sociology, and the humanities. All reacted with shock and disbelief.

In recent years, the NRM research community displayed a general agreement on a *hierarchy of credibility* (Becker 1967), according to which self-presentation by NRMs was epistemologically and logically superior to all outside accounts and observations. The NRM research community will give more credence to the claims of NRM members and leaders than to claims by former members, outside observers (e.g., the media), and government officials (especially law-enforcement officials). This has led, over the past twenty years, to a pattern of collaboration with NRMs, reaching its culmination, and logical conclusion, in the Aum episode reported above. I would like to look at the origins of the conceptual consensus and its derivatives. What might be the muse that has inspired it, and, if we follow the allusion to the Shakespearean sonnet, how do beauty and truth match? To use the sonnet's idiom, I would like to suggest that what we have here is a case of the neglect of truth in favor of beauty. The happy consensual discourse, shared by colleagues whose scholarship I admire and to whom I am in debt, turns out to be, on closer examination, a rhetoric and a logic of advocacy, apologetics, and propaganda. When the advocacy and apologetics agenda defines the rhetoric and the logic of research it creates an impoverished discourse, which denies the madness, passion, and exploitation involved in NRMs, and leads to an intellectual dead end. I would like to discuss some critical incidents which will serve as case studies in the esthetics and ethics of NRM scholarship, and then attempt some explanations for the development of the happy consensus.

The essence of the consensus has been described in a most elegant way by two leading sociologists of religion as follows: 'The pattern of various debates and positions adopted appear to represent something of a consensus that where there is a significant erosion of traditional religious liberties, litigation is likely to turn on evidence which conflicts with the prevailing corpus of knowledge represented by the professional societies, individual and collective activism is potentially appropriate' (Robbins and Bromley 1991: 199). The prevailing consensus has created norms around the tasks to be performed by NRM scholars and the rewards to be allocated to them. The felicitous phrasing hints at two separate issues. The first, more general, had to do with conflicts between NRM and society; the second had to do with court cases in which the (groundless) 'mind control' arguments had been raised.

The assumption of a 'significant erosion of religious liberties' which warrants 'activism' seems to cover the whole planet earth. No national boundaries are mentioned, though the context is clearly the United States. The automatic reaction on the part of some scholars in the cases of David Koresh and Aum Shinrikyo proves the seriousness with which this assumption is held. If we look around us and check the status of NRMs in 1970 and today, and the level of tolerance they have enjoyed over the years, we will be forced to conclude that this erosion of religious liberties is nonexistent. Not only do we find hundreds of unmolested NRMs in North America, but in Europe, Africa, and Asia, in countries which lack U.S. constitutional guarantees, NRMs are not only surviving in the face of the significant erosion, but some are thriving, a development which NRM scholars are happy to report on. It is clear that an organization such as the Solar Temple was not subject to any such 'erosion' in Europe or Canada, despite the attention it received from anti-NRM groups and the criminal activities of its members. Globally, it is the rise in tolerance which enabled NRMs to expand and survive. Intolerance is very much part of life everywhere, but today its impact is being checked by economic and cultural globalization.

There has been little explicit discussion of scholarly activism and collaborationism. One leading scholar has issued a striking appeal for greater activism which goes even beyond collaboration, when he stated:

> I propose that we become religious engineers ... Sociologists of religion are among the most ethical and high-minded of scholars, and there is no reason why they should not apply their knowledge to the creation of new religions. The world needs them. We have roles to play as consultants to existing new religions, helping them solve problems that our research has permitted us to understand. But we must be prepared to launch cults of our own invention, a task I admit is both hazardous to one's own welfare and outrageous in the eyes of people who refuse to admit that all religions are human creations. But it is far better for honest religious engineers to undertake the creation of new religions for the sake of human betterment than to leave the task to madmen and wealth-hungry frauds. (Bainbridge 1993: 289)

This suggestion from an eminent scholar runs counter to the party line. Here the elimination of a possible role conflict between that of a researcher and that of a consultant is easily achieved. As far as I know, this call has gone unheeded for the most part. NRM scholars have continued to serve as consultants to the same NRMs that Bainbridge regards as being led by 'madmen and wealth-hungry frauds,' but have refrained from starting their own religions.

'Activism' in Action – The Consensus

The Aum Shinrikyo incident can only be explained by assuming that an overall ideological commitment is involved. What we witness is a sentiment of solidarity with NRMs. Some scholars seem to be saying, paraphrasing John F. Kennedy in 1961: 'We will go anywhere, make any sacrifice' to defend NRMs in trouble. Looking at the history of collaboration with NRMs over the past thirty years takes us from the curious to the bizarre and then to the disgraceful performance described earlier. But it all started with benevolence and mutual curiosity, as researchers and NRMs were eyeing each other. The consensus started developing back in the 1970s, when some NRMs were fighting for recognition and legitimacy, and were eager to gain academic allies. Some NRM researchers willingly obliged, joined their side, and supported their claims. The mere fact of being recognized as a religious movement worthy of study seemed like an achievement for some groups. For other groups, the 'religious' label was crucial. As Greil (1996: 49) has suggested, being considered a religious movement is 'a cultural resource over which competing interest groups may vie ...' giving 'privileges associated in a given society with the religious label.' Moreover, 'the right to the religious label is a valuable commodity' (52). By applying the religion label consistently and generously to any group that asked for it, NRM scholars provided support that was not forthcoming from any other quarters. Not only is the 'religion' label worth money; so is support from sociologists who offer PR advice (see below). Harnessing scholarly prestige and enlisting scholars for unpleasant court cases was in the groups' clear interest.

When we take a closer look at the practices involved, we must realize that the issue is not our relations with groups we have done research on, but most often the collaboration with groups we have never done any research on. Normally, when we do research on human behavior, the issue may be one of empathy, sympathy, or the lack of both. Here we have not only sympathy and empathy, but complete identification. What we have is a practice of collaboration and an ideology of collaborationism, a perceived and experienced symbiosis, an alliance of mutual dependence. It seems that the strong and total identification of scholars with NRMs or groups claiming to be NRMs is deeply tied to their own identity as scholars. This description of the way collaborationist scholars feel is based on their own statements.

NRM PR Campaigns
What is PR? PR is different from the direct approach to selling your products and assumed under the heading of advertising. Here the action is subtle, selling people on something which is intangible, such as image or a reputation, and doing it gently, imperceptibly. Bits of information are manipulated to shape public perceptions and public opinion. The language of public relations includes such products (sold by PR agencies) as 'reputation protection systems,' vulnerability

assessment, re-branding, 'image rescue,' and crisis management. We can speculate that if a religious movement decides that it is faced with an 'image problem,' a natural response would be a religious one (e.g., praying to the gods for an improvement). What can we say about an NRM (or a group claiming such a label) which engages in a PR campaign, sometimes with paid help from professionals? Just that it probably feels the need for reputation protection and crisis management, and that it is quite atypical. Most NRMs have never engaged in such efforts, and have never tried to enlist scholars in their PR efforts. What is also clear is that in those rare cases in which NRMs have chosen to start PR campaigns, scholars were enthusiastic in their collaboration. We cannot generalize about NRMs, and any theoretical generalization about NRMs must be an empty abstraction, but it is clear that most NRMs do not spend money on publicity campaigns. At the same time, generalizing about NRM scholars is quite easy. When publicity campaigns have been engaged in, these scholars have come to the aid of those groups initiating them. The problem, as has become evident over the past few years, is that PR has become professionalized, and scholars have remained rank amateurs. The age of professionalism demands much more than academic imprimaturs.

The Unification Church in Search of Respectability: A Case Study
The 'Moonies' were the first to appreciate the value of having professors on their side. Since the 1970s, they organized a variety of front organizations and held numerous conferences, of which the best known were the Unity of Science conferences. At these conferences academics from all over the world met to discuss what united them, which was obviously the readiness to accept a free trip, no questions asked. Most academics attending the conferences were not religion scholars, but came from all fields. Those who had a scholarly interest in religion were clearly aware of their worth in the coin of legitimacy and respectability to the Moonies. There was criticism of academics who were ready to provide recognition to the Moonies by attending the conferences (Horowitz 1978), but these critical voices were decisively ignored by NRM scholars. There is a red thread that connects the cozy relationship with the Moonies in the 1970s and the events of the 1990s. In 1977, an organization calling itself Americans for the Preservation of Religious Liberty (APRL) was founded, one of many front organizations financed by groups seeking legitimacy as religions. The same groups that started it, the Unification Church, The Family, and

Scientology, have remained the most active in spending money and cultivating contacts with the NRM research community. One does not need to have access to the financial records of these groups to realize that many millions of dollars have been spent to achieve legitimacy and goodwill for such groups, through numerous front organizations, publications, public conferences, and less public transfers of funds. Has this spending been justified? This kind of cost-benefit analysis has to be done by the groups involved, using their own criteria. We can only state here that the money spent has been highly correlated with the level of friendly contacts with scholars. One may wonder about the financial resources which enable some NRMs, and not others, to spend many millions of dollars on publicity efforts. In terms of spending, the Unification Church and Scientology are probably the leaders, followed by The Family.

The Family (formerly Children of God) and Scholars
The case of The Family PR campaign is quite interesting. It seems that in the early 1990s, David Moses Berg decided that his group was in need of a PR face-lift in the form of an image change. (We can speculate that what was involved was not just a superficial PR change, but a change of heart as well, as Berg was removed from active leadership.) Contacts were developed with the NRM research community, and money was spent on publications, 'media houses' (i.e., the only Family dwellings which outsiders may enter), mass mailings, and visits to academic conferences. The amounts spent must have been significant. One may note that spending by The Family has brought about much in the way of goodwill and positive testimonials in writings, one film in 1994, appearances at scholarly conferences, and public statements in support of the group at such conferences. I myself attended a presentation of the film *The Love Prophet and the Children of God* at the 1998 meeting of the SSSR (Society for the Scientific Study of Religion). The film was followed by a discussion, in which three scholars who had benefited from The Family largesse spoke. Only one disclosed a financial relationship on that occasion. The Family is of course much different from Aum Shinrikyo, but the principle is the same: what Shils called 'publicistic and political activities' (1978: 183).

The historical continuity in the collaborationist network is quite evident. Some of the same scholars who were happy to enjoy the hospitality of the Unification Church in the 1970s are happy to appear in a videotape for The Family in 1994. What is most impressive is that no group is ever refused the scholarly imprimatur, and the usual suspects are always there. In the case of the Family video, the scholars giving their imprimatur were Bryan Wilson, Eileen Barker, Charlotte Hardman, Lawrence Lilliston, Gary Shepherd, Anson Shupe, J. Gordon Melton, James Lewis, and Evelyn Oliver. We run across the same names in the Church Universal and Triumphant (CUT) (Lewis and Melton 1994a) and The Family (Lewis and Melton 1994b) volumes, as well as in other NRM public relations efforts. To the best of my knowledge, most of these scholars have never done any research on the Family. The problem is, of course, that the usual suspects are our distinguished colleagues, those who define the field of NRM research.

An Operative Consensus

It seems that the operative consensus started forming in the late 1970s, and was well in place by the early 1980s. Leading scholars in the field decided to take a stand in the propaganda war over the legitimacy and reputation of certain NRMs (or groups claiming to be NRMs), and to work together with them in order to give them much needed public support. It was felt that in the struggle for legitimacy, anything perceived as weakening the public stand and harming the public image of NRMs should be avoided. We can hypothesize that public opinion is formed in many ways, and influenced by the deliberate efforts of government, the media, political leaders, cultural productions, educational institutions, and scholarship. In this case scholars tried their hand at influencing events outside the ivory tower. A defensive discourse has grown to protect any seeming indiscretion or transgression. Fifty years from now, when the archives are opened up and private letters read, historians will be able to answer better the questions raised here and explain the development of the late twentieth-century consensus among NRM scholars. In the meantime we can work only on the basis of public documents, but from time to time confidential documents see the light of day and provide additional insights into the behavior of our colleagues.

To illustrate and discuss the ideology of collaborationism we are going to look at a couple of pages from the memo written by Jeffrey K. Hadden on 20 December, 1989. This memo has been widely circulated and can be found on the Internet, but I thought it worthwhile to present it. It is significant that this memo was sent to numerous colleagues, and was not kept secret. The author's assumption was that there was nothing to hide, because of the overwhelming support for his point of view. I know that some of our colleagues do prefer a no-name policy, and just want me to say 'a prominent sociologist of religion.' I have used this kind of language before, but today I decided that I must use full names first because scholars should be held accountable for their actions. One important reason to look at this text is that Jeffrey Hadden is by no means a marginal figure. Some of his colleagues have been trying to tell me that he is some kind of a loose cannon ... At the same time, Hadden has not directly researched some of the groups he is willing to defend.

This emblematic document reports on a series of meetings and activities involving several leading NRM scholars (two of which have been presidents of the Society for the Scientific Study of Religion), NRM attorneys, NRM leaders, and some other scholars. Many future plans are discussed, most of which never materialized. The agenda and the commitments expressed are very clear. The memo proves, beyond a shadow of a doubt, that there exists not only behind-the-scenes contacts between scholars and NRMs, but also the coordinated effort on the part of leading NRM scholars to work with NRMs. What is striking is the clear sense in which the leading members of the NRM research network regarded NRMs as allies, not subjects of study. Three distinguished NRM scholars met privately with NRM representatives, not to discuss a research project or to interview them, but to discuss what was presented as a common cause. We find here the essence of collaborationism: the notion that scholars and NRMs are allies, and that there is no role conflict between being an ally and a researcher.

It seems that the scholars were more eager than the NRMs to lead the fight for NRM legitimacy. 'Our meetings with the members of the Unification Church confirmed our earlier impressions that while they may assent to the value of a long-range strategy for dealing with the anticultist and their forensic consultants, their response is very substantially confined to ad hoc responses to crises. I pressed them on the question of whether it might be possible for the UC in collaboration with several other NRMs to raise a significant amount of money – no strings attached – to an independent group, which in turn would entertain proposals and fund research on NRMs.' NRMS were less than enthusiastic, the writer thought, and 'The cooperative funding of the *American Conference on Religious Freedom* would appear to be about as far as they are prepared to go at this time' (Hadden 1989: 4). The collaborationism ideology, as revealed here, is somewhat paternalistic. We know what's good for the NRMs, which cannot recognize their own best interest. And it is in their own best interest to defend every single group claiming to be an NRM.

In addition to the idea of creating an NRM-funded research organization, '... we spent a good deal of time considering whether the time might be right to import ... INFORM, or create a U.S. organization that would perform a similar function ... In spite of having some bad experiences with the media ... INFORM has taken a very significant step in neutralizing anticult movements in the U.K.' (Hadden 1989: 5). Over the years, INFORM has been accused of acting as an NRM apologist (e.g., Usher 1997), and this memo seems to confirm some of the suspicions. Another striking aspect of the activities discussed in the memo is the orientation towards litigation: 'On the issue of the value of research and litigation, our legal consultant ... was not particularly sanguine about the prospects of social scientists coming up with findings that would be of great value. In so many words, he told us that the most important think [sic] we could do is prepare a statement that refutes the claim that social science can be helpful. I interpreted this as the agnostic statement we discussed in Salt Lake. Which brings us back to the question of a resolution for ASA Council consideration' (Hadden 1989: 6). We have not seen any similar documents written since 1989, but the public record over the past few years does indicate that leading NRM scholars have been involved in litigation as expert witnesses, consultants, or authors of amicus curiae briefs, always on the side of NRMs. These leading scholars became available to those groups that were interested in their support and services. The NRM advocacy consensus led to a broad propaganda effort, and had a significant effect on research. It looks like anti-NRM groups became a major interest, and that for some scholars more effort went into studying anti-NRM groups than into studying NRMs. This started quite early on (Shupe and Bromley 1980; Shupe, Bromley, and Oliver 1984).

Three years after the meeting reported in the 1989 memorandum, in 1992, the Association of World Academics for Religious Freedom (AWARE), which described itself (Lewis 1994a: 94) as '... an information centre set up to propagate objective information about non-traditional religions,' came on the scene. Each and every NRM scholar undoubtedly considers him- or herself an information centre propagating objective information about non-traditional religions, so there must be some real reasons for the creation of another such centre. 'The primary goal of AWARE is to promote intellectual and religious freedom by educating the general public about existing religions and cultures, including, but not limited to, alternative religious groups ... AWARE's orientation is scholarly and non-sectarian; the organization is not religious and does not have a religious ideology to propagate ... AWARE also educates the scholarly community and the general public about the severe persecution that religious and cultural minorities experience in the United States as well as abroad, and to support the United States government in its efforts to heal the prejudice that exists in our country and in the world' (214).

AWARE, led by James R. Lewis, has become a contractor for operations that can no longer claim any semblance or resemblance to research. One symptomatic product of the post-Waco NRM consensus is the Lewis volume titled *From the Ashes: Making Sense of Waco* (1994a). It seems like a typical apologetic pamphlet, a collection of 47 statements, authored by 46 individuals and 3 groups. Of the 46 individuals, 34 are holders of a PhD degree, and 19 are recognized NRM scholars. One cannot claim that this collection of opinion-pieces is unrepresentative of the NRM research network; quite the contrary. Most of the top scholars are here. The most significant fact is the participation by so many recognized scholars in this propaganda effort. In addition to *From the Ashes* we now have *Church Universal and Triumphant in Scholarly Perspective* (Lewis and Melton 1994a) and *Sex, Slander, and Salvation: Investigating the Children of God / The Family* (Lewis and Melton 1994b). The last two are clearly made-to-order PR efforts (with a few scholarly papers which got in by honest mistakes on the part of both authors and editors). The Family and Church Universal and Triumphant were interested in academic character witnesses, and many NRM scholars were happy to oblige. Balch and Langdon (1996) provide an inside view of how AWARE operates by offering a report on the fieldwork, if such a term can be used, which led to the AWARE 1994 volume on CUT (Lewis and Melton 1994a). What is described is a travesty of research. It is much worse than anybody could imagine, a real sellout by recognized NRM scholars. Among the contributors to the Family volume we find Susan J. Palmer, James T. Richardson, David G. Bromley, Charlotte Hardman, Massimo Introvigne, Stuart A. Wright, and John A. Saliba. The whole NRM research network is involved, the names we have known over the past thirty years, individuals with well-deserved reputations lend their support to this propaganda effort. There must be some very good reasons (or explanations, at least) for this behavior. The PR documents produced for groups such as Church Universal and Triumphant or The Family are but extreme examples of the literature of apologetics which has dominated NRM research for many years. Another aspect of these cases is that the reporting of financial arrangements is less than truthful. The fact that CUT financed the whole research expedition to Wyoming is not directly reported. We learn that CUT provided only room and board, while AWARE covered all other costs (Lewis 1994b). The fact that The Family volume was financed by the group itself is never reported anywhere, although it is clear to the reader that the whole project was initiated by Family leaders (Lewis 1994c). The Family volume has been recognized for what it is: a propaganda effort, pure and simple, paid for by the group (Balch 1996).

Lewis (1994c: vii), reporting on The Family, states that he 'found the young adults to be balanced, well-integrated individuals, and the children to be exceptionally open and loving.' In reporting on the Church Universal and Triumphant, Lewis (1994b: ix) states that he 'found the adults to be balanced, well-integrated individuals, and the children to exceptionally bright and open.' As a copywriter, James Lewis clearly leaves something to be desired, but so many copywriters have used the innocence of children to sell us anything from carpeting to laundry detergents. As these lines are being written, another volume of scholarly propaganda is being produced by the Lewis-Melton team, with the help of some distinguished scholars. The subject is the group known as MSIA (Movement for Spiritual Inner Awareness), led by John-Roger. The readers can expect another encounter with well-integrated adults and exceptionally open children. But what is the intended audience for such publications? Who is being addressed? In the case of the Lewis-Melton volumes, it is quite clear that the intended audience is not strictly academic. The intended non-academic audience is revealed through the press release style of the introductions. The audience in mind is very clearly the leaders of CUT and the Family, those who are paying for the product.

The issue of the conflict of interest created by financial support from corporations is one of the hottest in academic life today. The conflict is obvious to all except NRM researchers, who claim to be immune to it, and suggest that receiving money does not affect their activities or commitments in any way (e.g., Barker 1983). Such claims certainly sound strange when coming from social scientists. The norm of reciprocity is considered one of the building blocks of all human interaction, and it is clear that gifts are nearly always given with an expectation of reciprocity in mind (Arrow 1972). This norm, observed by most humans and conceptualized by some of the greatest names in sociology and anthropology (Gouldner 1960; Homans 1974; Levi-Strauss 1965; Mauss 1954; Titmus 1970), is suddenly ignored when the time comes to explain the behavior of real sociologists in the real world. Early theorists (Exod. 23: 8; Deut. 16: 19) were quite as decisive in their views concerning the possible effects of gifts on scholarly judgment: 'Thou shall take no gift: for the gift blindeth the wise, and perverth the words of the righteous.' This ancient opinion, possibly 2,500 years old, has not been heeded.

The Great Denial

The problem with the new dogma, and the new Inquisition guarding it, is that it obviously stifles curiosity and is likely to have a debilitating impact on research. The practice of apologetics is tied, causally or not, to the Great Denial. It starts with an emphatic denial of the pain, suffering, and hardships which characterize not only NRMs, but much of human existence. Pathology, deception, and exploitation can be found in many human interactions. In NRMs they may be more or less prevalent, but they are surely present. Does the literature reflect that? Not very often. What we deny is the madness, the oppression, and the deception, which create the totalitarian nature of many NRMs. The Great Denial offers those who accept it a sanitized, euphemistic, and sterilized view of humanity, an exclusion of tragedy, passion, sadness, frustration, brutality, and death. This is the great fear. It goes without saying that psychopathology and deception are excluded as explanations of any acts or events in NRMs.

How do we explain religious conversion? Conversion is an exceptional (some may say anomalous) behavior, occurring in a tiny proportion of religious believers. In old religions it has become rare; in new religions it is even rarer. It is also a mostly modern phenomenon, but even in modern times this behavior is highly unusual (Argyle and Beit-Hallahmi 1975; Beit-Hallahmi and Argyle 1997). Exceptional acts may be connected to exceptional situations, populations, personalities, or personality traits (cf. Anthony and Robbins 1997). Various motivations have been proposed to account for conversion, including serious psychopathology (e.g., borderline conditions, schizophrenia, depression) or vulnerability in the seeker (Beit-Hallahmi 1992a), as well as 'normal' psychodynamic factors of narcissism, dependency needs, or counter-dependent impulses. Some of the individuals involved may be judged by clinicians to be 'deeply disturbed,' 'seriously paranoid,' or 'having an immature ego.' It has often been argued, not only in the case of religion but also in the case of other significant ideologies, that early psychic wounds and the need for healing and compensation are the engines behind strong personal commitment. The question is that of judging whether the individual resorts to adaptive or maladaptive coping strategies, and whether the cognitive processes involved may be abnormal. Not too surprisingly, psychiatrists, psychoanalysts, and clinical psychologists have tended to mention biographical factors and psychopathology more often. Thus, Laing (1959) regarded those who would join NRMs as engaged in a desperate defence against psychotic breakdown. Similar suggestions have been made by Linn and Schwartz (1958) and Schimel (1973). Observations regarding psychopathology in NRM members, referring to groups by name, have appeared in the first part of this century (Bender and Spalding 1940; Yarnell 1957).

The Great Denial starts with denying the reality of distress in the seekers who join NRMs. While sociologists ignore psychopathology as an explanation for any behavior in formal writings, they refer to it in the real world. In most of the writings, conversion becomes a rational, intellectual process of creating a conscious ideology (or acquiring it). There are no personal or personality factors. No love or madness or pathology are encountered on the road to salvation. It should be noted that the use of psychopathology labels is never an explanation; it is only a starting point and a guide to further analysis. The language of psychopathology is too limited even just to describe the reality of life in groups such as Aum Shinrikyo or Heaven's Gate.

Viewing a cognitive search for a differing world view as the basis for the process of conversion is a starting point which creates a sterilized view of NRMs. The Great Denial naturally continues with describing the internal workings of NRMs as virtually untouched by any pathology and by any motives except religious beliefs. There is little emotion or psychological upheaval. There is no drama, only abstract social forces and conscious decisions by individuals. The deprivations and tragedies of the real world are left behind. The Black women, who were the majority of the victims in Jonestown, and a significant minority in Waco, are ignored by NRM researchers (with some welcome exceptions; cf. Anthony and Robbins 1997), who should be most alert to their presence.

Any discussion in terms of psychopathology or deception will stigmatize all NRMs, and cause incalculable damage to their public image.

Terms having to do with psychodynamics, psychopathology, or psychoanalysis frighten sociologists. But we are not talking about psychosis, pathologizing everybody, or 'medicalization.' Psychoanalysis is a theory of 'normal' universal motives: we all are given to the same pressures and needs. We all have narcissistic ideas and apocalyptic dreams – various needs leading to what Charles Rycroft (1991) has called pathological idealization. It is possible to hold on desperately to this pathological idealization in order to avoid disillusionment. In everyday life, and in the lyrics of the blues, we call that crazy love.

The denial of madness, so common to sociologists, is the denial of crazy love. The followers of David Koresh and Marshall Applewhite were not just following a totalitarian ideology. They were madly in love with their leaders. The denial of madness in general is tied to the denial of pathology in groups, but the pathology is visible to all, except NRM researchers. Marshall Applewhite was crazy, as was David Koresh. This has to be noted, while not being a complete explanation for the group's behavior. How did a madman become a group leader? We have to look at his followers, few in number, whose pathology miraculously matched his. Why did Applewhite castrate himself, with six of his disciples following suit? Rich (1998) suggested that this was a radical and total reaction to homosexual urges. To have this insight come from a journalist demonstrates again the poverty of scholarly discussion on the reality of NRMs, so often filled with horrors and anxieties. And this reality isn't new. Applewhite was a late twentieth-century version of George Rapp (1785–1847), founder of the Harmony Society, who castrated himself and his own son, and forced several of his followers to be castrated. And the idea of castration and genital mutilation is nothing new in the history of religion.

Defending NRMs and denying psychopathology in the seekers are connected. Denying evil deeds ascribed to NRMs is tied to denying the stigma of pathology in NRM members. The important idea of social constructivism may be taken too far, towards a radical critique which suggests (à la Michel Foucault) that all pathology (physical or mental) is a social construction, another instrument of oppression in the service of an evil establishment. Unfortunately schizophrenia is not a social construction, and can be found in all human societies at a constant ratio of around 1 to 100. Other serious psychopathologies add to a rate of prevalence, which means that the human psyche is less resilient than we would wish to believe. As a result, in every generation and in every culture, a significant minority of humanity does reach a point of self-destructive regression in its attempts to cope with reality.

Nevertheless, the denial goes on. Some NRM researchers have suggested that mental health professionals in the United States serve as social control agents in suppressing NRMs, through 'the medicalization of deviant religious behavior' (Hadden 1990; Robbins and Anthony 1982). Richardson (1994: 36) stated that the '... effort to "medicalize" participation in newer religious groups has been relatively successful.' And in the bluntest presentation of this thesis, Hadden (1990) compared the actions of these professionals to Soviet psychiatrists acting against political dissidents, and to Nazi atrocities. He then even suggested that 'the time is right for the United States to be visited by an international team of psychiatrists and social scientists for the purpose of investigating the role of American mental health professionals in their dealings with New Religious Movements' (13). Such a research team would easily discover that the vast majority of mental health professionals in the United States (and elsewhere) have little interest in NRMs, and even less knowledge. The 'medicalization of NRMs' never took place, and Hadden himself admits in a footnote that 'the proportion who are actively engaged in anticult activities [sic] is almost certainly very small' (20). As we all know, it was a mere handful of psychiatrists, and a few clinical psychologists, who have been active in looking at NRMs and their members. Benign neglect is the attitude of 99 per cent of the world's mental health professionals towards NRMs, for two simple reasons: first, NRMs involve a small minority of the general population, and a minority of mental health clients; second, these professionals are extremely individualistic in orientation. Despite the fact that religion (old or new) and psychotherapy offer individuals competing models of conceiving meaning and personal destiny (Beit-Hallahmi 1992a; Kilbourne and Richardson 1984), most psychotherapists seem to be happily oblivious to the existence of NRMs. We see that the medicalization thesis is totally irrelevant to reality.

Another critical claim regarding the use of psychopathology labels suggests that there is a common anti-religious prejudice in psychiatric nosology and diagnosis (Richardson 1993). If such a prejudice does exist, it has not affected the research on the relationship between religiosity and psychopathology, which neither assumes nor finds this prejudicial connection (Argyle and Beit-Hallahmi 1975; Beit-Hallahmi and Argyle 1997; Lowenthal 1995). Houts and Graham (1986), among others, have demonstrated that in clinical practice, religiosity is not judged as being tied to pathology; the opposite may be true (Shafranske 1997). Many researchers rather point to the therapeutic effects of religiosity, especially in the case of NRMs (Beit-Hallahmi and Argyle 1997). Early in this century it was a Viennese physician named Sigmund Freud who noted that it was not '... hard to discern in that all the ties that bind people to mystico-religious or philosophico-religious sects and communities are expressions of crooked cures for all kinds of neuroses' (Freud 1921: 142), and whether the cures are temporary or permanent is indeed a researchable issue. The opposite of the therapeutic effect is madness escalation within the group, mentioned above in reference to Koresh and Applewhite. Assessing psychopathology in the seekers who join NRMs is problematic, because it requires the use of control groups as well as retrospective and prospective biographical assessment. Comparing seekers and converts to matched controls, who are similar in all other respects save conversion, has rarely been reported (Beit-Hallahmi and Nevo 1987; Ullman 1989). In retrospective life history interviews, however, you can assess such things as drug addiction, prior hospitalizations, bereavement, and other relevant events, which then can be verified. Much better than any biographical reconstruction is prospective research, where a cohort of individuals is assessed at the starting point, and then followed up over time. Life events, such as joining an NRM, are recorded as they happen.

The study by Stone (1992) is one of a handful of relevant prospective studies. It traced the histories of 520 mostly borderline and schizophrenic patients who were hospitalized between 1963 and 1976, ten to twenty-five years after being discharged. This study was not designed to look at religious involvements, and it came as a surprise to the researcher that 7 of the 520 individuals had a conversion to an old religion, while 25 joined NRMs, for a total conversion rate of 6 per cent. This confirms many anecdotal observations and some systematic surveys (Beit-Hallahmi and Argyle 1997) about the involvement of former mental patients in NRMs. Stone's (1992) interpretation of the data, by the way, is wholly sympathetic to religion, NRMs, and their therapeutic benefits for psychiatric patients.

'So Many Rascals?': Deception, Money, and the Great Denial

An issue that is even more sensitive than that of psychopathology in NRMs is a rarely discussed aspect of charisma: the reality of cynical manipulation on the part of NRM entrepreneurs, hustlers engaged in self-invention in the service of greed. Charisma is, among other things, an odourless and colourless substance that enables con artists to prey on wealthy widows, and religious hustlers to exploit those seeking, and finding, salvation. You can be both deranged and a hustler, as shown by Luc Jouret. He taught people that there was more to life than money, and to prove their triumph over materialism they had to turn over their money to him, a little like David Koresh carrying the burden of sexuality all by himself for all (male) members of the Branch Davidians. In the novel *S.*, which is a *roman à clef* by John Updike (1988) about the Rajneesh movement, a similar point is made about material possessions, which are clearly a burden, and so the group is ready to shoulder this burden for its members, by asking them to sign over their financial assets.

In response to a question about the motivation of 'gurus,' Idries Shah, a man who has been often called a guru, says: 'Some are frankly phonies, and they don't try to hide it from me. They think I am one too, so when we meet they begin the most disturbing conversations. They want to know how I get money, how I control people, and so on ... They actually feel there is something wrong with what they are doing, and they feel better if they talk to somebody else who is doing it' (Hall 1975: 53). Are NRM researchers being conned by NRM entrepreneurs, or are they in reality willing shills for the con men (and women) at the top (cf. Zablocki 1997)? There are just a few references in the NRM literature to deception, manipulation, and greed.

What I have personally observed in some NRMs are two aspects of financing which create a great deal of opposition but are rarely discussed in the NRM literature. The first is deception in the solicitation of funds in public places. I can recall four incidents over twenty-five years, during which I have observed members of ISKCON (International Society for Krisha Consciousness) using false claims to collect money from innocent members of the public. The first was in Colorado in 1975, the second on the New York City subway in 1986, the third at the Los Angeles Airport in 1991, and the fourth was on my own campus in Haifa in 1998. On three occasions the claim was made that funds were being collected for homeless children, and on one occasion for 'retired priests.' The second aspect of financing which creates much opposition is the large amounts of money paid by NRM members as membership fees. In the case of one NRM I know, Emin, it has been observed that the group's demands for money have forced group members to become highly responsible and productive members of

society. Most outside observers, however, have still regarded the exor-
bitant sums as evidence of cynical exploitation.

We may want to differentiate between tactical and strategic deception in groups claiming the NRM label. When a member of ISKCON
(in street clothes) approaches us and asks for a donation for a shelter
housing homeless children, we may dismiss the incident, if we wish, as
simply instrumental or tactical deception. It is simply a way of getting
money out of kind strangers, and it works better than getting into a
discussion about the Vedas. It is also a non-threatening entree to a
recruitment effort. Some have regarded this kind of deception as triv-
ial. I do not, because the way a group presents itself to outsiders must
be symptomatic. One becomes suspicious of groups or individuals
who choose to present themselves to the world fraudulently even on
selected occasions. But beyond these behaviors, encountered in public
places in many cities around the world, there is also the spectre of strategic deception, in which the whole existence of a group presenting
itself as an NRM is an easy way of getting money out of kind strangers
(some of whom become members). The notion of strategic deception is
quite common in non-academic discussions of NRMs, but rarely mentioned in academic discourse. In the latter, strategic deception is never
considered, though there are references to tactical deception. Zaretsky
and Leone (1974) described 'spiritual leaders' as the last frontier for
entrepreneurs in the 'helping' professions, as no diplomas were necessary, but the concept of the entrepreneur has been absent from recent
NRM literature. Samuel L. Clemens, an observer of the U.S. scene in
the nineteenth century, reported on the lucrative practices of 'workin'
camp-meetin's, and missionaryin' around' (Twain 1884/1965: 107). Little seems to have changed since then, and such practices can still earn
you a decent living.

NRM researchers give all groups claiming the religion label their
imprimatur, and it is quite interesting to note that no group has ever
been refused this seal of approval. As far as I know, there has never
been a case where a claim to be recognized as an NRM was rejected by
scholars. The one axiom uniting all researchers (at least publicly) is that
all groups that claim to be NRMs are indeed NRMs. The possibility of
strategic deception is never considered by NRM researchers, even
when the commercial nature of a group's operations is highlighted by
the use of registered trademarks and official claims of 'trade secrets'
(Behar 1991; Passas and Castillo 1992). A naive observer, upon encountering the web site of such a group – (for example, MSIA) – with its

slick merchandising, using the language of 'goods and services' openly, and offering books, courses, booklets, workshops, trinkets, and videotapes, may think that this site represents a commercial enterprise. It takes a sophisticated NRM scholar, with a PhD and numerous publications, to figure out that behind this commercial glimmer hides the Sacred, with a capital S. Most of us will keep wondering why a religious movement feels it has got behind a commercial facade. Is it because of persecution?

Someone once said that the only two sure things in life are death and taxes. All religions promise us eternal life, and thus deal with the first existential issue facing humanity. Some so-called NRMs are doing something about the second, seemingly insurmountable, issue of taxes. How can one assume that in among thousands of groups worldwide there isn't a single case of strategic deception? It takes some faith, and what seems logically impossible is the reality of granting legitimacy to any group wishing to enjoy the benefits of tax-free operations. In one of the most memorable scenes from one of the greatest films of all time, *The Third Man* (1949, directed by Carol Reed, screenplay by Graham Greene), on the Ferris wheel above Vienna, Harry Lime (played by Orson Welles) proclaims what I have dubbed 'Harry Lime's First Law of Business Dynamics': 'Free of income tax, old man, free of income tax. The only way you can save money nowadays.' Harry Lime's Law has been put to good use by such moral paragons as Roy Cohn, and one must wonder whether it has occurred to anybody in the world of tax-free NRMs. Barker (1991: 11) noted the 'considerable economic advantages to be gained from being defined as a religion,' but has not suggested that this may motivate any specific NRMs or their leaders. Considerable economic advantages are to be gained from the support offered by NRM researchers to groups under fire, and these groups may show their appreciation by rewarding the researchers with some of their profits.

I have always thought that Anton Szandor LaVey's Church of Satan, which was actually liquidated as part of his divorce, had been a commercial enterprise, and it was not included in my reference works on NRMs (Beit-Hallahmi 1993, 1998). When LaVey died in November 1997 there was at least one obituary, by someone with an intimate knowledge of the man, one that described the Church of Satan as 'a cash cow' (Cabal 1997: 16). LaVey apparently did not inspire much respect, nor did he seek it. Anton Szandor LaVey was an operator. He made up his biography as a lion tamer and carnival barker (Knipfel

1998) and did not try to hide the fact that he was just out to make a living by attacking conventional wisdom. In terms of faith he was clearly an atheist, and still, such an eminent scholar as Melton (1989), in the most authoritative source on religions in the United States, was ready to take seriously and list as a 'religion' the Church of Satan and its various offshoots.

In the real world, far from NRM scholars, numerous works of fiction (and some of nonfiction) portray NRM founders and leaders as cynical hustlers and fakes. Adams (1995: 50) states: 'The career of Aimee Semple McPherson provided new chapters in the history of American hypocrisy, and Bruce Barton taught his readers to combine (however improbably) the principles of Jesus Christ with those of hucksterism.' This kind of analysis is a great U.S. cultural tradition. Henry James, an early critic of NRMs in the nineteenth century, does a good job of mocking both NRMs and the 'New Age' (yes, New Age) in *The Bostonians* (James 1877/1956). As we know, in the nineteenth century many cultural precedents were set, regarding both NRMs and their critics, such as Mark Twain, and in the absence of academic researchers. The literary tradition of mockery and critique directed at both old and new religions seems to be alive a century later, without much effect on academics. Elmer Gantry (Lewis 1927) seems to be reborn and technologically amplified in the shape of modern televangelists. *Reborn*, a 1979 grade B film by Bigas Luna, describes a joint scheme by the mafia and a televangelist, and gives a backstage view of televangelism as hustling.

In a *New Yorker* article discussing the positive role of inner-city churches in the United States in saving youngsters from a life of crime and self-destruction, a call is made for greater support of these churches. In addition to much well-deserved agreement from several observers of the inner-city scene, a cautionary note is sounded by Representative Tony Hall, described as 'a Democrat who has been active with religious charities.' 'We do have to be careful,' he says. 'There are some real thieves in this business' (Klein 1997: 46). Gates (1989) referred, in passing, to no less a figure than Father Divine as 'that historic con man of the cloth' (44). This assessment radically challenges social science and history of religion accounts (cf. Burnham 1979; Cantril 1941; Fauset 1944; Harris 1971; Parker 1937; Weisbrot 1983). Another observer stated that '... a Spiritualist cult is a house of religious prostitution where religion is only the means for the end of commercialization' (Washington 1973: 115). The U.S. NRM known as the United Church and Science Of Living Institute, founded in 1966 by former Baptist minister Frederick Eikerekoetter II, also known as Reverend Ike, is widely regarded as a con game. Most members are African Americans. In these instances the reality of hustling is thus well-acknowledged in the life of poor African Americans (cf. Baer 1981). We must wonder about its prevalence in other groups which cater to clients in search of religious salvation. But then Martin Marty (1987) called Rajneesh a con man, and the Attorney General of Oregon said that the Rajneesh organization had committed the number one crimes in several categories in the history of the United States: the largest network of fraudulent marriages, the most massive scheme of wiretapping, and the largest mass poisoning (Gordon 1987). Updike (1988), in a thinly veiled *roman à clef*, gives us a description of Rajneesh as a lecherous hustler, preying on the easy marks of Western bourgeoisie, and provides a glossary of Hindu terms, in case any of the readers wants to start an ashram somewhere. The novel is a literary failure, but probably a reliable ethnography. If we look at the world of NRMs according to Updike or Mehta (1990) we must ask ourselves whether they are such unsophisticated observers, or whether they are more sophisticated than the crowds of scholars who have observed the same world and found only idealism and the sacred. Why is there such a distance between the non-academic literary observers and NRM researchers? The former always describe this combination of sincere illusions (and delusions) together with the cynical manipulation of easy marks.

Even NRM researchers must be aware of the existence of groups that owe their survival to fraudulent claims of miracle cures. The group known as Cultural Minorities Spiritual Fraternization Church Of The Philippines, founded by Philip S. Malicdan in the 1960s, is a business which sells 'psychic surgery' to gullible (and terminally ill) foreigners. And then a book titled *218 Tax Havens* (Kurtz 1993) offers advice, according to its publisher, on 'What it takes to set up your own church or – eveñ better – open up an *independent branch of an existing church in California* – no matter in what part of the world you're living – and subsequently do all your business under the tax number of that church (DO-1599959) – *thus staying completely tax free'* (Privacy Reports 1993). Where did Mr Kurtz get these ideas?

Prediction and Retrodiction

'The prediction/retrodiction may be 'testable' in some sense, i.e., experiment or future observations may test the prediction, the acquisition of additional information about the past may test the retrodiction' (Saperstein 1997: 7). Recent NRM tragedies allow us to test the consensus through retrodictions. In these cases we have more data and we can perform an in-depth examination. Here tragedy becomes an opportunity. When disaster strikes, the backstage is exposed, not just the tragic ending itself but the whole mechanics and history of the group, its hidden anatomy and physiology. The tragedies offer us a unique vantage point, that of the behavioral autopsy. Following each of them we get more information about the inner workings of NRMs, and sometimes we obtain almost complete histories. Just as in a medical autopsy, these cases can demonstrate where observers went wrong in their diagnosis and treatment.

The brief history of the Order of the Solar Temple by Hall and Schuyler (1997) ties us immediately to the real world of salvation hustlers and their victims. Here members of the francophone bourgeoisie, in scenes which could have been staged by Luis Bunuel and Federico Fellini, seek escape by any means from their lives of quiet desperation. There is not only demand but also some supply, and various con artists are right there to take advantage of the growing market. Hall and Schuyler (289) cite Max Weber, who wrote that Joseph Smith 'may have been a very sophisticated swindler.' In the case of the Solar Temple, we may be dealing with less sophisticated swindlers, but they still can get away with a lot. Its two leaders, Joseph DiMambro and Luc Jouret, had between them a wide repertoire of fraudulent practices, from bad checks to homeopathy. The official belief system of the group, combining claims about 'ancient Egypt,' 'energy fields,' reincarnation, and the 'Age of Aquarius,' is so widely offered in hundreds of groups all over the world (cf. Beit-Hallahmi 1992a) as to be banal and harmless.

Most of those who make a living marketing this rather used merchandise will never commit violence. But this was a high-involvement group, not just a series of lectures. By the late 1980s, the Solar Temple was a target for anti-NRM groups. In 1993, it became the target for police attention (for illegal weapon charges) and sensational media reports in both Canada and Australia. In July 1993 Jouret and two associates received light sentences from a judge in Quebec for their attempts to buy pistols with silencers. The early warnings were not heeded. The most sensational media reports, calling the Solar Temple a 'doomsday cult,' turned out to be on the mark. It is possible that DiMambro, terminally ill, wanted to take as many with him as he could. It is clear that many of the dead at this going-away party were murdered, some for revenge, while others were willing victims. Of course, Jouret and Di Mambro were more than just hustlers. It is likely that they at least actually believed in some of the ideas they propagated (Mayer 1999).

There are other NRM disasters which remain less well-known, even though they involve real horrors. A case in point is that of the Faith Assembly, led by Hobart E. Freeman. In this group 100 members and their children were reported to have died between 1970 and 1990, because of their refusal to seek medical care. Freeman himself, a scholar of Hebrew and Greek and the author of ten books which were well received within the evangelical Christian community, has been described as schizophrenic, but was able to control his followers and persuade them to continue risking their own and their children's lives. He died in 1984, but his ideas live on among some (Beit-Hallahmi 1998; Hughes 1990). Freeman's victims are less known than those of other deranged leaders, but some of his followers were convicted and sent to prison for what some observers called infanticide. Richardson and Dewitt (1992: 561) note that public opinion '... seems to favor protection of children over parental rights and freedom of religion,' and it certainly should. The protection of powerless children must take priority over any other consideration.

Another NRM tragedy which has received little notice is the story of Osel Tendzin (formerly Thomas Rich of Passaic, N.J.). He was the Vajra Regent who died in 1990 after knowingly infecting some of his followers with the HIV virus. He is rarely mentioned in studies of this group (cf. Beit-Hallahmi 1998; Cartwright and Kent 1992; Rubin 1997). This story is quite astounding and deserves close scrutiny, even though the NRM involved refuses to do that, and remembers Osel Tendzin only in his status as a great teacher, 'Radiant Holder of the Teachings.' Osel Tendzin became leader of Vajradhatu in 1987, upon the death (by cirrhosis of the liver) of Chogyam Trungpa, who appointed him as successor. Both leaders shared the habit of enjoying sex and alcohol with followers. Osel Tendzin had had AIDS since 1985, and this was known to Chogyam Trungpa and to at least two other members of the Vajradhatu board. In December 1988, the world, together with the group's members, learned of Osel Tendzin's trail of death by sex (Butler 1990). He died in 1990, still nominally the leader, surrounded by admiring disciples. The case of Osel Tendzin and his behaviour provides less than an autopsy, but a dramatic backstage glimpse. Here, not only a Buñuel and a Fellini were required to stage the scenes, but also

Ingmar Bergman and Orson Wells. There are less tragic cases where no
deaths are involved, but criminal activities and various scandals provide openings into backstage activities. In the case of the Love Family
(Balch 1988) no lives were lost, but some lives were misspent, wasted,
and destroyed.

Melton and Moore (1982: 171) criticized anti-NRM sources as 'shallow and full of errors.' Following the Waco tragedy we have much
knowledge about everyday life in the Branch Davidians, just as we
have gained some insider views of the Solar Temple and Heaven's
Gate. Not only that, but it is now quite clear that without these horren-
dous tragedies we would have never known about the reality of backstage life among the Branch Davidians or in the Solar Temple. Recent
historical-behavioral autopsies enable us to realize that in every single
case allegations by hostile outsiders, critics, and detractors have sometimes been closer to the reality than any other accounts. The party line
has been that '... defectors are involved in either conscious or unconscious self-serving behavior' (Richardson 1980: 247), as opposed to
members and leaders, who are totally selfless. Ever since Jonestown,
statements by ex-members turned out to be just as accurate, or more so
than those of apologists and NRM researchers. While it is true that
organizations (and individuals) look less than perfectly appetizing
with their entrails exposed, the reality revealed in the cases of People's
Temple, Nation of Yahweh, Rajneesh International, the Branch Davidians, the Solar Temple, or Heaven's Gate is much more than unattrac-
tive; it is positively horrifying, confirming our worst nightmares. Each
one of these cases may be unrepresentative, deviating from the norm
in the majority of NRMs, but the cumulative record must be considered. Aum Sinhrikyo was an aberration, and the Solar Temple was an
aberration, and David Koresh was an aberration, and Osel Tendzin
was an aberration, and so on and on. But aberrations are piling up, and
we do have a representative sample, because the groups involved
come from differing backgrounds and traditions. One group is in
Japan, another is a branch of a mainstream Protestant denomination,
another is a schismatic millenarian group, another is UFO-oriented,
one Tibetan Buddhist, and another Rosicrucian. Our overall failure
in retrodiction is tied to our bias and ignorance, and the NRM consensus seems totally out of touch with the realities uncovered in these
autopsies.

In every case of NRM disaster over the past fifty years, starting with
Krishna Venta (Beit-Hallahmi 1993), we encounter a hidden reality of

madness and exploitation, a totalitarian, psychotic reality which is actually worse than detractors' allegations. The dynamics we discover in these social movements are not just of ideological and organizational totalism, but of totalitarianism and fascism. Exposing the inside workings of an NRM reveals a leader even more deranged than anybody could have imagined at the head of a small-scale dictatorship system similar to the well-known dictatorships of the twentieth century. The questions we ask about these groups should be similar to the ones raised about historical twentieth-century totalitarian regimes (Adorno et al. 1950; Fromm 1941). We are now better informed about the leaders that have been exposed, but this invokes some sobering thoughts about leaders in groups whose inner workings are still hidden from sunlight. Of course, most religious organizations are undemocratic by definition (and by claimed revelation), but in recent times not all have been totalitarian dictatorships.

Accuracy in the Mass Media and in Scholarly Writings

The moral of recent well-publicized NRM tragedies, such as the Branch Davidians case or the Heaven's Gate case, as far as reporting and analysis is concerned, is that reading *Newsweek*, *Time*, or the *New York Times* may be just as profitable, or more, as reading scholarly works. Media reporting in general is quite limited, but investigative reporting by major media, when time and effort are put in, and wire-service reports, are worth at least taking seriously. There are sometimes real errors in the media, but this happens in academic works too. Reading the scholarly literature, with a few notable and commendable exceptions, does not result in a better understanding of what the Branch Davidians at Waco were all about. The most basic human questions are left unanswered. *Newsweek* reported quite accurately on who David Koresh really was, and at the same time was severely critical of U.S. government authorities and their outrageous mishandling of the case. If you were just to rely on *Newsweek* to understand what happened at Waco, you would reach the conclusion that a group of deranged victims, led by a manipulative madman, was being decimated by superior federal firepower in a senseless and tragic confrontation ignited by the illegal acts of some group members. Would you miss out on some fine points of scholarly analysis? Not if such analysis consisted of a scholarly defence of indefensible behavior. One way of looking at the Mt Carmel tragedy is by comparing it to the many tragic confrontations between deranged individuals and insensitive or unaware members of police forces around the world. The only acceptable defence for David Koresh may be the insanity defence, and this is something you will gather soon enough from the media, which have proven themselves just as accurate in the cases of Krishna Venta, Benjamin Purnell, Aum Shinrikyo, the People's Temple, the Solar Temple, and Heaven's Gate. As we have demonstrated in the case of the Branch Davidians and Aum Shinrikyo, sensational media reports never die; they don't even fade away. They just come back reincarnated as scholarly data, to be interpreted or euphemized.

Note

I wish to thank L.B. Brown, Yoram Carmeli, Avner Falk, Mark Finn, Maxine Gold, A.Z. Guiora, Stephen A. Kent, Roslyn Lacks, Michael Langone, James R. Lewis, J. Gordon Melton, Jean-Francois Mayer, Dan Nesher, Tom Robbins, Leonard Saxe, Israel Shahak, Zvi Sobel, Roger O'Toole, and Benjamin Zablocki for generous help and advice. Whatever remaining faults are still found in this chapter are the author's sole responsibility.

References

Adams, R.M. 1995. 'Wonderful Town?' *The New York Review of Books*, 20 April.
Adorno, T., et al. 1950. *The Authoritarian Personality.* New York: Harper & Row.
Alper, G. 1997. *The Dark Side of the Analytic Moon.* Bethesda, Md.: International Scholars Publications.
Anthony, D., and T. Robbins, 1997. 'Religious Totalism, Exemplary Dualism, and the Waco Tragedy.' In *Millennium, Messiahs, and Mayhem*, edited by T. Robbins and S.J. Palmer. New York: Routledge.
Argyle, M., and B. Beit-Hallahmi. 1975. *The Social Psychology of Religion.* London: Routledge & Kegan Paul.
Arrow, K.J. 1972. 'Gifts and Exchanges.' *Philosophy and Public Affairs* 1: 343–62.
Baer, H.A. 1981. 'Prophets and Advisors in Black Spiritual Churches: Therapy, Palliative, or Opiate?' *Culture, Medicine and Psychiatry* 5: 145–70.
Bainbridge, W.S. 1993. 'New Religions, Science and Secularization.' *Religion and the Social Order* 3A: 277–92.
Balch, R. (1988). 'Money and Power in Utopia: An Economic History of the

Love Family.' *Money and Power in the New Religions*. J.T. Richardson. Lewiston, N.Y.: Edwin Mellen.

Balch, R.W. 1996. Review of *Sex, Slander, and Salvation: Investigating the Children of God / The Family,* edited by J.R. Lewis, and J.G. Melton. *Journal for the Scientific Study of Religion* 36: 35, 72.

Balch, R.W., and S. Langdon, 1996. 'How Not to Discover Malfeasance in New Religions: An Examination of the AWARE Study of the Church Universal and Triumphant.' University of Montana, unpublished.

Barker, 1983. 'Supping with the Devil: How Long a Spoon Does the Sociologist Need?' *Sociological Analysis* 44: 197–205.

– 1991. 'But Is It a Genuine Religion?' *Report from the Capitol* (April): 10–11, 14.

Becker, H.S. 1967. 'Whose Side Are We On?' *Social Problems* 14: 239–47.

Behar, R. 1991. 'The Thriving Cult of Greed and Power.' *Time*, 6 May, 32–9.

Beit-Hallahmi, B. 1974a. 'Salvation and Its Vicissitudes: Clinical Psychology and Political Values.' *American Psychologist* 29: 124–9.

– 1974b. 'Psychology of Religion 1880–1930: The Rise and Fall of a Psychological Movement.' *Journal of the History of the Behavioral Sciences* 10: 84–90.

– 1975. 'Encountering Orthodox Religion in Psychotherapy.' *Psychotherapy: Theory, Research and Practice* 12: 357–9.

– 1976. 'On the 'Religious' Functions of the Helping Professions. *Archive fur Religionpsychologie* 12: 48–52.

– 1977a. 'Humanistic Psychology – Progressive or Reactionary?' *Self and Society* 12: 97–103.

– 1977b. 'Curiosity, Doubt and Devotion: The Beliefs of Psychologists and the Psychology of Religion. In *Current Perspectives in the Psychology of Religion,* edited by H.N. Malony. Grand Rapids, Mich.: Eerdmans Publishing.

– 1981. 'Ideology in Psychology: How Psychologists Explain Inequality.' In *Value Judgment and Income Distribution,* edited by R. Solo and C.H. Anderson. New York: Praeger.

– 1987. 'The Psychotherapy Subculture: Practice and Ideology.' *Social Science Information* 26: 475–92.

– 1989. *Prolegomena to the Psychological Study of Religion*. Lewisburg, Pa.: Bucknell University Press.

– 1991. 'More Things in Heaven and Earth: Sharing the Psychoanalytic Understanding of Religion.' *International Journal of the Psychology of Religion* 1: 91–3.

– 1992a. *Despair and Deliverance: Private Salvation in Contemporary Israel.* Albany, N.Y.: SUNY Press.

– 1992b. 'Between Religious Psychology and the Psychology of Religion. In *Object Relations, Theory and Religion: Clinical Applications,* edited by M. Finn and J. Gartner. New York: Praeger.

- 1993. *The Annotated Dictionary of Modern Religious Movements.* Danbury, Conn.: Grolier.
- 1995. 'Ideological and Philosophical Bases for the Study of Personality and Intelligence. In *International Handbook of Personality and Intelligence,* edited by D.H. Saklofske and M. Zeidner. New York: Plenum.
- 1996a. 'Religion as Pathology: Exploring a Metaphor.' In *Religion, Mental Health, and Mental Pathology,* edited by H. Grzymala-Moszczynska, and B. Beit-Hallahmi. Amsterdam: Rodopi.
- 1996b. *Psychoanalytic Studies of Religion: Critical Assessment and Annotated Bibliography.* Westport, Conn.: Greenwood Press.
- 1998. *The Illustrated Encyclopedia of Active New Religions.* New York: Rosen Publishing.
Beit-Hallahmi, B., and M. Argyle. 1977. 'Religious Ideas and Psychiatric Disorders.' *International Journal of Social Psychiatry* 23: 26–30.
- 1997. *The Psychology of Religious Behaviour, Belief, and Experience.* London: Routledge.
Beit-Hallahmi, B., and B. Nevo. 1987. '"Born-again" Jews in Israel: The Dynamics of an Identity Change.' *International Journal of Psychology* 22: 75–81.
Bender, L., and M.A. Spalding. 1940. 'Behavior Problems in Children from the Homes of Followers of Father Divine. *Journal of Nervous and Mental Disease* 91: 460–72.
Burnham, K.E. 1979. *God Comes to America.* Boston: Lambeth.
Butler, K. 1990. 'Encountering the Shadow in Buddhist America.' *Common Boundary* (May/June): 14–22.
Cabal, A. 1997. 'The Death of Satan.' *New York Press* (12–18 November).
Cantril, H. 1941. *The Psychology of Social Movements.* New York: Wiley.
Cartwright, R.H., and S.A. Kent. 1992. 'Social Control in Alternative Religions: A Familial Perspective.' *Sociological Analysis* 53: 345–61.
Fauset, A.H. 1944. *Black Gods of the Metropolis.* Philadelphia: University of Pennsylvania Press.
Freud, S. 1921. 'Group Psychology and the Analysis of the Ego.' *The Standard Edition of the Complete Psychological Writings of Sigmund Freud* 18: 69–143.
Fromm, E. 1941. *Escape from Freedom.* New York: Rinehart.
Gates, H.L., Jr. 1989. 'Whose Canon Is It, Anyway?' *New York Times Book Review* 26 February.
Gordon, J.S. 1987. *The Golden Guru: The Strange Journey of Bhagwan Shree Rajneesh.* Lexington, Mass.: Stephen Green Press.
Gouldner, A. 1960. 'The Norm of Reciprocity: A Preliminary Statement.' *American Sociological Review* 25: 161–78.

Greil, A.L. 1996. 'Sacred Claims: The "Cult Controversy" as a Struggle over the Right to the Religious Label.' *Religion and the Social Order* 6: 47–63.

Hadden, J.K. 1989. 'Memorandum' (20 December).

– 1990. 'The Role of Mental Health Agents in the Social Control of Religious Deviants: A Comparative Examination of the U.S.S.R. and the United States.' Paper prepared for presentation at a conference on Religion, Mental Health, and Mental Pathology. Cracow, Poland (December 1990).

Hall, E. 1975. 'A conversation with Idries Shah.' *Psychology Today* (July).

Hall, J.R., and P. Schuyler. 1997. 'The Mystical Apocalypse of the Solar Temple.' In *Millennium, Messiahs, and Mayhem*, edited by T. Robbins and S.J. Palmer. New York: Routledge.

Harris, S. 1971. *Father Divine*. New York: Macmillan.

Haworth, A. 1995. 'Cults: Aum Shinrikyo.' *The Guardian* (14 May).

Homans, G.C. 1974. *Social Behavior: Its Elementary Forms*. New York: Harcourt Brace Jovanovich.

Horowtiz, I.L., ed. 1978. *Science, Sin, and Scholarship: The Politics of Reverend Moon and the Unification Church*. Cambridge, Mass.; MIT Press.

Houts, A.C., and K. Graham, 1986. 'Can Religion Make You Crazy? Impact of Client and Therapist Values on Clinical Judgments. *Journal of Consulting and Clinical Psychology* 54: 267–71.

Hughes, R.A. 1990. Psychological Perspectives on Infanticide in a Faith Healing Sect. *Psychotherapy* 27: 107–15.

James, H. (1877/1956). *The Bostonians*. New York: Modern Library.

Keita, L. 1998. *The Human Project and the Temptations of Science*. Amsterdam: Rodopi.

Kilbourne, B., and J.T. Richardson. 1984. 'Psychotherapy and New Religions in a Pluralistic Society.' *American Psychologist* 39: 237–51.

Klein, J. 1997. 'In God They Trust.' *New Yorker*, 16 June.

Knipfel, J. 1998. 'The Devil, You Say!' *New York Press* (4–10 Nov.).

Kowner, R. 1997. 'On Ignorance, Respect and Suspicion: Current Japanese Attitudes towards Jews.' Acta No. 11. Jerusalem: Vidal Sassoon International Center for the Study of Antisemitism, Hebrew University of Jerusalem.

Kurtz, G. 1993. *218 Tax Havens*. Hong Kong: Privacy Reports.

Laing, R.D. 1959. *The Divided Self*. London: Tavistock.

Levi-Strauss, C. 1965. The Principle of Reciprocity. In *Sociological Theory*, edited by L.A. Coser and L. Rosenberg. New York: Macmillan.

Lewis, J.R. (1994b). Introduction: On Tolerance, Toddlers, and Trailers: First Impressions of Church Universal and Triumphant. In *Church Universal and Triumphant in Scholarly Perspective*, edited by J.R. Lewis and J.G. Melton. Stanford, Calif.: Center for Academic Publication.

- 1994c. 'Introduction.' In *Sex, Slander, and Salvation: Investigating the Children of God / The Family*, edited by J.R. Lewis and J.G. Melton. Stanford, Calif.: Center for Academic Publication.
- 1995. 'Self-Fulfilling Stereotypes: The Anticult Movement, and the Waco Confrontation.' In *Armageddon in Waco*, edited by S.A. Wright. Chicago: University of Chicago Press.

Lewis, J.R., ed. 1994a. *From the Ashes: Making Sense of Waco*. Lanham, Md.: Rowman & Littlefield.

Lewis, J.R., and J.G. Melton, eds. 1994a. *Church Universal and Triumphant in Scholarly Perspective*. Stanford, Calif.: Center for Academic Publication.
- 1994b. *Sex, Slander, and Salvation: Investigating the Children of God / The Family*. Stanford, Calif.: Center for Academic Publication.

Lewis, S. 1927. *Elmer Gantry*. New York: Harcourt Brace.

Linn, L., and L.W. Schwartz. 1958. *Psychiatry and Religious Experience*. New York: Random House.

Lowenthal, K.M. 1995. *Mental Health and Religion*. London: Chapman & Hall.

Lurie, A. (1967/1991). *Imaginary Friends*. New York: Avon Books.

Marty, M. (1987). *Religion and Republic*. Boston: Beacon.

Mauss, M. 1954. *The Gift*. Glencoe, Ill.: The Free Press.

Mayer, J.F. 1999. 'Les chevaliers de l'apocalypse: L'Ordre de Temple Solaire et ses adeptes.' In *Sectes et Société*, edited by F. Champion amd M. Cohen. Paris: Seuil.

Mehta, G. 1990. *Karma Cola: Marketing The Mystic East*. New York: Vintage.

Melton, J.G. 1989. *Encyclopedia of American Religions*. Detroit: Gale.

Melton. J.G. and R. Moore. 1982. *The Cult Experience*. New York: Pilgrim Press.

Mullins, M.R. 1997. 'Aum Shinrikyo as an Apocalyptic Movement.' In *Millennium, Messiahs, and Mayhem*, edited by T. Robbins and S.J. Palmer. New York: Routledge.

Parker, R.A. 1937. *The Incredible Messiah*. Boston: Little, Brown.

Passas, N. and M.E. Castillo. 1992. 'Scientology and Its "Clear" Business.' *Behavioral Sciences and the Law* 10: 103–16.

Pastore, N. 1949. *The Nature-Nurture Controversy*. New York: King's Crown Press.

Privacy Reports, Inc. 1993. How the Rich Get Richer: Their Secrets Revealed (flyer).

Reid, T.R. 1995 'U.S. Visitors Boost Cause of Japanese Cult.' *Washington Post*, 9 May.

Reader, I. 1995. 'Aum Affair Intensifies Japan's Religious Crisis: An Analysis.' *Religion Watch* (July/August): 1–2.

Reuters News Service (1998). 'Life Sentence to Aum Member for the Poison Gas Attack, 27 May.

Rich, F. 1998. 'Lott's Lesbian Ally.' *New York Times*, 22 July, A19.

Richardson, J.T. 1980. 'People's Temple and Jonestown: A Corrective Comparison and Critique.' *Journal for the Scientific Study of Religion* 19: 239–55.

– 1993. 'Religiosity as Deviance: Negative Religious Bias and Its Misuse of the DSM-III.' *Deviant Behavior* 14: 1–21.

– 1994. 'Update on "The Family": Organizational Change and Development in a Controversial New Religious Group.' In *Sex, Slander, and Salvation: Investigating the Children of God / The Family*, edited by J.R. Lewis and J.G. Melton. Stanford, Calif.: Center for Academic Publication.

Richardson, J.T. and J. Dewitt. 1992. 'Christian Science, Spiritual Healing, the Law, and Public Opinion.' *Journal of Church and State* 34: 549–61.

Robbins, T. 1983. The Beach Is Washing Away. *Sociological Analysis* 44: 207–13.

Robbins, T., and D. Anthony. 1982. 'Deprogramming, Brainwashing: The Medicalization of Deviant Religious Groups. *Social Problems* 29: 283–97.

Robbins, T., and D.G. Bromley (1991). 'New Religious Movements and the Sociology of Religion.' *Religion and Social Order* 1: 183–205.

Rubin, J.B. 1997. 'Psychoanalysis Is Self-Centered.' In *Soul on the Couch: Spirituality, Religion, and Morality in Contemporary Psychoanalysis*, edited by C. Spezzano and G. Garguilo. Hillsdale, N.J.: Analytic Press.

Rycroft, C. 1991. *Psychoanalysis and Beyond*. London: Hogarth.

Saperstein, A.M. 1997. 'Dynamical Modeling in History.' *Physics and Society* 26, no. 4: 7–8.

Schimel, J.L., ed. 1973. 'Esoteric Identification Processes in Adolescence and Beyond.' *The Journal of the American Academy of Psychoanalysis* 1: 403–15.

Shafranske, E., 1997. *Religion and the Clinical Practice of Psychology*. Washington, D.C.: APA.

Shils, E. 1978. 'The Academic Ethos.' *The American Scholar* (spring): 165–90.

Shupe, A., and D. Bromley. 1980. *The New Vigilantes: The Anti-Cult Movement in America*. Beverly Hills: Sage.

Shupe, A., D.G. Bromley, and D. Oliver. 1984. *The Anti-Cult Movement in America: A Bibliographical and Historical Survey*. New York: Garland.

Spengler, O. 1926. *The Decline of the West*. New York: Knopf.

Stone, M.H. 1992. 'Religious Behavior in the Psychiatric Institute 500.' In *Object Relations Theory and Religion: Clinical Applications*, edited by M. Finn and J. Gartner. Westport, Conn.: Praeger.

Titmus, R. 1970. *The Gift Relationship*. London: Allen & Unwin.

Twain, M. 1884/1965. *The Adventures of Huckleberry Finn*. New York: Harper & Row.

70   Benjamin Beit-Hallahmi

Ullman, C. 1989. *The Transformed Self: The Psychology of Religious Conversion.* New York: Plenum.

Updike, J. 1988. *S.* New York: Fawcett Crest.

Usher, R. 1997. 'Cult Control.' *Time* (27 January).

Washington, J., Jr. 1973. *Black Sects and Cults.* Garden City, N.Y.: Doubleday.

Weisbrot, R. 1983. *Father Divine and the Struggle for Racial Equality.* Urbana: University of Illinois Press.

Weisstub, D.N. 1998. *Research on Human Subjects.* Amsterdam: Pergamon.

Yarnell, H. 1957. 'An Example of the Psychopathology of Religion: The Seventh Day Adventist Denomination.' *Journal of Nervous and Mental Disease* 125: 202–12.

Zablocki, B. (1997). 'Distinguishing Front-Stage from Back-Stage Behavior in the Study of Religious Communities.' San Diego, Society for the Scientific Study of Religion.

Zaretsky, I.I., and M.P. Leone, eds. 1974. *Religious Movements in Contemporary America.* Princeton: Princeton University Press.

2. Balance and Fairness in the Study of Alternative Religions

Thomas Robbins

'Alternative religions' have often tended to get a bad press, and indeed have been derided throughout history by outstanding intellectual and literary figures such as Charles Dickens and Mark Twain (1993). There have been those, however, who have defended unconventional and controversial movements – even disinterestedly, in the narrow sense that the defenders may not be true believers themselves. The relatively disinterested defenders of stigmatized 'cults' such as The Family (formerly the Children of God), the Church Universal and Triumphant, the Unification Church or the Church of Scientology have tended recently to be professional scholars from religious studies and sociology departments. A critical and occasionally vituperative literature has been emerging which employs somewhat of a *J'accuse* mode, and charges the scholarly defenders of controversial movements with grave derelictions of professional ethics, departures from scholarly objectivity, institutionalized biases, corruption, and naive or manipulative distortions of reality in behalf of noxious cults (Allen 1998; Balch and Langdon 1998; Beit-Hallahmi 1998; Horowitz 1983; Kent and Krebs 1998; West 1990; Zablocki 1997). An earlier genre, which peaked around a decade ago, levelled somewhat similar charges against those mental health professionals, journalists, clerics, lawyers, ex-devotees and concerned citizens who appeared to be spearheading the growing 'anticult' crusade (Anthony 1990; Anthony and Robbins 1982; Coleman 1985; Introvigne 1998; Kilbourne and Richardson 1984; Malony 1987; Robbins 1984).

Notwithstanding the recent spate of attacks on scholars deemed overly partial to controversial movements, the attack on 'cult apologists' has been building up for some time (Horowitz 1983). In 1982 an eminent psychiatrist and 'brainwashing expert' denounced the 'many apologists for the cults':

> These apologists, whose motivations are varius or mixed, undoubtedly contribute to the veneer of respectability behind which strange and ugly things are happening. Some of the apologists appear to be romantics, projecting into the cults some of their own hopes for religious reform, spiritual rebirth, a rejection of materialism, or even escape from the dangers of the thermonuclear age. Other apologists ... [believe that freedom of religion precludes countermeasures against cults] ... Still other apologists have been successfully gulled by charismatic cult leaders or their representatives ... (West 1982: 11)

Since it has recently become fashionable to evoke abuses of the McCarthy era such as blacklisting (Zablocki 1997) in discussing recent scholarly conflicts over cults, I will note that the above discourse seems to manifest at least some limited resemblance to the 'McCarthyite' rhetoric of the 1950s in which 'fellow travellers,' 'Communist sympathizers' and 'well-meaning dupes' were identified as fronting for sinister American Stalinism. The premise is that the evil of a certain movement (or movements) is so palpable and unambiguous that no tolerance or defence (even if seemingly disinterested) of the demonic malefactors can possibly be legitimate. Perspectives on the miscreants which fall short of the standards of Cassandra must thus be explained in terms of guilty collaboration, foolish romanticism, misguided idealism, gullibility, extremist First Amendment absolutism or scholarly opportunism.[1]

However, the 'other side' has played somewhat similar games. As a long-time 'cult apologist,' I recall how my colleagues and I have often sought to explain the crusade against cults in terms of the presence in the crusading ranks of clergy who could be said to be retaliating against upstart competitors, therapists, and clinicians who also see gurus as competitors (and, moreover, see career opportunities in the rehabilitation of ex-devotees), self-justifying apostates, etc. (e.g., Robbins 1984; Robbins and Anthony 1979, 1982). The assumption seemed to be that some special and probably invidious reason had to underlie hostility to certain innovative religious movements. We wished to deny that the religious groups themselves could be at least partly responsible for eliciting such animosity through actual abuses.

To some extent Dr West has a point when he claims that 'strange and ugly things are happening' in some alternative religions. In a recent essay, 'Religious Movements and Violence,' the present writer noted, 'it is worth keeping in mind that authoritarian sects with messianic leadership are likely to have some sort of problematic underside ... reflecting a lack of accountability and other factors' (Robbins 1997: 23). Such groups tend to have a small membership base and therefore may need to elicit financing from the general public, which is likely to be effected through methods such as street solicitation or commercial enterprises which are more questionable and legally precarious than internal membership funding. Messianic sects are unlikely to survive unless high levels of commitment and solidarity are cultivated such that a small, disciplined 'Gideon's army' substitutes for a larger, more flaccid mass membership. In this context no free riders or limited-liability investors should apply, and dissidents, independent thinkers, and potential rival leaders may also not be welcome. But the necessarily somewhat manipulative indoctrinational techniques for building and maintaining strong commitment will be readily labelled 'brainwashing' and 'mind control' by critics. The anticult rhetoric of mind control is, in this writer's view, overblown. Still, intensive indoctrination, strong solidarity, plus the close-knit and relatively isolated nature of some authoritarian sects do facilitate the crystallizing and consolidating of an institutional 'separate reality' in which the ethical orientation of group members may diverge significantly from the prevailing norms of the society. Thus, 'as the commitment of members increases, along with their investment of time and money, their sense of responsibility is defined increasingly by the overall religious authority of the group rather than by any values they may have previously entertained' (Pye 1996: 265). This effect can facilitate violence or other kinds of deviant behavior, particularly as it interfaces with the intrinsic precariousness and volatility of charismatic leadership (Robbins and Anthony 1995; Wallis and Bruce 1986).

The above considerations do not, in my view, justify the intense antipathy of some writers towards 'cults' in general (and towards their 'apologists'), which in some quarters approaches the demonological. Some of the allegations against 'destructive cults' may be exaggerated; for example, the alleged 'overpowering of the will' of converts by brainwashing.[2] While apocalyptic worldviews and 'messianic' forms of authoritarian charismatic leadership may amount to 'risk factors' regarding the possibility of violence (Robbins and Anthony 1995; Robbins and Palmer 1997), the majority of unconventional religious movements which possess these and other risk factors have not evinced violent (homicidal or suicidal) tendencies. The non-violent majority even includes some highly excoriated and notorious 'destructive cults.' There is also the problem of evaluating the impact of environmental hostility and persecution, and thus of weighing the relative significance of 'endogenous' and 'exogenous' factors contributing to catastrophic, violent outcomes (Hall and Schuyler 1998; Kaplan 1997; Robbins 1997; Robbins and Anthony 1995). The sexual seduction and exploitation of devotees by gurus and other leaders of esoteric groups is unfortunately rather common,[3] but the same might be said with respect to conventional churches. This parallelism can also be seen respecting the horror of child molestation, which, however, is allegedly becoming semi-institutionalized as the most promising area for attacking cults (Richardson 1999). In short, *ambiguity* pervades controversies over cults, which is why *objectivity*, although it can never be fully actualized, is so important, and why a crusading and absolutist 'countersubversive' orientation is as inimical to the responsibility of professional scholars as is a blatant apologetic or whitewashing proclivity.

It has been stated that many or most highly authoritarian sects may be expected to have some sort of negative underside. But this does not mean that any group is guilty of *all* charges which someone might level against it; for example, David Koresh sexually exploited minors in his sect, but the violence at Waco was not exclusively his responsibility (Wright 1995). Actual abuses and transgressions notwithstanding, the odds are generally weighted against 'cults' in the courts of popular and media opinion. There may be several reasons for this, but I think one of these is that the cognitive rigidity, intolerance of ambiguity, and tendency to see things in black and white, which have been said to pertain to the 'cult indoctrinee syndrome' (Delgado 1977), may actually represent a broader characteristic of the general population, which does not easily perceive notorious groups as complex and ambiguous entities or perceive highly emotional issues as involving shades of grey. It is suggested here that the initial response of the public to controversies over excoriated cults (or other stigmatized groups) might be said to be totalistic, in the sense that it is initially assumed that one of two things is likely to be true: either a particular embattled group (or a broader category of such groups) is innocent of all claims against it, such that the latter are largely malicious or bigoted, or else smoke must denote fire, and practically all damaging allegations are more or less valid. But this preliminary dualism or totalism tends to work against controversial alternative religions. It is not terribly difficult to discover that there are at least some questionable or objectionable elements (even aside from provocative beliefs) in the past or current operations of groups such as the Unification Church, the Church of Scientology, The Family, or the Church Universal and Triumphant. Thus the total innocence and martyred purity option is quickly discarded, and, one polarity having been rejected, the other now looms attractive. All claims against controversial and esoteric groups may subsequently tend to be *viewed as presumptively valid*. This predilection, however, may not arise from initial hostility. From our perspective, what might be desirable is not greater 'pro-cult' attitudes so much as an enhanced *sensitivity to ambiguity*.

Origins of Intense Scholarly Partisanship and Recrimination

As we have seen, considerable animosity seems to raise its head as scholars on different 'sides' of the 'cult wars' accuse each other of bias, manipulation, corruption, and irresponsible gullibility. 'Inter-expert' hostility even led to two civil suits in the 1990s in which a sociologist and a clinical psychologist, who regularly testified against religiotherapeutic movements and their leaders in civil suits, unsuccessfully sued a number of scholars known to be defenders of cults, plus two large scholarly associations. The high level of inter-expert hostility in cult controversies may be related to a number of factors, including the circumstances under which some sociologists of religion and religious-studies scholars initially became involved in defending heterodox religious movements from perceived persecution in the 1970s.

In the early years of the cult wars the major legal and policy issue appeared to involve *coercive deprogramming* (Bromley and Robbins 1993). Many scholars were shocked that young adult devotees of new movements were actually being physically seized and held captive for re-education. While most abductive deprogrammings were extra-legal in the sense that they did not proceed under explicit court orders, they were very difficult to prosecute or deter through civil suits brought by unsuccessfully deprogrammed escapees from captivity. Defences of necessity and 'choice of evils' often appeared persuasive. However, a significant number of physically coercive episodes were sanctioned explicitly by conservatorship and guardianship orders issued to the parents of adult converts by local judges. The latter accepted the views of clinical 'experts,' who, in support of relatives seeking to have their adult children seized or to justify prior extra-legal abductions, informed the courts that the rights of abducted ('rescued') devotees were not really being violated because their capacity to exercise free-dom had been destroyed by overpowering psychological conditioning within cults producing depersonalization, dissociation, infantile regression, and so on. What might appear to the untrained eye of an observer lacking in 'cult awareness' to be an outrageous, physically coercive imposition on movement participants was said to amount in reality to a salutary liberation from cultic slavery and a restoration of mental and moral autonomy (Delgado 1977).

Many students of religion were deeply disturbed by the use of blatant, tangible physical coercion to redress alleged (and surely somewhat ambiguous) 'psychological coercion.' They apprehended a persecutory potential implicit in treating traditional sectarian and revivalist spiritual intensity (including intolerance, dogmatism, and authoritarianism) as a medical and psychopathology issue calling for forcible confinement. They foresaw an undermining of religious liberty and the emergence of an inquisitorial process (Coleman 1985; Richard-son 1982; Robbins 1979; Robbins and Anthony 1982; Shapiro 1978; Shepherd 1982).

On the other hand, the parents of converts and their allies among mental health professionals and concerned citizens were shocked and outraged that their righteous efforts to rescue brainwashed 'cult slaves' and to punish seemingly vicious and deceptive organizations through criminal prosecutions and civil actions (often involving novel crimes and torts such as 'menticide,' 'psychological kidnapping,' false impris-onment via mind control, etc.) were sometimes frustrated due to the intervention of scholars whose testimony in courtrooms and legislative committees appeared to confer respectability on sinister and danger-ous groups. Such 'experts' were viewed by crusaders against cults as sleazy fellow travellers, duplicitous agents, or naive, well-meaning dupes (West 1982, 1990). Thus the ongoing dispute over alleged cultic brainwashing largely originated in the intensely emotional and dra-matic controversy over *who were the real kidnappers*: cult indoctrinators or abductive deprogrammers (Allen 1998; Robbins 1998)? 'Experts' on each side were perceived on the other side as ethical delinquents pandering to sinister and destructive forces.

The Cult of Expertise

If the controversy over cults and brainwashing is uniquely heated because of its origins in the emotional deprogramming/kidnapping issue, some other factors appear to operate to polarize numerous controversies and policy disputes in modern American society, especially cult controversies. Among these factors is the modernist conviction that these issues have a significant scientific and technical quality and are thus susceptible to arbitration by putatively objective experts. This scientistic 'cult of expertise' has become rather incongruously superimposed on a basic *adversarial* system of law and government. The result of this combination is continual politicization and polarization of ubiquitous expertise.

There is a continual tension in American legal and policy realms between *advocacy* and *objectivity*. This tension is particularly conspicuous as it relates to what we term the American *cult of expertise*. It is difficult these days for an advocate to carry any point in either a legal or policy context without an auxiliary support structure of 'experts' whose putatively objective and 'scientific' expertise is marshalled in support of a litigating or lobbying client. The 'cult wars' afford an example of the dependence of legal and policy advocacy on specialized expertise and its mystique, but there are several other recent examples. In many cases and issues, expertise appears to be conspicuously polarized and partisan, and there is mutual denigration of experts with opposing views.

In 1997 a particularly raucous battle of the experts erupted in connection with the sensational trial in Boston of the British nanny accused of second-degree murder in connection with the death of a child in her care. Experts testifying for both the prosecution and the defence elicited fervent critics and defenders, many of whom were themselves medical or scientific personnel. Sympathizers with defense or prosecution experts labeled the views of opposing experts 'junk science' such that both sets of expert witnesses were explicitly attacked in this manner.

In the broader realm of policy advocacy and public opinion, a spirited battle of experts currently rages with respect to estimations of the imminence, seriousness, causes, and appropriate remediation of the 'global warming' which is said to threaten the quality of life on the planet and which supposedly is associated with massive consumption of fossil fuels. Experts on one side are accused, in effect, of becoming whores kept by wealthy corporations that want to escape the costs of curtailing the use of fossil fuels, while advocates and experts supporting the global warming thesis are excoriated for sacrificing objectivity and scientific standards on behalf of environmentalist zealotry and quasi-religious visions of apocalypse.

As we have noted, scholars defending cults are often denigrated as 'cult apologists' responding to some combination of naive romanticism and self-serving opportunism. Likewise 'anticult' experts are viewed by their opponents (e.g., Anthony 1990) as bigots and crusading demonologists who are sometimes involved in absolutist countersubversive ideologies and possess latent prejudices against religious diversity or against non-rational faith claims. Our adversarial legal system may encourage such (sometimes inflammatory and distorted) attacks on scholars and scientists, but it also may create conditions under which there is likely to be some truth to these impassioned criticisms.

In the context of the cult of expertise, it is possible for persons with scholarly or scientific credentials to carve out lucrative careers as 'professional witnesses,' lobbyists, or expert consultants to various advocates and entities embroiled in adversarial processes in law and government. Rewards may involve money as well as media attention and public name recognition. Ideological commitment and commitment to remunerative career enhancement will often reinforce each other, such that many experts will become consistently associated with one 'side' of a controversial issue and will develop persisting connections with interested parties. Acrimony increases as such experts become stigmatized as either blind and narrow partisans or mercenary opportunists and hired guns. Acrimony and polarization is further enhanced by the tendency for experts 'performing' in courtrooms to allow their testimony to be shaped by the requirements of the legal situation as communicated to them by lawyers. Aside from the possibility of out-and-out mendacity, this tendency surely results in cruder and more extreme and exaggerated claims.

To take one example, legal defenses for coercive deprogramming as well as certain kinds of civil suits by ex-devotees against cults and their leaders often require that responsibility for the sustained involvement of a 'cult victim' in a formally voluntary association be treated as belonging *entirely* to the manipulative practitioners of cultic mind control. Experts appearing on behalf of either plaintiffs against cults or defendants accused of coercive abduction of a convert will duly testify about the cult victim's 'overwhelmed will' and coercively induced severe incapacity. Anthony (1990), a critic of such testimony, maintains that such theories are too extreme to be plausible with regard to almost all formally voluntary associations, although some of the latter might be analysed meaningfully in terms of somewhat more moderate notions of manipulative social influence in social movements.[4] The latter approaches, however, would not meet the legal requirements of certain civil causes of action or legal defences. Legal imperatives necessitate cruder and more sensational theories which affirm clear causal sequences. Experts who affirm extreme theories in court often write more moderately in professional journals and conference papers. However, experts appearing in court will be speaking to a lay audience. The need to simplify and frame propositions in terms which are understandable to laypersons will tend to enhance the crudity and the extremism of assertions. It has been frequently alleged that irresponsible expert witnesses will make assertions in courtrooms which they would not dare make in a reputable scholarly journal or in front of a scholarly audience.

The mystique of decisive specialized expertise combines with the overall adversarial context of legal and policy debates in the United States to create distortions of discourse and to seduce engaged scholarly and scientific experts into ethical lapses. Ethical norms, however, are not easily imposed on experts' courtroom performances under the present system (Shuman and Greenberg 1998).

The polarization and politicization of expertise in the area of potentially violent religious movements is reflected in the otherwise highly praiseworthy effort by some religious-studies scholars to cultivate a connection with the FBI for the purpose of 'educating' the latter and thus hopefully preventing 'another Waco' (Rosenfeld 1997). My colleagues currently compete with anticultists for the attention of the bureau, each scholarly faction hoping to become the favored experts who will be consulted when the next dangerous confrontation erupts. The feds, it appears, cannot be expected to act appropriately in potentially violent situations unless they comprehend the nature of millennialist religion, one set of scholars proclaims. According to their competitors, it is the sinister dynamics of 'destructive cultism' which must be understood.

The Double Standard

One thing which becomes clear upon considering the role of experts in this area and in associated problems of objectivity is the pervasiveness of *double standards* employed in the evaluation of experts and their contributions. It is currently more reputable to be a scientific expert testifying or crusading against tobacco companies than to be an expert mobilized in their defence. Nevertheless, the apparent past duplicity of these corporations notwithstanding, there still may be a few telling points which might be ventured on behalf of the contentions of tobacco moguls; for example, is the addictiveness of nicotine really equivalent to that of heroin or cocaine? Similarly, it is also now perceived as substantially more legitimate to be a scholar who is exposing the ravages and depredations of cults than one who is supporting such groups against alleged persecution and countering the claims of their critics. Recent catastrophic events in Waco, Japan, southern California, and other places is likely to intensify this effect. Nevertheless, the issues entailed in cult controversies are not always black and white. One-sided, prejudicial climates of public opinion discourage the perception of ambiguities which might otherwise be seen to surround certain issues. Objectivity is inhibited by hegemonic demonology.

The notion of 'objectivity' is not without its own ambiguities and is only with difficulty applied in the area of religion, particularly as the latter increasingly becomes an object of controversy (Robbins and Robertson 1991). Objectivity naturally becomes highly precarious when controversy rages, hurts go deep, and feelings become inflamed. In this context a kind of ambivalence about objectivity may emerge. Lapses of objectivity on the part of investigators who are perceived as sympathizing with rotten miscreants are deplored, while any departure from objectivity associated with demonological or countersubversive approaches is either ignored or somehow not perceived. In any case, objectivity in the sense of *neutrality* often does not appear to be considered mandatory in order to legitimate the status of an 'expert' on disvalued groups. There are definitely some current models for legitimate activist expertise in the realm of controversial social movements.

Consider the hated KKK. Who are popularly considered to be the legitimate experts on the Ku Klux Klan? Is it not researchers such as the crusading lawyer Morris Dees and persons associated with organizations such as Klanwatch and the Southern Poverty Law Center? Is not the Anti-Defamation League (ADL) widely viewed as a legitimate – perhaps the premier – source of expertise on authoritarian racist, anti-Semite, and neofascist groups? Similarly, the media has long conferred the mantle of helpful-expertise-on-behalf-of-the public-interest on (anticult) 'cultwatchers' and 'cult experts,' and particularly persons associated with the former Cult Awareness Network (CAN). Scholars who have been critical of CAN and anticult constructions of reality are often labeled 'cult apologists.' This labelling game is at least slightly reminiscent of the 1950s when critics of certain anticommunist programs were called Communist sympathizers (comsymps) or 'well-meaning dupes.' The underlying dynamic entails the widespread perception that certain groups represent *known malefactors*, miscreants, and public enemies. In this context crusading activists denouncing these groups become generally accepted as the authentic and more or less exclusive repositories of legitimate, objective expertise. Investigators with divergent perspectives are shunted aside as naive and fatuous, and may even be branded subversive and treated as suspect!

An illustration of this phenomenon may be afforded by the declining status of the 'Old China Hands' (experts in East Asian studies) in the late 1940s and early 1950s. In the context of the emerging Cold War (and the eruption of a bloody 'hot war' in Korea) a number of Old China Hands experienced a decline in their academic prestige and a loss of their positions and/or influence with the State Department. Their sin was to be insufficiently alarmist about the threat of Maoist totalitarianism and unduly critical of the corrupt (but anticommunist) nationalist regime of Chiang Kai-shek. A rigidly one-sided climate of opinion crystallized, which limited diplomatic options.[5] Will today's excoriated cult apologists go the way of the Old China Hands?

Are crusading, countersubversive experts on alternative religions objective? Are they accurate? Jeffrey Kaplan has noted that public information on cults and 'hate groups' often seems to be controlled by antagonistic 'watchdog' groups such as the ADL or CAN, which can actually develop strange symbiotic relationships with the stigmatized movements they monitor (Kaplan 1997). Exaggerations or worst-case scenarios purveyed by the watchdogs with respect to extremist groups often tend for various reasons to become self-fulfilling prophecies. Hence the importance of not allowing watchdog and countersubversive submissions to totally dominate public and scholarly opinion even with respect to generally discreditable groups. It is also worthwhile to note the subjectivity of the clinical methods employed by critics of induced psychopathology in cults. Psychotherapy itself is very much a *persuasive* enterprise, which has even been compared to thought reform (Frank 1961; Coleman 1985). Some counsellors and therapists will elicit information from a devotee or former devotee regarding life within a controversial movement while concurrently revealing to the counselee the *real* nature of his or her involvement in the group and the underlying, insidious reality of mind control, enslavement, ego destruction, and so on. The accounts of ex-devotee subjects who have been involved in such persuasive therapeutic relationships are then treated as data. The persuasive clinician may subsequently appear as a remunerated expert witness in the ex-devotee's civil suit against the group for 'intentional infliction of emotional distress,' and so on (Malony 1987). Some 'experts' are engaged so frequently in litigation sequences as to be plausibly designated professional witnesses.

Dilemmas of Objectivity and Partisanship

Ethically dubious behaviour and departures from objectivity can be found 'on both sides of the line.' But *Tu Quoque* is not an adequate defense for overly partisan scholars. The study of alternative religions is now deplorably politicized, and we 'cult apologists' bear some of the responsibility. It has been noted that strong feelings arose among some scholars when 'brainwashing' notions were used to justify shocking abductions and coercive deprogrammings. As noted by the writer over a decade ago, the scholarly reaction to deprogramming 'has probably distorted scholarly discourse and pushed scholars ... into downplaying manipulative and coercive elements in some movements' (Robbins 1988: 73). But neither these strong feelings nor the haunting spectre of persecution, or even the state suppression of unpopular sects, can justify a partisan engagement that sacrifices objectivity, any more than concern for the way in which some exploitative groups ravage the lives of members – and the way some leaders manipulate followers – can justify a narrow, one-sided countersubversive approach.

The late religious studies scholar Barbara Hargrove pointed out some time ago that the concentration by scholars on the controversial aspects of movements such as the Unification Church, whether writing in a prosecutorial or defensive mode, has had reductive consequences. The quality of scholarship suffers when studying a movement such as the Unification Church or Scientology becomes a *political act*. She noted that most studies of the UC in the 1970s 'tended to be less studies of the group as a religion than of the civil liberties of their members, whether in terms of loss of freedom to an authoritarian leader or of rights to free choice of religion thwarted by deprogrammers' (Hargrove 1982: 212).[6] Extrapolating Hargrove's point, the present writer has noted that in the current politicized climate, 'the Unification Church is "reduced" to its "coercive" indoctrination processes or its right-wingedness or even to its "persecuted" status' (Robbins 1988: 201). However, 'the purpose of social scientific research should not be to defend or criticize but to describe and explain social phenomena' (Balch and Langdon 1998: 207).

Since the early impassioned conflicts over deprogramming, liaisons between scholars and cults have expanded and become diversified. Abuses have crept in. Benjamin Zablocki (1997) has critically evaluated the tendency for scholars associated with the 'scientific study of religion' and the sociology of religion to close ranks protectively in support of movements facing million-dollar civil suits related to claims of brainwashing, and thus to exclude by fiat the latter conjecture and discriminate against its adherents. Dr Zablocki may have a valid point, but his overheated blacklisting metaphor notwithstanding, the *Journal for the Scientific Study of Religion* did not become the *Red Channels* of the 1980s.[7]

Sympathetic researchers sometimes appear to assume that a stigmatized and arguably persecuted religious movement is somehow more virtuous, straightforward, and above-board than groups in general. Citing Goffman (1958), Balch and Langdon (1998: 207) note that 'virtually all groups have secrets to hide. Police officers band together to protect each other from charges of brutality and corruption; academic departments soft-pedal rumors of infighting during accreditation reviews; and family members stop arguing when neighbors come to visit.' The authors suggest that 'the study of religious movements could profit immensely from research designs that combine traditional sociological methods with the model of investigative journalism' (Balch and Langdon 1998: 193). This is an excellent suggestion, but the model of journalism may simplify the epistemology of 'facts.' Some issues, such as 'mind control,' may be complicated and conceptually subtle. Because an investigative reporter exposes certain manipulative procedures in a group may not necessarily mean that the followers have lost their capacity to make decisions and exercise autonomy.

Some scholars have been accused of taking money from cults to support their research. It probably should be a general norm that sources of financial support should always be *disclosed*, even if the double standard leads to a one-sided stigmatization of researchers with controversial associations. This may be unfortunate, since moral entrepreneurial zealots and their movements may be just as partisan as the controversial religious movements or cigarette companies they attack. It is also unfortunate as well as misleading that an exaggerated mythology may now be developing about vast funds flowing from cultic coffers into the scholarly study of religious movements. Traditionally, research in the sociology of religion has often been funded by churches. Zablocki (1997) suggests that funding from controversial cults should not be treated the same way as subventions from the Methodist or the Episcopal Church. But *where precisely should the line be drawn?* For example, how about support from Jehovah's Witnesses, Mormons, Bahai, a fringe Pentecostal fellowship, or a televangelical ministry? Disclosure would allow the consumers of studies to make their own judgments even if some take a narrow, censorious attitude or adhere to a politically correct double standard.

It has also been suggested that some studies have been more or less designed to defend or whitewash an embattled group, and have been carried out in such a way as to avoid any engagement with a group's 'underside' (Balch and Langdon 1998). Shoddy research intended from the outset to exculpate (or indict) a particular group will probably ultimately discredit the researchers. Nevertheless, students of religious movements may face a credibility problem related to what has been called the 'philomanderin' (or pro-scholarly) pose affected by some religious movements, who play up to scholars of religion and eagerly solicit (and may seek to guide) research on their communities (Robbins and Robertson 1991). In some cases, religious institutions which invited or funded studies may actually have been carefully precluded from interfering with the actual process of the study and thus influencing the findings. However, the mere *appearance* of a cozy collaboration of scholars with controversial movements reputed to be highly manipulative may be damning in the eyes of many observers and consumers of scholarship. Certain groups such as INFORM in the United Kingdom and AWARE in the United States, which attempt to mediate disputes between alternative religions and the anxious friends and relatives of devotees, have been denounced as puppets of objectionable cults. This writer is not sufficiently knowledgeable to definitively adjudicate these disputes, although I have great admiration for Eileen Barker, the founder of INFORM. In our view, there is a need for such mediating groups, which, however, will not maintain credibility if they are seen to be controlled by or dependent on controversial groups.

In any case, there will continue to be many difficult ethical dilemmas arising in the study of controversial religious movements. It is a reflection of the polarization and politicization which infects this area that partisan (or 'committed') scholars may actually end up becoming gatekeepers with regard to research opportunities for other scholars. They may control access to research subjects and data. Thus some devotees of a particular group may only cooperate with a researcher whose sympathy or fairness is certified by leaders of the group, while some ex-devotees who are involved in supportive networks may only participate in a study when its appropriate character and auspices can be vouched for by certain counsellors trusted and admired by ex-member support groups. What then is the ethical responsibility of a researcher who has good relations with a controversial or close-knit group and *fears that some other researcher who wants to study them might end up writing about the group very negatively or even testifying against them in court*? Should the first researcher warn the group about the second researcher and thus torpedo the latter's research? Should a researcher sacrifice his credibility with a controversial group by not alerting them to the agenda or bias of another scholar? These are not easy questions to answer. Some projects may appear conceptually or methodologically 'loaded,' such that subjects would be participating in research which would inevitably defame them or their group or subject them through the process of the study to attacks on their group and their beliefs. Research projects in which groups with sharply conflicting values are both participating may prove difficult to organize; moreover, the responsibility for a breakdown may not be exclusively associated with one party. There may not be easy answers and prescriptions in this area.

Objectivity and Commitment

Ultimately the meaning of *objectivity* is the underlying issue which must be probed. To what degree are objectivity and deep commitment (e.g., to freedom of religion or against mind control and exploitation) compatible? Is it improper for the citizen and scientist to exist in the same body, and must the total personality of the scholar become fragmented into 'objective' and 'subjective' components, even in situations in which a basic value such as religious liberty is under attack?

To some extent the answer must be yes. When a scholar declines to manufacture false data which would help the 'cause,' or when he or she straightforwardly reports data regardless of the impact of disclosure on ideological conflicts, the scholar is properly subordinating his religiopolitical value commitments to the regulation of norms of scholarly objectivity and integrity. But in a broader context it does not appear dishonourable per se for 'critical' schools of thought (such as the Frankfurt School of sociology) to dedicate their scholarship to the critical analysis of a sinister movement or a tendency such as fascism or racism. Of course it will generally be debatable as to which party embodies or is analogous to the spectre of 'fascism' in a particular situation; for example, one in which an authoritarian and reputedly highly manipulative 'cult' is faced with becoming the object of repressive regulatory measures which arguably undermine religious liberty.

As we have suggested above, a controversy has developed regarding sponsorship of research by controversial cults. More heat than light has so far been produced. Several considerations need to be kept in mind. All sorts of institutions such as corporations and public agencies routinely hire social scientists for various purposes. The American Sociological Association recognizes a sub-area of applied sociology, and has been considering certification procedures. Psychologists are particularly ubiquitous in applied practice. I can envision a sociologist, psychologist, or student of religion being hired by esoteric groups to help them revise their practices to meet cultural norms and avoid being subject to certain kinds of stigmatization. The sociology of religion has traditionally been subsidized by churches, and, owing to the relative absence of social programs and policies in the area of religion, it might not have survived if government or other 'neutral' entities were considered to be the exclusive legitimate supporters of research on religion (or controversial religion) as proposed by Horowitz (1983). Large churches, such as the Catholic and the Mormon, have legions of in-house scholars which they support. The supposed qualitative difference between the Methodist Church and the Unificationist Church subsidizing scholarship needs to be considered more thoughtfully and articulated more clearly. Even if a policy of 'Methodists *si*, Moonies *no*' is agreed upon, where should the cutting point be? What about Jehovah's Witnesses (currently embattled in France), Mormons, or Bahai?

It is worth noting that a piece of research should not be discredited and dismissed simply because an ideological involvement or 'bias' on the part of the researcher has been discerned, or because of research funding. It is definitely necessary for the critic to actually pinpoint flaws or dubious manipulations in the scholar's methodology and handling of data to make his case. Too often the allegations of bias and expressive commitment serve as a glib substitute for a careful critique of a study which has produced unwelcome conclusions.

At this point the issue of *credibility* must be considered. Rightly or wrongly, someone critically evaluating in 1952 the House Un-American Activities Committee or the work of Senator Joseph McCarthy would have faced a sizeable credibility problem if his or her research were known to be subsidized by the Communist Party. In the 1980s, however, the phenomenon of scholars contributing articles to volumes published by the Unification Church attained a substantial magnitude. Volume after volume appeared. At the very least the appearance was created of scholars maintaining a rather cosy relationship with a highly controversial movement. Assuming the legitimacy of scholars of religion defending freedom of religion, is their ability to defend a controversial movement's rights helped or hurt by a visibly close relationship with the reputedly hyper-manipulative group? The opportunities which the group provides for scholars to publish will probably suggest to suspicious minds the possibility of a quid pro quo.

Is the credibility issue merely a tactical concern? Much of the audience for scholarship in the social sciences presupposes that the scholar is a social scientist first and the fighter for religious freedom or against cultic authoritarianism only afterwards. If the audience loses faith in an expert's objectivity, it will not find him or her persuasive. Of course there are, as our earlier discussion has implied, reasons for doubting the objectivity of some polarized, policy-oriented experts. Yet scholars seeking to persuade the authorities necessarily present themselves as worshippers at the shrine of objectivity. Indeed experts on cults pay homage to this deity when they frequently accuse opposing experts of lacking objectivity (Allen 1998). Thus perspectives which place the ultimate value on commitment and recognize no overarching regulatory norms of objectivity are partly *furtive* orientations, at least with respect to public discourse. Should scholars have divergent public and private philosophies?

It has been stated above that more heat than light is being produced by recent attacks upon the ethics of cult apologists. Scholars are assailed for receiving support from noxious cults, but they have not been given a carefully thought-out statement regarding the conditions under which support can be accepted from which or what kinds of groups. In order to expose allegedly compromised scholars, documents are purloined and placed on the Internet, where they appear detached from their original context such that persons who did not create the document but might be named therein are inadvertently defamed. Both religious movements and their opponents have created numerous websites on the Internet where quantities of fervent testimonials or atrocity accounts are provided to investigators. As ready-made surrogates for interviews, these materials are extremely useful to writers, who are quickly presented with enough material to compose a short book. However, the material is relatively decontextualized; that is, the scholar or journalist doesn't know under what conditions the testimonials were produced or even whether each separate testimonial or account was composed by a separate individual. Polemical attacks on cults, cult apologists, and cult bashers are grounded increasingly in Internet 'research,' which increasingly may supplant traditional fieldwork.

Some of the criticisms of the alleged unethical behavior of cult apologists appear to crucify scholars on the cross of an austere and pristine standard of neutrality and detachment, which is generally ignored when unpopular cults or other politically incorrect entities are not under consideration. 'Women's studies,' notes Timothy Miller, 'is populated by persons of feminist conviction, and African-American studies is inseparable from an agenda of combating racism' (1998: 12). American sociology itself appears to have a nearly official agenda of opposing inequality, class domination, and racism. Where advocacy and engagement is the norm rather than the aberration, it behooves critics of apologists to recognize the predominance of double standards and the possibility that the implicit standards which they want to impose on academic supporters of the rights of religious movements are unrealistic if not hypocritical, and expressive of their own engagement. On their part, scholarly votaries of religious freedom and minority rights must recognize the pervasive power of ubiquitous double standards.

Errors of judgment may have lain some scholars open to attacks on their credibility. Nevertheless a large body of multigenerational scholarship on new religious movements exists, and there is at least a whiff of McCarthyism associated with a strategy of attempting to discredit existing scholarly research based on accusations about relationships of scholars to religious groups. As stated above, it is not a sufficient criticism of a scholar's work to simply point to a scholar's relationships and allege a bias. Thus the funding of tests of new medicines by pharmaceutical companies does not automatically discredit the findings though critics' eyebrows may be raised.

Recently a journalistic article (Allen 1998) on controversies over brainwashing referred (actually in the journal issue's table of contents) to 'cult-sponsored scholars' as if certain very eminent scholars referred to in the piece were wholly owned subsidiaries of Scientology or the Unification Church and could not publish or fund their work or gain tenure or promotion without the assistance or sponsorship of cults. In the text of her piece Ms Allen refers to 'cult-friendly' scholars; however, one of those she refers to has published a penetrating and revealing analysis of the financial practices of the Unification Church which did not please the church (Bromley 1985). The increasingly popular term 'cult apologist' implies that certain writers are *all-purpose supporters or defenders of cults*, which is generally a misleading premise. A number of scholars to whom that term has been applied have published implicitly critical pieces on groups whose rights they have defended (e.g., Anthony and Robbins 1978).

There seems to be more than a hint in Allen's (1998) piece that there is something dubious about being an expert witness in behalf of a cult in litigation, or attending a conference sponsored by such a movement. This chapter has criticized the 'cult of expertise' and the polarization and politicization of expertise which results from the combination of the exaggerated deference to scientific expertise with the underlying adversarial system which pervades law and government. Nevertheless one cannot simply assume that any expert witness for a controversial manipulative group must necessarily be either an unprincipled whore or an all-purpose sympathizer with the group or its creed. Partisan litigators, lobbyists, and policy groups do not always hire either unprincipled whores or 'kept' dependents or puppets; rather they may end up hiring highly principled, independent experts whose *known commitments* with regard to certain issues may render their testimony predictable and dependable. For example, it is usually not a secret which scientists are fervent about global warming or the perils of silicone implants and which experts are sceptical.

Ultimately the attack on 'cult-sponsored' and 'cult-friendly' scholars bears some resemblance to the earlier (1950s) attack on Communist sympathizers, or 'comsymps.' Both formulations share an underlying absolutism and flight from ambiguity. If it is assumed that a certain group is a totally wretched and vicious malefactor, which is probably the guilty party with regard to all conflicts in which it may be enmeshed, then any involvement with the group or support of it on the part of a non-member necessarily amounts to a species of corruption. But if more ambiguity is allowed, then it may be seen that it is not necessarily dishonorable to testify on behalf of or to support the claims of a flawed movement with some objectionable elements. Thus we return to our main theme: *the need to acknowledge ambiguity.*

Conclusion

The reader of this essay may have noted that it is pervaded to some degree by an analogy which may appear disconcerting, farfetched, or tedious. I refer to a comparison between contemporary controversies over deviant religious movements, or cults, and the anticommunist hysteria of the late 1940s and early 50s. My own objections to Dr Zablocki's use of the blacklisting metaphor notwithstanding, I think the analogy can be useful if it is not reduced to a simplistic, rhetorical assertion; for example, that alternative religions such as the Moonies are persecuted today as the 'Commies' and other leftists were persecuted earlier by McCarthyites. Although such a claim is not really wrong, it is incomplete when rhetorically posed. What is more significant is that a crucial ambiguity which pervaded the domestic hysteria of the early cold war bears some similarity to the ambiguity of the more recent cult wars.

It is ironic that the indictments proclaimed in the one-dimensional perspectives of countersubversive crusaders often contain substantial elements of truth, notwithstanding the deficiencies of such perspectives. Thus J. Edgar Hoover is definitely not this writer's idea of an objective expert on communism, yet arguably many party cadres were indeed the 'masters of deceit' he branded them (Hoover 1958). This should not, however, be taken as a recommendation for heavy-handed countersubversive perspectives which are blind to ambiguity, subtlety, and nuance, and restrict their empathy and compassion to one set of oppressed – for example, the victims of communist totalitarianism but not the victims of McCarthyism or the victims of authoritarian anti-communist regimes, or 'cult victims' and 'cult slaves' but not persons and groups deprived of freedom of religion or devotees compelled to sacrifice other rights (such as custody or visitation of children) as the cost of their exercising freedom of religion. Students of cult controversies should develop *pluralistic compassion* for victims on both 'sides.'

McCarthyism[8] threatened American civil liberties and reeked of unfairness and persecution. Yet some of the allegations by Hoover, Nixon, and even McCarthy against the 'Communist conspiracy' were true (Powers 1995). Similarly, some alternative religious movements have manifested disturbing elements as even staunch opponents of persecutions such as Barker (1989) have acknowledged and warned against. Indeed, it has been stated above and elsewhere by the author that highly authoritarian religious sects are likely to have some sort of 'problematic underside' (Robbins 1997) which is related ultimately to the absence of accountability and perhaps to the precariousness and volatility of charismatic leadership (Wallis and Bruce 1986). The underside of extreme authoritarian groups may feature any number of dubious items, including violence-prone volatility (not very frequent), quasi-totalitarian regimentation, sexual or material exploitation of members, manipulative indoctrination, severe denigration of outsiders, and so on. But not all of these elements are or ought to be legally proscribed or actionable. Moreover, groups which possess one or more of these features are not necessarily guilty of all claims which might be made against them (even objectionable groups can be slandered!). More importantly, groups perpetrating abuses or possessing objectionable attributes are not necessarily also characterized by the routinely involuntary participation of mind-raped 'cult slaves.' The followers of even intolerant, authoritarian, totalistic, and seemingly exploitative movements may nevertheless develop rewarding socioreligious experiences and feel spiritually fulfilled.

One deficiency associated with crusading countersubversive and demonological approaches, particularly in the area of cults, is a tendency to treat various objectionable or miscreant groups as more or less *interchangeable*. The Branch Davidians, the Solar Temple, Heaven's Gate, Jonestown, and others have become part of a litany of demonic groups which are implicitly equated with each other, notwithstanding the very different circumstances featured in their various violent actions. David Koresh, for example, did not engage in the terrorism (attacks on innocent, anonymous civilians) which characterized Aum Shinrikyo's subway gas episode; rather he (wrongly) defended his compound against a militarized assault by federal agents. Koresh may have a lot to answer for, but it should, in this writer's view, be possible to say certain things in his defence without signalling that one is a craven apologist bereft of objectivity. The recruitment patterns of certain groups such as the People's Temple or the Branch Davidians were unique and distinctive and did not conform to cult stereotypes involving lonely guys picked up in bus stations (Maaga 1998; Gallagher 2000). On the other hand, religious libertarians and 'cult apologists' may tend to see disparate groups as interchangeable 'victims.'

Countersubversive approaches also tend to equate groups which have not had violent episodes with notorious groups such as Heaven's Gate or Aum. The Unification Church, Scientology, the Branch Davidians, the Solar Temple, Aum ... they are all denounced as essentially interchangeable mind-controlling destructive cults. Some of the most excoriated groups such as Scientology or the Moonies have shown little propensity for actual violence. They are the usual suspects who are symbolically rounded up when an obscure group such as Heaven's Gate enacts mass mayhem.

In short, where religious movements are concerned *ambiguity abounds*, in part because of the subjective quality of spiritual experience and its rewards.[9] It is partly for this reason that extreme countersubversive and quasi-demonological perspectives which treat conversion to esoteric groups (or 'cultism') as a disease or epidemic (Conway and Siegelman 1978; West 1990) are not constructive.[10] Of course, something similar might be said about one-sided whitewashes and apologetics, which are, moreover, often conspicuously unpersuasive. Conspicuously naive or manipulative apologists will generally function as straw men whose easy refutation reinforces hegemonic proscriptions.

Since this writer's inclination is more towards the cult apologists than the 'cult bashers,' it seems appropriate to explain that the seeming one-sidedness of the former is often rooted in a deep anxiety over the spectre of persecution and the prospect that the United States, which was partly founded and built by heterodox and stigmatized religious groups (e.g., Puritans, Mormons), may be evolving into an overregulated, repressive society in which dynamic religious innovation is smothered by a thickening web of legal liability.[11] Thus Anthony and Robbins (1995) have asked whether the Second Great Awakening would have survived if wild and emotionally manipulative revivalists could have been sued for 'Intentional (or Negligent) Infliction of Emotional Distress' as easily as are contemporary gurus and high-pressure spiritual movements. In this writer's view, this may be a legitimate argument for tolerating at least some abuses. Nevertheless, this consideration must still be balanced by the acknowledgment that abuses in some groups may blight lives (or occasionally threaten public order), as well as by the recognition that while it may sometimes be appropriate to defend the rights of even abusive groups, this need not and should not entail 'gilding the lily,' in the sense of denying or inaccurately minimizing those excesses which have transpired.

Notes

1 A more recent article by the same Dr West contains a rather similar passage but adds the observation that 'The grateful cults have been known to reward them [scholarly apologists] with grants, awards, published praise, and even "research" opportunities' (1990: 134).

2 For critiques of theories of cultic brainwashing by the author and his colleague Dick Anthony, see Anthony (1990) and Anthony and Robbins (1992, 1994, 1995).

3 It is ironic that, according to Robert Balch, who is more or less the leading sociological authority on Heaven's Gate, sexual exploitation of participants did not characterize this notorious, suicidal community. The point is that crusading countersubversive perspectives tend to treat various objectionable or transgressive groups as *more or less interchangeable*, thereby implicitly equating transgressive groups such as the Branch Davidians with the worst possible groups (e.g., Aum Shinrikyo).

4 Anthony, it should be acknowledged, is himself an expert who works as a paid consultant to lawyers contending against claims of mind control.

5 One scholar, who may have been very left-leaning, was ludicrously attacked by Senator McCarthy as the 'top Russian espionage agent in the country' (Powers 1995: 242–4).

6 Hargrove (1982) argued that the scholarship on the UC which appeared in the 1970s was inferior to the John Lofland's pioneering 1966 study (Lofland 1977), and that the intense politicization of the research context was partly responsible.

7 *Red Channels* was a periodical published in the early 1950s by entrepreneurs who pandered to McCarthyism by listing the names of television entertainers with leftist backgrounds. Its exposés were crucial to the development of unacknowledged industry blacklists.

8 This term embraces not only themes and tactics associated with the controversial senator, but also excessive hysteria over domestic subversion in the half decade preceding the senator's initial splash in 1950. For differing evaluations of American Communism and the anticommunist crusades of the 1940s and 50s, see Powers (1995), and Shrecker (1997).

9 Space will not permit an extended philosophical inquiry into what are appropriate or non-arbitrary criteria for 'abuse' in close-knit movements. Do unconventional and unpopular social practices (e.g, 'free love,' arranged marriage, corporal punishment) qualify? Alienation of converts from their original families is a long-standing charge against cults. Yet the Gospels of Mark, Matthew and Luke contain various passages in which Jesus reveals to actual or would-be followers that the imperative of follow-ing the Messiah is greater than worldly filial and familial obligations. 'Jesus is not the champion of family life that his present day followers would have us believe' (Storrs 1997: 122). The social unconventionality of movements should not produce a decisive condemnation except with regard to certain particular practices, such as adult-child sexual interaction, which are almost universally condemned.

10 For comparisons between contemporary controversies over cults and past countersubversive agitation (e.g., against Mormons, Catholics, etc.) in American religious history, see Robbins and Anthony (1979) and Bromley and Shupe (1981).

11 Over two decades ago two anthropologists argued that proliferating eso-teric religious movements tended to manifest an entrepreneurial quality, partly in response to bureaucratic rigidity in dominant social institutions, which suppress innovation and flexibility. Religion had become 'the only place where social experimentation was possible. It is the folk answer to a system that is over-diplomatted, over-certified ... It is the last voice for decentralization and the free enterprise system' (Zaretsky and Leone 1974: xxxxi). See also Robbins and Bromley (1992).

References

Allen, Charlotte. 1998. 'Brainwashed: Scholars of Cults Accuse Each Other of Bad Faith.' *Lingua Franca* (Dec.–Jan.): 26–37.

Anthony, Dick. 1990. 'Religious Movements and Brainwashing Litigation: Evaluating Key Testimony.' In *In Gods We Trust: New Patterns of Religious Pluralism in America*. 2d ed. Edited by T. Robbins and D. Anthony. New Brunswick, N.J.: Transaction.

Anthony, Dick, and Thomas Robbins. 1978. 'The Effect of Detente on the Growth of New Religions: Reverend Moon and the Unification Church.' In *Understanding New Religions*, edited by J. Needleman and G. Baker. New York: Seabury.

- 1992. 'Law, Social Science and the "Brainwashing" Exception to the First Amendment.' *Behavioral Sciences and the Law* 10 (1): 5–27.
- 1994. 'Brainwashing and Totalitarian Influence.' In *The Encyclopedia of Human Behavior*. Vol. 1. San Diego, Calif.: Academic Press.
- 1995. 'Negligence, Coercion and the Protection of Religious Belief.' *Journal of Church and State* 37(3): 509–36.
- 1997. 'Religious.Totalism, Exemplary Dualism and the Waco Tragedy.' In *Millennium, Messiahs, and Mayhem*, edited by T. Robbins and S. Palmer. New York: Routledge.
Balch, Robert, and Stephan Langdon. 1998. 'How the Problem of Malfeasance Gets Overlooked in Studies of New Religious Movements.' In *Wolves within the Fold: Religious Leadership and Abuses of Power*, edited by A. Shupe. New Brunswick, N.J.: Rutgers.
Barker, Eileen. 1989. *New Religious Movements: A Practical Introduction*. London: Her Majesty's Stationery Office.
Beit-Hallahmi, Benjamin. 1997. 'Advocacy and Research in New Religious Movements.' Paper presented to the Annual Meeting of the Society for the Scientific Study of Religion. San Diego, November.
Bromley, David. 1985. 'Financing the Millennium: The Economic Structure of the Unificationist Movement.' *Journal for the Scientific Study of Religion* 24: 253–75.
Bromley, David, and Thomas Robbins. 1993. 'The Role of Government in Regulating New and Nonconventional Religions.' In *The Role of Government in Monitoring and Regulating Religion in Public Life*, edited by J. Wood and D. Davis. Waco, Tex.: Dawson Institute for Church State Studies.
Bromley, David, and Anson Shupe. 1981. *Strange Gods: The Great American Cult Hoax*. Boston: Beacon.
Coleman, Lee. 1985. 'Using Psychiatry to Fight "Cults": Three Case Histories.' In *Scientific Research on New Religions*, edited by B. Kilbourne. Proceedings of the Annual Meeting of the Pacific Division of the American Association for the Advancement of Science and the 59th Meeting of the Rocky Mountain Div. San Francisco: AAAS.
Conway, Flo, and Jim Siegelman. 1978. *Snapping: America's Epidemic of Mass Personality Change*. Philadelphia: Lippincott.
Delgado, Richard. 1977. 'Religious Totalism: Gentle and Ungentle Persuasion Under the First Amendment.' *So. California Law Review* 51: 1–99.
Frank, Jerome. 1961. *Persuasion and Healing*. Baltimore: John Hopkins Press.
Gallagher, Eugene. 2000. 'Theology Is Life and Death: David Koresh on

Violence.' In *Millennialism, Persecution and Violence: Historical Cases*, edited by Catherine Wessinger. Syracuse: Syracuse University Press.

Goffman, Erving. 1958. *The Presentation of Self in Everyday Life*. New York: Doubleday.

Hall, John and Philip Schuyler. 1998. 'Apostasy, Apocalypse and Religious Violence: An Exploratory Comparison of the Peoples Temple, the Branch Davidians and the Solar Temple.' In *The Role of Apostasy in Transforming Religious Movements*, edited by D. Bromley. Westport, Conn.: Praeger.

Hargrove, Barbara. 1982. 'On Studying the "Moonies" as a Political Act.' *Religious Studies Review* 8 (3): 1–4.

Hoover, J. Edgar. 1958. *Masters of Deceit*. New York: Henry Holt.

Horowitz, Irving. 1983. 'Universal Standards Not Uniform Beliefs: Further Reflections on Scientific Method and Religious Sponsors.' *Sociological Analysis* 44 (3): 179–82.

Introvigne, Massimo. 1998. 'Blacklisting or Greenlisting? A European Perspective on the New Cult Wars.' *Nova Religio* 2 (1): 16–23.

Kaplan, Jeffrey. 1997. *Radical Religions in America*. Syracuse: Syracuse University Press.

Kent, Steven, and Theresa Krebs. 1998. 'Academic Compromise in the Social Scientific Study of Alternative Religions.' *Nova Religio* 2 (1): 44–54.

Kilbourne, Brock, and James Richardson. 1984. 'Psychotherapy and New Religions in a Pluralistic Society.' *American Psychologist* 39 (3): 237–51.

Lofland, John. 1977 (1966). *Doomsday Cult: A Study of Conversion, Proselytization and Maintenance of Faith*. New York: Irvington.

Maaga, Mary. 1998. *Hearing the Voices of Jonestown*. Syracuse: Syracuse University Press.

Malony, H. Newton. 1987. 'Ethics of Psychologists' Reactions to New Religions.' Paper presented to the Annual Meetings of the American Psychological Association, New York, August.

Miller, Timothy. 1998. Introduction to the 'Symposium on Academic Integrity and the Study of New Religious Movements.' *Nova Religio* 2 (1): 8–16.

Powers, Richard. 1995. *Not Without Honor: The History of American Anti-Communism*. New York: Free Press.

Pye, Michael. 1996. 'Aum Shinrikyō: Can Religious Studies Cope?' *Religion* 26: 261–70.

Richardson, James. 1982. 'Conversion, Brainwashing and Deprogramming.' *The Center Magazine* (March/April): 18–24.

Richardson, James. 1999. 'Social Control of New Religions: From Brainwashing Claims to Child Abuse Accusations.' In *Children in New Religions*, edited by S. Palmer and C. Hardman. New Brunswick, N.J.: Rutgers University Press.

Robbins, Thomas. 1979. 'Cults and the Therapeutic State.' *Social Policy* (May/June): 42–6.

– 1984. 'Constructing Cultist "Mind Control."' *Sociological Analysis* 45 (3): 241–56.

– 1988. *Cults, Converts and Charisma*. London: Sage.

– 1997. 'Religious Movements and Violence: A Friendly Critique of the Interpretive Approach.' *Nova Religio* 1 (1): 13–29.

– 1998. 'Objectivity, Advocacy, and Animosity.' *Nova Religio* 2: 24–30.

Robbins, Thomas, and Dick Anthony. 1979. 'Cults, Brainwashing and Countersubversion.' *Annals of the American Association of Political and Social Science* 446 (November): 78–90.

– 1982. 'Deprogramming, Brainwashing and the Medicalization of New Religious Movements.' *Social Problems* 29 (3): 283–97.

– 1995. 'Sects and Violence: Factors Enhancing the Volatility of Marginal Religious Movements. In *Armageddon in Waco*, edited by S. Wright. Chicago: University of Chicago Press.

Robbins, Thomas, and David Bromley. 1992. 'Social Experimentation and the Significance of American New Religions: A Focused Review Essay.' In *Research in the Social Scientific Study of Religion*. Vol. 4. Edited by M. Lynn and D. Moberg. Greenwich, Conn.: JAI Press.

Robbins, Thomas, and Susan Palmer. 1997. 'Patterns of Contemporary Apocalypticism.' In *Millennium, Messiahs and Mayhem*, edited by T. Robbins and S. Palmer. New York: Routledge.

Robbins, Thomas, and Roland Robertson. 1991. 'Studying Religion Today: Controversiality and "Objectivity" in the Sociology of Religion.' *Religion* 21: 319–37.

Rosenfeld. Jean. 1997. 'The Importance of the Analysis of Religion in Avoiding Violent Outcomes: The Justus Freemen Crisis.' *Nova Religio* 1 (1): 72–95.

Schrecker, Ellen. 1997. *Many Are the Crimes: McCarthyism in America*. New York: Little, Brown.

Shapiro, Robert. 1978. 'Mind Control or Intensity of Faith: The Constitutional Protection of Religious Beliefs.' *Harvard Civil Rights–Civil Liberties Review* 13: 751–97.

Shepherd, William. 1982. 'The Prosecutor's Reach: Legal Issues Stemming from the New Religious Movements.' *Journal of the American Academy of Religion* 50 (2): 187–214.

Schuman, Donald, and Stuart Greenberg. 1998. 'The Role of Ethical Norms in the Admissibility of Expert Testimony.' *The Judges Journal* (winter): 5–9, 42–3.

Storrs, Anthony. 1997. *Feet of Clay: A Study of Gurus*. New York: Simon and Schuster (Free Press Paperbacks).

Twain, Mark. 1993. *Christian Science*. Buffalo, N.Y.: Prometheus.

Wallis, Roy, and Steven Bruce. 1986. 'Sex, Violence and Religion.' In *Sociological Theory, Religion and Collective Action*, edited by R. Wallis and S. Bruce. Belfast: Queens University.

West, Louis J. 1982. 'Contemporary Cults – Utopian Image, Infernal Reality.' *The Center Magazine* (March/April): 10–13.

– 1990. 'Persuasive Techniques in Contemporary Cults: A Public Health Approach.' *The Cultic Studies Journal* 7 (2): 126–49.

Wright, Stuart. 1995. *Armageddon at Waco*. Chicago: University of Chicago Press.

Zablocki, Benjamin. 1997. 'The Blacklisting of a Concept: The Strange History of the Brainwashing Conjecture.' *Nova Religio* 1 (1): 96–121.

Zaretsky, Irving, and Marc Leone. 1974 'The Common Foundation of Religious Diversity.' In *Religious Movements in Contemporary America*, edited by I. Zaretsky and M. Leone. Princeton: Princeton University Press.

3. Caught Up in the Cult Wars: Confessions of a Canadian Researcher

Susan J. Palmer

'It would seem, Dr Palmer, that you have acquired a bit of a reputation for being "soft on the cults". Are you indeed ... a cultlover?'

— High Solicitor

I was standing nervously in the carved oak witness box in the High Court, Lincoln's Inn in London, when the High Solicitor asked this question. It was in 1994, when I became embroiled in what the Children of God's lawyer described as 'the longest and second most expensive custody battle in the history of the British Empire.' I protested that I strove to be an objective, value-free social scientist when I studied new religions – but then admitted I also felt a sneaking aesthetic appreciation for 'the cults.' This made the judge smile, but it made me wonder – are the two approaches really incompatible?

As a mature researcher, somewhat scarred from my forays into that embattled terrain known as the cult wars, I am now ready to make a confession. I do see myself as a *connoisseur*. For me, NRMs are beautiful life forms, mysterious and pulsating with charisma. Each 'cult' is a mini-culture, a protocivilization. Prophets and heretics generate fantasy worlds that rival those of Philip K. Dick or L. Frank Baum. When I venture into the thickets of wild home-grown spirituality, and explore the rich undergrowth of what society rejects as its 'weed' religions, I sometimes think of Dorothy's adventures in *The Emerald City of Oz*. Dorothy follows the yellow brick road that leads her through Utensia, a city whose inhabitants are kitchen utensils. Managing to escape King

Kleaver (who threatens to chop her), she wanders into Bunbury where houses are made of crackers with bread-stick porches and wafer-shingles and are inhabited by living buns with currant eyes. She ventures on to meet the evil headless Scoodles, then continues on down the yellow brick road.

New religions are no less phantasmagorical. Immersed in the *Oz* books as a malingering schoolgirl, I wanted to 'have adventures' when I grew up. My wish came true. Today I find myself in the not-quite-respectable, morally problematic, and impecunious field of 'cult' studies. Travelling the 'yellow brick road' of social scientific research, I encounter oddly coherent worldviews constructed higgledy-piggledy out of the most incongruous elements: songs of Solomon, UFO lore, electric bulbs, biofeedback machines, gnostic creation myths – all welded into one seamless syncretism. I drop in on dreams of Utopia and discover quaint communes like Puritan villages, the brothers and sisters marching to a tasteful percussion of Bible-thumping. I have felt trapped in nightmares – racist compounds, parodies of Paradise, Nietzchean dystopias.

Each new religion I encounter evokes in me a sense of awe not unlike what my art historian mother feels when she beholds Greek ruins, German cathedrals, or Renaissance paintings. I see heretical religions as 'totems' or testaments – not necessarily of Ultimate Truth, but rather of the creative power of the collective human imagination. Their prophets I approach cautiously, and with respect, as artists of the most radically experimental sort: unpredictable conceptual artists at best, semi-opaque con artists at worst.

This approach seems to aggravate almost everybody; they find it frivolous, irresponsible. One Sufi lady at the Abode of the Messenger stopped me mid-interview and said accusingly, 'You're not *really* interested in the spiritual path. I get the impression you have more of a *literary* interest in what we're doing!'

Another time I was effervescing on the sheer *fun* of researching NRMs when a psychologist at a lunchtime lecture for the psychologists at the Montreal General Hospital interrupted: 'So I suppose you think it's fun and OK for groups like the Solar Temple to go around killing each other!' I was irritated, since I had just spent ten minutes explaining that each 'cult' is different, and statistics showed that only a tiny handful engaged in criminal acts, so I responded: 'You must excuse me, I prepared this talk for the doctors; I didn't realize that the psychiatric *patients* would be invited here as well.' I don't expect to be invited back.

When asked to define a cult, I explain that it is a baby religion. Personally, I find cults (and babies) attractive. Babies can be heartbreakingly adorable or intensely annoying, depending on the beholder's perspective – but also on the baby's mood and stage of development. So infant religions are not quite toilet-trained, like MOVE, a cult that annoyed neighbours by throwing garbage on the street; toddler NRMs, like the Rajneesh, run around naked in the park and knock over tea trays; and teenage missionary movements, like The Family, mooch off their parent society, refuse to get a job, and flaunt their pimply sexuality.

I have heard mothers excuse their obstreperous infants by saying, 'It's only a *phase* he's going through!' (teething, bed-wetting, screaming). NRMs also go through phases, shutting out the surrounding culture to form their own identity. NRM scholars may sound like over-indulgent mommies making excuses for their spoiled brats when they protest that communal experiments, sexual innovations, and apocalyptic expectations are merely developmental phases, and that society should grit its teeth and give these budding religions a chance to grow up.

Having confessed to singular tastes, perhaps I should explain how I got into 'cult studies.' My formal debut as a researcher of new religious movements commenced in the 1970s, when meditations – like 100 per cent cotton wear or silk – were Oriental imports, and most of my cool friends had already left for India to seek the right guru. At that time we were, of course, wary of false gurus who sold useless *sadhanas* (spiritual guidelines), or leched after American blondes, but the notion of the charismatic cult leader as obligatory pederast, oppressor of women, and designer of mass suicide had not yet been forged in the media.

Professor Fred Bird was my MA adviser at Concordia University when the department received a grant to study new religious movements in Montreal. I was one of four students hired as research assistants, and was actually paid $60 a week to choose a cult, spy on it, and write up field reports. When I look back on this period the word 'halcyon' comes to mind; we researchers were light-hearted and naive, fancying ourselves spiritual PIs. We swopped bizarre anecdotes about our chosen groups and boasted of mild vicarious spiritual highs. As young, counter-cultural types we could easily pass as typical spiritual seekers, and, indeed, that's what we were in our own wishy-washy ways.

Like many of my fellow scholars, I have been called a closet cultist.
Perhaps there *is* a grain of truth to this allegation, for although I have
never joined a group I've researched, I did start out hanging around
meditation centres as a spiritual seeker, and only ended up in the
microsociology of NRMs by default – as a failed meditator. I tried
many systems, but never got the hang of it. I realize, of course, that the
whole point is not to try to be 'good' at meditating ... but I kept trying.

So I began *doing* sociology of religion inadvertently, simply because I
was bored with trying to concentrate on my mantra or third eye.
Sitting in lotus posture at 4:00 a.m. on a scratchy grey woolen blanket in Swami Vishnu Devananda's quonset hut in Morin Heights, Quebec, I would peek around at my fellow meditators chanting
'AUMMMMMM,' and observe their subtle social interactions. Making
beds and washing sheets, understood as karma yoga, I would question
my fellow *chelas* regarding their conversions. At the visiting swamis'
evening lectures, I paid more attention to the jocular rivalry between
these shrewd old disciples of Swami Sivanada than I did to Hindu philosophy. Had I been able to make honest progress in my meditation
practice, I would perhaps be living happily in the Himalayas – probably in Swami Shyam's Canadian enclave in Kulu – celibate, sattvic
(pure), probably childless, my consciousness percolating up towards
my seventh chakra.

Researching NRMs has its pleasures. I meet delightful people. I hear
the intimate spiritual confessions of peaceful meditators, unselfish
communalists, and disciplined ascetics. But there are disadvantages to
taking on the public role of 'cult scholar.' Courted by the media as an
offbeat academic who represents the 'other view,' TV stations have
offered me free travel and luxurious sojourns in Canadian Pacific Rail-
way hotels; but then they edit my interview so I come across as a
caricature of a misguided civil libertarian. In anticult circles I am dismissed as a naive dupe, or a closet cultist. In France my name has been
listed with the other 'revisionists' who deny atrocities *dans les sectes*. As
for my Mormon relatives, they urge me to return to the fold lest I end
up in the 'telestial sphere.'

Many cults also look askance at me. Grossed out by the social-
scientific method and sick of a sociologist's depressingly secular scrutiny, leaders have denounced me to their disciples as a hireling of a
corrupt society. A Rajneesh therapist warned the other 'supermoms'
not to give me interviews because 'she's coming from her head, not
from her heart.' E.J. Gold (the gnostic guru whose declared mission is

'the education of the universe, one idiot at a time'), upon reading my MA thesis (about him), reportedly said, 'This lady has the consciousness of a rubber duck!' When I asked a barefoot missionary from the Free Daist Communion for an interview, she explained she must first collect all my writings and send them to Fiji to be vetted. 'Do you mean *Da Free John* is going to read my articles?' I asked, thrilled. 'Not exactly,' she replied. 'He *handles* them, and whatever wisdom they contain he absorbs through his fingertips.' Da Free John never got back to me.

Excluded from Black Hebrew assemblies as a 'leprous pale-eyed Amorite,' shunned by the Asatru (racialist Druids) for looking 'slightly jewish,' and dismissed by *les sectes Quebecois* as a *carré tête* (square-head or anglophone), I continue the struggle to present myself in such a way that my research attentions will be welcome. But what can be even more disconcerting is when I am beseiged by groups *overly eager* to be studied, and subjected to that special kind of 'love bombing' that is a product of what sociologist Roland Robertson dubbed philomandarin-ism: 'Susan, we just *love* you! You're so *beautiful* – and so *objective!*' Aside from that sticky feeling of entering a fly-trap, I can foresee the day when they will all turn on me. In fifty years or so, after achieving the status of minority churches with the assistance of the dull ethno-graphics of academics like myself who function as alkaline neutralizers of the more acid anticult/media reports, these once controversial cults will loose their church historians on me and my peers, and they will *condemn* our careful writings – all because we tried to include reason-able but unflinching explanations for their bad news, and neglected to indulge in what my Mormon relatives call 'faith-promoting incidents.'

Covert Researcher – or Closet Convert?

One obvious solution is to resort to covert research. When I first began to 'spy on cults' back in the 1970s, on Professor Fred Bird's research team, we four graduate students started out as strictly *covert*. We infil-trated our chosen groups, danced with sufis, hyperventilated with yogis, chanted with devotees. This created delicate dilemmas in eti-quette later on. Once we got together and designed our questionnaires and interview schedules, the prospect of unmasking our real selves as ambitious academics in front of our fellow-seekers-on-the-path was daunting, and threatened an embarrassing loss of face. All four stu-dents had by now *joined* their chosen groups and some had 'gone native.' Steve was initiated into TM and refused to reveal his mantra to

our team. Bill balked at handing out questionnaires to his fellow meditators in Integral Yoga, for he feared it would interfere with his spiritual path. Hugh had completely disappeared into a nine-week Arica
training seminar; he was *incommunicado* and had mumbled something
before he left about 'how my energy has moved beyond academia.'

We all got together after Hugh resurfaced in his new swashbuckling
persona as an Arican space cowboy, and wrote up a manifesto justifying the 'phenomenological' approach over the 'quantitative' method,
and confronted Professor Fred Bird. He threatened to fire us all and
replace us with more docile graduate students who were less spiritually squeamish. We backed down and crassly proceeded to hand out
questionnaires, thereby compromising our hard-won spiritual credentials.

Today, covert research is generally considered *extremely* unethical
and methodologically unsound. It is something investigative journalists did to the Moonies in the 1980s to expose their 'brainwashing'
methods. French reporters still do it to the Raelians, pointing hidden
cameras at rows of chubby nudists, so their photos can appear (eyes
blacked out), as they did in an article on *les sectes dangereuses* in
Echo Vedettes. Scholars criticize covert research as psychologically
unhealthy, morally compromising, potentially dangerous, and methodologically inefficacious, and yet ... I often find myself doing it still.
There is always that ambiguous stage when I stumble across a new
group and am trying to decide whether there is anything there worth
studying. It is less bother to simply show up at the meetings, thereby
placing oneself in the role of potential recruit rather than to formally
introduce oneself as a professor of religion (organized religion often
gets a bad reaction), or a teacher of a course titled Cults and Controversy (which sets off the 'we are not a cult' speech).

Now, when I decide to unmask my secular identity, I confront quite
a different reaction than I did as a sociology student. Since I am now
perceived as a professor who is open-minded and charitably inclined
towards religious minorities, I am relentlessly hustled to perform
dreary tasks: 'Can you write us a letter of recommendation?'; 'Can you
phone the Hindu professor at McGill and tell her to invite us to her
class?'; 'CNN is making an unflattering documentary about us. They
promised they would interview you if we gave them a list of our enemy
ex-members. Can you phone up the television station and tell them
how harmless and wonderful we are?'; 'Can you find out for us at
Dawson College how to organize free vegetarian cooking classes for

the students?' My position also allows me deeper access to information in some ways. I was able to interview the elusive Eugene Elbert Spriggs, founder of the Twelve Tribes movement, at dawn in the Basin Valley farm. The ex-nun who channels sexy angels let me sit in on her group therapy session for free, and I didn't even have to do their silly exercises. When I researched the Children of God, I met 'King Peter,' the successor of the late David Berg, who is normally *selah* (hidden), and he played me a tape of the reclusive Queen Maria's scratchy southern voice.

But in other ways my role as 'cult scholar' impedes my research. The wide range of strange groups I have investigated appear in my books, and some straitlaced groups assume I must be immoral to hang out with the Rajneeshees, the Raelians, and The Family, whom they perceive as sinners and sex maniacs. Others feel a little queasy about my overly tolerant attitude towards atheistic or 'heretical' groups who claim Jesus was a space alien, and wonder how I can bear to sit down and sup with a mystical pope or a vampire. I received a letter from a Krishna devotee complaining she felt 'quite nauseous' that her interview appeared in the same book as a Moonie. Several core-group leaders have expressed jealousy and feelings of abandonment – that since I stopped researching their community I have flitted off to some silly UFO group that even I must realize does not possess the Truth.

When I meet young graduate students researching NRMs today, I envy them their freedom, their naive enthusiasm, their straightforward, unpoliticized curiosity. I recall how effortless it used to be to blend into a following. Even after declaring oneself a researcher, the response was often, 'Oh well, you'll soon get over that!' I miss the intensity of real participant observation, the altered states, the gruelling ordeals I was subjected to!

I recall how, in the late 70s, I was among a group of neo-gnostics who jumped out of a van at 8:15 a.m. in front of a suburban supermarket. We all wore skin-tight grey leotards, transparent plastic gloves, grey bathing caps, bare feet (painted grey) – and shaved-off eyebrows! We formed a huddle around our core group leader, who instructed us that we were all 'hungry ghosts' and our mission was to enter the supermarket by following a customer through the revolving door – 'Make sure you touch nothing. If any part of your body makes contact with anything or anybody, go back outside immediately and start over.' Having fasted for three days we were hungry, but our exercise was to wander the aisles staring longingly at our favorite food, but to take nothing. After one hour we were meant to leave by shadowing a customer. We didn't last the hour, for one of the cashiers called the police. ('Who are all those weirdos?' we overheard the staff muttering. 'They look like a biker gang ... planning a robbery.') We leaped into the van and squealed off before the police arrived. We lay on the rusty floor, doubled up, holding onto each other as we lurched around corners, hysterical with laughter. The same group, a month before, had me crawling around a giant playpen wearing diapers, undershirt, and bonnet for an entire day, gurgling incoherently, sucking huge bottles of warm milk and playing with building blocks with my fellow 'babies.' Anticultists might be onto something when they claim an important stage of mind control is to 'humiliate the victim' by 'reinforcing childish behaviour.'

Today I am never invited to humiliate myself. I wear suits and shoulder pads and am taken on decorous tours, like visiting royalty. My eyebrows have grown in again, though they've never been quite the same!

Kai Erikson (1967: 373) has argued that 'it is unethical for a sociologist to deliberately misrepresent his identity for the purpose of entering a private domain to which he is not eligible; and second, that it is unethical for a sociologist to deliberately misrepresent the character of the research in which he is engaged.' I find it difficult *not* to misrepresent my identity, since most of my informants ignore my staunch protests that I am merely a dreary academic, a boring social scientist doing my job. They insist that, deep down, I am a lost soul desperately struggling towards the light. It is often counterproductive to protest *too* vigorously, so I just let them think I am on the brink of a conversion – and, indeed, part of me secretly hopes I *am* still capable of what C.S. Lewis called being 'surprised by joy.'

Too Close to the Cults?

I have been asked to justify my getting 'too close to the cults.' I have been criticized for staying in a commune for a week or two, for travelling on the road with a missionary team, for having private conferences with charismatic leaders, for participating in meditation retreats, and so on. I felt a blast of criticism when I attended a meeting of the American Family Foundation in May 1997, attracted by the theme Cults and Children. The director of the Watchman Fellowship, a Christian counter-cult organization in Alabama, came up and introduced himself to me in the following disconcerting fashion: 'Are you *the* Susan Palmer who wrote that *positive* chapter on The Family in *Sex, Slander and Salvation*? Why do you bother to go *into* these groups and talk to them. Don't you know they always lie?'

I was astonished. For a researcher to avoid the living community and to rely exclusively on data supplied by ex-members and the group's literature would be like an anthropologist claiming to be an expert on an Aboriginal tribe, but who only interviews Aborigines once they have migrated to the city; one who has never ventured into the outback let alone visited or lived with the tribe. Suppose Jane Goodall had never ventured into the Kenyan masai *mara*, but studied chimpanzees in zoos? It seems to me that any serious researcher who has the vocation to learn about new religions must seek them out in their purest form, and be present during their earliest, vital stages of development.

Anticultists have accused scholars of being *paid* by cults to say nice things about them, or accepting bribes to keep their mouths shut about the supposed atrocities ongoing in cultland. Any information centre on NRMs – CESNUR in Italy, INFORM in London, ISAR in Santa Barbara – that is not specifically set up to warn worried parents or concerned Christians about new religious horrors and heresies, is routinely accused by anticultists of receiving their funding from the cults. This very assumption – that NRMs are *capable* of networking with each other, or that they have heard and approve of the sociology of religion – reveals a profound ignorance of new religions in all their staggering diversity.

For certain large, international movements like the Unification Church, Scientology, International Society for Krishna Consciousness (ISKCON), the Family, the word *sociologist* has an auspicious ring. For most groups, it denotes a boring, depressingly secular, time-wasting, spiritually contaminated nerd. When I told the *sannyasis* at my neighbourhood Rajneesh Meditation Center in 1985 that I wished to do a sociological study of their commune, they rolled their eyes. 'Talk about missing the point!' one remarked. One swami who had an MA in Sociology commented, 'It's a good way to avoid looking inside yourself and get your energy stuck.'

As a Quebec scholar, I have had a great deal of difficulty explaining my academic intentions to the small anglophobic right-wing Catholic sectarian groups as well as to the magical-arcane lodges that make up a significant proportion of our French-Canadian groups. I tend to prefer virgin turf untouched by other researchers, and so I have had to start from square one trying to educate these adepts in the scientific study of religion. I have wasted much time trying in vain to convince them of the innocuous nature of my research plans and have often been igno-miniously driven away.

That Elusive Thing Called Objectivity

Objectivity is not a fixed, eschatological state from whence unworthy and corrupt scholars plunge from grace. It is an ongoing balancing act, a kind of gradual sensitivity training. Any experienced scholar knows it is not easy to collect and analyse data on controverial movements, or to navigate the subtle terrain of real research situations. In the course of my own participant-observation studies I have experienced intense moments of aesthetic revulsion, emotional attraction, or cultural bias. My initial impressions of a group have often been erroneous, and my hypotheses and hunches have frequently proven false upon further investigation. Rather than recoil sanctimoniously at external assaults upon one's objectivity, or castigate oneself for receptivity to un-scholarly emotions or unwelcome mystical cognitions, the serious researcher will forge ahead knowing the adventure is just beginning.

Nevertheless, there is clearly a need for constructive suggestions concerning a new code of ethics, or at least some recognized guide-lines, for the complex, nuanced situations field researchers encounter inside 'world rejecting' NRMs. In 1967, in response to the controversy over the infamous Milgram experiment, the American Psychological Association's Ad Hoc Committee on Ethical Standards in Psychologi-cal Research recommended that 'members of the profession them-selves should supply ethical problems as the raw material for discussion.' They hoped that through this inductive approach ethical principles would emerge that were relevant to contemporary research (Palys 1992: 83). Until recently, the exchange of concrete examples and discussion of these dilemmas among NRM scholars has been largely informal and interpersonal. We need more open forums along the lines of Catherine Wessinger's sessions at the American Academy of Reli-gion (AAR), where researchers exchange anecdotes that illustrate the unforeseen challenges met in the field.

There has been a mounting concern over the problem of *trusting* the published research of NRM scholars, whose work may be contami-nated by making deals with the cult leaders, or by closet conversion experiences, not unlike the Patty Hearst 'Stockholm syndrome,' or – worst of all – through bribes or cult funding to 'say nice things.' Irving Horowitz (1983: 180) first identified an academic weakness he called 'slippage into unabashed support for groups and the quality of publications produced by academics who attended expenses paid Unificationist Church sponsored conferences.' Robert Balch and Stefan Langdon (1996:72) criticized the design of the AWARE group study of the then-controversial CUT, arguing that the scholars were willing victims of the group's 'impression management' (Goffman 1959). Balch's critique has been cited repeatedly by anticultists as evidence that *any* research undertaken on NRMs with the knowledge and cooperation of the cult leaders is by nature contaminated.[1] In my conversations with Rob Balch, he has expressed surprise that what he hoped was a constructive criticism to raise research standards within the academy was taken up and brandished by anticultists as evidence that any published research on NRMs that isn't of the explicitly cult bashing sort is suspect, and the researcher's objectivity has been corrupted!

Cult research poses its own peculiar set of problems. This was noted in the textbook I use for my course, *Research Methods in the Social Sciences*. The authors, Del Balso and Lewis (1997:222) claim that 'certain social groups, such as religious cults or extremist political, groups, require covert observation.' Other textbooks compare cults to motorcycle gangs and quasi-criminal, racist, or anarchist groups that are so difficult and dangerous to study that covert research and snowballing techniques are recommended as the appropriate means to gather data.

Stephen A. Kent and Theresa Krebs (1998) also raise the issue of the ethics appropriate for researchers in NRMs, and proceed to outline the dangers that await scholars in the field, dangers that are seemingly insurmountable and so morally contaminating as to cast doubt upon the personal integrity and efficaciousness of field researchers. They relate a series of anecdotes of how cults gain legitimacy by using, manipulating, or making deals with scholars, then sound the alarm for the future respectablity and credibility of the discipline. There are several assumptions in their argument that I find disquieting: assumptions about the character of NRMs, about the brains of researchers, and about research methodology in general.

First, they imply that a new religion's gradual acquisition of public acceptance is gained through *sneaky means* – that they somehow 'got away with it,' and that it is undeserved. I have heard this argument before, most recently from the director of an anticult organization who

spoke to my class, warning them that cults resort to underhand strategies to appear respectable or to gain legitimacy. They set up lectures at
McGill University; their leaders are photographed shaking hands with
politicians and respectable religious leaders. He was saying NRMs
don't deserve social acceptance and tolerance because *we know* they are
intrinsically evil, or at least socially dysfunctional. The underlying
message was, '*we know* they are quasi- or proto-criminal organizations,
so their slimy efforts to suck up to us respectable people must be
exposed!'

These authors (Kent and Krebs 1998) actually imply that a religious
minority's newfound freedom from stigma and cult stereotyping
in the media or exoneration in court constitutes a kind of *litmus test*
for the objectivity of the scholarly research cited in the affadavits
and the news reports. I would agree heartily, as I assume my fellow
researchers would, that academics should not be *partisans* in a religious
movement's missionary efforts, charisma-building, millenarian prepa-
rations, or eschatological aspirations. Whether a young religion's reputation thrives or dives *should be irrelevant* to the pursuit of accurate
knowledge and should not concern the scholar. But Kent and Krebs's
emphasis seems to imply that *if* a researcher's findings *just so happen* to
contribute to the NRM's struggle for social legitimacy, then the findings themselves are suspect.

History tells us that those new religions that managed to survive the
death of their founder, weather persecution, and schisms, and to
socialize their second and third generations, *inevitably* work out a more
civil and mutually accomodating relationship with society. The Mormons, the Christian Scientists, the Lutherans, and the Anabaptists all
managed to do this without the assistance of 'cult-sponsored scholars.'

The third assumption – that researchers are naive and easily duped –
could be made only by scholars who occupy a bleak and marginal out-
post in this field. Kent and Krebs (1998) warn scholars that they are
often the targets of public relations and 'impression management'
when they begin to study a community that is in dire need of outside
support for their legal and media battles. These are realities of which
active researchers are *already* (trust me!) acutely aware. Most NRMs
have an outer vestibule where they can check out prospective initiates,
where charming host/hostesses speak to the media and provide information to visiting scholars. Surely even an inexperienced undergradu-
ate student would not mistake this vestibule for the group's innermost
sanctuary. Any discerning anthropologist expects to wade through

opening courtesies and cermonial PR before unearthing more interest-ing data. It is quite understandable that NRMs with a history of con-flict with society and of stigmatization in the media are wary of admitting researchers and will try to feed them the 'relevant' informa-tion, hide discrediting literature, and reinterpret embarrassing events. Often these PR efforts are so poorly organized and transparent that they reveal more than they hide, drawing the inquisitive researcher's eye to the vulnerable points in the group's armour.

Kent and Krebs broaden the stigma surrounding cults to include the cult scholars who embark on first-hand research in the field. In the end they veer away from the thorny task of thrashing out ethical guidelines for researchers going into controversial groups. Instead of grasping the nettle by the thorns, they brandish it. Some might even mistake their message to be 'Researchers beware! *Avoid* challenging research projects *entirely*, lest your objectivity suffer irremediable erosion!' Thus the scholar's overriding concern should be to preserve her/his *reputation* at all costs. This new 'ethical' development in the field would be lamentable, as research would come to a screeching halt in areas that badly need elucidation, such as racialist, survivalist, and apocalyptic movements.

Weird Ethical Dilemmas beyond Your Wildest Dreams

But the real ethical dilemmas and challenges to objectivity are encoun-tered *after* the PR phase, once the researcher has won the trust of the leaders and received permission to engage in research. These *actual* threats to scholarly objectivity are beyond your wildest dreams! Ten-ured professors, experts in the microsociology of NRMs who read the latest cult scandal in the news, then knowingly quote Toqueville while gazing out at their lawn sprinklers, have no idea what fasci-nating adventures they are missing by avoiding the strenuous, time-consuming work of field research. Scholars who rely exclusively on ex-members or on second-hand research for their data understandably lack any sense of the complex political situations and serious ethical decisions that confront the more energetic, less squeamish scholars who are willing to go into controversial communities. Each group poses unforeseen challenges, and every researcher presumably has dif-ferent chinks in his/her armour. Problematic situations might be encountered in the course of sleeping inside a commune, participating in rituals designed to induce altered states of consciousness, interviewing rival leaders who try to enlist the researcher in their struggle over the succession, or talking to rebellious teens who tell you stuff their parents really should know about ... These challenges can be complex and dramatic, requiring the researcher to improvise ethical guidelines as these situations come up.

I will now relate some of my adventures.

Why I Don't Consider Myself a 'Kept Scholar'

In 1992 I received two grants to study children in new religions. I approached two different sects in Quebec and was refused permission to interview their members (they suspected I was a spy sent by the Catholic school board to undermine their home schooling). Then two international NRMs heard about me and called me up, offering plane tickets to 'come on out and study *our* kids!' I turned them down. The situation made me nervous, for several reasons. First, I was concerned about preserving my 'scholarly virginity.' Second, I feared that if in the future I did not cooperate with their agenda, they might resort to blackmail (no doubt this is pure paranoia). Finally, I like to feel I am unhampered as a writer, free to poke fun at the group delicately if I feel like it, or mention stuff that is embarrassing. In short, I don't like being censored. I was aware that by choosing to study controversial child-rearing methods in NRMs, I would be vulnerable to criticism, but I didn't realize that I was stepping into the front line of a new battleground in the Cult Wars.

April 1994 I was standing in the witness box at the High Court, Family Division, in Lincoln's Inn to testify during the *Turle vs. Turle* custody battle over the grandson of a millionairess whose mother joined The Family. The same official solicitor who wanted to know if I were 'soft on the cults' asked: 'Who *paid* for your trip to San Diego to study The Family's home-school?' Fortunately I was able to respond: 'I paid for it out of my SSSR grant' – and could have produced the receipts if necessary.

I have never accepted money from an NRM to study them, but I have had to make deals with leaders who have curtailed the areas I was allowed to go into. I have managed to preserve my scholarly virginity, but have engaged in mutual flattery and love-bombing, if not heavy petting (figuratively speaking), with charismatic leaders and their top aides. Personally, I don't know of any kept scholars in real life, but I am unsuited for the job since I prefer my NRMs wild and virgin. I seek out groups that are almost inaccessible and unselfconscious, groups that know *they* are not a cult, but I naively swallow what the newspapers say about other cults – groups that have never heard of the term *NRM*, groups that are suspicious of researchers and assume a sociologist is just a pretentious variety of journalist. Once they start sending out PR reps to conferences wearing suits, groomed hair, and name tags, they're no fun anymore. Well, that's not true. They can still be interesting, but suddenly they seem tame, almost domesticated. Other scholars horn in and conduct schmaltzy interviews in the hotel breakfast nook and arrange visits.

If NRMs are baby religions, scholarly conferences provide the venues to set up *petting zoos*.

A Condominum on the Outskirts of Heaven

I have been offered bribes, so I keep all my receipts and correspondance to make it more convenient to sue anyone who suggests my research efforts or opinions can be bought. But I never turn down otherworldly rewards. Three different apocalyptic sects have awarded me a sort of last-minute squeezed-in salvation when the cosmic countdown comes. 'We want you to know you will be *blessed* when Our Saviour returns,' a bearded elder told me. Technically I deserve to be consigned to eternal oblivion or fall into the pit amidst other soulless beer-swilling sinners, but I have been promised a condominium on the outskirts of Heaven, according to 'The Chosen People.' I have been assured by another 'biblically based' group that I will be beamed up before Armageddon gets too nasty. I was informed that Da Free John (currently known as Adidam) 'meditated me' long before I appeared on their scene. An infamous 'cult leader' prophesied I was 'one of the three wise women sent by God to assist the Prophet in opening the seventh seal at the end of time.' One Raelian guide suggested I might be eligible for cloning when the extraterrestrials arrive. And if linear time is indeed an illusion, I can look forward to a better rebirth, according to a member of Hare Krishna who suggested that I am a devotee of Swami Prahupada 'in my heart.'

Oddly enough, these assurances make me feel more secure on airplanes when I travel to conferences.

I also receive quite a lot of flattery. I am so accustomed to lovebombing that I have stopped blushing and now courteously return the blast: 'I love you too! If I were even one tenth as beautiful as you are, I would be so happy!' My own children have accused me of sycophantic behaviour in the presence of charisma: 'That's my mom sucking up to Rael,' I overheard my daughter say as she showed my photo album, Quebec Sect Tours, to a friend. I don't 'suck up!' Prophets are fascinating people – although my excitement in their presence might more closely resemble a manic butterfly collector than a sincere spiritual seeker.

The Sociologist as Hired Gun

To agree to appear in court as a witness to help a NRM (or a member) win or defend their case is *not* the same as being a 'cult-sponsored scholar.' Charlotte Allen (1999) lumps kept scholars and court witnesses together, but since we live in a society where even religious minorities actually enjoy the right to a fair trial, expert witnesses are generally considered to be legitimate. Nevertheless, going to court raises a whole new spectrum of problems for the researcher who nurtures objectivity.

Personally, when I first accepted the gig of hired gun, I experienced it as a traumatic loss of innocence. Courts are scary. I felt dragged into an adversarial situation and the anticult newsletters were soon taking potshots at me. I felt uncomfortable when asked to name my fee. Then, later (when I found out what the *other* witnesses got), I was annoyed at myself for requesting so little.

Just asking about fees was an education in itself. I called one eminent British scholar who replied, 'I would never agree to go to court, I would find it compromising to my scholarship.' Another European scholar who had appeared in court on occasion said, 'I never accept money as a witness, it looks and feels too much like a bribe.' One French professor insisted, 'in France an expert witness who accepts money is considered ineligible as a witness by the court.' Then I phoned several American scholars and noticed a very different view. 'You must establish a substantial fee, or you will be perceived as a closet member of the cult, and your testimony won't be taken seriously,' one scholar advised me. Another seasoned expert witness counselled, 'Charge as much as you can – $150 an hour just for reading the affadavits – because lawyers talk to each other, and if it becomes known that you charge a low fee, your testimony won't be valued, and you won't get asked back.'

The next time I was asked to appear in court by a different NRM, I told their lawyer I wouldn't charge anything because it would not require extra research, the group was not rich, and I could see the defendant had been unfairly treated. All I asked was that my expenses be covered. Initially I felt comfortable with that, but soon realized that my relationship with the group leaders had begun to take on a 'covenantal' as opposed to a 'contractual' character (Bromley and Busching 1988). They were now firmly convinced I had been sent by God to aid them in their battle against the Prince of Darkness. That was OK, I told myself, I don't mind accommodating their worldview, but the real problem was that they now expected me to be constantly on the alert and ready to jump into the fray. I flew out for the pretrial hearing, then they wanted me to fly out *again* for the last day of the trial, and now expect me to be on call for more upcoming cases. I am currently trying to figure out how I can gracefully bow out of their mythic landscape.

The Sociologist as Undercover Agent

Three months after the Solar Temple perpetrated their shocking mass suicide/homicide ritual 'transit' to Sirius, I found myself in an office being grilled by two policemen from the Securité Quebec concerning my belated and rather tentative research efforts into this controversial and criminal order. They wanted me to hand over a list of the Templars or ex-Templars I had met or interviewed. (It was impossible to tell the difference since none of them would admit to a current affiliation.) I refused, saying that to reveal the names of one's informants contravened ethics in the social sciences. 'Excuse me, Madame,' said one official, 'What is that?' It was difficult to explain. Finally the 'good cop' in the tweed suit joked, 'Be very careful, Madame. But, if you find yourself on Sirius, send us a postcard.'

The Sociologist as Soft Deprogrammer

I have noticed that the visit of a researcher is sometimes welcomed by NRM adherents as an opportunity for hedonism, a chance to gain access to luxuries and indulgences not normally available within the strict regimen of a commune or the work space of even the more secularized religious institutions. This particular ethical problem has never been identified or discussed in anticult circles, because they view cultists as obedient robots incapable of rebelling. In my experience, the brainwashed are quite capable of sneakiness, of pursuing their own individualistic whims or vices.

The kind of situation I am talking about has occurred quite often, where the people assigned to host me and facilitate my reseach *very* often suggest we go outside to a local bar or restaurant and order a drink or a meal. Somehow, many NRMs seemed to have gained the impression that most sociologists are borderline alchoholics. After one round of beers (paid for by the cult budget) they have suggested we order another round. The first time this happened I unthinkingly and selfishly said 'No thanks,' and then saw the anxious, disappointed looks on their faces. I realized this was perhaps their *only* opportunity to indulge in alcoholic beverages for the next few years, so I said, 'OK, maybe I will,' and paid for the second round. When I left half a glass, I noticed one of them swilled it down quickly as we got up to leave.

Since I privately feel many of the new religions I study are too strict and overly spartan, I am inclined to collude with my interviewees and encourage their secret rebellions – which places me in a morally dubious position, since I genuinely respect their religious principles and realize the rules are based on sound economics or communal ideals of humility and equality – or necessary measures to avoid assimilation. It puts sociologists like me rather in the position of being a 'soft deprogrammer,' – by encouraging members to disobey leaders, break out of their conditioning, and place their own selfish desires before the group goals – perhaps the first tentative steps towards eventually leaving?

On one occasion I had arranged to spend a few days living with a rather puritanical, biblically based commune in order to interview members and study communal patterns. Two members in their forties, who had recently been given the exciting task of dealing with the public, picked me up in a car to drive me to the commune four hours away in the countryside. On the way they suggested we stop off at a beautiful hotel by a lake to get some refreshment and so that I could admire the prospect of the mountains. I agreed, still feeling jet-lagged. Upon our arrival at the hotel front desk it became clear they had booked rooms – one for the two women, and the other for the man. Then they turned to me and said, 'Susan, you must be really tired with all your teaching and travelling, we thought it would be great for you if we all stayed here for three days. You could interview us, and catch up with your writing projects. We'll double up and give you the private room so you can work in peace.' It became clear that their *real* agenda was to indulge a secret passion they had been harbouring for years. It turned out their love affair had started years ago, but had been squelched by the leaders, and they had been encouraged to marry more suitable partners. I was not unsympathetic to their romance, and I could appreciate their need for a little holiday away from the crowded commune.

In this situation we find the sociologist-as-chaperone. The two would no doubt later report to their leaders: 'Dr Palmer *insisted* on stopping at a hotel for three days en route,' and they probably had been instructed to indulge a decadent sociologist. I had no problem personally with facilitating their affair, except that I really *did* want to conduct as many interviews as possible and realized if the situation became public this would not be good for my rep.: I would very much look like a jet-setting, kept scholar using research trips to enjoy luxurious holidays. So I had to play the priggish spoilsport and say no, although I sat by the lake and reviewed my notes while they went to the room to 'rest from the drive.' Thus sociologists can have a corrupting effect upon the morals of members.

The Real Ethical Question: Who Gets Hurt by Whom?

Ever since the Milgram experiment in 1963, the concern has been exclusively for the rights and dignity of the human subjects in experiments. And yet, all the recent discussion on research ethics in the microsociology of NRMs has focused on the potential harm to the discipline (due to sleazy researchers) and to the general public who might mistake a cult for a respectable enterprise. I feel it is time we exhibited some concern for the informants in NRMs, who already have been stripped of dignity through being labelled brainwashed cultists.

Baker (1988: 74) notes that 'It has more often been the case that social researchers have studied those with lower status than themselves rather than higher. Indigent and poorly educated people do not have the resources or knowledge, the lawyers, or the "I'm too busy" excuses to fend off social researchers.' Many members of NRMs feel so outcast, so marginalized, that they exhibit a pathetic gratitude that here at last is someone who is willing to listen to their side of the story. In some instances they have been told by the leaders to cooperate with sociologists, since scholarly articles on their movements tend to be more balanced and accurate than news reports. Thus they are in a vulnerable position to be exploited and manipulated by the researcher.

Sometimes this happens in the process of writing. It is only too easy for sociologists to make their informants sound less educated and articulate than themselves. Obviously there is a difference in the way even PhDs express themselves verbally and on paper. What we find in many scholarly studies of new religions (including my own, I confess) are many indented passages in which the informant spills his or her guts in less than grammatical fashion. The informants' responses in interviews (often to touchy and impertinent quesions concerning intimate conversion experiences, sensations while meditating, the group's controversial sexual mores, and their own deeply emotional first encounter with their God-in-flesh leader) are often liberally sprinkled with 'like,' 'um,' 'kind of,' 'you know.' On concluding the indented quote as a specimen of cultic thinking, the sociologist then lunges into an interpretation of the statement in the industrial Latin of American 'sociologese,' leaving the reader stunned by the disparities in the two prose styles.

Often it is quite evident to the reader that the 'cultists' statements might be interpreted in several ways and are applicable to more than one hermeneutic context, but the impatient sociologist ignores these subtleties and proceeds to pounce upon the odd sentence that fits the theory presented in the article. References to Durkheim, Levi Strauss, or Eliade unconsciously underscores the portrait of the modern urban 'cultist' with the 'Savage Mind' – as a sort of naive neo-primitive. In the end, the sociologist comes across as smarter than she/he might actually be, and the cultist as stupider, less self-aware than he or she probably would strike you in a real life situation. By scrupulously including all the 'ums' and 'well, it's like, ...' the sociologist gets extra points for being a rigorous and accurate recorder of naturalistic data, while at the same time demonstrates his or her intellectual superiority to – and distance from – the informant.

Scholars and researchers play an important role as educators in the global process of the proliferating new religious pluralism. Often they are the only go-betweens, the ones who have traversed that no man's land between the 'cult' and 'normal society.' In this situation it is tempting to fancy oneself as a 'freedom fighter' or a *deus ex machina* who advises cult leaders on how to get out of trouble.

I find myself torn between the need to educate and the desire to entertain. By highlighting spiritual weirdnesses I grab my students' attention and please journalists, but I undermine the groups' struggle for respect. It is only too easy to forget that cult members are human beings too, and that many have found happiness, learned social graces, received spiritual gifts participating in less than respectable religions.

Recently I invited a Knight of the Golden Lotus to speak to my class, after giving the students a rather unfeeling satirical sketch of the late leader's eccentricities. Our speaker appeared in the knights' orange and yellow garments, with mirrors fastened on his headband. His companion wore amulets of swans, rainbows, and mandalas pinned to her ample bosom. I stifled a smirk, and was feeling particularly frazzled – the VCR wasn't working and the audiovisual man refused to help, and he launched into a tirade on the college cutbacks that robbed him of his assistant. My daughter had refused to brush her hair before leaving for school, and my students were now behaving badly, lurching in late and babbling at the back. My Knight of the Golden Lotus stepped forward: 'Please be quiet! We have come to present to you our religion and would appreciate respect.' The students immediately calmed down and he launched into a fascinating lecture.

Afterwards, walking down the hall beside him, I reflected that, in spite of his leader's execrable taste in architecture, here was an admirable human being. His swift social responses had shown considerable insight and intelligence. I suspected that on this particular day his mental health was superior to my own. In fact, he'd put me in a good mood – perhaps an altered state?

Learning How to Navigate the Cult Wars

Over thirty-odd years, the controversial field of what Thomas Robbins (1988) dubbed the 'microsociology of new religions' has blossomed, waxed in complexity, and come to resemble a German late-Romantic string quartet in all its dark, foreboding dissonances. In the past five years, since Waco, we have witnessed a heightened awareness of religious liberty issues, the sudden demise of the Cult Awareness Network, and a softening of the boundaries separating NRM scholars from anticultists. Former deprogrammers present papers at the SSSR, and NRM researchers who have debunked the brainwashing theory are finally permitted to attend the American Family Foundation conferences. As the no man's land that recently separated the anticultists from the 'cult scholars' is tamed by footprints, and new, uneasy alliances are formed, each side shows signs of fissiparousness as various schools of thought – and backbiting – threaten the collegiality of cult scholars.

All the evidence at hand points to a future filled with a dizzying abundance of ever-proliferating new religions. This phenomenon begs to be studied and offers stimulating hands-on research opportunities for young scholars. And yet, inexperienced and ambitious aspiring academics are likely to be deterred by a kind of miasma hovering around the field, a miasma arising from rumours and stereotypes as well as occasional errors and poor judgment on the part of NRM researchers. Will the young field researcher who wishes to write about the vampire subculture and its rituals hesitate to embark on this project lest she later find herself *branded* as a morbid blood-drinker once she becomes a famous sociologist? Young scholars may feel reluctant to embark on the study of NRMs like the Church Universal and Triumphant, the Unification Church and The Family, groups that in the past have been known to exhibit 'philomandarin' tendencies – to eagerly court, and even pay, scholars to study them. These groups continue to mature, mutate, and institutionalize charisma in fascinating ways ... but by associating with these groups, are young researchers compromising their most precious commodity: objectivity? Or, even more important, are they compromising their *reputations* as objective social scientists?

Paradoxically, there is pressure in the academy to steer clear of cults, but the news media exerts considerable pressure on scholars to comment on, and hence to study, the more controversial, outrageous, or dangerous groups – and these are precisely the areas of unpredictable pitfalls. What NRM scholar does not feel trepidation upon hearing the following cautionary, but true tales? (1) A Japanese professor who wrote an encyclopedia entry on Aum Shinrikyo, and whose graduate student was recruited into the movement, was fired by the university – the rationale being, if he knew his stuff he should have been able to recognize danger signals and warn the proper authorities; and (2) an Oregon high-school teacher was fired after inviting two sannyasis from Rajneeshpuram to talk to his class.[2]

Like Dorothy on the yellow brick road, young researchers will occasionally lose their barking 'Totos' of objectivity. They will rely on their Cowardly Lions (academic caution) and rusty Tin Woodmen (quantitative methods) as they wander off into the yet undreamt-of spiritual landscapes of the future. Perhaps in a few years it will be considered quite as respectable to receive research funding from NRMs as it is from the Vatican. Perhaps 'religious minority' will have the same earnest ring to it as 'sexual minority' or 'women of colour.' The best advice I can offer to my students who aspire to spiritual espionage is this: Be open about what you're doing, don't apologize for mistakes, grow a rhinoceros-hide, but cultivate an empathetic ear for spiritual confessions.

Notes

1 I heard Balch's 'findings' cited four times at the American Family Foundation meeting in May 1997.
2 From *The Oregonian*, a special issue on Rajneeshpuram, August 1985.

References

Allen, Charlotte. 1999. 'Brainwashed! Scholars of Cults Accuse Each Other of Bad Faith.' *Lingua Franca* (January): 26–37.
Baker, Theresa L. 1988. *Doing Social Research*. New York: McGraw Hill.
Balch, Robert, and Stephen Langdon. 1998. 'How the Problem of Malfeasance Gets Overlooked in Studies of New Religions: An Examination of the AWARE Study of the Church Universal and Triumphant.' In *Wolves within the Fold*, edited by Anson Shupe, 191–211. New Brunswick, N.J.: Rutgers University Press.
Barker, Eileen. 1996. 'The Scientific Study of Religion? You Must be Joking!' In *Cults in Context*, edited by Lorne L. Dawson, 5–27. Toronto: Canadian Scholars Press.
Baum, L. Frank. 1910. *The Emerald City of Oz*. Chicago: Reilly & Lee.
Bromley, David, and Bruce Busching. 1988. 'Understanding the Structure of Contractual and Covenantal Social Relations.' *Sociological Analysis* 49: 15–32.
Del Balso, Michael, and Alan D. Lewis. 1997. *First Steps: A Guide to Social Research*. Toronto: ITP Nelson.
Erikson, Kai T. 1967. 'A Comment on Disguised Observation in Sociology.' *Social Problems* 14 (14): 367–73.
Goffman, Irving. 1961. *Asylums*. New York: Doubleday.
Horowitz, Irving. 1983. 'Unusual Standards NOT Uniform Beliefs.' *Sociological Analysis* 44: 179–82.
Kent, Stephen, and Theresa Krebs. 1998. 'Academic Compromise in the Social Scientific Study of Alternative Religions.' *Nova Religio* 2: 44–54.
Milgram, Stanley. 1965. 'Some Conditions of Obedience and Disobedience to Authority,' *Human Relations* 18: 57–75.
Palmer, Susan J. 1994. *Moon Sisters, Krishna Mothers, Rajneesh Lovers: Women's Roles in New Religions*. Syracuse, N.Y.: Syracuse University Press, 105–36.
– 1995. 'Women in the Raelian Movement.' In *The Gods Have Landed: New Religions from Other Worlds*, edited by James R. Lewis. New York: SUNY.

122   Susan J. Palmer

Palys, Ted. 1992. *'Research Decisions: Quantitative and Qualitative Perspectives.'* Toronto: Harcourt and Brace.

Robbins, Thomas. 1988. *Cults, Converts and Charisma.* New Jersey: Transaction Press.

Singer, Margaret Thaler, with Janja Lalich. 1995. *Cults in Our Midst: The Hidden Menace in Our Everyday Lives.* San Francisco: Jossey-Bass.

4. Pitfalls in the Sociological Study of Cults

Janja Lalich

One of the things that cults do well is the construction of inspiring and exciting alternative worldviews. They do this passionately and with great skill, and the most successful of them are also skilled at creating internally consistent social and cultural contexts to make these worldviews visible and attractive both to their members and to their audiences. Consequently, researchers attempting to study cults are confronted with a set of problems beyond those encountered by ethnographers studying other types of social organizations. Researchers of cults are faced with a kind of hall of mirrors in which they must contend with multiple layers of reality construction. In this chapter I address the potential pitfalls inherent in doing research on such groups.

First, let me attempt to define what I mean by *cult*, that problematic word. The definition I shall be using is drawn primarily from the works of Robert Jay Lifton (1979, 1987, 1991, 1999) and Benjamin Zablocki (1971, 1980, 1997a, 1999). This usage and my understanding of this interactive dynamic has also been informed by my own work – both research and practical – during the past decade and by my life experience, having spent more than ten years as a member of the Democratic Workers Party (DWP), a highly restrictive political cult.[1] The reader should be aware at the outset that I bring to this definition (and, indeed, to this entire chapter) the specific insights and the specific biases of a former cult member and not merely the more detached curiosity of a general social scientist. I define a cult as follows:

A cult can be either a sharply bounded social group or a diffusely bounded social movement held together through shared commitment to a charismatic leader. It upholds a transcendent ideology (often but not always religious in nature) and requires a high level of personal commitment from its members in words and deeds.

There are three clarifying points that need to be made about this definition. One is that a cult can take the form of either a social group or a social movement. Analytically, the concept is applicable to either of those social forms as long as the cohesiveness of the entity is provided by shared loyalty to a charismatic leader in pursuit of a set of transcendent ideological goals. Indeed, a number of cults have switched back and forth between those two forms of organization, sometimes on more than one occasion in order to accommodate changes in size and/or shifts in recruitment strategies or proselytization tactics. Thus, at certain times in its history a cult can be a precisely defined group with clear boundaries separating members from outsiders, and at other times it can take the form of a more amorphous social movement with fuzzy concentric boundaries shading off imperceptibly from totally committed inner-circle members to fellow travellers to vaguely interested spectators. This point is particularly germane to this book because scholars have often been confused by those different forms of social organization, which in turn has led to some basic misunderstanding of cults. For example, scholars have argued for years over the question of whether membership turnover in cults is high or low. Although it would appear that, empirically, both sides can't be right, an examination of their empirical sources reveals that one side is drawing its conclusions of low turnover from studies of cults as tightly knit social groups, whereas the other side is drawing its conclusions of high turnover from studies of cults as loosely knit social movements (see, for example, Barker 1995a and Langone 1993). This is a typical (and, alas, all too common) example of cult scholars as blind men examining the elephant.

A second important point about my definition is that it contains no mention of two features of cults that have attracted great attention in the mass media: the systems of totalistic social control that cults frequently impose upon their members, and the separatism or withdrawal from the larger society that frequently make cults appear so alien and threatening. I recognize that cults are frequently totalistic and separatist. But to be an aspect of the definition of *cult*, a feature must always be present in every instance. It is more useful, I think, to

treat totalism and separatism as analytically interesting aspects of cultic organization rather than explaining them away by treating them as
part of the definition.

My third and final clarifying point is that my definition is not meant
to be in opposition to Stark and Bainbridge's excellent but very different definition. Stark and Bainbridge (1996: 24) define a cult as 'a deviant *religious* organization with novel beliefs and practices' [emphasis
mine]. I do not believe in the proliferation of definitions, and Stark and
Bainbridge do the job well for the meso- and macro-sociological issues
with which they are primarily concerned. But their definition is not of
the right type to serve the intensely micro-sociological aspects that are
at the heart of my concerns in this chapter. When one turns the viewing lens on a single cult in order to extract a thick definition of the
forces that hold it together, one inevitably sees charismatic relationships and devotion to transcendent ideology as the important defining
features. In addition, Stark and Bainbridge are interested in defining
cults within the framework of the sociology of religion, whereas I see
cults as an analytic category that can be usefully applied to political
groups, business organizations, psychotherapy and self-help groups,
as well as groups and movements within other social institutional
categories.

Cults differ in their particular ruling ideologies and in their specific
requirements, practices, and behaviours; a single group may even differ over its lifetime or across different locations. These groups exist on
a continuum of influence (regarding a particular group's effect on its
members and on society, and vice versa) and a continuum of control
(from less invasive to all-encompassing).

Cults Try to Prevent You from Coming Backstage after the Show

Often cults are found to be mystical, grandiose, secretive, and multilayered. Such characteristics have been noted by various researchers
(Balch 1985; Balch and Langdon 1998; Barker 1995b; Carter 1990;
Singer 1995; Tobias and Lalich 1994; Wilson 1988; Zablocki 1997b).
There is no way to know how many times researchers have been successfully 'fooled' by such groups, in the sense that the researchers were
shown a version of reality that either differed from the typical daily life
or hid from view the negative or controversial aspects. But if we
assume that a researcher wants to present a thorough descriptive
account (Geertz 1973), then how best achieve that goal? Whether doing
content analysis of documents, participant observation, or interviews,

in addition to abiding by generally accepted standards of research in the social sciences, an important first step would be for the researcher to acknowledge that there might be some distortion going on, meant either to impress or to hide, or both.

I do not mean to imply here, or elsewhere throughout this chapter, that all such groups are the same; nevertheless, over the years there has been a surprising likeness in reports of systems of control and influence used in cultic groups, which have served to misinform, disinform, or obfuscate in one way or another. Those efforts at information control and impression management might be called the group's 'mask of normalcy.' This mask can serve to keep researchers at arm's length, impeding an inside look at what really transpires. For that reason a researcher must be methodical, thorough, and grounded, and have a solid but flexible plan or approach.

An initial task involves acquiring basic knowledge of the group in question. Know as much as possible about the group beforehand (its doctrine, practices and rituals, lingo, history, lineage, controversies, and crises); then be ready to entertain various interpretations of findings. A central challenge, of course, is gaining access. I will not address here the related issue of a group's efforts at converting the researcher, for the topic of researcher as potential convert has been adequately covered by Ayella (1990). Other possible obstructions, discussed below, primarily arise in the areas of information control and impression management. I offer here a glimpse of the various strategies used some of the time by some groups, with examples of the types of occurrences that might derail the researcher. Some of the examples are taken from my own experience of having been in a cult's upper-level leadership ranks. These manipulative strategies pose four categories of problems for the researcher who would not be deceived: (1) tricks and setups; (2) demands, restrictions, and intimidation; (3) informants as spin masters; and (4) researcher susceptibility to the cult's appeal. I will discuss each of them in turn.

Problem 1: Tricks and Setups
Researchers must remember the ease with which a group can trick visitors and outsiders. This can happen through selected interviewees, selected topics of discussion, and staged events.

Selected Interviewees   '
When visiting a group facility or location, a researcher may believe

that she is free to interview or observe whomever is there, and as a result may feel that she has been given free reign. In many cases, however, only trusted members are allowed in those locations during the time the researcher (or, in some cases, the public) will be there. As a result, 'outsiders' end up talking to or interviewing only those group members who were preselected by the gatekeeper, or were preassigned and trained as spokespersons for the group (Hammersley and Atkinson 1996). Another way this type of control occurs is through either overt or indirect censoring of responses and interactions. Carter (1990), for example, described certain conversations with Rajneeshis that were interrupted by fellow adherents when a devotee was overheard saying 'too much' to the research team during its data-gathering visits to Rajneeshpuram in Oregon.

Selected Topics of Discussion
Researchers or journalists who want to interview a group leader may quickly learn that this is not so easy. One evasive strategy has been to ask researchers to submit their questions in writing to the leader, who then (either himself or through his aides) selectively chooses the questions he wants to answer. Sometimes the questions are rewritten so the leader can talk about his own favourite topics. That type of manoeuvring occurred, for example, when a journalist from India wanted to interview Marlene Dixon, the leader of the DWP (the group referred to earlier, of which I had been a member). It took months to finalize the questions and carefully structure the answers into interview format for the Indian paper (Chatterjee 1985). None of the negotiations and little of the actual composition were done by Dixon. Top-level DWP 'intellectuals' and aides handled the entire episode, which Dixon vetted (or criticized) all along the way. The result was a tightly structured document filled with rhetoric, which eventually was distributed to the group's 'political officers,' such as myself. We were to use the document in our weekly meetings to train members in the party line and to bolster morale – for here was evidence that our leader had been sought out and interviewed by a foreign correspondent, further proof that she was working hard to spread our message far and wide. In the end, the journalist was used for our own gain.

Staged Events
These events occur for a variety of reasons: to gain credibility for the group, to recruit, to fund-raise, to keep members busy, or simply to put

forth a public face. Many such episodes have been written about in the literature. Carter (1990) described 'carefully scripted tours' of Rajneesh-puram, acknowledging that his entire research team felt manipulated. Also, Kent and Krebs (1998a) commented on 'media homes' set up by The Family (formerly the Children of God) for public display to give a good impression: 'Hand-picked individuals living in these well-funded facilities went through rehearsals about how to portray themselves and the group to media, scholars, and others who might scruti-nize them' (45). Maaga (1998) described Jim Jones and his People's Temple leadership circle staging fake healings as a means of recruit-ment; similarly, Jones 'would instruct his audience on the proper image to project when strangers of any significance were to be present' (157).

There were many occasions in the DWP when we put on a good face, at times erecting a sort of Potemkin village in order to impress a visit-ing dignitary, or for some other reason. Oftentimes, most of the mem-bers working on such a project were not informed of the purpose – and given the group's very strict need-to-know policy, naturally, one dared not ask. Let me illustrate this type of impression management with a classic example of a DWP Potemkin village – the time we put on a show for academics and sociologists.[2]

In 1982 the American Sociological Association (ASA) held its annual meeting in San Francisco, where the DWP was headquartered. Dixon saw the conference as an opportunity to bring important contacts to our 'research institute,' named the Institute for the Study of Labor and Economic Crisis (ISLEC). I use quotation marks because ISLEC was one of many DWP front groups;[3] ISLEC's brochure described it as an independent leftist think-tank, and it was not affiliated publicly with the DWP. ISLEC's purpose was to attract scholars and academic sup-porters and to be an outlet for our political ideas. The institute's letter-head sported an impressive list of board members, including some of the more well-known intellectuals on the Left at the time. Before her efforts at establishing a revolutionary cadre party, which is how the DWP viewed itself, Dixon, with a PhD in sociology, had been a college professor. But she left academia after controversial partings from fac-ulty positions at two universities. As a result, she felt and expressed a great deal of conflict about academicians in general, and about pro-gressive-minded sociologists and historians in particular. She often tar-geted for harsh criticism those whom she considered to be 'petty-bourgeois intellectuals' and 'traitors to the working class' (see, for example, Dixon 1977a, b, 1978, 1979). At the same time, she curried the favor of certain Left-leaning, influential academics and tried to induce them to be on one or another advisory board of our various front groups or to contribute to our publications, such as the journal *Contemporary Marxism*. The fact that ASA was going to be held on the DWP's home turf was recognized as a key event, and determining exactly how to take advantage of it became the subject of many strategy sessions and late-night meetings among Dixon and her top lieutenants. Some DWP members were academics (or had been deemed by Dixon to be party intellectuals); several were already members of the ASA's Marxist section and were scheduled to present papers at various sessions. We planned to pack the sessions with our own members, as well as have literature to sell and give away. But the final grand idea was to host an open house at our new 'institute.'

At the time I was in an upper-level administrative position and also in charge of the DWP's publishing house, Synthesis Publications. It was my job, along with other inner-circle leaders, to see that everything Dixon wanted happened without a hitch. We worked at a feverish pitch, and no excuse was accepted to lighten anyone's load. I and others in leadership pushed ourselves and those below us to the max. Rank-and-file 'militants' assigned to our twenty-four-hour print shop designed, produced, and mailed off fancy invitations and created other special documents for the occasion. Meanwhile, other militants planned the details of a formal cocktail party and tour of the institute. Remaining members (whether of full-time or part-time status) were assigned to many hours of work late into the night and on weekends to fix up the two-storey building recently rented to house the institute. The project involved a complete overhaul, to Dixon's specifications, including redoing walls, painting, scrubbing, installing fixtures, organizing and installing a multivolume research library, setting up a vast clipping database, decorating with art and posters, furnishing, and all the other fine-tuning required in a total refurbishment.

One DWP member who was a sociologist at a large university was instrumental in organizing this event – under Dixon's command, of course. When asked recently about this episode, he replied, 'The event was a huge success. ASA visitors were given a tour of the building, were chatted up by the party intellectuals, and were wooed with good wine and specially prepared food. It was all very impressive. But little did they know,' he added, 'that it was all built at the expense of "underlings" who would never be seen or recognized for their hard work' (personal communication, 27 September, 1998).[4]

Beneath the facade there is often a hidden layer – and, in this case, more than one. While the performance itself is sociologically interesting, equally important is what is being hidden: the backstage, the secret nature of the organization, its purpose, and the control of its membership. For, in this instance, in addition to the unrecognized labor of the many unseen militants, what was also not known by the visiting sociologists, who were so impressed with our very academic-looking institute, was that at same time Dixon's top leadership (myself included) was orchestrating a purge of 'petty bourgeois parents.'

Earlier in the week, some DWP members who were parents of young children had requested permission not to work all day on the Sunday just before the ASA event. They had wanted to spend a few hours with their children. When word of this got back to Dixon, all hell broke loose. At one point, Dixon and her entourage, including bodyguards and Rottweiler dogs, arrived at the institute, where she lashed out with harsh rebukes and warnings of expulsion, accusing any laggard of being a traitor to the working class. As a result, alongside the ASA planning, another operation was being staged: a Stalinist-type trial and purge. While the 'external relations' department was in a frenzy over the imminent arrival of friendly and/or curious sociologists, the DWP's 'internal' apparat was attending to many dedicated members who, at the snap of a finger, had just been declared selfish, self-centred, and anti-revolutionary. One by one, these so-called criminals and traitors were brought before their comrades to be accused, criticized, humiliated, and, for some, ejected from the organization. So, that week, besides hosting – and charming – scholars from around the world, the DWP executed one of its largest purges at any one time, expelling the 'lazy, self-indulgent' parents, and in some cases requiring spouses to make a choice: their partner or the DWP. Many couples were broken up permanently over this incident, while other members learned the hard lesson that it was not smart to ask for time off. Needless to say, the admiring audience from the American Sociological Association meetings never became aware of the purge.

Now, is it inappropriate to compare the fake healings of a Jim Jones, as mentioned earlier, with pulling the wool over some sociologists' eyes in an academic setting? I think not. In effect, each was a manipulative strategy devised for a particular context. The purpose was to impress and recruit, and in both groups the members' dedication, commitment, and idealism were taken advantage of, both to put on a good front and to hide certain less desirable aspects. As we know, Jones used other types of guile in settings with politicians, just as Dixon used dumbed-down language when appealing to the masses. See, for example, *The People Make History* (n.d.), a picture book with captions issued by the DWP. It is that talent for presenting a different face to different audiences that not only treads a fine ethical line, but also covers up backstage behavior that might be quite revealing. And researchers in these contexts should be looking for such inconsistencies, not clapping their hands at the performance.

An antidote to the types of tricks and setups that researchers might encounter would be to try to establish beforehand some ways to ensure getting unadulterated data. For example, whenever possible, and, if the setting permits, arrive unannounced or early. Try to visit a group's various locations, including members' residences, the leaders' quarters, and any other special facilities. Also request that you be allowed to randomly select interview subjects, and ask permission to speak with members of different ranks, positions, functions, and lengths of time in the group. If at all possible, conduct your interviews off-site, which may allow members to speak more freely. Naturally, all of this must be done within ethical research standards and in a way that maintains good relations with your subjects. Be sensitive as well to the potential emotional, psychological, or physical risks that may befall your informants – whether they are current or former members. And take that same care yourself.

Problem 2: Demands, Restrictions, and Intimidation
Researchers must be alert to a group's attempt to put demands on them by restricting visiting times, locations, and access to members, and sometimes even requesting to review and approve the researcher's results or final reports. If a group so desires and is unable to put its stamp of approval on a report, or if a negative or critical report should surface, harassment of the authors and/or publishers is always a possibility.

Ayella (1990) advises that researchers be critical of the kind of access they are given. Why is the group allowing you in? Is it looking for a clean bill of health or stamp of approval? Has it been criticized recently and is now seeking outside aid in impression management? Does the group understand and agree with scientific norms of research? And possibly most critical, did the group invite you to do the research? Honest answers to such questions may reveal that a researcher is slated to become an unwitting pawn in someone else's project, perhaps with a questionable goal, and, potentially, with just as questionable an outcome.

Cultic groups with controversial and secret practices are unlikely to be open to scrutiny. It is not unusual for such groups to work against the airing of information that might be detrimental. Jim Jones was by no means the only leader of a controversial group who encouraged the disruption of a free press. Some of his antics – such as having his followers picket newspaper offices (Maaga 1998) – seem mild-mannered in contrast to other, more aggressive approaches used today. The ante has been upped considerably, with researchers, authors, and reporters more likely to be hit with a lawsuit or other types of harassment and unpleasantries. Groups much prefer positive puff pieces. Some will expend vast resources to launch public relations campaigns – using either in-house or external resources, and sometimes both. Muster's (1997) account of her publicity work in the Hare Krishna movement offers one such example.

In some research textbooks the effort at derailing Wallis's work on Scientology has become a case example of meddling in a researcher's results and conclusions (see, for example, Hammersley and Atkinson 1996: 283–4). Being the target of one of these campaigns is never fun. Such experiences have been described by Rubin (1998). According to Rubin, because the leadership was displeased with what they considered to be critical reports of their group, Rubin was characterized as an enemy and sued for defamation, and other attempts were made to discredit him. (Rubin describes these and related incidents in detail in chapter 12.) In another instance, when Kent's study on the leader of the Children of God (now The Family) was at the page proof stage, the article was withdrawn from an academic, peer-reviewed, annual publication because of aggressive actions and threats towards the publisher (Kent and Krebs 1998b).[5] Other incidents of harassment and intimidation of researchers and critics are recounted by Singer (1995). Efforts such as these, whose aim is the control and suppression of information, tend to have a chilling effect on research.

My only suggestion in this regard is to be cautious, be savvy, and seek legal counsel if you have any doubts.

Problem 3: Informants as Spin Masters
Researchers may encounter trained behaviour on the part of cult members and adherents. Therefore, while acknowledging this front-stage activity, researchers must also be prepared to seek out backstage behaviours and attitudes. Researchers might also consider ways in which they might evoke a fuller picture of what is going on in the member-informant's mind. Such investigation requires perseverance, creativity, and critical thinking.

As noted earlier, some cults allow only carefully selected members to speak with the press or outsiders. On audiotapes discovered in Jonestown after the mass deaths, for example, listeners can hear Jones quizzing and rebuking his followers concerning how to answer questions from reporters or other visitors: 'That's right, say "we." Never say "family,"' Jones says. Before a visit by a Soviet representative, Jones briefed his followers to call him and each other 'comrade.' They were told to refrain from calling him 'Dad' or his wife, Marceline, 'Mother,' as had been their practice. 'Comrade, comrade, comrade,' Jones made them repeat *en masse*. Elsewhere on the tape, using no uncertain terms and harsh language, Jones expresses disgust with some of his followers' perceived inability to catch on: 'I'm sick of this shit,' he says. And, snidely, 'You can't ask *her*,' in reference to a woman who falters during the role-play. Clearly not satisfied with another's responses, he instructs the woman to stay away from the press: 'You should avoid the reporters like the plague, honey, because you don't think well on your feet. You just say "Hi,"' Jones admonishes (original audiotape in Reston and Adams, n.d.).

The type of briefing, grilling, and role-playing that occurs in some groups is intended to train members to respond in desired ways, rather than as they feel. As Barker so aptly described:

> Some members of some movements have gone further than concealing the truth – they have denied the truth, blatantly lying to potential converts and 'outsiders.' Furthermore, some members of some movements lie to other members of the same movement. It is not unusual for members of certain NRMs not to know what their leaders get up to – how the money is spent, exactly who issues the orders, or what the long-term goals of the leaders are.
>
> Sometimes members have been instructed to say that they are collecting money, food or other goods for the aged, for young people on drugs, or for poor people in underdeveloped countries. Sometimes these state-

ments are downright lies; at other times, they are twisting the truth; at yet
other times, the members may convince themselves that they are telling
the truth. (1995b: 49–50)

In researching cultic groups, the text is perhaps not so important as
the subtext and nonverbal cues.

Planting members trained to 'spin' in the group's front organizations
is a common tactic among cults concerned about their public image.
The research institute described earlier was not the DWP's only front
group. Another, formed in the 1980s, was named U.S. Out of Central
America (USOCA). It was designed to harvest recruits, funds, and
positive press – all possible because of public interest at that time in
political events in Central America. Among other activities, USOCA
sponsored tours to Nicaragua. Participants in one of those tours may
or may not have figured out who the DWP 'plants' were. Each tour
group included a certain number of DWP members; some were supposed to be open about their affiliation and 'exemplary' in their behaviour and attitude, whereas others were instructed to hide their DWP
membership and pretend to be ordinary citizens. Their job was to wax
enthusiastic about what they were seeing in the Sandinistas' Nicaragua, and to model being supportive of the USOCA tour guide (who
was, of course, a DWP member). Each evening, after the other tour
members were in bed, DWP members would have a secret meeting to
review the day's events, share information about and assess the
recruitability of others in the tour group, and criticize any mistakes
made during the day. Once again, several layers of activity were going
on simultaneously. Things were never exactly what they seemed.

Similar situations might occur when visitors stay at certain ashrams
or communes, when unsuspecting tourists go on tours of 'sacred'
locales in such places as Sedona (Arizona) or Mount Shasta (California), when people sign up for certain retreats or seminar trainings, or
when visitors come to any site that may be a front operation for a secretive group.

Astute researchers who want to be comprehensive will take into
account such multilayered reality construction of group scenarios.
They will seek it out, and incorporate all of it into their findings.

Problem 4: Researcher Susceptibility to the Cult's Appeal
*Researchers of cultic groups are treading into charismatic environments.
Many of these groups have great appeal – through the belief system, the activ-*

ities and interactions, the members, and, of course, the leaders. Researchers must learn how not to be overly influenced by the charismatic performance of a leader – whether it consists of showing off, or feigned humility, or both. Being dazzled by the leader's glamour is something many a researcher has experienced, if only momentarily. But the savvy researcher will acknowledge his vulnerabilities and guard against succumbing to this very human foible.

I realize how difficult it is to gain access to a cultic group, let alone remain disinterested. Barker (1995c) spoke of the dangers of getting too close to one's subject; she cautioned against favouritism in reporting, or researchers acting to protect members from experiencing bad press. Spending time with these groups, attending their services or meetings or events, observing members interact, sitting with them while their leader is lecturing – certainly only someone made of stone would not feel drawn in. How else can the researcher expect to gather data and draw interpretations? A researcher must both yield and hold back – a sometimes tricky mix in what are often extraordinary settings.

Operating with the authority of charisma, some leaders of charismatic groups go so far as to fancy themselves to be above and beyond human. (Marshall Applewhite of Heaven's Gate is but one recent example.) Not surprisingly, then, a charismatic leader's behavior may be exaggerated and flamboyant, although there are some who have preferred a low profile, at least in relation to the outside world. Bhagwan Shree Rajneesh, with his more than ninety Rolls Royces, fit the flamboyant image, whereas someone like Gino Perente, leader of a small political group, who reportedly lived in a room the size of a closet in a Brooklyn brownstone, better fit the low-profile image. Many cult leaders, however, appear to be prone to attention-seeking behaviour that is often exemplified by opulent lifestyles, a multitude of abodes, and extravagant international travel. One common approach is to mingle with the rich and famous, indulging in lavish entertaining of important people, dining with them, and sometimes even creating events at which to present awards or pose in photo opportunities with such luminaries as Mother Teresa, Nelson Mandela, current and former government officials, entertainment celebrities, professional sports personalities, or Sanskrit scholars. One end-product of such events is the increased credibility and stature of the group and its leader. Being invited to such momentous events can be impressive to a researcher, who on these occasions must always be attentive to backstage activities and the motivations and purposes of such events.

Many cult leaders are quite gifted at their public performances. It is not surprising, then, that the researcher, a mere mortal, finds herself responding to the charismatic lure. Naturally, the wise cult leader counts on such a response – it is not only self-validating but also likely to achieve some desired outcome. A researcher who finds himself swayed by the prowess, magical powers, wisdom, or flattery of a cult leader is less likely to be 'objective' in his recording and reporting. Therefore, the researcher might want to put into place certain safe-guards against those automatic emotional responses. The first would be, of course, to admit to one's susceptibility to that charismatic pull. The next would be to institute checkpoints and outside reminders to help bring you back to earth. For example: (1) ensure that you have sufficient time alone, away from group rituals, practices, and para-phernalia; (2) place regular phone calls home or to colleagues who can give you a reality check; (3) stay on a good diet with plenty of liquids, nourishment, and protein; (4) surround yourself with reminders of your usual life; and (5) engage in regular reviews of your research objectives. It is important to remember that the objective is not to get recruited, or even to have a good time, but to collect data and report on your findings.

How Not to Become a Mere Apologist for the Cult You Are Studying

No researcher wants to become a pawn of the group that he or she is studying, but it is all too easy and tempting to fall into just that trap. Cultural anthropologists have long been known to become protective of the tribes they study. The more they come to understand tribes from the inside, the more they realize how vulnerable those distant cultures are to misunderstanding back home. Similarly, with cults, many aspects of their behavior that seem weird to outsiders are much more understandable within the cult's own milieu. It is only human nature for the researcher, having worked so hard to become familiar with the cult's context, to wish to parade this expertise by explaining to the world why certain outrageous cult behaviours really do make sense when looked at from the appropriate perspective. Add to all this the fact that the leaders of totalistic cults are in a position to grant the researcher complete access to the cult with a mere wave of the hand, or just as easily to take it all away, as we have seen. Thus, the urge to ingratiate compounds itself upon the urge to protect the cult. Under such circumstances, it is no wonder that some researchers have found it difficult to resist the pressure to become apologists rather than unbiased observers.

The secrecy that often envelops cultic organizations makes that pressure all the more of an obstacle to objective research. Wilson (1988: 238) was explicit in advising researchers that the 'tendency toward secrecy is intensified' in cults and sects.[6] Investigators who are not aware of (or turn a blind eye to) this reality will be doing a disservice to their field and to their research subjects. When researchers don't make efforts to look at what might be going on behind the scenes or when they accept the front stage at face value, the results will stack up alongside some of the weaker studies and analyses in this field.

Balch's critiques of two relatively recent research projects are cases in point. A volume edited by Lewis and Melton (1994a), claiming to be a comprehensive study of The Family (Children of God), is described as being 'fundamentally an apology rather than an objective, scholarly investigation' (Balch 1996: 72) because of overt researcher bias, lack of triangulation in most of the articles, and superficiality. In another instance, Lewis and Melton's study (1994b) of the Church Universal and Triumphant was criticized for failing 'to dig into the issues that made the Church so controversial in the first place' (Balch and Langdon 1998: 198). Balch and Langdon, who had been asked to participate, reported that the study lacked a critical perspective and its design 'virtually assured that if malfeasance existed within the Church, it would not be discovered' (192). Their criticisms included the following: (1) most participants on the research team were unfamiliar with the church's belief system and knew little about the controversies surrounding the church; (2) no effort was made to inform the team of church beliefs or the controversies; (3) sharing of information during data collection was not possible because of logistical and scheduling difficulties; (4) many team members could stay only a short time, and some chose to sightsee or hang around with each other rather than learn about the church; and (5) informants consisted primarily of church officials, and the study included no former members. With such limitations as those, the study and its published results serve as another clear example of the need for an investigative and critical mind-set when researching new religions and cults.

Another instance of whitewashing occurred recently when a sociologist of religion was flown out to the West Coast as an expert to do a report on a local controversial group for a lawyer and public relations firm hired by the group (or rather, a member of the group). After two or three days in the area, the scholar asserted in writing that the group was not a cult and there was no evidence of brainwashing. His report was sent to both local and national media, as well as to some families of group members who were being affected by the brewing controversy. The report helped to stave off (and water down) media exposés, and put another wedge between some of the families and their relatives in the group. The scholar's findings, however, were at odds with other evidence from cross-corroborated, first-hand reports from almost a dozen former members and families of members, documentation from a lawsuit filed several years earlier, and extensive research done by a local investigative reporter, which included access to internal group materials and videotapes that gave direct evidence to support some of the allegations. Nevertheless, the scholar's report, based on a couple of days of visits orchestrated by the group, and supported by a well-paid public relations campaign, as well as legal threats, made it more difficult to shed light on this group's controversial backstage behaviour.

Some apologists are quick to say that everything from the 913 Jonestown deaths to the allegations of child abuse or sexual improprieties in other groups are nothing but the result of the 'bigoted and criminal' anticult movement and a handful of 'disgruntled and vengeful' former cult members. Yet, I would argue that such mud merely sullies the waters but does not change the facts. Over the years there has been enough evidence that at least some cultic groups have engaged in illegal or harmful activities, and, on a lesser scale, have created environments held together by intense forms of enforced conformity and rigid methods of controlling and constraining their members. These situations and these aspects of organizational control must not be overlooked if we are to understand these groups and their behaviors, as well as attempt to comprehend the lives and choices of the individual members. We must not be guided by 'the norms of academia [that] make us reluctant to believe or to disseminate negative facets of controversial groups' (Carter 1998: 229). Rather it is vital to look beyond the surface appeal of any group in order to examine and assess both the individual and societal ramifications and implications. Then, as Barker suggested, one's interpretation of raw data might 'become a basis for social action' (1995b: xi) that is preferably positive in nature as opposed to simply being favourable to the group's perspective.

The work of scholars in this field can and does have real-life implications. Apologies and whitewashing based on inadequate or biased research may help perpetuate harm by glossing over or covering up questionable practices and activities, and, at worst, a variety of improprieties, abuses, or crimes. A researcher's job is to produce knowledge and minimize distortion (Hammersley and Atkinson 1996). Data provided by a cultic group should never be taken at face value, and being courted or toured about by the leadership is probably not a reliable avenue to anything other than a superficial view. Every charismatic group has gatekeepers who control the group's environment, and many groups have vast public relations operations that send out polished views of their corporate world or public face. Similarly, claims by those who appear to be opponents of the group or merely are taking a critical stance must also be verified and cross-corroborated; but they should not be ignored or discounted. If Lofland and Lofland's (1995) 'questioning mind-set' is recommended in everyday research of 'ordinary' situations, then it seems only obvious that such an attitude would be all the more necessary when investigating cultic groups.

Use of Whistle-Blowers in Cult Research

Another important issue in researching cultic groups relates to the use of former members as informants and/or as researchers. Generally, in other contexts, a researcher will pursue information and insights from previous participants or other affiliated persons (e.g., consultants, business partners, investors, project collaborators, fellow-travellers, relatives). But in cult research, whether or not to use former members as sources of information has been a subject of much controversy. This controversy has raised such basic questions as the following: Should former member accounts be sought out, ignored, or overtly discounted and discredited? Are such accounts valid and reliable? Why or why not? Do all former cult members express negativity about their experiences, or just the ones who have been 'deprogrammed'? Do all former cult members who speak critically about their experiences have an unworthy agenda? Why are some scholars adamant about deriding the accounts of those who are critical of their former group?

Central to this discussion is the issue of the reliability and validity of so-called apostate accounts. According to Merriam-Webster's Collegiate Dictionary (10th ed.), *apostasy* merely means 'abandonment of a previous loyalty' or 'renunciation of a religious faith.' Yet some scholars appear determined to discredit the testimony of any and all former cult members (see, for example, Bromley 1998b). They label former-member accounts as atrocity tales, and promote the idea that they should never be taken seriously. Instead, such researchers tend to rely on the accounts of leaders and current members, as well as accepting at face value the group's literature (when it exists) and explanations.

However, other scholars do believe in the truthfulness and the value of the accounts of former members. There is a risk in doing so, however – such as being accused of being an anticult-movement sympathizer, not getting published in certain academic journals, not being accepted as a conference participant, being pressured to conform, or, as discussed earlier, being threatened or harassed by the cult in question (Ayella 1990; Balch and Langdon 1998; Kent 1994; Singer 1995; Zablocki 1997c, 1998).

Zablocki (1996) supports the use of former-member accounts. He studied a sample of 281 members of communal religious movements and cults: 176 were still believers, and 105 were apostates. They were compared with 109 members of a control group of individuals who were members of non-religious communes. Zablocki found no significant differences between the reliability of believer accounts and apostate accounts, with neither group's accounts being less reliable than the control-group accounts. Also, both believer and apostate accounts had a similar moderate level of validity. Balch and Langdon (1998) further supported this when they concluded that 'defectors are more trustworthy than sociologists like to believe' (201). They reported that Balch found few inconsistencies between his field-note observations and ex-member accounts about the same events months later; similarly, he found that ex-member accounts were able to be corroborated against each other.

In fact, former-member reports could be regarded as vital to obtaining a more comprehensive picture of certain cults. Especially taking into account the level at which a person functioned while in the group, a former-member informant who was in leadership or had other kinds of access to privileged locations or information is a valued source of information (Carter 1998). Wilson (1988) noted that the lack of cooperation on the part of leaders or members will influence '*what* can be discovered and *how* what is discovered is understood' (230). In this vein, Zablocki (1996) reminds us that ethnographers rarely see anything but front-stage behaviour. The implication of Wilson's and Zablocki's comments is that it is even more crucial to gather data from those who have participated in and left a group. Seeing only front-stage behaviour typically means that a researcher will not get to hear members talk about what is really on their minds.

Many researchers in this field insist on the need for triangulation (using multiple sources of varying viewpoints), although few seem to practise what they preach (Zablocki 1996). This lack of thoroughness has been reinforced by those who strive to delegitimate the entire category of former-member accounts. For such researchers there are two types of former members: (1) 'good' former members (called leave-takers) who leave the group quietly, and (2) 'bad' former members (labeled apostates) who voice discontent about their experiences (Zablocki 1997a). Here is but one example of this crude typology:

> The apostate is a defector who is aligned with an oppositional coalition in an effort to broaden a dispute, and embraces public claimsmaking activities to attack his or her former group. Unlike typical leavetakers whose responses range from indifference to quiet disenchantment, the apostate assumes a vituperative or hostile posture and pursues a moral campaign to discredit the group. (Wright 1998: 109)

Bromley (1998a), Wright (1995a, 1998), Lewis (1995), and others put forth the notion that so-called career apostates (those bad former members) have won over and influenced the views of journalists, commentators, and, hence, the general public. Yet, I have seen no evidence of any solid effort on the part of those scholars to ascertain, for example, what percentage of former members actually even speak out about their groups, much less in the exaggerated form attributed to them. It is my contention that the image of the vengeful, fabricating apostate has a shabby foundation.

In fact, in my experience it is extremely difficult to put together a panel of even three or four former members for a public education program. In most cases, former members are reluctant to speak about their experiences or participate in public forums – not because they do not have important experiences and insights to share, but rather because they are self-critical, cautious, stigmatized, and fearful of lawsuits. In many instances, those who have decided to speak publicly or write about their experiences have chosen not to identify the group or name the leader.[7] Sometimes this has been done out of respect for the privacy and confidentiality of other group members; but also, such an approach has been taken because the aim was not to point fingers or name names, as the following illustrates.

One former cult member, who had been exploited sexually for more than sixteen years by her self-proclaimed 'celibate' swami, exemplified such magnanimity when she wrote, 'I do not want to obscure my primary purpose of helping others understand manipulative influence processes by making this article appear to be a mere exposé of the deeds of somebody who hurt me' (Betz 1997: 85). Describing first being seduced at age twenty-three by her spiritual teacher, twenty years her senior, the author did not simply lambast his improprieties and the violation of his role as her minister. Instead, she presented a heartfelt and complex picture of what was going on in her own mind at the time and how she rationalized in order to satisfy her own spiritual longing and survival needs, and, in so doing, adopted the leader's justification for his actions, which he attributed to a '7,000-year-old yogic secret.' She also discussed in the article her own inner torment until she finally spoke out about the 'harmful secret,' only to feel the hostility of other group members who were annoyed that she was revealing the misdeeds. This led to her departure from the group, after twenty-one years of membership, and eventually to some disintegration of the group itself. In the end, former members have provided invaluable insights into complex phenomena, making important contributions to our understanding of cults and charismatic relationships (see, for example, A Collective of Women 1997; Lalich 1992, 1993, 1996, 1997a, 2000, forthcoming; Layton 1998; MacDonald 1988; Siskind 1995; Stein 1997; Tobias and Lalich 1994; Weishaupt and Stensland 1997; Winocur et al. 1997).

The Issue of Reflexivity Bias

Reflexivity bias can occur when the researcher is also a member or an ex-member of the cult being studied and therefore sees the cult in part as reflected through his or her own internalized cult worldview and/ or memories of cult experiences. Clearly, such researchers have the benefit of having had an inside look, which can provide insight into other similar situations and is a vantage point not often shared by others. Yet, the insider perspective can also color what the researcher sees and the conclusions she draws. Along with the opportunities afforded by insider status, doing research on a cult with which one had been affiliated poses a set of unique challenges. Some examples from my own experience – as a former cult member and now researcher – will illustrate some of these challenges and how they can be met.

First, and most obviously, it is important to openly acknowledge any personal interest in the subject in general, any personal experiences that may influence objectivity, any residual cult or anticult point of view, as well as any bias one may have concerning the group being studied. (See Burawoy et al. 1991; Sobo and de Munck 1998; Steier 1995, for general discussions of reflexivity; see Rochford 1994 for a specific instance.) In my own case, I have never hidden the fact that I had a professional interest as a practitioner and consultant, having worked with families of individuals involved in cultic groups or relationships, and with former members of such groups to help them find balance in their assessment of their experiences and regain a sense of future. I also lecture and perform other public education services related to this broad topic. Certainly my interest in this whole subject stems in part from having been a member of a cult; but it is also rooted in my concern as a member of society who has always been critical of human injustices, bigotry, and indecencies, and has looked for solutions to them, as well as seeking positive alternative ways of living.

I am well aware of the possibility that others might claim that my conclusions are influenced by my own subjective perspectives. Therefore, I am careful to use standard research methodologies and practices that will enhance objectivity, authenticity, and verification. Seeking out multiple sources of data, requesting peer review, engaging in prolonged study or observation, and checking perceptions with informants are the types of insurance policies that I adopt, to the extent possible. This is no different, of course, from what is recommended for any type of qualitative study (Creswell 1998; Lofland and Lofland 1995; Miles and Huberman 1994; Robson 1993; Silverman 1993; Yin 1994).

Researchers who have been members of the groups they are studying have the considerable advantage of already knowing the cult's private 'language.' They know what the leader means by his or her often-coded utterances. They know where to look, and what veils to shake loose. They are familiar with the effect of the leader's words (spoken or written) on the devotees. They have lived with and shared the group's attitudes towards outsiders. They may even be aware of the false claims, the tricks, the devices used to sway and convince. For example, in one group, words were manipulated to serve the leader's sexual urges, so that 'meditating with swami' meant engaging in sexual activities with him (Betz 1997). That usage was understood only by those in his inner circle who were expected to participate in the sexual behavior. Someone from outside listening to an adherent of this particular swami, or observing behavior around the ashram, probably would not catch on to the subterranean world of words, glances, gestures, relationships, and so on, whereas a former-member researcher stands to grasp more precisely the meanings of statements and actions. Just as Peoples Temple leaders knew how Jones was orchestrating fake healings (Maaga 1998), manipulating outsiders to gain political influence (Hall 1987), and hiding church funds (Layton 1998), so did Muster (1997) know how the ISKCON public relations department was being used to help cover up misdeeds, and so did I know that DWP internal documents were hidden under floorboards in our administrative facility, that we had 'safe' houses whose locations were to be kept secret, and that on occasion goon squads were sent to mess up someone's life – surely not features the DWP would have been likely to disclose publicly.

The ability to comprehend a cult's literature or spoken word is also enhanced by having shared the insider perspective. For example, in the DWP we were fond of saying, 'The children are our future,' which implied that we loved children. Yet, DWP members were discouraged from having children, and those who already had them were discriminated against in terms of types of assignments and other 'rewards,' while the children themselves were treated as second-class citizens, shuffled around in the evenings to party-organized child care, and given little attention from the adults.

Naturally, as with any research, a former member's memories and perceptions must be corroborated, and triangulation becomes critical. But having been there lends a perspective and provides insights not otherwise possible. Ultimately, I see no problem in former cult members conducting research on their own group or any other so long as 'experiences prior to entering the field [are] subjected to analytic reflection' (Hammersley and Atkinson 1996: 29).

How to Get a Peek Backstage When the Cult Doesn't Want You To

Cults are private organizations and deserve respect for their privacy. It follows from this that when a cult says 'No, thank you' to a request for research access, the 'no' response should be respected. And, perhaps even more obviously, a researcher does not have the ethical right to infiltrate a cult's circles by pretending to be a devotee. However, it does not follow from this that cults have the right to play it coy with researchers and show the pretty side while hiding the ugly. Researchers have rights too; and, once a researcher has been invited in, there is nothing wrong with trying to see behind the masks and the façade. Doing so during any but the briefest stay at a cult is far from impossible, but it does require that the researcher keep her wits about her.

Various scholars have presented useful suggestions to help pave the way. More than a decade ago, Balch (1985) offered a comprehensive guide for the kind of data needed in the studies of these groups. His hope was that these categories would become standard. The categories are (1) demographic characteristics of membership, (2) historical development, (3) structure and content of belief system, (4) leadership, (5) social organization, (6) relationship between members and outsiders, (7) economic system, (8) material culture, (9) patterns of everyday life, (10) talk, (11) sexual relationships, (12) child-rearing, (13) deviance and social control, (14) recruitment strategies, (15) commitments demanded of members, (16) socialization techniques, (17) conversion experiences, and (18) defection. Balch argued that too often in published studies many of those topics were ignored or touched on too lightly to be useful for comparative purposes. In agreement with that perspective, I believe that researchers would be making a far greater contribution to the study of cults if they kept those categories in mind as they went about their work.

More recently, Balch and Langdon (1998) had these suggestions: 'First, scholars who study alternative religions need to be familiar with the charges against them before they begin collecting data. Second, they should not take members' claims at face value, however reasonable they seem. Third, they need to interview defectors and other critics to get different viewpoints, although here too they must be aware of hidden agendas. Finally, whatever the source of information, statements presented as fact need to be corroborated and verified with independent evidence' (207). Those four points, in my opinion, could serve as an invaluable guide for researchers of cults and controversial new religious and social movements.

Here are some of my own pointers:

1 *Watch how people relate to each other, and especially how they act around the leader.* For example, in one Heaven's Gate recruitment video, the leader, Do, is lecturing about their beliefs and *raison d'être* (*Beyond Human* 1991). He states that two of his students (followers) are there with him to ask questions, but they rarely get a chance to speak because Do talks all the way through as the students sit quietly and

smile. The interaction in that video indicates quite a lot about the power relations in that group. Do was not simply a soft-spoken, fatherly type who occasionally got teary-eyed; he was also the one in control (Lalich 1997b, 2000, forthcoming).

2 *Ask tough questions – about money, about sex, about decision-making procedures, about time away from the group, about independent thinking.* Be ready with specific questions, and don't let them get deflected or turned back on you. Insist on specific answers, and don't accept digressions or evasions. Get examples. Consider speaking with former members beforehand, so that you as the researcher will be armed with the types of probes that should generate some useful data.

3 *Look carefully at all mechanisms of conformity and control.* Study the living quarters, clothing style, and speech and mannerisms to assess the extent of individual expression. Find out about group dynamics, criticism sessions, confessionals, or other means of using group processes to enforce conformity through humiliation, guilt, shame, and various means of influence and peer pressure.

4 *Determine how the group tolerates – or does not tolerate – dissent.* Assess how former members are regarded, whether current members have access to former members or critical reports, and how much contact there is with families and other 'outsiders.' Also, find out if there is an internal justice system, a mechanism for feedback, and also one for appeals.

5 *When evaluating documents, use the same reflexive and critical thinking as in any other project.* Be sure to review both external (for public consumption) and internal (for members only) documents; in the latter category, there are likely to be tiers of documents meant for members at ascending levels of commitment or trust. Using questions such as those posed in basic research texts would be a good start: 'How are documents written? How are they read? Who writes them? Who reads them? For what purposes? On what occasions? With what outcomes? What is recorded? What is omitted? What does the writer seem to take for granted about the reader(s)? What do readers need to know in order to make sense of them? The list can be extended readily, and the exploration of such questions would lead the ethnographer inexorably towards a systematic examination of each and every aspect of everyday life in the setting in question' (Hammersley and Atkinson 1996: 173–4).

6 *Fact-check everything you can.* For example, DWP leader Dixon repeatedly boasted that she had been a leader in the Civil Rights move-

ment. However, based on my research after I left the group, all I could gather was that she went *once* with a busload of students to a demonstration in the South, and possibly worked with one of the activist organizations at the time. Group lore transforms easily into self-perpetuating myths that serve the cult's image. It is important to look beyond the obvious, and use multiple sources of information and verification, including going outside the confines of the information provided by the cult and/or its archives.

Overall my advice is, be more like state investigators who drop in on nursing homes unannounced. Assume that things will be hidden, or prettied up. Be on the lookout for less-than-obvious findings and nonverbal cues. Charismatic leaders don't need to hold a gun to their followers' heads to get them to comply, but charismatic magic does only part of the job. Thus, explore specifically how the system works to bind members to the group and/or leader. Who are the key players and what are the crucial interactions? Where and when do they take place? How can you, the researcher, gain access to that?

As Lofland and Lofland (1995) cautioned, 'The researcher is bound to doubt and to check and to hold *all* claims as simply claims. This creates an unavoidable tension between social scientists, group members, and any champions of those members' (154–5). An objective look that does not gloss over what is there requires being aware of the ways in which cultic groups can cover up or tone down. To reveal or write about these realities is not an attack on religious deviance or non-mainstream behaviour; rather, it is offering a more complete look at complex phenomena. Whether or not a researcher takes the next step of also providing a critique of certain social practices is an individual choice.

Conclusion: Deviance Amplification vs. Deviance Whitewashing

Delving into another person's social reality in the pursuit of scientific observation is a risky business by any measure. My aim here was not to claim that I know better how to fathom the 'truths' of another person's world. Rather my objective has been to highlight some of the difficulties one can expect in researching a cultic milieu. In that regard I have addressed issues pertinent to the intellectual virginity of the young scholar, as well as the intellectual integrity of the more seasoned scholar. Cults are about charisma, power, transcendent belief, and complex social relations; they are also about impression management, and, in many instances, about secrets, concealment, and obfuscation. Going into the field with some sense of what might be going on backstage, or even that there might be something going on backstage, is a first step towards gathering solid data for a useful knowledge base. Then, being keenly aware of the ways in which a group may attempt to obstruct your view is not necessarily a guarantee of learning about the reality of that group, but it is certainly a more likely approach to coming out with the ability to construct reliable and accurate representations.

I don't think any of us can claim to be 'more "scientific"' or 'more balanced, objective, and accurate' or even 'less biased, subjective, and wrong' (Barker 1995c: 288) – unless we have looked at as big a picture as possible of any one group. That means looking in, under, through, and around; looking before, during, and after; it means not limiting informants to only active participants and supporters, nor to only former members and detractors; it means being cognizant of personal biases and susceptibilities; and it means seriously weighing features and factors that might make one side or another less pleased with the final result. Protecting one's intellectual integrity can become almost everyday fare in the heated atmosphere of a controversial group. Others have also discussed the ethical dilemma inherent in glossing over the dark side (see, for example, Balch and Langdon 1998; Carter 1998; Kent and Krebs 1998a, 1998b; Zablocki 1997c). A researcher must remain committed to the scientific community, not to the cult or some other special-interest group.

Sometimes it appears as though we scholars ourselves and our motivations have become more the objects of inquiry than the cults that piqued our curiosity in the first place. Not long ago Barker (1995c) raised the concern that researchers of what she called the 'cult scene' were letting others define the research agenda. She was referring to academic researchers responding to the activities (and perceived victories) of the anticult movement.[8] Evidently, some scholars feared that emotional stories of distress were being heard over and above the scholars' objective analyses. Hence, some scholars began working overtime to get the upper hand in what they regarded as a volatile situation, and, as a result, in some cases, their research suffered. Wright (1995b), for example, concluded that anticultists have made a bad situation worse by creating a public hysteria about the cult issue. From his perspective, this was a case of 'deviance amplification.' Wright (1995a) bolstered his argument by citing Max Weber, who believed that sectarian movements were the driving force for reform and change, and that they would necessarily be unstable, volatile, and explosive. Perhaps true. But that does not mean the groups should be spared incisive inquiry.

It is my conclusion that one of the major blockage points in resolving this problematic rests in the utilization of the wrong overall paradigm. This is why I hold firm on the use of the word *cult* rather than the term *new religious movement* to describe these objects of our study. There is a widespread misconception that 'cults' are a phenomenon inextricably bound up in religion and that negative findings about cults, therefore, give religion as a whole a black eye. That idea not only sets up obstacles to carrying out meaningful research, but also potentially contributes to both the researcher and society turning a blind eye to certain groups' practices that sometimes result in injuries to children and adult members, and to social ramifications (like the stockpiling of weapons) that could be considered pathological or antisocial. Because of this propensity to regard all cults as religious entities, there has come to be a professional and public tendency to excuse the aberrant behavior of certain groups in deference to our society's principle of freedom of religion. Yet, there are serious consequences if we continue to regard these groups only as religious and their behaviours as manifestations of a 'growth phase.' For then, at the extreme end of the spectrum, those groups engaged in activities that violate ordinary civil or criminal law will continue to function as though they are above the law, believing themselves to be sheltered by a First Amendment privilege which they hope will shield them from scrutiny. For accountability's sake, these groups should be held to the same standards of civil behaviour as secular organizations and social movements. And researchers of cultic groups – be they benign or harmful – would do well to bear this in mind.

The polar opposites in the 'misunderstanding cults' debate can be caricatured as those on the one side who look at any cult and say, 'Oh, horrors,' and those on the other side who look at the same groups in an extremely sympathetic manner and explain away the causes for concern. The flip side of deviance amplification is deviance whitewashing. Neither is a desirable course. In studying a controversial ideological social group or movement, ideally a researcher wants to construct an objective portrayal – of its normalcy and of its deviance. It is my hope that the ideas presented in this chapter will contribute to that end.

Notes

The author thanks Richard Appelbaum, Trude Bennett, Marny Hall, John Horton, Michael Langone, and Fred Steier for their commentaries and feedback on draft versions of this chapter. Also, I acknowledge with much appreciation Ben Zablocki, who pushed me to clarify my ideas with his astute comments and unrelenting red pen.

1   I joined the DWP in 1975, shortly after its founding in 1974. Almost immediately I was put into leadership, and most years I was also part of the leader's inner circle. The DWP was Marxist-Leninist in orientation; its stated aim was to bring about a workers' state, although we did not believe that would occur in our lifetimes. We saw ourselves as martyrs for the cause. I was still in the group at the time of its demise, which began in late 1985 and culminated in the sale of all assets and the disbursement of funds among members in 1987. For more details see Lalich (1992, 1993, 2000, forthcoming) and Siegel et al. (1987).

2   The relating of this incident is based on my recollection of the events. I have corroborated this account with others who also were members at the time and were present for these events.

3   I recognize that some scholars assert that referring to a group's organizational affiliates as front groups is the hallmark of an incorrigible apostate stance (see, for example, Bromley 1998a: 42). On the other hand, I contend that it is somewhat naive not to consider as well the possibility that some groups have been very deliberate in their establishment of a variety of venues, with an array of names that serve an assortment of organizational purposes, from recruitment to fundraising to money laundering to public relations to civic participation to any range of services and functions. That a group-sponsored association or event does some good does not necessarily preclude the fact that concomitantly it is serving a hidden organizational purpose with less than honest, or less upfront motives. The fact that in many instances the relationship between the two (the parent organization and the affiliate) is not spelled out is not insignificant.

4   For reasons of confidentiality and privacy, I am not naming my source here.

5   The article was eventually published in the *Cultic Studies Journal* (Kent 1994).

6   In the article Wilson uses 'religious minorities,' although it is clear that he is referring to new religious movements, cults, and sects.

7   This statement is not meant to imply that I support only total anonymity in personal accounts. I am merely recognizing the dilemma, as well as

acknowledging that lessons can be learned without naming names. In actuality, I believe that both types of accounts are valuable.

8 The very fact that some scholars have consistently called this movement the anticult movement as opposed to the cult-awareness movement, which is how it referred to itself, is somewhat indicative of the warrior mind-set of certain scholars.

References

A Collective of Women. 1997. 'Sex, Lies, and Grand Schemes of Thought in Closed Groups.' *Cultic Studies Journal* 14 (1): 58–84.

Ayella, Marybeth. 1990. '"They Must Be Crazy": Some of the Difficulties in Researching "Cults."' *American Behavioral Scientist* 33 (5): 562–77.

Balch, Robert W. 1985. 'What's Wrong with the Study of New Religions and What We Can Do about It.' Paper read at annual meeting of the Pacific Division of the American Association for the Advancement of Science. San Francisco, October.

– 1996. Review of *Sex, Slander, and Salvation: Investigating The Family/Children of God*, edited by J.R. Lewis and J.G. Melton. *Journal for the Scientific Study of Religion* 35: 72.

Balch, Robert W., and Stephan Langdon. 1998. 'How the Problem of Malfeasance Gets Overlooked in Studies of New Religions: An Examination of the AWARE Study of the Church Universal and Triumphant.' In *Wolves within the Fold: Religious Leadership and Abuses of Power*, edited by A. Shupe. New Brunswick, N.J.: Rutgers University Press.

Barker, Eileen. 1995a. '*Plus ça change.*' In *20 Years On: Changes in New Religious Movements*. Special edition of *Social Compass* 42, edited by E. Barker and J.-F. Mayer, 165–80.

– 1995b. *New Religious Movements: A Practical Introduction*. London: HMSO.

– 1995c. 'The Scientific Study of Religion? You Must Be Joking!' *Journal for the Scientific Study of Religion* 34: 287–310.

Betz, Katherine E. 1997. 'No Place to Go: Life in a Prison Without Bars. *Cultic Studies Journal* 14 (1): 85–105.

Beyond human: The Last Call. 1991. Videocassette, sessions 1 and 2, produced by Total Overcomers Anonymous.

Bromley, David G. 1998a. 'The Social Construction of Contested Exit Roles.' In *The Politics of Apostasy: The Role of Apostates in the Transformation of Religious Movements*, edited by D.G. Bromley. Westport, Conn.: Praeger.

– ed. 1998b. *The Politics of Apostasy: The Role of Apostates in the Transformation of Religious Movements.* Westport, Conn.: Praeger.

Burawoy, Michael, Alice Burton, Ann Arnett Ferguson, Kathryn J. Fox, Joshua Gamson, Nadine Gartrell, Leslie Hurst, Charles Kurzman, Leslie Salzinger, Josepha Schiffman, and Shiori Ui, eds. 1991. *Ethnography Unbound: Power and Resistance in the Modern Metropolis.* Berkeley: University of California Press.

Carter, Lewis F. 1990. *Charisma and Control in Rajneeshpuram: The Role of Shared Values in the Creation of a Community.* New York: Cambridge University Press.

– 1998. 'Carriers of Tales: On Assessing Credibility of Apostate and Other Outsider Accounts of Religious Practices.' In *The Politics of Apostasy: The Role of Apostates in the Transformation of Religious Movements,* edited by D.G. Bromley. Westport, Conn.: Praeger.

Chatterjee, Suman. 1985. *Suman Chatterjee Interview with Marlene Dixon on the U.S. Left Today.* N.p.

Creswell, John W. 1998. *Qualitative Inquiry and Research Design: Choosing Among Five Traditions.* Thousand Oaks, Calif.: Sage.

Dixon, Marlene. 1977a. 'The Rise and Demise of Women's Liberation.' *Synthesis* II (1, 2): 21–38.

– 1977b. 'The Sisterhood Ripoff.' *Synthesis* II (1,2): 39–47.

– 1978. 'What's in a Name?: A Critical Review of Barbara and John Ehrenreich's "Professional-Managerial Class."' *Synthesis* II (3): 68–89.

– 1979. 'Statement of the General Secretary Introducing the Workers Party.' In *The Founding of the Workers Party.* San Francisco: Synthesis Publications.

Geertz, Clifford. 1973. *The Interpretation of Cultures.* New York: Basic Books.

Hall, John R. 1987. *Gone from the Promised Land: Jonestown in American Cultural History.* New Brunswick, N.J.: Transaction Books.

Hammersley, Martyn, and Paul Atkinson. 1996. *Ethnography: Principles in Practice.* 2d ed. London: Routledge.

Kent, Stephen A. 1994. 'Lustful Prophet: A Psychosexual Historical Study of the Children of God's Leader, David Berg.' *Cultic Studies Journal* 11 (2): 135–88.

Kent, Stephen A., and Theresa Krebs. 1998a. 'Academic Compromise in the Social Scientific Study of Alternative Religions.' *Nova Religio* 2 (1): 45–54.

– 1998b. 'When Scholars Know Sin: Alternative Religions and Their Academic Supporters.' *Skeptic* 6 (3): 36–44.

Lalich, Janja. 1992. 'The Cadre Ideal: Origins and Development of a Political Cult.' *Cultic Studies Journal* 9 (1): 1–77.

– 1993. 'A Little Carrot and a Lot of Stick: A Case Example.' In *Recovery from Cults: Help for Victims of Psychological and Spiritual Abuse,* edited by M.D. Langone. New York: Norton.

- 1996. 'Repairing the Soul after a Cult Experience.' *Creation Spirituality Network Magazine*, 12 (1): 30–33.
- 1997a. *Women under the Influence: A Study of Women's Lives in Totalist Groups.* Special edition of the *Cultic Studies Journal* 14 (1).
- 1997b. 'Mimesis and Metaphors in the Discourse of Heaven's Gate Students.' Paper read at the annual meeting of the Society for the Scientific Study of Religion. San Diego, Calif. (November).
- 2000. 'Bounded Choice: The Fusion of Personal Freedom and Self-renunciation in Two Transcendent Groups.' PhD diss., Fielding Institute, Santa Barbara, Calif.
- Forthcoming. *Bounded Choice: True Believers and Charismatic Commitments.* Berkeley: University of California Press.
Langone, Michael D. 1993. 'Introduction.' In *Recovery from Cults: Help for Victims of Psychological and Spiritual Abuse*, edited by M.D. Langone. New York: Norton.
Layton, Deborah. 1998. *Seductive Poison: A Jonestown Survivor's Story of Life and Death in the Peoples Temple.* New York: Anchor Books.
Lewis, James R. 1995. 'Self-fulfilling Stereotypes, the Anticult Movement, and the Waco Conflagration.' In *Armageddon in Waco: Critical Perspectives on the Branch Davidian Conflict*, edited by S.A. Wright. Chicago: University of Chicago Press.
Lewis, James R., and J. Gordon Melton, eds. 1994a. *Sex, Slander, and Salvation: Investigating The Family / Children of God.* Stanford, Calif.: Center for Academic Publication.
- 1994b. *Church Universal Triumphant in Scholarly Perspective.* Stanford, Calif.: Center for Academic Publication.
Lifton, Robert Jay. 1979. 'The Appeal of the Death Trip.' *The New York Times Magazine* (7 January): 26–7, 29–31.
- 1987. *The Future of Immortality and Other Essays for a Nuclear Age.* New York: Basic Books.
- 1991. 'Cult Formation.' *Harvard Mental Health Letter* 7 (8).
- 1999. *Destroying the World to Save It: Aum Shinrikyo, Apocalyptic Violence, and the New Global Terrorism.* New York: Metropolitan Books.
Lofland, John, and Lyn H. Lofland. 1995. *Analyzing Social Settings: A Guide to Qualitative Observation and Analysis.* 3d ed. Belmont, Calif.: Wadsworth.
Maaga, Mary McCormick. 1998. *Hearing the Voices of Jonestown.* Syracuse, N.Y.: Syracuse University Press.
MacDonald, Jerry Paul. 1988. '"Reject the Wicked Man" – Coercive Persuasion and Deviance Production: A Study of Conflict Management.' *Cultic Studies Journal* 5 (1): 59–121.

Melton, J. Gordon. 1998. 'Mea culpa! Mea culpa!: J. Gordon Melton Answers His Critics.' Available online at www.cesnur.org/melton98.htm.

Miles, Matthew B., and A. Michael Huberman. 1994. *Qualitative Data Analysis*. 2d ed. Thousand Oaks, Calif.: Sage.

Muster, Nori J. 1997. *Betrayal of the Spirit: My Life Behind the Headlines of the Hare Krishna Movement*. Urbana: University of Illinois Press.

The People Make History: The Practice of the Workers Party, Rebel Workers Organization and Grass Roots Alliance. Np, nd.

Reston, James, Jr., and Noah Adams. N.d. *'Father Cares': The Last of Jonestown*. Audiocassette. Washington, D.C.: National Public Radio.

Robson, Colin. 1993. *Real World Research: A Resource for Social Scientists and Practitioner-Researchers*. Cambridge, Mass.: Blackwell.

Rochford, Burke E. 1994. 'Field Work and Membership with the Hare Krishna. In *Constructions of Deviance: Social Power, Context, and Interaction*, edited by P.A. Adler and P. Adler. Belmont, Calif.: Wadsworth.

Rubin, Julius H. 1998. 'Techniques for Suppressing Information Used by New Religious Groups. Paper read at the annual meeting of the Society for the Scientific Study of Religion, Montreal, Canada, November.

Siegel, Peter, Nancy Strohl, Laura Ingram, David Roche, and Jean Taylor. 1987. 'Leninism as Cult: The Democratic Workers Party.' *Socialist Review* 17 (6): 60–85.

Silverman, David. 1993. *Interpreting Qualitative Data: Methods for Analysing Talk, Text and Interaction*. London: Sage.

Singer, Margaret Thaler. 1995. *Cults in Our Midst: The Hidden Menace in Our Everyday Lives*. San Francisco: Jossey-Bass.

Siskind, Amy B. 1995. 'The Sullivan Institute/Fourth Wall Community: The Relationship of Radical Individualism and Authoritarianism.' PhD diss. New School for Social Research, New York.

Sobo, Elisa J., and Victor C. de Munck. 1998. 'The Forest of Methods.' In *Using Methods in the Field: A Practical Introduction and Casebook*, edited by V. C. de Munck and E. J. Sobo. Walnut Creek, Calif.: Alta Mira Press.

Stark, Rodney, and William Sims Bainbridge. 1996. *A Theory of Religion*. New Brunswick, N.J.: Rutgers University Press.

Steier, Frederick. 1995. 'Reflexivity, Interpersonal Communication, and Interpersonal Communication Research.' In *Social Approaches to Communication*, edited by W. Leeds-Hurwitz. New York: Guilford Press.

Stein, Alexandra. 1997. 'Mothers in Cults: The Influence of Cults on the Relationship of Mothers to Their Children.' *Cultic Studies Journal* 14 (1): 40–57.

Tobias, Madeleine Landau, and Janja Lalich. 1994. *Captive Hearts, Captive Minds: Freedom and Recovery from Cults and Abusive Relationships*. Alameda, Calif.: Hunter House.

Weishaupt, Kaynor J., and Michael D. Stensland. 1997. 'Wifely Subjection: Mental Health Issues in Jehovah's Witness Women.' *Cultic Studies Journal* 14 (1): 106–44.

Wilson, Bryan R. 1988. 'Methodological Perspectives in the Study of Religious Minorities.' *Bulletin of the John Rylands University Library of Manchester* 70 (3): 225–40.

Winocur, Nadine, Jonibeth Whitney, Carol Sorenson, Peggy Vaughn, and David Foy. 1997. 'The Individual Cult Experience Index: The Assessment of Cult Involvement and Its Relationship to Postcult Distress.' *Cultic Studies Journal* 14 (2): 290–306.

Wright, Stuart A. 1995a. 'Introduction: Another View of the Mt. Carmel Stand-off.' In *Armageddon in Waco: Critical Perspectives on the Branch Davidian Conflict*, edited by S.A. Wright. Chicago: University of Chicago Press.

– 1995b. 'Construction and Escalation of a Cult Threat.' In *Armageddon in Waco: Critical Perspectives on the Branch Davidian Conflict*, edited by S.A. Wright. Chicago: University of Chicago Press.

– 1998. 'Exploring Factors that Shape the Apostate Role.' In *The Politics of Apostasy: The Role of Apostates in the Transformation of Religious Movements*, edited by D.G. Bromley. Westport, Conn.: Praeger.

Yin, Robert K. 1994. *Case Study Research: Design and Methods.* 2d ed. Thousand Oaks, Calif.: Sage.

Zablocki, Benjamin D. 1971. *The Joyful Community.* Baltimore, Md.: Penguin Books.

– 1980. *Alienation and Charisma: A Study of Contemporary American Communes.* New York: Free Press.

– 1996. 'Reliability and Validity of Apostate Accounts in the Study of Religious Communities.' Paper read at the annual meeting of the Association for the Sociology of Religion, New York.

– 1997a. 'A Sociological Theory of Cults.' Paper read at annual meeting of the American Family Foundation, Philadelphia, May.

– 1997b. 'Distinguishing Front-stage from Back-stage Behavior in the Study of Religious Communities.' Paper read at the Society for the Scientific Study of Religions at San Diego, Calif. (November).

– 1997c. 'The Blacklisting of a Concept: The Strange History of the Brainwashing Conjecture in the Sociology of Religion.' *Nova Religio* 1 (1): 96–121.

– 1998. 'Reply to Bromley.' *Nova Religio* 1 (2): 267–71.

– 1999. 'Hyper Compliance in Charismatic Groups.' In *Mind, Brain and Society: Toward a Neurosociology of Emotion*, edited by D.D. Franks and T.S. Smith. Stamford, Conn.: JAI Press.

Part Two

HOW CONSTRAINED ARE THE PARTICIPANTS?

5. Towards a Demystified and Disinterested Scientific Theory of Brainwashing

Benjamin Zablocki

Nobody likes to lose a customer, but religions get more touchy than most when faced with the risk of losing devotees they have come to define as their own. Historically, many religions have gone to great lengths to prevent apostasy, believing virtually any means justified to prevent wavering parishioners from defecting and thus losing hope of eternal salvation. In recent centuries, religion in our society has evolved from a system of territorially based near-monopolies into a vigorous and highly competitive faith marketplace in which many churches, denominations, sects, and cults vie with one another for the allegiance of 'customers' who are free to pick and choose among competing faiths. Under such circumstances, we should expect to find that some of the more tight-knit and fanatical religions in this rough-and-tumble marketplace will have developed sophisticated persuasive techniques for holding on to their customers. Some of the most extreme of these techniques are known in the literature by the controversial term 'brainwashing.' This chapter is devoted to a search for a scientific definition of brainwashing and an examination of the evidence for the existence of brainwashing in cults. I believe that research on this neglected subject is important for a fuller understanding of religious market dynamics.[1] And, ultimately, research on this subject may yield a wider dividend as well, assisting us in our quest for a fuller understanding of mass charismatic movements such as Fascism, Nazism, Stalinism, and Maoism.

Do We Need to Know Whether Cults Engage in Brainwashing?

The question of why people obey the sometimes bizarrely insane commands of charismatic leaders, even unto death, is one of the big unsolved mysteries of history and the social sciences. If there are deliberate techniques that charismatic leaders (and charismatically led organizations) use to induce high levels of uncritical loyalty and obedience in their followers, we should try to understand what these techniques are and under what circumstances and how well they work.

This chapter is about nothing other than the process of inducing ideological obedience in charismatic groups. Many people call this process brainwashing, but the label is unimportant. What is important is that those of us who want to understand cults develop models that recognize the importance that some cults give to strenuous techniques of socialization designed to induce uncritical obedience to ideological imperatives regardless of the cost to the individual.

The systematic study of obedience has slowed down considerably within the behavioural sciences. Early laboratory studies of obedience-inducing mechanisms got off to a promising start in the 1960s and 1970s, but were correctly criticized by human rights advocates for putting laboratory subjects under unacceptable levels of stress (Kelman and Hamilton 1989; Milgram 1975; Zimbardo 1973). Permission to do obedience-inducing experiments on naive experimental subjects became almost impossible to obtain and these sorts of laboratory experiments virtually ceased. However, large numbers of charismatic cultic movements appeared on the scene just in time to fill this vacuum left by abandoned laboratory studies. Being naturally occurring social 'experiments,' obedience-induction in such groups could be studied ethnographically without raising the ethical objections that had been raised concerning laboratory studies.

Social theorists are well aware that an extremely high degree of obedience to authority is a reliably recurring feature of charismatic cult organizations (Lindholm 1990; Oakes 1997). But most social scientists interested in religion declined this opportunity. For reasons having more to do with political correctness than scientific curiosity, most of them refused to design research focused on obedience-induction. Many even deny that deliberate programs of obedience-induction ever occur in cults.

The existence of a highly atypical form of obedience to the dictates of charismatic leaders is not in question. Group suicides at the behest of a

charismatic leader are probably the most puzzling of such acts of obedience (Hall 2000; Lalich 1999; Weightman 1983), but murder, incest,
child abuse, and child molestation constitute other puzzling examples
for which credible evidence is available (Bugliosi and Gentry 1974; Lifton 1999; Rochford 1998). Moreover, the obedience reported is not limited to specific dramatic actions or outbursts of zeal. Less dramatic
examples of chronic long-term ego-dystonic behaviour,[2] such as criminal acts, abusive or neglectful parenting, and promiscuous sexual
behaviour have also been documented (Carter 1990; Hong 1998; Layton 1998; Rochford 1998; Williams 1998). However, agreement on these
facts is not matched, as we shall see, by agreement on the causes of the
obedience, its pervasiveness among cult populations, or the rate at
which it decays after the influence stimuli are removed.

But given the fact that only a small proportion of the human population ever join cults, why should we care? The answer is that the
sociological importance of cults extends far beyond their numerical
significance. Many cults are harmless and fully deserving of protection
of their religious and civil liberties. However, events of recent years
have shown that some cults are capable of producing far more social
harm than one might expect from the minuscule number of their
adherents. The U.S. State Department's annual report on terrorism for
the year 2000 concludes that 'while Americans were once threatened
primarily by terrorism sponsored by states, today they face greater
threats from loose networks of groups and individuals motivated more
by religion or ideology than by politics' (Miller 2000: 1).

In his recent study of a Japanese apocalyptic cult, Robert Jay Lifton
(1999: 343) has emphasized this point in the following terms:

> Consider Asahara's experience with ultimate weapons ... With a mad guru
> and a few hundred close followers, it is much easier to see how the very
> engagement with omnicidal weapons, once started upon, takes on a psy-
> chological momentum likely to lead either to self-implosion or to world
> explosion ... Asahara and Aum have changed the world, and not for the
> better. A threshold has been crossed. Thanks to this guru, Aum stepped
> over a line that few had even known was there. Its members can claim the
> distinction of being the first group in history to combine ultimate fanati-
> cism with ultimate weapons in a project to destroy the world. Fortunately,
> they were not up to the immodest task they assigned themselves. But
> whatever their bungling, they did cross that line, and the world will never
> quite be the same because, like it or not, they took the rest of us with them.

Potentially fruitful scientific research on obedience in cultic settings has been stymied by the well-intentioned meddling of two bitterly opposed, but far from disinterested, scholarly factions. On the one hand, there has been an uncompromising outcry of fastidious naysaying by a tight-knit faction of pro-religion scholars. Out of a fear that evidence of powerful techniques for inducing obedience might be used by religion's enemies to suppress the free expression of unpopular religions, the pro-religion faction has refused to notice the obvious and has engaged in a concerted (at times almost hysterical) effort to sweep under the rug any cultic-obedience studies not meeting impossibly rigorous controlled experimental standards (Zablocki 1997). On the other hand, those scholars who hate or fear cults have not been blameless in the pathetic enactment of this scientific farce. Some of them have tried their best to mystically transmute the obedience-inducing process that goes on in some cults from a severe and concentrated form of ordinary social influence into a magic spell that somehow allows gurus to snap the minds and enslave the wills of any innocent bystander unlucky enough to come into eye contact. By so doing, they have marginalized themselves academically and provided a perfect foil for the gibes of pro-religion scholars.

Brainwashing is the most commonly used word for the process whereby a charismatic group systematically induces high levels of ideological obedience. It would be naively reductionistic to try to explain cultic obedience entirely in terms of brainwashing. Other factors, such as simple conformity and ritual, induce cultic obedience as well. But it would be an equally serious specification error to leave deliberate cultic manipulation of personal convictions out of any model linking charismatic authority to ideological obedience.

However, the current climate of opinion, especially within the sociology of new religious movements, is not receptive to rational discussion of the concept of brainwashing, and still less to research in this area. Brainwashing has for too long been a mystified concept, and one that has been the subject of tendentious writing (thinly disguised as theory testing) by both its friends and enemies. My aim in this chapter is to rescue for social science a concept of brainwashing freed from both mystification and tendentiousness. I believe it is important and long overdue to restore some detachment and objectivity to this field of study.

The goal of achieving demystification will require some analysis of the concept's highly freighted cultural connotations, with particular regard to how the very word *brainwash* became a shibboleth in the cult wars. It is easy to understand how frightening it may be to imagine that there exists some force that can influence one down to the core level of basic beliefs, values, and worldview. Movies like *The Manchurian Candidate* have established in the popular imagination the idea that there exists some mysterious technique, known only to a few, that confers such power. Actually, as we will see, the real process of brainwashing involves only well-understood processes of social influence orchestrated in a particularly intense way. It still is, and should be, frightening in its intensity and capacity for extreme mischief, but there is no excuse for refusing to study something simply because it is frightening.

The goal of establishing scientific disinterest will require the repositioning of the concept more fully in the domain of behavioural and social science rather than in its present domain, which is largely that of civil and criminal legal proceedings. It is in that domain that it has been held hostage and much abused for more than two decades. The maxim of scholarly disinterest requires the researcher to be professionally indifferent as to whether our confidence in any given theory (always tentative at best) is increased or decreased by research. But many scholarly writers on this subject have become involved as expert witnesses, on one side or the other, in various law cases involving allegations against cult leaders or members (where witnesses are paid to debate in an arena in which the only possible outcomes are victory or defeat). This has made it increasingly difficult for these paid experts to cling to a disinterested theoretical perspective.

In my opinion, the litigational needs of these court cases have come, over the years, to drive the scientific debate to an alarming degree. There is a long and not especially honourable history of interest groups that are better armed with lawyers than with scientific evidence, and that use the law to place unreasonable demands on science. One need only think of the school segregationists' unreasonable demands, fifty years ago, that science prove that any specific child was harmed in a measurable way by a segregated classroom; or the tobacco companies' demands, forty years ago, that science demonstrate the exact process at the molecular level by which tobacco causes lung cancer. Science can serve the technical needs of litigation, but, when litigation strategies set the agenda for science, both science and the law are poorer for it.

My own thirty-six years of experience doing research on new religious movements has convinced me beyond any doubt that brainwashing is practised by some cults some of the time on some of their members with some degree of success. Even though the number of times I have used the vague term *some* in the previous sentence gives testimony to the fact that there remain many still-unanswered questions about this phenomenon, I do not personally have any doubt about brainwashing's existence. But I have also observed many cults that do not practise brainwashing, and I have never observed a cult in which brainwashing could reasonably be described as the only force holding the group together. My research (Zablocki 1971; 1991; 1996; Zablocki and Aidala 1991) has been ethnographic, comparative, and longitudinal. I have lived among these people and watched the brainwashing process with my own eyes. I have also interviewed people who participated in the process (both as perpetrators and subjects). I have interviewed many of these respondents not just one time but repeatedly over a course of many years. My selection of both cults and individuals to interview has been determined by scientific sampling methods (Zablocki 1980: app. A), not guided by convenience nor dictated by the conclusions I hoped to find. Indeed, I have never had an axe to grind in this field of inquiry. I didn't begin to investigate cults in the hope of finding brainwashing. I was surprised when I first discovered it. I insist on attempting to demonstrate its existence not because I am either for or against cults but only because it seems to me to be an incontrovertible, empirical fact.

Although my own ethnographic experience leads me to believe that there is overwhelming evidence that brainwashing is practised in some cults, my goal in this chapter is not to 'prove' that brainwashing exists, but simply to rescue it from the world of bogus ideas to which it has been banished unfairly, and to reinstate it as a legitimate topic of social science inquiry. My attempt to do so in this chapter will involve three steps. First, I will analyse the cultural misunderstandings that have made brainwashing a bone of contention rather than a topic of inquiry. Second, I will reconstruct the concept in a scientifically useful and empirically testable form within the framework of social influence theory. Third, I will summarize the current state of evidence (which seems to me to be quite compelling) that some cults do in fact engage in brainwashing with some degree of success.

Cultural Contention over the Concept of Brainwashing

That Word 'Brainwashing'
The word brainwashing is, in itself, controversial and arouses hostile

feelings. Since there is no scientific advantage in using one word rather than another for any concept, it may be reasonable in the future to hunt around for another word that is less polemical. We need a universally recognized term for a concept that stands for a form of influence manifested in a deliberately and systematically applied traumatizing and obedience-producing process of ideological resocialization.

Currently, brainwashing is the generally accepted term for this process, but I see no objection to finding another to take its place. There are in fact other terms, historically, that have been used instead, like 'thought reform' and 'coercive persuasion.' Ironically, it has been those scholars who complain most about 'the B-word' who have also been the most insistent that none of the alternatives is any better. As long as others in the field insist on treating all possible substitute constructions as nothing more than gussied-up synonyms for a mystified concept of brainwashing (see, for example, Introvigne 1998: 2), there is no point as yet in trying to introduce a more congenial term.

An overly literal reading of the word brainwashing (merely a literal translation of the accepted Chinese term *shi nao*) could be misleading, as it seems to imply the ability to apply some mysterious biochemical cleanser to people's brains. However, the word has never been intended as a literal designator but as a metaphor. It would be wise to heed Clifford Geertz's (1973: 210) warning in this connection, to avoid such a 'flattened view of other people's mentalities [that] more complex meanings than [a] literal reading suggests [are] not even considered.'

Thus, please don't allow yourself to become prejudiced by a visceral reaction to the word instead of attending to the underlying concept. There is a linguistic tendency, as the postmodernist critics have taught us, for the signified to disappear beneath the signifier. But the empirically based social sciences must resist this tendency by defining terms precisely. The influence of media-driven vulgarizations of concepts should be resisted. This chapter argues for the scientific validity of a concept, not a word. If you are interested in whether the concept has value, but you gag on the word, feel free to substitute a different word in its place. I myself have no particular attachment to the word brainwashing.

But if all we are talking about is an extreme form of influence, why do we need a special name for it at all? The name is assigned merely for convenience. This is a common and widely accepted practice in the social sciences. For example, in economics a recession is nothing more

than a name we give to two consecutive quarters of economic contrac-
tion. There is nothing qualitatively distinctive about two such consecutive quarters as opposed to one or three. The label is assigned
arbitrarily at a subjective point at which many economists begin to get
seriously worried about economic performance. This label is nevertheless useful as long as we don't reify it by imagining that it stands for
some real 'thing' that happens to the economy when it experiences precisely two quarters of decline. Many other examples of useful definitions marking arbitrary points along a continuum could be cited. There
is no objective way to determine the exact point at which ideological
influence becomes severe and encompassing enough, and its effects
long lasting enough, for it to be called brainwashing. Inevitably, there
will be marginal instances that could be categorized either way. But
despite the fact that the boundary is not precisely defined, it demar-
cates a class of events worthy of systematic study.

The Reciprocal Moral Panic
Study of brainwashing has been hampered by partisanship and tendentious writing on both sides of the conflict. In one camp, there are
scholars who very badly *don't* want there to be such a thing as brainwashing. Its nonexistence, they believe, will help assure religious liberty, which can only be procured by defending the liberty of the most
unpopular religions. If only the nonexistence of brainwashing can be
proved, the public will have to face up to the hard truth that some citizens choose to follow spiritual paths that may lead them in radical
directions. This camp has exerted its influence within academia. But,
instead of using its academic skills to refute the brainwashing conjecture, it has preferred to attack a caricature of brainwashing supplied by
anticult groups for litigational rather than scientific purposes.

  In the other camp, we find scholars who equally badly *do* want there
to be such a thing as brainwashing. Its existence, they believe, will give
them a rationale for opposition to groups they consider dangerous. A
typical example of their reasoning can be found in the argument put
forth by Margaret Singer that 'Despite the myth that normal people
don't get sucked into cults, it has become clear over the years that
everyone is susceptible to the lure of these master manipulators'
(Singer 1995: 17). Using a form of backward reasoning known as the
ecological fallacy, she argues from the known fact that people of all
ages, social classes, and ethnic backgrounds can be found in cults
to the dubious conclusion that everyone must be susceptible. These

scholars must also share some of the blame for tendentious scholarship. Lacking positions of leadership in academia, scholars on this side of the dispute have used their expertise to influence the mass media, and they have been successful because sensational allegations of mystical manipulative influence make good journalistic copy.

It's funny in a dreary sort of way that both sides in this debate agree that it is a David and Goliath situation, but each side fancies itself to be the David courageously confronting the awesome power of the opposition. Each side makes use of an exaggerated fear of the other's influence to create the raw materials of a moral panic (Cohen 1972; Goode and Ben Yehudah 1994). Thus, a disinterested search for truth falls victim to the uncompromising hostility created by each side's paranoid fear of the power of the other.

The 'cult apologists' picture themselves as fighting an underdog battle against hostile lords of the media backed by their armies of 'cult-bashing' experts. The 'cult bashers' picture themselves as fighting an underdog battle for a voice in academia in which apologists seem to hold all the gatekeeper positions. Each side justifies its rhetorical excesses and hyperbole by reference to the overwhelming advantages held by the opposing side within its own arena. But over the years a peculiar symbiosis has developed between these two camps. They have come to rely on each other to define their own positions. Each finds it more convenient to attack the positions of the other than to do the hard work of finding out what is really going on in cults. Thomas Robbins (1988: 74) has noted that the proponents of these two models 'tend to talk past each other since they employ differing interpretive frameworks, epistemological rules, definitions ... and underlying assumptions.' Most of the literature on the subject has been framed in terms of rhetorical disputes between these two extremist models. Data-based models have been all but crowded out.

Between these two noisy and contentious camps, we find the curious but disinterested scientist who wants to find out if there is such a thing as brainwashing but will be equally satisfied with a positive or a negative answer. I believe that there can and should be a moderate position on the subject. Such a position would avoid the absurdity of denying any reality to what thousands of reputable ex-cult members claim to have experienced – turning this denial into a minor cousin of holocaust denial. At the same time, it would avoid the mystical concept of an irresistible and overwhelming force that was developed by the extremist wing of the anticult movement.

One of the most shameful aspects of this whole silly affair is the way pro-religion scholars have used their academic authority to foist off the myth that the concept of brainwashing needs no further research because it has already been thoroughly debunked. Misleadingly, it has been argued (Introvigne forthcoming; Melton forthcoming) that the disciplines of psychology and sociology, through their American scholarly associations, have officially declared the concept of brainwashing to be so thoroughly discredited that no further research is needed. Introvigne, by playing fast and loose with terminology, attempts to parlay a rejection of a committee report into a rejection of the brainwashing concept by the American Psychological Association. He argues that 'To state that a report "lacks scientific rigor" is tantamount to saying that it is not scientific' (Introvigne 1998: 3), gliding over the question of whether the 'it' in question refers to the committee report or the brainwashing concept.[3] Conveniently, for Introvigne, the report in question was written by a committee chaired by Margaret Singer, whose involuntarist theory of brainwashing is as much a distortion of the foundational concept as Introvigne's parody of it.

The truth is that both of these scholarly associations (American Psychological Association and American Sociological Association) were under intense pressure by a consortium of pro-religion scholars (a.k.a. NRM scholars) to sign an amicus curiae brief alleging consensus within their fields that brainwashing theory had been found to be bunk. This was in regard to a case concerning Moonie brainwashing that was before the United States Supreme Court (*Molko v Holly Spirit Ass'n.*, Supreme Court of Calif. SF 25038; *Molko v Holy Spirit Ass'n.*, 762 p.2d 46 [Cal. 1988], *cert. denied*, 490 U.S. 1084 [1989]). The bottom line is that both of the associations, after bitter debate, recognized that there was no such consensus and refused to get involved. Despite strenuous efforts of the NRM scholars to make it appear otherwise, neither professional association saw an overwhelming preponderance of evidence on either side. Both went on record with a statement virtually identical to my argument in this chapter: that not nearly enough is known about this subject to be able to render a definitive scientific verdict, and that much more research is needed. A few years later, the Society for the Scientific Study of Religion went on record with a similar statement, affirming 'the agnostic position' on this subject and calling for more research (Zablocki 1997: 114).

Although NRM scholars have claimed to be opposed only to the most outrageously sensationalized versions of brainwashing theory, the result, perhaps unintended, of their campaign has been to bring an entire important area of social inquiry to a lengthy halt. Evidence of this can be seen in the fact that during the period 1962 to 2000, a time when cults flourished, not a single article supportive of brainwashing has been published in the two leading American journals devoted to the sociology of religion, although a significant number of such articles have been submitted to those journals and more than a hundred such articles have appeared in journals marginal to the field (Zablocki 1998: 267).

The erroneous contention that brainwashing theory has been debunked by social science research has been loudly and frequently repeated, and this 'big lie' has thus come to influence the thinking of neutral religion scholars. For example, even Winston Davis, in an excellent recent article on suicidal obedience in Heaven's Gate, expresses characteristic ambivalence over the brainwashing concept:

> Scholarship in general no longer accepts the traditional, simplistic theory of brainwashing ... While the vernacular theory of brainwashing may no longer be scientifically viable, the general theory of social and psychological conditioning is still in rather good shape ... I therefore find *nothing objectionable* [sic] in Benjamin Zablocki's revised theory of brainwashing as 'a set of transactions between a charismatically led collectivity and an isolated agent of the collectivity with the goal of transforming the agent into a deployable agent.' The tale I have to tell actually fits nicely into several of Robert Lifton's classical thought reform categories. (Davis 2000: 241–2)

The problem with this all too typical way of looking at things is the fact that I am not presenting some new revised theory of brainwashing but simply a restatement of Robert Lifton's (1989, 1999) careful and rigorous theory in sociological terms.

There are, I believe, six issues standing in the way of our ability to transcend this reciprocal moral panic. Let us look closely at each of these issues with an eye to recognizing that both sides in this conflict may have distorted the scientifically grounded theories of the foundational theorists – Lifton (1989), Sargant (1957), and Schein (1961) – as they apply to cults.

The Influence Continuum
The first issue has to do with the contention that brainwashing is a

newly discovered form of social influence involving a hitherto unknown social force. There is nothing about charismatic influence and the obedience it instills that is mysterious or asks us to posit the existence of any new force. On the contrary, everything about brainwashing can be explained entirely in terms of well-understood scientific principles. As Richard Ofshe has argued: 'Studying the reform process demonstrates that it is no more or less difficult to understand than any other complex social process and produces no results to suggest that something new has been discovered. The only aspect of the reform process that one might suggest is new, is the order in which the influence procedures are assembled and the degree to which the target's environment is manipulated in the service of social control. This is at most an unusual arrangement of commonplace bits and pieces' (1992: 221–2).

Would-be debunkers of the brainwashing concept have argued that brainwashing theory is not just a theory of ordinary social influence intensified under structural conditions of ideological totalism, but is rather a 'special' kind of influence theory that alleges that free will can be overwhelmed and individuals brought to a state of mind in which they will comply with charismatic directives involuntarily, having surrendered the capability of saying no. Of course, if a theory of brainwashing really did rely upon such an intrinsically untestable notion, it would be reasonable to reject it outright.

The attack on this so-called involuntarist theory of brainwashing figures prominently in the debunking efforts of a number of scholars (Barker 1989; Hexham and Poewe 1997; Melton forthcoming), but is most closely identified with the work of Dick Anthony (1996), for whom it is the linchpin of the debunking argument. Anthony argues, without a shred of evidence that I have been able to discover, that the foundational work of Lifton and Schein and the more recent theories of myself (1998), Richard Ofshe (1992), and Stephen Kent (Kent and Krebs 1998) are based upon what he calls the 'involuntarism assumption.' It is true that a number of prominent legal cases have hinged on the question of whether the plaintiff's free will had been somehow overthrown (Richardson and Ginsburg 1998). But nowhere in the scientific literature has there been such a claim. Foundational brainwashing theory has not claimed that subjects are robbed of their free will. Neither the presence nor the absence of free will can ever be proved or disproved. The confusion stems from the difference between the word *free* as it is used in economics as an antonym for *costly*, and as it used in philosophy as an antonym for *deterministic*. When brainwashing theory speaks of individuals losing the ability to freely decide to disobey, the word is being used in the economic sense. Brainwashing imposes costs, and when a course of action has costs it is no longer free. The famous statement by Rousseau (1913, p.3) that 'Man is born free, and everywhere he is in chains,' succinctly expresses the view that socialization can impose severe constraints on human behaviour. Throughout the social sciences, this is accepted almost axiomatically. It is odd that only in the sociology of new religious movements is the importance of socialization's ability to constrain largely ignored.

Unidirectional versus Bi-directional Influence
The second issue has to do with controversy over whether there are particular personality types drawn to cults and whether members are better perceived as willing and active seekers or as helpless and victimized dupes, as if these were mutually exclusive alternatives. Those who focus on the importance of the particular traits that recruits bring to their cults tend to ignore the resocialization process (Anthony and Robbins 1994).[4] Those who focus on the resocialization process often ignore personal predispositions (Singer and Ofshe 1990).

All this reminds me of being back in high school when people used to gossip about girls who 'got themselves pregnant.' Since that time, advances in biological theory have taught us to think more realistically of 'getting pregnant' as an interactive process involving influence in both directions. Similarly, as our understanding of totalistic influence in cults matures, I think we will abandon unidirectional explanations of cultic obedience in favour of more realistic, interactive ones. When that happens, we will find ourselves able to ask more interesting questions than we do now. Rather than asking whether it is the predisposing trait or the manipulative process that produces high levels of uncritical obedience, we will ask just what predisposing traits of individuals interact with just what manipulative actions by cults to produce this outcome.

A number of the debunking authors use this artificial and incorrect split between resocialization and predisposing traits to create a divide between cult brainwashing theory and foundational brainwashing theory as an explanation for ideological influence in China and Korea in the mid-twentieth century. Dick Anthony attempts to show that the foundational literature really embodied two distinct theories. One, he claims, was a robotic control theory that was mystical and sensationalist. The other was a theory of totalitarian influence that was dependent for its success upon pre-existing totalitarian beliefs of the subject which the program was able to reinvoke (Anthony 1996: i). Anthony claims that even though cultic brainwashing theory is descendant from the former, it claims its legitimacy from its ties to the latter.

The problem with this distinction is that it is based upon a misreading of the foundational literature (Lifton 1989; Schein 1961). Lifton devotes chapter 5 of his book to a description of the brainwashing *process*. In chapter 22 he describes the social *structural conditions* that have to be present for this process to be effective. Anthony misunderstands this scientific distinction. He interprets it instead as evidence that Lifton's work embodies two distinct theories: one bad and one good (Anthony and Robbins 1994). The 'bad' Lifton, according to Anthony, is the chapter 5 Lifton who describes a brainwashing process that may have gone on in Communist reindoctrination centres, but which, according to Anthony, has no applicability to contemporary cults. The 'good' Lifton, on the other hand, describes in chapter 22 a structural situation that Anthony splits off and calls a theory of thought reform. Anthony appears to like this 'theory' better because it does not involve anything that the cult actually *does to* the cult participant (Anthony and Robbins 1995). The cult merely creates a totalistic social structure that individuals with certain predisposing traits may decide that they want to be part of.

Unfortunately for Anthony, there are two problems with such splitting. One is that Lifton himself denies any such split in his theory (Lifton 1995, 1997). The second is that *both* an influence process and the structural conditions conducive to that process are necessary for any theory of social influence. As Lifton demonstrates in his recent application of his theory to a Japanese terrorist cult (Lifton 1999), process cannot be split off from structure in any study of social influence.

Condemnatory Label versus Contributory Factor

The third issue has to do with whether brainwashing is meant to replace other explanatory variables or work alongside them. Bainbridge (1997) and Richardson (1993) worry about the former, complaining that brainwashing explanations are intrinsically unifactoral, and thus inferior to the multifactoral explanations preferred by modern social science. But brainwashing theory has rarely, if ever, been used scientifically as a unifactoral explanation. Lifton (1999) does not attempt to explain all the obedience generated in Aum Shinrikyō by the brainwashing mechanism. My explanation of the obedience generated by the Bruderhof relies on numerous social mechanisms of which brainwashing is only one (Zablocki 1980). The same can be said for Ofshe's explanation of social control in Synanon (1976). Far from being unifactoral, brainwashing is merely one essential element in a larger strategy for understanding how charismatic authority is channelled into obedience.

James Thurber once wrote a fable called *The Wonderful O* (1957), which depicted the cultural collapse of a society that was free to express itself using twenty-five letters of the alphabet but was forbidden to use the letter O for any reason. The intellectual convolutions forced on Thurber's imaginary society by this 'slight' restriction are reminiscent of the intellectual convolutions forced on the NRM scholars by their refusal to include brainwashing in their models. It is not that these scholars don't often have considerable insight into cult dynamics, but the poor mugs are, nevertheless, constantly getting overwhelmed by events that their theories are unable to predict or explain. You always find them busy playing catch-up as they scramble to account for each new cult crisis as it develops on an ad hoc basis. The inadequacy of their models cries out 'specification error' in the sense that a key variable has been left out.

The Thurberian approach just does not work. We have to use the whole alphabet of social influence concepts from Asch to Zimbardo (including the dreaded B-word) to understand cultic obedience. Cults are a complex social ecology of forces involving attenuation effects (Petty 1994), conformity (Asch 1951), crowd behaviour (Coleman 1990), decision elites (Wexler 1995), deindividuation (Festinger, Pepitone et al. 1952), extended exchange (Stark 1999), groupthink (Janis 1982), ritual (Turner 1969), sacrifice and stigma (Iannaccone 1992), situational pressures (Zimbardo and Anderson 1993), social proof (Cialdini 1993), totalism (Lifton 1989), and many others. Personally, I have never seen a cult that was held together only by brainwashing and not also by other social psychological factors, as well as genuine loyalty to ideology and leadership.

Arguments that brainwashing is really a term of moral condemnation masquerading as a scientific concept have emerged as a reaction to the efforts of some anticultists (not social scientists) to use brainwashing as a label to condemn cults rather than as a concept to understand them. Bromley (1998) has taken the position that brainwashing is not a variable at all but merely a peremptory label of stigmatization – a trope for an ideological bias, in our individualistic culture, against people who prefer to live and work more collectivistically. Others have focused on the obverse danger of allowing brainwashing to be used as an all-purpose moral excuse (It wasn't my fault. I was brainwashed!), offering blanket absolution for people who have been cult members – freeing them from the need to take any responsibility for their actions (Bainbridge 1997; Hexham and Poewe 1997; Introvigne forthcoming; Melton forthcoming). While these allegations represent legitimate concerns about potential abuse of the concept, neither is relevant to the scientific issue. A disinterested approach will first determine whether a phenomenon exists before worrying about whether its existence is politically convenient.

Obtaining Members versus Retaining Members

The fourth issue has to do with a confusion over whether brainwashing explains how cults obtain members or how they retain them. Some cults have made use of manipulative practices like love-bombing and sleep deprivation (Galanti 1993), with some degree of success, in order to obtain new members. A discussion of these manipulative practices for obtaining members is beyond the scope of this chapter. Some of these practices superficially resemble techniques used in the earliest phase of brainwashing. But these practices, themselves, are not brainwashing. This point must be emphasized because a false attribution of brainwashing to newly obtained cult recruits, rather than to those who have already made a substantial commitment to the cult, figures prominently in the ridicule of the concept by NRM scholars. A typical straw man representation of brainwashing as a self-evidently absurd concept is as follows: 'The new convert is held mentally captive in a state of alternate consciousness due to "trance-induction techniques" such as meditation, chanting, speaking in tongues, self-hypnosis, visualization, and controlled breathing exercises ... the cultist is [thus] reduced to performing religious duties in slavish obedience to the whims of the group and its authoritarian or maniacal leader' (Wright 1998: 98).

Foundational brainwashing theory was not concerned with such Svengalian conceits, but only with ideological influence in the service of the retaining function. Why should the foundational theorists, concerned as they were with coercive state-run institutions like prisons, 're-education centres,' and prisoner-of-war camps have any interest in explaining how participants were *obtained*? Participants were obtained at the point of a gun.[5] The motive of these state enterprises was to *retain* the loyalties of these participants after intensive resocialization ceased. As George Orwell showed so well in his novel *1984*, the only justification for the costly indoctrination process undergone by Winston Smith was not that he love Big Brother while Smith was in prison, but that Big Brother be able to retain that love after Smith was deployed back into society. Nevertheless, both 'cult apologists' and 'cult bashers' have found it more convenient to focus on the obtaining function.

If one asks why a cult would be motivated to invest resources in brainwashing, it should be clear that this can not be to obtain recruits, since these are a dime a dozen in the first place, and, as Barker (1984) has shown, they don't tend to stick around long enough to repay the investment. Rather, it can only be to retain loyalty, and therefore decrease surveillance costs for valued members who are already committed. In small groups bound together only by normative solidarity, as Hechter (1987) has shown, the cost of surveillance of the individual by the group is one of the chief obstacles to success. Minimizing these surveillance costs is often the most important organizational problem such groups have to solve in order to survive and prosper. Brainwashing makes sense for a collectivity only to the extent that the resources saved through decreased surveillance costs exceed the resources invested in the brainwashing process. For this reason, only high-demand charismatic groups with totalistic social structures are ever in a position to benefit from brainwashing.[6]

This mistaken ascription of brainwashing to the obtaining function rather than the retaining function is directly responsible for two of the major arguments used by the 'cult apologists' in their attempts to debunk brainwashing. One has to do with a misunderstanding of the role of force and the other has to do with the mistaken belief that brainwashing can be studied with data on cult membership turnover.

The widespread belief that force is necessary for brainwashing is based upon a misreading of Lifton (1989) and Schein (1961). A number of authors (Dawson 1998; Melton forthcoming; Richardson 1993) have based their arguments, in part, on the contention that the works of foundational scholarship on brainwashing are irrelevant to the study of cults because the foundational literature studied only subjects who were forcibly incarcerated. However, Lifton and Schein have both gone on public record as explicitly denying that there is anything about their theories that requires the use of physical force or threat of force. Lifton has specifically argued ('psychological manipulation is the heart of the matter, with or without the use of physical force' [1995: xi]) that his theories are very much applicable to cults.[7] The difference between the state-run institutions that Lifton and Schein studied in the 1950s and 1960s and the cults that Lifton and others study today is in the obtaining function not in the retaining function. In the Chinese and Korean situations, force was used for obtaining and brainwashing was used for retaining. In cults, charismatic appeal is used for obtaining and brainwashing is used, in some instances, for retaining.

A related misconception has to do with what conclusions to draw from the very high rate of turnover among new and prospective recruits to cults. Bainbridge (1997), Barker (1989), Dawson (1998), Introvigne (forthcoming), and Richardson (1993) have correctly pointed out that in totalistic religious organizations very few prospective members go on to become long-term members. They argue that this proves that the resocialization process cannot be irresistible and therefore it cannot be brainwashing. But nothing in the brainwashing model predicts that it will be attempted with all members, let alone successfully attempted. In fact, the efficiency of brainwashing, operationalized as the expected yield of deployable agents[8] per 100 members, is an unknown (but discoverable) parameter of any particular cultic system and may often be quite low. For the system to be able to perpetuate itself (Hechter 1987), the yield need only produce enough value for the system to compensate it for the resources required to maintain the brainwashing process.

Moreover, the high turnover rate in cults is more complex than it may seem. While it is true that the membership turnover is very high among recruits and new members, this changes after two or three years of membership when cultic commitment mechanisms begin to kick in. This transition from high to low membership turnover is known as the Bainbridge Shift, after the sociologist who first discovered it (Bainbridge 1997: 141–3). After about three years of membership, the annual rate of turnover sharply declines and begins to fit a commitment model rather than a random model.[9]

Membership turnover data is not the right sort of data to tell us whether a particular cult practises brainwashing. The recruitment strategy whereby many are called but few are chosen is a popular one among cults. In several groups in which I have observed the brainwashing process, there was very high turnover among initial recruits. Brainwashing is too expensive to waste on raw recruits. Since brainwashing is a costly process, it generally will not pay for a group to even attempt to brainwash one of its members until that member has already demonstrated some degree of staying power on her own.[10]

Psychological Traces

The fifth issue has to do with the question of whether brainwashing leaves any long-lasting measurable psychological traces in those who have experienced it. Before we can ask this question in a systematic way, we have to be clear about what sort of traces we should be looking for. There is an extensive literature on cults and mental health. But whether cult involvement causes psychological problems is a much more general question than whether participation in a traumatic resocialization process leaves any measurable psychological traces.

There has been little consensus on what sort of traces to look for. Richardson and Kilbourne (1983: 30) assume that brainwashing should lead to insanity. Lewis (1998: 16) argues that brainwashing should lead to diminished IQ scores. Nothing in brainwashing theory would lead us to predict either of these outcomes. In fact, Schein points out that 'The essence of coercive persuasion is to produce ideological and behavioral change in a fully conscious, mentally intact individual' (1959: 437). Why in the world would brainwashers invest scarce resources to produce insanity and stupidity in their followers? However, these aforementioned authors (and others) have taken the absence of these debilitative effects as 'proof' that brainwashing doesn't happen in cults. At the same time, those who oppose cults have had an interest, driven by litigation rather than science, in making exaggerated claims for mental impairment directly resulting from brainwashing. As Farrell has pointed out, 'From the beginning, the idea of traumatic neurosis has been accompanied by concerns about compensation' (1998: 7).

Studies of lingering emotional, cognitive, and physiological effects on ex-members have thus far shown inconsistent results (Katchen 1997; Solomon 1981; Ungerleider and Wellisch 1983). Researchers studying current members of religious groups have found no significant impairment or disorientation. Such results have erroneously been taken as evidence that the members of these groups could, therefore, not possibly have been brainwashed. However, these same researchers found these responses of current members contaminated by elevations on the 'Lie' scale, exemplifying 'an intentional attempt to make a good impression and deny faults' (Ungerleider and Wellisch 1983: 208). On the other hand, studies of ex-members have tended to show 'serious mental and emotional dysfunctions that have been directly caused by cultic beliefs and practices (Saliba 1993: 106). The sampling methods of these latter studies have been challenged (Lewis and Bromley 1987; Solomon 1981), however, because they have tended to significantly over-sample respondents with anti-cult movement ties. With ingenious logic, this has led Dawson (1998: 121) to suggest in the same breath that cult brainwashing is a myth but that ex-member impairment may be a result of brainwashing done by deprogrammers.

All this controversy is not entirely relevant to our question, however, because there is no reason to assume that a brainwashed person is going to show elevated scores on standard psychiatric distress scales. In fact, for those for whom making choices is stressful, brainwashing may offer psychological relief. Galanter's research has demonstrated that a cult 'acts like a psychological pincer, promoting distress while, at the same time, providing relief' (1989: 93). As we shall see below, the brainwashing model predicts impairment and disorientation only for people during some of the intermediate stages, not at the end state. The popular association of brainwashing with zombie or robot states comes out of a misattribution of the characteristics of people going through the traumatic brainwashing process to people who have completed the process. The former really are, at times, so disoriented that they appear to resemble caricatures of zombies or robots. The glassy eyes, inability to complete sentences, and fixed eerie smiles are characteristics of disoriented people under randomly varying levels of psychological stress. The latter, however, are, if the process was successful, functioning and presentable deployable agents.

Establishing causal direction in the association between cult membership and mental health is extremely tricky, and little progress has been made thus far. In an excellent article reviewing the extensive literature in this area, Saliba (1993: 108) concludes: 'The study of the relationship between new religious movements and mental health is in its infancy.' Writing five years later, Dawson (1998: 122) agrees that this is still true, and argues that 'the inconclusive results of the psychological study of members and ex-members of NRMs cannot conceivably be used to support either the case for or against brainwashing.' Saliba calls for prospective studies that will establish baseline mental health measurements for individuals before they join cults, followed by repeated measures during and afterward. While this is methodologically sensible, it is impractical because joining a cult is both a rare and unexpected event. This makes the general question of how cults affect mental health very difficult to answer.

Fortunately, examining the specific issue of whether brainwashing leaves psychological traces may be easier. The key is recognizing that brainwashing is a traumatic process, and, therefore, those who have gone through it should experience an increasing likelihood in later years of post-traumatic stress disorder. The classic clinical symptoms of PTSD – avoidance, numbing, and increased arousal (American Psychiatric Association 1994: 427) – have been observed in many ex-cult members regardless of their mode of exit and current movement affiliations (Katchen 1997; Zablocki 1999). However, these soft and somewhat subjective symptoms should be viewed with some caution given recent controversies over the ease with which symptoms such as these can be iatrogenically implanted, as, for example, false memories (Loftus and Ketcham 1994).

In the future, avenues for more precise neurological tracking may become available. Judith Herman (1997: 238) has demonstrated convincingly that 'traumatic exposure can produce lasting alterations in the endocrine, autonomic, and central nervous systems ... and in the function and even the structure of specific areas of the brain.' It is possible in the future that direct evidence of brainwashing may emerge from brain scanning using positron emission tomography. Some preliminary research in this area has suggested that, during flashbacks, specific areas of the brain involved with language and communication may be inactivated (Herman 1997: 240; Rauch, van der Kolk et al. 1996). Another promising area of investigation of this sort would involve testing for what van der Kolk and McFarlane (1996) have clinically identified as 'the black hole of trauma.' It should be possible to determine, once measures have been validated, whether such traces appear more often in individuals who claim to have gone through brainwashing than in a sample of controls who have been non-brainwashed members of cults for equivalent periods of time.

Separating the Investigative Steps

The final issue is a procedural one. There are four sequential investigative steps required to resolve controversies like the one we have been discussing. These steps are concerned with attempt, existence, incidence, and consequence. A great deal of confusion comes from nothing more than a failure to recognize that these four steps need to be kept analytically distinct from one another.

To appreciate the importance of this point, apart from the heat of controversy, let us alter the scene for a moment and imagine that the scientific conflict we are trying to resolve is over something relatively innocuous – say, vegetarianism. Let us imagine that on one side we have a community of scholars arguing that vegetarianism is a myth, that nobody would voluntarily choose to live without eating meat and that anyone who tried would quickly succumb to an overpowering carnivorous urge. On the other side, we have another group of scholars arguing that they had actually seen vegetarians and observed their non-meat-eating behavior over long periods of time, and that, moreover, vegetarianism is a rapidly growing social problem with many new converts each year being seduced by this enervating and debilitating diet.

It should be clear that any attempt to resolve this debate scientifically would have to proceed through the four sequential steps mentioned above. First, we would have to find out if anybody ever deliberately *attempts* to be a vegetarian. Maybe those observed not eating meat were simply unable to obtain it. If nobody could be found voluntarily attempting to follow a vegetarian diet, we would have to conclude that vegetarianism is a myth. If, however, we find at least one person attempting to follow such a diet, we would next have to observe him carefully enough and long enough to find out whether he succeeds in abstaining from meat. If we observe even one person successfully abstaining from meat, we would have to conclude that vegetarianism *exists*, increasing our confidence in the theory of the second group of researchers. But the first group could still argue, well, maybe you are right that a few eccentric people here and there do practise vegetarianism, but not enough to constitute a social phenomenon worth investigating. So, the next step would be to measure the *incidence* of vegetarianism in the population. Out of every million people, how many do we find following a vegetarian diet? If it turns out to be very few, we can conclude that, while vegetarianism may exist as a social oddity, it does not rise to the level of being a social phenomenon worthy of our interest. If, however, we find a sizeable number of vegetarians, we still need to ask, 'So what?' This is the fourth of our sequential steps. Does the practice of vegetarianism have any physical, psychological, or social *consequences*? If so, are these consequences worthy of our concern?

Each of these investigative steps requires attention focused on quite distinct sets of substantive evidence. For this reason, it is important that we not confuse them with one another as is so often done in 'apologist' writing about brainwashing, where the argument often seems to run as follows: Brainwashing doesn't exist, or at least it shouldn't exist, and even if it does the numbers involved are so few, and everybody in modern society gets brainwashed to some extent, and the effects, if any, are impossible to measure. Such arguments jump around, not holding still long enough to allow for orderly and systematic confirmation or disconfirmation of each of the steps.

Once we recognize the importance of keeping the investigative steps methodologically distinct from one another, it becomes apparent that the study of brainwashing is no more problematic (although undoubtedly much more difficult) than the study of an advertising campaign for a new household detergent. It is a straightforward question to ask whether or not some charismatic groups attempt to practise radical techniques of socialization designed to turn members into deployable agents. If the answer is no, we stop because there can be no brainwashing. If the answer is yes, we go on to a second question: Are these techniques at least sometimes effective in producing uncritical obedience? If the answer to this question is yes (even for a single person), we know that brainwashing exists, although it may be so rare as to be nothing more than a sociological oddity. Therefore, we have to take a third step and ask, How frequently is it effective? What proportion of those who live in cults are subjected to brainwashing, and what proportion of these respond by becoming uncritically obedient? And, finally, we need to ask a fourth important question: How long do the effects last? Are the effects transitory, lasting only as long as the stimulus continues to be applied, or are they persistent for a period of time thereafter, and, if so, how long? Let us keep in mind the importance of distinguishing attempt from existence, from incidence, from consequences.

Brainwashing as a Scientific Concept

What I am presenting here is not a 'new' theory of brainwashing but a conceptual model of the foundational theory developed in the mid-twentieth century by Lifton, Schein, and Sargant as it applies to charismatic collectivities. Because its scientific stature has been so frequently questioned, I will err on the side of formality by presenting a structured exposition of brainwashing theory in terms of eight definitions and twelve hypotheses. Each definition includes an operationalized form by which the trait may be observed. If either of the first two hypotheses is disconfirmed, we must conclude that brainwashing is not being attempted in the cult under investigation. If any of the twelve hypotheses is disconfirmed, we must conclude that brainwashing is not successful in meeting its goals within that cult.

I do not pretend that the model outlined here is easy to test empirically, particularly for those researchers who either cannot or will not spend time immersing themselves in the daily lives of cults, or for those who are not willing, alternatively, to use as data the detailed retrospective accounts of ex-members. However, it should be clear that the model being proposed here stays grounded in what is empirically testable and does not involve mystical notions such as loss of free will or information disease (Conway and Siegelman 1978) that have characterized many of the extreme 'anticult models.'

Nor do I pretend that this model represents the final and definitive treatment of this subject. Charismatic influence is still a poorly understood subject on which much additional research is needed. With few exceptions, sociology has treated it as if it were what engineers call a 'black box,' with charismatic inputs coming in one end and obedience outputs going out the other. What we have here is a theory that assists in the process of opening this black box to see what is inside. It is an inductive theory, formed largely from the empirical generalizations of ethnographers and interviewers. The model itself presents an ideal-type image of brainwashing that does not attempt to convey the great variation among specific obedience-inducing processes that occur across the broad range of existing cults. Much additional refinement in both depth and breadth will certainly be needed.

Definitions
D1. *Charisma* is defined, using the classical Weberian formula, as a condition of 'devotion to the specific and exceptional sanctity, heroism, or exemplary character of an individual person, of the normative patterns or order revealed or ordained by him' (Weber 1947: 328). Being defined this way, as a condition of devotion, leads us to recognize that charisma is not to be understood simply in terms of the characteristics of the leader, as it has come to be in popular usage, but requires an understanding of the relationship between leader and followers. In other words, charisma is a relational variable. It is defined operationally as a network of relationships in which authority is justified (for both superordinates and subordinates) in terms of the special characteristics discussed above.

D2. *Ideological Totalism* is a sociocultural system that places high valuation on total control over all aspects of the outer and inner lives of participants for the purpose of achieving the goals of an ideology defined as all important. Individual rights either do not exist under ideological totalism or they are clearly subordinated to the needs of the collectivity whenever the two come into conflict. Ideological totalism has been operationalized in terms of eight observable characteristics: milieu control, mystical manipulation, the demand for purity, the cult of confession, 'sacred science,' loading the language, doctrine over person, and the dispensing of existence (Lifton 1989: chap. 22).[11]

D3. *Surveillance* is defined as keeping watch over a person's behaviour, and, perhaps, attitudes. As Hechter (1987) has shown, the need for surveillance is the greatest obstacle to goal achievement among ideological collectivities organized around the production of public goods. Surveillance is not only costly, it is also impractical for many activities in which agents of the collectivity may have to travel and act autonomously and at a distance. It follows from this that all collectivities pursuing public goals will be motivated to find ways to decrease the need for surveillance. Resources used for surveillance are wasted in the sense that they are unavailable for the achievement of collective goals.

D4. *A deployable agent* is one who is uncritically obedient to directives perceived as charismatically legitimate (Selznick 1960). A deployable agent can be relied on to continue to carry out the wishes of the collectivity regardless of his own hedonic interests and in the absence of any external controls. Deployability can be operationalized as the likelihood that the individual will continue to comply with hitherto ego-dystonic demands of the collectivity (e.g., mending, ironing, mowing the lawn, smuggling, rape, child abuse, murder) when not under surveillance.

D5. *Brainwashing* is an observable set of transactions between a charismatically structured collectivity and an isolated agent of the collectivity, with the goal of transforming the agent into a deployable agent. Brainwashing is thus a *process* of ideological resocialization carried out within a *structure* of charismatic authority.

The brainwashing process may be operationalized as a sequence of well-defined and potentially observable phases. These hypothesized phases are (1) identity stripping, (2) identification, and (3) symbolic death/rebirth. The operational definition of brainwashing refers to the specific activities attempted, whether or not they are successful, as they are either observed directly by the ethnographer or reported in official or unofficial accounts by members or ex-members. Although the exact order of phases and specific steps within phases may vary from group to group, we should always expect to see the following features, or their functional equivalents, in any brainwashing system: (1) the constant fluctuation between assault and leniency; and (2) the seemingly endless process of confession, re-education, and refinement of confession.

D6. *Hyper-credulity* is defined as a disposition to accept uncritically all charismatically ordained beliefs. All lovers of literature and poetry are familiar with 'that willing suspension of disbelief for the moment, which constitutes poetic faith' (Coleridge 1970: 147). Hyper-credulity occurs when this state of mind, which in most of us is occasional and transitory, is transformed into a stable disposition. Hyper-credulity falls between hyper-suggestibility on the one hand and stable conversion of belief on the other.[12] Its operational hallmark is plasticity in the assumption of deeply held convictions at the behest of an external authority. This is an other-directed form of what Robert Lifton (1968) has called the protean identity state.

D7. *Relational Enmeshment* is a state of being in which self-esteem depends upon belonging to a particular collectivity (Bion 1959; Bowen 1972; Sirkin and Wynne 1990). It may be operationalized as immersion in a relational network with the following characteristics: exclusivity (high ratio of in-group to out-group bonds), interchangeability (low level of differentiation in affective ties between one alter and another), and dependency (reluctance to sever or weaken ties for any reason). In a developmental context, something similar to this has been referred to by Bowlby (1969) as anxious attachment.

D8. *Exit Costs* are the subjective costs experienced by an individual who is contemplating leaving a collectivity. Obviously, the higher the perceived exit costs, the greater will be the reluctance to leave. Exit costs may be operationalized as the magnitude of the bribe necessary to overcome them. A person who is willing to leave if we pay him $1,000 experiences lower exit costs than one who is not willing to leave for any payment less than $1,000,000. With regard to cults, the exit costs are most often spiritual and emotional rather than material, which makes measurement in this way more difficult but not impossible.

Hypotheses

Not all charismatic organizations engage in brainwashing. We therefore need a set of hypotheses that will allow us to test empirically whether any particular charismatic system attempts to practise brainwashing and with what effect. The brainwashing model asserts twelve hypotheses concerning the role of brainwashing in the production of uncritical obedience. These hypotheses are all empirically testable. A schematic diagram of the model I propose may be found in figure 1.

This model begins with an assumption that charismatic leaders are capable of creating organizations that are easy and attractive to enter (even though they may later turn out to be difficult and painful to leave). There are no hypotheses, therefore, to account for how charismatic cults obtain members. It is assumed that an abundant pool of potential recruits to such groups is always available. The model assumes that charismatic leaders, using nothing more than their own intrinsic attractiveness and persuasiveness, are initially able to gather around them a corps of disciples sufficient for the creation of an attractive social movement. Many ethnographies (Lofland 1966; Lucas 1995) have shown how easy it is for such charismatic movement organizations to attract new members from the general pool of anomic 'seekers' that can always be found within the population of an urbanized mobile society.

The model does attempt to account for how some percentage of these ordinary members are turned into deployable agents. The initial attractiveness of the group, its vision of the future, and/or its capacity to bestow seemingly limitless amounts of love and esteem on the new member are sufficient inducements in some cases to motivate a new member to voluntarily undergo this difficult and painful process of resocialization.

H1. *Ideological totalism* is a necessary but not sufficient condition for the brainwashing process. Brainwashing will be attempted only in groups that are structured totalistically. However, not all ideologically totalist groups will attempt to brainwash their members. It should be remembered that brainwashing is merely a mechanism for producing deployable agents. Some cults may not want deployable agents or have other

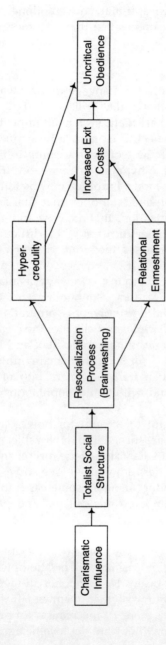

Figure 1: The Effect of Charismatic Influence on Uncritical Obedience

ways of producing them. Others may want them but feel uncomfortable about using brainwashing methods to obtain them, or they may not have discovered the existence of brainwashing methods.

H2. The exact nature of this resocialization process will differ from group to group, but, in general, will be similar to the resocialization process that Robert Lifton (1989) and Edgar Schein (1961) observed in Communist re-education centres in the 1950s. For whatever reasons, these methods seem to come fairly intuitively to charismatic leaders and their staffs. Although the specific steps and their exact ordering differ from group to group, their common elements involve a stripping away of the vestiges of an old identity, the requirement that repeated confessions be made either orally or in writing, and a somewhat random and ultimately debilitating alternation of the giving and the withholding of 'unconditional' love and approval. H2 further states that the maintenance of this program involves the expenditure of a measurable quantity of the collectivity's resources. This quantity is known as C, where C equals the cost of the program and should be measurable at least at an ordinal level.

This resocialization process has baffled many observers, in my opinion because it proceeds simultaneously along two distinct but parallel tracks, one involving cognitive functioning and the other involving emotional networking. These two tracks lead to the attainment of states of hyper-credulity and relational enmeshment, respectively. The group member learns to accept with suspended critical judgment the often shifting beliefs espoused by the charismatic leader. At the same time, the group member becomes strongly attached to and emotionally dependent upon the charismatic leader and (often especially) the other group members, and cannot bear to be shunned by them.

H3. Those who go through the process will be more likely than those who do not to reach a state of hyper-credulity. This involves the shedding of old convictions and the assumption of a zealous loyalty to these beliefs of the moment, uncritically seized upon, so that all such beliefs become not mere 'beliefs' but deeply held convictions.

Under normal circumstances, it is not easy to get people to disown their core convictions. Convictions, once developed, are generally treated not as hypotheses to test empirically but as possessions to value and cherish. There are often substantial subjective costs to the individual in giving them up. Abelson (1986: 230) has provided convincing linguistic evidence that most people treat convictions more as valued possessions than as ways of testing reality. Cognitive dissonance theory predicts with accuracy that when subject to frontal attack, attachment to convictions tends to harden (Festinger, Riechen et al. 1956; O'Leary 1994). Therefore, a frontal attack on convictions, without first undermining the self-image foundation of these convictions, is doomed to failure. An indirect approach through brainwashing is often more effective.

The unconventional beliefs that individuals adopt when they join cults will come to be discontinuous with the beliefs they held in precult life. What appears to happen is a transformation from individually held to collectively held convictions. This is a well-known phenomenon that Janis (1982) has called groupthink. Under circumstances of groupthink, the specific content of one's convictions becomes much less important than achieving the goal that all in the group hold the same convictions. In elaboration likelihood terms we can say that the subject undergoes a profound shift from message processing to source processing in the course of resocialization (Petty and Wegener 1998).

When the state of hyper-credulity is achieved, it leaves the individual strongly committed to the charismatic belief of the moment but with little or no critical inclination to resist charismatically approved new or contradictory beliefs in the future and little motivation to attempt to form accurate independent judgments of the consequences of assuming new beliefs. The cognitive track of the resocialization process begins by stripping away the old convictions and associating them with guilt, evil, or befuddlement. Next, there is a traumatic exhaustion of the habit of subjecting right-brain convictions to left-brain rational scrutiny. This goes along with an increase in what Snyder (1974) has called self-monitoring, implying a shift from central route to peripheral route processing of information in which the source rather than the content of the message becomes all important.

H4. As an individual goes through the brainwashing process, there will be an increase in relational enmeshment with measurable increases occurring at the completion of each of the three stages. The purging of convictions is a painful process and it is reasonable to ask why anybody would go through it voluntarily. The payoff is the opportunity to feel more connected with the charismatic relational network. These people have also been through it, and only they really understand what you are going through. So cognitive purging leads one to seek relational comfort, and this comfort becomes enmeshing. The credulity process and the enmeshing process depend on each other.

The next three hypotheses are concerned with the fact that each of the three phases of brainwashing achieves plateaus in both of these processes. The stripping phase creates the vulnerability to this sort of transformation. The identification phase creates realignment, and the rebirth phase breaks down the barrier between the two so that convictions can be emotionally energized and held with zeal, while emotional attachments can be sacralized in terms of the charismatic ideology. The full brainwashing model actually provides far more detailed hypotheses concerning the various steps within each phase of the process. Space constraints make it impossible to discuss these here. An adequate technical discussion of the manipulation of language in brainwashing, for example, would require a chapter at least the length of this one. Figure 2 provides a sketch of the steps within each phase. Readers desiring more information about these steps are referred to Lifton (1989: chap. 5).

H5. The stripping phase. The cognitive goal of the stripping phase is to destroy prior convictions and prior relationships of belonging. The emotional goal of the stripping phase is to create the need for attachments. Overall, at the completion of the stripping phase, the situation is such that the individual is hungry for convictions and attachments and dependent upon the collectivity to supply them. This sort of credulity and attachment behaviour is widespread among prisoners and hospital patients (Goffman 1961).

H6. The identification phase. The cognitive goal of the identification phase is to establish imitative search for conviction and bring about the erosion of the habit of incredulity. The emotional goal of the identification phase is to instill the habit of acting out through attachment. Overall, at the completion of the identification phase the individual has begun the practice of relying on the collectivity for beliefs and for a cyclic emotional pattern of arousal and comfort. But, at this point this reliance is just one highly valued form of existence. It is not yet viewed as an existential necessity.

H7. The symbolic death and rebirth phase. In the death and rebirth phase, the cognitive and emotional tracks come together and mutually support each other. This often gives the individual a sense of having

Figure 2: The Stages of Brainwashing and Their Effect on Hyper-credulity and Emotional Enmeshment

Phase	Stage	Hyper-credulity	Relational enmeshment
Stripping	Assault on identity	Destruction of prior peripheral beliefs; attainment of new ones	Destruction of prior emotional relations; arousal of hope for unconditional love
	Establishment of guilt	Association of a guilt reaction with any independent thinking	Learning to feel guilty
	Self-betrayal	Destruction of prior core convictions	Humility: willingness to accept help; beginning of acting out on basis of relational dependency
	Breaking-point	Blurring of boundaries between sensed empirical reality and ideologically mediated reality	Traumatic Hyper-arousal. Learning to avoid feelings that could threaten the relational bond
Identification	Leniency and opportunity	Hope that it might be possible to find 'correct' convictions	Establishment of state of anxious attachment; becomes a partner in brainwashing
	Compulsion to confess	Active involvement in purge of old convictions from own point of view	Acting out becomes compulsive; active involvement in purge of old feelings and values from own point of view
	Channelling of guilt	Purge of old convictions from cult's point of view	Purge of old feelings and values from cult's point of view; old identity seen as repulsive
	Re-education logical dishonouring	Development of a new worldview into which to pour convictions as they are received	Relationships established with other cult members on the basis of dependency needs (need to be nurtured)
	Progress and harmony	Cultivation of non-attachment to received convictions; sense of groupthink	Intimacy on the basis of dependency needs (need to be valued)

Figure 2: The Stages of Brainwashing and Their Effect on Hyper-credulity and Emotional Enmeshment—(*concluded*)

Phase	Stage	Hyper-credulity	Relational enmeshment
Rebirth	Ultimate confession: summing up	Convictions become ideology (deeply shared, emotionally charged, not to be questioned)	Cutting residual ties of loyalty to the old identity; full and unequivocal commitment made to the new identity
	Cognitive and emotional rebirth	Return of old cognitive processes under new ideological worldview	Resumption of emotional liberty under conditions of ideological zeal

emerged from a tunnel and an experience of spiritual rebirth.[13] The cognitive goal of this phase is to establish a sense of ownership of (and pride of ownership in) the new convictions. The emotional goal is to make a full commitment to the new self that is no longer directly dependent upon hope of attachment or fear of separation. Overall, at the completion of the rebirth phase we may say that the person has become a fully deployable agent of the charismatic leader. The brainwashing process is complete.

H8 states that the brainwashing process results in a state of subjectively elevated exit costs. These exit costs cannot, of course, be observed directly. But they can be inferred from the behavioral state of panic or terror that arises in the individual at the possibility of having his or her ties to the group discontinued. The cognitive and emotional states produced by the brainwashing process together bring about a situation in which the perceived exit costs for the individual increase sharply. This closes the trap for all but the most highly motivated individuals, and induces in many a state of uncritical obedience. As soon as exit from the group (or even from its good graces) ceases to be a subjectively palatable option, it makes sense for the individual to comply with almost anything the group demands – even to the point of suicide in some instances. Borrowing from Sartre's insightful play of that name, I refer to this situation as the 'no exit' syndrome. When demands for compliance are particularly harsh, the hyper-credulity aspect of the process sweetens the pill somewhat by allowing the individual to accept uncritically the justifications offered by the charismatic leader and/or charismatic organization for making these demands, however farfetched these justifications might appear to an outside observer.

H9 states that the brainwashing process results in a state of ideological obedience in which the individual has a strong tendency to comply with any behavioral demands made by the collectivity, especially if motivated by the carrot of approval and the stick of threatened expulsion, no matter how life-threatening these demands may be and no matter how repugnant such demands might have been to the individual in his or her pre-brainwashed state.

H10 states that the brainwashing process results in increased deployability. Deployability extends the range of ideological obedience in the temporal dimension. It states that the response continues after the stimulus is removed. This hypothesis will be disconfirmed in any cult within which members are uncritically obedient only while they are being brainwashed but not thereafter. The effect need not be permanent, but it does need to result in some measurable increase in deployability over time.

H11 states that the ability of the collectivity to rely on obedience without surveillance will result in a measurable decrease in surveillance. Since surveillance involves costs, this decrease will lead to a quantity S, where S equals the savings to the collectivity due to diminished surveillance needs and should be measurable at least to an ordinal level.

H12 states that S will be greater than C. In other words, the savings to the collectivity due to decreased surveillance needs is greater than the cost of maintaining the brainwashing program. Only where S is greater than C does it make sense to maintain a brainwashing program. Cults with initially high surveillance costs, and therefore high potential savings due to decreased surveillance needs [S], will tend to be more likely to brainwash, as will cults structured so that the cost of maintaining the brainwashing system [C] are relatively low.

Characteristics of a Good Theory

There is consensus in the social sciences that a good inductive qualitative theory[14] is one that is falsifiable, internally consistent, concrete, potentially generalizable, and has a well-defined dependent variable (King, Keohane et al. 1994). I think it should be clear from the foregoing that this theory meets all of these conditions according to prevailing standards in the social and behavioral sciences. However, since brainwashing theory has received much unjustified criticism for its lack of falsifiability and its lack of generalizability, I will briefly discuss the theory from these two points of view.

The criterion of falsifiability, as formulated primarily by Popper (1968), is the essence of what separates theory from dogma in science. Every theory must be able to provide an answer to the question of what evidence would falsify it. If the answer is that there is no possible evidence that would lead us to reject a so-called theory, we should conclude that it is not really a theory at all but just a piece of dogma.

Although Dawson (1998) and Richardson (1993) have included the falsifiability problem in their critiques of brainwashing, this criticism is associated mainly with the work of Dick Anthony (1996). Anthony's claim that brainwashing theory is unfalsifiable is based upon two related misunderstandings. First, he argues that it is impossible to prove that a person is acting with free will so, to the extent that brainwashing theory rests on the overthrow of free will, no evidence can ever disprove it. Second, he applies Popper's criterion to cults in a way more appropriate for a highly developed deductive theoretical system. He requires that either brainwashing explain all ego-dystonic behaviour in cults or acknowledge that it can explain none of it. But, as we have seen, brainwashing is part of an inductive multifactorial approach to the study of obedience in cults and should be expected to explain only some of the obedience produced in some cults.

With regard to generalizability, cultic brainwashing is part of an important general class of phenomena whose common element is what Anthony Giddens has called 'disturbance of ontological security' in which habits and routines cease to function as guidelines for survival (Cohen 1989: 53). This class of phenomena includes the battered spouse syndrome (Barnett and LaViolette 1993), the behaviour of concentration camp inmates (Chodoff 1966), the Stockholm Syndrome (Kuleshnyk 1984; Powell 1986), and, most importantly, behaviour within prisoner of war camps and Communist Chinese re-education centres and 'revolutionary universities' (Lifton 1989; Sargant 1957; Schein 1961). There exist striking homologies in observed responses across all of these types of events, and it is right that our attention be drawn to trying to understand what common theme underlies them all. As Oliver Wendell Holmes (1891: 325) attempted to teach us more than a century ago, the interest of the scientist should be guided, when applicable, by 'the plain law of homology which declares that like must be compared with like.'

Evidence for Brainwashing in Cults

I have attempted to test the model as much as possible with the limited data that currently exist. I have relied on three sources of evidence. The first and most important of these consists of ethnographic studies of a wide variety of contemporary American charismatic cults conducted by myself and others. The first-hand opportunities I have had to watch (at least the public face of) charismatic resocialization in numerous cult situations has convinced me of the need to theorize about this phenomenon. The second source of data consists of interviews with former leaders of charismatic groups. Although I have only a handful of such interviews, they are particularly valuable for elucidating the process from the perspective of 'management,' rather than from the perspective of the subjects. The third source of data consists of reports of ex-members of cults, drawing heavily on scientifically sampled interviews that my students and I have conducted. Most of these respondents were interviewed at least twice over a roughly twenty-five-year period.

Because evidence in this field of study tends to be so bitterly contested, it is perhaps necessary to point out that my own studies in this area were all subject to rigorous and competitive peer review. Five of my studies were reviewed and funded by three organizations – the National Institute of Mental Health (2), the National Science Foundation (2), and the National Institute of Health (1) – over a period extending from 1964 to 2001. On all of these I was the principal investigator, and the research designs are in the public record. During this same period, other research of mine in this same field of study was funded by peer-reviewed faculty research grants from all of the universities with which I have been affiliated: the University of California at Berkeley, the California Institute of Technology, Columbia University, and Rutgers University. It is a strange anomaly that this body of work seems to be generally respected throughout the social and behavioural sciences, with the exception of a small field, the sociology of new religious movements, where some try their best to hold it up to ridicule and disesteem.

Ethnographic Accounts
Bainbridge (1997) has argued that most ethnographic studies of cults have failed to find evidence of brainwashing. But it is more accurate to say that ethnographers have been divided on this subject. Lalich, Ofshe, Kent, and myself have found such evidence abundantly (Kent and Krebs 1998; Lalich 1993; Ofshe, Eisenberg et al. 1974; Zablocki 1980). Even Barker, Beckford, and Richardson, who are among the most hostile to the brainwashing conjecture, have found evidence of attempted brainwashing, although they have claimed that these attempts are largely or entirely unsuccessful (Barker 1984; Beckford 1985; Richardson, Harder et al. 1972). Still other ethnographers (Balch 1985; Rochford, Purvis et al. 1989) seem ambivalent on the subject and not sure what to make of the evidence. Others such as Palmer (1994)

and Hall (1987, 2000) have been fairly clear about the absence of brain-washing in their observations.

Such disparity is to be expected. There is no reason to believe that all cults practise brainwashing any more than that all cults are violent or that all cults make their members wear saffron robes. Most ethnographers who did discover evidence of brainwashing in the cults they investigated were surprised by the finding. The fact that evidence of this sort has been repeatedly discovered by researchers who were not particularly looking for it suggests that the process really exists in some cults. I have observed fully developed brainwashing processes in some cults, partially developed ones in others, and none whatsoever in others. As ethnographic work in cults continues to accumulate, we should expect to find a similar degree of heterogeneity in published reports. Certainly, there is abundant evidence of uncritically obedient behaviour in charismatic cults (Ayella 1990; Davis 2000; Katchen 1997; Lalich 1999; Lifton 1999; Wallis 1977), and this behaviour needs to be explained. The presence or absence of brainwashing may ultimately turn out to contribute to such an explanation.

When I first studied the Bruderhof thirty-five years ago, using ethnographic methods, I noticed a strong isomorphism between the phases of Bruderhof resocialization and the phases of brainwashing in Chinese re-education centres described by Lifton. Since I could think of no other reason why the Bruderhof would support such a costly and labour-intensive resocialization program if it were not to create deployable agents with long-term loyalty to the community, I hypothesized that something akin to brainwashing must be going on. My observations over the next thirty-five years have only strengthened my confidence in the correctness of this hypothesis. Bruderhof members were never kept from leaving by force or force threat. But the community put a lot of time and energy into assuring that defections would be made rare and difficult by imbuing in its members an uncritical acceptance of the teachings of the community and a terror of life outside the community.[15]

Some (but not all) of the other cultic groups I have lived with as a participant-observer have shown signs of a brainwashing process at work. Individuals being plucked suddenly out of the workaday routine of the group, appearing to become haggard with lack of sleep for prolonged periods, secretiveness and agitation, alternating periods of shunning and warm communal embrace, all suggest the presence of such a process. Some of these people, years later, having left the cult, have confirmed to me that such a process is what they went through when I observed them under this stress. According to my ethnographic observations, some sort of fully or partially developed brainwashing process figures in the resocialization of at least half of the cults I have studied during at least some phases of their history.

Leader Accounts
A second source of evidence may be found in reports given by people who were actually responsible for practising brainwashing with their fellow cult members. Several cult leaders who left their groups have since apologized to other ex-members for having subjected them to brainwashing methods. One such former cult leader put it this way:

> What you have to understand is that, for us, breaking the spirit ... emptying out the ego, is very very important. And any means to that end ... well, we would have said it was justified. And over the years we developed [by trial and error] ways of accomplishing this [task]. It was only after I was finished with [the cult] and living in the world again that I did some reading and realized how similar [our techniques] were to what the Communists did – to brainwashing. I think you would have to say that what we did was a kind of brainwashing even if we didn't mean it to be so.

In another case I interviewed the widow of a cult leader who had died and whose cult had disbanded soon thereafter. She said the following:

> Those kinds of things definitely happened [on quite a few occasions]. It's not like we ever sat down and said, hey we're going to brainwash everybody. That would have been crazy. It's more like we knew how important our mission was and how [vulnerable it was] to treachery. I think we got a little paranoid about being overcome by treachery within, especially after Gabe and Helen left and starting saying those things about us. So everybody had to be tested. I had to be tested. Even he [the leader] had to be tested. We all knew it and we all [accepted it]. So we would pull a person out of the routine and put him in solitary for awhile. Nobody could talk to him except [my husband] and maybe a few others. I couldn't even talk to him when I brought him his meals. That was usually my job ... At first it was just isolation and observation and having deep long talks far into the

night about the mission. We didn't know anything about brainwashing or any of that stuff. But gradually the things you describe got in there too somehow. Especially the written confessions. I had to write a bunch of them towards the end when [X] was sick. Whatever you wrote was not enough. They always wanted more, and you always felt you were holding out on them. Finally your confessions would get crazy, they'd come from your wildest fantasies of what they might want. At the end I confessed that I was killing [my husband] by tampering with his food because I wanted to – I don't know – be the leader in his place I guess. All of us knew it was bullshit but somehow it satisfied them when I wrote that ... And, even though we knew it was bullshit, going through that changed us. I mean I know it changed me. It burned a bridge ... [T]here was no going back. You really did feel you changed into being a different person in a weird sort of way.

Perhaps the closest thing I have found to a smoking gun in this regard has to do with a sociology professor who became a charismatic cult leader. Two of this cult leader's top lieutenants independently spoke to me on this subject. Both of these respondents described in great detail how they assisted in concerted campaigns to brainwash fellow cult members. Both felt guilty about this and found the memory painful to recount. One of them indicated that the brainwashing attempt was conscious and deliberate:

During her years in academia, Baxter became very interested in mass social psychology and group behavior modification. She studied Robert Jay Lifton's work on thought reform; she studied and admired 'total' communities such as Synanon, and directed methods of change, such as Alcoholics Anonymous. She spoke of these techniques as positive ways to change people. (Lalich 1993: 55)

In this cult, which has since disbanded, there seems to be general consensus among both leaders and followers that systematic brainwashing techniques were used on a regular basis and were successful in their aim of producing deployable agents.

Ex-Member Accounts
Our third source of evidence is the most controversial. There has been a misguided attempt to deny the validity of negative ex-member accounts as a source of data about cults. They've been condemned as

'atrocity tales' (Richardson 1998: 172), and Johnson (1998: 118) has dismissed them categorically by alleging that 'the autobiographical elements of apostate narratives are further shaped by a concern that the targeted religious groups be painted in the worst possible light.'

The apostate role has been defined by Bromley (1997) largely in terms of the content of attitudes towards the former cult. If these attitudes are negative and expressed collectively in solidarity with other negatively disposed ex-members, they constitute evidence that the person must be not an ordinary ex-member but an 'apostate.' This is a direct violation of Robert Merton's (1968) admonition that role sets be defined in terms of shared structural characteristics, not individual attitudes. What if this same logic were used to denigrate abused spouses who choose to be collectively vocal in their complaints? Nevertheless, this perspective on so-called 'apostate accounts' has been widely influential among cult scholars.

David Bromley is a sociological theorist of great personal integrity but limited field experience. I think that if Bromley and his followers could just once sit down with a few hundred of these emotionally haunted ex-members whom they blithely label 'apostates,' and listen to their stories, and see for themselves how badly most of them would like nothing more than to be able to put the cult experience behind them and get on with their lives, they would be deeply ashamed of the way they have subverted role theory to deny a voice to a whole class of people.

Dawson (1995) has correctly pointed out that there are methodological problems involved in using accounts of any kind as data. We need to be careful not to rely *only* on ex-member accounts. Triangulation of data sources is essential. But even the reports of professional ethnographers are nothing more than accounts, and thus subject to the same sort of limitations. Ex-member accounts have been shown to have reliability and validity roughly equivalent to the accounts given by current cult members (Zablocki 1996).

Solomon (1981) has provided some empirical support for the argument that those with stormy exits from cults and those with anticult movement affiliations are more likely to allege that they have been brainwashed than those with relatively uneventful exits and no such affiliation. 'Cult apologists' have made much of the finding that ex-members affiliated with anticult organizations are more likely to allege brainwashing than those who are not. Their hatred of the anticult movement has blinded them to two important considerations: (1) The causal direction is by no means obvious – it is at least as likely that those who were brainwashed are more likely to seek out anticult organizations as support groups as that false memories of brainwashing are implanted by anticult groups into those ex-members who fall into their clutches; and (2) Although the percentages may be lower, some ex-members who don't affiliate with anticult groups still allege brainwashing.

Many ex-members of cults find brainwashing the most plausible explanation of their own cult experiences. While some might be deluding themselves to avoid having to take responsibility for their own mistakes, it strains credulity to imagine that all are doing so. Here, just by way of example, are excerpts from interviews done with five ex-members of five different cults. None of these respondents was ever affiliated, even marginally, with an anticult organization:

'They ask you to betray yourself so gradually that you never notice you're giving up everything that makes you who you are and letting them fill you up with something they think is better and that they've taught you to believe is something better.'

'What hurts most is that I thought these people were my new friends, my new family. It wasn't until after that I realized how I was manipulated little step by little step. Just like in Lifton; it's really amazing when you think of it ... couldn't just be a coincidence ... I don't know if you can understand it, but what hurts most is not that they did it but realizing that they planned it out so carefully from the beginning. That was so cold.'

'I've never been able to explain it to people who weren't there. I don't really understand it myself. But black was white, night was day, whatever they told us to believe, it was like a test. The more outrageous the idea the greater the victory, when I could wrap my mind around it and really believe it down to my toes. And, most important, be prepared to act on it just like if it was proven fact. That's the really scary part when I look back on it.'

'In the frame of mind I was in [at the time], I welcomed the brainwashing. I thought of it like a purge. I needed to purge my old ways, my old self. I hated it and I felt really violent toward it ... I wanted to wash it all away and make myself an empty vehicle for [the guru's] divine plan ... [Our] ideal was to be unthinking obedient foot soldiers in God's holy army.'

Many wax particularly eloquent on this subject when interviewed in the aftermath of media events involving cultic mass suicides or murders. The fifth respondent said the following:

'It makes me shudder and ... thank God that I got out when I did. 'Cause that could have been me doing that, could have been any of us. [I have] no doubt any one of us would have done that in the condition we all were in – killed ourselves, our kids, any that [the leaders] named enemies.'

I have quoted just five ex-members because of limitations of space. Many more could be found. Thousands of ex-members of various groups (only a small minority of whom have ever been interviewed by me) have complained of being brainwashed. Contrary to the allegations of some 'cult apologists,' very few of these are people who had been deprogrammed (and presumably brainwashed into believing that they had been brainwashed). The accounts of these people tend often to agree on the particulars of what happened to them, even though these people may never have talked with one another.

Another striking aspect of these brainwashing accounts by ex-members is that they are held to consistently for many years. I have interviewed many ex-cult members twenty to thirty years after leaving the cult, and have yet to have a single case of a person who alleged brainwashing immediately after leaving the cult, later recant and say it wasn't true after all. More than anything else, this consistency over extended periods of time convinces me that ex-member accounts often may be relied on. Even if some of the details have been forgotten or exaggerated with the passage of time, the basic outline of what happened to them is probably pretty accurate. All in all, therefore, I think it is fair to conclude, both from accumulated ethnographic and ex-member data, that brainwashing happens to at least some people in some cults.

Incidence and Consequences

Finally, we come to the aspect of brainwashing theory for which our data are sketchiest, the one most in need of further research. How often does brainwashing actually occur (incidence)[16] and how significant are its consequences?

Defining what we mean by incidence is far from a simple matter. In the reporting of brainwashing there are numerous false positives and false negatives, and no consensus as to whether these errors lead to net underestimation or net overestimation. Several factors can produce false positives. Unless the term is precisely defined to respondents, some answers will reflect folk definitions of the term. It might mean little more to them than that they believe they were not treated nicely by their former cults. Other respondents may share our definition of the term, but answer falsely out of a desire to lay claim to the victim role or out of anger towards the cult. False negatives also can occur for several reasons. Most significantly, current members (as well as ex-members who still sympathize with the cult) may deny brainwashing to protect the cult. Others may understand the term differently than do the interviewers, and still others may be embarrassed to admit that they had been brainwashed. These errors can be minimized but hardly eliminated by in-depth interviewing in which respondents are asked not merely to label but to describe the process they went through.

There is insufficient space in this chapter to discuss these important methodological issues. I will therefore merely state the criteria upon which I base my own measurement. I treat incidence as a ratio of X to Y. In Y are included all those who were fully committed members of a cult for a year or more, but who are currently no longer affiliated with any cult.[17] In X are included those members of the Y set who both claim to have been brainwashed and who are able to give evidence of the particulars of their own brainwashing experience (at least through phase 2) consistent with those discussed in the previous section of this chapter.

In the handful of systematic studies that have been done, estimates of brainwashing incidence seem to cluster around 10 per cent (plus or minus 5 per cent) of former cult members (Katchen 1997; Wright 1987; Zablocki, Hostetler et al. in press). However, there is tremendous variation in estimates for this number given by people working in this field. Ignoring those scholars who deny that brainwashing is ever attempted or ever successful, I have heard anecdotal estimates as low as <0.1 per cent and as high as 80 per cent, given by ethnographers.

Stuart Wright's (1987) data on voluntarily exiting ex-members indicate that 9 per cent say they had been brainwashed. This study is noteworthy because it examined ex-members of a variety of different cults rather than just one. It relied, however, on each respondent's own definition of what it meant to be brainwashed.

My national longitudinal study (Zablocki 1980) relied primarily on a two-stage sampling procedure in which geographical regions were first selected and groups then sampled within these regions. I have followed 404 cases, most of them surveyed at least twice over intervals extending up to twenty-five years. Of those who were interviewed, 11 per cent meet the criteria for having been brainwashed discussed above. Interestingly, all those in my sample who claim to have been brainwashed stick to their claims even after many years have passed. My own study is the only one that I know of that has repeatedly interviewed members and former members over several decades.

Another issue is whether overall incidence among the ex-member population is the most meaningful statistic to strive for given the heterogeneity among cults and types of cult member. Cults vary in the proportion of their members they attempt to brainwash from 0 per cent to 100 per cent. Since brainwashing significantly increases exit costs (according to hypothesis 8), it follows that examples of brainwashed individuals will be somewhat over-represented among current cult members and somewhat under-represented among ex-members.

The incidence, among ex-members, is higher (24 per cent in my sample) when the relevant population is confined to a cult's 'inner circle,' the core membership surrounding the leader. In an important and neglected article, Wexler (1995) makes the point that it is simplistic to think of a cult as comprising only a leader and a homogeneous mass of followers. Most cults have a third category of membership, a corps of lieutenants surrounding the leader, which Wexler refers to as a 'decision elite.' It follows from the hypotheses discussed earlier that we should expect attempts to brainwash to be concentrated among members in this category.

One study suggests that incidence is also higher among adults who grew up in cults (Katchen 1997). My own ethnographic observation supports this last point, and further suggests that cults under extreme stress become more likely to engage in brainwashing or to extend already existing brainwashing programs to a much wider circle of members.

With regard to consequences, we must distinguish between obedience consequences and traumatic consequences. Uncritical obedience is extinguished rapidly, certainly within a year of exiting if not sooner. The popular idea that former cult members can be programmed to carry obedience compulsions for specific acts to be performed long after membership in the cult has ceased is, in my opinion, wholly a myth based largely on a movie, *The Manchurian Candidate*. I know of nobody who has ever seen even a single successful instance of such programming. However, many brainwashed ex-members report that they would not feel safe visiting the cult, fearing that old habits of obedience might quickly be reinstilled.

There is evidence, in my data set, of persistent post-traumatic effects. The majority of those who claim to have been brainwashed say that they never fully get over the psychosocial insult, although its impact on their lives diminishes over time. The ability to form significant bonds with others takes a long time to heal, and about a third wind up (as much as a quarter of a century later) living alone with few significant social ties. This is more than double the proportion of controls (cult participants who appeared not to have been brainwashed) that are socially isolated twenty-five years later. Visible effects also linger in the ability to form new belief commitments. In about half there is no new commitment to a belief community after two years. By twenty-five years, this has improved, although close to twenty-five per cent still have formed no such commitment. Occupationally, they tend to do somewhat better, but often not until having been separated from the cult for five to ten years.

Conclusions

We can conclude from all of the above that those who claim that cultic brainwashing does not exist and those who claim it is pandemic to cults are both wrong. Brainwashing is an administratively costly and not always effective procedure that some cults use on some of their members. A few cults rely heavily on brainwashing and put all their members through it. Other cults do not use the procedure at all. During periods of stressful confrontation, either with external enemies or among internal factions, or in attempts to cope with failed apocalyptic prophecies, it is not uncommon for brainwashing suddenly to come to play a central role in the cult's attempts to achieve order and social control. At such times, risk of uncritically obedient violent aggression or mass suicide may be heightened.

Hopefully, it will be clear from this chapter that brainwashing has absolutely nothing to do with the overthrow of 'free will' or any other such mystical or nonscientific concept. People who have been brainwashed are 'not free' only in the sense that all of us, hemmed in on all sides as we are by social and cultural constraints, are not free. The kinds of social constraints involved in brainwashing are much more intense than those involved in socializing many of us to eat with knives and forks rather than with our hands. But the constraints involved differ only in magnitude and focus, not in kind. Any brain-washed cult member always retains the ability to leave the cult or defy the cult as long as he or she is willing to pay the mental and emotional price (which may be considerable) that the cult is able to exact for so doing.

As I finish this chapter, a number of European nations are debating the advisability of anti-brainwashing laws, some of which eventually may be used to inhibit freedom of religious expression. In light of this trend a number of colleagues have criticized me, not on the grounds that my facts are incorrect, but that my timing is unfortunate. One socked me with the following, particularly troubling, complaint: 'Ben, if you had discovered evidence, in 1942, of a higher prevalence among Jews than among non-Jews of the Tay-Sachs genetic defect, would you have published your findings in a German biology journal?' Ultimately, although I respect the sentiments behind my colleagues' concerns, I must respectfully disagree with their fastidious caution. It never works to refuse to look at frightening facts. They only become larger, more frightening, and more mystically permeated when banished to one's peripheral vision. A direct, honest acknowledgment of the limited but significant role that brainwashing plays in producing uncritical obedience in some cults will serve, in the long run, to lessen paranoid reactions to 'the threat of the cults,' rather than to increase them.

Notes

1 Most of the examples in this chapter will be drawn from studies of religious cults because these are ones with which I am most familiar through my research. But it should be noted that cults need not be religious, and that there are plenty of examples of brainwashing in political and psychotherapeutic cults as well.

2 When I speak of ego dystonic behaviour, I refer to behaviour that was ego dystonic to the person before joining the cult and after leaving the cult.

3 I have no doubt that Introvigne, who is a European attorney, is sincere in his desire to stifle brainwashing research out of a fear that any suggestion that brainwashing might possibly occur in cults will be seized on by semi-authoritarian government committees eager to suppress religious liberty. Personally, I applaud Introvigne's efforts to protect the fragile tree of religious freedom of choice in the newly emerging democracies of Eastern

Europe. But I don't appreciate his doing so by (perhaps inadvertantly) sticking his thumb on the scales upon which social scientists attempt to weigh evidence.

4 The Anthony and Robbins article cited demonstrates how little we really know about traits that may predispose people to join cults. They say '... some traditionally conservative religious groups attract people who score highly on various measures of totalitarianism, e.g., the F scale or Rokeach's Dogmatism scale ... It seems likely that these results upon certain Christian groups would generalize to alternative religious movements or cults, as many of them have theological and social beliefs that seems similar to those in some fundamentalist denominations' (1994: 470). Perhaps, but perhaps not. No consensus has yet emerged from numerous attempts to find a cult personality type, but this seems like a promising area of research to continue.

5 Some, it is true, were nominally volunteers into re-education programs. However, the power of the state to make their lives miserable if they did not volunteer cannot be ignored.

6 Unfortunately, however, uncritical obedience can be wayward and dangerous. It can be useful to a cult leader when the cult is functioning well. But it often has been perverted to serve a destructive or self-destructive agenda in cults that have begun to disintegrate.

7 Some confusion on this subject has emerged from the fact that Lifton has distanced himself from those attempting to litigate against cults because of alleged brainwashing. He has consistently argued (and I wholeheartedly agree) that brainwashing, in and of itself, where no force is involved, should not be a matter for the law courts.

8 Formal definitions for this and other technical terms will be presented in the next section of this chapter.

9 In other words, the probability of a person's leaving is inversely dependent upon the amount of time he or she has already spent as a member.

10 The 'cult-basher' version of brainwashing theory has played into this misunderstanding by confounding manipulative recruitment techniques (like sleep deprivation and 'love-bombing') with actual brainwashing. While there may be some overlap in the actual techniques used, the former is a method for obtaining new members, whereas brainwashing is a method for retaining old members.

11 Because of space limitations, I cannot give this important subject the attention it deserves in this chapter. Readers not familiar with the concept are referred to the much fuller discussion of this subject in the book by Robert Lifton as cited.

12 Students of cults have sometimes been misled into confusing this state of hyper credulity with either hyper suggestibility on the one hand or a rigid 'true belief' system on the other. But at least one study has shown that neither the hyper-suggestible, easily hypnotized person nor the structural true believer are good candidates for encapsulation in a totalist cult system (Solomon 1981: 111–12). True believers (often fundamentalists who see in the cult a purer manifestation of their own world view than they have seen before) do not do well in cults and neither do dyed-in-the-wool sceptics who are comfortable with their scepticism. Rather it is those lacking convictions but hungering for them that are the best candidates.

13 Hopefully, no reader will think that I am affirming the consequent by stating that all experiences of spiritual rebirth must be caused by brainwashing. This model is completely compatible with the assumption that most spiritual rebirth experiences have nothing to do with brainwashing. The reasoning here is identical to that connecting epilepsy with visions of the holy. The empirical finding that epileptic seizures can be accompanied by visions of the holy does not in any way imply that such visions are always a sign of epilepsy.

14 The theory outlined here is basically a qualitative one, although it does call for the measurement of two quantities, C and S. However, it will frequently be sufficient if these two quantities can be measured at just an ordinal level, and indeed that is generally all that will be possible in most circumstances.

15 Bruderhof members, particularly those in responsible positions, are never fully trusted until they have gone through the ordeal of having been put into the great exclusion (being sent away) and then spiritually fought their way back to the community. Such exclusion serves as the ultimate test of deployability. Is the conversion deep enough to hold even when away from daily reinforcement by participation in community life? The degree to which the Bruderhof stresses the importance of this ideal serves as additional evidence that the creation of deployable agents is a major aim of the socialization process.

16 A related question is what portion of those a cult attempts to brainwash actually get brainwashed. No data have been collected on this issue to the best of my knowledge.

17 I do not distinguish between voluntary and involuntary mode of exit in my measure because my sample includes only an insignificant number (less than one-half of one per cent) who were deprogrammed out of their cults.

References

Abelson, R. 1986. 'Beliefs are Like Possessions.' *Journal for the Theory of Social Behaviour* 16: 223–50.

American Psychiatric Association. 1994. *Diagnostic and Statistical Manual of Mental Disorders* 4th ed. Washington D.C.: American Psychiatric Association.

Anthony, D. 1996. 'Brainwashing and Totalitarian Influence: An Exploration of Admissibility Criteria For Testimony in Brainwashing Trials.' Berkeley, Calif.: Graduate Theological Union.

Anthony, D., and T. Robbins. 1994. 'Brainwashing and Totalitarian Influence.' *Encyclopedia of Human Behavior.* New York: Academic Press, 1.

– 1995. 'Religious Totalism, Violence, and Exemplary Dualism: Beyond the Extrinsic Model.' *Terrorism and Political Violence* 7 (3): 10–50.

Asch, S. 1951. 'Effects of Group Pressure upon the Modification and Distortion of Judgments.' In *Groups, Leadership, and Men,* edited by H. Guetzknow. Pittsburgh: Carnegie.

Ayella, M. 1990. '"They Must Be Crazy": Some of the Difficulties in Researching "Cults."' *American Behavioral Scientist* 33 (5): 562–77.

Bainbridge, W.S. 1997. *The Sociology of Religious Movements.* New York: Routledge.

Balch, R.W. 1985. '"When the Light Goes Out, Darkness Comes": A Study of Defection from a Totalistic Cult.' In *Religious Movements: Genesis, Exodus, and Numbers,* edited by R. Stark. New York: Paragon.

Barker, E. 1984. *The Making of a Moonie: Choice or Brainwashing.* Oxford: Basil Blackwell.

– 1989. *New Religious Movements: A Practical Introduction.* London: Her Majesty's Stationery Office.

Barnett, O.W., and A.D. LaViolette. 1993. *It Could Happen to Anyone: Why Battered Women Stay.* Newbury Park, Calif.: Sage.

Beckford, J.A. 1985. *Cult Controversies: The Societal Response to the New Religious Movements.* London: Tavistock.

Bion, W.R. 1959. *Experiences in Groups.* New York: Basic Books.

Bowen, M. 1972. 'Toward the Differentiation of a Self in One's Own Family.' In *Family Interaction,* edited by J. Framo. New York: Springer.

Bowlby, J. 1969. *Attachment and Loss: Attachment.* New York: Basic Books.

Bromley, D. 1998. 'Listing (in Black and White) Some Observations on (Sociological) Thought Reform.' *Nova Religio* 1: 250–66.

– 1997. 'The Social Construction of Religious Apostasy.' In *The Politics of Religious Apostasy,* edited by D.G. Bromley. New York: Praeger.

Bugliosi, V., and C. Gentry. 1974. *Helter Skelter: The True Story of the Manson Murders*. New York: Norton.

Carter, L.F. 1990. *Charisma and Control in Rajneeshpuram: The Role of Shared Values in the Creation of a Community*. New York: Cambridge University Press.

Chodoff, P. 1966. 'Effects of Extreme Coercive and Oppressive Forces: Brainwashing and Concentration Camps.' In *American Handbook of Psychiatry*. Vol. 3, edited by S. Arieti, 384–405. New York, Basic Books.

Cialdini, R. 1993. *Influence: The Psychology of Persuasion*. New York: William Morrow.

Cohen, I. 1989. *Structuration Theory*. New York: St Martin's.

Cohen, S. 1972. *Folk Devils and Moral Panics*. Oxford: Basil Blackwell.

Coleman, J.S. 1990. *Foundations of Social Theory*. Cambridge, Mass.: Harvard University Press.

Coleridge, S.T. 1970. *Biographia Literaria*. New York: Random House.

Conway, F., and J. Siegelman. 1978. *Snapping: America's Epidemic of Sudden Personality Change*. Philadelphia: Lippincott.

Davis, W. 2000. 'Heaven's Gate: A Study of Religious Obedience.' *Nova Religio* 3: 241–67.

Dawson, L. 1995. 'Accounting for Accounts: How Should Sociologists Treat Conversion Stories.' *International Journal of Comparative Religion and Philosophy* 1: 51–68.

– 1998. *Comprehending Cults: The Sociology of New Religious Movements*. New York: Oxford University Press.

Farrell, K. 1998. *Post-traumatic Culture*. Baltimore: Johns Hopkins University Press.

Festinger, L., A. Pepitone, et al. 1952. 'Some Consequences of Deindividuation in a Group.' *Journal of Abnormal and Social Psychology* 47: 382–9.

Festinger, L., H. Riechen, et al. 1956. *When Prophecy Fails*. Minneapolis: University of Minnesota Press.

Galanter, M. 1989. *Cults: Faith, Healing, and Coercion*. New York: Oxford University Press.

Galanti, G.-A. 1993. 'Reflections on "Brainwashing."' In *Recovery From Cults: Help for Victims of Psychological and Spiritual Abuse*, edited by M.D. Langone. New York: Norton.

Geertz, C. 1973. *The Interpretation of Cultures*. New York: Basic Books.

Goffman, E. 1961. *Asylums*. Garden City, N.Y.: Anchor Books.

Goode, E., and N. Ben Yehudah. 1994. *Moral Panics*. Cambridge, Mass.: Blackwell.

Hall, J.R. 1987. *Gone from the Promised Land*. New Brunswick: N.J.: Transaction.

210   Benjamin Zablocki

- 2000. *Apocalypse Observed: Religious Movements and Violence in North America, Europe, and Japan.* New York: Routledge.
Hechter, M. 1987. *Principles of Group Solidarity.* Berkeley: University of California Press.
Herman, J. 1997. *Trauma and Recovery: The Aftermath of Violence – From Domestic Abuse to Political Terror.* New York: Basic Books.
Hexham, I., and K. Poewe. 1997. *New Religions as Global Cultures: Making the Human Sacred.* Boulder, Colo.: Westview.
Holmes, O.W. 1891. *Crime.* Boston: Houghton Mifflin.
Hong, N. 1998. *In the Shadow of the Moons.* Boston: Little, Brown.
Iannaccone, L.R. 1992. 'Sacrifice and Stigma: Reducing Free-Riding in Cults, Communes, and Other Collectives.' *Journal of Political Economy* 100: 271–91.
Introvigne, M. 1998. 'Liar, Liar: Brainwashing, CESNUR, and APA,' Center for Studies on New Religions: http://www.cesnur.org/testi/se_brainwash.htm
- Forthcoming. '"Brainwashing": Career of a Myth in the United States and Europe.' In *The Brainwashing Controversy: An Anthology of Essential Documents,* edited by J.G. Melton and M. Introvigne. Stanford, Calif., Center for Academic Publications.
Janis, I. 1982. *Groupthink: Psychological Studies of Policy Decisions and Fiascos.* Boston: Houghton Mifflin.
Johnson, D.C. 1998. 'Apostates Who Never Were: The Social Construction of Absque Facto Apostate Narratives.' In *The Politics of Apostasy: The Role of Apostates in the Transformation of Religious Movements,* edited by D.G. Bromley. Westport: Conn.: Praeger.
Katchen, M.H. 1997. 'The Rate of Dissociation and Dissociative Disorders in Former Members of High Demand Religious Movements.' PhD diss., Sociology department, Sydney University, Sydney, Australia.
Kelman, H.C. and V.L. Hamilton. 1989. *Crimes of Obedience: Toward a Social Psychology of Authority and Responsibility.* New Haven: Yale University Press.
Kent, S.A., and T. Krebs. 1998. 'Academic Compromise in the Social Scientific Study of Alternative Religions.' *Nova Religio* 2: 44–54.
King, G., R.O. Keohane, et al. 1994. *Designing Social Inquiry: Scientific Inference in Qualitative Research.* Princeton: Princeton University Press.
Kuleshnyk, I. 1984. 'The Stockholm Syndrome: Toward an Understanding.' *Social Action and the Law* 10: 37–42.
Lalich, J. 1993. 'A Little Carrot and a Lot of Stick: A Case Example.' In *Recovery From Cults: Help for Victims of Psychological and Spiritual Abuse,* edited by M.D. Langone. New York: Norton.
- 1999. 'Bounded Choice: The Fusion of Personal Freedom and Self-Renuncia-

tion in Two Transcendent Groups.' *Human and Organizational Systems.* PhD diss. Fielding Institute, Santa Barbara, Calif.

Layton, D. 1998. *Seductive Poison: A Jonestown Survivor's Story of Life and Death in the Peoples Temple.* New York: Doubleday.

Lewis, J.R. 1998. *Cults in America.* Santa Barbara, Calif.: ABC-CLIO.

Lewis, J.R., and D.G. Bromley. 1987. 'The Cult Withdrawal Syndrome: A Case of Misattribution of Cause?' *Journal for the Scientific Study of Religion* 26: 508–22.

Lifton, R.J. 1968. 'Protean Man.' *Partisan Review* 35: 13–27.

– 1989. *Thought Reform and the Psychology of Totalism.* Chapel Hill: University of North Carolina Press.

– 1995. Foreword to *Cults in Our Midst,* by M. Singer. San Francisco: Jossey-Bass.

– 1997. 'Reflections on Aum Shinrikyo.' In *The Year 2000: Essays on the End,* edited by C.B. Strozier and M. Flynn. New York: New York University Press.

– 1999. *Destroying the World to Save It: Aum Shinrikyo, Apocalyptic Violence, and the New Global Terrorism.* New York: Henry Holt.

Lindholm, C. 1990. *Charisma.* Cambridge: Basil Blackwell.

Lofland, J. 1966. *Doomsday Cult: A Study of Conversion, Proselytization and Maintenance of Faith.* Englewood Cliffs, N.J.: Prentice Hall.

Loftus, E. and K. Ketcham 1994. *The Myth of Repressed Memory: False Memories and Allegations of Sexual Abuse.* New York: St Martin's.

Lucas, P.C. 1995. *The Odyssey of a New Religion: The Holy Order of MANS from New Age to Orthodoxy.* Bloomington, Ind.: Indiana University Press.

Melton, J.G. forthcoming. 'Brainwashing and the Cults: The Rise and Fall of a Theory.' In *The Brainwashing Controversy: An Anthology of Essential Documents,* edited by J.G. Melton and M. Introvigne. Stanford, Calif.: Center For Academic Publication.

Merton, R.K. 1968. *Social Theory and Social Structure.* New York: Free Press.

Milgram, S. 1975. *Obedience to Authority.* New York: Harper & Row.

Miller, J. 2000. 'South Asia Called Major Terror Hub in a Survey by U.S.' *New York Times,* 30 April, 1.

Oakes, L. 1997. *Prophetic Charisma: The Psychology of Revolutionary Religious Personalities.* Syracuse: Syracuse University Press.

Ofshe, R. 1976. 'Synanon: The People Business.' In *The New Religious Consciousness,* edited by C. Glock and R. Bellah, 116–37. Berkeley: University of California Press.

– 1992. 'Coercive Persuasion and Attitude Change.' In *The Encyclopedia of Sociology,* edited by E. Borgatta and M. Borgatta. New York: Macmillan.

Ofshe, R., N. Eisenberg, et al. 1974. 'Social Structure and Social Control in Synanon.' *Voluntary Action Research* 3: 67–76.

O'Leary, S.D. 1994. *Arguing the Apocalypse: A Theory of Millennial Rhetoric.* New York: Oxford University Press.

Palmer, S.J. 1994. *Moon Sisters, Krishna Mothers, Rajneesh Lovers: Women's Roles in New Religions.* Syracuse: Syracuse University Press.

Petty, R. 1994. 'Two Routes to Persuasion: State of the Art.' In *International Perspectives on Psychological Science,* edited by G. d'Ydewalle, P. Eelen, and P. Bertelson. Hillsdale: N.J.: Erlbaum.

Petty, R.E., and D.T. Wegener 1998. 'Attitude Change: Multiple Roles For Persuasion Variables.' In *The Handbook of Social Psychology.* Vol. 1, edited by D.T. Gilbert, S.T. Fiske, and G. Lindzey, 323–90. New York: McGraw-Hill.

Popper, K.R. 1968. *The Logic of Scientific Discovery.* New York: Harper & Row.

Powell, J.O. 1986. 'Notes on the Stockholm Syndrome.' *Studies in Symbolic Interaction* 7: 353–65.

Rauch, S.L., B. van der Kolk, et al. 1996. 'A Symptom Provocation Study of Post-traumatic Stress Disorder Using Positron Emission Tomography and Script-Driven Imagery.' *Archives of General Psychiatry* 53: 380–7.

Richardson, J.T., 1993. 'A Social Psychological Critique of "Brainwashing" Claims about Recruitment to New Religions.' Pt. B of *Religion and the Social Order: The Handbook on Cults and Sects in America,* edited by D.G. Bromley and J.K. Hadden. Greenwich, Conn.: JAI.

– 1998. 'Apostates, Whistleblowers, Law, and Social Control.' In *The Politics of Apostasy: The Role of Apostates in the Transformation of Religious Movements,* edited by D.G. Bromley. Westport, Conn.: Praeger.

Richardson, J.T., and G. Ginsburg. 1998. 'A Critique of "Brainwashing" Evidence in Light of Daubert: Science and Unpopular Religions.' In *Law and Science: Current Legal Issues.* Vol. 1, edited by H. Reece, 265–88. New York: Oxford University Press.

Richardson, J.T., and B. Kilbourne. 1983. 'Classical and Contemporary Applications of Brainwashing Models: A Comparison and Critique.' In *The Brainwashing/Deprogramming Controversy: Sociological, Psychological, Legal, and Historical Perspectives,* edited by D.G. Bromley and J.T. Richardson. New York: Edwin Mellen.

Richardson, J.T., M. Harder, et al. 1972. 'Thought Reform and the Jesus Movement.' *Youth and Society* 4: 185–202.

Robbins, T. 1988. *Cults, Converts, and Charisma: The Sociology of New Religious Movements.* Beverly Hills: Sage.

Rochford, E.B., Jr., S. Purvis, et al. 1989. 'New Religions, Mental Health, and Social Control.' In *Research in The Social Scientific Study of Religion.*

Vol. 1, edited by M.L. Lynn and D.O. Moberg, 57–82. Greenwich, Conn.: JAI.

- 1998. 'Child Abuse in the Hare Krishna Movement: 1971–1986.' *ISKCON Communication Journal* 6: 43–69.

Rousseau, J. 1913. *The Social Contract and Discourses*. London: J.M. Dent.

Saliba, J.A. 1993. 'The New Religions and Mental Health.' Pt. B of *Religion and the Social Order: The Handbook on Cults and Sects in America*, edited by D.G. Bromley and J.K. Hadden. Greenwich: Conn.: JAI.

Sargant, W. 1957. *Battle for the Mind: A Physiology of Conversion and Brainwashing*. Westport, Conn.: Greenwood.

Schein, E. 1959. 'Brainwashing and Totalitarianization in Modern Society.' *World Politics* 2: 430–41.

- 1961. *Coercive Persuasion*. New York: Norton.

Selznick, P. 1960. *The Organizational Weapon*. Glencoe, Ill.: Free Press.

Singer, M. 1995. *Cults in Our Midst*. San Francisco: Jossey-Bass.

Singer, M., and R. Ofshe. 1990. 'Thought Reform Programs and the Production of Psychiatric Casualties.' *Psychiatric Annals* 20: 188–93.

Sirkin, M., and L. Wynne. 1990. 'Cult Involvement as a Relational Disorder.' *Psychiatric Annals* 20: 199–203.

Snyder, M. 1974. 'The Self-Monitoring of Expressive Behavior.' *Journal of Personality and Social Psychology* 30: 526–37.

Solomon, T. 1981. 'Integrating the "Moonie" Experience: A Survey of Ex-Members of the Unification Church.' In *In Gods We Trust*, edited by T. Robbins and D. Anthony. New Brunswick, N.J.: Transaction.

Stark, R. 1999. 'Micro Foundations of Religion: A Revised Theory.' *Sociological Theory* 17: 264–89.

Thurber, J. 1957. *The Wonderful O*. New York: Simon & Schuster.

Turner, V.W. 1969. *The Ritual Process*. Hardmondsworth, England: Penguin Press.

Ungerleider, J.T. and D.K. Wellisch. 1983. 'The Programming (Brainwashing)/ Deprogramming Religious Controversy.' In *The Brainwashing/Deprogramming Controversy: Sociological, Psychological, Legal and Historical Perspectives*. Vol. 5, edited by D.G. Bromley and J.T. Richardson, 205–11. New York: Edwin Mellen.

van der Kolk, B.A., and A.C. McFarlane. 1996. 'The Black Hole of Trauma.' In *Traumatic Stress: The Effects of Overwhelming Experience on Mind, Body, and Society*, edited by B.A. van der Kolk, A.C. McFarlane, and L. Weisaeth. New York: Guilford.

Wallis, R. 1977. *The Road to Total Freedom: A Sociological Analysis of Scientology*. New York: Columbia University Press.

Weber, M. 1947. *The Theory of Social and Economic Organization*. New York: Free Press.

Weightman, J.M. 1983. *Making Sense of the Jonestown Suicides*. New York: Edwin Mellen.

Wexler, M. 1995. 'Expanding the Groupthink Explanation to the Study of Contemporary Cults.' *Cultic Studies* 12: 49–71.

Williams, M. 1998. *Heaven's Harlots: My Fifteen Years as a Sacred Prostitute in the Children of God Cult*. New York: William Morrow.

Wright, S. 1998. 'Exploring Factors That Shape the Apostate Role.' In *The Politics of Apostasy: The Role of Apostates in the Transformation of Religious Movements*, edited by D.G. Bromley. Westport, Conn.: Praeger.

– 1987. *Leaving Cults: The Dynamics of Defection*. Washington, D.C.: Society for the Scientific Study of Religion.

Zablocki, B.D. 1971. *The Joyful Community*. Chicago: University of Chicago Press.

– 1980. *Alienation and Charisma: A Study of Contemporary American Communes*. New York: Free Press.

– 1980. *The Joyful Community*. Chicago: University of Chicago Press.

– 1996. *Reliability and Validity of Apostate Accounts in the Study of Religious Communities*. New York: Association for the Sociology of Religion.

– 1997. 'The Blacklisting of a Concept: The Strange History of the Brainwashing Conjecture in the Sociology of Religion.' *Nova Religio* 1: 96–121.

– 1998. 'Exit Cost Analysis: A New Approach to the Scientific Study of Brainwashing.' *Nova Religio* 1: 216–49.

– 1998. 'Reply to Bromley.' *Nova Religio* 1: 267–71.

– 1999. 'Hyper Compliance in Charismatic Groups.' In *Mind, Brain, and Society: Toward a Neurosociology of Emotion*, edited by D. Franks and T. Smith. Stamford, Conn.: JAI.

Zablocki, B.D., A. Aidala, et al. 1991. 'Marijuana Use, Introspectiveness, and Mental Health.' *Journal of Health and Social Behavior* 32: 65–89.

Zablocki, B.D., J. Hostetler, et al. In press. *Religious Totalism*. Syracuse: Syracuse University Press.

Zimbardo, P. 1973. 'On the Ethics of Investigation in Human Psychological Research: With Special Reference to the Stanford Prison Experiment.' *Cognition* 2: 243–56.

Zimbardo, P., and S. Anderson. 1993. 'Understanding Mind Control: Exotic and Mundane Mental Manipulations.' In *Recovery From Cults: Help for Victims of Psychological and Spiritual Abuse*, edited by M.D. Langone. New York: Norton.

6. Tactical Ambiguity and Brainwashing Formulations: Science or Pseudo-Science?[1]

Dick Anthony

Introduction

Zablocki's Brainwashing Formulation

This chapter will evaluate the scientific status of cultic brainwashing formulations, with special focus upon the recent formulations of Benjamin Zablocki (1993, 1997, 1998, 1998b; 1999).[2] Zablocki's recent articles concerning brainwashing do not report concrete research, but rather attempt to clarify the conceptual outline of the brainwashing idea and to defend its authentically scientific character.[3] Therefore the scientific status of his attempted clarification and defense of the brainwashing idea crucially depends upon the accuracy of his characterization of the previous empirical research upon which he claims that it is based. Consequently, I will also focus upon older publications by Zablocki (1971, 1980), as well as publications by Margaret Singer and Richard Ofshe (Mitchell, Mitchell, and Ofshe 1980; Ofshe 1992; Ofshe and Singer 1986; Singer with Lalich 1995) and by Steven Kent (1997), all of which Zablocki claims are reports of the cultic brainwashing research which provides the empirical foundation for his more recent articles.

In addition, Zablocki claims that his recent brainwashing articles are based upon the empirical foundation provided by research on Communist thought reform published in books by Edgar Schein (1961) and Robert Lifton (1961). I will also evaluate the relationship of his recent cultic brainwashing articles to the data reported in these books.

In his recent articles, Zablocki claims that brainwashing is a valid scientific concept that has been supported by considerable research both upon Communist coercive persuasion and upon coercive influence tactics in new religions or cults (1997: 104–7). He acknowledges, however, that brainwashing is a concept that is widely regarded in sociology and psychology as being without scientific foundation (Zablocki 1997: 96–7, 1998a: 217), and says that many scholars in those disciplines regard it as being an evaluative rather than a scientific concept which is empirically untestable because of its definitional imprecision and other epistemological flaws.[4]

He contends that such a pejorative view of the brainwashing concept is based upon a misunderstanding of its true nature and of the validly scientific research supporting it (1997: 100). According to Zablocki, such misunderstanding of the concept was brought about by the use of a distorted caricature of the concept the development of which was motivated by legal and pecuniary goals rather than by an honest concern with the scientific understanding of the phenomenon (100–1).[5] He claims that his recent articles straighten out this misperception of the nature of the brainwashing concept and that they restore it to its proper scientific status (102, 106).

According to Zablocki the primary ideologically motivated misinterpretation of the scientific brainwashing concept is that it has to do with illicit recruitment mechanisms when it is really a concept concerning influence processes which bring about addictive commitments to worldviews to which the targets of brainwashing have already been converted prior to their being brainwashed. He states: 'Popular usage has come to imply that brainwashing has something to do with recruitment mechanisms when, on the contrary, it has mostly to do with socio-emotional exit costs. An examination of any of the foundational literature makes it very clear that what these researchers were attempting to explain was the persistence of ideological conversion after the stimulus was removed, not how subjects were initially hooked into the ideology' (1997: 100).

In his recent brainwashing articles, Zablocki refers to his approach to interpreting such 'foundational literature' as 'exit cost analysis,' and in the subtitle to his 1998 article he refers to such exit cost analysis as a 'new approach to the scientific study of brainwashing.' (His claim that his approach is new is somewhat confusing since he also claims that it is well known that such exit cost analysis has always been the primary theme of validly scientific brainwashing theory and research.) Zablocki claims that his formulation has identified the moderate and scientifically testable essence of the brainwashing paradigm (1997: 106), as opposed to the caricature of the brainwashing model which has been misused for ideological and legal purposes.

Zablocki (1997: n.8) identifies the foundational literature of the brainwashing concept as the books by Robert Lifton (1961) and Edgar Schein (1961), in which they reported their research upon Communist thought reform in China around the time of the Korean War. These are also the books that are normally claimed as the primary theoretical foundation for anticult brainwashing testimony in legal trials. Thus a primary burden of Zablocki's approach would seem to be that he make good on his claim that his interpretation of this foundational literature is different in kind from the epistemologically spurious version used in legal trials.

As we will see, I do not believe that he has met this burden. In my view, from an epistemological or scientific perspective his brainwashing formulation is not significantly different from that of the ideologically based anticult brainwashing theory that he claims to reject. His approach is merely one of a number of recent attempts to cosmetically alter the brainwashing concept so as to evade the force of (1) legitimate research which has, insofar as the brainwashing concept is scientifically testable at all, disconfirmed it; and (2) valid epistemological analysis, which has come to the conclusion that the brainwashing concept is pseudo-scientific.

Evaluation of Zablocki's Formulation

In the course of this chapter I will describe the grounds for my conclusion that the scientific disconfirmation and epistemological critiques of other brainwashing formulations also apply to Zablocki's approach. In evaluating Zablocki's brainwashing formulation I will apply a 'totalitarian influence' interpretation of the theoretical and empirical foundation which Zablocki claims as the basis for his point of view (Anthony 1996; Anthony and Robbins 1994; Richardson and Kilbourne 1983).

I have previously used this approach in evaluating other brainwashing formulations, and it has become the primary basis for my consultation and testimony in anticult brainwashing legal cases in which I have criticized the scientific standing of anticult brainwashing perspectives such as Zablocki's. In addition, this approach has served as the primary basis for legal briefs (motions to exclude testimony, summary judgment motions, appeal briefs) designed to convince judges to exclude cultic brainwashing testimony because of the unscientific character of the brainwashing formulations upon which it is based.

See Anthony (1990) for the original statement of the argument which has become the primary basis for legal briefs and testimony arguing the unscientific character of cultic brainwashing testimony; see Anthony 1996 and 1999, and Anthony and Robbins 1992 and 1995a, for elaborations of this basic argument and descriptions of its effects upon cultic brainwashing legal cases.

As stated above, Zablocki has criticized such testimony and legal briefs as unscientific and motivated primarily by pecuniary rather than scientific motives. In that I have developed the primary argument of this type, and in that as a forensic psychologist I have served most often as the expert witness and consultant critiquing cultic brainwashing formulations such as his as unscientific,[6] our dialogue, described in note 2, has proved an interesting exploration of radically opposed viewpoints. This chapter, evaluating his brainwashing formulation, and his chapter in this volume evaluating my totalitarian influence perspective,[7] should give the reader fertile ground for evaluating each side in this debate; that is, for deciding which of our apparently contradictory perspectives has scientific merit, or whether either or both of them do.

All brainwashing formulations claim to provide criteria for identifying social influence that results in involuntary conduct from social influence that does not result in involuntary conduct.[8] In addition, as I stated above, authors of brainwashing formulations claim that research upon Chinese and North Korean Communist coercive indoctrination practices around the time of the Korean War provides the primary theoretical foundation for their theories of involuntary cultic commitment. Given these claims, the following are the primary questions to answer with respect to the scientific status of these formulations: (1) Do they provide testable or falsifiable criteria for distinguishing coer-cive influence from non-coercive influence? (2) Have such criteria been confirmed through methodologically valid scientific research?

The primary contexts in which brainwashing concepts have been scientifically evaluated have been (1) research funded and supervised by the American CIA, which attempted to develop procedures capable of transforming the worldviews of foreign nationals of enemy countries into ones sympathetic to the United States (thereby transforming them into 'deployable agents' of the United States); (2) research which evaluated Chinese and Korean Communist attempts to transform the worldviews of American prisoners to Communist worldviews, thereby transforming them into Communist agents; and (3) research upon new religious movements. This article will evaluate the issue of testability/

falsifiability, and the issue of confirmation/disconfirmation of brainwashing formulations, in each of these three contexts.

Moreover, it is conceivable that even if falsifiable brainwashing formulations capable of differentiating voluntary from involuntary worldview transformations have not yet been evaluated and confirmed in any of these contexts, Benjamin Zablocki and/or other theorists may have formulated a falsifiable cultic brainwashing theory that might be confirmed through future research. I will also evaluate that possibility below.

CIA Research on Brainwashing

In earlier publications (Anthony and Robbins 1994; Anthony 1996: chap. 2) I reviewed research on the relationship between cultic brainwashing formulations and the original development and testing of brainwashing theory by the American CIA. As I demonstrate therein, the core idea of brainwashing formulations is that worldviews can be transformed to their polar opposites through techniques that create disorientation and hypersuggestibility followed by intensive indoctrination. The key idea for brainwashing theory – that is, the use of specialized procedures to induce an altered, hypersuggestible, state of consciousness combined with intensive indoctrination – was developed originally by the German Nazi intelligence services, the Gestapo and the SS, during the Second World War.[9] Psychedelic drugs, such as mescaline, and sedatives, such as barbiturates, were combined with hypnosis and forceful interrogation and indoctrination procedures in the Nazi research.

Following the Second World War, the American OSS (the predecessor of the CIA) recovered records of Nazi research on innovative coercive persuasion methods. With the development of the Cold War between the United States and its allies on the one hand and the Communist states on the other, the American CIA began to fund and supervise ambitious research programs designed to build upon and extend the Nazi research. The CIA brainwashing research program lasted from the 1940s until the early 1970s (Scheflin and Opton 1978: 103; Marks 1980: 11). The primary intent of such research was to develop methods capable of transforming foreign nationals of Communist countries hostile to the United States into reliable American 'deployable agents' who could then be used to spy upon or otherwise undermine the Communist regimes.

The covert CIA brainwashing research was conducted both by its own employees and also by prominent American social and behavioral scientists in university settings. The basic model that was being explored consisted of two stages: (1) a 'deconditioning stage' intended to wipe out previous ideological loyalties through the imposition of a disoriented, hyper-suggestible state of consciousness; (2) a 'conditioning stage' intended to implant new loyalties and a new self through specialized conditioning procedures based upon behaviourist psychology (Scheflin and Opton 1978: 13, 86, 293, 451–5; Marks 1980: 136–7, 140).

The CIA attempted many different experimental techniques in addition to hypnosis in attempting to operationalize this vision of involuntary conversion by means of a hyper-suggestible, disoriented state of consciousness. These included drugs,[10] sensory deprivation and isolation,[11] electroshock,[12] narcotherapy (Marks 1980: 23, 26, 40, 134), lobotomy, and other forms of psychosurgery (Lee and Schlain 1985: 38; Scheflin and Opton 1978: 243–324, esp. 274 and 285; Marks 1980: 26, 212), and so on. None of these attempts to produce a primitive, suggestible consciousness enabled the CIA to develop a workable brainwashing technique.

The second stage of brainwashing explored by the CIA research involved post-hypnotic suggestions as well as specialized conditioning procedures, such as playing recorded indoctrination tapes in continuous loops for twenty-four hours a day, for many days in a row, to subjects who were continuously kept in a deeply disoriented state through the administration of a combination of drugs and also a series of intensive electroshock treatments (Marks 1980: 131–41; Anthony 1996: 76–80).

In spite of the scope and ambitiousness of these German and American mind-control research programs (the American research program went on for over twenty-five years [Scheflin and Opton 1978: 103; Marks 1980: 11]), in terms of their original goals of improving interrogation and coercive indoctrination tactics beyond that obtainable with physical coercion or other traditional methods, they were complete failures. Neither the German nor the American programs ever learned how to change people's minds about their political orientations, much less turn them into so-called deployable agents. Like the German program before it, the American program never developed reliable alternatives to extreme physical coercion in interrogation and indoctrination procedures (Lee and Schlain 1985: 23; Marks 1980: 5, 12, 28–9, 144–6).

Cultic Brainwashing Formulations

History

As we saw in the previous section, the CIA's own research indicated that brainwashing is not effective in accomplishing involuntary world-view transformations. In spite of its disconfirmation in its own research program, the two-stage brainwashing model was disseminated by the CIA as an explanation of the Communist bloc's influence upon its own citizens as well as upon Western soldiers and civilians imprisoned by Chinese and Korean Communists during the Korean War. The CIA perspective was offered as an explanation of alleged conversions to Communist worldviews in articles and books ostensibly written by Edward Hunter, a covert propaganda specialist of the CIA with a cover identity as a journalist. (Anthony 1996: n. 37; Hunter 1951; Scheflin and Opton 1978: 226–8). His publications on brainwashing probably should be viewed more as an aspect of an anti-Communist misinformation campaign by the CIA than as a serious attempt to account for Communist influence from a scientific perspective.

Moreover, the brainwashing model was disconfirmed in generally accepted research on Communist forceful indoctrination of Western civilians and POWs conducted by, among others, Robert Lifton (1954,1961), Edgar Schein (1956, 1957a, 1957b, 1959, 1961, 1973), Albert Biderman (1962, 1963), and Hinkle and Wolff (1956). (In their 1961 books, both Schein and Lifton proposed their own theories of Communist influence referred to, respectively, as *coercive persuasion* and *totalism*.)

To return to the issue at the beginning of this chapter, the results of the CIA's own research program, as well as the results of the research disconfirming the brainwashing model with respect to Korean War–era Communist forceful indoctrination by Lifton and others, indicated that brainwashing is not a viable method of producing involuntary commitments to new worldviews. The primary scientific problem with cultic brainwashing formulations is that they are actually based upon the discredited CIA brainwashing model while they claim to be based upon generally accepted research upon Korean War–era Communist indoctrination practices, especially the research of Schein, Lifton, and Hinkle and Wolff. (It is thus perhaps understandable that expressions of cultic brainwashing theory do not discuss the body of evidence disconfirming the brainwashing model produced by the CIA's own research program.)

In earlier publications (Anthony 1990, 1996, 1999; Anthony and Robbins 1992, 1994, 1995a, 1995b) I demonstrated that cultic brainwashing theory, particularly statements concerning it by Margaret Singer and Richard Ofshe, is actually based upon Hunter's CIA brainwashing theory rather than its claimed theoretical foundation of generally accepted research upon Communist forceful indoctrination practices. As with Hunter's theory, the core proposition of cultic brainwashing theory is that brainwashing consists of the use of techniques which place its victims into a disoriented state of consciousness in which their normal capacity to rationally evaluate social influence has been suspended, and in which they have become hyper-suggestible and therefore unable to resist propaganda advocating alternative totalitarian worldviews.

In addition, brainwashing formulations contend (1) that such influence occurs without pre-existing motives or character traits which predispose those who are influenced to respond positively to the new worldviews; (2) that once converted to the new worldview, a brainwashed convert has difficulty repudiating it, so that in effect the new worldview has become a sort of addiction; and (3) that such brainwashed conversion and commitment to new worldviews overwhelms the free will of its victims without the use of physical coercion. (As I have demonstrated elsewhere [Anthony 1990, 1996], and as we will see below, generally accepted research on Communist indoctrination practices disconfirmed each of these alleged characteristics of Communist thought reform.)

Since its publication, my 1990 article has become widely accepted as an accurate analysis of the conflict between cultic brainwashing formulations and the research on Communist thought reform. Generally, cultic brainwashing formulations have not been used as the basis for systematic research with respect to involuntary influence, in new religious movements. Publications and testimony utilizing cultic brainwashing theory have focused rather upon the speculative transfer of principles of involuntary influence allegedly discovered in research by many scholars upon Communist coercive persuasion. Consequently, the scientific claims of cultic brainwashing formulations have depended crucially upon their now discredited contention that they involve an accurate transfer of the principles of involuntary influence, discovered originally in such research on Communist influence.

In that cultic brainwashing theory has neither been used as the basis for systematic research nor is accurately based on research upon Communist thought reform, its primary purpose seems to have been ideological and practical rather than scientific. Ideological in that it has been used as the central ideology of a social movement that has been primarily concerned with protecting conservative forms of mainstream beliefs from being supplanted by novel worldviews.[13] Practical in that cultic brainwashing theory has been the primary basis for testimony in court trials and other appeals for governmental action, which have attempted to make belief in novel worldviews illegal. As a result of the research by many scholars disconfirming cultic brainwashing theory, and also as a result of my 1990 article, my later publications, and those co-authored with Tom Robbins' (Anthony 1996, 1999; Anthony and Robbins 1992, 1994, 1995a, 1995b), as a basis for legal motions and testimony asking for the exclusion of cultic brainwashing testimony as having no scientific basis, cultic brainwashing theory has decreased its viability as a social weapon.

Tactical Ambiguity
If the contradictions between cultic brainwashing formulations and their claimed theoretical/empirical foundation are as glaring as I claim, why do they continue to influence segments of the general public and even to be used in some instances as a basis for testimony in legal trials? The secret of their continuing influence is the ambiguity with which they are stated.

Cultic brainwashing formulations are stated in a fashion that is essentially ambiguous and which thus tends to render them immune to empirical evaluation. Such skilful ambiguity allows them to conceal the contradictions which I have described above, to evade the many disconfirmations of their predictions by valid research on NRMs, and to appear plausibly scientific to a non-specialist audience. As the philosopher of science, Karl Popper has argued, non-falsifiable theories are 'pseudo-scientific' ideologies rather than scientific theories. (Hacohen 2000; Magee 1985; O'hear 1980; Popper 1959, 1963). Among the forms such ambiguity takes in cultic brainwashing formulations are the following: (1) internal contradictions; (2) unfalsifiable identifying characteristics for key variables and predictions; and (3) connotative rather than denotative use of language; that is, the use of emotionally charged buzz words rather than precisely defined terminology which is capable of being operationalized.

I refer to the ambiguity of cultic brainwashing formulations as 'tactical' ambiguity because their creators tend to shift their statements of the formulation from context to context depending on the tactical requirements of the situation they are in at the time.[14] Their guiding principle is to render their formulation plausible given the particular hermeneutic characteristics of the situation in which they are restating them without maintaining the internal and external consistency from context to context, which is the hallmark of well-stated scientific theory. In this way these formulations tend to seem plausible even to some specialists, who evaluate them only in a particular context, and their artful ambiguity may tend to conceal their pseudo-scientific character even to non-specialists who review them in a variety of contexts.

The most glaring source of ambiguity in cultic brainwashing formulations develops from their attempt to simultaneously affirm the brainwashing argument and also to affirm the research on Communist coercive persuasion, which flatly contradicts it with respect to a number of core issues; for example, the presence or absence of predisposing motives, involuntary versus voluntary influence, defective cognition versus full cognitive capacity, and so on. As I have documented elsewhere (Anthony 1990, 1996; Anthony and Robbins 1995a), Margaret Singer and Richard Ofshe, who were until recently the most influential exponents of cultic brainwashing theory, switch back and forth between the two traditions as the tactical requirements of particular contexts demand. In their testimony they have tended to express the brainwashing side of these polarities more explicitly than in their publications; for instance, they say unequivocally that a particular convert was hypnotized or otherwise put in a disoriented state during conversion, and, as a result had no free will with respect to making decisions after conversion, particularly with respect to deciding whether to stay or leave the groups, and so on. In their publications, on the other hand, they have presented a more ambiguous argument, expressing some *totalitarian influence* (see below) principles mixed with brainwashing ideas, and expressing the brainwashing ideas more equivocally, often through innuendo rather than direct statement.

My deconstruction of the Singer-Ofshe version of cultic brainwashing theory appears to have effectively uncovered its underlying ambiguities and thus, for the most part, to have rendered it inoperative as an explicit basis for testimony in brainwashing cases. However, revisions of the Singer-Ofshe theory continue to appear and to be used as attempted foundations for testimony in brainwashing trials.

Third-stage Brainwashing Formulations
In a recent article Thomas Robbins and I (Anthony and Robbins 1995a) described three successive stages of the development of the brainwash-

ing paradigm. The first stage (1940s through early 1970s) was the CIA's creation of the two-part brainwashing model as a basis both for research on involuntary worldview transformation and also for anti-Communist propaganda as described above. The second stage was the transformation of the CIA brainwashing model into an ideology which rationalized coercive deprogrammings, cultic brainwashing lawsuits, and other practical aims of the anticult movement during the late 1970s and 1980s.

The third stage of the implementation of brainwashing theory, which is still going on, emerged as a result of practical and academic repudiations of the cultic brainwashing theory in the late 1980s and early 1990s. This stage involves attempts to refashion the cultic brainwashing theory into a form that transcends scholarly and legal criticisms. For instance, in most of the brainwashing legal cases in which I have served as an expert in the 1990s, brainwashing experts have attempted to base their proposed testimony upon one or the other of various revisions of the brainwashing model, which have attempted to transcend the argument I had originally presented in my 1990 article.

In the second stage, brainwashing testimony tended to assert straightforwardly that research on Communist coercive persuasion, discussed above provided a scientific basis for distinguishing between social influence that caused involuntary worldview transformation and social influence that did not. In the light of the argument expressed in my 1990 article, as well as other research evaluating the cultic brainwashing argument, such exclusive assertions no longer tend to be accepted by the courts. Third-phase arguments, therefore, tend to make such assertions in a more ambiguous fashion, and to supplement them with additional theoretical foundations upon which to ground claims of involuntary worldview transformation. Such supplementary scientific foundations for testimony of involuntary worldview transformation, in brainwashing trials in which I have served as an expert, include putative research on hypnosis, addiction, the psychoanalytic transference concept, charisma, the attitude-change literature, disorientation, male chauvinism/ gender bias, and so on. As the reader of Zablocki's articles may recognize, his approach includes several of such supplementary foundations for allegations of involuntary worldview transformation; that is, addiction, transference, hypnosis, and disorientation.

The discussion of the differential characteristics of second- and third-phase cultic brainwashing arguments in Thomas Robbins, and my 1995 article is based primarily upon an analysis of testimony in cultic brainwashing cases rather than upon the publications of cultic brainwashing formulations that have been used to give a putative academic foundation to such testimony. In this chapter I will extend the analysis of differences between second- and third-stage testimony in brainwashing suits to an analysis of publications of third-stage brainwashing formulations. Benjamin Zablocki's recent articles are an example of this trend. Others include Abgrall 1996 1999a, 1999b; Kent 1997; Martin et al. 1998; Ofshe 1992; Singer and Addis 1992; and Winell 1993.

Zablocki's Third-Stage Brainwashing Formulation

Disorientation, Defective Thought, Suggestibility, and the False Self

The following list represents the individual elements or hypotheses within Zablocki's definition of his supposedly 'new approach to the scientific study of brainwashing.' (In later sections I will evaluate the relationship of these individual elements/hypotheses to the theoretical foundation which Zablocki contends supports their role in brainwashing.)

1 *Absence of pre-motives:* People who join new religions cults are not seeking alternatives to mainstream worldviews prior to their membership in the new group.
2 *Disorientation:* New religions or cults induce irrational altered states of consciousness as the core technique in seducing people into giving up their existing worldview. (Zablocki and other brainwashing theorists have referred to it as hypnosis, dissociation, trance, and so on. However, there is no meaningful distinction between these various terms for primitive consciousness as they are used by brainwashing theorists; that is, they are functional synonyms within the brainwashing worldview.)
3 *Defective cognition:* In the disoriented state essential to brainwashing, the person has a significantly reduced cognitive capacity to evaluate the truth or falsity of worldviews with which he or she is confronted.
4 *Suggestibility:* As a result of externally induced disorientation and defective cognitive capacity, the victim of brainwashing is highly 'suggestible'; that is, prone to accept as her/his own, ideas and worldviews which are recommended by the person or organization that has induced the defective cognitive state.

5 *Coercive or involuntary imposition of a defective or false worldview.* The above sequence of criteria for brainwashing results in the involuntary imposition of a defective or false worldview, which anyone in a rational state of mind would have rejected.

6 *Coercive imposition of a false self.* As a result of the brainwashing process, the person manifests a pseudo-identity or shadow self which has been involuntarily imposed upon him/her by brainwashing.

7 *Deployable agency.* The involuntarily imposed false self and defective worldview persist after the brainwashing process has been completed and as a result the brainwashed person retains his commitment to the new self and worldview even when he or she is not in direct contact with the group doing the brainwashing.

8 *Exit costs:* It is extremely difficult for the person to later repudiate his new worldview and false self-conception because he or she no longer has the capacity to rationally evaluate these choices.

All of these hypotheses were aspects of the original, generally discredited CIA brainwashing model which Zablocki claims he is replacing with his 'new approach.' As we shall see, all of them were disconfirmed by generally accepted research on Communist thought reform, including the research which Zablocki claims supplies the primary theoretical foundation of his formulation.

Basically, Zablocki's statement concerning the CIA brainwashing theory conflicts with generally accepted research on Communist thought reform in the same ways as did second-stage perspectives, but he has added a new level of tactical ambiguity to his argument.

At its core, Zablocki's publications on brainwashing affirm the same characteristics of allegedly involuntary influence as did first- and second-stage brainwashing formulations, for example, those of Hunter, Singer, and Ofshe. For instance, he asserts that disorientation and a suspension of critical rationality are essential to the brainwashing process. He states:

> The core hypothesis is that, under certain circumstances, an individual can be subject to persuasive influences so overwhelming that they actually restructure one's core beliefs and worldview and profoundly modify one's self-conception. The sort of persuasion posited by the brainwashing conjecture is aimed at somewhat different goals than the sort of persuasion practiced by bullies or by salesman and teachers ... *The more radical sort of persuasion posited by the brainwashing conjecture utilizes extreme stress and disorientation along with*

ideological enticement to create a conversion experience that persists for some time after the stress and pressure have been removed ... To be considered brainwashing this process must result in (a) effects that persist for a significant amount of time after the orchestrated manipulative stimuli are removed, and (b) an accompanying dread of disaffiliation which makes it extremely difficult for the subject to even contemplate life apart from the group. (Zablocki 1997: 104–5, emphasis mine)

Within this statement, in which Zablocki defines the core of his brainwashing formulation, the reader may recognize the very same altered states/suggestibility/overwhelmed-will concept that (1) constituted the essence of the CIA brainwashing theory described above; (2) is typically used as the primary basis for cultic brainwashing legal suits.

The 'profoundly modified self' referred to by Zablocki in the above statement as characteristic of brainwashing is essentially the same as the false self or 'pseudo-identity' which Singer with Lalick (1995: 60, 61, 77–9), West and Martin (1994), and other brainwashing theorists regard as an essential aspect of brainwashing. The new identity is viewed as false because it is allegedly imposed wholly by extrinsic influence, and thus is seen as discontinuous with the pre-existing values and self-conception of the person, that is, as being 'ego-dystonic' to use Zablocki's appropriation of psychoanalytic terminology. (Within psychoanalysis the term *ego-dystonic* refers to distortions of rational thought processes, such as delusions, hallucinations, obsessive thoughts, or compulsive behaviours, produced by eruptions of primitive unconscious materials into consciousness.)

Zablocki discusses the false self imposed by brainwashing, which he refers to as a 'shadow self,' in his 1998a article (223, 226, 244). He states:

The result of this [brainwashing] process, when successful, is to make the individual a deployable agent of the charismatic authority. This is not merely commitment but a form of commitment that does not depend on continuous surveillance by the group. A rational choice perspective on the brainwashing model conceives of this process as a fundamental restructuring of the self through a reorganization of preferences. We are talking about change on a deep although not necessarily permanent level ... This 'doubling' or creation of a shadow self is something that I have often observed but cannot pretend to understand on more than a metaphoric level. (1998a: 223)[15]

At a later point, Zablocki states:

> In these terms, brainwashing can be operationalized as an influence process orchestrated towards the goal of charismatic addiction ... The identification stage creates the biochemical alignment and the rebirth stage creates the fully addicted shadow self. (1998a: 244)

As Zablocki has said in his definition of brainwashing (previously quoted above, 1997: 104–5) in his view the cult is able to overwhelm – and replace with a shadow self – the pre-existing authentic self of the person only by inducing an altered, primitive state of consciousness in which the person is unable to resist indoctrination. He refers to this alleged state of primitive consciousness as 'disorientation,' one of several terms used by brainwashing theorists to refer to the allegedly primitive state of consciousness induced by brainwashing techniques, the other most common ones being hypnosis and dissociation.

It is important to realize that neither disorientation, as Zablocki uses the term, nor any of the other terms that brainwashing theorists commonly use to describe the primitive state of consciousness that they allege is essential to brainwashing – trance, hypnosis, loose cognition – are defined specifically enough to differentiate them from each other or from normal consciousness. (For instance, Zablocki doesn't provide a definition for his use of the disorientation term, nor does he supply any citation to scientific research or other literature which could explain to his readers what scientific meaning he intends by the term.)[16] These terms thus are functionally equivalent as used by brainwashing theorists, and are in effect synonyms.[17]

Elsewhere, Zablocki elaborates upon the disoriented state which he considers to be the core of the brainwashing process. He states that those in the throes of the brainwashing process

> are, at times, so disoriented that they do appear to resemble zombies or robots: glassy eyes, inability to complete sentences, and fixed eerie smiles are characteristics of disoriented people under randomly varying levels of psychological stress ...
>
> I, myself, happened to witness an entire building full of several hundred highly disoriented Moonies, and it is not an experience that I will ever be able to forget. These people, though gentle and harmless, were frightening in their disjointed affect and loose cognition. (1998: 232)

In this passage, in addition to an extreme level of disorientation resembling that of 'zombies or robots,' Zablocki refers to the 'loose cognition' which he believes to be characteristic of those who are in the process of being brainwashed. He also elaborates in a later section of the same article upon the loose cognition and suspension of critical rationality referred to in this passage, which he regards as essential to the brainwashing process (1998a: 241–4). He states:

> My argument is that his transition to the biological [essential to brain-washing] involves both *a suspension of incredulity* and an addictive orientation to the alternation of arousal and comfort comparable to the mother-infant attachment ...
>
> At the cognitive level this relationship [between the charismatic cult and its brainwashed victim] involves the *suspension of left-brain criticism of right-brain beliefs such that the beliefs are uncritically and enthusiastically adopted ... By preventing even low-level testing of the consequences of our convictions, the [brainwashed] individual is able rapidly to be convinced of a changing flow of beliefs, accepted uncritically.* (1998: 241–2, emphasis mine)[18]

This passage defines the 'suggestibility' which Hunter and other brainwashing theorists contend results from the inducement of a primitive state of consciousness in brainwashing ('the suspension of left-brain criticism of right-brain beliefs such that the beliefs are uncritically and enthusiastically adopted'). As should be clear from my discussion above, the notion that brainwashing uses the induction of a primitive state of consciousness and a resulting inability to resist indoctrination – leading in turn to an addictive or compulsive attachment to a new worldview and a false self – is the heart of the CIA brainwashing paradigm. (In Zablocki's formulation, the conversion to the new worldview is regarded as involuntary and compulsive because it follows from the absence of even 'low-level testing of the consequences of our convictions,' and thus the new worldview is 'accepted uncritically.')

Disconfirmation of the Primitive Consciousness Hypothesis
As I discussed in the introduction to this chapter, Zablocki claims to base his brainwashing formulation upon research on Communist thought reform at the time of the Korean War, particularly the research of Schein and Lifton. Contrary to Zablocki's claims that such research supports his formulation, however, with its central proposition that

brainwashing results from the induction of a primitive state of defective cognition and resulting suggestibility, these and other researchers found that such Communist influence did not result from diminished cognitive competence. Schein states:

> There is always a certain amount of distortion, sharpening, leveling, and false logic in the beliefs and attitudes which other people acquire. Because people are ambivalent on many issues it is easy to play up some 'facts' and play down others when our value position or feeling changes. Coercive persuasion involves no more or less of such distortion than other kinds of influence, but our popular image of 'brainwashing' suggests that somehow the process consists of extensive self-delusion and excessive distortion. We feel that this image is a false one: it is based on our lack of familiarity with or knowledge about the process and the fact that so much publicity was given to the political influence which resulted in a few cases. (Schein 1961: 239)

In addition, Schein found in his research that Communist coercive persuasion did not result from the induction of hypnosis or other forms of dissociation. He states:

> Given these considerations, it is difficult to see how Meerloo and Huxley can be so sure of the effectiveness of brainwashing and of their interpretation of it as a process based on hypnosis and Pavlovian psychology. The chief problem with the hypnotic interpretation [of Communist coercive persuasion] is that the relationship between hypnotist and subject is to a large degree a voluntary one, whereas the coercive element in coercive persuasion is paramount (forcing the individual into a situation in which he must, in order to survive physically and psychologically, expose himself to persuasive attempts). A second problem is that as yet we do not have an adequate theoretical explanation for the effects seen under hypnosis, and hence there is little to be gained by using it as an explanatory concept. Third, and most important, all hypnotic situations that I know of involve the deliberate creation of a state resembling sleep or dissociation. *The essence of coercive persuasion, on the other hand, is to produce ideological and behavioral changes in a fully conscious, mentally intact individual.* (Schein 1959: 437, emphasis mine; see also Schein 1959: 437)

Such statements indicate that cultic brainwashing formulations such as Zablocki's which highly resemble the CIA mind-control theory on the issue of whether brainwashing is based upon the induction of primitive states of consciousness, explicitly contradict their claimed theoretical/empirical foundation of generally accepted research on Communist thought reform. The central scientific question that remains with respect to the primitive states of consciousness hypothesis, then, is whether falsifiable, primitive states of consciousness are instrumental in producing involuntary conversion and commitment to new religions, even though they were not involved in Communist thought reform.

Third-generation cultic brainwashing formulations claim that they are. See for instance Ofshe and Singer (1986), where *they claim that cults use brainwashing techniques that are different from and more effective than techniques used in Communist thought reform.* (Zablocki 1998: 222n21 specifically claims that Ofshe and Singer's article is part of the empirical basis of his own brainwashing formulation.) According to Ofshe and Singer (1986: 15–17), such new and more effective techniques in so-called second-generation brainwashing include various techniques such as hypnosis for inducing primitive states of consciousness. Such claims focused specifically on 'hypnosis' have become central to other third-generation brainwashing formulations (e.g., those of Abgrall 1996: 179–90; West and Martin 1994: 273; and, most relevantly with respect to this article, Zablocki 1998a: 237).

Claims that brainwashing is based upon hypnosis and/or dissociation are also central to almost all testimony in brainwashing legal trials (see, for example, Abgrall 1990: 42–59; Ofshe 1989: 3–8; Singer 1983: 5, 325). There are many other examples (see discussions in Anthony 1990: 313–16, 1996: 228–30, Anthony and Robbins 1995a: 528–9).

Surprisingly, on this issue contemporary cultic brainwashing formulations are very similar to earlier mind-control formulations that were used as a basis for attacks on American religious movements in the nineteenth and earlier twentieth centuries (Taves 1999; Jenkins 2000). As with contemporary cultic mind-control formulations, such formulations were based primarily on the contention that alternative movements induced primitive stages of consciousness, variously referred to as 'hypnosis', 'dissociation', 'trance', and so on. Also, as with Zablocki's and other contemporary formulations, nineteenth-century dissociative formulations were primarily speculative, and they provided no empirical criteria by which religious experience and conversions could be distinguished from each other with respect to whether they were voluntary or involuntary.[19]

Many theories of the distinctive character of religious meaning, as opposed to other realms of cultural knowledge and understanding such as science, emphasize that religious knowledge and faith distinctively depend upon altered states of consciousness which cannot be meaningfully evaluated by epistemological criteria relevant to other realms of meaning. (See Hood 1995, for a collection of articles on the experiential dimension of a variety of religious traditions.) From this point of view, attacks upon religious conversion as being involuntary because they involve 'irrational' states of mind are evaluative rather than scientific because they are tautological; that is, they simply define all non-rational states of consciousness involved in religious conversions as undesirable without providing falsifiable empirical criteria for evaluating this assumption.

Contemporary cultic brainwashing theorists attempt to provide falsifiable empirical support for their claim that brainwashing induces primitive states of consciousness in order to produce involuntary commitment to religious movements by citing research on 'hypnosis' that supposedly demonstrates that hypnosis can force people to engage in unethical or illegal behavior that they would not do of their own free will. Abgrall, for instance, adopts this strategy when he claims that the work of T.X. Barber (1969), a leading researcher on hypnosis, is the scientific basis for his claim that alleged mental manipulation by new religions is based upon hypnosis (Abgrall 1996 chap. 8, n. 15). Similarly, West and Martin (1994: 273) and Miller (1986) claim that the hypnotic research of Milton Erikson (1939, 1980) demonstrates that hypnosis can force individuals to engage in unacceptable behavior against their will.

Finally, Zablocki (1998a: 227) claims that the research of Orne (1972) as reported in his article, 'Can a Hypnotized Subject Be Compelled to Carry Out Otherwise Unacceptable Behavior?' provides scientific support for the idea that hypnosis can be used to compel involuntary behavior. In the section of his article on mental or physical impairment as an explanation for cult membership Zablocki states: 'Orne has done some interesting experimental work on the extent to which subjects can be hypnotized to do things against their will.' In the same paragraph he also cites Katchen's article entitled 'Brainwashing, Hypnosis and the Cults' for the idea that hypnosis can be used to force individuals susceptible to it to submit to cultic membership.

However, contrary to the contentions of Zablocki, Abgrall, and the other anticult brainwashing authors, it is well established in the relevant scientific communities – i.e., psychology and psychiatry – that hypnosis is not an effective technique for causing people to engage involuntarily in conduct that is immoral, illegal, or against their own self-interest. (See Conn 1982; Orne 1961, 1962, 1972; Orne and Evans 1965; M. Erikson 1939, 1980, vol. 1, 46; Moss 1965: 32–6; Barber 1961; Fromm and Shor 1979: 6, 12; and Spanos 1996: 52. Several of these authors, such as T.X. Barber, Martin Orne, Milton Erikson, and Nicholas Spanos, are among the foremost scientists who have studied the hypnotic phenomenon.)

The hypothesis that hypnosis can be used to overwhelm free will is one of the most well-researched questions in the history of hypnosis research, and because of this it is the consensus of informed scientific opinion that hypnosis cannot be used effectively for the purpose of overwhelming free will or for substituting the will of the hypnotist for the will of the hypnotized. The myth of overwhelmed will by means of hypnosis is a staple of stage hypnotism that has long been repudiated by scientific research. Moreover, the idea that hypnosis could be used to impose a false personality on another and to establish long-lasting control over their whole lifestyle is so far-fetched that it is found only in popular science fiction, such as the book, and subsequent film, *The Manchurian Candidate*.

Strangely, several of the prominent scientists who did the most highly regarded research on the issue of whether hypnosis can be used to overwhelm free will and compel otherwise unacceptable behavior are the same authors whom cultic brainwashing authors cite in favour of this long-discredited myth. For instance, Abgrall (1990) cites Barber (1969) in support of the idea that hypnosis can overwhelm free will, even though Barber's research on this topic (1961) has been among the most influential in disconfirming the hypnosis/overwhelmed-will myth. Similarly, West and Martin (1994: 273) and Miller (1986) both cite the work of Milton Erikson in support of this myth, even though Erikson also did some of the most highly regarded research repudiating this notion (M. Erikson 1939; 1980, 1: 46).

Zablocki makes this same fundamental error in support of the notion that hypnosis and other primitive states of concsciouness form the basis for brainwashed involuntary commitment to religious groups; that is, *Orne's research, which Zablocki cites in support of his hypnosis/ overwhelmed-will hypothesis, actually flatly contradicts it.* For instance, in the abstract to the article that Zablocki cites in support of his hypothesis, Orne states: 'Further, no evidence is available to indicate that hypnosis increases the behavioral control of the hypnotist over that already present prior to its induction. Certainly, the popular view which holds that hypnosis is able to exert a unique form of control over the hypnotized individual, which can compel him to carry out otherwise repugnant actions, must be rejected' (1972: 101).

Significantly, Milton Orne's program of research on this topic, which he conducted over a long period (1961, 1962, 1972; Orne and Evans 1965), was originally undertaken in an attempt to evaluate the CIA theory that hypnosis is an effective tool for brainwashing (1961). Orne's research on this topic became among the most influential disconfirmations of the CIA brainwashing theory. *In this instance also, then, as with Zablocki's claim that the research of Schein (1961) and Lifton (1961) supports the brainwashing idea, the claimed empirical foundation for his brainwashing formulation actually disconfirms it rather than confirms it.*

In this connection, Nicholas Spanos, perhaps the most distinguished scientific researcher on hypnosis in the recent past, has evaluated the claimed role of hypnosis in causing involuntary influence, especially as it has been alleged to occur in the CIA brainwashing theory and in cultic brainwashing formulations such as Zablocki's. See Spanos (1996: 49–53) where he criticizes Hunter as the originator of the CIA brainwashing paradigm, and also the use of the CIA paradigm as a basis for allegations that cults brainwash converts by using hypnosis. He states (52):

> The idea that people can be transformed into robots in this manner [i.e., through brainwashing] is a cultural myth that grew out of the Korean conflict and subsequent cold war tensions. The myth was reinforced both by simplistic notions concerning Pavlovian conditioning and by even older cultural myths concerning the coercive 'power' of hypnosis. The robot mythology was maintained because it served a number of useful propaganda purposes, and it continues to serve such purposes today for those who use notions like 'brainwashing,' 'mind control,' 'spot hypnosis,' and 'cult programming' to explain why people sometimes join new religious movements such as the Unification Church (Moonies) and the Hare Krishna sect. (Anthony and Robbins 1992)

Note that in this passage Spanos cites in support of his viewpoint Anthony and Robbins (1992), one of Tom Robbins's and my articles critiquing the scientific standing of cultic brainwashing formulations.

Note also that Spanos's book was published by the American Psychological Association. These two facts should go far in demonstrating that the viewpoint expressed in this section – that is, that social influence in new religions is not based upon hypnosis and other alleged primitive states of consciousness such as *disorientation* – reflects a strong consensus among scientists who are qualified to speak on this topic.

Exit Costs, Pre-motives, and Totalitarian Influence

Brainwashing as Exit Costs and Absence of Pre-motives

The novel feature of Zablocki's version of the CIA model, when compared to previous versions of the cultic brainwashing model, is the surprising claim that research on thought reform did not demonstrate involuntary conversion of its victims to a new Communist worldview but rather *the coercive intensification of commitment to a Communist worldview to which the victims of thought reform were already committed.* Zablocki states: 'An examination of any of the *foundational literature* makes it very clear that what these researchers were attempting to explain was *the persistence of ideological conversion after the stimulus was removed, not how subjects were initially hooked into the ideology*'[8] (1997: 100).

In endnote 8, Zablocki also cites both Lifton's and Schein's 1961 books on Communist thought reform. But none of Schein's or Lifton's subjects were Communists before they were subjected to thought reform in the sense of having adopted, provisionally or otherwise, the Communist worldview. What could Zablocki possibly mean when he makes it so central to his formulation of a brainwashing argument?

Could he be implying that because their Western subjects were imprisoned in Communist thought reform prisons, and Lifton's Chinese subjects were living within a Communist society, that these conditions were somehow equivalent to their having provisionally adopted a Communist worldview, and thus that they had already been 'hooked into the ideology' before being subjected to thought reform. But how does that follow? In my reading, none of their subjects had adopted a Communist worldview before they were subjected to thought reform. (This is particularly obvious with their Western subjects, who were imprisoned during the thought reform process; if they were already seeing the world through the lens of Communist ideology, why would they have had to be imprisoned in order to undergo thought reform?)

Elsewhere Zablocki seems to be saying that Lifton's and Schein's subjects were already Communists prior to thought reform in the sense of already having joined a Communist organization. He states:

> Brainwashing may be defined as a set of transactions between a charismatically led collectivity and an isolated agent of the collectivity with the goal of transforming the agent into a deployable agent. In the terminology I am using here, there exist three levels of affiliation in such collectivities: recruits, agents, and deployable agents. A recruit is a person who is considering membership in the group and perhaps is also being courted by the group. An agent is a person who has already made the commitment to become a member of the group and accept its goals. A deployable agent is a person who has internalized the group's goals to such an extent that he or she can be counted on with high probability to act so as to implement those goals even when free of direct surveillance and even when those goals run counter to the individual's personal goals.
>
> The target of brainwashing is always an individual who has already joined the group. (1998: 221)

It seems clear that Zablocki is claiming here that brainwashing is only used with respect to people who have already adopted an alternative worldview; that is, 'agents' or 'ordinary members,' 'who have already joined the group' but who have not yet become so-called deployable agents. Thus, Zablocki seems to be contending that Schein's and Lifton's subjects had already joined Communist groups because they were existing within Communist prisons or living in a Communist society. But that doesn't follow either. None of their subjects ever joined Communist organizations, either before or after they were subjected to thought reform.

As we will see below, none of Schein's or Lifton's subjects ever became recruits, agents, or deployable agents of Communism by adopting Communist worldviews or joining Communist organizations, even *after* they had been subjected to thought reform much less before. And as we will see also, none of them ever had trouble repudiating any degree of interest they may have had in Communism after they left the thought reform environment; the only kind of exit costs they encountered were the difficulty of getting out of prison.

Thus, the assumptions that Zablocki adopts in defining a supposedly 'new' *exit costs* definition of brainwashing, in an attempt to differentiate his perspective from earlier cultic brainwashing arguments, does not hold up to any kind of informed scrutiny.

Pre-motives: It would seem that Zablocki's insistence that Lifton's and Schein's subjects were Communists (recruits or agents) before being brainwashed involves a strained analogy between Communist imprisonment and becoming a member of a new religion. This analogy doesn't hold up. Imprisonment does not indicate that a person has adopted a worldview or joined a group, whereas those who voluntarily become members of new religions have accepted, at least provisionally the worldview of the group they have joined.

Zablocki's insistence that brainwashing consists of coercive change in *level of commitment* to totalistic ideology, rather than coercive *conversion* to totalistic ideology in the first place, is all the more puzzling when other passages are taken into account, such as those in which he seems clearly to define brainwashing as coercive conversion to a new worldview. See for instance, Zablocki (1971: 239, 243–6, 251–2, 257, 282; 1980: 7–10, 357; 1997: 104–5, and throughout).

It seems likely to me that Zablocki's tactical ambiguity on this key aspect of his theory can be explained by his attempt to evade the implications of a body of research on both Communist indoctrination practices and new religious movements [NRMs], which disconfirmed the contention of both first- and second-stage brainwashing formulations that brainwashing produces, purely through extrinsic techniques of influence, involuntary conversion to a new worldview.

Research with respect to Communist indoctrination practices as well as a considerable body of research on NRMs (Wuthnow 1979, Richardson 1993, Zimbardo and Hartley 1985, Barker 1984, Anthony and Robbins 1974, and many others) seems to have rather conclusively established that the 'invasion of the body snatchers' view of conversion to NRMs as having resulted primarily from the efficacy of extrinsic techniques of proselytization is inaccurate. The research demonstrates that the overwhelming majority of converts to NRMs (including most plaintiffs in brainwashing trials) fit a profile of a 'seeker': a person who is disillusioned with mainstream worldviews and is searching actively for alternative worldviews prior to his or her conversion to NRMs.

Clearly, if brainwashing perspectives were to survive such voluminous disconfirmations, and the repeated findings by the courts that cultic brainwashing testimony could not be allowed because of its lack of scientific support, some revision of the involuntary conversion aspect of the CIA brainwashing model was necessary.

According to Zablocki and other brainwashing theorists, brainwashing consists of overwhelming or irresistible 'extrinsic' influence to which the inner qualities of the person are irrelevant, as opposed to normal 'intrinsic' influence, resulting from an interaction between the inner characteristics of the person and outside influence. (For a book-length discussion and analysis of the difference between extrinsic and intrinsic psychological paradigms of influence and motivation, see Pervin 1984. For a discussion of the application of this distinction to brainwashing versus totalitarian influence approaches to social influence see Anthony (1996: 221–5).

Zablocki (1998: 225) repeatedly claims that the brainwashing paradigm does not take into account individual differences between people who are being exposed to brainwashing, in accounting for how such influence occurs or which person will be successfully brainwashed. He states: 'it is situational and relational factors rather than predispositions that help us to predict this [successful brainwashing] phenomenon. (See also Zablocki 1998: 222, 235; 1993: 83–4; 1997: 101; Singer and Lalich 1995: 15–20.)

The extrinsic influence character of brainwashing formulations is essential to establish that such influence is 'involuntary.' Sociologists have demonstrated that contemporary 'postmodern' (pluralistic, multicultural) society is characterized by a focus upon individual autonomy as the prime determinant of authentic personhood. While unreflective conformity is the mark of the inauthentic or 'false' self (Winnicott 1960).

In order to be a genuine person in a contemporary, multicultural society, individuals are expected to independently reflect upon and consciously choose their own identities and worldviews from among the pluralistic mixture of alternatives with which they are presented. Consequently, if a person is viewed as having passively accepted an identity and worldview without having evaluated it in relation to their own distinctive inner characteristics and organic development of authentic personhood, he/she is viewed as not being a 'real' or authentic person. However, in practice all of us choose our identities, worldviews, and lifestyles as a result of an indeterminate mixture of outside influence and inner reflection and choice. Thus, most of us are unsure of the degree to which we are conformists or authentic 'self-actualizers.'

One function of the brainwashing myth may be that it provides its believers with a line at which social influence overwhelms inner authenticity. By doing so this myth creates for its believers a definition of false personhood, thus creating a stereotype which, by contrast, will reaffirm their own supposedly authentic personhood. Unfortunately for the scientific credibility of the brainwashing idea, this aspect of the paradigm has been disconfirmed by three important sources of data: research on conversion to Communist and other totalitarian political ideologies, research upon conversion to alternative religions, and statements by brainwashing theorists themselves upon intrinsic motivation for joining new religions.

The question of whether internal motivation for joining new religions is an important predictor of who responds favorably to attempts at proselytization, has been repeatedly answered in the affirmative by the very same anticult brainwashing authors who elsewhere (often in the same publications in which they also deny it) claim that conversion and commitment is solely determined by extrinsic influence. The types of pre-existing motivation for joining new religions affirmed by brainwashing theorists fall into two broad categories: (1) alienation or anomie relative to mainstream values and social institutions, resulting in a pattern of 'seeking' for non-traditional alternatives; and (2) family dysfunction combined with characterological predispositions to respond favourably to totalitarian ideologies.

Virtually all authors who have written about brainwashing describe widespread social change since the 1960s as resulting in widespread alienation or anomie, which in turn motivates young people to seek for and join non-traditional religions (see Zablocki, 1980). Such authors do not seem to realize that accounting for responsiveness to proselytization in this way essentially negates the claim that people involuntarily join new religions primarily for extrinsic reasons. Obviously, even in periods of social turmoil, not all members of society are equally alienated from traditional values and institutions. Alienation, therefore, differs in degree from person and person, and the more alienated are more apt to seek alternative worldviews and institutions.

Zablocki's recent brainwashing articles are theoretical and speculative rather than being accounts of actual research on new religions. He claims, however, to base his brainwashing theory upon research on minority religions and communes which he conducted and described in earlier books (1971, 1980). Both books adopt the *social change-producing individual differences in anomie/alienation* view of why particular people are more likely to join new religions (1971, 1980).

Indeed, in Zablock's book, *Alienation and Charisma* (1980), alienation is one of the two master concepts (the other being charisma) by which he organizes his data. In this book, alienation is clearly treated as a motive which predisposes individuals to being influenced by charismatic social movements, with higher levels of alienation predisposing individuals to choose more authoritarian movements, or, in Zablocki's current terminology, 'cults.' (In his basic thesis in this book, alienation is cured by involvement in a charismatic social movement, with more extreme degrees of alienation requiring more authoritarian and extreme forms of charismatic organization for its cure.)

Thus Zablocki himself is, in this former guise as the author of these earlier publications, a proponent of what he now labels the 'seekership conjecture' school of new religions scholarship (1998: 234–6), a theoretical orientation that he now sees as conflicting with his current brainwashing perspective. In one of the theoretically incoherent and self-contradictory twists characteristic of his brainwashing articles, he now claims that his earlier seekership tomes are actually the empirical basis for his new brainwashing formulation.

Interestingly, in note 43 in the seekership section of his 1998a article, which lists a number of publications he considers to be reputable scientific instances of the seekership conjecture, Zablocki includes Robert Lifton's 1968 article entitled 'Protean Man,' as one of the examples. Here, as Zablocki acknowledges in this note, Lifton views *proteanism* – that is, anomic, relativistic cultural tendencies and the confused and ambiguous self-concepts that result from them – as the source of motives for conversion to alternative religious movements. (In his later books on new religious movements [1993: 10–11, and throughout; 1999: 5, 236–8] Lifton uses the proteanism concept as a master concept, along with totalism, to explain pre-existing motives, i.e., 'seekership,' as an explanation for why people convert to join new religions and totalistic fundamentalistic Christian sects [1993: 177–87].) Thus, at that point in his brainwashing article, Zablocki appears to be acknowledging Lifton as a proponent of the seekership explanation of conversion to new religions, whereas elsewhere he views Lifton's work as the primary theoretical foundation for the brainwashing explanation which he regards as contradictory to the seekership explanation.

These various indications that Zablocki both repudiates and embraces what he refers to as the seekership explanation for conversion to new religions are further examples of the theoretical incoherence of his brainwashing formulation, a trait that I discussed above under the rubric of *tactical ambiguity.*

Totalitarian Influence Theories

Erikson's Totalism Theory

Research on Communist thought reform by Lifton and Schein affirmed totalitarian influence theories (Anthony 1996, 2000; Anthony and Robbins 1994, 1998). In positing totalism as an interaction of, as Lifton put it, an 'immoderate ideology and immoderate character traits' (1961: 419), the books by these authors reflected a school of thought which was concerned with describing and accounting for the development of individual motives for totalitarianism. This school had developed out of the broader concern with the nature of totalitarian societies. Interdisciplinary studies of totalitarianism (e.g., the work of Hannah Arendt 1951, and Friedrich and Brzezinski 1956) both led to and resulted from studies of the intra-psychic sources of support for the totalitarian 'escape from freedom,' and of the salient psychological dimensions of totalitarianism as epitomized in the work by Adorno et al. (1950), Bob Altemeyer (1981, 1988), Erik Erikson (1942, 1954), Eric Fromm (1941, 1984), Wilhelm Reich (1970, 1972), Milton Rokeach (1960, 1973), and many others.

The best-known example of such a theory was the concept of the authoritarian personality, described in the research of Adorno et al. (1950). Such theories describe a pattern of psychological characteristics, developing in childhood and adolescence, that predispose individuals to respond favourably to totalitarian ideologies, social movements, or governments. Erik Erikson's (1954) totalism concept was his version of the psychological predisposition to respond favourably to totalitarian ideologies, which was described by all the authors in this tradition of thought. In his 1961 book, Lifton applied Erikson's totalism concept in explaining why only a small percentage of his interview subjects were influenced by the thought reform indoctrination process that they had undergone. Authors in this tradition also describe totalitarian ideologies as all-encompassing ideologies which interpret the world in terms of a comprehensive set of polarized, black versus white categories, typically designed to legitimate a totalitarian state. (See Anthony 1996: 156–220, and Anthony and Robbins 1994 for general discussions of the class of totalitarian influence theories and of the relation of Erikson's and Lifton's totalism concept to this school of thought.)

According to authors in this tradition, people reared in certain types of circumstances tend to have a *polarized self-sense* in which a precariously maintained, unrealistically positive (*grandiose*) self-concept is always on the verge of being overthrown by a powerful but largely unconscious negative self-image. Such persons are 'extra-punitive,' that is, they are always on the lookout for someone to blame when things go wrong. Totalitarian ideologies appeal to such people because they rigidly divide the world into the saved and the damned, and thus support the maintenance of unrealistically positive self-concepts by encouraging the projection onto scapegoated contrast categories of the disowned negative self-concept.

Although Erikson's concept of totalism was influenced by this tradition, and shares its key assumptions, Erikson himself had earlier strongly influenced the theory of psychological *authoritarianism* described in the important study *The Authoritarian Personality* (Adorno et al. 1950). Early in the Second World War, Erikson published a now classic article on the development of Hitler's own authoritarianism and the general cultural and familial circumstances that created widespread authoritarianism in Germany (Erikson 1942). The conception of the relationship between child-rearing practices and the development of an authoritarian personality expressed in the book *The Authoritarian Personality* owes much to Erikson's earlier article.

Erikson's later concept of totalism broadens the concept of authoritarianism from Fascist to Communist types of totalitarianism, and to other types of totalitarian influence as well. Erikson's thoughts on the relationship between personality formation and attraction to totalitarianism both contributed to and drew from the larger psychoanalytic tradition concerned with these issues. Neither Lifton's nor Erikson's use of the totalism concept can be properly understood outside of its relationship to this larger tradition of thought and research.

As we suggested above, the totalitarian influence paradigm – for example, the Adorno et al. theory of the authoritarian personality or the Lifton/Erikson totalism concept, encompass theories of *intrinsic* influence. In this chapter I will focus primarily on the totalism concept, since Zablocki claims to base his neo-brainwashing theory primarily on the theoretical and empirical foundation of Robert Lifton's use of totalism to explain influence in Communist thought reform prisons.

In the article in which he originated the concept of totalism, Erikson maintained that persons with certain personality characteristics are particularly attracted to movements, governments, and ideologies which manifest a characteristically totalitarian ideological and persuasive style. According to Erikson, totalism is a feature of individual personality structure, whereby the person has a tendency to undergo 'all or nothing emotional reorganization' in which he or she assumes a new identity and a new totalitarian worldview. He further defined totalism as 'man's inclination, under certain conditions, to undergo ... that sudden total realignment and, as it were, co-alignment which accompanies conversion to the totalitarian conviction that the state may and must have absolute power over the minds as well as the lives and the fortunes of its citizens' (Erikson 1954: 159). Note that Erikson defines totalism as a *predisposition* to convert to totalitarian ideology; that is, as the 'inclination to undergo ... conversion to the totalitarian conviction.' Thus, in Erikson's usage, the totalism concept contradicts the extrinsic brainwashing model by defining totalism as a longing for totalitarianism that long predates contact with an actual totalitarian movement or ideology.

He further specifies: 'It is, then, the psychological need for a totality without further choice or alternation, even if it implies the abandonment of a much desired wholeness, which I would invite you to consider. To say it with one sentence: when the human being, because of accidental or developmental shifts, loses an essential wholeness, he restructures himself and the world by taking recourse to what we may call totalism' (162, emphasis his).[20]

Again, Erikson defines totalism as an inner predisposition that predates contact with totalitarian movements, in other words as an intrapsychic defence mechanism; that is, 'a psychological need for a totality without further choice or alternation.' He contends that as a transitory phenomenon in adults, totalistic reorganization of the personality actually belongs to normal psychology, that it becomes a psychiatric issue only when the totalistic state persists beyond its functional utility in helping the individual negotiate a psychological emergency.[21]

Erikson maintains that totalitarian movements appeal to such persons by providing support to the narcissistically grandiose definition of self, and by giving collective support to the projection of the polarized evil self-image onto a scapegoated contrast group. Moreover, the article on totalism (E. Erikson 1954) also goes beyond Erikson's earlier paper on Hitler (1950), and beyond the book *The Authoritarian Personality* (Adorno et al. 1950), which it had influenced, in describing predispositions towards totalitarianism as developing, not only at the Oedipal stage, but at other developmental stages as well.

As is generally well-known, one of Erikson's primary contributions to psychoanalytic ego-psychology was in broadening and extending the psychoanalytic scheme of psycho-sexual ['libidinal'] development. The orthodox psychoanalytic scheme had only three primary developmental stages: the oral, the anal, and the Oedipal, all of which occur in early childhood. Erikson extended this scheme into a description of eight developmental stages: the three classic Freudian ones plus five others that encompass the whole human life cycle. These eight stages are (1) Basic Trust vs. Basic Mistrust (the oral stage); (2) Autonomy vs. Shame and Doubt (the anal stage); (3) Initiative vs. Guilt (the Oedipal Stage); (4) Industry vs. Inferiority (the latency period); (5) Identity vs. Role Diffusion (the stage of the identity crisis); (6) Intimacy vs. Isolation (young adulthood); (7) Generativity vs. Stagnation (middle age); and (8) Ego Integrity vs. Despair (old age) (Erikson 1950, chap. 7, 247–74, 1954: 166).

According to Erikson, each of these eight stages involves a crisis in which one developmental polarity is resolved in more or less of one direction than of its opposite. In his paper on totalism, Erikson maintains that personality may be organized in either a totalistic pattern or a wholistic one, and unfavourable versus favourable resolutions of these basic dichotomies that comprise human development may contribute either to the totalistic or to the wholistic pattern.

As indicated above, in this article, unlike that of the authors of *The Authoritarian Personality*, Erikson does not give exclusive responsibility for the development of totalitarian tendencies to a poor resolution of the Oedipus complex.[22] Erikson discusses, in addition to the role of a poor resolution of the Oedipal complex in the development of totalism, the contributions of improper resolutions of the oral stage as well as the stage of the identity crisis.

Erikson explicitly indicates that the other childhood stages – Autonomy vs. Shame and Doubt (the anal stage) and Industry vs. Inferiority (the latency period) – can also play a role in the development of totalism (Erikson 1954: 166). However, in this article he chooses to discuss only the contributions of the stages of Basic Trust vs. Basic Mistrust (the oral stage), Initiative vs. Guilt (the Oedipal stage), and Identity vs. Role-Diffusion (the stage of the identity crisis).

Lifton's Application of the Totalism Theory
Lifton's 1961 book reported the results of an interview study of forty subjects (25 Western, 15 Chinese) who had undergone Communist thought reform in China, the process that Hunter and Zablocki con-

sider to be the most clear-cut example of brainwashing. Lifton explicitly attempted to evaluate the brainwashing concept in his study, and
finished by repudiating both the brainwashing term and the concept of
overwhelmed will which it signified (Lifton 1961: 4). Lifton replaced
the brainwashing concept with the concept of 'totalism' in describing
the thought reform process.

Erikson's totalism theory was applied by Lifton to explain why only
two of his forty subjects responded favorably to totalistic influence in
Chinese thought reform prisons (Lifton 1961: 117–32, 207–21, esp. 117–
19). (Even these subjects did not convert to Communism, but they did
become somewhat more sympathetic to Communist ideology.)

Erikson and Lifton had a long and intimate relationship, with Erikson playing the role of mentor and Lifton as apprentice. Their relationship began when Erikson helped Lifton extensively in writing his first
book; that is, the 1961 book in which Lifton used Erikson's totalism
concept to help him explain why so few people were responsive to
thought reform. The following passage from a new biography of Erikson describes the beginning of their relationship and the key role that
Erikson's concepts played in helping Lifton understand why only two
of his forty subjects were significantly influenced by their thought
reform experiences.

> [Lifton's and Erikson's] friendship can be traced back to 1956, when Lif-
> ton had completed a psychiatric residency in New York City and was
> researching his first book concerning Maoist 'brainwashing' in China. *He
> was not entirely clear why 'brainwashing' techniques affected some victims but
> not others.* After he read Erikson's article, 'The Problem of Ego Identity,' in
> the *Journal of the American Psychoanalytic Association*, he announced,
> 'That's my answer.' ... Hastily, Lifton wrote to Erikson explaining his
> project and requesting an appointment. (Friedman 1999: 356–7, emphasis
> mine)[23]

Erikson granted Lifton the appointment and became intimately
involved in helping him interpret his interviews and write his book.
After Erikson had explained to Lifton his theory that responsiveness to
totalitarian propaganda resulted from a pre-existing totalistic personality structure, Lifton came to see that his thirty-eight other subjects
didn't respond favorably to totalistic influence because, unlike the two
totalistic subjects, they did not have totalistic personalities which had
developed during their childhoods.[24]

In the article on the development of totalism discussed above (Erikson 1954), Erikson argues that child-rearing practices that foster a polarized, black or white, all or nothing emotional and cognitive style (i.e., 'intolerance of ambiguity') are the primary cause of the development of totalism. (The intolerance of ambiguity concept was developed originally by Else Frenkel-Brunswick 1949, 1951, 1954.) In Robert Lifton's extrapolation of Erik Erikson's totalism concept he also locates the essence of totalism in a polarized emotional and cognitive style (1961). For instance Lifton, following Erikson, defines individual totalism as a 'form of all or nothing emotional alignments' (419). For more on emotional and cognitive polarization as the essence of totalism, see Lifton 1961: 419–37, especially 420 and 436. (I discuss more fully Lifton's use of the intolerance of ambiguity concept in defining totalism in my 1996 dissertation [287–90], and in Zygmunt, 1999, and Anthony and Robbins, 1984.)[25]

Lifton referred to the predisposition of two of his thirty-eight thought reform subjects to respond favorably to totalitarian ideology during the thought reform process, as 'individual totalism.' (1961: 129–31, 150–1, 419, 436). Lifton states: 'In all cases of apparent conversion (the two I studied in detail, the two I met briefly, and two others I heard of), similar [pre-existing] emotional factors seemed to be at play: a strong and readily accessible negative identity fed by an unusually great susceptibility to guilt; a tendency toward identity confusion (especially that of the cultural outsider); a profound involvement in a situation productive of historical and racial guilt; and, finally, a sizeable element of [individual totalism]' (1961: 130).

At a later point, Lifton again summarizes the character traits that were common to two of his forty interview subjects whom he designated as 'apparent converts,' because they had expressed some sympathy for Communism upon their initial appearance in Hong Kong after their release from thought reform prisons. (Lifton designated these two subjects as only *apparent* converts rather than *actual* converts because neither of them actually converted to Communist worldviews, although after having been thought-reformed they did express more sympathy for Communist ideology than they had prior to their participation in thought reform.) Lifton states: 'This authoritarian priest shared with the liberal missionaries' daughter [pre-existing] psychological traits characteristic of the apparent convert: strong susceptibility to guilt, confusion of identity, and most important of all, a longstanding pattern of [individual] totalism' (1961: 219–19).[26]

Schein's and Hinkle and Wolff's Research
In his research on Communist thought reform of Western civilians, Schein also found that only those rare prisoners who were strongly predisposed to respond favourably to Communist ideology prior to the point that they were subjected to thought reform were influenced by the thought reform process (Schein 1961: 62–110, especially 104–10; 1973: 295). Only one or two of Schein's fifteen subjects showed any substantial influence as a result of thought reform (157–66). As with Lifton's subjects, none of Schein's subjects actually converted to the Communist worldview (164–6). Schein's results are all the more significant as a disconfirmation of Hunter's brainwashing theory, in that Schein chose as his subjects those ex-prisoners who had been the most responsive to the thought reform process (13). Schein states:

> *Successful brainwashing,* in the sense of the repatriate espousing Communist attitudes and reiterating his crimes following release from Communist China, *was a rare outcome. Genuine attitude change could only occur if there were already a predisposition in the prisoner* and if he encountered a highly effective prison regimen built around the use of the group cell. (1973: 295, emphasis mine)

Other researchers on Communist thought reform also found that only those few subjects who were strongly predisposed to respond favourably to totalitarian ideology prior to thought reform showed any degree of approval of Chinese Communism after their thought reform experiences. Prior to Schein's (1961) and Lifton's (1961) research projects upon the Communist thought reform of Western civilians, a CIA-sponsored research project upon Communist forceful indoctrination of western civilians, which included extensive interviews of those who apparently had been most influenced by thought reform in Chinese prisons, indicated that (1) brainwashing as defined by the CIA model was not used in the Communist forceful indoctrination process, (2) Communist forceful indoctrination practices (sometimes referred to as thought reform, or coercive persuasion) were not effective in establishing commitment to the Communist worldview in people who were not previously attracted to it, and (3) those few Westerners who emerged from this process affirming Communist ideas had already been strongly attracted to such ideas prior to their imprisonment and subjection to the thought reform program (Hinkle and Wolff 1956).

Hinkle and Wolff state:

The people who have been described in the public press as 'brainwashed' have been prisoners suddenly released after as long as four years in Chinese detention prisons. Such persons have appeared at the border at Hong Kong, looking calm, fit, and sane. They praise their captors, praise Communism, and damn 'American imperialism' ... A number of people called 'successfully brainwashed' have been studied intensively ... The study of these people reveals that they possessed certain characteristics in common before they were imprisoned ... They were people who, long before their imprisonment, were in rebellion against their parents and the way of life and segment of society to which their parents belonged, including many of its standards, beliefs, and practices ... Several of them had been members of Communist and fellow-traveller groups [before being thought reformed], and at least one of them is known to have been a Party member ... These people had been offered repatriation after the Communist Revolution, but they had elected to remain in China, most of them primarily because they were both sympathetic to the Chinese Communist Revolution and curious to see how it would work out. They were anxious to help develop the new China, if they were allowed to do so. For months prior to their imprisonment, several of them were engaged in studying Chinese Communist literature and translating it into other languages. (1956: 162–3)

The research of Schein and Lifton on Westerners in thought reform prisons, upon which Zablocki claims to base his brainwashing theory, confirmed and extended Hinkle's and Wolff's earlier findings.

The Erikson/Lifton Totalism Perspective as a Psychoanalytic Theory
It is important to recognize, in differentiating the totalism concept, from the brainwashing concept that according to both Erikson and Lifton such individual totalism is a personality characteristic that develops as a result of certain childhood influences and it is present long before a person encounters the totalitarian ideology to which he or she is predisposed to respond favourably. Lifton states:

'The degree of individual totalism involved [in a person ho is likely to convert to totalitarian ideology] depends greatly upon factors in one's personal history: early lack of trust, extreme environmental chaos, total domination by a parent or a parent representative, intolerable burdens of guilt, and severe crisis of identity. Thus an early sense of confusion and dislocation, or an early experience of unusually intense family milieu control, can produce later a complete intolerance for confusion and dislocation, and a longing for the reinstatement of milieu control.' (1961: 436)

From this point of view, Lifton's two moderately totalistic subjects may have been just as apt to respond favourably to Communist ideology if they had studied it in settings other than that of the thought reform process.

Thus, the theory of totalism is first of all a *psychoanalytic theory* which locates the causes of behaviour in the internal mental structures and the developmental history of the person who converts. (Both Erikson and Lifton are psychoanalitic theorists and the totalism theory draws substantially from the larger psychoanalytic tradition within which it was developed.)[27] Unlike the brainwashing paradigm, the totalism theory does not interpret the contemporary influence situation of the person as the primary cause of his religious or political choices.

This approach is clearly contradictory to Zablocki's attempt to explain involuntary religious conversions exclusively on the basis of social influence which is independent of the pre-existing character of the person who is being influenced. (For instance, Zablocki states: ... 'the brainwashing model does not focus primarily on characteristics of the subject. The assumption is that many different kinds of people can with enough effort, be brainwashed' [1998a: 222]). Thus, Zablocki's version of the CIA brainwashing idea, like all brainwashing formulations, is a theory of extrinsic social influence. Like other brainwashing formulations, Zablocki's perspective conflicts with totalitarian influence theories such as the Erikson/Lifton theory of totalism, which account for individual differences in responsiveness to totalitarian influence on the basis of individual personality characteristics which develop in childhood.

The Brainwashing Term
Another obvious indication that Zablocki's articles express the CIA brainwashing paradigm rather than the totalitarian influence paradigm is that he refers to the perspective he is advocating as a 'brainwashing' theory. Both Schein and Lifton repudiate the brainwashing term because it designates the CIA brainwashing theory which their research had disconfirmed. (Schein 1961: 18; Lifton 1961: 4; 1987: 211).

In his testimony in the Patty Hearst trial, Lifton several times repudiated the brainwashing term and distanced his own totalism theory from Hunter's brainwashing theory. For instance, Lifton stated: 'I wrote a book entitled *Thought Reform, A Psychology of Totalism*, whose subtitle is *A Study of "Brainwashing" in China*, brainwashing in quotes I hasten to add ... At the time I began [studying thought reform] there were a couple of very popular and somewhat inaccurate books, one of them by a journalist, Edward Hunter – a couple of them by Edward Hunter, who, as I think has been mentioned before, was the first to use the term (dubiously, I fear) 'brainwashing,' but there hadn't been any systematic psychiatric or medical knowledge about thought reform prior to my studies' (1976: 314).

As this passage indicates, when Lifton uses the term brainwashing, he puts it in quotes as he did in the title of his 1961 book, and by doing so he means to indicate that it stands for Hunter's inaccurate theory rather than his own account of thought reform, which he views as contradicting Hunter in important respects. (Lifton uses the term brainwashing a number of other times in his 1961 totalism book, in addition to the title, i.e., on pages 3, 4, 117, 420, and 435, and each time he places it in quotes.)

As my 1990 article demonstrates, research on totalitarian influence contradicted the brainwashing paradigm with respect to each dimension discussed briefly above. Consequently, Lifton and Schein objected to the brainwashing term because it inaccurately indicated that Communist thought reform accomplished involuntary worldview transformation. In addition, they objected to the term because it stood for a paradigm that was so ambiguously stated that it resisted scientific refutation and tended to be used for ideological rather than scientific purposes.

Zablocki, on the other hand, asserts that the brainwashing term accurately stands for the tradition represented by Lifton's and Schein's research. He invariably uses it to refer both to the original research on Communist thought reform and to the anticult brainwashing paradigm that claims to be based upon it.[28]

At one point Zablocki defends his preference for the brainwashing term (rather than terms such coercive persuasion or totalism which were preferred by researchers on totalitarian influence) thusly:

I have chosen to use the term *brainwashing* because it has the widest public recognition. It may also be the most misunderstood of all these [mind control] terms, but I see that as an advantage, since using the term impels us to face these misunderstandings head-on instead of avoiding them with linguistic sleight of hand. (1997, n.17)

In this passage Zablocki acknowledges that brainwashing is the most misunderstood, and presumably misleading, of the terms that are used to refer to Communist and cultic indoctrinational practices. However he believes that its use is justified because (1) the term has the widest public recognition, and (2) its use impels us to face these misunderstandings head-on.

If, as I believe, the brainwashing term refers to a pseudo-scientific paradigm that has been repudiated by legitimate researchers, why is widespread public recognition grounds for its use? Doesn't its use simply tend to perpetuate the false conception that the paradigm it refers to is a legitimately scientific explanation of social influence by Communists and new religions? Zablocki addresses this issue by contending that use of the brainwashing term forces us to repudiate the inaccurate paradigm it stands for.

Does this make sense? Doesn't it sound like *double-talk*: the simultaneous affirmation of contradictory assertions as if they mean the same thing? Have the critics of other pseudo-scientific concepts continued to employ the terms that refer to them as acceptable scientific designations for the superior theories that have replaced them? Following this principle, geographers would continue to refer to the *flat earth* because that would enable them to explain that the earth is really round, biologists would use the term *creationism* to refer to the theory of evolution because that would better enable them to explain why creationism is both a false and a pseudo-scientific theory, and so on.

It seems likely that Zablocki continues to use the brainwashing term in contradiction to its repudiation by Schein and Lifton for the same reason that they have rejected it: because the brainwashing term is actually defined in terms of the involuntary worldview transformation which the research of Schein and Lifton demonstrated did not occur as a result of Communist thought reform.

It is well-established in authoritative commentary on Lifton's and Schein's research that they both repudiated the brainwashing term, and that when they did use it they placed it in quotes as an indication that the term, with its meaning of involuntary worldview transformation, had been discredited by serious academic research upon Communist coercive persuasion. See, for instance, the commentary on this issue by Albert Biderman, who was himself one of the most respected researchers on Communist coercive persuasion. He says the following, in an ambitious review essay on Schein's and Lifton's 1961 books:

> While the social scientists pondered their case histories of released prisoners, *popular writings established an image of 'brainwashing' as, in the words of Lifton, 'an all-powerful, irresistible, unfathomable, and magical method of achieving total control over the human mind'* (1961: 4). As both Lifton and Schein concede, these almost ineradicable [involuntarist] connotations make 'brainwashing' a term that is far from precise and of questionable utility. Nonetheless, it has become so much a fixture of the vocabulary that *the authors of both books have used it in their titles, albeit only in the subtitles and with the note of disdain that is conveyed by the quotation marks with which these authors fence the word off.* (Biderman 1962: 549, emphasis mine)

There seems little doubt that Schein and Lifton were correct in viewing the brainwashing term as the name for the involuntarist paradigm which their research had disconfirmed. Hunter, who coined the brainwashing term, clearly intended it to indicate a form of involuntary worldview transformation that is qualitatively different from other forms of social influence with respect to the involuntarism issue (Hunter 1957: 26–7). Even Ofshe and Singer, whose testimony was repeatedly excluded from legal cases because of its unscientific involuntarist claims regarding cultic influence, acknowledge in one of their publications that the brainwashing term is scientifically inaccurate, and thus misleading, because of the extreme degree of involuntary influence that the term normally stands for. They comment: 'Brainwashing' is the least satisfactory of the common names for the [mind control] phenomenon. It conjures up, at least for the non-professional reader, ideas of mindless automatons deprived of their capacity for decision-making (Ofshe and Singer 1986: 20).

Moreover, psychological and psychiatric dictionaries consistently define brainwashing as a model of social influence that asserts significant reduction in the voluntary character of mental operations. See for instance *The Concise Dictionary of Psychology* (Statt 1990), which defines brainwashing as 'an attempt to *coerce* someone into radically changing his beliefs or behavior by using physical, psychological, or social pressures.' See also Chaplin's *Dictionary of Psychology* (1985) which defines brainwashing as the 'conversion of an individual from one established orientation (usually political) to another. The word is derived from two

Chinese words meaning "to wash the brain" and implies the use of physical or psychological *duress*.' (emphasis in these definitions is mine). The terms for involuntarily influencing someone used in these definitions of brainwashing; that is, *coerce* and *duress* (as indicated, in turn, by the definitions of those terms), denote influences or activities that produce a significant reduction of the voluntary character of decisions or actions.

In view of the unequivocal meaning of the brainwashing term as designating a form of social influence that produces an extreme reduction in the voluntary character of belief and action, and in view of the fact that generally accepted research on Communist thought reform did not demonstrate that the process produced such involuntary consequences, it seems to me that the strategy of Lifton, Schein, and other researchers in rejecting *both* the CIA brainwashing paradigm and the term that refers to it, and adopting other terms for their very different formulation are correct; that is, Scheim and Lifton's replacement of the brainwashing term with alternative terminology is more likely to eliminate the widespread misinformation about the nature of Communist and religious influence than is Zablocki's use of the brainwashing term to refer to their research. Zablocki's use of Hunter's brainwashing term (while simultaneously claiming to repudiate Hunter's brainwashing theory) is more likely to be an instance of *tactical ambiguity* in the service of surreptitiously *advocating* Hunter's theory than it is to be a valuable technique for *repudiating* Hunter's theory.

Equation of Brainwashing and Totalitarian Influence Perspectives

Against the explicit repudiation of the brainwashing term by Schein, Lifton, and virtually all of those who conducted generally accepted research on Communist coercive persuasion, Zablocki offers this additional rationale for his use of the term.

> Throughout this paper, I have used the term brainwashing to describe a process that has gone by many names in the scientific and popular literature. This process has been called *thought reform* (Lifton [1961], *Thought Reform and the Psychology of Totalism; menticide* (Joost Meerloo [1956], *The Rape of the Mind); coercive persuasion* (Edgar Schein [1961], *Coercive Persuasion); mind rape* (Meerloo [1956], *The Rape of the Mind); debility, dependency, and dread* (L.E. Farber, H.F. Harlow, and L.J. West [1957], 'Brainwashing, Conditioning, and DDD' [Debility, Dependency and Dread]. Singer has

preferred the longer phrase, *systematic manipulation of psychological and social influence* ('Group Psychodynamics' [1987]). *All of these terms are roughly synonymous.* (Zablocki 1997, n.17)

This passage nicely illustrates the essential disagreement between Zablocki's brainwashing approach and that of the totalitarian influence scholars whose research he claims to be summarizing.[29] It equates perspectives that are restatements of the CIA brainwashing model – that is, those of Farber et al., Meerloo, and Singer – with the totalitarian influence perspectives of Schein and Lifton.[30]

As we saw above, respected research on Communist indoctrination practices repudiated both the brainwashing model and the brainwashing term that referred to it. Those who conducted such research chose alternative terminology precisely because they had found that the brainwashing model was both inaccurate and too ambiguous to constitute a legitimate scientific theory. In their minds the brainwashing term and the terms they preferred were not at all 'roughly synonymous,' as Zablocki claims, but actually contradicted each other.

In affirming that such terms are roughly synonymous, Zablocki is informing us that in his mind the CIA brainwashing paradigm as expressed by Meerloo, Singer, Ofshe, and Farber et al. on the one hand, and the totalitarian influence perspectives of Schein, Lifton et al. on the other, are essentially the same. This disagreement of Zablocki with totalitarian influence authors on terminology, therefore, signals a crucial substantive disagreement as well: Zablocki believes that the CIA model and totalitarian influence perspectives are essentially in agreement about the nature of Communist thought reform, whereas those who conducted totalitarian influence research asserted that the two traditions are contradictory.

Voluntary vs. Involuntary Influence

One feature of third-stage brainwashing theory which was never present in second-stage publications is an acknowledgment of the existence of a pseudo-scientific brainwashing model which is inferior to generally accepted research on Communist indoctrination practices. Conforming to this third-stage characteristic, Zablocki states: 'The brainwashing conjecture has never been subjected to such (scientifically valid) refutation. Instead *a caricature of the brainwashing conjecture supplied by various anticult groups for litigational rather than scientific reasons* has been put on trial in its place' (1997: 106, emphasis mine).

In this statement, Zablocki acknowledges the existence of a pseudo-scientific brainwashing paradigm ('a caricature of the brainwashing conjecture'), and that it has typically been used as the basis for testimony in cultic brainwashing trials. (Elsewhere he states that this caricature of a scientifically valid brainwashing conjecture, presumably based on Hunter's CIA theory, 'totally distort[s] the foundational literature' (1997: 110).

Such acknowledgments of the existence of the pseudo-scientific brainwashing paradigm in third-stage brainwashing publications typically do not describe the paradigm in any detail, and thus are too ambiguous to enable the reader to determine whether the author's own perspective is actually a pseudo-scientific robot perspective itself. For instance, Zablocki's statement raises the question of what exactly the nature of the pseudo-scientific brainwashing perspectives are, such that they distort the foundational literature. Zablocki's mere acknowledgment of the existence of such an unscientific brainwashing paradigm, without further describing it, appears to conform to this tendency.

However, at another point, Zablocki states: 'Attempts were made to frighten the American public by claiming that the Communists had discovered in brainwashing a powerful and mysterious new weapon that could rob ordinary people of their free will. Although these claims totally distorted the foundational scholarship on brainwashing, they left a bad odor attached to the concept which lingered for a long time, particularly for intellectuals who opposed McCarthyism and anti-Communist hysteria' (1997: 110).[31]

In this passage, we get the impression that Zablocki feels that the characteristic that distinguishes the pseudo-scientific CIA brainwashing perspective from the valid brainwashing perspective, which he claims to advocate, is that the CIA perspective claims that brainwashing 'rob[s] ordinary people of their free will,' whereas his own perspective does not. Accordingly, he also states elsewhere:

One of the major arguments for the assertion that brainwashing is not intrinsically a scientific concept is the claim that the conjecture is based on questions of 'free will' which are not scientifically verifiable even in principle. But the brainwashing conjecture does not assert that subjects are robbed of their free will. Free will is a philosophic concept that has no place in scientific theory building. Neither the presence nor the absence of free will can ever be proved or disproved ...

The brainwashing conjecture does assert that resocialization remaps the values and preferences of the subject so that the subject voluntarily chooses to do what the group wants him to do. The goal of brainwashing is to create deployable agents. A deployable agent is one who evaluates his self-interest rationally as the group would wish. *It [the brainwashing conjecture] does not argue the elimination of choice but rather the modification of the preference structure on which choice is based.* The brainwashed individual remains capable of rational choice and action but over a transformed substrate of values and preferences remapped to conform to the collective ideology.[32] (1997: 102, emphasis mine)

I think that we have more double-talk here. On the one hand, Zablocki says that brainwashing does not claim that its victims are robbed of their free will. On the other, he says that the goal of brainwashing is the modification of the preference structure on which choice is based. The question then becomes whether a brainwashing account of how such a modification is accomplished indicates that the modification is voluntary or involuntary. The central theme of Zablocki's brainwashing articles is to show that the accomplishment of such a modification of preferences by brainwashing is involuntary, and that once the modified preference structure is accomplished, the person becomes stuck in it against their will. In other words, the central assertion of Zablocki's brainwashing model is that cult membership is a compulsive habit, a form of addiction.

In the latter part of his 1998 article (241–4), Zablocki develops quite explicitly his contention that brainwashing produces a compulsive attachment to a totalistic worldview, group, and false or shadow self. As we saw above, Zablocki contends that brainwashing involves 'an addictive orientation to the alternation of arousal and attachment comparable to the mother-infant attachment.' He continues: 'In these terms, brainwashing can be operationalized as an influence process orchestrated towards the goal of charismatic addiction. My hypothesis is that each of the three stages of brainwashing achieves a plateau in this addictive process. The stripping stage creates the vulnerability to this sort of transformations. The identification stage creates the biochemical alignment, and the rebirth stage creates the fully addicted shadow self' (1998a: 244).

Zablocki and I have had several discussions and e-mail interchanges on the question of whether his brainwashing argument is centrally organized around the theme of involuntary commitment to cults. His argument that the brainwashing perspective is not concerned with involuntarism boils down to two assertions. The first is that his articles are not concerned with the voluntarism/involuntarism dimension because he doesn't use the terms *voluntary* or *involuntary* in them. The second is that the distinction between voluntary or involuntary is a qualitative one (i.e., either/or), whereas the brainwashing perspective as he articulates it merely demonstrates a reduction in voluntary choice rather than its complete loss.

Actually in the penultimate draft of his 1998 article he did use the voluntarism term in defining an essential dimension of the brainwashing paradigm. He stated:

> In this paper, *I attempt to lay the foundation for brainwashing as a useful and well defined scientific concept.* An essential part of this effort is to cut away some of the more grandiose claims that have been made for this concept *and to locate it simply as one among many constraints on religious voluntarism.* (penultimate draft of Zablocki 1998: 2, emphasis mine)

As this statement illustrates, the voluntarism/involuntarism dimension is not necessarily an either/or or qualitative variable. Zablocki is clearly referring to it in this passage as a continuous variable. The more important question, however, is whether Zablocki's paradigm is concerned with the concept of voluntarism, not whether it is treated either as a qualitative or as a continuous variable.

In the final draft of his 1998a paper Zablocki eliminated these sentences, but there are many other passages in his works on brainwashing in which he contends, as in this passage, that the brainwashing paradigm is concerned with demonstrating that brainwashed conversion and commitment to social groups is (at least relatively) involuntary. See for instance this statement in the abstract to his 1998 article:

> In contrast to some of the more grandiose claims sometimes made for brainwashing as the sole explanation of cult movement behavior, I argue instead that brainwashing is only one of the factors that needs to be examined in order to understand the more general phenomenon of exit costs as a barrier to free religious choice. (216)

> Relational networks and dependence on specific religions as life support systems both work powerfully to limit freedom of choice in switching decisions. (219)

... exit cost analysis is primarily concerned with the paradox of feeling trapped in what is nominally a voluntary association. It asks not 'Why did they leave?' but rather, 'What prevents them from leaving?' (1998: 220)

As we will see below, there are many other examples of passages in which Zablocki asserts that brainwashing diminishes voluntary religious choice without actually using the words *voluntary* or *involuntary*.

The question of whether Zablocki's brainwashing argument is concerned with the voluntarism/involuntarism dimension of social influence cannot be settled according to whether Zablocki uses the involuntarism *term* or not; the question is not primarily whether he uses the term, but rather whether his paradigm is concerned with the *concept* of involuntarism, which can be asserted in various ways. In my view Zablocki contends repeatedly that brainwashing accomplishes involuntary influence of cult members even if he doesn't always use the voluntarism term in affirming this proposition.

Nevertheless, as we have seen, at times Zablocki does use the voluntary/involuntary terminology. In one of his publications, which he regards as a scientific study of cultic brainwashing, he made the following statement:

Change of worldview is possible, although rare and difficult. It can occur in a religious conversion and in psychoanalysis. Both of these processes are undergone voluntarily. *Classic thought reform [as defined by Lifton] is an involuntary method of changing a person's worldview.* I am going to compare the Bruderhof novitiate with the thought reform process in order to locate *the points of structural similarity which are common to all forms of worldview socialization, whether voluntary or coercive, religious or secular.* (1971: 247, emphasis mine)

In this passage, at least, Zablocki uses variants of the voluntary/involuntary *terminology* to refer to the voluntary/involuntary *dimension* of worldview transformation. He also seems in this passage to be referring to the voluntarism dimension as an either/or variable, asserting without qualification that thought reform [brainwashing] is an involuntary method of changing a person's worldview.

At the time Zablocki wrote this passage, he apparently believed that Lifton had demonstrated that thought reform, as conducted by the

Chinese Communists, accomplished involuntary worldview transformation of its victims, whereas conversion and commitment to NRMs such as the Bruderhof (the subject of his book) was essentially voluntary and thus didn't really constitute thought reform or brainwashing, even though it might be 'structurally similar' to it in certain ways. Furthermore, as he clearly says in this passage, at that time Zablocki believed that (1) all forms of worldview [re]socialization are structurally similar to thought reform; (2) some forms of worldview resocialization, such as thought reform, are involuntary, whereas other forms, such as conversion to the Bruderhof, and presumably to other new religions or so-called cults, are voluntary.

Careful review of his 1971 book reveals that Zablocki believed at the time he wrote it that conversion to NRMs such as the Bruderhof community is voluntary whereas the Communist thought reform process as described by Lifton was involuntary. This is further illustrated by the following statement, as well as by many other passages in his 1971 book.

> The similarities between Bruderhof socialization and involuntary means of world-view change raise disturbing questions about the compatibility of freedom and community ...
>
> *There is a danger, however, in making structural comparisons among totally different processes.* A fault of the comparative method is an inevitable tendency to stress similarities and neglect differences. As I mentioned earlier, thought reform and Bruderhof resocialization are poles apart phenomenologically. *One is coercive, rigid, and exploitive* [sic]. *The other is voluntary, flexible, and loving.* Thought reform sacrifices its victims for the sake of future generations. The Bruderhof, although concerned with the future, offers its members a deeply rewarding life in the present. (1971: 265–6, emphasis mine)

It seems obvious from this and similar passages that Zablocki, at the time he wrote the book, believed that even though conversion to new religious worldviews shares certain 'structural similarities' to the process of Communist thought reform as described by Lifton, nevertheless the resocialization processes in the Bruderhof and other new religions do not result in involuntary commitment to the new worldviews, whereas in Communist thought reform it did result in involuntary commitment to Communist ideology.

As I have discussed above, and will discuss further below, Zablocki was wrong in believing that Lifton's research demonstrated that Communist thought reform resulted in involuntary commitment to Communism, but at least he was correct in contending that vague 'structural similarities' between Bruderhof conversion and Communist thought reform does not indicate that the Bruderhof influence is an involuntary process. From my point of view, Zablocki's understanding of the similarities and differences in conversions to NRMs and Communist indoctrination processes was more nearly correct in 1971 than it is in his current brainwashing articles.

Furthermore, since Zablocki says (in the passage from his 1971 book quoted earlier) that all worldview resocialization is structurally similar to brainwashing, this would presumably mean that he now thinks, at some level, that all worldview resocialization in involuntary. This in turn would seem to support the conclusion, which has been advanced by various critics of the cultic brainwashing theory, that the concept of involuntary worldview resocialization (brainwashing) is an evaluative rather than an empirical concept in that it cannot be falsified; that is, any and all occurrences of worldview resocialization are treated as confirmation of the notion that the person concerned has become involuntarily committed to an NRM, that is, brainwashed. (See below on the testability/falsifiability of Zablocki's perspective.)

Moreover, Zablocki's current account of how brainwashing accomplishes worldview transformation and commitment asserts such an extreme *degree* of involuntarism, compulsivity, or impaired will as intrinsic to brainwashing that the question of whether such loss of capacity is absolute or only relative becomes not very important.

The following statement suggests that Zablocki is attempting to show in his writing that brainwashing produces a rather extreme degree of the loss of the voluntary capacity to control one's own actions.

> Within family sociology, it used to be the tendency to say of battered wives, 'Why don't they just leave the abusive situation? Nobody is holding them there by force.' Now it is much better understood that chronic battering *can wear down* not only the body but *the capacity to make independent decisions about leaving*. I fail to see any significant differences between this phenomenon and the phenomenon *of the charismatically abused participant in a cult movement*. (1998: 231, emphasis mine)

Consider, as well, similar statements by Zablocki (1997: 99, 101) which contend that converts to new religions are unable to leave them, or at least find it very difficult to leave them even when they want to. See also the statements in the section evaluating the testability of Zablocki's *exit costs* version of the brainwashing paradigm below. In these passages Zablocki unequivocally asserts that brainwashing produces a severe compulsion to remain in cults once one has joined, and, in this sense, produces a loss of free will. This is the primary distinctive feature of his 'exit costs' interpretation of the brainwashing and totalitarian influence literature. Passages throughout his brainwashing articles make this same point from a variety of angles. It seems obvious, then, that Zablocki's assertion that his perspective on brainwashing does not address the issue of free will is an example of tactical ambiguity rather than an internally consistent characteristic of his argument. This in turn would seem to indicate that, in this respect at least, Zablocki's brainwashing argument is congruent with the CIA brainwashing paradigm that he claims to repudiate.

To sum up, it seems to me that both Zablocki's paradigm, and the CIA brainwashing paradigm from which it is derived, are primarily aimed at demonstrating the loss of free will of the alleged victims of brainwashing.

Brainwashing vs. Totalitarian Influence: Summary of Empirical Conflicts

As we have shown, the CIA brainwashing model which had been disconfirmed by the CIA research program, as well as by the research of Lifton, Schein, and others, provides the actual theoretical foundation for all statements of brainwashing theory including cultic brainwashing formulations such as Zablocki's. Consequently, his cultic brainwashing theory, like the earlier statements of this theory, such as those of Singer and Ofshe, is contradicted by its own claimed theoretical foundation, that is the research of Schein and Lifton. My 1990 article demonstrated that eight variables differentiate Singer's and Ofshe's brainwashing theory from Schein's and Lifton's research. The present chapter has demonstrated the same set of conflicts between Zablocki's approach and generally accepted research on Communist thought reform as characteristic of the Ofshe-Singer formulation.

As I have shown above, the research of Schein and Lifton on Westerners in thought reform prisons, upon which Zablocki claims to base his brainwashing formulation, confirmed and extended Hinkle's and

Wolff's earlier findings. As I argued in my 1990 article, their research on Communist forceful indoctrination practices disconfirmed the CIA model with respect to eight variables:

1 *Conversion.* None of Schein's and Lifton's subjects became committed to Communist worldviews as a result of the thought reform program. Only two of Lifton's forty subjects and only one or two of Schein's fifteen subjects emerged from the thought reform process expressing some sympathy for Communism, with neither of them actually becoming Communists. In the remaining subjects, Communist coercive persuasion produced behavioural compliance but not increased belief in Communist ideology (Lifton 1961: 117, 248–9; Schein 1958: 332, 1961: 157–66, 1973: 295).

2 *Predisposing motives.* Those subjects who were at all influenced by Communist indoctrination practices were predisposed to be so before they were subjected to them (Lifton 1961: 130; Schein 1961: 104–10, 140–56 1973: 295).

3 *Physical coercion.* Communist indoctrination practices produced involuntary influence only in that subjects were forced to participate in them through extreme physical coercion (Lifton 1961: 13, 1976: 327–8; Schein 1959: 437,[33] 1961: 125–7).

4 *Continuity with normal social influence.* The non-physical techniques of influence utilized in Communist thought reform are common in normal social influence situations and are not distinctively coercive. (Lifton 1961: 438–61; Schein 1961: 269–82, 1962: 90–7, 1964: 331–51).

5 *Conditioning.* No distinctive conditioning procedures were utilized in Communist coercive persuasion (Schein 1959: 437–8, 1973: 284–5; Biderman 1962: 550).

6 *Psychophysiological stress/debilitation.* The extreme physically-based stress and debilitation to which imprisoned thought reform victims were subjected did not cause involuntary commitment to Communist worldviews (Hinkle and Wolff 1956; Lifton: 117, 248–9; Schein 1958: 332, 1961: 157–66, 1973: 295). Moreover, no comparable practices are present in new religious movements (Anthony 1990: 309–11).

7 *Deception/defective thought.* Victims of Communist thought reform did not become committed to Communism as a result of deception or defective thought (Schein 1961: 202–3, 238–9).

8 *Dissociation/hypnosis/suggestibility.* Those subjected to thought reform did not become hyper-suggestible as a result of altered states of con-

sciousness; for example, hypnosis, dissociation, disorientation, and so on (Schein 1959: 457; Biderman 1962: 550).

The primary basis for Zablocki's 'exit costs,' third-stage brainwashing perspective is the notion that the research of Lifton and Schein had demonstrated that Communist thought reform could bring about a conversion to the Communism worldview which: (1) did not result from predisposing motives to respond favourably to Communist ideology; (2) resulted rather from disorientation, suppression of critical thought, hyper-suggestibility, and the resulting inability to resist propaganda advocating an alternative worldview; (3) persisted once the thought reform process had been completed; and (4) was difficult for the convert to Communism to repudiate even at the point at which he or she desired to do so.

As we have seen however, all of these research positions were disconfirmed by the research of Schein, Lifton, and other experts on Communist thought reform. None of Scheim's or Lifton's subjects became Communists at any point and only a very small number of them showed any degree of increased sympathy for Communist ideas. Those few who became more sympathetic to Communism did so because of predisposing motives to respond favourably to Communist ideology rather than because of a disoriented state, decreased cognitive ability, hyper-suggestibility, or a resulting inability to resist ideas to which they were not naturally attracted. Furthermore, there was no evidence that those few subjects felt trapped or mentally imprisoned by their sympathy for some Communist ideas. It would seem that like Singer's and Ofshe's account of the brainwashing paradigm, Zablocki's 'exit costs' brainwashing theory conflicts in fundamental ways with its claimed theoretical and empirical foundation of generally accepted research upon Communist thought reform. If there is any scientific support for Zablocki's brainwashing perspective, it would have to come from sources other than its alleged relationship to Communist thought reform.

Falsifiability/testability of Zablocki's Formulation

Demarcation of Science from Pseudo-science
As we saw above, Zablocki's earlier empirical research on new religions such as the Bruderhof conflicts dramatically with his later claim that commitments to new religions are involuntary because of brain-

washing. Given that Zablocki's exit costs brainwashing theory is not really based upon research upon Communist thought reform, and given that his earlier research is not really supportive of his brainwashing theory either, what basis does Zablocki have for claiming that his brainwashing theory is a genuinely scientific perspective? It would seem that the most he can claim is that he has developed a testable theory which could serve in the future as the basis for scientific research. Surprisingly, when his brainwashing articles are read carefully, this turns out to be all that he is really claiming. Consequently, the scientific status of Zablocki's exit costs brainwashing model stands or falls upon its testability.

Early in his brainwashing articles Zablocki (1997: 101) does boldly claim that his brainwashing theory is falsifiable; that is, testable. He acknowledges that majority opinion among social scientists engaged in research on new religions is that the brainwashing perspective is an evaluative rather than a scientific viewpoint. Contrary to such generally accepted opinion, however, he argues that the criticisms of NRM scholars that the brainwashing concept is an evaluative rather than a scientific concept because it is not testable are flatly wrong (101), and he claims that his articles will prove that his brainwashing concept is a testable scientific concept (104). He states:

> It is my ... modest aim [in his 1997 and 1998a articles on brainwashing] to show that brainwashing is a precise and empirically testable conjecture about a very important social-psychological process that has been treated shabbily within the sociology of religion. My argument is that the brainwashing conjecture has been convicted and dismissed without a fair scientific trial. It is this shabby treatment that I have called "blacklisting" and that we turn to in the next section of this paper.

As I have argued in other publications, previous brainwashing formulations do not provide reliable criteria for differentiating brainwashing from other forms of social influence (Anthony 1999; Ginsburg and Richardson 1998). In other words, they are not falsifiable and they lead to *irrefutable allegations*. When such formulations are applied to particular religious worldviews and organizations, therefore, their real effect is to evaluate the religious authenticity of these particular religious beliefs and practices. This is so because it is the minority status of their non-mainstream worldviews that triggers the application of the brainwashing allegation rather than anything distinctively coercive

about their techniques of influence. In other words, brainwashing formulations are evaluative rather than scientific perspectives, which cannot even in principle be evaluated empirically.[34]

Does Zablocki's recent brainwashing formulation fulfil his promise
to do a better job than previous formulations in providing an empirically testable theory which is scientific rather than evaluative? It seems
to me that the answer is no. Like many perspectives that claim scientific status, the brainwashing viewpoint has two principle components,
sometimes referred to in textbooks on scientific methodology as the
independent and dependent variables. In other words, the brainwashing theory claims that certain sorts of social influence techniques (the
independent variable) cause certain sorts of effects – that is, involuntary commitment to worldviews and organizations, including a false
or shadow self and exit costs – in the people to whom they are applied
(the dependent variable).

It seems to me that in Zablocki's definition of them, neither the independent variable (the coercive cause) nor the dependent variable (the
involuntary effect) of his brainwashing formulation are falsifiable. In
other words, he has not supplied criteria which clearly differentiate
brainwashing techniques and their allegedly involuntary effects from
components of normal social influence, in particular from other forms
of religious conversions and commitments.

Falsifiability and the Independent Variable of Brainwashing
Zablocki primarily identifies brainwashing techniques – the independent or causal variable – with Lifton's accounts of the twelve *psychological steps* which Lifton (1961: 65–85) found to characterize the
Communist thought reform process for his subjects. It is Zablocki's
application of this model of conversion to the Bruderhof which constitutes his only concrete empirical application of thought reform research
to a new religion. (Zablocki also claims that this process usually must
occur in the context of a totalistic social organization in order to constitute brainwashing, but he is somewhat ambiguous with respect to this
aspect of brainwashing,[35] and he supplies no evidence that the Bruderhof is a totalistic organization, nor that its ideology is totalistic.)

As we saw above, Zablocki interprets such psychological steps as
occurring through techniques that impose a primitive state of consciousness (and resulting suggestibility) that he variously describes as
disorientation, hypnosis, transference, the suspension of critical ratio-

nality, and so on. But as we also saw, he supplies no criteria or generally accepted empirical foundation which differentiates these different terms for primitive consciousness in a falsifiable way from other forms of religious experience (see Anthony 1999, 443–5, 445–51 for demonstrations that the *hypnosis, transference,* and *addiction* concepts as used by Zablocki and other authors of brainwashing formulations are not falsifiable). Consequently, the case for his having provided a falsifiable definition of the independent variable in his brainwashing formulation stands or falls upon his characterization of Lifton's twelve psychological steps as illustrated by his application of this model to the Bruderhof.

It seems to me, however, that Zablocki's application of the twelve psychological steps model to the Bruderhof does not supply a falsifiable way of differentiating a brainwashing process of religious conversion from other forms of religious conversion. To make this point in a brief way, I will return to a quote which I discussed formerly in the section upon Zablocki's characterization of the brainwashing process as one embodying involuntary influence. (I think anyone who goes to the trouble of reviewing the entire chapter in Zablocki's Bruderhof book [in which he applies the Lifton's twelve steps model to the Bruderhof conversion process] will agree that Zablocki does not therein provide criteria that falsifiably differentiate brainwashed religious conversions from other types.) Zablocki states: 'Change of worldview is possible, although rare and difficult. It can occur in a religious conversion and in psychoanalysis. Both of these processes are undergone voluntarily. *Classic thought reform [as defined by Lifton's 12 psychological steps] is an involuntary method of changing a person's worldview.* I am going to compare the Bruderhof novitiate with the thought reform process in order to locate *the points of structural similarity which are common to all forms of worldview socialization, whether voluntary or coercive, religious or secular'* (1971: 247, emphasis mine).

Zablocki states quite clearly in this passage that the twelve psychological steps described by Lifton as characteristic of thought reform are structurally similar to 'all forms of worldview socialization.' Zablocki could hardly say it any more clearly, that in his mind the twelve psychological steps describe a universal process of conversion to a new worldview; that is, they describe worldview conversion per se, rather than a distinctively involuntary form of conversion; therefore they could not possibly constitute falsifiable criteria for differentiating coercive or involuntary conversions (brainwashing) from other types.

The reader may recall that in another statement from that chapter, supplied earlier, Zablocki states that 'structural comparisons' between 'totally different processes' are dangerous ('There is a danger, however, in making structural comparisons among totally different processes.' (1971: 265–66) In the same passage he insists that the reader be careful not to equate voluntary conversion processes, such as those he has described in the Bruderhof, with coercive influence as described by Lifton in his twelve psychological steps as characteristic of thought reform, simply because they are 'structurally similar.'

These earlier statements by Zablocki agree with my impression that Lifton's twelve psychological steps, shorn of their enforcement by extreme physical coercion, would describe a very broad class of conversion experiences, perhaps as Zablocki states, all conversion (worldview resocialization) experiences, of which coercive conversion experiences would constitute, at most, only a small and distinctive percentage. Zablocki's interpretation of any conversion that includes the twelve psychological steps as brainwashing in his recent articles, therefore, tends to confirm my impression that this brainwashing interpretation of Lifton's research is an evaluative rather than a scientific perspective, intended to call into question the authenticity of religious conversion experiences simply because they are experiential in nature.

Confirming this interpretation of Zablocki's assertions in these passages, the rest of the chapter in his 1971 book makes clear that Zablocki characterizes the thought reform process as described by Lifton as involuntary. On the other hand, Zablocki describes the Bruderhof conversion process as voluntary, primarily because in the case of thought reform as described by Lifton, the twelve steps were enforced through the use of extreme physical coercion, a condition that was not present in the Bruderhof conversion process. This is consistent with the way Lifton generalizes, or refuses to generalize, the twelve steps model to other contexts.

Lifton generalizes the totalism concept to other contexts many times in a number of different books. But he generalizes the twelve steps component of his description of thought reform only once – i.e., to the influence process that was applied upon Patty Hearst by the Symbionese Liberation Army (Lifton 1976: 314–35). In that use of the twelve psychological steps model to describe the influence upon Patty Hearst by the SLA, he says very explicitly that the process only produces involuntary conduct when it is combined with 'life and death coercion' (327–8, and throughout). Thus, it would seem that both Lifton and Zablocki (at the time that Zablocki originally wrote his book on the Bruderhof) agreed that the twelve psychological steps do not in themselves provide criteria for differentiating coercive from non-coercive influence, and that only their combination with extreme physical coercion describes a distinctively coercive process of influence. Zablocki's brainwashing formulation thus lacks falsifiable criteria for differentiating coercive techniques of influence (the independent variable of this theory) from non-coercive techniques of influence.

Falsifiability and the Dependent Variable of Brainwashing

Zablocki's brainwashing formulation has no better luck in defining a falsifiable dependent variable. In the course of his two articles, it becomes clear that he has not been able to provide a testable criterion for involuntary belief and conduct, the so-called exit costs that he maintains are the outcome of brainwashing. As we saw above, the novel feature of this third-stage brainwashing argument is to claim that brainwashing does not lead to involuntary *conversions*, but rather to involuntary *commitments* to a new worldview after conversion has already occurred. But what is the testable or falsifiable criterion of involuntary commitment to the new worldview, such that an objective outsider could determine that Zablocki's brainwashing theory has been either confirmed or disconfirmed?

As we saw above, neither Lifton's nor Schein's thought reform subjects became Communists, only a few of them were influenced at all by the process, and none of these latter few experienced their moderately changed attitudes towards Communism as compulsive, ego alien, or difficult to get rid of in the fashion that Zablocki describes as characteristic of those who have been brainwashed.

Even if we were to interpret more of their subjects as having been influenced during the course of thought reform rather than after it was finished, that still wouldn't satisfy Zablocki's definition of brainwashing. As we saw above, he specifies that deployable agency and exit costs result from 'the persistence of ideological conversion after the stimulus [the thought reform process] has been removed' (Zablocki 1997: 105), and it is unquestionable that this substantial influence was not present in most of their subjects after they left the thought reform environment, and none of them 'converted' to Communism.

Also as we have seen, none of these subjects satisfied the criteria for 'deployable agency' as Zablocki defines it: 'A deployable agent is a person who has internalized the group's goals to such an extent that he or she can be counted on with high probability to act so as to implement those goals even when free of direct surveillance and even when those goals run counter to the individual's personal goals' (1998: 221).

As we saw above, it is questionable whether any of their subjects ever became 'deployable agents' in this sense, and it is certain that none but the few who were characterized by individual totalism *before* they underwent thought reform, could by any stretch of the imagination be accurately described as deployable agents of Communist China after they were released from China.

But even without its claimed theoretical foundation in Lifton's and Schein's research, does Zablocki's brainwashing formulation provide falsifiable criteria for measuring exit costs in new religions? According to Zablocki the exit costs idea depends upon his finding that converts to totalistic new religious movements find it more difficult to leave than they would if they had converted to other movements. This is the whole basis for his exit costs reinterpretation of the brainwashing paradigm. He states:

> The brainwashing conjecture is concerned with whether something happens to a member while he or she is in a group to make it emotionally not impossible, but very difficult to get out again. Does something occur to create, in the mind of the person, a socio-psychological prison without guards or walls?' (1997: 101, emphasis mine)

Moreover, according to Zablocki, the brainwashed convert is aware that he wants to leave the

> socio-psychological prison, but is unable to do so in very much the same way as someone who is addicted to drugs or other undesirable habits. The attachment to the cultic worldview has become *compulsive*. (See above; also Zablocki 1998a: 241–4).[36]

Zablocki states:

> When the time came that he and others [brainwashed cult members] became thoroughly disillusioned with the group's goals and methods, *they nevertheless found it emotionally impossible to leave. They felt trapped.* (1997: 99, emphasis mine)

But what is measurable about this feeling of being trapped such that we could scientifically determine that converts to totalistic new religious worldviews are more apt to have difficulty leaving their religion than are those committed to other types of worldviews? It is by no means intuitively obvious that converts to totalistic new religions have more difficulty leaving such groups than do converts to non-totalistic new religions. In fact my impression is that converts to totalistic religions are if anything more apt to leave such groups than converts to non-totalistic groups.

As Zablocki acknowledges, both proponents and critics of the brainwashing perspective agree that a certain number of ex-members of new religions, particularly those who have had substantial contact with the anticult movement, claim that they had been mentally imprisoned or trapped in a cult. But as Zablocki also acknowledges, there are a number of alternative ways of explaining this pattern of biographical reconstruction other than his brainwashing theory, and so this fact in itself doesn't provide a significant test of his theory.

It would seem that a minimum test of his theory would be if Zablocki could show that totalism as an independent variable could differentially predict the dependent variable of lower defection rates than in non-totalistic groups, particularly if such lower turnover rates were combined with evidence that members consciously wanted to leave but had great difficult doing so while they were still members of the group. Demonstration of such a differential pattern compared to non-totalistic NRMs would seem to provide some support for his claim that brainwashed commitments are a form of compulsivity or addiction. Certainly, similar patterns are present in the other habits and commitments – for example, to drugs or to abusive families – that Zablocki claims are compulsive in a manner that is essentially identical to that of attachments to totalistic worldviews.

In Zablocki's only systematic discussion of this issue, he acknowledges that there is no evidence that totalistic NRMs have a lower turnover rate than other new religions, and he even contends that such differential rates of defection are irrelevant to testing his exit costs hypothesis (1998a: 228–9). That would seem to leave a purely subjective criterion, that is the criterion of 'feeling trapped,' as the only prediction of his exit costs theory which would conceivably differentiate involuntarily brainwashed attachments from non-brainwashed attachments to alternative worldviews. But this criterion is also rather difficult to measure in a fashion that would satisfy brainwashing theorists.

For example, brainwashing theorists tend to discount claims of satisfaction with new religions by current members on the grounds that they are brainwashed so you can't believe them. On the other hand, feeling trapped is such a common complaint of those who are in the process of defecting from previous attachments, such as those who are undergoing or about to undergo a divorce, that even if it were measurable it wouldn't provide a very interesting confirmation of the brainwashing idea.

Zablocki's Admission Brainwashing Not Testable/Falsifiable

Surprisingly, even Zablocki, towards the end of his second brainwashing article, (Zablocki 1998a) acknowledges that he has failed to make good on his original intent to demonstrate that his exit costs interpretation of the brainwashing idea is a testable scientific concept. In this article (227) he admits that so-called scientific 'conjectures' such as the brainwashing concept, are not testable after all and are merely 'plausible,' a characteristic he defines as telling a story that makes some kind of sense to its audience. Yet he provides no criterion which would differentiate scientific plausibility from pseudo-scientific plausibility, and he fails to provide any authority for his notion that plausibility is an interesting criterion for differentiating science from pseudo-science. Surely pseudo-scientific concepts often meet this test, which is why scientists and philosophers of science have sought to develop criteria which can differentiate scientific concepts from mere prejudices.

By the point at which he wrote this passage, as opposed to the earlier passage in 'The Blacklisting of a Concept' (1997: 106) in which he promised to demonstrate that his brainwashing perspective is testable, Zablocki apparently has come to believe that there is a well-recognized difference in the epistemological requirements for scientific *conjectures* as opposed to scientific *theories*, whereby the former must only tell a 'plausible story,' whereas actual scientific theories must be falsifiable or testable. Furthermore, by the end of his 1998 article, *Zablocki very clearly admits that his own formulation of the brainwashing idea is only a plausible conjecture and not a testable theory.* He states:

> The brainwashing conjecture is based on a theory of preference modification. Since there is no direct way to observe or measure the process of preference transformation, we can currently test this conjecture only at the level of plausibility (1998a, 232–3).

At a later point he also states:

These sorts of comparisons [between his brainwashing formulation and other explanations of commitment to NRMs] can only be made on the basis of plausibility. If we want a theory we can actually test, we need to model the phenomenon in terms of measurable changes to persons and relationships. At the present time I believe we are still far away from such an achievement. This is why I have repeatedly referred to arguments concerning brainwashing as conjectures rather than as theories (1998: 239).

There is no question, then, that contrary to the bold testability claim in his 1997 'blacklisting' article, Zablocki finishes his two brainwashing articles (1997, 1998a) by admitting that his brainwashing formulation is not testable after all. Nothing could better illustrate the tactical ambiguity of Zablocki's whole model of involuntary influence than his contradictory position, and thus his theoretical incoherence, on the question of whether his brainwashing formulation is testable.

Zablocki has painted himself into a corner with respect to this testability claim. He is damned when he claims that brainwashing is testable, and damned when he admits that it is not testable. In the section of his formulation where he claims it is testable, he has no option but to provide explicit empirical predictions, which, as I have shown, previous voluminous research has already disconfirmed, thus indicating that brainwashing is no longer a viable scientific concept. On the other hand, when he admits, as in the passage above, that his brainwashing formulation is not testable, he is in effect agreeing with critics of the brainwashing idea who contend that it is an evaluative rather than a scientific perspective.

The confusion in Zablocki's mind over these issues may stem partially from his confusion over the meanings of the philosophy of science terms which he uses repeatedly in his articles, especially the terms *conjectures, theories, falsifiability, testability,* and *plausibility.*

The first four of these terms are associated with the philosophy of science of Sir Karl Popper (1959, 1963). Zablocki's only citation of a philosophy of science reference in these articles is to a book (Phillips 1992) that repeatedly discusses and cites Popper's work on these topics. Consequently I think it is reasonable to hold Zablocki to the definitions for these terms in Popper's work and also to the interpretations of Popper's work in the book which Zablocki cites.

In Popper's use of these terms, there is no real difference between the concepts of *conjectures* and *theories*, nor between *falsifiability* and *testability* (Popper 1963: 33–9). In Popper's use of these terms, in order for allegedly scientific ideas (which he alternatively refers to as either *conjectures* or *theories*) to qualify as scientific rather than *pseudo-scientific*, they must be testable, which, according to Popper's understanding, means that they must be *falsifiable*, which is his particular notion of testability.

Unfortunately, Zablocki's misunderstanding of these terms is far from an isolated case. In his brainwashing articles Zablocki sprinkles reputed philosophy of science jargon throughout, and he frequently attempts to base his defence of the scientific status of his brainwashing approach upon the concepts that these terms allegedly stand for. However, careful attention to such scientistic window-dressing reveals that Zablocki frequently misunderstands the normal academic meaning of such terms and concepts, or, on some occasions, actually imputes a technical philosophy of science meaning to terms and distinctions which have no recognized meaning within that discipline.[37]

For instance, with respect to the term and concept of *plausibility*, I have been unable to find this term used as one which is relevant in differentiating scientific from pseudo-scientific concepts in any of Popper's works, nor in any commentaries on Popper's work, including the one (Phillips 1992) cited by Zablocki. Moreover, it seems to me that the idea that telling a plausible story is a meaningful criterion of acceptable science is wholly foreign to Popper's thought, and indeed to any generally accepted criterion of the differentiation of scientific from non-scientific concepts.

It seems to me that pseudo-scientific concepts which have been used to rationalize religious or racial prejudice typically seem plausible to those who advocate them, and it was partially as an attempt to differentiate such merely plausible ideological concepts from authentically scientific ones that Popper proposed his falsifiability criterion for differentiating science from pseudo-science in the first place. It is ironic that one of Popper's primary concerns in developing the falsifiability criterion was to differentiate totalitarian ideologies – for instance, fascism and communism – from genuinely scientific theories (Popper 1945; Hacohen 2000: 6–7), whereas Zablocki has arguably used the terms associated with his perspective in defence of a perspective that is ideological rather than scientific.

At any rate, Zablocki at several points in his 1998a article acknowledges that his brainwashing theory, at least as currently formulated, is not 'testable.' (Zablocki 1998: 216, 239–40, 244). In his last reference to this issue he states:

> At some point in the future, brainwashing theory will be testable at the chemical level of the brain. Until then, hopefully I have at least traced the outlines of a viable agenda for theory building' (244).

As stated above, in the latter sections of his 1998a article Zablocki admits that his original aim – to demonstrate that brainwashing is a testable scientific concept – has failed. It also seems to me that the more modest claim that he is making for his approach in this passage – that is, to have 'traced the outlines of a viable agenda for theory building' – is also rather questionable. To fall back on the reductionistic hope that brainwashing will someday become a testable scientific theory by attaining falsifiability through neurochemistry seems too speculative to provide brainwashing with any current scientific credibility.

It is undoubtedly true that all forms of social influence have bio-chemical substrates, but so do all other forms of human mental func-tioning. I am unaware of any credibly scientific research which differentiates voluntary from involuntary forms of social influence on the basis of differential neurophysiological variables, and I think it unlikely that such falsifiable differential criteria with be discovered any time soon. To base the allegedly scientific status of brainwashing theory on such an utopian hope seems a very questionable basis for the claim that brainwashing theory is a scientific rather than an ideological concept. It would seem that Zablocki in effect is agreeing with the crit-ics of the brainwashing concept that it, at least as currently formulated, is an evaluative rather than a scientific concept.

Conclusion: Brainwashing vs. Totalitarian Influence

Unfalsifiable Brainwashing Formulations and Civil Liberties

I return now to the question that began this article: Is Zablocki's brain-washing formulation a scientific or an ideological perspective? For the reasons discussed above, his approach appears to me to be ideological rather than scientific. To recapitulate: Insofar as his viewpoint has been specified unequivocally enough that it can be scientifically evaluated, it has been disconfirmed in each of the several contexts in which it has been evaluated. These contexts include (a) CIA research which attempted to develop techniques for creating 'deployable agents,'

(b) research on Korean War era Communist coercive persuasion, (c) research upon the use of hypnosis for coercing otherwise unacceptable conduct, and (d) research upon conversion and commitment to alternative religious movements.

The latter three contexts were claimed by Zablocki as empirical foundations for his brainwashing formulation. As we have seen, on closer inspection his brainwashing formulation is actually a version of the CIA brainwashing argument that was disconfirmed in each of those contexts.

Research upon new religions is particularly conclusive in disconfirming Zablocki's brainwashing formulation in the following sense. Zablocki claims his own earlier research upon new religions (1971, 1980) as one of the primary scientific bases for his expertise on this topic. As we have seen, however, his own research not only is inconsistent with his more recent brainwashing formulation, but it also actually disconfirms it in central respects. Nothing could be clearer in showing that the cultic brainwashing perspective is a wholly abstract one which has not served as a basis for scientific research. Its only real use has been in supplying a rationale for practical actions against new religions.

Which brings me to the remaining question with which I started this exercise; that is, the question of whether Zablocki's formulation is clearly stated enough so that it could serve as the basis for future scientific research that might eventually confirm it or conclusively disconfirm it. As we have seen, Zablocki's formulation is stated very ambiguously, a characteristic that results in its being impervious to definitive empirical disconfirmation. In other words, it is not falsifiable, a quality which by contemporary philosophy of science criteria differentiates scientific theories from pseudo-scientific ideologies.

Even Zablocki admits that his brainwashing formulation does not constitute a testable scientific theory. (Although he contradicts himself on this point, as on many others, he finishes his most recent attempt at stating a brainwashing theory by admitting that he has failed to formulate a testable theory, a conclusion with which I agree.)

Civil Liberties and Scientists' Duties as Citizens: Testimony

The question of the scientific status of the brainwashing idea has significant real-world consequences. The brainwashing idea has been used as the rationale for a variety of social activities that embody a serious level of religious prejudice. I don't wish to go into any great detail about this issue here, but it seems obvious that if the brainwashing concept is a pseudo-scientific myth rather than a scientifically testable theory, then action based upon it which seriously interferes with religious belief and practice is a social problem that should be remedied.

The fact that the brainwashing concept is non-falsifiable means that in practice its application results in *irrefutable allegations*; that is, allegations of brainwashing cannot be disconfirmed in its application to any particular religious or political viewpoint. Consequently it can be, and in my experience often has been, used as the basis for legal actions against new religions which are not at all totalistic.

It is true that in cases in which I serve as an expert and consultant, and in which I apply the totalitarian influence perspective discussed herein in my reports and testimony, or assist lawyers in using this perspective as the basis for motions in limine and other briefs, brainwashing testimony is often excluded in advance of a trial. Nevertheless, these cases are so expensive to fight, even in the pre-trial phase, that the expense of fighting them often serves as a serious impediment to the religious practice and association of small religious organizations.

In one case in which I recently served as an expert, involving an organization that in my judgment was not at all totalistic, the defence lawyers managed with my assistance to exclude brainwashing testimony in advance of the trial, and consequently the damages assessed at trial were relatively minor. But the expense of fighting the case was itself so large that as a result the organization was forced into bankruptcy. When it is realized that, as a result of the use of brainwashing testimony as the keystone for legal cases which otherwise would have no viable 'cause of action,' it takes only one disgruntled former member to catastrophically interfere with the religious practice and association of the other members of a small religious organization, it can be seen that the legal use of brainwashing formulations seriously restricts religious civil liberties.

Also, in both the United States and other countries, the widespread public acceptance of the anticult brainwashing concept often results in non-governmental instances of religious prejudice; for example, the shunning of members of alternative religions in residential neighbourhoods, discriminatory treatment in hiring and promotion policies in work settings, and so on.

In Europe and Asia, the use of the brainwashing theory to legally restrict the religious freedom of alternative religions often results in consequences that are even more extreme than in the United States; for instance, using it as the basis for criminal charges that result in imprisonment of members of alternative groups (e.g., in France with members of the Church of Scientology; in China with members of the Falun Gong).

In China many imprisoned Falun Gong members have reportedly been beaten in an attempt to force them to repudiate the Falun Gong worldview in favour of the atheistic Communist worldview, and there have been some deaths (*New York Times* 30 April 2000, 4: 1, 4). It is ironic that in China, cultic brainwashing allegations against the Falun Gong are used as the rationale for imprisonment and forceful resocialization of its members; whereas in the United States, on the other hand, authors of brainwashing formulations such as Zablocki view Chinese thought reform and imprisonment similar to that endured by members of Falun Gong as the classical foundation for their own brainwashing formulations.

How different is the legal use of brainwashing formulations in the United States to interfere with religious civil liberties from that in China relative to the Falun Gong? Surely the difference is only one of degree and not of essence; the brainwashing formulations used as a rationale for such penalties are basically the same in these other countries and in the United States. (See Anthony 1999 for a demonstration that the brainwashing formulation used as a basis for criminal charges against new religions in France is basically the same as third-stage brainwashing formulations such as Zablocki's, published in the United States.

In view of the seriousness of the civil liberties abuses resulting from the use of pseudo-scientific brainwashing formulations, is it too much to say that scientists who are experts on this topic have a civic duty to make their expertise available to the agencies which are concerned with determining whether social action that interferes with religious activities should be based upon this putatively scientific theory?

Zablocki himself has claimed that he is opposed to the form of the brainwashing idea that is used as a basis for testimony in brainwashing trials against new religions. Presumably he is also against the legal actions that are based primarily upon this unscientific brainwashing concept. On closer inspection, however, his claims on this topic turn out to be as ambiguous as several of his other attempts to differentiate his own brainwashing formulation from unscientific brainwashing formulations. As we have seen, his theory is essentially the same as the theory which has been used as the primary basis for such brainwashing legal actions and other forms of religious prejudice against new religions.

We have demonstrated this in considerable detail by comparing the substantive elements of his formulation to the ones used as the basis for legal actions. Examples include Zablocki's claim that brainwashing is based upon the induction of primitive states of consciousness, or the claim that brainwashing produces involuntary commitment to alternative worldviews. The equivalence of Zablocki's formulation to the ones used as a basis for legal testimony is also obvious when we consider the fact that he claims that the published formulations of prominent brainwashing experts who testify in these trials – formulations such as those of Margaret Singer, Richard Ofshe, and Steven Kent – constitute a share of the empirical base for his own formulation.

As we have seen, the fact that published brainwashing formulations of such experts are stated more ambiguously than their actual testimony is not therefore an indication that such publications are not pseudo-scientific. The ambiguous manner in which such formulations are stated misleadingly enables them to appear to untutored eyes as consistent with both the CIA brainwashing model used for testimony and with credible scientific research upon Communist thought reform and new religious movements. To the extent that advocates of the brainwashing idea are successful in accomplishing such a fusion of contradictory models of influence, they capture the prestige of science for the CIA model and thus are able to persuade courts to allow it to be used as a basis for their testimony. Similarly, to the extent that Zablocki is successful in reviving the credibility of the brainwashing idea, to that extent also his formulation will tend to encourage cultic brainwashing trials and other forms of religious prejudice, and will serve as the theoretical foundation for actual testimony in such trials.

That such is the case is demonstrated by the fact that Steven Kent's professionally presented version of the brainwashing idea (1997) is similar to Zablocki's own formulation, in that it emphasizes exit costs rather than involuntary conversion as the core of the brainwashing idea. Kent has repeatedly used this exit costs approach as the basis for his own brainwashing testimony in legal trials against the new religions.

Zablocki's criticism of my formulation of the totalitarian influence perspective – a formulation which has been the primary basis for successful legal briefs and testimony, excluding brainwashing testimony in legal trails – is another indication that his viewpoint will, to the extent that it is influential, work in favour of further brainwashing trials.[38] In addition, he has argued that the viewpoints of NRM scholars such as myself, who testify against cultic brainwashing arguments in legal trials for that very reason, lack scientific merit and objectivity (1997: 100).

Zablocki contends therein that payment for our services as forensic expert witnesses motivates us to present testimony that is unscientific and to distort our review of the evidence on the scientific standing of brainwashing accounts of involvement in new religions. (See 1997: 100 n. 5, which summarizes Zablocki's viewpoint on this issue.)

But if cultic brainwashing testimony is unscientific, and therefore tends to undermine religious civil liberties, it would seem that testimony pointing that out is necessary to protect such liberties. Zablocki has never provided a systematic analysis of the totalitarian influence perspective which has been the primary basis for such testimony. In view of the serious civil liberties effects of cultic brainwashing testimony, it would seem that Zablocki would have to come up with a better reason than the fact that the totalitarian influence perspective has served as the basis for testimony and briefs in legal trials if he expects his criticism of it as motivated by pecuniary rather than scientific considerations to be taken seriously.

If Zablocki's brainwashing formulation is ever to be taken seriously as an argument against the use of brainwashing testimony in legal trials, he would have to specify in much more detail than he has up to now what there is about the theoretical foundation of such testimony that renders it pseudo-scientific, and how his own formulation differs from it in ways that would prevent its use for practical forms of religious prejudice. As we have seen, Zablocki has a long way to go in differentiating his own approach from the unscientific model that is used as a basis for such testimony. In view of the essential identity of his own formulation with the one that is used as the basis for testimony, it seems unlikely that he will ever be able to accomplish this minimum requirement for giving the brainwashing idea scientific credibility. It is my view that the brainwashing idea in all of its formulations is intrinsically an exercise in propaganda rather than science, and that no amount of rehabilitation will ever turn it into a law-abiding citizen of the scientific community.

Research on Harm in NRMs

General Research on Harm

Which brings me to another issue raised by Zablocki. In his 1997 article, he gives the impression that NRM scholars and cultic brainwashing authors are polarized, not only on the scientific status of the brainwashing concept but also on whether new religions are psychologically or socially harmful. As Zablocki sees it, the brainwashing concept is the only valid approach to evaluating why, or if, new religions have harmful social or psychological consequences. Such is not the case. Many of the same scholars who have been instrumental in critiquing the brainwashing concept have also been instrumental in developing theories and conducting research intended to help individuals and social agencies to understand and predict when and how some new religions may have undesirable consequences both socially and psychologically.[39]

Totalitarian Influence and Research on Harm

Contrary to Zablocki's 1997 article, this is true even with respect to scholars who are active as expert witnesses and consultants for the defence in brainwashing trials. For instance, I have served more often as an expert in such cases than any other scholar, and the general approach to evaluating the cultic brainwashing theory I have expressed in this chapter and elsewhere has been the primary basis for my reports and testimony, as well as for motions in limine and appeal briefs which have limited the use of brainwashing testimony in legal trials against new religions. But I have also been very active in developing theories and conducting research concerned with differentiating pathological from beneficial alternative religious practices.[40]

The lack of falsifiability of the brainwashing perspective in effect renders it irrefutable when applied to any religious orientation in which religious experience plays a role. Zablocki's and other brainwashing authors' emphasis on altered states of consciousness and charisma as the hallmarks of involuntary, pathological influence is stated at such a level of generality that it in effect rules out of bounds and therefore vulnerable to extreme forms of religious prejudice such as brainwashing trials all forms of experiential religion. In my view, what is needed as an alternative to such pseudo-scientific ideology targeting all experiential religion is a critical theory of experiential religiosity that falsifiably differentiates harmful from beneficial forms.

It is also the case that my own interpretation of the totalitarian influence literature, which brainwashing theorists claim as the chief theoretical foundation for their approach, is central to my own attempts to produce such a critical theory. Much of my work has been concerned with demonstrating that the credible scientific literature on Communist indoctrination practices is part of a larger totalitarian influence tradition, one which is both scientifically falsifiable and relevant to developing a critical theory of alternative religious involvements.[41]

As I have indicated above, totalitarian influence theories, unlike their distorted interpretations in brainwashing formulations, explore a distinctive interaction between a certain type of person and a certain type of ideology. The key idea in totalitarian influence theories is rather simple. From the point of view of such theories, what is distinctive about totalitarian institutions is not their techniques of influence (except, in some instances, for the use of extreme physical coercion to enforce compliance), but rather the structure and content of totalitarian beliefs.

Totalitarian ideologies promise the creation of a utopia through the control of all facets of social life in conformity with their content. The structure of such beliefs is distinctive in that they are organized as a hierarchy of black and white polar contrasts between good and evil, with one overarching polarity (e.g., communists vs. capitalists, or Aryans vs. Jews) giving force and meaning to subordinate oppositions. When such totalitarian ideology is used to rationalize religious practices and organizations, the contrast becomes some version of the contrast between the saved and the damned. Thus totalitarian ideologies are highly dualistic.

According to Erikson's theory of totalism, to take the example of a totalitarian influence psychological theory that was employed by Lifton in making sense of his interviews of victims of thought reform, those attracted to such dualistic ideologies have a polarized sense of self; that is, a sense of self that is polarized between conflicting images of themselves as both extremely good and extremely bad. Such polarization frequently results in identity confusion, particularly during the period when adolescents and young adults are expected to achieve a sense of ego-identity separate from that of their families of origin. One solution to this crisis of identity, according to Erikson, is to adopt a totalitarian ideology and join a totalistic social movement. Totalism helps an individual to crystallize a regressive but coherent totalistic identity. Such an identity confirms the grandiose side of the person's split sense of self, and projects the negative aspect of a polarized sense of self onto a designated contrast category or scapegoat.

It seems to me that at least some of the new religious movements that have manifested social and psychological pathology (e.g., The People's Temple, Aum Sinrikyo) had/have a totalitarian ideology of this type. Anticult brainwashing theorists such as Zablocki and I tend to be in essential agreement about this point. Where we part company is in the explanation of why people join such movements. It seems to me that a totalitarian influence explanation which emphasizes an interaction between predisposing characteristics of the person and the nature of totalitarian ideologies and institutions is more faithful to the theoretical tradition each of us claims as a key influence in our own formulations. In addition, it seems to me that thus interpreted, the totalitarian influence tradition has produced testable theories (e.g., Rokeach's dogmatism scales or Adorno et al.'s authoritarian personality measures), while even Zablocki admits that the brainwashing interpretations of this tradition currently do not constitute testable theories (Zablocki 1998a: 232, 239, 244).

Research on pre-motives in NRMs. In addition, it seems to me that the totalitarian influence interpretation of this tradition of research handles more parsimoniously the range of research currently available on new religions. For instance, there is a considerable body of research that indicates that very few people exposed to it are influenced by proselytization by new religions, and that only a very small percentage of those so influenced end by converting to the theology to which they have been exposed (Barker 1984). Such research also tends to show that those who do convert are actively searching for alternatives to mainstream beliefs before they encounter the new religion that they join. (As we have seen, even Zablocki's own research (1971, 1980) strongly supports this generalization.) In view of these generally accepted findings, it seems obvious to me that a theory that hopes to explain conversion to new religions, as well as their psychological impact on individuals and the evolution of such movements in either positive or pathological directions, must take individual differences into account as a central aspect.

In that many of the more pathological of the new religions seem to have highly dualistic ideologies, similar to those described by previous studies of totalitarian organizations, it seems to me a reasonable hypothesis that the small percentage of people attracted to them are likely to have predisposing characteristics (for example, a polarized sense of self, identity confusion, alienation from mainstream values) typical of those attracted to totalistic political orientations such as Fascism or Communism. At least this approach, unlike the brainwashing approach of Zablocki and others, is testable by currently available scientific methods, and so could not be used as a basis for arbitrary, irrefutable allegations against new religions. (It also could not be used as a basis for arbitrary legal actions against new religions, since according to it, those joining new religions do so because they are authentically attracted to them, and so become jointly responsible with other members for their own religious choices.)

I don't mean necessarily that currently available dogmatism or authoritarianism scales would be optimal measures of personality traits that predispose individuals to being influenced by contemporary totalitarian religious ideologies. But such scales could be useful starting points in developing measures more relevant to contemporary religious movements. In addition, the whole theoretical tradition of totalitarian studies provides rich theoretical resources for developing falsifiable re-search methods for identifying totalitarian religious institutions.

Related theoretical and empirical resources. In addition, there are several other contemporary schools of thought that provide rich theoretical and empirical resources that are highly relevant to developing falsifiable research tools for exploring the nature of totalitarian religion. For instance, contemporary psychiatric diagnostic categories, as expressed for instance in the *Diagnostic and Statistical Manual of Mental Disorders* (*DSM-IV*), describe the whole range of personality disorders (e.g., borderline, narcissistic, and schizoid), as being centrally defined by the characteristic of *splitting*, that is, rigidly dividing the world into all bad and all good categories, as well as other characteristics that tend to be associated with splitting; that is, tendencies to all or nothing emotional reorganization, identity confusion, a polarized self-sense, extrapunitiveness, and so on. All of these related personality characteristics are features that Adorno et al., Erikson, Lifton, and other authors and researchers within the totalitarian influence tradition found to be characteristic of those people likely to be influenced by totalitarian ideology.

Also, schools of contemporary psychoanalysis – for example, object relations theory and self-psychology – tends to take these same characteristics as central to contemporary theories of psychopathology and therapy. In object relations theory, the concept of the *paranoid schizoid position* describes an arrested state of development characterized by splitting, as well as the other features associated with a predisposition to being influenced by totalitarian ideologies.

In addition, the object relations concept of *projective identification*, which is viewed as characteristic of those stuck in the paranoid schizoid state of development, is useful in explaining the tendencies of those attracted to totalitarian ideologies to project their disowned qualities onto scapegoats, and to interact with such contrast individuals or groups in such a way that they trigger the very actions and attitudes of which they are accusing them. These related object relations concepts thus may be useful in generating public policy guidelines which could help agencies to interact with totalistic groups more skilfully, and perhaps avoid triggering tragedies such as happened in Jonestown or Waco. (It is possible that such tragedies occurred partially as a result of unskilful government confrontations with these groups, rationalized by brainwashing formulations.) See Anthony and Robbins (1995b) for an attempt to integrate these contemporary psychodynamic and diagnostic concepts in modifying and expanding the totalism and authoritarianism ideas so as to make them more relevant to developing a critical theory of contemporary experiential religions.

Other theoretical schools are also relevant to developing such a critical theory. For instance, there is a tradition of thought which explains stages of cultural development in terms that are very similar to how object relations theorists explain personality development. See Webb 1993, Burkett 1983, Joy 1992, and Girard 1972, 1987, for discussions of related theories which describe more primitive levels of cultural development in terms that are very similar to the concepts of splitting, the paranoid-schizoid position, projective identification, and so on, which are central to both object relations and totalitarian influence theories of psychological and social pathology.

See also (1) attempts within the history of religion to differentiate genuinely transcendent from regressive religious experiences and conversions (Zaehner 1957); (2) attempts within transpersonal psychology (e.g., Wilber 1987) to distinguish so-called *trans-rational* from *pre-rational* contemporary alternative religions; and (3) a rich research tradition within the psychology of religion which attempts to differenti-

ate benevolent religious conversions and commitments from pathological ones (Koenig 1977; Pullum 1989). Some of this research literature in
the psychology of religion is based upon the use of totalitarian influence concepts and measures, for example, authoritarianism and dogmatism. (Altemeyer 1988: 200–38; Anthony and Robbins 1995b: 23–7;
Rokeach 1970; Kirkpatrick et al. 1991).

Brainwashing Ideology as Totalism: Apostate Tales
There remains one additional finding of research upon new religions,
which, to my mind, the totalitarian influence approach accounts for
more convincingly than does the brainwashing explanation. It is well
established that a certain percentage of ex-members of new religions,
primarily those who have some involvement in the anticult movement,
view themselves as formerly having been brainwashed and thus as
formerly having converted and remained committed to a new religion
for some time against their will. On the other hand, former members of
new religious movements who do not become affiliated with the anticult movement tend not to view themselves as having been brainwashed. (See Dawson, this volume, for an overview of the research
literature on this topic.)

As we have seen, brainwashing is an interpretive rather than an
empirical concept; it is not falsifiable, and cannot be conclusively disconfirmed on empirical grounds.[42] This fact is consistent with the finding that people may be exposed to the same empirical situation –
conversion to and membership in a particular new religious movement
– and yet radically disagree about whether they were brainwashed or
not, and also about whether their membership in the religion was
intentional or against their will.

On these facts, both authors whose subject is brainwashing and
NRM scholars critical of the brainwashing explanation agree. However, they explain them differently. NRM scholars view these findings
as an indication that the brainwashing claims of ex-members result
from their socialization into the anticult movement and are adopted as
an exculpatory mechanism for re-entering mainstream institutions
without being blamed for having rejected them in the first place.
Brainwashing authors adopt various explanations for defending the
scientific accuracy of the brainwashing claims of some ex-members; for
example, some members of the same group were brainwashed and
some were not, or ex-members associated with the anticult movement
have learned to understand their past memberships correctly, whereas

those not associated with it remain in denial about why they were members in the first place.

However, I would suggest yet another way of viewing this data about discrepant interpretations of responsibility for former membership in new religions. This approach is more consistent with the one sketched above advocated by new religious scholars than it is with the one offered by brainwashing authors, but it integrates the NRM resocialization explanation with the totalitarian influence tradition. My idea is that the anticult movement itself, and the brainwashing ideology which rationalizes it, have many of the characteristics that the totalitarian influence tradition describes as characteristic of totalistic organizations and ideologies.

For instance, like other totalitarian ideologies, brainwashing formulations are highly dualistic; that is, they divide the world into their version of the saved and the damned. Only non-brainwashed people are really people, whereas brainwashed people are non-people with *shadow selves* because they lack the essential characteristics of authentic personhood, that is, rationality and free will. (Erikson refers to this tendency of totalistic ideologies to dualistically divide humanity into people and non-people as 'pseudo-speciation,' a terminology Lifton also sometimes adopts.)

Other totalistic characteristics of anticult brainwashing ideology and the social movement for which it provides a dualistic worldview include (1) a bias in favour of cultural uniformity and a definition of alternative worldviews as heretical, irrational and unworthy of respect (see Langone 1986; Singer 1976, 1984, Anthony 1990, Anthony and Robbins 1995a); (2) attempts to enforce a uniform worldview within the culture by extending state power and evading the absolute protection of freedom of religious belief, and (3) willingness to use physical force to suppress heretical beliefs (e.g., forcible deprogrammings, conservatorships, etc.). (Lifton himself has suggested that at least some of these practices and beliefs within the anticult movement are totalistic (Lifton 1987: 219).

Hunter's original formulation of the brainwashing idea was quite explicit about this pseudo-speciation characteristic of the brainwashing ideology, describing brainwashed individuals as insects or machines rather than genuine people. In their published formulations, brainwashing authors tend to be more restrained in making these assertions, qualifying them in various ways to escape criticism. But even in such ambiguous publications, the robot or zombie imagery tends to leak through, although often in modified form, as in Zablocki's claim that brainwashed people are characterized by 'glassy eyes' and a 'hollow beaming smile' (1980: 332), and that while undergoing the brainwashing process converts to new religions 'resemble zombies or robots' (1998a: 232).

If I am correct about brainwashing ideology being a form of totalitarian influence, it would presumably serve the function of ministering to a polarized self-sense and curing identity confusion by enabling converts to it to shift responsibility for undesirable aspects of their personalities and former behaviour onto a scapegoated contrast category, in this case the new religious movement of which they were formerly a member. As we saw above, Erikson described those individuals characterized by totalism as having a predisposition to undergo 'all or nothing emotional reorganization' of a dualistic type, and thus they tend to be relatively fickle with respect to their allegiances.

In addition, much research in the totalistic influence tradition has indicated that those with totalistic/authoritarian personal characteristics tend to be highly ambivalent towards authority even while they are conforming to its demands. What better way for a totalistic person who has affiliated with the anticult movement to act out the hostile pole of such ambivalence than by suing their former authority figures and reference group.

Of course, because totalism is a characteristic of individuals as well as groups, it is quite possible for one reason or another for a totalistic person to be a member of a non-totalistic group. Given the tendency of totalistic persons to undergo all or nothing emotional reorganization, and given the irrefutable, non-falsifiable character of brainwashing allegations, it is quite likely that at least some of the legal actions based upon anticult brainwashing formulations are brought by a totalistic person against a non-totalistic group. My impression is that this has been true in a number of the cases in which I have served as an expert or consultant.

As I have said above, even in those cases in which a totalistic person is suing a totalistic group, from the totalitarian influence perspective the essential premise of such actions (i.e., involuntary conversion and commitment) is not really present. Consequently, freedom of belief and practice should be protected by constitutional safeguards, even when it is totalistic or authoritarian belief and practice that is at issue. This is all the more obvious when it is realized that totalism/authoritarianism, either that of an individual or of a group, is not an either/or characteristic, and that almost any human organization or individual is totalistic to some degree and in some circumstances.

Conclusion of the Conclusion: Future Prospects for Totalitarian Research on NRMs.
While extreme forms of totalism/authoritarianism may be associated with undesirable social or personal consequences, according to some authorities, such as W. Erikson (1954), such tendencies may also have positive consequences in some situations (e.g., as a temporary cure for identity disorder), while the person develops the inner resources to achieve a more mature form of selfhood. It seems likely that totalism/ authoritarianism in NRMs has unequivocally harmful consequences only when combined with other variables, some of which are being explored in the current literature on features associated with the occurrence of violence in contemporary religious groups (Anthony and Robbins 1997).

I don't wish to give the impression that any of the hypotheses I am discussing about the possible utility of totalitarian influence theories in helping to develop a critical theory of new religions are definitive or set in stone. I am making these suggestions as heuristic devices intended to serve as stimuli to further research. These are very complicated and subtle matters, and it seems to me that we are at a relatively early stage in their scientific exploration.

It does seem quite clear, however, that the appropriation of totalitarian influence theory and research as the theoretical foundation for brainwashing formulations is mistaken. The brainwashing concept has been an ideological weapon rather than a falsifiable scientific theory in all the contexts in which it has been advocated as an explanation for worldview resocialization. I do not think that its ideological character is likely to change.

Totalitarian influence theories, on the other hand, have served as the basis for interesting scientific research, and they may yet play a productive role in aiding our understanding of why new religions sometimes aid the benevolent transformation of individuals, and sometimes have less desirable consequences.

Notes

1 Generally, in this chapter, I have adopted the convention of designating brainwashing perspectives as 'formulations' because they do not have the

generally accepted characteristics of scientific theories, e.g., clarity of meaning, flasifiability, testability, etc. 'Formulation' seems to me to be a more
appropriate term than 'theory' because it is consistent with the variability
in relation to tactical considerations in concrete contexts which, as I will
argue below, characterizes brainwashing perspectives.

2 My assessment of Benjamen Zablocki's brainwashing formulation is not
based upon his article in this volume, which I had not see prior to my writing of this article. However, as part of the format for the preparation of our
article in this book, he and I engaged in a dialogue comparing our respective approaches to evaluating the scientific standing of the cultic brainwashing perspective over a period of about a year and a half. This dialogue
was carried on through long e-mail messages, telephone conversations, and
one five-hour meeting. During this dialogue, most of my criticisms of his
previous 'brainwashing publications' were discussed directly with him,
and my treatment of them herein reflects these discussions as well as my
review of his prior publications on this topic. Presumably his chapter in this
volume reflects these discussions as well.

3 Zablocki's attempted clarification of the brainwashing concept and his
defense of its scientific status have influenced some scholars. See Allen
1998–99, throughout; and Davis 2000: 242. On the other hand, Zablocki's
recent articles have received some criticism. See Bromley 1998, and
Zablocki's reply, 1998b.

4 Zablocki states: 'Many of the harshest critics of the brainwashing conjecture
assume it to be an evaluative concept for the existence of which it is impossible, even in principle, to marshal empirical evidence' (1997: 101).

5 Zablocki explains the development and use of a distorted definition of
brainwashing and a misinterpretation of the research literature that supports his correct definition of brainwashing thusly:

> How may we explain *this shift in the definition of brainwashing* from a con-
> cern with difficulty in extricating oneself after joining to a concern with
> deception in recruitment before joining? I believe it *is an example of how
> the debased currency of litigation can all too easily drive out the honest currency
> of science.* Lucrative stipends to expert witnesses were offered by mem-
> bers of both sides of this dispute in court cases involving allegations of
> deception in recruiting. And so it came to be in the mutual interest of
> both extreme camps in this debate to perpetuate a common distortion of
> the phenomenon, while at the same time arguing in favour of opposite
> positions as to whether or not the phenomenon itself was real or an illu-
> sion. (Zablocki 1997: 100, emphasis mine)

Zablocki seems to be saying in this passage that both expert witnesses who are proponents of the cultic brainwashing explanation of involvement in new religions, and those who are critics of the brainwashing perspective, offer an incorrect definition of the brainwashing idea, not because they believe it but because their professional integrity and honesty have been compromised by the fact of their having been paid for their testimony. In traditional logic and rhetoric, this claim would be viewed as an *ad hominem* argument, considered to be a 'logical fallacy' because it tends to be used as a replacement for an actual demonstration of the incorrectness of the argument that is being criticized.

In addition, his reasoning that service as an expert witness necessarily distorts the expression of scientific opinion, and that payment for such services necessarily distorts the content of such opinion, if correct, would seem generally to invalidate the integrity and competence of the related professions of forensic psychology and forensic psychiatry, and the other forensic specialties as well. Such forensic professions have their own divisions within leading professional associations (e.g., the American Psychological Association and the American Psychiatric Association) and their own professional journals. They also offer advanced degrees and training in university departments, and provide their members with standards intended to insure the objectivity and correctness of the evaluations of scientific arguments provided by their members in a courtroom setting.

Thus, Zablocki's sweeping generalization about the 'debased currency of litigation' driving out the 'honest currency of science' is a rather large claim that conflicts with the claims to professional standards and competence within these professions. His argument calls into question the possibility of noble motives and the expression of honest opinions by all professionals who are paid for their services in a legal context, and as such seems too general to provide much help in evaluating the criticisms of brainwashing perspectives offered in a courtroom setting by myself and other experts. At a minimum his argument would require considerably more elaboration than he gives in these articles before it could be taken seriously as a defence and justification of his own brainwashing formulation. See the conclusion of this chapter for further commentary on this issue.

6 As a psychologist at the University of North Carolina at Chapel Hill, Department of Psychiatry, and later at the Center for Research on New Religions in Berkeley, I supervised research programs on alternative religious movements funded by government agencies (e.g., the National Institute of Mental Health, the National Institute of Drug Abuse, the National Endowment for the Humanities), and by private philanthropic organizations such

as the Ford, Rockefeller, and San Francisco Foundations. Since 1981 I have also conducted a private forensic psychology practice specializing in cases involving minority religions and other organizations accused of so-called brainwashing, or other forms of coercive influence. I have served as an expert and/or consultant both in criminal and civil cases, and both for the defence and the prosecution.

7 Prior to the beginning of our dialogue and the writing of our pieces for this volume, Zablocki had repudiated the scientific standing of my totalitarian influence perspective. He states: 'Most of the scholarship during this period [1987–1997] was nothing more than cultural interpretation with the goal of deconstructing and thereby marginalizing opposing points of view'. (1997: 112). In note 59, in which he gives examples of such 'cultural interpretation,' he includes my 1990 article, which has been the primary basis for legal briefs intended to exclude cultic brainwashing testimony from being presented in court. He also includes an article by Thomas Robbins and I, 'Religious Totalism, Violence and Exemplary Dualism: Beyond the Extrinsic Model (Anthony and Robbins 1995b), as well as articles by other scholars such as J. Gordon Melton and James Lewis. Apparently, by referring to these articles as 'cultural interpretation' intended only to marginalize opposing points of view, he means that they are not actually meaningful as statements of social or behavioural science. It is hard to know why Zablocki dismisses their scientific value, since he does not expand upon his dismissal of them beyond his one sentence critique. I don't think this judgment is correct with respect to my 1990 article or these other publications for reasons that are too complicated to state in a note, but should become evident during the course of this chapter.

   In addition, this evaluation of Robbins's and my 1995 article is particularly difficult for me to understand. This article consists primarily of an attempt to integrate the totalism concept with other types of social scientific theory and research, e.g., contemporary psychoanalytic theory and psychology of religion research, in the service of developing a synthesis that would be useful as the theoretical foundation for research on violence and other problematic aspects of new religions.

8 I am aware that Zablocki, at a certain point of his recent brainwashing articles, claims that his version of cultic brainwashing theory is not intended to demonstrate that brainwashing overwhelms 'free will.' (Zablocki 1997: 102). On the other hand, at many other points he claims that brainwashing produces involuntary belief and behaviour. See discussion below for many examples of such claims by Zablocki. Such contradictions, especially on this key point, constitute a characteristic of brainwashing arguments that

I refer to as 'tactical ambiguity'; see below for a fuller discussion of this concept.

9 The view of the brainwashing concept as originating through research conducted by German and American intelligence agencies is quite well documented at present. However, from its inception in the 1940s until the American research petered out in the early 1970s, the existence of such brainwashing research was a closely guarded secret by both American and German intelligence agencies (Marks 1980: 11). In the aftermath of the widespread criticism of CIA covert operations in the 1960s, and after the passage of the U.S. Freedom of Information Act in 1974 (Ranelagh 1986: 11, 12, 845), researchers and journalists were able to ferret out a fairly complete picture of such research. The best general overviews of such research include *The Mind Manipulators* by Scheflin and Opton (1978: especially chaps. 3, 4, 5, 11) and *The Search for the Manchurian Candidate* by John Marks (1980 throughout) The Scheflin and Opton book is more complete, but the Marks book is better organized and easier to absorb. Briefer but still valuable overviews of such research also are presented in *Acid Dreams*, by Martin Lee and Bruce Shlain (1985, especially chap. 1) and in *The Agency: The Rise and Decline of the CIA*, by John Ranelagh (1986; 1987, especially p. 216).

10 Drugs were, from the beginning, at the centre of German and American mind-control research focused upon creating technology-based enhancements to interrogation methods. Such drug-based interrogation methods were also actually used in field operations. (Ranelagh 1987, 205: Scheflin and Opton 1978, 132, 149–50; Lee and Schlain 1985, XVI–XXI, 23–48).

11 Explicit research on sensory deprivation in the laboratory was a natural, putatively scientific attempt to measure the effect, in an intensified and purified form, of isolation and solitary confinement of individuals during interrogation, a process known to be a prominent feature of Communist (and American, cf. Marks 1980: 145–6) interrogation methods, e.g., during the Moscow show trials. Such research is described by Lee and Schlain 1985: 39, and Marks 1980: 137–8, 143, 148. According to Scheflin and Opton, many of the hundreds of mind-control research projects on hypnosis were carried out in conjunction with sensory deprivation and/or drugs (1978: 149). Scheflin and Opton also refer to voluminous CIA-funded research on sensory deprivation (104), and give references to some of the published literature resulting from that research in n. 247, p. 494.

12 According to Marks (1980: 26), an ambitious mind-control research program utilizing electroshock was conducted with unwitting mental patients (133–6). Scheflin and Opton (1978: 387–92) describe this research as

attempting to convert 'deviants,' e.g., homosexuals, drug abusers, political dissidents, and youthful drug abusers to normality (360).

13 See Anthony (1990: 317–22) for examples and discussion of Margaret Singer's statements condemning new religions on ideological rather than behavioural grounds. See Anthony and Robbins (1995a: 524–34) for examples of testimony in religious brainwashing cases which attack religious beliefs rather than behaviour as evidence of brainwashing. See Langone 1986, 1994, 1993a, 1993b, for publications arguing that new religions are objectionable because their theologies conflict with traditional American values and beliefs. (Langone is executive director of the American Family Foundation, which is the leading anticult organization, an organization which promotes the cultic brainwashing perspective as its primary ideology).

   Later, I will argue that Zablocki's brainwashing formulation is actually in line with Langone's, Singer's, Ofshe's, and other anticult brainwashing formulations in being covertly targeted at new religious beliefs rather than at scientifically testable coercive conduct.

14 Although I refer to the ambiguity of cultic brainwashing as tactical, I do not thereby intend to claim that their creators are consciously altering them according to tactical characteristics of situations with full awareness that they are doing so. Rather I think that such theories are 'theoretically incoherent,' and as a result their creators apply them to the best of their ability to specific situations without being conscious that they are using such incoherence in this tactical way. My impression is that such unconsciously tactical character of such theoretically incoherent theories is characteristic of the putatively scientific ideologies which Popper refers to as 'pseudoscientific.'

15 On p. 223 Zablocki quotes Lifton as arguing that cults produce 'doubling' in their converts: 'Intense milieu control can contribute to a dramatic change of identity which I call "doubling": the formation of a second self which lives side by side with the former one, often for a considerable period of time' (Lifton 1993: 2). I am not sure what Lifton intended his readers to understand by this statement, but he could not accurately be claiming, as Zablocki interprets him as claiming, that his 'doubling' concept is equivalent to the brainwashing notion of a false or shadow self. Lifton developed the concept of *doubling* – he meant the simultaneous existence of two radically dissimilar selves in the same person, selves which would express themselves in contradictory manners in different social contexts – to account for the behaviour of Nazi doctors who engaged in inhumane medical research in a professional context, but who were, during the same

period humane and decent individuals with their families (Lifton 1986; 1987: 195–208).

Doubling, as Lifton defines it may be seen as an extreme example of the very different interpersonal styles which people in modern industrialized nations express in their professional and their personal lives. In the former they may be highly competitive (and metaphorically bloodthirsty) capitalists, whereas in the personal context they may be humane and loving. The difference in ethical and interpersonal character of the same people in the economic vs. the personal spheres is a much remarked upon characteristic of modern societies, and has served as a central organizing principle of major sociological theories, e.g., those of Parsons 1951 and Habermas (1984, 1987).

On the other hand, the conception of the false or shadow self proposed by Zablocki and other brainwashing theorists is very different from the concept of doubling, in that it involves the notion of a new but inauthentic self which replaces the original and authentic self rather than living side by side with it at the same time in the same person. If the brainwashed person as described by Zablocki, Singer, and other cult brainwashing theorists were characterized by doubling, they should be able to move smoothly back and forth between the cult and the pre-cult or familial contexts without apparent difficulty. But Zablocki and his cohorts describe the brainwashed person as being unable to do this except with great difficulty. See for instance Zablocki's discussion of what he refers to as the 'shadow self imbued with the cult ideology,' on pp. 236 and 237 of his 1998 article. See also West and Martin 1994.

Doubling as Lifton defines it, no matter how extreme, could not reasonably be interpreted as implying the involuntary, compulsive, or addictive attachment to a false self that Zablocki imputes to it. According to Lifton, doubling is the normal means by which people choose to engage in immoral activity. As such it is voluntarily chosen by the person rather than being imposed upon him/her by an external agent or institution. In addressing the involuntariness issue relative to the doubling concept, Lifton says:

In sum, doubling is the psychological means by which one invokes the evil potential of the self. That evil is neither inherent in the self nor foreign to it. To live out the doubling and call forth the evil is a moral choice for which one is responsible, whatever the level of consciousness involved. By means of doubling, Nazi doctors made a Faustian choice for evil: in the process of doubling, in fact, lies an overall key to human evil. (1986: 423 – Lifton repeats this statement in his 1987 article, p. 201).

16 Disorientation has an accepted and well-defined scientific meaning only
within two interrelated scientific fields: psychiatry and neurology. In these
fields, disorientation refers only to the specific lack of awareness of one's
identity, the time and date, and one's geographical location. See Campbell
1981: 180, 434. See also *Webster's Unabridged Dictionary*, 1996, for 'disorient
Psychiatry: to cause to lose perception of time, place or one's personal identify.' In these definitions, personal identity refers only to literal awareness
of one's name and of one's status as a specific psychological/physical
entity with a specific physical and social history. It does not refer to the sub-
tler and more controversial discontinuities in selfhood which are alleged to
be a consequence of brainwashing. Testing for 'orientation' with respect to
personal identity, place, and time is generally the first test conducted in a
standard psychiatric interview or mental status examination. Disorientation in this sense is considered to indicate that the patient is suffering from
a neurological rather than a psychological disorder, e.g., one of the senile
dementias, or a toxic brain condition induced by drugs or physical disease.

   In defining brainwashing as a process that is accomplished primarily by
means of disorientation, Zablocki appears to be giving the disorientation
term a more metaphorical and less precise meaning than its scientific meaning in psychiatry, as a way of disputing the allegedly transcendent or mystical character of the altered states of consciousness in which religious
influence often occurs. In this less precise form, however, disorientation is
an evaluative rather than a scientific term, as it is unfalsifiable. Thus used,
the term has no clear operational definition such that its presence could be
disconfirmed in research on the conversion process. In discussing this issue
with Zablocki, he also was unable to give me a precise scientific definition
for his usage, such that its absence in a specific instance could be empirically determined, and he questioned whether the term has the restricted
meaning in psychiatry which I have specified above. However, he also was
unable to give me a citation to any other well-accepted and falsifiable usage
in psychiatry or any other science.

   As I have indicated, in psychiatry or neurology lack of orientation with
respect to person, place, and time is considered to be diagnostic of some
form of organic brain dysfunction, as opposed to the sorts of mental disease
that have social-environmental and psychodynamic causes. In the latter
part of his 1998 article, Zablocki claims that brainwashing has an organic
basis (neuroendocrinological or neurophysiological), and thus is distinguishable from other forms of social influence on this basis. In using the
term *disorientation* rather than *hypnosis* or *trance*, Zablocki may have been
implying this speculative organic basis for brainwashing. As I will discuss

below, he bases his hopes that the brainwashing concept will some day be falsifiable on the assumption that it has a distinctively organic basis. However, as he admits in that section, he cannot provide any scientific or empirically falsifiable basis for this speculation, and his vague and unfalsifiable use of the disorientation term seems consistent with this admission.

17 Zablocki does supply a scientific citation for his use of the term. On page 237 of his 1998 brainwashing article he claims that Orne's 1972 article reports research demonstrating that people *can be hypnotized to do things against their will.'* As I will discuss below, however, Orne's article demonstrates findings which are exactly the opposite of the conclusion that Zablocki imputes to it; that is, Orne's research demonstrated that *hypnosis cannot be used to get people to do things against their will.* In Zablocki's case, as is typical for brainwashing theorists, the terms for primitive consciousness viewed as essential for brainwashing are either so vaguely defined that they are unfalsifiable, or when they are defined through a claimed basis in scientific research that research is misinterpreted.

18 In his 1980 book Zablocki describes the disorientation and cognitive deficiency which he believes to be characteristic of the imposition of the brainwashed state thusly:

> The *cognitive disorder* associated with type 5, or absolute, charisma is submissiveness. The common manifestations of this among cult members, *the glassy eyes, the hollow beaming smile,* are too well known to need examples here. As many accounts of cult experiences have indicated (e.g., Edwards 1979), *these exaggerated symptoms of extreme cognitive submissiveness (turning off the mind)* are a conditioned response, among cult members, to any challenge to the absolute truth of the cult reality. (1980: 332, emphasis mine)

On the next page Zablocki describes the transition of a group from being a legitimate Christian group to a brainwashed cult:

> It was at this time also that *the glassy-eyed, frozen smile look* began to appear on the faces of the Waystation members. In terms of our model this was a symptom of a crisis of *self-estrangement.* A sense of legitimate total commitment to the charismatic leader had given way *to an artificial forced total commitment, maintained only through adherence to the mind-emptying discipline of submissiveness'* (Zablocki 1980: 333, emphasis mine).

In his 1998 article Zablocki acknowledges that research has demonstrated that such disorientation and defective cognition are not characteristic of allegedly brainwashed members of so-called cults (232), but he attempts to get around this by claiming that these qualities are only essential characteristics of cult converts during the process of brainwashing, rather than after they have been successfully brainwashed: 'The popular association of brainwashing with zombie or robot states comes out of a confusion between the physical characteristics of people *going through* the brainwashing process and the characteristics of those who have completed the process' (232, emphasis his). In his earlier book, however, he appears to be saying that such cognitive defects are continuing characteristics of cult members, i.e., 'an artificial forced total commitment, maintained only through adherence to the mind-emptying discipline of submissiveness.' It is likely that this shift (from viewing disorientation and extreme cognitive defects as essential to the ongoing maintenance of brainwashed 'forced total commitment' to the cult, to viewing disorientation and extreme cognitive defects as characteristic only of the process of brainwashing but not of continuing commitment to the cult) is an example of tactical ambiguity in the face of disconfirming evidence.

19 The brainwashing notion as applied to religion seems an aspect of a centuries-old conflict, beginning with the enlightenment, between secularized models of idealized rational consciousness, identities, and worldviews on the one hand, and models of optimal consciousness, identities, and worldviews that prioritize experiential religious states of consciousness on the other. See Armstrong 2000 for a book-length account of this conflict. According to Armstrong, in the United States this conflict has played out primarily in relation to Evangelical Christian groups which emphasize the 'born again' conversion experience as the mark of being 'saved.' (However, Armstrong views the renaissance of experiential religiosity in the United States since the 1960s as simply the current version of this centuries-old conflict. According to Armstrong, this 'third great awakening' has included Asian and *de novo* religions, quasi-religious therapeutic movements, the revival of evangelical/born again Christianity, and also the various social critiques of this efflorescence, such as the brainwashing ideology of the anticult movement.)

In the nineteenth century, during one period of this conflict described by Armstrong, American nativists attacked Mormons, Catholics, and Masons for engaging in the mind control of their members in terms that are very similar to the contemporary cult brainwashing formulations of Zablocki and others (Davis 1960: 28; Cox 1978: 127). (See Robbins and Anthony 1979 for a discussion of the parallels between the nativist religious mind-control formulation of the nineteenth century and current anticult brainwashing formulation.)

Most relevantly to the CIA and other contemporary brainwashing formulation, nineteenth-century mind-control formulations were focused primarily upon the hypothesis that religious brainwashing created addictive
attachments by inducing trance states in which victims were highly suggestible and powerless to resist new worldviews and a new, false self. See
Taves's 1999 book *Fits, Trances, and Visions: Experiencing Religion and
Explaining Experience from Wesley to James* for a fascinating and very detailed
book-length account of the nineteenth- and early twentieth-century use of
mind-control formulations emphasizing 'hypnosis' and 'dissociation' for
disputing the authenticity and voluntariness of evangelical 'born again'
and other religious conversions that centrally involved altered states of
consciousness.

See also Jenkins's book-length account of the interplay between experiential religious movements and anticult movements in American history (Jenkins 2000). According to Jenkins, beginning in the early nineteenth-century
such historical anticult movements anticipated the CIA brainwashing theory and the contemporary anticult movement in every respect, e.g., claiming that the induction of hypnotic trance and other dissociative states
resulted in the involuntary conversion and commitment of participants in
such movements. Jenkins states: 'Every element of the modern anticult
polemic was a familiar component of American culture by about 1840, and
the critique was powerfully reinforced from the upsurge of outré religious
groups between about 1830 and 1860' (2000: 31).

20 By *wholeness* Erikson refers to a quality of the personality in which the often
repressed, rejected poles of the opposites of experience (e.g., aggressive-
ness) have remained, or become, conscious. Therefore, they are not available for projection onto scapegoated contrast categories and do not lead to
the persecution of minorities and other cultures which are treated as *the
enemy* within a dualistic worldview. Erikson's affirmation of the desirability
of wholeness as an antidote to totalism/authoritarianism is part of a tradition of thought in the social sciences, i.e., holism, which has links to *dialectical* perspectives in philosophy, e.g., existentialism, phenomenology,
hermeneutics, or deconstructionism, and to mystical orientations in religion. See Phillips 1976 for discussions of holistic traditions in social and
behavioural science.

21 Erikson states:

It would be wise to abstain from considering this totalism a merely
regressive or infantile mechanism. It is an alternate, if more primitive,
way of dealing with experience, and thus has, at least in transitory states,

a certain adjustment and survival value. It belongs to normal psychology. Any possible psychiatric inquiry is restricted to these questions: Can the transient means of emergency adjustment be prevented from becoming fixed ends? Can totalism reverse itself when the emergency is over? Can its elements be resynthesized in a wholeness which is then possible?

22 Erikson states: 'Only in passing do I wish to make reference here to that aspect of infantile development which in the psychoanalytic literature on totalitarianism has received the greatest, if not an exclusive emphasis: I mean that infantile [Oedipal] period (around the age of five) when the child gets ready to develop not only a more goal-directed and rebellious initiative, but also a more organized conscience (1954: 166).' In this article, Erikson devoted only two pages to discussion of the contribution of the Oedipal period to totalism because he had already expressed himself at greater length on this topic (1942), and also because he considered his own point of view on this topic to be in essential agreement with that of Adorno et al. (1950), Fromm (1941, 1984), Reich (1970), etc. Therefore his discussion could be brief because he had nothing new to contribute on the relationship between the Oedipal period and totalism at this point. For instance, as a transition from his discussion of the Oedipus complex in totalism to his discussion of the role of the identity crisis, he says: I shall now proceed from *this relatively better-known fact* [Oedipus complex and totalism] to considerations pertaining to the end of childhood and to what seems to me the third, and more immediately political, crisis of wholeness [identity crisis] (1954: 168, emphasis mine).

23 The author's use of quotation marks around the brainwashing term in this paragraph follows Lifton's own practice, by which he intended to indicate that the brainwashing term commonly used to refer to Communist thought reform was a misleading and inaccurate way of designating the thought reform phenomenon. See below for a fuller discussion of this issue.

24 For discussions of Erikson's and Lifton's mentorship/apprenticeship relationship and its relationship to Lifton's use of the totalism concept, see Lifton 1974 and 1961: xii–xiii; Anthony 1996: 209–10; Mazlish 1987; and Friedman 1996, 1999.

25 Also following Erikson, and Frenkel-Brunswick (1949, 1951, 1954), Lifton locates the cause of the development of such a totalistic, polarized style of personality organization in early childhood socialization (Lifton 1961: 436). (For a discussion of the relationship of Frenkel-Brunswick's concept of 'intolerance of ambiguity' to Erikson's and Lifton's concept of 'totalism' and to Adorno et al.'s concept of the 'authoritarian personality,' see

Anthony 1996: 183–6 and 213–14.) Thus, there appears to be complex and intimate interconnections between the work of Erikson, Frenkel-Brunswick, and Lifton with respect to the role of child-rearing practices in the development of a polarized, all or nothing interpersonal style, which all three of them see as the essence of the predisposition to convert to totalitarian ideologies.

26 The terminology and concepts of a 'strong susceptibility to guilt, confusion of identity, and most important of all, a long-standing pattern of [individual] totalism' were all key concepts in the article in which Erikson originally defined totalism. As with the term and concept of 'totalism,' Erikson originated the concepts of and terms for 'negative identity,' 'identity confusion,' 'crisis of identity,' and 'negative conscience,' which Lifton uses throughout his discussion of individual totalistic tendencies in his subjects. Erikson was also responsible for the psychoanalytic development of the concept of 'ego identity,' which is central to both his and Lifton's analysis of totalism. Erikson and Lifton also both made the concept of 'splitting,' or 'split identity,' central to their analysis of totalism. Nine entries for the specifically Eriksonian concept of 'negative identity' are given in the index to Lifton's book, eight entries to the related Eriksonian concepts of identity crisis and identity diffusion, six references to the concept of splitting, a key reference to the concept of negative conscience, and eighty-five additional entries to the concept of identity that is generally used in the psychoanalytic sense, which originated with Erikson (Lifton 1961: 505–10).

The key role of Eriksonian concepts in Lifton's analysis of thought reform is illustrated by the paragraph summarizing his book, on the back cover of the 1989 quality paperback edition. The first sentence of this overview of the book is as follows: '*Informed by Erik Erikson's concept of the formation of ego identity,* this book, which first appeared in 1961, is an analysis of the experiences of fifteen Chinese citizens and twenty-five Westerners who underwent "brainwashing" by the Communist Chinese government' (emphasis mine).

27 The theoretical conflict of cultic brainwashing perspectives with the Lifton/Erikson psychoanalytic theory of psychological totalism is illustrated by a recent book co-authored by Richard Ofshe (Watters and Ofshe 1999), whose articles on brainwashing Zablocki describes (like his own brainwashing articles) as being based upon the theoretical foundation of the Lifton/Erikson theory. Ofshe's co-authored book is an extended critique of psychoanalytic theory and other similar psychodynamic perspectives. (Ofshe perceives psychoanalytic theory as wholly false and attributes its influence to a social influence process which in his eyes is essentially iden-

tical to cultic brainwashing [136–42, 159–92]. This raises the question of how Ofshe's claim that his brainwashing articles and testimony are based upon the theoretical foundation of the Erikson/Lifton psychoanalytic theory could possibly be accurate, given his sweeping opposition to psychoanalytic theories of human development. Zablocki's endorsement of Ofshe's cultic brainwashing theory as essentially equivalent to his own, raises also the question of whether his own brainwashing articles are actually in conflict with the Lifton/Erikson theory which he claims as their theoretical foundation.

28 See Zablocki 1998n4 as well as Zablocki 1997n17.

29 Elsewhere Zablocki even more unequivocally makes the claim that the brainwashing term (and presumably other terms for the CIA model, such as menticide) are synonymous with Lifton's thought reform term:

> My concern is with the [brainwashing] concept and I don't care what word is used to describe it. In fact, in my earliest work on the subject (a study of the Bruderhof)), I described the phenomenon without using the word *brainwashing* at all. Instead I used the *synonymous term 'thought reform'* favoured by Robert Lifton in his foundational work on the subject. Many *synonymous terms for roughly the same phenomenon* can be found in the literature. (1997: 105)

It is clear in this passage that Zablocki is asserting not only that the brainwashing term and its variants, such as *menticide*, are synonymous with the term 'thought reform,' but also that the brainwashing and thought reform models ('roughly the same phenomenon') are equivalent also.

30 Elsewhere (1997n30) Zablocki claims that Ofshe's (1974, 1976, 1992) and Ofshe's and Singer's (1986) publications also are compatible with the foundational scholarship of which he approves.

31 Note 43 in this passage cites Hunter's *Brainwashing in Red China* (1951) as an example of the robot brainwashing paradigm that, Zablocki acknowledges, misleadingly claimed that Communist indoctrination practices could 'rob people of free will.' However, Zablocki doesn't mention that the brainwashing term itself was coined by Hunter, and that virtually all respected researchers on Communist practices repudiated both the term and the CIA paradigm to which it referred.

32 The assertion in this passage that the goal of the brainwashing is to create 'deployable agents' implicitly contradicts Zablocki's assertion in the same passage that brainwashing is not concerned with the issue of free will. The deployable agent term is used only by advocates of the CIA brainwashing model and indicates that the person so designated has become an involun-

tary mental prisoner of the group to which he is committed. See below and Anthony (1996: 58–127).

33 Schein states: 'the coercive element in coercive persuasion is paramount (forcing the individual into a situation in which he must, in order to survive physically and psychologically, expose himself to persuasive attempts' [1959: 437]). Notice that Schein says 'physically *and* psychologically,' not 'physically *or* psychologically,' thus establishing that, in his mind, physical coercion is a necessary component of distinctively involuntary coercive persuasion.

34 See Anthony (1990: 317–22) for examples and discussion of Margaret Singer's statements condemning new religions on ideological rather than behavioural grounds. See Anthony and Robbins 1995a: 524–34 for examples of testimony in religious brainwashing cases which attacks religious beliefs rather than behaviour as evidence of brainwashing. See Langone 1986, 1993a, 1993b, 1994, for publications arguing that new religions are objectionable because their theologies conflict with traditional American values and beliefs. (Michael Langone is the executive director of the American Family Foundation, which is the leading anticult movement organization, and is the editor of its *Cultic Studies Journal*, the leading publication promoting the cultic brainwashing perspective. Margaret Singer has long served on the board of advisors of the journal published by this organization, and Richard Ofshe also served on the journal's board of advisers for a number of years.) In one of his articles on this topic Langone states: 'I make no apologies for evaluating cults in terms of fundamental American cultural values, which I have imbibed, examined, and accepted' (1986: 159).

See also Langone 1993a, which is a transcript he edited of a discussion between himself and other American anticult figures with the Danish anticultist Johannes Aagaard. Within this discussion, Langone repudiates contemporary political correctness and multiculturalism because they allegedly cause anomie, which in turn allegedly serves as a fertile breeding ground for cults. He claims that the integrity of American culture depends upon our adherence to what is in effect an American civil religion which limits religious pluralism and toleration to Protestantism, Catholicism, and Judaism. He states:

> There are rules to pluralism. There are boundaries to [acceptable American] pluralism ... [American] pluralism is in fact a religion that has within it various strands – Protestantism, Catholicism, Judaism – but nonetheless has a common coding system ... and that pluralism is not the doctrine that says we can embrace everyone. (1993a 107)

This 1993 discussion makes clear that the primary concern of at least some American anticultists is that new religions are in conflict with traditional Western values and beliefs. See especially the introduction (Ecksteian 1986) and pages 103–12. In an article published in the same issue of his journal (Langone 1993b), which expands upon his attack on contemporary American multiculturalism in the discussion with Aagaard, Langone states:

> ... this contemporary notion of pluralism is a pseudopluralism and a 'bad' religion because it is impossible to live in good faith with its contradictory propositions ... This conceptual disorder has many destructive consequences, not the least of which is providing fertile ground for the growth and proliferation of cults ... Charismatic charlatans, frauds, and megalomaniacs need only devise a specious argument or an emotionally persuasive rhetorical system in order to win over and control minds, because these minds are either not trained or unwilling to look beneath the surface. (199)

35 For instance, Zablocki (1998a) says that all of the eight themes of totalism do not have to be present in order for an environment to be considered totalistic. Thus he doesn't provide a clear dividing line between totalistic and non-totalistic organizations, and concrete allegations of totalism by him would be difficult to falsify.

In addition, in my experience in evaluating allegations of totalism made against specific groups in brainwashing trials, the criteria brainwashing experts use for claiming that any one of the eight themes is actually present in a given environment, as well as for claiming that an environment is totalistic as a whole, are rather arbitrary and subjective, to put it mildly. Given such amorphous criteria of application, in the minds of brainwashing experts almost any environment might be considered totalistic. Thus, it is questionable whether the criteria of application of the totalism concept in its present form have been formulated explicitly enough, so that it is a falsifiable concept.

The totalism concept remains of heuristic value, but it may be that it needs to be further developed before it would be falsifiable, particularly when applied to groups as opposed to individuals. (Authoritarianism [Adorno et al. 1951] and dogmatism scales [Rokeach 1960, 1973] provide important precedents for the falsifiable application of totalitarian influence concepts to individuals.) In addition, in Lifton's original 1961 statement of it, as well as in his application of the concept in a variety of other books, he tends to treat totalism as a continuous variable with rather indefinite boundaries rather than as a qualitative, i.e., either/or, variable. It seems that in Lifton's mind, many if not most groups are totalistic to one degree or another. (See Anthony [1990: 305–7]) for indications that the totalism and coercive persuasion concepts as utilized by Lifton and Schein respectively, have broad and rather amorphous boundaries.

At any rate, as I say in the text, as far as I have been able to determine Zablocki himself has never applied the totalism concept to any of the groups upon which he has actually done research, e.g., Zablocki 1971, 1980, and neither does he spell out in any detail in his brainwashing articles how he would actually apply it in conducting research. Consequently we have no way of knowing for sure whether his actual use of the concept would achieve a falsifiable degree of rigor. Given his admission that his brainwashing formulation as a whole is not falsifiable, I think we are probably safe in assuming that he has not solved the problem of how to apply the totalism concept to groups in a falsifiable way.

36 See Anthony 2000: 449–51, for an overview of addiction research which indicates that the use of the addiction concept, in the vague sense in which Zablocki and other authors of third-stage brainwashing formulations use it, is not falsifiable.

37 In my discussion of these issues with him, Zablocki seemed surprised that the falsifiability concept was associated primarily with the philosophy of science of Karl Popper. He also seemed to misunderstand the actual meaning of the falsifiability concept, and claimed that Popper was a proponent of positivism, a perspective to which Zablocki claims allegiance, but of which Popper has been one of the most prominent critics. Zablocki's misunderstanding of Popper's falsifiability concept is further illustrated by the section of his 1998 article in which he claims to demonstrate that his brainwashing formulation is falsifiable (Zablocki 1998: 224). It is hard to know what to make of this section, since in later sections of the same article Zablocki repeatedly acknowledges that his brainwashing formulation has not described a falsifiable/testable scientific theory or model. At any rate, the examples that Zablocki gives of allegedly falsifiable predictions of his formulation of the brainwashing idea (224) clearly do not meet Popper's standard for scientifically significant falsifiability. For instance, Zablocki claims that his formulation is falsifiable because it predicts that some apostates from totalistic new religions will complain that they had been brainwashed, and that if no apostates ever complained, that would falsify the brainwashing theory. According to Popper, however, scientifically meaningful falsifiability must involve novel predictions that differentiate competing theories from each other. (Popper 1963: 33–9). Since, by Zablocki's own admission, all the competing explanations for conversion and commit-

ment to new religions acknowledge the fact that some apostates complain they had been brainwashed and also include explanations within their own frameworks of this feature of the new religions data base (Zablocki 1998: 220–1), the brainwashing explanation of such complaints by apostates clearly does not provide a falsifiable characteristic which distinguishes it from other explanations of the same empirical pattern. Thus this feature of the brainwashing explanation fails to demonstrate that it is falsifiable in a scientifically meaningful sense. And so on.

38 As indicated above, Zablocki has previously repudiated the scientific standing of the totalitarian influence perspective used in my consulting and testimony (1997: 112 and n59).

39 For instance, there is a considerable literature by NRM scholars opposed to the cultic brainwashing formulations which attempts to develop criteria that differentiate new religions which are potentially violent or have other pathological attributes from benevolent or at least benign ones. See for instance Anthony and Robbins 1998; Dawson 1998: 128–57; Galanter 1999; Hall et al. 2000; Juergensmeyer 2000; Mills 1998: 385; Robbins and Palmer 1997; Shupe 1998; and Wessinger 2000a, 2000b. There are many other examples. It would seem that contrary to Zablocki's 1997 'blacklisting' article, repudiation of the scientific status of the brainwashing concept is not correlated with unrealistically positive evaluations of minority religions, nor with a lack of involvement in research and scholarship exploring the dark side of such movements.

40 See for instance Anthony et al. 1987, which is a book-length attempt to develop criteria which can help religious 'seekers' to discriminate between benevolent and harmful minority religions. Included in the book is an eight-cell typology which describes the advantages and disadvantages of eight different types of minority religions. This book, especially the typological section, received a very favourable review in *Cultic Studies Journal*, the primary journal of the anticult movement (Brauns 1988), which indicates to me that even some anticultists regard the approach to discriminating harmful from helpful religion that I have developed as a reasonable alternative to anticult brainwashing formulations such as Zablocki's.

41 See Anthony 1989; Anthony and Ecker 1987; Anthony and Robbins 1978, 1982a, 1982b, 1995b; Robbins and Anthony 1978; Robbins and Anthony et al. 1977. The Anthony and Robbins 1995b article specifically expands and modifies the totalism concept as developed by Erikson and Lifton and applies it in an analysis of problematic factors in some contemporary new religious movements. The other articles listed apply more general totalitarian influence perspectives, e.g., that developed by the authors of *The*

Authoritarian Personality (Adorno et al. 1950), to explorations of problematic features of some new religions.

42 See Dole 1991 for a fascinating review of Stuart Wright's book describing his research on ex-members of controversial new religions. This study found that most such ex-members did not view themselves as having formerly been brainwashed. In his review Dole, without realizing it, actually makes the point that brainwashing is an interpretive rather than a falsifiable empirical concept. He points out that at least some of Wright's subjects described characteristics of their former religious commitments that participants in the anticult movement would interpret as definitive evidence that they had been brainwashed. These primarily include statements by ex-members that their former religious worldviews asserted their superiority to other worldviews, that they might not be 'saved' if they joined a different church, that they should conform to the directives of the leaders of their own religion on matters of faith and morals, etc. In the minds of most NRM scholars these are common characteristics of evangelical religions and are not uniquely associated with involuntary conversion or commitment, that is, with brainwashing. *However, in Dole's mind the view of these ex-members that they had not been brainwashed simply indicates that they are interpreting these characteristics of their former religious involvements incorrectly.* Dole states:

> *Obviously, since the defectors had not experienced exit counselling or rehabilitation, and since neither defectors nor cultists had much exposure to CAN or AFF (the leading anticult organizations at that time) they did not use terms like mind control or brainwashing.* (1991: 88)

In other words, ex-members of the same groups may have experienced the same empirical phenomena, but they interpret them differently depending on how they are taught to interpret them subsequent to their experience. In Dole's mind, then, brainwashing is not an empirical phenomenon that can be identified correctly simply by observing it firsthand. Rather its proper identification requires specialized training and rehabilitation by anticult organizations in how to interpret the raw data of one's history, which, when properly interpreted, constitute the evidence for brainwashing having occurred. In view of the highly dualistic character of the brainwashing ideology which is inculcated through such training, participation in anticult worldview resocialization processes seems more likely to constitute a conversion process than it does to constitute simple technical training in identifying a falsifiable empirical phenomenon. Dole continues: 'To sum up Wright's commitment theory and his various propo-

sitions about defection ... [are] based on an admittedly biased interpretation of raw data; yet, in fact, *if examined closely, the raw data can be construed
as consistent with theories of social control, manipulation and intense persuasion.
Far from evidence about the absence of brainwashing, examples of mind control
can be easily found in the words of the study participants'* (1991: 89–9, emphasis
mine).

In my mind, Dole's interpretation of Wright's research is more consistent
with the view that retrospective accusations of brainwashing by ex-
members result from processes of resocialization and biographical reconstruction within the anticult movement than they are with the view that
they constitute falsifiable evidence for the factual reality of the brainwashing concept. His review nicely illustrates my contention that brainwashing
formulations of religious involvement are cultural, i.e., inter-pretive, constructions rather than falsifiable scientific theories, and that the research on
attitudes of defectors from minority religions is more consistent with my
totalitarian influence viewpoint than it is with Zablocki's and other brainwashing formulations.

References

Abgrall, J.-M. 1990. *Rapport sur 'L'Eglise de Scientologie': Les techniques de la Scientologie, la doctrine Dianetique, leurs consequences médico-legales* (Report on the
Church of Scientology: The Techniques of Scientology and the Doctrine of
Dianetics, Their Medical-Legal Consequences). Submitted in 'Case for Criminal Prosecution for Fraud,' no. 90:6119074. *Isabelle Archer et al. v. Higher
Court of Marseilles* (also submitted in another case in Lyon).
– 1996. *La Mécanique des Sectes*. Paris: Documents Payot.
– 1999a. *Les sectes de l'apocalypse: Gourous de l'an 2000*. Paris: Calmann-Levy.
– 1999b. *Soul Snatchers: The Mechanism of Cults*. English translation of *La Méca-
nique des Sectes*. New York: Algora.
Adorno, T., et al. 1950. *The Authoritarian Personality*. New York: Norton.
Allen, C. 1998–99. 'Brainwashed!: Scholars of Cults Accuse Each Other of Bad
Faith.' *Lingua Franca* (December/January): 26–37.
Altmeyer, B. 1981. *Right-Wing Authoritarianism*. Winnipeg: University of Mani-
toba Press.
– 1988. *Enemies of Freedom*. New York: Jossey-Bass.
American Psychiatric Association. 1994. *Diagnostic and Statistical Manual of
Mental Disorders: [DSM IV]: Washington, D.C.: American Psychiatric Associa-
tion.

Anthony, D., 1989. Spiritual Authenticity: Separating the Wheat from the Chaff, (interview). *Clarion Call*, Oct., 1989.

– 1990. 'Religious Movements and "Brainwashing" Litigation: Evaluating Key Testimony.' In *Gods We Trust*. 2d ed., Edited by Thomas Robbins and Dick Anthony. Reprint (in German) in *The Brainwashing Controversy: An Anthology of Essential Documents*, edited by Gordon Melton and Massimo Introvigne. Marburg, Germany: Remid, 2000.

– 1996. *Brainwashing and Totalitarian Influence: An Exploration of Admissibility Criteria for Testimony in Brainwashing Trials*. Ann Arbor: UMI Dissertation Services.

– 1999. 'Pseudoscience and Minority Religions: An Evaluation of the Brainwashing theories of Jean-Marie Abgrall.' *Social Justice Research* 12: 421–56

Anthony, D., and B. Ecker. 1987. 'A Typology of Contemporary Religious Movements.' In *Spiritual Choices: The Problem of Recognizing Authentic Paths to Spiritual Transformation*, edited by D. Anthony, B. Ecker, and K. Wilbur. New York: Paragon Books.

Anthony, D., and T. Robbins. 1974. 'The Meher Baba Movement: Its Effect on the Alienation of Youth.' In *Contemporary American Religious Movements* edited by Irving Zaretsky and Mark Leone. Princeton: Princeton, University Press, 1974.

– 1978. 'The Effect of Detente on the Growth of New Religions: Reverend Moon and the Unification Church.' In *Understanding the New Religions*, edited by Jacob Needleman and George Baker. New York: Seabury Press.

– 1982a. 'The Growth of Moral Absolutism in an Age of Anxious Relativism.' In *Observations of Deviance*, 2d ed. Edited by Jack Douglas. Boston: Allyn and Bacon.

– 1982b. 'Contemporary Religious Movements and Moral Ambiguity.' In *New Religious Movements: A Perspective for Understanding Society*, edited by Eileen Barker. Lewiston, N.Y.: Edwin Mellon.

– 1992. 'Law, Social Science and the "Brainwashing" Exception to the First Amendment.' *Behavioral Sciences and the Law* 10: 5–30.

– 1994. 'Brainwashing and Totalitarian Influence.' In *Encyclopedia Of Human Behavior*, edited by V.S. Ramachandran. San Diego, Calif.: Academic Press (division of Harcourt Brace Jovanovich). Reprint in the *Encyclopedia of Mental Health*, edited by Howard Friedman.

– 1995a. 'Negligence, Coercion, and the Protection of Religious Belief.' *Journal of Church and State* 37.

– 1995b. 'Religious Totalism, Violence and Exemplary Dualism.' In *Millennialism and Violence*, special issue of *Terrorism and Political Violence* 7 (Autumn), edited by Michael Barkun. Reprint, London and Portland: Frank Cass, 1996.

- 1997. 'Religious Totalism, Exemplary Dualism, and the Waco Tragedy.' In *Millennium, Messiahs and Mayhem*, edited by Thomas Robbins and Susan Palmer New York and London: Routledge Books.

Anthony, D., B. Ecker, and K. Wilbur, eds. 1987. *Spiritual Choices: The Problem of Recognizing Authentic Paths to Spiritual Transformation*. New York: Paragon Books.

Arendt, H. 1951. *The Origins of Totalitarianism*. San Diego, New York, London: Harcourt Brace Jovanovich.

Armstrong, K. 2000. *The Battle for God*. New York: Knopf.

Barber, T.X. 1961. 'Antisocial and Criminal Acts Induced by Hypnosis: A Review of Experimental and Clinical Findings.' *Archives of General Psychiatry* 5.

- 1969. *Hypnosis: A Scientific Approach*. New York: Litton.

Barker, E. 1984. *The Making of a Moonie: 'Brainwashing' or Choice?* New York: Basil Blackwell.

Biderman, A. 1962. 'The Image of Brainwashing.' *Public Opinion Quarterly* 26: 547–63.

- 1963. *March to Calumny*. New York: Macmillan.

Brauns, T. 1988. Review of *Spiritual Choices: The Problem of Recognizing Authentic and Inauthentic Paths to Inner Transformation*, edited by Dick Anthony, Bruce Ecker, and Ken Wilbur. *Cultic Studies* 5: 145–9.

Bromley, D. 1998. 'Listing (in Black and White): Some Observations on (Sociological) Thought Reform.' *Nova Religio* 1 (3): 250–67.

Burkett, W. 1983. *Homo Necans: The Anthropology of Ancient Greek Sacrificial Ritual and Myth*. Berkeley: University of California Press.

Burkett, W., R. Girard, and J. Smith. 1987. *Violent Origins: Ritual Killing and Cultural Formation*. Stanford: Stanford University Press.

Campbell, R. 1981. *Psychiatric Dictionay*. New York: Oxford University Press.

Chaplin, J. 1985. *Dictionary of Psychology*. New York: Dell.

Davis, R. 1960: 'Some Theories of Counter-Subversion: An Analysis of Anti-Masonic, Anti-Catholic, and Anti-Mormon Literature' *Mississippi Historical Review* 48: 205–24.

Davis, W. 2000. 'Heaven's Gate: A Study of Religious Obedience.' *Nova Religio* 3 (2): 241–67.

Dawson, L. 1998. *Comprehending Cults: The Sociology of New Religious Movements*. Toronto: Oxford University Press.

Eckstein, P. 1993. Introduction to Symposium with Johannes Aagaard.' *Cultic Studies Journal* 10: 100–2.

Edwards, C. 1979. *Crazy for God*. Englewood Cliffs, N.J.: Prentice-Hall.

Erikson, E. 1942. 'Hitler's imagery and German Youth.' *Psychiatry* 5: 475–93.

Reprint chap. 9, 'The Legend of Hitler's Childhood.' In *Childhood and Society*, edited by E. Erikson. New York: Norton, 1950.

- 1950. *Childhood and Society.* New York: Norton.
- 1954. 'Wholeness and Totality: A Psychiatric Contribution.' In *Totalitarianism: Proceedings of a Conference Held at the American Academy of Arts and Sciences*, edited by Carl Friedrich. Cambridge, Mass.: Harvard University Press.
- 1958. *Young Man Luther: A Study in Psychoanalysis and History.* New York: W.W. Norton.

Erikson, M. 1939. 'An Experimental Investigation of the Possible Anti-Social Use of Hypnosis.' *Psychiatry* 2: 391–414.

- 1980. *The Collected Papers of Milton H. Erikson on Hypnosis*. Vol. 1. Edited by E.L. Rossi. New York: Irvington.

Farber, I.E., H.F. Harlow, and L.J. West. 1957. 'Brainwashing, Conditioning and the DDD (Debility, Dependency and Dread) Syndrome.' *Sociometry* 29: 271.

Frenkel-Brunswick, E. 1949. 'Intolerance of Ambiguity as an Emotional and Perceptual Personality Variable.' *Journal of Personality XVIII.*

- 1951. 'Patterns of Social and Cognitive Outlook in Children and Parents.' *American Journal of Orthopsychiatry XXI.*
- 1954. 'Environmental Controls and the Impoverishment of Thought.' In *Totalitarianism: Proceedings of a Conference Held at the American Academy of Arts and Sciences* (March 1953), edited by C. Friedrich. Cambridge: Harvard University Press.

Friedman, Lawrence J. 1999. *Identity's Architect: A Biography of Erik H. Erikson.* With an introduction by Robert Coles. New York: Scribner.

Friedrich, C., and Z. Brzezinski. 1956. *Totalitarian Dictorship and Autocracy.* New York: Praeger.

Fromm, E. 1941. *Escape from Freedom.* New York: Rinehart.

- 1984. *The Working Class in Weimar Germany: A Psychological and Sociological Study.* Translated by Barbara Weinberger. Cambridge, Mass.: Harvard University Press.

Galanter, M. 1999. *Cults: Faith, Healing, and Coercion.* 2d ed. New York: Oxford University Press.

Gilbert, R. 1991. *The Element of Mysticism.* Boston: Element Books.

Girard, R. 1972. *Violence and the Sacred.* Baltimore: Johns Hopkins University Press.

- 1987. *Things Hidden Since the Foundation of the World.* Stanford: Stanford University Press.

Ginsburg, G., and J.T. Richardson. 1998. '"Brainwashing" Evidence in Light of Daubert.' In *Law and Science*, edited by H. Reece, 265–88. Oxford: Oxford University Press.

Habermas, J. 1984–87. *The Theory of Communicative Action: Two Volumes.* Boston: Beacon.

Hacohen, M. 2000. *Karl Popper: The Formative Years, 1902–1945.* Cambridge: Cambridge University Press.

Hall, J., P. Schuyler, and S. Trinh. 2000. *Apocalypse Observed: Religious Movements and Violence in North America, Europe, and Japan.* New York: Routledge.

Hinkle, L.E, Jr., and H.E. Wolff. 1956. 'Communist Interrogation and the Indoctrination of "Enemies of the State."' *A.M.A. Archives of Neurology and Psychiatry* (76): 117.

Hood, R. 1995. *Handbook of Religious Experience.* Birmingham: Religious Education Press.

Hunter, E. 1951. *Brainwashing in Red China.* New York: Vanguard.

– 1960. *Brainwashing: From Pavolov to Powers.* New York: The Bookmaster.

Jenkins, P. 2000. *Mystics and Messiahs: Cults and New Religions in American History.* Oxford: Oxford University Press.

Joy, N. 1992. *Throughout Your Generations Forever: Sacrifice, Religion, and Paternity.* Chicago: University of Chicago Press.

Juergensmeyer, M. 2000. *Terror in the Mind of God: The Global Rise of Religious Violence.* Berkeley: University of California Press.

Katchen, M. 1992. 'Brainwashing, Hypnosis and the Cults.' *Australian Journal of Clinical and Experimental Hypnosis* 20: 79–88.

Kent, S. 1997. 'Methodological Problems Studying Brainwashing in Scientology's Rehabilitation Project Force.' Paper presented at the annual meeting of the Society for the Scientific Study of Religion, San Diego, Calif.

Kirkpatrick, L., R. Hood, and G. Hartz. 1991. 'Fundamentalist Religion Conceptualized in Terms of Rokeach's Theory of the Open and Closed Mind; New Perspectives on Some Old Ideas.' *Research in the Social Scientific Study of Religion* 3: 157–80.

Koenig, H. 1997. *Is Religion Good for Your Health: The Effects of Religion on Physical and Mental Health.* New York: Haworth.

Langone, M. 1986. 'Cultism and American Culture.' *Cultic Studies Journal* 3: 157–72.

– 1993a. ed. 'Symposium with Johannes Aagaard.' *Cultic Studies Journal* 10: 103–94.

– 1993b. 'Pluralism, Deeds, Creeds and Cults.' *Cultic Studies Journal.* 10: 195–206.

– 1994. 'Are Sound Theology and Cultism Mutually Exclusive?' *Cult Observer* 11: 9–10, 21–2.

Lee, M., and B. Shlain. 1985. *Acid Dreams: The CIA, LSD, and the Sixties Rebellion.* New York: Grove Press.

Lifton, R. 1954. 'Home by Ship: Reaction Patterns of American Prisoners of

War Repatriated from North Korea.' *American Journal of Psychiatry* 110: 732–9.

- 1961. *Chinese Thought Reform and the Psychology of Totalism.* 2d ed. New York: W.W. Norton. With a new introduction by the author, 1989. Chapel Hill: University of North Carolina Press.
- 1968. 'Protean Man.' *Partisan Review* 35: 13–27.
- 1974. Preface. In *Explorations in Psychohistory: The Wellfleet Papers*, edited by R. Lifton. New York: Simon & Schuster.
- 1976. 'Testimony in Patty Hearst Trial.' In *The Trial of Patty Hearst*, 314–35. San Francisco: Great Fidelity Press.
- 1986. *The Nazi Doctors: Medical Killing and the Psychology of Genocide.* New York: Basic Books.
- 1987. 'Cults, Religious Totalism and Civil Liberties.' In *The Future of Immortality and Other Essays for a Nuclear Age.* New York: Basic Books.
- 1993. *The Protean Self: Human Resilience in an Age of Fragmentation.* New York: Basic Books
- 1999. *Destroying the World to Save It: Aum Shinrikyo, Apocalytic Violence, and the New Global Terrorism.* New York: Metropolitan Books, Henry Holt.

Magee, B. 1985. *Philosophy and the Real World: An Introduction to Karl Popper.* LaSalle Ill.: Open Court.

Marks, J. 1980. *The Search for the Manchurian Candidate.* New York: Random House.

Martin, P. 1998. 'Overcoming the Bondage of Revictimization: A Rational/Empirical Defense of Thought Reform.' *Cultic Studies Journal* 15: 151–91.

Mazlish, B. 1987. 'Group Psychology and Problems of Contemporary History.' In *Psychohistory: Readings in the Method of Psychohistory, Psychoanalysis, and History,* edited by G. Cocks and T. Crosby. New Haven: Yale University Press.

Meerloo, J. 1956. *The Rape of the Mind: The Psychology of Thought Control, Menticide, and Brainwashing.* Cleveland: World Publishing.

Miller, J. 1986. 'The Utilization of Hypnotic Techniques in Religious Conversion.' *Cultic Studies Journal* 3: 243–50.

Mills, E. 1998. 'Cult Extremism: The Reduction of Normative Dissonance.' In *Cults in Context: Readings in the Study of New Religious Movements,* edited by L. Dawson. New Brunswick: Transaction.

Mitchell, D., C. Mitchell, and R. Ofshe. 1980. *The Light on Synanon: How a Country Weekly Exposed a Corporate Cult – and Won the Pulitzer Prize.* New York: Seaview.

Moss, C. 1965. *Hypnosis in Perspective.* New York: Macmillan.

Ofshe, Richard. 1976. 'Synanon: The People Business.' In *The New Religious Consciousness,* edited by Glock and Bellah, 116–37. Berkeley: University of California.

– 1989. 'Report Regarding Steven Fishman.' In *U.S. v. Fishman.* April 23.

– 1992a. 'Coercive Persuasion and Attitude Change.' In *The Encyclopedia of Sociology,* edited by E. Borgatta and M. Borgatta. New York: Macmillan.

Ofshe, R., and M. Singer. 1986. 'Attacks on Central vs. Peripheral Elements of Self and the Impact of Thought Reforming Techniques.' *Cultic Studies Journal* 3(1): 3–24.

Ofshe, Richard, et al. 1974. 'Social Structure and Social Control in Synanon.' *Journal of Voluntary Social Action* 3: 67–76.

O'Hear, A. 1980. *Karl Popper.* London: Routledge & Kegan Paul.

Orne, M. 1961. 'The Potential Uses of Hypnosis in Interrogation.' In *The Manipulation of Human Behavior,* edited by A. Biderman and H. Zimmer. New York: Wiley.

– 1962. 'Antisocial Behavior and Hypnosis.' In *Hypnosis: Current Problems,* edited by G. Estabrooks. New York: Harper & Row, 137–92.

– 1972. 'Can a Hypnotized Subject Be Compelled to Carry Out Otherwise Unacceptable Behavior?' *International Journal of Clinical and Experimental Hypnosis* 20: 101–17.

Orne, M., and F. Evans. 1965. 'Social Control in the Psychological Experiment: Anti-social Behavior and Hypnosis. *Journal of Personality and Social Psychology* I: 189–200.

Paloutzian, R., Richardson, J.T., and Rambo, L. 1999. 'Religious Conversion and Personality Change.' *Journal of Personality* 67: 1047–79.

Parsons, T. 1951. *The Social System.* Glencoe: The Free Press.

Peele, S. 1989. *Diseasing America: Addiction Treatment Out of Control.* Lexington, Mass.: Lexington Books

Pervin, L. 1984. *Current Controversies and Histories in Personality.* New York: John Wiley.

Phillips, D. 1976. *Holistic Thought in Social Science.* Stanford, Calif.: Stanford University Press.

– 1992. *The Social Scientist's Beastiary: A Guide to, and Defense of, Naturalistic Social Science.* Oxford: Pergamon Press.

Popper, K. 1945. *The Open Society and Its Enemies.* London: Routledge & Kegan Paul.

– 1959. *The Logic of Scientific Discovery.* New York: Harper Torchbooks.

– 1963. *Conjectures and Refutations: The Growth of Scientific Knowledge.* London and New York: Routledge & Kegan Paul.

Pullum, R. 1989. 'Cognitive Styles of Hypocrisy? An Explanation of the Religious-Intolerance Relationship.' In *Social Consequences of Religious Belief,* edited by W. Garrett. New York: Paragon House.

Ranelagh, John. 1986. *The Agency: The Rise and Decline of the CIA.* New York: Simon & Schuster.

Reich, W. 1970. *The Mass Psychology of Fascism*. New York: Noonday/Farrar, Straus & Giroux.

– 1972. *Sex-Pol: Essays, 1929–1934*. New York: Vintage/Random House.

Richardson, J. 1993. 'A Social Psychological Critique of "Brainwashing" Claims about Recruitment to New Religions.' In *The Handbook of Cults and Sects in America*, edited by J. Hadden and D. Bromley, 75–97. Greenwich, Conn.: JAI Press.

Richardson J., and B. Kilbourne. 1983. 'Classical and Contemporary Applications of Brainwashing Models: A Critique and Comparison.' In *The Brainwashing/Deprogramming Controversy*, edited by D. Bromley and J. Richardson, 29–45.

Richardson, J., and M. Stewart. 1977. 'Conversion Process Models and the Jesus Movement.' *American Behavioral Scientist*. 20: 819–38.

Robbins, T., and D. Anthony. 1978. 'New Religious Movements and the Social System: Integration, Transformation or Disintegration.' *Annual Review of the Social Sciences of Religion. Vol. II.*

– 1979. '"Cults," "Brainwashing" and Counter Subversion,' *The Annals of the American Academy of Political and Social Science*. Vol. 449 (Special Issue on Church and State).

Robbins, T., and S. Palmer. 1997. *Millennium, Messiahs, and Mayhem: Contemporary Apocalyptic Movements*. New York: Routledge.

Robbins, T., D. Anthony, M. Doucas, and T. Curtis. 1977. 'The Last Civil Religion: Reverend Moon and the Unification Church.' *Sociological/Analysis* 17:2–19.

Rokeach, M. 1960. *The Open and Closed Mind*. New York: Basic Books.

– 1970. 'Faith, Hope, and Bigotry.' *Psychology Today* 11: 33–7.

– 1973. *The Nature of Human Values*. New York: Free Press.

Scheflin, A., and E. Opton. 1978. *The Mind Manipulators*. Washington, D.C.: Paddington.

Schein, E. 1956. 'The Chinese Indoctrination Program for Prisoners of War: A Study of Attempted "Brainwashing."' *Psychiatry* 19: 149–72.

– 1957a. 'Reaction Patterns to Severe, Chronic Stress in American Army Prisoners of War of the Chinese.' *Journal of Social Issues* 13: 21–9.

– 1957b. Epilogue to 'Something New In History?' *Journal of Social Issues* 13: 56–60.

– 1958. 'The Chinese Indoctrination Program for Prisoners of War: A Study of Attempted "Brainwashing."' In *Readings in Social Psychology*, edited by Macoby et al. New York: Holt.

– 1959. 'Brainwashing and Totalitarianization in Modern Society.' *World Politics* 2: 430–41.

– 1961. *Coercive Persuasion*. New York: Norton.

- 1962. 'Man Against Man's Brainwashing.' *Corrective Psychiatry* and *Journal of Social Therapy* 8: 86–100.
- 1964. 'Management Development as a Process of Influence.' In *Readings in Managerial Psychology,* edited by H. Leavitt and L. Pondy. Chicago: University of Chicago Press.
- 1973. 'Brainwashing.' In *Interpersonal Dynamics: Essays and Readings on Human Interaction,* edited by W. Bennis, D. Berlew, E. Schein, and F. Steele. Homewood, Ill.: Dorsey Press.
Shupe, A., ed. 1998. *Wolves within the Fold: Religious Leadership and Abuses of Power.* New Brunswick: Rutgers University Press.
Singer, M. 1978. 'Therapy with Ex-Cult Members.' *Journal of the National Association of Private Psychiatric Hospitals* 9: 14–18.
- 1983. 'Testimony in *Robin and Marcia George v. International Society of Krishna Consciousness of California et al., 25–75–65.'* Orange County: California Superior Court.
- 1984. Interview. In *Spiritual Counterfeits Newsletter* 10: 2–4.
- 1987. 'Group Psychodynamics.' In *Merck Manual,* edited by R. Berkow. Rahway, N.J.: Merck Sharp and Dohme Research Laboratories.
Singer, M., and M. Addis. 1992. 'Cults, Coercion, and Contumely.' In *The Mosaic of Contemporary Psychiatry in Perspective,* edited by A. Kales et al. Zurich: Springer Verlag, 130–42.
Singer, M. and J. Lalich. 1995. *Cults in Our Midst: The Hidden Menace in Our Everyday Lives.* San Francisco: Jossey-Bass.
Spanos, N.P. 1996. *Multiple Identities and False Memories: A Sociocognitive Perspective.* Washington, D.C.: American Psychological Association.
Statt, David A. 1990. *The Concise Dictionary of Psychology.* London and New York: Routledge & Kegan Paul.
Taves, A. 1999. *Fits, Trances and Visions: Experiencing Religion and Explaining Experience from Wesley to James.* Princeton: Princeton University Press.
Watters, E., and R. Ofshe. 1999. *Therapy's Delusions: The Myth of the Unconscious and the Exploitation of Today's Walking Worried.* New York: Scribner.
Webb, E. 1993. *The Self Between: From Freud to the New Social Psychology of France.* Seattle, Wash.: University of Washington.
Wessinger, C. 2000a. *How the Millennium Comes Violently: From Jonestown to Heaven's Gate.* New York: Seven Bridges Press.
Wessinger, C., ed. 2000b. *Millenialism, Persecution, and Violence: Historical Cases.* Syracuse, N.Y.: Syracuse University Press.
West, L., and Martin, P. 1994. 'Pseudo-Identity and the Treatment of Personality Change in Victims of Captivity and Cults.' In *Dissociation: Clinical and*

Theoretical Perspectives, edited by S. Lynne and J. Rhine. New York: Guilford.

Wilber, K. 1987. 'The Spectrum Model.' In *Spiritual Choices: The Problem of Recognizing Authentic Paths to Inner Transformation,* edited by D. Anthony et al. New York: Paragon House.

Winell, M. 1993. *Leaving the Fold: A Guide for Former Fundamentalists and Others Leaving Their Religions.* Oakland, Calif.: New Harbinger.

Winnicott, D. 1960. 'Ego Distortion in Terms of True and False Self.' In *The Maturational Process and the Facilitating Environment,* 15–20. London: Routledge.

Zablocki, B. 1971. *The Joyful Community: An Account of the Bruderhof, a Communal Movement Now in Its Third Generation.* Baltimore: Penguin Books.

– 1980. *Alienation and Charisma: A Study of Contemporary Communes.* New York: Free Press.

– 1993. 'Rational Models of Charismatic Influence.' In *Social Theory and Social Policy: Essays in Honor of James S. Coleman,* edited by S. Lynne and J. Rhine. Westport, Conn.: Praeger.

– 1996. 'Reliability and Validity of Apostate Accounts in the Study of Religious Communities.' Paper presented to the Association for the Sociology of Religion, New York, August.

– 1997. 'The Blacklisting of a Concept: The Strange History of the Brainwashing Conjecture in the Sociology of Religion.' *Nova Religio* 1: 96–121.

– 1998a. 'Exit Cost Analysis: A New Approach to the Scientific Study of Brainwashing.' *Nova Religio* 2: 216–49

– 1998b. 'Reply to Bromley.' *Nova Religio* 1 (2): 267–71.

– 1999. 'Why Most Sociologists are Cult Apologists.' Presentation to *CULTinfo,* Stamford Connecticut. Reported as a cult observer report in *The Cult Observer: A Review of Press Reports on Cultism and Unethical Social Influence* 16 (7): 1, 5.

Zaehner, R. 1961. *Mysticism Sacred and Profane: An Inquiry into Some Varieties of Praeternatural Experience.* Oxford: Oxford University Press.

– 1972. *Drugs, Mysticism and Make-Believe.* New York: Collins.

Zimbardo, P., and C. Hartley, C. 1985. 'Cults Go to High School: A Theoretical and Empirical Analysis of the Initial Stage in the Recruitment Process.' *Cultic Studies Journal* 2: 91–47.

Zygmunt, Daryl. 1999. *A Theory of Cults.* New York: Random House.

7. A Tale of Two Theories: Brainwashing and Conversion as Competing Political Narratives

David Bromley

The controversy over the cohort of movements referred to alternatively as new religious movements and cults has yielded intellectual and political polarization in academe. The movements at issue have been described as unfairly maligned new religious groups on the one hand, and as destructive cults on the other. The countermovements opposing these groups have been depicted as unjustly denigrated self-help movements composed of concerned families and citizens and also as the latest incarnation of anti-religious bigotry. Scholars have divided into two camps, offering what appear to be dramatically different interpretations of the same organizations, actors, and events. Suspicions run deep on each side concerning the logic and loyalties of the other.

In this chapter I take an analytic step back from the controversy to inquire why this debate has been so intractable. After all, disputation has now traversed three decades. Written works on contemporary religious movements surely number in the thousands at this point, and affiliation-related behaviours are the most intensively researched issues (Rambo 1993; Saliba 1990; Snow and Machalek 1984). Yet, little progress has been achieved in resolving what may be the most volatile dispute in this area of scholarship: the appropriate theoretical framework through which to explain affiliations with contemporary religious movements. I offer two alternative explanations for the current impasse: (1) the investigation of religious movement affiliations is an empirical thorny thicket that does not easily lend itself to empirical resolution; and (2) the actual debate is not empirical at all, but rather is a political imbroglio. I shall argue the second position against the first while allowing that the two positions are not mutually exclusive. The terms *brainwashing* and *conversion* are employed here to summarize the political positions of the disputants, whether or not specific actors and narratives employ that terminology.

To summarize my argument briefly, the dispute centres on individual-group relationships, specifically the appropriate nature and degree of individual embeddedness in religious organizations. Conversion is a symbolic designation that positively sanctions embeddedness while brainwashing negatively sanctions embeddedness. The dispute is a political imbroglio that involves two major coalitions, which I term the *religion coalition* and the *mental health coalition*. The disagreement between the coalitions, however, is not nearly as great as rhetorical positioning on both sides would suggest. The protagonists are all professional-managerial representatives of dominant institutions, and the coalitions with which they are associated both are committed to high levels of individual autonomy, voluntarism, and self-directedness. Paradoxically, it is *because* both coalitions are converging around this commitment that the conflict has intensified. Since both coalitions have formidable institutional power bases and high legitimacy, it appears unlikely that either will achieve total victory. For social scientists involved in the dispute, acknowledging and openly discussing its political basis is important irrespective of the settlement reached. Such an exchange would explore the political dimensions of science and identify the social forces that shape not only the patterning of the social order but also social science accounts as an integral element of that order.

The Empirical Thorny Thicket Thesis

The case that the conversion-brainwashing dispute is not amenable to empirical resolution rests on a number of problems of theory, methods, and data. I shall illustrate, rather than exhaustively review, this position by briefly outlining several empirical problems in reconciling conversion and brainwashing interpretations. These problems include (1) empirical complexity, (2) observability, (3) theoretical pluralism, and (4) organizational diversity and change.

Empirical Complexity
Both what are termed conversion and brainwashing traditionally have

been treated as if their referents are unitary phenomena. Recent theorizing in each area has resulted in the development of typologies that
distinguish subcategories of brainwashing and conversion, although
these initiatives have been much more extensive for the latter than the
former. One example in the case of brainwashing theory is work by
Richard Ofshe and Margaret Singer (1986). They designate two types
of thought reform techniques, which they term first and second generations of interest. This typology appears intended to distinguish
degrees of invasiveness, and identifies the second generation as more
destructive because it attacks 'core sense of being' (18). Another relatively clear distinction has been drawn between religiously based concepts of deception, which emphasize symbolic manipulation (i.e., false
theology), and secular concepts of brainwashing, which emphasize
social and psychological behavioural manipulation (Shupe and Bromley 1980). There have been few other attempts to develop typologies
for brainwashing, although there is no a priori reason why distinctions
cannot be drawn. For example, references to different types of group
processes that constitute brainwashing techniques – such as ritual
chanting, isolation, and authoritarian leadership – might constitute the
grounds for developing typologies. The existing typologies tend to
share in common a presumption of compromised voluntarism. It
appears that for the moment, however, the primary thrust of scholars
pursuing a brainwashing argument is to establish the existence and
parameters of a process that is categorically different from other influence processes and therefore deserving of separate terminological
status.

Over the last several decades there have been a number of conversion models that identify different categories of conversion. For example, Lofland and Skonovd (1981) identify five of the conversion types
based on degree of pressure, temporal duration, affective arousal,
affective content, and belief-participation ordering. 'Coercive' is one of
these modes, although the authors conclude that it is a rare empirical
event. Lofland and Richardson (1984) delineate four major types and
eleven subtypes of conversion organized by level of analysis and
degree of individual agency. Travisano (1970) distinguishes between
alternation and conversion as 'qualitatively different transformations.'
Most of the categories of conversion contained in these typologies pre-
sume a substantial measure of convert voluntarism.

The implication in all of these typologies is that brainwashing and
conversion have multiple empirical referents. If there are a number of

analytically separable processes sharing a 'family resemblance,' then the irresolvability of the present debate might be attributable in part to observation of different empirical phenomena. There simply are not single positions to be compared to one another. While it might be possible to conduct comparisons of particular types of conversion and brainwashing, any binary choice resolution of the debate would be unlikely.

Observability

There are two associated observability problems, one related to observation of the processes themselves and the other to observation of the individuals participating in those processes. At the core of both conversion and brainwashing theories is the concept of a qualitative, holistic transformation. Snow and Machalek (1984:169) capture this point nicely in summarizing the theory and research on conversion when they write that 'The one theme pervading the literature on conversion is that the experience involves *radical personal change* ... a turning from one viewpoint to another, or a return to principles from which one has strayed' (emphasis mine). A variety of social and psychological indicators may be used to measure this putative transformation empirically. Snow and Machalek (1984: 172–4) summarize these as changes in membership status, demonstration events, and rhetorical indicators (biographical reconstruction, adoption of a master attributional scheme, suspension of analogical reasoning, and embracement of the convert role).

A similar notion is found in theories of brainwashing. One of the primary proponents of the brainwashing approach, Margaret Singer, conveys the sense of a qualitative shift in terms of loss of free will. In legal testimony (Bromley 1988a: 276) concerning a former member of the Hare Krishna (Robin George), Singer at one point concluded that 'It's my opinion that she was not at that point freely using her *own will and volition*' (emphasis mine). The process through which individual volition is compromised Singer terms the 'systematic manipulation of social influence' (SMSI). Indicators that an individual has undergone SMSI experiences include what she refers to as the five d's: *deception* of the person, *dependence* on the organization, *debilitation* of the individual through group controls and routines, *dread* (both within the group and of the outside world), and *desensitization* such that individuals no longer utilize their 'old conscience' (1988a: 276).

Whatever the set of empirical indicators used on either side of the argument, one pivotal fact remains: the transformation itself is not directly observable. Since the phenomenon is beyond direct observation, the battle revolves around surrogate indicators, most notably individual accounts and behavioural changes. The observability problem is exacerbated by the fact that few, if any, social science studies of brainwashing or conversion actually are based on cases for which the entire process was recorded. At best, observations are of segments of the processes, and usually they are for different individuals at those various points in the process. Data are particularly thin for certain parts of these processes, most tellingly of the actual 'moment of transformation' itself. One surrogate indicator commonly employed by researchers is individual accounts, which are used to 'fill in the blanks' where observation is segmental. Conversion narratives typically are more strongly bolstered by individuals with movement affiliations and brainwashing narratives by individuals with countermovement affiliations. Each side in essence concludes that the other is relying on the wrong data and is therefore accepting an erroneous view. Shifts in behavioural patterns constitute a second surrogate indicator. Group affiliation typically is accompanied by observable behavioural change, which is then attributed alternatively to manipulated change in internal states or adoption of group-appropriate role behaviour.

These problems do not mean that there are no means for evaluating accounts (Carter 1998; Zablocki 1996) or identifying the source of behaviour change. Rather, the point is that because researchers on both sides rely on a patchwork of individual cases, behavioural change, and individual accounts, each possesses the capacity to marshall data of a technically comparable nature. If the essential qualities of the putative transformations are not directly observable, and reliance is on accounts and behaviour in which various parties have an interest, then alternative interpretations seem likely indeed. In theory these problems could be resolved by improving the validity and reliability of indices and conducting more systematic observation of individuals, but both resolutions obviously encounter a myriad of practical difficulties.

Organizational Diversity and Change

One of the most common observations about religious movements is the diversity they exhibit organizationally and the rapidity with which they change. Organization varies on a number of dimensions that influence the nature of the individual-group relationships. Some movements are very tightly organized; this is most evident for collectivistic movements that attempt to create self-contained social worlds. Other movements, such as New Age groups, typically are much more loosely organized networks. The potential for individual embeddedness and organizational control probably are greatest in the former conditions. Closely related to this factor is distancing from the social order. Individual-group relationships are likely to be stronger where neither individuals nor groups are linked to multiple social networks. Movement case studies indicate that organizational intensity and distancing vary considerably among movements and across specific movement histories. However encompassing social movements may be as entire entities, there will also inevitably be organizational layering. One of the most common forms this takes is what might be described in terms of a series of concentric circles denoting degree of movement involvement. At the centre of the movement is a relatively small coterie of leadership and highly committed followers, surrounded by a series of other groups of individuals with successively lower degrees of involvement, commitment, and exposure to movement control. Political and geographic divisions constitute other sources of sectorization within movements. Organization and lifestyle may diverge dramatically in different sectors of movements. Movements also vary in size, and membership sometimes shifts dramatically over relatively short time spans as a product of recruitment and defection. Individual-group relationships can be significantly determined by group size; increases in membership yield more complex organization and formal social control mechanisms, for example. The level of charismatic authority varies among movements and within movements over time. There is a significant difference between spiritual mediums, priestly leaders, and prophetic revolutionaries in terms of moral claimsmaking vis-à-vis movement members.

Any of these characteristics may change both in direction and rapidity. It is therefore difficult to characterize movements as overall entities or across time with any precision. This problem is exacerbated by the fact that a relatively small proportion of religious movements have been studied at all, and even for those that have been studied, research tends to be for specific periods and sectors of the movement. It is probably fair to state that there is no movement that has been researched continuously and exhaustively through its history. Scholars of a brainwashing persuasion are likely to infer more modal tendencies in individual-group relationships for religious movements than would those of a conversion persuasion, but the empirical evidence that would definitively confirm descriptions of these relationships across movements and movement histories simply does not exist. Generalizations are unlikely to be either valid or reliable. These difficulties would multiply, of course, for generalizations applied across movements.

Theoretical Pluralism

If individual-group relationships vary because religious movements are heterogeneous and rapidly changing, the theories employed to explain those relationships are equally diverse. There is no single theory of either conversion or brainwashing. Rather, both designations encompass sets of theories, and the within-set variance is as pronounced as the between-set variance. In the case of conversion designations, for example, some theories describe this process in terms of social role behaviour. Individuals simply learn and adopt the normative behavioural patterns of the movement with which they affiliate (Bromley and Shupe 1979, 1986). Other theories define conversion in cultural terms, as a change in symbolic presentation. From this perspective conversion is a change in one's 'universe of discourse' (Snow and Machalek 1984). Conversion is also interpreted as a change in social context. The influential Lofland and Stark theory (1965) depicts conversion in terms of diminishing interpersonal ties in one social network and intensifying them in another network. One important feature of all these theories is that they essentially bracket the question of a holistic personal change that underpins traditional religious conceptions of conversion. Each emphasizes individual initiative but also allows both individual and group influence.

There is a corresponding diversity among brainwashing theories. The most general frameworks are related to thought reform and coercive persuasion theories (Lifton 1989; Schein and Baker 1961). These theories describe religious movement affiliations as the product of a deliberate, systematic, manipulative, authoritarian program of social and physical environment control (Cushman 1986; Singer and Ofshe 1990). Other theories of movement affiliation are constructed around control over mental/cognitive functioning. Conway and Siegelman (1982), for example, have offered an 'information disease' theory that attributes affiliation to a cybernetic trauma that compromises normal cognitive functioning. Several theories are based on the exercise of influence over affiliates through manipulative use of trance and hypnotic states (Katchen 1992; Verdier 1977). Finally, there are theories that define and analyse affiliations as inappropriate types of social relationships. Sirkin and Wynne's (1990) concept of 'relational disorder' and Zablocki's (1998) concept of 'high exit costs' exemplify this type. All of these theories share in common a focus on group-induced, deleterious effects on individuals affiliated with religious movements. While they admit some measure of both individual and group influence, the latter is asserted to be more powerful and determinative of outcomes.

For both conversion and brainwashing theories, then, there is limited agreement on the core process that is being observed, the dynamics involved in the process, or the consequences of process. If the dynamics of individual-group relationships are complex and fluid, it is difficult to define what constitutes the essential or most relevant data. It seems perfectly possible that a number of theories on both sides would receive empirical support in their own terms. Under these conditions, it is difficult indeed to envision any 'critical experiments' that would yield an empirical resolution of the debate.

All four of these problems, or others that could be added, surely are legitimate, and they complicate the problem of fashioning and confirming summary statements about individual-movement relationships. A more comprehensive analysis of these issues might well yield a conclusion that this is an area of inquiry awash in unanswered questions, methodological disagreements, and conflicting findings. But these are 'normal problems' that pervade many areas of scientific inquiry. Some of these problems may be resolved, and efforts in that direction are useful. Again, the argument pursued here is not that reliability and validity questions are beyond resolution, but that the intractability of the conversion-brainwashing debate does not derive from these issues. Rather, I shall argue that while the debate is oriented to disagreements on methodological procedures and empirical findings, these issues actually provide a veneer of scientific objectivity in a dispute that is fundamentally political in nature.

The Political Imbroglio Thesis

The argument I am developing does not challenge the actuality of individual transformative experiences. There is compelling evidence that such events do occur, that they are pivotal in the lives of individuals who experience them, and that they play a significant role in the social dynamics of some groups. There is also convincing evidence that both individuals and organizations are integrally involved in accomplishing such transformative experiences. And the empirical problems I have

delineated do not preclude descriptive and interpretive agreement
with respect to transformative experiences in specific groups. However, the current conversion-brainwashing debate is about much more
than these matters. It concerns morally advantaging and disadvantag-
ing certain kinds of individual-group relationships by designating
them as conversion or brainwashing. Cast in political terms, the issue
is not about the nature of transformative experiences, it is about the
moral assessment of those experiences.

Brainwashing and conversion share a common heritage that traces
historically to the concepts of spiritual conversion and demonic possession. Both concepts describe individual embeddedness in agentic
relationships. In each case individuals are defined as having encountered a transcendent power, an 'otherness' that reshapes their intentionality such that it becomes coterminous with the intention and
purpose of the other (Swanson 1978). It is the nature of the 'otherness'
that distinguishes the spiritual and demonic. In the former, individuals
are defined as unifying with an emancipating transcendent power,
which facilitates their progress towards expressing what they ultimately are or should be. In the latter, individuals are defined as unifying with a subjugating transcendent power, which progressively
alienates them from what they ultimately are or should be. Historically, agentic relationships in the Judaeo-Christian tradition involved
individuals embedding themselves in religious communities unified
around commitments to transcendent purpose. This tradition juxta-
posed communities founded on spiritual unity with alternative,
demonically centred communities that posed a constant threat to any
loss of individual or collective commitment.

Tracing the meanings of conversion and possession as those have
been understood during various historical periods is beyond the mandate of this chapter, but the contemporary legacy of these designations
is central to my argument. In its current usage, religious conversion
continues to refer to uniting with a liberating transcendent power. In
moral terms, to label an event as conversion is to assert (1) a change
from less desirable to more desirable conduct, and (2) that the convert
is now more capable of appropriate self-regulation as a result of
coincidence of individual and positive transcendent purpose. These
conversion designations are religiously authorized. While possession
designations continue to be applied in some religious traditions,
brainwashing is a secular designation that derives specifically from
Cold War–era political conflict. In its current usage, brainwashing

refers to uniting with a subjugating transcendent power. The nature and degree of transcendence is more limited in most brainwashing theories, and transformations are the product of human agents. In moral terms, to label an event as brainwashing is to assert (1) a change from more desirable to less desirable conduct, and (2) that the brain-washed individual is now less capable of acceptable self-regulation as a result of coincidence of individual and negative transcendent purpose. These symbolic designations, labels if you will, are employed to positively or negatively sanction individual-group connections of a particular kind – individual embeddedness in agentic relationships. Each designation commands the highest level of authority when individual, organizational, and external network interpretations of individual-group connections coincide. In the case at hand, of course, there is contention rather than agreement between various parties over the proper designation of individual-group relationships in religious movements.

There are several components to the political imbroglio thesis. First, I present evidence indicating the political nature of the conversion-brainwashing debate. I then identify the core issue in the debate as embeddedness in agentic relationships. There is a pronounced contemporary trend towards problematizing agentic relationships across social institutions. I link the intensification of the brainwashing-conversion debate to this trend. Finally, I define the mental health and religion coalitions as the two sets of disputants. The rhetoric in the debate notwithstanding, scholars in the two coalitions occupy similar social locations and defend comparable positions within their respective coalitions. It is because the coalitions occupy similar locations but defend different institutional interests that the debate remains intractable.

The Politics of Science in the Brainwashing-Conversion Debate

Despite efforts to maintain the brainwashing-conversion debate as a scientific disagreement, there are a number of indications of its political character. I make this case by re-analysing the empirical thorny thicket explanation in political terms; contending that brainwashing and conversion are historically rare designations, which are the product of particular political circumstances; maintaining that conversion and brainwashing are uncommon individual events even within the current sociopolitical context; demonstrating that the actual usage of the two designations is highly ideological in character; presenting evidence that high descriptive agreement does not necessarily yield interpretive agreement; and, correspondingly, showing that theoretical consonance does not produce descriptive convergence.

Let us begin by reformulating the empirical complexity arguments to reflect a political interpretation. First, if there are not single processes or patterns of behaviour that correspond to what are termed brainwashing and conversion, then what the terms provide are symbolic umbrellas that positively or negatively sanction diverse phenomena. The umbrellas can be deployed to privilege a broader or narrower range of relationships. For example, some scholars argue that physical coercion is the requisite division point between the two processes, while others contend that psychological coercion is admissible (Anthony and Robbins 1992). The former position encompasses more relationships under the conversion umbrella, and the latter expands the coverage of the brainwashing umbrella. To put the matter more pointedly, to either disregard empirical diversity under one umbrella or empirical similarities between symbolic designations is a political act. Second, if the putative phenomena cannot be observed but rather must be inferred, very different inferences about the same events are possible. This, of course, is precisely what has occurred. In some cases dramatically opposed interpretations are offered for the same individual's experiences, and the same individuals offer opposed interpretations of their own experiences at different times. These competing accounts are a product of the social locations in which they are framed, and privileging one set over another is a political act. Third, if social scientists are proposing an array of processes under the rubric of each of the two concepts, then some or all may occur empirically in different degrees, for different groups and individuals, and at different moments and locations. This would mean that there are a variety of routes by which the same outcome may be reached. What individuals share, then, are destination points and the evaluative labels that are attached to them. Fourth, if socialization and control practices vary substantially within subunits of movements, across time in the same movement, and among different movements, then summarizing them through either lens is to prospectively apply a single, evaluative label to disparate events. Attributing specific, limited patterns of either type to an entire movement or set of movements constitutes political sanctioning rather than interpretation. In sum, I would argue that what have been treated as empirical complexities actually serve as proxies for political disagreements.

Brainwashing and conversion as important social and psychological designations are the product of a very specific historical context, and in that sense reflect a particular set of political arrangements. For example, such designations make little sense in culturally homogeneous tribal groups where there are no alternative groups with which to ally. In contemporary society, neither designation in its traditional usage is likely to apply to mainline churches since theological variations are minimal and individual commitment levels are modest. Indeed, brainwashing and conversion designations are most likely in a religious economy in which individuality is pronounced; there is some degree of religious pluralism, with no single group holding hegemonic control; legitimacy is granted to a range of religious groups, so that shifts in loyalty are acceptable; and there are contesting groups that are accorded less legitimacy, such that moral ranking is called for. This set of conditions must be relatively unique historically. There is very good evidence that the foundational element of both designations, conceiving of individuals as autonomous entities and as the constituent building blocks of the social order, is unique to modern, Western societies (Geertz 1974). The implication is that these designations have emerged as political settlements between various political coalitions.

Both conversion and brainwashing, as described in the ideal types of these designations, probably are also empirically rare as individual events even within their specific historical contexts. The scenario in which individuals experience a sequence of events that constitutes a major transformative moment, and this moment thematizes identity and activity across the remainder of an individual's biography, is exceptional. Each thus constitutes an archetypal event or sequence that is used to symbolize and to positively or negatively sanction the range of actually occurring individual-group connections. Further, attributing subsequent behavior to conversion or brainwashing begs key motivational questions. The reality is that individual-group connections vary greatly, and the reasons for their stability or change shift over time. As we have already noted, research on conversion indicates that there are a variety of modes through which that process occurs, and that individual-group connections involve different types and levels of involvement. Similarly, research on influence processes indicates a variety of techniques and that these have quite variable effects (Cialdini 1985). From this perspective both brainwashing and conversion serve as metanarratives, political narratives that privilege certain relational forms over others.

The way in which conversion and brainwashing are actually

employed as designations is revealing. There are numerous institutional arenas through the social order in which high control, encapsulation, and identity transformation occur that do not evoke a brainwashing designation. These settings are considered 'functional' to the social order, and assessments of individual participation range from rehabilitative to honorific. In each case there is a considerable body of research that discusses organizational practices and individual impact in neutral to favourable terms. Examples include military training (Dornbusch 1955; Endleman 1974; Zurcher 1967), convents and monasteries (Ebaugh 1984; Hillery 1969), secular and religious communes (Kanter 1972), medical training (Becker and Greer 1958; Davis 1968), mental hospitals (Karmel 1969), and prisons (Etzioni 1961). Even where outcomes contravene legitimate institutional objectives, such as police interrogation methods that elicit false confessions, coercive processes have been tolerated until quite recently, and have avoided a brainwashing designation (Hepworth and Turner 1982; Zimbardo 1971). By contrast, where the form of organization is contested and deemed illegitimate, organizational settings receive brainwashing designations. Examples include socialist regimes, POW camps (Lifton 1989; Schein and Baker 1961), religious movements, controversial therapies, shepherding movements within established churches, and some conservative churches (Danzger 1989; Estruch 1995; Tobias and Lalich 1994; Yalom and Lieberman 1971). One clue to the political nature of these designations is that for each concept there is a conspicuous absence of positive terminology that refers to the reciprocal condition. What, for example, is the language for describing favorable brainwashing or desirable deconversion in their traditional meanings?

Another way of glimpsing the political nature of this debate is to pose the question of what would happen if members of the opposed camps could agree on the empirical observations. Would observational agreement yield interpretive agreement? I think not. In fact I would argue that empirical agreement already is greater than either side cares to acknowledge. The problem in arguing this point is that there are few cases in which any group-affiliation practices have been studied by an array of different researchers. The Oakland Family of the Unificationist Movement is one case for which a number of social scientists and other individuals have produced accounts of the affiliation process during the same time period (Ayella 1975; Barker 1984; Edwards 1979; Kemperman 1981; Lenz 1982; Lofland 1977; Robbins 1984; Taylor 1983). This is an important case because the Oakland Family clearly was the

Unificationist's most productive unit in terms of producing affiliates, and it was also the most controversial component of the movement, both internally and externally. What is most striking about the accounts of this setting is the degree of basic descriptive agreement on matters such as the nature of the initial recruitment process, the setting in which designated events occur, the sequence of events, the roles specific actors play, the methods of exerting influence, the orchestration of events, and even the outcomes. The descriptive agreement on events contrasts dramatically with the interpretive disagreement on the meaning of those same events. To put the matter another way, in the accounts produced by observers and participants alike, the variance is primarily in the *adjectives* rather than the *nouns*. In some accounts authors conclude on the basis of roughly comparable information that individual-group relationships constitute conversion, while in others they are deemed brainwashing.

In some respects at least, the theoretical frameworks through which social scientists interpret the organizational and individual patterns as brainwashing and conversion are not as opposed as they appear. For example, the central elements of transformative social movements (Bittner 1963; Bromley 1997a, 1997b; Kanter 1972; Kornhauser 1962) are quite similar to what Robert Lifton (1989) refers to as thought reform. Briefly, transformative movements engage in deconstruction and reconstruction of the cultural legitimation system and destructuring and restructuring of the dominant institutional order. With respect to cultural legitimation, these movements proclaim an ultimate reality that clashes dramatically with the reality constructed by the dominant social order. Constructing a vision of ultimate reality (Lifton's 'sacred science') typically involves developing a special language that recasts conventional meanings, creates a symbolic universe that adherents share, and serves as the lens through which the dominant social order is viewed (Lifton's 'language loading'). This vision of the ultimate contrasts sharply with the realities of the dominant social order, which is described in morally derogatory terms (Lifton's 'demand for purity') and sometimes condemned to destruction (Lifton's 'dispensing of existence').

The future social order that transformative movements seek to model is proclaimed against the existing social order. In order to maintain this proposed order against the power of existing realities, these movements typically establish strong, relatively impermeable boundaries (Lifton's 'milieu control') and engage in heavily ritualized lifestyles. Some rituals are organized to morally distance affiliates from the social order against which resistance is being mounted, and to eliminate the corrupting effects of participation in that order (Lifton's 'cult of confession'). Others are intended to demonstrate the active intervention of transcendent power in everyday life (Lifton's 'mystical manipulation') and to remove the 'pollution' associated with a corrupted social order through purification rituals. The high level of mobilization and vision of imminent transformation yield a sense of urgency and commitment in such movements, which legitimates asserting movement ideology against the apparent reality of individual experience and movement demands against individual needs (Lifton's 'doctrine over person'). There is not even disagreement on the attribution of intentionality to the implementation of these processes. Transformative religious movements clearly reject the dominant social order and seek to create a social environment in which the alternative reality is sustained against the dominant social reality. One component of this process is fostering identity transformation in affiliates that is consistent with the model of social reality being constructed. The two theoretical frameworks, therefore, do not differ nearly as much in their respective analyses of the structure and dynamics of religious movements as in the language employed in the analysis.

The difference in linguistic patterns between the two camps, in terms of both observational and theoretical accounts, is informative. Where the brainwashing theorists see individuals being disciplined, conversion theorists observe disciples. What the former regard as captivity, the latter perceive as captivation. What is humiliation to brainwashing theorists is humility from the perspective of conversion theorists. Brainwashing theorists describe religious movements as coercive communities, penitentiaries, while conversion theorists describe communities of penitents. Whether affiliates of these movements are assessed as thralls or enthralled is a function of the political location from which the narratives are constructed. The theories serve as political narratives in the sense that they are working from conclusions to data.

If the disagreement is political rather than observational and theoretical, it becomes clearer why it is not easily resolvable. The problem is not the absence of some set of crucial experiments. The differences are of political commitments rather than 'scientific' observations. Efforts on both sides to invoke the imprimatur of science and politics are predictable. As the primary knowledge legitimation system of the contemporary social order, science is a major source of power. If either side can cloak itself with the mantle of scientific legitimacy, knowledge and power are seamlessly united.

This argument does not, however, lead to the conclusion that the debate is intractable because there are profound differences between the two sides. To the contrary, what makes this case intriguing is that while there are differences, the commonalities between the protagonists far outweigh the differences. And further, there is evidence that the differences between the two sides are narrowing. Paradoxically, perhaps, it is *because* the differences have narrowed that conflict has intensified. In order to develop this argument, it is necessary to identify the core issue and convergence of the two coalitions around that issue.

Agentic Relationships: The Core Issue
The core issue in the brainwashing-conversion debate is agentic relationships that are developed and sustained through individual embeddedness.

One of the foundational processes in the historical development of what I refer to as contractually based social order (or, alternatively, 'modernity') is disembedding of individuals from tight-knit communities, which creates heightened individuation (Bromley 1997a). Individuation describes a structural situation in which there is a high level of organizational and role differentiation as well as consciousness of self vis-à-vis the roles one plays and the environment in which one operates. The normative attributes around which individuality is currently defined and defended across the social order include autonomy, voluntarism, and self-directedness (London 1969: 12). Preserving autonomy means avoiding personal embeddedness in any relational context that might compromise independent selfhood. Voluntarism involves exercising choice; individuals are defined as free when they have options and exercise choice between those options. Self-directedness involves the rational pursuit of individual interests or self-actuation. As institutions move in this direction, agentic relationships that involve individual embeddedness in any social context are suspect, and require evidence that they meet these three standards. Any relational form that embeds individuals by compromising these attributes is defined as detrimental to individual well-being and therefore as illegitimate. The common referent that links conversion and brainwashing is agentic relationships.

In its strongest form, conversion connotes unifying with a positive transcendent force. For example, the narrative of Paul on the road to Damascus continues to be invoked as the archetype of conversion. As Richardson (1983: 1) observes, 'Traditional views of Paul's conversion attribute agency or cause to an omnipotent God ... it was assumed that Paul did not act under his own volition, but was temporarily incapacitated by the actions of some outside force.' The implications are that an external force operated unilaterally to reorient Paul's volition and behaviour and that the result was an agentic relationship. Swanson (1978: 255) adopts similar language in defining charismatic influence. He writes that such influence is 'experienced through our having a special kind of relationship to the superordinate entity that we encounter. The entity has an existence and a creative role apart from our own. We can participate in its existence and activity if we make its purposes our own or if those purposes, by some means, replace our own vision of reality in the shaping of our action.' Concerted efforts to create such relationships by religious groups are at least implicit in typologies of conversion. The 'revivalist' motif in Lofland and Skonovd's (1981) conversion typology is defined as a transformation that occurs in a short time, with a high level of emotionality involving love and/or fear, in the context of a high level of group pressure. More broadly, the notion of agentic relationships is integral to a number of religious roles such as monks, nuns, missionaries, disciples, and devotees.

Brainwashing theories also revolve around agentic relationships, simply from the opposite position. Brainwashing involves unifying with a negative transcendent force that reorients individual volition and purpose. Since brainwashing is a secular theory, the nature of the transcendent force is not quite parallel to its counterpart in conversion theory. The forces at work are powerful secular forces that exceed the individual's capacity to cope with them. Singer and Ofshe (1990:190), for example, assert that thought reform programs 'are organized to destabilize individuals' sense of self by getting them to drastically reinterpret their life's history, radically alter their worldview, accept a new version of reality and causality, and develop dependency on the organization, thereby being turned into a *deployable agent* of the organization operating the thought reform program' (emphasis mine). Similarly, Zablocki (1998: 220) states that 'The brainwashing conjecture argues that there are conditions under which members of a religious organization may be systematically resocialized to become *deployable agents* of that organization with strong internalized disincentives for leaving' (emphasis mine).

From a political perspective, one of the major means through which the positive and negative sanctioning of conversion and brainwashing is accomplished is through connecting those designations to legitimate and illegitimate organizations and activities. The positive sanctioning of conversion is achieved by linking religious movements to the morally advantaged category of 'religion' (represented as 'churches'). As positively sanctioned institutions, churches are presumptively prosocial in character. Problematic episodes tend to be treated as uncharacteristic of the essential purposes of the institutional form, and do not in and of themselves undermine their legitimate standing. Contemporary movements are linked to the status of 'church' through various theories, such as the church-sect theory. Radical forms represent revitalization or the first stage in the process of institutionalization. The negative sanctioning of brainwashing is attained by connecting religious movement to the morally disadvantaged category of 'pseudo-religion' (represented as 'cults'). As a negatively sanctioned form, cults are presumptively antisocial in character. Problematic events are treated as characteristic of their essential purposes and confirm their illegitimate standing. Movements are linked to the status of cult through various theories of entrepreneurial and pathological formation. Radical forms represent the development of organized subversion.

Problematizing Embeddedness
The brainwashing-conversion debate has intensified, because over the last several decades agentic relationships created through embeddedness have become a source of increasing contention. The dominant institutions within American society have moved rapidly in the direction of disembedding individuals from the social contexts in which they operate. These various developments throughout the social order have the effect of preserving autonomy, expanding requirements for voluntarism, and promoting self-directedness. Consider the following.

One of the most important developments in fostering individual autonomy is increasing constraint on the legitimate use of coercion. For example, armed-forces boot camps have dramatically reduced the amount of physical 'intimidation' allowed, traditional fraternity 'hazing' has been all but eliminated, corporal punishment in public school systems has been prohibited, pressure is mounting to designate any physical punishment of children in families as abusive, physical force by one marriage partner against the other is legally actionable, and use of deadly force by police officers is more closely monitored and more often challenged (Bromley and Cress 1998; Cohen 1998; Thompson 1997).

In a variety of areas in which voluntarism is regarded as potentially problematic, more explicit evidence of assent is being mandated. Recent judicial rulings requiring that individuals be informed of their rights before police interviews, and legislation establishing requirements for 'truth in advertising' and 'truth in lending,' are examples of this trend. These kinds of initiatives are visible particularly in sexually related behaviors. Sexual harassment regulations hold organizations accountable for a 'hostile working environment,' institutions of higher education have adopted policies requiring evidence of explicit agreement in dating intimacy, and recent reforms in rape statutes have shifted the burden of proof from victim to perpetrator by basing judgments on degree of coercion used rather than on amount of resistance offered.

The mandate for self-directedness is evident in the creation of a new spectrum of disorders and syndromes through which individuals are evaluated as having lost this attribute. For example, 'compulsions' or 'addictions' to work, sex, food, money, drugs and alcohol, exercise, religion, and even the Internet have been identified. Most notable is 'codependence,' or addiction to relationships. These designations define new forms of inappropriate embeddedness in which identity and sense of worth are too closely tied to another individual. Books with titles such as *Codependent No More* (Beattie 1987), *Painful Affairs: Looking for Love through Addiction and Co-dependence* (Cruse 1989), and *Leaving the Enchanted Forest: The Path from Relationship Addiction to Intimacy* (Covington and Beckett 1988) offer analyses, warning signs, symptoms, and treatments designed to reassert selfhood. The most recent versions of therapy correspondingly diminish the power of therapists and expand the power of clients as a means of insuring self-directedness. For example, contemporary 'brief therapy' shortens the treatment period and attributes individual problems of living to a 'bad story' through which clients are thematizing their lives. The task of the therapist becomes to assist the client in developing a better, more empowering narrative (Bauer and Kobos 1987).

Parallel developments are occurring in mainstream churches. There has been a pronounced decline in institutional authority and a corresponding increase in parishioner autonomy, voluntarism, and self-directedness vis-à-vis churches. Sacred narratives are being loosened to emphasize individual empowerment, fulfilment, and freedom. Rituals do not invoke transformative encounters with transcendent power but rather tend to be constructed as aesthetic dramas that urge participants to live moral lives and engage in moral activities. The churches themselves organize as voluntary associations, with a service orientation towards parishioners; clerics function in a therapeutic role that is designed to accommodate a high level of individuation. Roof and McKinney (1987: 67) observe that 'the subjective aspects of faith have expanded as ascriptive and communal attachments have declined.' For their part, parishioners make decisions about religious participation voluntaristically on grounds of personal needs and preferences. As Hammond (1992: 169) puts it, 'Greater numbers of persons now ... legitimately look upon their parish involvement as their choice, to be made according to their standards. That involvement is now calculated as rewarding or not by individually derived equation.' By contrast, mainline denominations negatively sanction movements within their own ranks that accentuate individual embeddedness. For example, movements such as Opus Dei in the Catholic tradition, resurgent Orthodox Judaism, and shepherding in some Protestant denominations have met with denominational resistance (Blood 1985; Committee of Evangelical Theologians 1985; del Carmen Tapia 1998; Enroth 1992; Hume 1985). The language sanctioning embeddedness is that of authoritarianism, exploitation, and abuse rather than brainwashing, but the common denominator is individual disempowerment through embeddedness (Enroth 1992; Wellwood 1987). As Ronald Enroth writes in *Churches That Abuse* (1992: 30, 235), abusive religion 'fosters an unhealthy dependence of members on the leadership' and 'Unquestioning obedience and blind loyalty are its hallmarks.'

The shift in normative institutional relationships is accompanied by reassessment of different social forms by social scientists. Traditional forms of social organization that involved a high level of individual embeddedness have come under theoretical attack and contemporary forms are defended. For example, in his book *Sick Societies: Challenging the Myth of Primitive Harmony* (1992: 202–3), Robert Edgerton writes:

> the belief that folk societies ... were more harmonious and hence better adapted than larger, more urbanized societies is so ancient and deeply entrenched in Western thought that it has taken on the quality of a myth,

a sacred story not to be challenged. In this story, folk community was said to consist of emotional sharing, personal intimacy, moral commitment, social cohesion, and continuity over time. This sense of community, this harmony, was said to make possible the stable, positive adaptations that small-scale populations made to their environments. Due largely to the size and heterogeneity of urban centers, this sense of community – of common purpose – that had directed and united small-scale societies was lost.

Not so, he asserts. He concludes (1992: 15) that 'traditional beliefs and practices may be useful, may even serve as important adaptive mechanisms, but they may also be inefficient, harmful, and even deadly.' In a similar vein, Lewis Coser (1991: 19) refers to 'the modern conceit and the modern nostalgia of types of Gemeinschaft relationships whether it is found in Toennies' work or in that of modern cultural critics who, being alienated in the world of modernity, dream Rousseauistic dreams of the beauty of communities of noble savages.'

One of the seminal statements in contemporary sociology on strong and weak connections between individuals and groups is Mark Granovetter's widely cited article, 'The Strength of Weak Ties' (1973). Based on a study of two urban communities his argument is that 'weak ties' between individuals create more information availability, adaptability, opportunities, and mobility since individuals' knowledge-based and social network connections are more extensive. Rose Coser builds on the perspective reflected in the work of Edgerton and Granovetter in her book, *In Defense of Modernity*. She asserts (1991: 71) that 'In groups that offer complete security, in which role partners hardly change, and in which mutual expectations remain stable, there is relatively little opportunity to innovate or to weigh alternatives of thought and behavior. A gemeinschaft is such a group.' She then links embeddedness in folk and contemporary societies through Lewis Coser's (1974) concept of 'greedy institutions.' These social forms share in common the feature that 'individuals are cut off from current or prior cathectual relationships on the outside and thus are made dependent on the institution that claims their moral allegiance and the totality of their efforts' (1991: 73). She continues: 'The gemeinschaft is greedy to the extent that it absorbs individuals in unidimensional relationships, depriving them of the opportunities to confront multiple and contradictory expectations that would make them reflect about their roles' (74). Such groups, she claims, have less survival value in the modern world as they isolate individuals; limit opportunities, social mobility, and complex mental abilities; and are ineffective in dealing with crises. Wilbert Moore (1966) reaches much the same conclusion in his analysis of utopian groups, which he contends violate basic survivability principles by virtue of being sexless, too uniform, and overly static. The moral undesirability of embeddedness is clearly evident in the concepts of dependence, greediness, absorption, and low survivability.

There are, of course, voices of dissent and countertrends. The most persistent resistance emanates from conservative religious traditions that are constructed around a strong family-church network in which individuals are deeply embedded. In these traditions individual freedom is understood as 'freedom to' carry out the divine plan and is measured by individual commitment. Individuals can be protected and fulfilled only by being embedded in a strong community of believers where this connection to the divine can be continuously maintained. From their perspective, individuals can accomplish little on their own initiative; it is through submission to divine purpose as members of a community that all things are possible. In her description of conservative Christians, Ammerman (1987: 78) observes that conservative Christians 'expect church and friendship and everyday life will form a seamless whole. They expect the people and activities of the church to dominate and define their lives.' It is precisely the conservative religious groups that have been growing most rapidly over recent decades, and Dean Kelley (1972) argues that these churches are growing because they offer 'strong religion.' From the perspective being developed here, the characteristics of strong religion he enumerates (e.g., self-sacrifice, high demand, identification of individuals with collective goals) constitute embeddedness in agentic relationships. This is not the direction of the dominant institutions, of course, but it is important to note that resistance to that order extends well beyond contemporary religious movements.

Coalitions in Conflict

Although the dominant institutions in Western societies have moved rapidly towards rooting out individual disembeddedness, conflict remains over how individual essence and individual-group relationships will be authorized. Pursuant to the present argument, I distinguish two loosely organized coalitions, the religion and mental health coalitions. Constituent partners in the former coalition tend to include the religion movements, some denominational bodies, religious liberty organizations, and religion scholars working from a structural perspective. Institutional authorization derives from the assertion of a transcendent power that is the ultimate source of individual essence and social relationships. The constitutional privileging of religion presents a formidable obstacle to challenging this source of authorization. Constituent partners in the latter coalition tend to include the religion countermovements, a segment of mental health professionals, some regulatory institutions, and religion scholars working from a social-psychological perspective. Institutional authorization derives from the assertion of the individual as the fundamental reality upon which all social relationships are constructed. The recent expansion of provisions in state and national legislation defining and protecting individual rights against institutional claims has created strong momentum towards extension of such provisions across all institutional sectors. Although there are numerous individuals and groups that do not conform to this profile, the two coalitions do offer competing definitions of and authorization for individual-group relationships.

While there is potential for intense conflict between these two coalitions, several factors operate to reduce the actual conflict significantly. First, there has been a major accommodation between church – through which religious relationships are authorized – and state – through which therapeutic relationships are authorized (Williams and Demerath 1991). Mainline churches do not seriously challenge state legitimacy, and state agencies privilege religion.

Second, there has been convergence in the organization of therapy and religion. Most notably, mainline clergy have adopted pastoral counselling roles based on therapeutic principles, and a number of therapeutic traditions have moved towards sacralizing selfhood. The day-to-day practice of counselling, therefore, does not differ dramatically under the two sources of authorization. Tension is at the level expected between competitors offering similar services.

Third, there are major divisions within each coalition. For example, liberal and conservative denominations divide internally over the acceptable degree of religious authorization; conservative denominations support higher levels of embeddedness but reject the theological tenets of contemporary religious movements. The mental health coalition divides over the appropriate stance of therapy towards religion as well as the types of religious practice that are salubrious. Such divisions are critical to the dynamics of the brainwashing-conversion dispute because they have prevented either coalition from achieving sufficient cohesiveness to mount a major challenge to the other.

Fourth, the major actors in the religion and mental health coalitions share key attributes in common. They are credentialed by similar institutions, occupy professional-managerial positions in their respective institutions, and are linked into larger networks that operate on similar organizational principles. These similarities render the dispute even more perplexing to participants in both coalitions. Each side appears genuinely nonplussed at the position of the other, in part because there probably are few other issues on which they would divide so dramatically. Many participants in the religion coalition, for example, define themselves as ardent proponents of legal measures to prosecute various forms of abuse, and many participants in the mental health coalition regard themselves as dedicated defenders of religious liberty.

Finally, most scholars adopt moderate stances within their respective coalitions. There is a continuum of positions within each coalition on individual-group relationships. In the religion coalition, the definitions of conversion range from those asserting the absolute reality of a connection between the individual and spiritually liberating transcendent forces to those depicting conversions as socially constructed experiences forged jointly by convert and group. In the mental health coalition, the definitions of brainwashing range from those asserting the connection between transcendent enslaving forces to those depicting brainwashing as inappropriately constrained relationships. The 'strong conversion' and 'strong brainwashing' positions are held predominantly by movement and countermovement activists. For the most part, scholars on both sides do not defend those positions. Rather, the scholarly debate is being conducted in terms of 'weak conversion' and 'weak brainwashing' positions; that is, scholars on both sides tend to explain individual-group relationships in terms of some combination of personal and organizational characteristics. In the conversion model, individuals are depicted as in protest against the dominant social order, and the groups constitute vehicles of social protest. Models of individual-group relationships that are constructed in terms of role theory, experimentation, alternation, and conversion careers all reflect this orientation. In the brainwashing model, individuals are depicted as vulnerable, and the groups constitute inappropriate exploitive responses to this vulnerability. Models such as relational disorders, high exit costs, and spiritual abuse exemplify this perspective. Currently there appears to be consensus on the issue of physical coercion. Neither coalition will positively sanction behaviours or accounts that are directly attributable to such coercion.

The two coalitions continue to divide, however, on the key issue of authorization. As Sarbin (1973: 185) notes, relinquishment of one identity and formation of another is integral to all 'systems of conduct reorganization.' The dispute is over authorization of that process. The mental health coalition constitutes a threat to the religion coalition in (1) defining ultimate selfhood in secular terms, which poses a challenge to transcendent authorization, and (2) asserting the individual right to challenge institutional claims, including religious claims, in the name of defending selfhood. The religion coalition presents a threat to the mental health coalition by (1) asserting a transcendent authorization, which effectively trumps therapeutic authority; and (2) asserting the individual right to submit to institutional claims, particularly religious claims, in the name of expressing selfhood. In the present engagement the mental health coalition is on the offensive while the religion coalition seeks to preserve established privilege. The religion coalition cannot afford to concede much ground. Conversion is a foundational process in the logic of religious authorization; whether or not most mainline churches actually produce conversions is largely irrelevant. To submit conversion authenticity to mental health tests and to disclaim the right to prophetic protest would undermine religious authority. On the other side, the mental health coalition is unlikely to discontinue efforts to extend mental health claims. To privilege religious claims against the right of the individual to resist them or against damage to individual integrity would undermine therapeutic authority. Each is likely to attack the other at its point of greatest vulnerability, 'individual subjugation' and 'religious intolerance,' respectively.

Social science scholars in the religion coalition resonate with its logic in regarding religious movements as authentic resistance to the dominant social order. In this view, the source of protest is the contradictions in that order. Excesses by religious movements are tolerable only in the sense that they are preferable to an extension of state power against protest movements under a mental health banner. If there is a caution from the conversion scholars to the brainwashing scholars it is to avoid demonizing social protest. Social science scholars in the mental health coalition resonate with its logic in regarding religious movements as an exploitation of vulnerabilities in the conventional social order. From this perspective, the source of countermovement opposition is the contradictions within the movements themselves, which promise freedom and produce encapsulation under the protection of religious freedom. Excesses by countermovements are tolerable only as they constitute a defense of fundamental individual rights and a refusal to permit the blanket privileging of any group adopting a religious appellation. The caution from brainwashing to conversion scholars is to avoid sacralizing abuse.

Summary and Conclusions

The conversion-brainwashing debate has polarized scholars for several decades, purportedly as a result of intractable empirical issues. I have argued that while empirical problems abound, these are not the source of the protracted dispute. Rather, I contend that the conversion-brainwashing debate is a political imbroglio. As employed in the academic debate brainwashing and conversion have been used as symbolic umbrellas through which to morally advantage and disadvantage certain forms of individual-group relationships. The core issue in the debate is embeddedness in agentic relationships. The conflict has intensified as agentic relationships have been problematized across social institutions, and, paradoxically, because differences between the mental health and religion coalitions have narrowed.

There is more than a little irony in the conversion-brainwashing debate. At the end of the day, *both sides are endorsing individual autonomy, voluntarism, and self-directedness.* In the brainwashing camp this means resisting embeddedness that undermines those qualities, while in the conversion camp it means endorsing embeddedness as precisely the means for realizing those qualities. Key differences remain, of course, as the coalitions defend alternative sources of authorization and tacitly accept the different costs associated with expanded religious or state authorization. There is therefore likely to be resistance on both sides to reframing the issue, as I have suggested here. This analysis endangers both the professional dominance that conversion coalition scholars have achieved through amassing a major corpus of theoretical and empirical work, and the professional challenge being mounted by brainwashing coalition scholars on grounds that a meritorious scientific perspective is being deliberately 'blacklisted' (Zablocki 1997).

Although an early resolution of the dispute seems unlikely, even to debate the political differences openly rather than through the veil of scientific objectivity would constitute a measure of progress. It is just as important to reintegrate the brainwashing-conversion debate into the broader disciplinary and political conversations currently taking place over individual-group relationships. Unless this occurs, the sociology of religion will have relegated itself to an intellectual cul-de-sac and missed the opportunity to inform and be informed by the broader intellectual community.

References

Ammerman, Nancy. 1987. *Bible Believers: Fundamentalists in the Modern World*. New Brunswick, N.J.: Rutgers University Press.

Anthony, Dick, and Thomas Robbins. 1992. 'Law, Social Science and the "Brainwashing" Exception to the First Amendment.' *Behavioral Sciences and the Law* 10: 5–30.

Ayella, Marybeth. 1975. 'An Analysis of Current Conversion Practices of Followers of Reverend Sun Myung Moon.' Unpublished paper. Berkeley: University of California at Berkeley.

Barker, Eileen. 1984. *The Making of A Moonie*. Oxford: Basil Blackwell.

Bauer, Gregory, and Joseph Kobos. 1987. *Brief Therapy: Short-term Psychodynamic Intervention*. Northvale, N.J.: Aronson.

Beattie, Melody. 1987. *Codependent No More*. New York: Harper & Row.

Becker, Howard, and Blanche Greer. 1958. 'The Fate of Idealism in Medical School.' *American Sociological Review* 23: 50–6.

Bittner, Egon. 1963. 'Radicalism and Radical Movements.' *American Sociological Review* 28: 928–40.

Blau, Judith. 1991. 'When Weak Ties Are Structured.' In *Social Roles and Social Institutions: Essays in Honor of Rose Laub Coser*, edited by Judith Blau and Norman Goodman, 133–47. Boulder, Colo.: Westview Press.

Blood, Linda. 1985. 'Shepherding/Discipleship: Theology and Practice of Absolute Obedience.' *Cultic Studies Journal* 2: 235–45.

Bromley, David. 1988. 'ISKCON and the Anti-Cult Movement.' In *Krishna Consciousness in the West*, edited by David G. Bromley and Larry Shinn, 252–89. Lewisburg: Bucknell University Press.

– 1997a. 'A Sociological Narrative of Crisis Episodes, Collective Action, Culture Workers, and Countermovements.' *Sociology of Religion* 58: 105–40.

– 1997b. 'Constructing Apocalypticism: Social and Cultural Elements of Radical Organization.' In *Millennium, Messiah, and Mayhem*, edited by Thomas Robbins and Susan Palmer, 31–46. New York, N.Y.: Routledge.

Bromley, David, and Clinton Cress. 1998. 'Locating the Corporal Punishment

Debate in the Context of Conflicting Forms of Social Relations.' *Marriage and Family* 2: 152–64.

Bromley, David G., and Anson Shupe. 1986. 'Affiliation and Disaffiliation: A Role Theory Approach to Joining and Leaving New Religious Movements.' *Thought: A Review of Culture and Ideas* 61: 197–211.

– 1979. 'Just a Few Years Seem Like a Lifetime: A Role Theory Perspective on Conversion to a Marginal Religious Group.' In *Research in Social Movements, Conflict and Change*, edited by Louis Kriesberg, 169–96. Greenwich, Conn.: JAI Press.

Carter, Lewis. 1998. 'Carriers of Tales: On Assessing Credibility of Apostate and Other Outsider Accounts of Religious Practices.' In *The Politics of Religious Apostasy*, edited by David Bromley, 221–38. Westport, Conn.: Praeger.

Cialdini, Robert. 1985. *Influence: How and Why People Agree to Things*. New York: Quill.

Cohen, Adam. 1998. 'Is This a Camp or Jail?' *Time*, 26 January, 56–7.

Committee of Evangelical Theologians. 1985. 'A Statement of Evaluation Regarding Maranatha Campus Ministries/Maranatha Christian Ministries/Maranatha Christian Church.' *Cultic Studies Journal* 2: 278–83.

Conway, Flo, and Jim Siegelman. 1982. 'Information Disease: Have the Cults Created a New Mental Illness?' *Science Digest* (January): 86–92.

Coser, Lewis. 1974. *Greedy Institutions*. New York: Free Press.

– 1991. 'Role-Set Theory and Individual Autonomy.' In *Social Roles and Social Institutions: Essays in Honor of Rose Laub Coser*, edited by Judith Blau and Norman Goodman, 13–20. Boulder, Colo.: Westview Press.

Coser, Rose. 1991. In *Defense of Modernity: Role Complexity and Individual Autonomy*. Stanford: Stanford University Press.

Covington, Stephanie, and Liana Beckett. 1988. *Leaving the Enchanted Forest: The Path from Relationship Addiction to Intimacy*. San Francisco: Harper & Row.

Cruse, Joseph. 1989. *Painful Affairs: Looking for Love through Addiction and Co-dependence*. San Francisco: Heath Communications.

Cushman, Philip. 1986. 'The Self-Besieged: Recruitment-Indoctrination Processes in Restrictive Groups.' *Journal for the Theory of Social Behavior* 16: 1–32.

Danzger, M. Herbert. 1989. *Returning to Tradition: The Contemporary Revival of Orthodox Judaism*. New Haven: Yale University Press.

Davis, Fred. 1968. 'Professional Socialization as Subjective Experience: The Process of Doctrinal Conversion among Student Nurses.' In *Institutions and the Person*, edited by Howard Becker et al., 235–51. Chicago: Aldine.

del Carmen, Tapia. 1998. *Beyond the Threshold: A Life in Opus Dei*. New York: Continuum.

Dornbusch, Sanford. 1955. 'The Military Academy as an Assimilating Institution.' *Social Forces* 33: 316–21.

Ebaugh, Helen Rose. 1984. *Out of the Cloister*. Austin: University of Texas Press.

Edgerton, Robert. 1992. *Sick Societies: Challenging the Myth of Primitive Harmony*. New York: Free Press.

Edwards, Christopher. 1979. *Crazy for God*. Englewood Cliffs, N.J.: Prentice-Hall.

Endleman, Robert. 1974. 'The Military as a *Rite de Passage*.' In *Anthropology and American Life*, edited by Joseph Jorgensen and Marcello Truzzi, 282–9. Englewood Cliffs, N.J.: Prentice-Hall.

Enroth, Ronald. 1992. *Churches that Abuse*. Grand Rapids, Mich.: Zondervan.

Estruch, Joan. 1995. *Saints and Schemers: Opus Dei and Its Paradoxes*. New York: Oxford University Press.

Etzioni, Amitai. 1961. *A Comparative Analysis of Complex Organizations: On Power, Involvement, and Their Correlates*. New York: Free Press of Glencoe.

Geertz, Clifford. 1974. 'From the Native's Point of View.' *American Academy of Arts and Sciences Bulletin* 28: 26–43.

Granovetter, Mark. 1973. 'The Strength of Weak Ties.' *American Journal of Sociology* 78: 1360–80.

Hammond, Phillip. 1992. *Religion and Personal Autonomy: The Third Disestablishment in America*. Columbia: University of South Carolina Press.

Hepworth, Mike, and Bryan Turner. 1982. *Confession: Studies in Deviance and Religion*. London: Routledge & Kegan Paul.

Hillery, George. 1969. 'The Convent: Community, Prison, or Task Force?' *Journal for the Scientific Study of Religion* 8: 140–51.

Hume, Cardinal Basil. 1985. 'Guidelines for Opus Dei in Westminster Diocese.' *Cultic Studies Journal* 2: 284–5.

Kanter, Rosabeth. 1972. 'Commitment and the Internal Organization of Millennial Movements.' *American Behavioral Scientist* 16: 219–44.

Karmel, Madeline. 1969. 'Total Institution and Self-Mortification.' *Journal of Health and Social Behavior* 10: 134–40.

Katchen, Martin. 1992. 'Brainwashing, Hypnosis, and the Cults.' *Australian Journal of Clinical and Experimental Hypnosis* 20: 79–88.

Kelley, Dean. 1972. *Why Conservative Churches are Growing: A Study in Sociology of Religion*. New York: Harper and Row.

Kemperman, Steve. 1981. *Lord of the Second Advent*. Ventura, Calif.: Regal Books.

Kornhauser, William. 1962. 'Social Bases of Political Commitment: A Study of Liberals and Radicals.' In *Human Behavior and Social Processes*, edited by Arnold Rose, 321–39. Boston: Houghton Mifflin.

Lenz, Douglas. 1982. 'Twenty-Two Months as a Moonie.' *LCA Partners* (February): 12–15.

Lifton, Robert. 1989. *Thought Reform and the Psychology of Totalism*. Chapel Hill: University of North Carolina Press.

Lofland, John. 1977. *Doomsday Cult*. Rev. ed. New York: Irvington.

Lofland, John, and James Richardson. 1984. 'Religious Movement Organizations: Elemental Forms and Dynamics.' In *Research in Social Movements, Conflicts and Change*, edited by Lewis Kriesberg, 29–51. Greenwich, Conn.: JAI Press.

Lofland, John, and Norman Skonovd. 1981. 'Conversion Motifs.' *Journal for the Scientific Study of Religion* 20: 373–85.

Lofland, John, and Rodney Stark. 1965. 'Becoming a World-Saver: A Theory of Conversion to a Deviant Perspective.' *American Sociological Review* 30: 862–75.

London, Perry. 1969. *Behavior Control*. New York: Harper & Row.

Moore, Wilbert. 1966. 'The Utility of Utopias.' *American Sociological Review* 31: 765–72.

Ofshe, Richard, and Margaret Singer. 1986. 'Attacks on Peripheral Versus Central Elements of Self and the Impact of Thought Reforming Techniques.' *Cultic Studies Journal* 3: 3–24.

Rambo, Lewis. 1993. 'Understanding Religious Conversion.' New Haven, Conn.: Yale University Press.

Richardson, James. 1983. 'The Brainwashing/Deprogramming Controversy: An Introduction.' In *The Brainwashing/Deprogramming Controversy*, edited by David Bromley and James Richardson, 1–12. New York: Edwin Mellen Press.

Robbins, Thomas. 1984. 'Constructing Cultist "Mind Control."' *Sociological Analysis* 45: 241–56.

Roof, Wade Clark, and William McKinney. 1987. *American Mainline Religion: Its Changing Shape and Future*. New Brunswick: Rutgers University Press.

Saliba, John. 1990. 'Social Science and the Cults: An Annotated Bibliography.' New York: Garland Publishers.

Sarbin, Theodore. 1973. 'Self-Reconstitution Processes.' *Journal of Abnormal Psychology* 81: 182–98.

Schein, Edgar, and C.H. Baker. 1961. *Coercive Persuasion*. New York: Norton.

Shupe, Anson, and David Bromley. 1980. *The New Vigilantes*. Beverly Hills: Sage Publications.

Singer, Margaret, and Richard Ofshe. 1990. 'Thought Reform Programs and the Production of Psychiatric Casualties.' *Psychiatric Annals* 20: 188–93.

Sirkin, Mark, and Lyman Wynne. 1990. 'Cult Involvement as Relational Disorder.' *Psychiatric Annals* 20: 199–203.

Snow, David, and Richard Machalek. 1984. 'The Sociology of Conversion.' *Annual Review of Sociology* 10: 167–90.

Swanson, Guy. 1978. 'Trance and Possession: Studies of Charismatic Influence.' *Review of Religious Research* 19: 253–78.

Taylor, David. 1983. 'Thought Reform and the Unification Church.' In *The Brainwashing/Deprogramming Controversy*, edited by David G. Bromley and James T. Richardson, 73–90. New York: Edwin Mellen Press.

Thompson, Mark. 1997. 'Boot Camp Goes Soft.' *Time*, 4 August, 18–23.

Tobias, Madeleine, and Janja Lalich. 1994. *Captive Hearts-Captive Minds: Freedom and Recovery from Cults and Abusive Relationships*. Alameda, Calif.: Hunter House.

Travisano, Richard. 1970. 'Alternation and Conversion as Qualitatively Different Transformations.' In *Social Psychology Through Symbolic Interaction*, edited by G. Stone and M. Garverman, 594–606. Waltham, Mass.: Ginn-Blaisdell.

Verdier, Paul. 1977. *Brainwashing and the Cults*. Hollywood, Calif.: Institute of Behavioral Conditioning.

Wellwood, John. 1987. 'On Spiritual Authority: Genuine and Counterfeit.' In *Spiritual Choices: The Problem of Recognizing Authentic Paths to Inner Transformation*, edited by Dick Anthony, Bruce Ecker, and Ken Wilber, 283–304. New York: Paragon House.

Williams, Rhys, and N.J. Demerath III. 1991. 'Religion and Political Processes in an American City.' *American Sociological Review* 56: 417–31.

Yalom, Irvin, and Morton Lieberman. 1971. 'A Study of Encounter Group Casualties.' *Archives of General Psychiatry* 25: 16–30.

Zablocki, Benjamin. 1996. 'Reliability and Validity of Apostate Accounts in the Study of Religious Communities.' Paper presented at the annual meeting of the Association for the Sociology of Religion, New York.

– 1997. 'The Blacklisting of a Concept: The Strange History of the Brainwashing Conjecture in the Sociology of Religion.' *Nova Religio* 1: 96–121.

– 1998. 'Exit Cost Analysis: A New Approach to the Scientific Study of Brainwashing.' *Nova Religio* 1: 216–49.

Zimbardo, Philip. 1971. 'Coercion and Compliance: The Psychology of Police Confessions.' In *The Triple Revolution Emerging*, edited by Robert Perucci and Marc Pilisuk, 492–508. Boston: Little, Brown.

Zurcher, Louis. 1967. 'The Naval Recruit Training Center: A Study of Role Assimilation in a Total Institution: Recruits in Boot Camp.' *Sociological Inquiry* 37: 85–98.

8. Brainwashing Programs in The Family/ Children of God and Scientology

Stephen A. Kent

A recent attempt to renew the 'sociology of religion debate' about 'brainwashing' insisted that earlier academic dismissals of the term were premature, at least regarding its applicability to techniques and programs found within some alternative religions. Leading this attempt at renewal is sociologist Ben Zablocki, who stated that he disagreed with earlier definitional restrictions on the brainwashing concept. These earlier restrictions concluded that forcible confinement *had* to be part of a person's experience before it could receive the brainwashing label (see Zablocki 1998: 231–2; cf. Scheflin and Opton 1978: 40). In refutation, Zablocki argued that he had observed profound personality transformations among members of high-demand faiths without physical constraint having played a role (Zablocki 1997: 97, see 99), and that these profound transformations convinced him that in fact the brainwashing term did have utility for explaining these kinds of phenomena.

Scholars currently disagree about the appropriateness of applying the "brainwashing" term to situations where there is no physical force or force-threat. But, presumably, most would agree that the term is applicable to cultic situations in which members experience programs involving threats or force. My study of high-demand camps and programs in two groups – The Family (formerly the Children of God) and

---

*Please note that this is an historical analysis; it does not necessarily describe events as they exist in Scientology or The Family at the present time (eds.).

Scientology explores the effects of brainwashing in systems that did threaten and use force. Brainwashing is an appropriate descriptor of what these groups imposed upon hundreds of their members. Characteristics of these two systems of ideological reshaping were: (1) forcible confinement, (2) physical maltreatment (Anthony 1990: 304–5; see Anthony and Robbins 1992: 18; World Services 1993: 4, 20, 21; Zablocki 1997: 112–14), (3) social degradations and maltreatment, along with (4) intense study of ideology, coupled with (5) forced confessions, and (6) personal 'success' stories.

Social degradations and maltreatment were part of a brainwashing program's efforts to pressure selected individuals into renouncing fundamental aspects of their lives. Humiliation, social isolation, submission, public degradations, and confessions characterized such efforts. Their purpose was to shame individuals into renouncing aspects of their past in attempts to instill or renew leadership-sanctioned, 'acceptable' ideological teachings. Concurrently, group leaders conducted specific programs that provided the targeted individuals with the beliefs and behaviours that persons in charge required them to adopt and internalize. Individuals had to confess their reputed shortcomings by negatively comparing themselves to the imposed beliefs and behaviours. Finally, before leaders allowed members to leave these programs, the members had to produce stories that glorified the supposedly positive transformations that they underwent.

I build my case for the appropriateness of the brainwashing term by utilizing primary documents, publications, and policies from The Family and Scientology, combined with legal statements, media accounts, and personal interviews with former members of both groups who had been through the brainwashing programs. Much of this evidence was relatively easy to obtain, and a considerable portion of the Scientology information is available on the World Wide Web.

The Family operated what it called Victor programs in relation to its teen training centres in the 1980s and into the early 1990s, and discussion specifically of the centres and programs appears in Family publications (for example, Family Services 1990; see Home Services 1992: 10), several academic sources (Kent and Hall 1997: Melton 1994: 90; Millikan 1994: 229; Shepherd and Lilliston 1994: 63; Van Zandt 1991: 171–2), and one British court case (Ward 1995: 125–33). Thirteen former members, moreover, who were young teens in the organization during the period, spoke to me at length about their experiences in centres and Victor programs, and recently former members discussed or mentioned the Victor programs on an Internet website, <excognet.com> (for example, Cobra 1998; La Mattery 1998; McNeil 1998a, 1998b). An additional former member provided me with a written account about one particularly harsh punishment that she personally witnessed being imposed upon a teen in The Family's large Filipino facility (Priebe 1995).

Scientology refers to its Rehabilitation Task Force (RPF) and its more severe punishment system within the brainwashing program – the Rehabilitation Project Force's Rehabilitation Project Force (RPF's RPF) – in a widely circulated book (Hubbard 1976: 441–2, 451), and a few of the actual policies overseeing the program have become available (see, for example, Boards of Directors of the Churches of Scientology 1974, 1977, 1980). In addition, accounts of the RPF from former members have appeared in print since 1980, first in a court case (Burden 1980) and subsequently in additional court documents (Armstrong 1982; Aznaran and Aznaran 1988; Whitfield 1989, 1994; Young 1994) and in testimonies (*California Court of Appeal* 1989; *Royal Courts of Justice* 1984). Authors have reported similar accounts in numerous books, newspapers, and magazines in the United States (Behar 1986; Corydon 1996: 123–9, 136–7; Koff 1989; Shelor 1984; Welkos and Sappell 1990), England (Atack 1990; Barnes 1984; Bracchi 1994: 5; Miller 1987), and Germany (Bavarian State Ministry of the Interior 1997; Enquete Kommission 1998: 77 n. 135; Gruber and Kintzinger (interviewers) 1994; *Hessische Allgemeine* 1997; Kintzinger (interviewer) 1997: 52; Reichelt 1997: 284–5, see 273–85; Tongi 1998; Young 1995: 107). Eight former members have discussed with me their experiences in the RPF (and in some cases, the RPF's RPF), and some of these same people have posted accounts on the Internet. Recently an active Scientologist posted some of his RPF experiences on the Web's <alt.religion.scientology> newsgroup (SB 1998a, b, c, d, e, f, g, h, i). (I decided not to attempt to interview current Family members[1] or Scientologists[2] because I feared they likely would suffer unacceptable consequences if they were to reveal aspects about these camps and programs that their respective groups want to keep concealed.) All of the information tells a consistent set of stories, except for the RPF account that Scientology has on one of its websites (Church of Scientology International 1996).[3] In essence, the operation of forced labour and reindoctrination programs in both The Family and Scientology is well known, yet they have received scant academic attention.

Some differences exist between these programs in The Family as opposed to Scientology, and even within each facility or program in different locations and at different points in time. Nevertheless, the slight variations pale in comparison to the internal consistency within each program or facility and the parallels between the two of them. Initially The Family's Victor program targeted adolescents, but later it expanded to include adults (although we still know little about the adult program [see COUNTERCOG, n.d.; Dupuy, circa 1993: 8–14]). By contrast, from the inception of Scientology's RPF programs, teens and possibly younger children were subject to its harsh regime (Cohee 1989; Jebson 1997; Kent, Interview with Dale, 1997: 4; Kent, Interview with Pat, 1997a: 32; Kent, Interview with Pignotti, 1997: 30), even though a majority of inmates were adults (apparently with no upper age limit).

Brief Program Histories

Each of the respective organization's programs has its own unique genesis. The Family's teen centres and related Victor programs appear to have emerged in the mid-1980s, as a wave of young people born inside the group were maturing children or young teens. Many Family youth lacked the fervour and commitment that motivated their parents, which meant that The Family suffered the classic 'crisis of the second generation' that is common in many sects. As Maria (who was the long-time partner to The Family's founder) realized in 1990, converts *were willing to forsake all to join us, and were determined to give their lives* for what we stand for. But most of our JETTs [Junior End Time Teens, around 10 to 13 years old] have *not* volunteered to join The Family, and what we stand for' (Maria 1990a: 617 [emphasis Maria's]). In an attempt to socialize them more deeply into the group's ideology, Family leadership established instructional centres for them in various parts of the world. Leaders overseeing these instructional or educational centres sent young members to special disciplinary regimes – the Victor programs – if they did not adjust to their rules or expressed persistent doubts about the organization's teachings, practices, or leaders.

A Family publication, for example, commented on the beginning of the Japanese Victor Program:

Recently, different teens were brought in from many different field Homes to the Heavenly City School to be part of the 'Teen Ministry Training Program' where they were to receive special training in different ministries. At the same time the Shepherds wanted to help a number of teens who had serious problems & were greatly in need of very close oversight, discipline & intense retraining & rewiring in the Word.

To give this small group of problem teens the care & attention needed, the 'Teen Victor Program' was begun. These problem teens, now called the Teen Victors, were moved to a retraining centre where their Shepherds were able to zero in on their needs. (Family Services 1990: 10–11)

A separate document suggests that the Victor Program began some time during 1989 (Maria 1990c: 636).

What little we know about the subsequent inclusion of adults in Victor programs suggests that leaders sent them for intensive confessions and reindoctrination for similar reasons as they did to the youth (Dupuy circa 1993: 8, 10, 12–14). According to one researcher who had been close to the group, the last Victor program (in England) closed in 1992 (Millikan 1994: 229). Before their closure, however, Maria called for the attention and discipline that teens received in the Teen Centers and Victory Program to become part of regular home life (Maria 1990b: 626–7).

Scientology's RPF program began in January 1974 on a ship captained by Scientology's founder, L. Ron Hubbard. It had a number of antecedent programs, which in various degrees punished supposedly wayward members, trained them in particular skills, and extracted nearly free labour from them (Boards of Directors of the Churches of Scientology 1977: 1 [on the Estates Project Force]; Dagnell 1997: 3–4; Hubbard 1969 [on the Decks Projects Force]; Hubbard 1972, 1976: 501 [on the Stewards Project Force]; Hubbard 1976: 341 [on the mud box brigade]; Hubbard 1976: 429 [on the Pursers Project Force]; Hubbard 1977: 1). Hubbard himself almost certainly forged a brainwashing manual in the mid-1950s, which his organization distributed widely at the time (Hubbard [probable author] n.d. [circa 1955], 1955),[4] and ideas appearing in it likely influenced aspects of Scientology's subsequent forced labour and re-indoctrination programs (see, for example [Hubbard, L. Ron] 1969). The immediate incident, however, that propelled Hubbard to order an aide to design the program was an injurious motorcycle accident he suffered, and that he blamed on subversive elements working on the ship (Miller 1987: 321; see Kent, Interview with Ernesto, 1997: 1; with Pignotti, 1997: 6). Subsequently, Scientologists received RPF assignments if they gave indications on Scientology's

confessional and interrogation machine, the E-Meter, that they har-
boured dangerous thoughts against Scientology or its leader. People
also received RPF assignments if they were performing poorly on their
jobs, were showing negative personality indicators (presumably such
things as attitude, doubts, hostility, etc.), or were causing trouble
(Boards of Directors of the Churches of Scientology 1977: 1).

It appears that the first assignment to the RPF's RPF occurred on 24
April 1974 when someone thought that his or her 'RPF assignment was
amusing' and therefore 'was unable to recognize a need for redemption or any means to effect it,' which the regular RPF supposedly provided (Hubbard 1976: 451, see 627). (The Scientology source on the
RPF's RPF does not allow readers to determine either who made the
first assignment, or who was the first person assigned.) Inmates stayed
in this harsher program until they 'recognized this need [for redemp-
tion] and of their own self-determinism requested to be included in
RPF redemption actions ...' While in it they remained segregated from
the RPFers, received no pay for their work, did not receive auditing (a
type of Scientology counselling), but received no more than six hours
sleep and triple punishments for infractions (Hubbard 1976: 451).

Forcible Confinement

Both the Victor programs and various RPF programs operated within
larger organizational facilities, and both also had some programs that
functioned in relative isolation. Some of the Victor camp locations are
well documented, while others receive mention in accounts by one or
more people who claim to have been in them. Discussion about the Victor program (sometimes called a Teens Detention Camp [Ward 1995:
152]) in Macao, for example, received attention in a British court case
involving The Family (Ward 1995: 74, 131, 152, 157–62; see also Kent,
Interview with Frost, 1995; Interview with Lorna, 1996: 11–24), in which
'the children were subjected to a regime of physical and psychological
brutality' (Ward 1995: 158). Moreover, so many former members have
discussed the forced isolation and often harsh conditions within The
Family's facilities in the Philippines during the 1980s that their existence is beyond doubt (Ward 1995: 153–5; see Kent, Interview with
Cheryl, 1996: 70–113; Interview with Donovan, 1995; Interview with
Hendricks, 1995; Interview with Lorna, 1996: 10–11; Priebe 1995). Likewise, the Japanese facility is well documented (Ward 1995: 155; Kent,
Interview with Albert, 1997: 25–7, 33; Interview with Marleana, 1995b:

12–17; Interview with Stephanie, 1997: 2, 4). Similar accounts about teen training centres (sometimes with attached Victor programs) in Brazil (Kent, Interview with Stephanie, 1997: 7, 10), England (Kent, Interview with Donovan, 1995: 34), Hungary (Kent, Interview with Frost, 1995: 1), Mexico (Ward 1995: 135, 150, 157, 167; see Kent, Interview with Betty, 1996: 42, 45–6; Interview with Marleana, 1995a: 32–5, 37), Peru (see Kent, Interview with Betty, 1996: 34; Interview with Emily, 1995: 10), and Puerto Rico (Interview with Donovan, 1995: 30; Interview with Shawn, 1995: 27), suggest that Family teens experienced brainwashing conditions around the world (see Ward 1995: 167 [who mentions additional Victor programs in Switzerland, Italy, Denmark, and Thailand]).

Scientology's first RPF was aboard ship in the 1970s, when Hubbard oversaw his small fleet in the Mediterranean and the Atlantic Ocean. When the organization began its Clearwater, Florida, land operation in 1975 (Atack 1990: 209), the RPF also came ashore (Superior Court of the State of California 1984: 1461–3). On the other side of the American continent, RPF labour helped renovate Scientology's current facilities in Los Angeles (Kent, Interview with Pat, 1997a: 21; Interview with Prince, 1998: 15; see Aznaran and Aznaran 1988: 8) after the organization acquired an old Los Angeles hospital building in February 1977 (Church of Scientology of California 1978: 144). RPF labour helped build various desert facilities on Scientology's Gilman Hot Springs, California and La Quinta, California properties (Superior Court of the State of California 1984: 1473–4). Its RPF camp in Happy Valley (near the Soboba Indian reservation in southern California) seems to be the most isolated facility of this nature about which solid evidence exists (see Aznaran and Aznaran 1988: 11–12). Likewise, strong evidence exists for the operation of additional RPF programs in England (Royal Courts of Justice 1984: 27) and Denmark (Kintzinger [Interviewer] 1997; Schernekau/Elleby, n.d. 1990, 1989a, b; 1990a, b, c, d, e, f, g, h, i, j, k). All of these RPFs presumably still operate, except for the ones on the ships (since the small fleet no longer operates).

Scientology's RPF and RPF'S RPF

In The Family's and Scientology's programs, leadership of the respective organizations assigned people and confined them, often by force. The Scientology evidence about forcible confinement is somewhat modified by the fact that, apparently, many current RPF 'participants' sign releases which state that they are in the program voluntarily, having chosen it over the option of automatic Sea Org expulsion (see

Anonymous n.d.). Sufficient numbers of accounts also exist, however, of people indicating that they were sent to the RPF against their will. Consequently, they are most accurately called 'inmates' rather than mere participants. A typical scenario seems to be that two 'guards' arrive with instructions that they are to escort someone to the RPF, which is what happened to Pat in the late 1970s at the Los Angeles building complex (Kent, Interview with Pat, 1997a: 19) and Dennis Erlich in Clearwater, Florida. As Erlich indicated, he did not resist the guards' directive to proceed to the RPF, since 'it was sort of implicit that [if] you wanna [sic] fight you're gonna [sic] get the shit kicked out of you' (Kent, Interview with Erlich, 1997: 9). In 1974 former member Jesse Prince apparently did try to resist the five guards in 1977 whose directive was to accompany him to the RPF, since he recounted that these men literally had to drag him into it as he kicked and screamed (Kent, Interview with Prince, 1998: 15). More dramatically, former member David Mayo stated that in 1982 high ranking Scientologists 'kidnapped me and subsequently kept me captive and physically and mentally abused me for six months' (Mayo 1994: 2–3).

Once in the RPF (or its harsher companion, the RPF's RPF), at least a few inmates seem to have suffered severe restraint or confinement. Erlich, for example, claimed that he spent the first day or two of his RPF's RPF assignment locked in a metal cage (Kent, Interview with Erlich, 1997: 8). Moreover, four former members – Dennis Erlich, Hana Whitfield, Tonya Burden, and an anonymous Internet 'poster' calling herself Nefertiti – each wrote about seeing a woman chained to a pipe in the basement of Scientology's Fort Harrison Hotel in Clearwater, and at least two of the accounts appear to be of incidents that are roughly a decade apart (Burden 1980: 12; Nefertiti 1997: 3; Whitfield 1994: 42; WMNF 1996: 5).[5]

Final evidence about the forcible confinement issue comes from the fact that some former RPFers indicated that they escaped from RPF facilities. Julie Mayo, for example, reported that she snuck out of a guarded Scientology compound when a gate was momentarily open (Mayo 1996: 8–9). Similarly, Vicki Aznaran swore that she and two others fled from the RPF facility called Happy Valley, even though Scientology guards pursued them on motorcycles (Aznaran and Aznaran 1998: 12). Apparently Pat had to devise an elaborate ruse to escape, which culminated in her tricking her guard so that she had time to jump into the car of a friend she had arranged to meet (Kent, Interview with Pat, 1997b: 4).

Guards at some of the RPF facilities apparently were armed. For example, former high-ranking Scientologist Jesse Prince reported both that the guards at the Happy Valley RPF carried rifles (Kent, Interview with Prince, 1998: 42, 49), and that while he was in the Sea Org staff at Gilman Hot Springs (where RPFers worked), he and other Scientology executives had many guns (49). A more extensive discussion of the weaponry that the guards and others had at Gilman Hot Springs appeared in the affidavit of former member Andre Tabayoyon, who indicated that he helped design the security system for the facility (Tabayoyon 1994: 8 [par. 28]). The weapons stockpile allegedly included 'semi-automatic assault rifles (HK 91 assault rifles capable of firing 300 to 500 rounds of ammunition a minute[)], 45 caliber pistols, .380 automatic weapons, and twelve gauge shotguns ...' He further claimed that guards on motorcycles 'were trained to carry loaded cocked 45 caliber pistols,' and that a marksman sat at a location high above the base with 'a high powered rifle with a telescopic scope' (8 [par. 31–2]). The grounds themselves, Tabayoyon indicated, were secured with a perimeter fence, razor wire, lighting, electronic monitors, concealed microphones, ground sensors, motion sensors, and hidden cameras (8 [par. 28]).

Finally, from yet another Scientology RPF facility, the security conditions that existed during the renovations of the former hospital construction site in Los Angeles (which now is a Scientology complex) allegedly included a barbed wire fence patrolled by guards with dogs. Ostensibly security guards intended to keep out unauthorized people from the facility, but their presence also kept RPFers from leaving (with a few accounts of people actually having to escape in order to get out [Kent, Interview with Prince, 1998: 25–6, 28–9]). Taken together, these descriptions of RPF guards at various facilities strongly suggest that the RPF programs meet the necessary academic requirement that forcible confinement must be a factor before stating that inmates were participants in a brainwashing program.

The Family's Teen Training and Victor Programs
In contrast to some of the RPF accounts, no comparable escape stories exist regarding inmates fleeing either the teen camps or their harsher Victor programs. Leaders did prevent, however, the teens from leaving their respective programs and facilities. Indeed, the Filipino facility known as 'The Jumbo' (because of its size) contained (according to one estimate) up to three hundred and fifty people living within ten- to fifteen-foot walls – walls patrolled by armed guards at night (Kent, Interview with Donovan, 1995: 1–2; see also Interview with Hendricks,

1995: 18). In the year Ernest Donovan was there, he only left the compound five times, always under supervision (Kent, Interview with Donovan, 1995: 2). Cheryl indicated that she only went outside the compound three times during the year she was there, also only under supervision (Kent, Interview with Cheryl, 1996: 60). For the teens at least, they were confined within The Family compound.

Entering the teen program was far easier than leaving it. Thirteen-year-old Cheryl read about The Family's invitation for teens to receive training at the Jumbo, so she and her parents parted company and she travelled to the Philippines as they left for missionary work in other parts of the world (Kent, Interview with Cheryl, 1996: 55–6). Many months later she had grown tired of the physical and emotional demands of the program, so she asked the leaders in charge for permission to leave. Rather than granting it, one of the male leaders reputedly took her in a closet and beat her four or fives times with a paddle. As Cheryl remembered, he said something like, "'And now, this is for your own good. We're not going to let you go ... We're not going to let this be a failure. After all we've invested in you, we're not gonna let you just get off the hook so easily"' (Kent, Interview with Cheryl, 1996: 92).

A common experience for teens in the training camps was for supposedly deviant or disruptive teens to be confined in an area away from the others (Ward 1995: 167). Cheryl, for example, went into (what she called) 'isolation' for having expressed doubts about both the existence of God and The Family's founder, David Berg, being God's prophet (Kent, Interview with Cheryl, 1996: 69). She also found herself monitored by an adult 'shepherd' day and night. (See also Kent, Interview with Betty, 1996: 45.) Another young member named Sam Hendricks reported being confined in isolation for (he indicated) a month and a half (Kent, Interview with Hendricks, 1995: 21). By far, however, the most dramatic physical confinement allegedly took place in the Macao Victor program, in which Merry Berg, the granddaughter of the founder, spent six months in a locked room. During part of that time, she allegedly had to use a bucket containing disinfectant as a toilet (Kent, Interview with Berg, 1992a: 80).

Physical Maltreatment

As would be expected in brainwashing programs, Family members and Scientologists experienced a range of physically difficult, and often painful, assignments. Family youth in the Filipino Jumbo, for example, had to perform calisthenics – 'sit-ups, jumping jacks ... vigorous running, running up and down stairs, push-ups, and star jumps' (Kent, Interview with Cheryl, 1996: 100–3; Interview with Donovan, 1995: 10, 12). By far the most arduous (and potentially damaging) exercise was the 'duck-walk' that involved the teens walking around the compound while squatting (Kent, Interview with Donovan, 1995: 11; Interview with Cheryl, 1996: 101).

Scientology's RPFers often had to do calisthenics as punishment, but running was (and remains) a basic part of the program. RPFers were required to run everywhere (see Hartwell n.d.: 3), and former members who went through different RPF programs universally report having had to run in a variety of circumstances. People who were on the RPF on a Scientology ship in the mid-1970s report having to run laps around the deck (Pignotti 1989: 23). Similarly, former inmates from the Fort Harrison incarceration had to run up and down the ramp in the car park (Kent, Interview with Erlich, 1997: 16; Nefertiti 1997: 11; Rosenblum n.d.: 2). In Los Angeles, Pat indicated that RPFers ran stairs or did laps around the complex (Kent, Interview with Pat, 1997a: 27), and RPFers in Denmark experienced similar running punishments (Schernekau/Elleby 1990g: 2; 1990h; k; see 1990i). By far, however, the most extreme running punishments took place at the Happy Valley (and possibly the Gilman Hot Springs) RPF programs, where RPF inmates had to run around either a tree or a pole for up to twelve hours a day (with few breaks) in the hot sun (Aznaran and Aznaran 1988: 9; Kent, Interview with Prince, 1998: 45; D. Mayo 1994: 3; J. Mayo 1996: 7).

In addition to the physical demands running placed upon RPFers, they also performed hard physical labour, usually including maintenance and renovation. Cleaning, scraping paint, washing, and structure refurbishing were common assignments, sometimes involving extremely dirty and potentially dangerous chores. On the ship *Apollo*, for example, RPFer Monica Pignotti had to clean the muck and sludge from the bilges, and then paint the area (Kent, Interview with Pignotti, 1997: 26). A current Scientologist and former RPFer in the Los Angeles Scientology facility wrote about inmates having to clean a narrow, roach-infested tunnel beneath the food preparation area that was crisscrossed with hot pipes and smelled so badly that in one instance he passed out (SB 1998h: 2). The most extreme working conditions existed in the Los Angeles facility around 1977 and 1978, when RPFers were required to perform potentially dangerous renovation work for thirty hours at a time, followed only by three hours' sleep (Kent, Interview with Pat, 1997a: 25–26; Interview with Prince, 1998: 16).

Family teens likewise performed hard labour in the Victor programs, often in the hot sun of tropical or semi-tropical climates. Chores in the Victor program in Macao involved breaking up old concrete, pouring cement, cutting grass with sickles, doing farm chores, carrying away scrap metal, building septic tanks, and (like their RPF counterparts) working a considerable amount of time on construction sites and painting (Kent, Interview with Berg, 1992b: 8; see also Interview with Frost, 1995: 11, 34–6; Interview with Lorna, 1996: 19). Apparently these types of hard labour also took place in the Victor program in Brazil (Interview with Stephanie, 1997: 7). Concerning a Mexican teen home, Valerie spoke about people in it who were 'put on, like, hard labour for weeks and months on end, just out in the sun, you know, hauling rocks and digging holes and filling 'em back up again' (Interview with Valerie, 1996: 31; also Interview with Betty, 1996: 46). A very similar report also came from the RTC (Retraining Camp) in Japan, which a former member indicated 'was a predecessor to the Victor camps' (Interview with Albert, 1997: 37–8; see also Interview with Stephanie, 1997: 5). In fact, this former member blames the degeneration of his back on the 'excessive work' that The Family director allegedly forced him to do (Interview with Albert, 1997: 38).

Victor Program teens who supposedly misbehaved suffered a fate that did not befall adults on Scientology's RPF: Leaders reportedly beat them publicly. Young adults who were teens in various Victor programs (in Macao, the Philippines, and Japan) spoke about the (frequently public) beatings they received by leaders who used wooden paddles that had holes drilled in them to reduce wind resistance (Kent, Interview with Albert, 1997: 26; Interview with Berg, 1992a: 82; 1992b: 6; Interview with Donovan, 1995: 13–15; Interview with Stephanie, 1997: 2; see Ward 1995: 155). One young man who received a beating in the Filipino Jumbo later recounted that he had been hit repeatedly, so hard that afterward the bruises on his legs and buttocks thickened to the point that he could not sit or sleep on his back for a period of time (Interview with Hendricks, 1995: 24–5). I am not aware of anything comparable occurring in the RPF programs.

Social Degradations and Maltreatment

Coupled with the forms of physical maltreatment that occurred in the RPF and Victor programs was an array of social maltreatment. These degradations receive little attention in discussions about brainwashing, yet social maltreatment helps to reduce people's support networks while attacking the psychosocial dimensions of personality (such as status, self-esteem, and identity). Social maltreatment contributes to the coercive efforts by which groups attempt to reduce a person's resistance to the re-indoctrination efforts. Remarkably, both programs developed relatively similar forms of maltreatment involving restrictions on social interactions with others.

The most dramatic similarities between the two groups are the restrictions on communications that existed in the programs of each of them. Both programs placed severe restrictions on inmates' abilities to communicate with one another and with people who were not in the programs. The Scientology document, for example, which provides the directives for the RPF operation, specifically prohibits inmates from talking either to staff members who are not in the RPF or to members of the public unless they absolutely have to (Boards of Directors of the Churches of Scientology 1977: 10). Contact with the outside world was even more curtailed by the prohibition against radios, televisions, or taped music (11). Scientologists easily recognized RPF inmates by their garments: either dark boiler suits or blue work uniforms (1).

Family teenagers did not wear special uniforms, but teens receiving punishment were easily distinguishable by the signs that leaders placed around their necks announcing, 'Don't talk to me – I'm on silence restriction' (Kent, Interview with Albert, 1997: 25 [in Japan]; Interview with Donovan, 1995: 19 [in the Philippines]; Interview with Lorna, 1996: 19 [in Macao]; Interview with Marleana, 1995b: 15 [in Japan]; Interview with Shawn, 1995: 27 [in Puerto Rico]; Interview with Stephanie, 1997: 6 [in Japan], 9, 10 [in Brazil]; Interview with Valerie, 1996: 31 [in Mexico]). One former inmate reported being brought into a public meeting wearing a mask over his mouth (Interview with Hendricks, 1995: 24).

Additional forms of social maltreatment contributed to both groups' attempts to utilize social pressure to acquire conformity. Teens on The Family's Victor program had little if any contact with their birth families (Kent, Interview with Cheryl, 1996: 56; Interview with Donovan, 1995: 6; Interview with Lorna, 1996: 8; see also Interview with Frost, 1995: 2), and RPF inmates had limited and highly controlled family contact only after they had achieved a level of success on the RPF program (see Boards of Directors of Churches of Scientology 1977: 10). Access to mainstream media – television, magazines, radio, music, and so on – was prohibited on both programs, and the Victor program's teens did not receive payment for their hard physical labour (Kent, Interview with Berg, 1992b: 9). RPF policy, in contrast, stated that inmates were to receive a quarter or a half of their normal salaries (Boards of Directors of Churches of Scientology 1977: 10).[6] Inmates, however, of the RPF's RPF received no pay, regardless of what work they performed or how long they laboured (Hubbard 1975: 451). In reality, however, many RPF inmates received dramatically low weekly payments – well under eight dollars for as much as 100 hours' work a week in the late 1970s and 1980s (Superior Court of the State of California 1984: 1463; Kent, Interview with Pignotti, 1997: 17; Interview with Young, 1994: 24; Rosenblum, n.d.: 3; see Aznaran and Aznaran 1988: 8).

Ideological Study

Except during periods when pressing construction demands determined the schedules of RPFers, RPF inmates and Victor program teens had extended periods of time set aside each day for study of ideological tracts, especially ones written by their respective leaders. The assumption in both contexts seems to have been that the leader had uncovered or revealed the truth, and that the road to 'rehabilitating' supposedly deviant members was to expose them to that truth in a context that punished any other perspectives by imposing intense physical and social malfeasance. Brainwashing, therefore, entailed not only the adoption of the leaders' ideologies, but also the renunciation of previous ideas that might have indicated degrees of social or intellectual independence.

The schedule for 'auditing' (e.g., a form of counselling) and the study of various Scientology courses – filled with the founder's writings – was supposed to involve five hours a day over a period of months (and, it seems in some cases, years [Boards of Directors of Churches of Scientology 1977: 4]). For hundreds of hours, RPFers studied Hubbard's teachings, as they worked through combinations of readings, tapes, and exercises that all inmates had to undergo (Boards of Directors of Churches of Scientology 1974; 1980). By contrast, The Family imposed an unlimited number of study hours on 'deviant' young members who had to examine extensive accumulations of material to ensure that they internalized their leader's (often eccentric) instructions and worldview (Kent, Interview with Berg, 1992b: 9; Interview with Cheryl, 1996: 72–3). Teens who were in ordinary educational programs had periods of time set aside each day for reading or listening to their founder's writings, plus attending lectures and memorizing key ideological passages (Kent, Interview with Berg, 1992b: 3; Interview with Betty, 1996: 45–6; Interview with Cheryl, 1996: 66; Interview with Donovan, 1995: 20).

Forced Confessions and Success Stories

Amid environments in which forcibly confined people were physically and socially maltreated as they (re)studied group ideology, the use of forced confessions became an intricate aspect of the brainwashing process (Kent, Interview with Erlich, 1997: 10–11; Interview with Pat, 1997a: 30; Interview with Pignotti, 1997: 14; J. Mayo 1996: 7; Nefertiti 1997: 12). Through such confessions, people renounced crucial aspects of their lives prior to their entry into the brainwashing programs, as well as subjected themselves to often scathing self-criticism for both large and seemingly small behavioural or 'thought-crimes.' Indeed, RPFers frequently confessed to extraordinary crimes that they allegedly committed in past lives (Kent, Interview with Pignotti, 1997: 15). In both groups, the procedures for forced confessions were highly systematized.

RPF members were coupled or 'twinned' with specific partners, and the RPF leaders made the members feel responsible for their twins' progress in the program. Partners heard and recorded one another's confessions in counselling (or what Scientology calls 'auditing') sessions, and they charted one another's progress through the numerous readings they had to absorb (California Court of Appeal 1989: 9269; Kent, Interview with Dale, 1997: 8–9; Rosenblum, n.d.: 2, 4). The system placed additional pressure on RPFers to conform, since deviance damaged members themselves along with their twins (who would not be able to progress).

No such 'buddy' system existed in The Family, since no partner-obligations existed among the teens. Leaders expected them, however, to report one another if they knew or heard of infractions (including ones they learned about through supposedly private conversations [Kent, Interview with Cheryl, 1996: 105–6]). Adult leaders supposedly would assign deviant teens to Victor programs, and then collect daily confessions and personal reflections (called Open Heart Reports) from them (Kent, Interview with Berg, 1992b: 4; Ward 1995: 150, 154–5). These confessions required that teens report on what they supposedly had learned from the daily readings, often doing so in a context in which they spoke about alleged shortcomings that the readings had allowed them to overcome. The teens then shared their confessions in small groups (Kent, Interview with Donovan, 1995: 21; Interview with Frost, 1995: 44). Often in large public meetings, Family leaders who worked with teens criticized them either for items they had disclosed or for other alleged improprieties (Kent, Interview with Berg, 1992b: 3–4; Interview with Donovan, 1995: 21; see also Interview with Cheryl, 1996: 84).

The goal of these confessions, and indeed of the entire Family program, was to pressure teens to get 'the Victory,' which was a poorly defined experience (see Kent, Interview with Betty, 1996: 48) that seemingly involved one's self-acceptance as a sinner who needed the direction of Family leadership for salvation. Cheryl, for example, was in isolation when she apparently had a 'Victory' experience: 'it's hard to put it in words. I just couldn't stop crying and I thought, "the Family is right. I'm – I'm so wrong." And "how could I have been so presumptuous to think that I knew better than ... than God's prophet?"' (Kent, Interview with Cheryl, 1996: 79).

Similarly, the Scientology RPF experience intended to instill in inmates a belief that they had fallen off the 'bridge to total freedom,' but had been saved by the rehabilitation that the harsh program offered them (see Kent, Interview with Pat, 1997a: 24). Consequently, they spent what may have been hundreds of hours with their partners, supposedly 'discovering' misdeeds that date back thousands if not millions of years. After each reputed 'revelation,' the RPF program required that people state how much better and unburdened they felt (Nefertiti 1997: 12; see Forde 1996: 3). Their graduation from the RPF program coincided with – indeed, depended upon – their construction of written 'success stories' that praised the RPF program and gave thanks for the redemption that it provided (Kent, Interview with Pignotti, 1997: 19–20; Interview with Young, 1994: 17–18; Sea Organization 1977: 4–5).

Conclusion

Many social scientists seem reluctant to apply the brainwashing term to activities that 'religious' groups undertake, fearing in part that critics will use the term to justify acts of repression against those groups by authorities and the press. In the particular cases that this article analyses, however, 'brainwashing' is undeniably the appropriate academic term to describe what institutions have attempted to impose upon what may have been hundreds of their members. By embracing the brainwashing term to describe situations involving forcible confinement and physical and social maltreatment in the context of an indoctrination program, social scientists still can oppose repressive acts against (especially minority) faiths. At the same time, however, they also must acknowledge that ideological groups have operated brainwashing programs in the recent past that involved serious human rights abuses for which the groups themselves may be held accountable. Confinement and maltreatment violate basic rights concerning (among others) religious freedom, privacy, personal honour, fair wages and appropriate work conditions, and acceptable standards of mental and physical health (see United Nations 1996a; 1996b). These probable human rights issues are in addition to the strictly academic issues that also deserve attention.

Among the most important academic issues involved is the new direction that the current brainwashing debate has taken. No longer are the advocates of the brainwashing term using it to explain conversions, as some persons had attempted to do in the 1970s and early 1980s. Now its proponents see it as efforts by some controversial religions to *retain* members whom leadership fears are deviating or drifting away (Zablocki 1998: 218). Even Maria, who was the person closest to The Family's founder, saw the teen programs in this manner. When, for example, she addressed teens who had been through various programs, she stated, '[n]ow is your chance to *re-dedicate* your lives, to bring the best of your TTC [Teen Training Camp] training, the best of your Family training, the best of your Teen Combo training, the best of your Victor training, and the best of our new disciple babes training into our Homes!' (Maria 1991: 742). Similarly, Scientology's web page entry on the RPF refers to it as 'a second chance' for 'Sea Organization staff members who would otherwise be subject to dismissal for serious and/or continuous ecclesiastical violations' (Church of Scientology International 1996). Again, the RPF's purported purpose is to retain existing members.

This new focus on brainwashing as an effort to retain members adds a new dimension to existing brainwashing theory. According to Alan Scheflin and Edward Opton, Jr., all brainwashing programs strive to obtain *compliance* from inmates, but the goals of various programs have differed widely. Soviet brainwashing in the 1930s, for example, demanded *compliance and confession* from its victims, whom the state used in show trials as they confessed to 'crimes' (Scheflin and Opton 1978: 88). By contrast, Chinese Communist brainwashing in the early 1950s demanded *compliance and ideological conversion* from inmates. The Chinese Communists expected their victims to adopt the teachings of Chairman Mao (88). Finally, the North Koreans modified both Soviet and Chinese brainwashing systems and developed their own goals, which demanded *compliance and collaboration* from captured Western soldiers (89). The brainwashing systems that I have discussed in both The Family and Scientology, however, demand(ed) from their inmates *compliance and re-conversion or membership retention.*

Other high-demand ideologies containing strong religious overtones also may have implemented brainwashing programs in efforts at member retention in ways that resemble the RPF and Victor programs. Synanon, for example, in its third phase, used its 'Boot Camp' program[7]: 'not only to train newcomers but also to retrain old-timers, senior squares [i.e., persons who joined without drug histories], and even some [program] graduates, and to inculcate them with new soldierly devotion' (Gerstel 1982: 160).

Worth noting in this passage is mention that Synanon sent new members to Boot Camp, which may represent an exception to the general sociological conclusion that new religions do not use brainwashing as a recruitment device. In any case, former member David Gerstel highlighted the Boot Camp indoctrination for problem youths, which sounds a great deal like The Family's Victor program: '[Boot Camp] was being used, also, as a model for a new branch of the Synanon children's school. A dozen of the community's most recalcitrant adolescent boys had been placed in a "Punk Squad." For several months they were put through a regimen of marching, calisthenics, running, and hard physical work. They were made to address all adults as "Sir" or "Ma'am." They stood at rigid attention for inspection by their squad leaders. And they were subjected to physical punishment' (Gerstel 1982: 160). Gerstel added, '[i]n due course the Punk Squad was enlarged so that it served not only as a reform program for the most difficult kids, but [also] as "obedience training" for a wide range of Synanon children' (161). Indeed, the parallels with the Victor programs for Family youth around the world seem striking.

Other groups, about which we know comparatively little, may have placed children in what amount to brainwashing programs. For example, the 44-page indictment on involuntary servitude charges brought by the United States federal government against former leaders of the

Ecclesia Athletic Ass[ociatio]n provides glimpses into what may have been a brainwashing program. The religious-organization-turned-athletic-commune in Oregon allegedly had children who:

'were compelled to perform long hours of rigorous exercises and were drilled in how to present themselves to the public for marketing purposes,' the indictment stated.

The children who did not want to perform, who made mistakes and who did not fully comply with the defendants' orders were struck with long wooden paddles and whipped with razor straps, braided cords and rubber hoses ... and frequently were forced to watch other children being whipped and beaten,' the indictment continued.

Youngsters were isolated from their parents, other relatives and neighbors, forced to stand in line and remain silent for long periods, and subjected to 'inadequate diet and nutrition, inadequate school and systematic beatings,' to break their will, according to the indictment. (Timnick 1991: B6)

Children are easy brainwashing targets for totalistic groups, since they have fewer skills and resources that they can muster in opposition or in attempts at escape.

An even more dramatic brainwashing program seems to have operated within Colonia Dignidad [Dignity Colony] of German immigrants in Chile. An article in the respected British newspaper, the *Weekend Guardian*, identified the '[f]orced labour, religious obsession, homosexual abuse of children, drugs, electro-shock and experimental torture techniques for the Dina [i.e., the Chilean secret police] ...' that almost certainly went on in the colony (Coad 1991: 12). Finally, one must not forget Jonestown as a brainwashing site, where community members lived under the tight security of armed guards as they suffered public confessions and humiliation, running and hard-labour punishments, sensory deprivation, psychotherapeutic drugs, and occasional 'white night' suicide rehearsals (Hall 1987: 237–42, 245–6).

Returning, finally, to the brainwashing examples in Scientology and The Family, my discussion leaves unanswered the question about how 'effective' the RPF and the Teen and Victor programs were in forcing the retention of members. No figures about the RPF's 'success' come from Scientology, although the number of former members willing to speak about their RPF experiences suggests that the re-conversion and retention efforts do fail over the long run in a number of cases. From

The Family's perspective, a top leader lamented in 1991, 'many of these young people who left the Victor Program had a big problem when they went back home ... [T]hey fell back into their NWOs [i.e., 'need work-ons' or problems and doubts], backslid in their spiritual victories, and began to have some of the same serious problems that they'd had before, which of course was very disappointing and discouraging for them' (Maria 1991: 740). It well may be that this new goal of brainwashing people so that they remain members suffers the same basic shortcoming as did the Soviet and the Chinese efforts. In a phrase, '[t]he effectiveness of their techniques dissipates rapidly when the coercive environment is removed' (Scheflin and Opton 1978: 93). Upon leaving the Victor programs and the teen training facilities, youth in The Family may have had too many contacts with the outside world for the desired effects of the group's brainwashing efforts to last. By contrast, the relatively closed and totalitarian world of Scientology's Sea Org may be sufficiently self-contained that the effects on former RPFers from their organization's brainwashing efforts may last a considerable period of time.

Notes

1 The Family has a discussion about 'Offences Warranting Excommunication' in its members' 'charter of responsibilities and rights' (called *The Love Charter* [The Family 1995: 1]). 'Those who disobey them will be excommunicated from The Family fellowship and/or literature, according to the degree of disobedience, which will be determined by the Continental Office' (1995: 116). Among the offences that can lead to excommunication are '[t]he continual voicing of doubts, criticisms, or scepticism, in a destructive manner designed to foster strife or schism, of Dad, Maria, the Word or The Family' (120). The document added that if 'you continue airing matters which result in the spreading of doubts or bringing about contention or division, then this is unacceptable behaviour and will warrant excommunication' (120). Although honest but critical comments to an academic *may* be subject to interpretation, it seems probable that Family leadership would see them as grounds for dismissal.

  Knowing that groups such as Scientology and The Family have such punishment policies against honest criticism by their own members, researchers must be highly critical of information that current members provide when leadership knows what they are doing. Likewise, researchers should weigh carefully the ethics involved in interviewing people whose honest comments may elicit group punishment.

2 Current Scientologists, for example, are subject to being labelled 'suppressive persons' by their organization if they were to tell researchers negative things about the RPF or their experiences in it. Among many actions that the Scientology organization considers 'suppressive acts' are '[p]ublic statements against Scientology or Scientologists but not to Committees of Evidence duly convened' (Hubbard, assisted by LRH Technical Research and Compilations 1991: 875). (Committees of Evidence are internal Scientology courts that rule about people's deviations from Scientology 'tech' and assign penalties to the deviating members.) Another suppressive act involves 'pronouncing Scientologists guilty of the practice of standard Scientology' (875). A third suppressive act is '[w]riting anti-Scientology letters to the press or giving anti-Scientology or anti-Scientologist data to the press' (876). In general, '[o]utright or covert acts knowingly designed to impede or destroy Scientology or Scientologists is what is meant by acts suppressive of Scientology and Scientologists' (885). As a consequence of Committees of Evidence ruling that people committed these or other 'offences,' '[s]uppressive persons or groups relinquish their rights as Scientologists by their very actions and may not receive the benefits of the Codes of the Church' (874). Were Scientologists, therefore, to tell researchers *anything* that was critical of the RPF program and organizational leaders were to discover what had transpired, then the research process would have placed informants at unacceptable risk. Ethical considerations prohibit researchers from doing so to informants. Under the threat of punishment, therefore, current Scientology member informants (especially ones whom leadership know are speaking to researchers) are most likely to provide public relations material of questionable validity.

3 The nine-sentence statement says that the RPF is a 'second chance' for Sea Organization members ('who have signed a pledge of eternal service to Scientology and its goals') to get 'complete rehabilitation' rather than 'dismissal for serious and/or continuous ecclesiastical violations ...' It adds that RPFers 'both study and receive religious counselling on a daily basis to address areas of difficulty in their personal lives,' and they 'work eight hours per day as a team on tasks which improve the facilities of the Church by which they are employed ...' The work, which RPFers perform in teams, allegedly 'allows the individual to regain confidence in himself [sic] and the pride of accomplishment' [sic]. Apparently many of those members 'participating' in the RPF are experiencing 'personnel "burn out" ...' In contrast to portrayals by critics (whom the statement alleges 'cannot speak authenti-

cally from personal experience') RPF graduates 'attest to its enormous personal benefit, and express their appreciation for being able to avail themselves of redemption as opposed to dismissal' (Church of Scientology International 1996). All aspects of this statement – the implicitly voluntary nature of the RPF, the supposedly religious counselling, the work days, the nature of Scientology's employment, and the expressions of appreciation – receive very different interpretations by a number of persons who in fact speak from personal experience but do so outside of the organization's immediate controls.

4 Researchers have known for nearly three decades that the text is fraudulent (Kominsky 1970), but they did not know the author. Researchers on Scientology, however, are definite: '[t]he *Brainwashing Manual* is one of Scientology's most revealing [d]ocuments. I believe that this book was secretly authored by L. Ron Hubbard in 1955 and that he incorporated its methods into his organization in the mid 1960s and beyond' (Corydon 1996: 107). Hubbard's (now deceased) son, Ron, Jr., specified that his father was the sole author, and he identified two women (one of whom was his wife) who typed the manuscript from Hubbard's dictation. Moreover, former member John Sanborne indicated that he had given Hubbard the idea to write it (108). However, Ron Jr.'s statement about his father's authorship of the forged brainwashing manual first appeared in a book-length study of Scientology, on which he had been working as co-author until he made a cash settlement with Scientology 'to cease any assistance on the book and remove his name from it' (which the publisher refused to do [Corydon and Hubbard, Jr. 1987: 12]). Beyond these statements by people who worked closely with Hubbard in the 1950s, an analysis of the peculiar language of the brainwashing text (including such odd phrases as 'pain-drug-hypnotism') strongly indicates Hubbard's hand (compare Hubbard [probable author] 1955: 37, 39, with Hubbard 1975: 296). Mostly revealingly, different editions of the manual published by the Scientology organization contained mention of either Dianetics or the Church of Scientology in the actual text as targets for Communist, psycho-political attack (Hubbard [probable author] n.d.: 49; Hubbard [probable author] 1955: 49). Proof that Scientology distributed the brainwashing manual appears in the Church of Scientology of California 1978: 301. I am working with two original copies, as well as a later reprint by a non-Scientology organization.

5 Hana Whitfield indicated that, in 1978, she saw Lyn Froyland 'chained to a pipe down there [in the Fort Harrison basement] for weeks, under guard' (Whitfield 1994: 42). Dennis Erlich referred to the same person (*WMNF* 1996: 5), although with a different spelling of her last name. Tonya Burden

was in the RPF sometime between August and around November 1977
(Burden 1980: 9, 10; see Armstrong 1982: 3). Nefertiti did not give the dates
in which she was in the RPF, but she wrote her account in 1997, in which
she referred to her escape ten years earlier (i.e., 1987 [Nefertiti 1997: 12]).

6 By the mid-1990s, normal Sea Org pay was around $50 a week for a mini-
mum of about 50 hours or more of work, plus room and board (Harrington
1997a; 1997b). Excluding the value of the room and board, this amount
comes to around $1.00 per hour.

7 Gerstel described the origins of Synanon's boot camp as follows:

> Under [founder Charles] Dederich's guidance, the [newcomer] depart-
> ment evolved through several forms [in the early 1970s] until an experi-
> mental 'Synanon Boot Camp' was established at the Ranch. A select
> group of young men and women were put into a strict regime of exercise,
> physical work, and study ... They answered smartly to roll call, formed
> closed order ranks, and marched up the road toward the pond, their
> young voices echoing boisterously across the meadow as they shouted
> cadence. When they came near the pond, they broke into a jog and disap-
> peared into the hills. After their morning run, they worked menial chores
> in the gardens or shops ... Toward evening they gathered on circles of hay
> bales in the meadows and Gamed [i.e., participated in Synanon's process
> of intensive verbal confrontation, challenge, and defense].
>
> The Boot Camp seemed to have more power to hold new people than
> any previous form of the newcomer department. (Gerstel 1982: 139–40)

References

Anonymous. n.d. 'Rehabilitation Project Force[.] RPF Waiver.' [N.p.]. 1p.

Anthony, Dick. 1990. 'Religious Movements and Brainwashing Litigation:
Evaluating Key Testimony.' *In Gods We Trust: New Patterns of Religious Pluralism in America*. New Brunswick, N.J.: Transaction Books, 295–344.

Anthony, Dick, and Thomas Robbins. 1992. 'Law, Social Science and the
"Brainwashing" Exception to the First Amendment.' *Behavioral Sciences & the
Law* 10, no. 1 (winter): 5–29.

Armstrong, Gerry. 1982. 'Affidavit of Gerry Armstrong.' Filed in Orange
County, California, for the United States District Court, Middle District of
Florida, Tampa Division. *Tonya Burden, Plaintiff v. Church of Scientology of Cal-
ifornia, Defendants* (25 June): 8pp.

Atack, Jon. 1990. *A Piece of Blue Sky. Scientology, Dianetics, and L. Ron Hubbard
Exposed*. New York: Lyle Stuart.

Aznaran, Vicki J., and Richard N. Aznaran. 1988. United States District Court, Central District, State of California. *Vicki J. Aznaran and Richard N. Aznaran, Plaintiffs, v. Church of Scientology of California, Inc.; Church of Spiritual Technology, Inc.; Scientology Missions International, Inc.; Author Services, Inc.; Church of Scientology International, Inc.; Church of Scientology of Los Angeles, Inc.; Mission Office Worldwide; Author Family Trust; The Estate of L. Ron Hubbard; David Miscavige; and Norman Starkey.* 'Complaint for False Imprisonment, Intentional Infliction of Emotional Distress, Negligent Infliction of Emotional Distress ...' Case No. C1/88-178-WDK (EX). 29pp.

Barnes, John. 1984. 'Sinking the Master Mariner.' *London Sunday Times Magazine* [London]: 34–42.

Bavarian State Ministry of the Interior. 1997. 'Measures Undertaken by the Government of the State of Bavaria Against Scientology.' (15 January); <http://www.bayern.de/STMI/Scientology/e2197.htm> (1 February): 2pp.

Behar, Richard. 1986. 'The Prophet and Profits of Scientology.' *Forbes* (27 October): 314–22.

Boards of Directors of the Churches of Scientology. 1974. 'R.P.F. Tr's & Objectives Course.' *Flag Order 3434 – 16R.* Written by P. Brice, RPF training supervisor; revised by David Ziff and Glenn Samuels; authorized by AVU. 28 July (revised from 25 January): 7pp.

– 1977. 'The Rehabilitation Project Force.' *Sea Organization Flag Order* 3434RB. Revised by Ens. Susan Walker, I/C, and Lt. (jg) Art Webb, 2nd; re-revised by Commodore's Messenger; approved by L. Ron Hubbard, Commodore (7 January 1974; revised 21 August 1976; re-revised 30 May 1977): 14pp.

– 1980. 'RPF Graduation Requirements Checklist.' *Flag Order 3434-RC-56.* (Written by Tech Comps Pjt I/C and Snr C/S Int for Int Pgms Chief CMO Int; Approved by D/CO CMO Int and CO CMO Int). (March 17): 13pp.

Bracchi, Paul. 1994. 'Behind the Castle's Walls.' *Evening Argus* [Sussex, England] (28 March): 4–5.

Burden, Tonya. 1980. 'Affidavit.' Signed in Las Vegas, Nevada (25 January): 12pp.

California Court of Appeal. 1989. *'Larry Wollersheim v. Church of Scientology of California.* No. B023193 Super. Ct. No. Second Appellate District, Division Seven. 89 Daily Journal D.A.R. 9269. (Filed 19 July): 9269–79.

Church of Scientology of California. 1978. *What is Scientology?* Los Angeles: Publication Organization United States.

Church of Scientology International. 1996. 'What is the Rehabilitation Project Force?' <http://faq.scientology.org/ref_5.htm>

Coad, Malcolm. 1991. 'Symphony with the Devil.' *Weekend Guardian* [U.K.] (24–5 August): 12–13.

Cobra, 1998. 'UK Victor Programs.' <excognet.com> (29 July): 1p.

Cohee, Nedra. 1989. 'Kids Scene in PAC.' Memo (7 July): 1p.

Corydon, Bent. 1996. *L. Ron Hubbard, Messiah or Madman?* Fort Lee, N.J.: Barricade Books.

Corydon, Bent, and L. Ron Hubbard, Jr. 1987. *L. Ron Hubbard: Messiah or Madman?* Secaucus, N.J.: Lyle Stuart.

COUNTERCOG, n.d. 'The Cult Killed Rick.' *Newsletter #9*: 8pp.

Dagnell, Birgitta. 1997. 'My Story About Scientology.' <alt.religion.scientology> (18 August): 6pp.

Dupuy, Richard. circa 1993. 'Draft Notes of Interview with Richard, Dupuy.' 22pp.

Enquete Kommission. 1998. 'Endbericht der Enquete-Kommission "Sogenannte Sekten und Psychogruppen."' *Deutscher Bundestag* 13. Wahlperiode. Drucksache 13/10950.

The Family. 1995. *The Love Charter.* Zurich, Switzerland: The Family (January): xii, 218pp.

Family Services, 1990. 'Faithy's Deliverance from Alcoholism!' *Family Special News Magazine* FSM 162 (FN 271), DFO. March, 12pp.

Forde, Peter. 1996. 'In and Out of Scientology.' <pforde01.txt at home.icon.fi> (3 August): 6pp.

Gerstel, David U. 1982. *Paradise, Incorporated: Synanon.* Novato, Calif.: Presidio Press.

Gruber, Peter and Axel Kintzinger. 1994. '"Umfassende Unterwerfung."' Interview. *Focus* (12 December): 72ff.

Hall, John R. 1987. *Gone from the Promised Land: Jonestown in American Cultural History.* New Brunswick, N.J.: Transaction Books.

Harrington, Joe. 1997a. 'Current Sea Org Salaries?' <alt.religion.scientology> (2 December): 2pp., in response to Mark Dallara. 1997: 'Current Sea Org Salaries?' (1 December): 1p.

– 1997b. 'Current Sea Org Salaries? [more on Sea Org Salaries].' <alt.religion.scientology>, (3 December [*sic*]: 2 December]): 1p.; in response to: Mark Dallara. 1997. 'Current Sea Org Salaries?' (1 December): 1p.

Hartwell, Adelle. N.d. 'Affidavit of Adelle Hartwell.' 5pp.

Hessische Allgemeine. 1997. 'Abweichler in Arbeitslager?' (5 July): 3.

Home Services, 1992. 'False Accusers in the Last Days!' #2820 *Good News* (November): 16pp.

Hubbard, L. Ron [probable author]. 1955. *Brain-Washing[.] A Synthesis of the*

Russian Textbook on Psychopolitics. With an editorial note by Charles Stickley. Los Angeles: American Saint Hill Organization.

– n.d. [circa 1955]. *Brain-Washing[.] A Synthesis of the Russian Textbook on Psychopolitics*. With an editorial note by Kenneth Goff. South Pasadena, Calif.: Emissary Publications.

– 1969. 'Brainwashing.' *Freedom*. International U.S.A. 2d ed. (11 March): [4–5].

– 1969. 'Reorganization.' *Flag Order* 1889 (25 March): 2pp.

– 1972a. 'Handling of Clinical Assignments to SPF and DPF.' *Flag Order 3163* (6 April): 1p.

– 1975. *Dianetics and Scientology Technical Dictionary*. Los Angeles: Publications Organization.

– 1976. *Modern Management Technology Defined*. Copenhagen: New Era Publications.

– 1977. 'Estates Project Forces.' *Flag Order 3129R* (16 June 1977, rev. of 16 June 1972): 2pp.

Hubbard, L. Ron (assisted by LRH Technical Research and Compilations). 1991. 'Suppressive Acts[,] Suppression of Scientology and Scientologists.' Revision of *HCO Policy Letter* of 23 December 1965RB (Revised 8 January). In *The Organization Executive Course*, edited by L. Ron Hubbard, 873–905. HCO Division. Vol. 1. Los Angeles: Bridge Publications.

Jebson, Steve [pseudonym]. 1997. 'Subject: Stephen A. Kent (PhD) – Address Leipzig, Germany.' (14 September); <alt.religion.scientology>.

Kent, Stephen A. 1992a. 'Interview with Merry Berg,' 11 December: 84pp.

– 1992b. 'Interview with Merry Berg,' 14 December: 20pp.

– 1994. 'Interview with Robert Vaughn Young,' 13 August: 71pp.

– 1995. 'Interview with Ernest Donovan [pseudonym],' 17 May: 46pp.

– 1995. 'Interview with Danny Frost [pseudonym],' 25 May: 87 pp.

– 1995. 'Interview with Sam Hendricks,' 1 August: 37pp.

– 1995. 'Interview with Shawn [pseudonym], 15 November: 60pp.

– 1995. 'Interview with Emily [pseudonym],' 14 December: 43 pp.

– 1995a. 'Interview with Marleana [pseudonym],' 30 November: 57pp.

– 1995b. 'Interview with Marleana [pseudonym],' 3 December: 40pp.

– 1996. 'Interview with Betty [pseudonym],' 6 March; 1, 2 April: 88pp.

– 1996. 'Interview with Cheryl [pseudonym],' 9 February: 204pp.

– 1996. 'Interview with Lorna [pseudonym],' 16 January: 42pp.

– 1996. 'Interview with Valerie [pseudonym],' 14 March: 37pp.

– 1997. 'Interview with Albert [pseudonym],' 25 January, 59pp.

– 1997. 'Interview with Dale [pseudonym],' 1 April: 18pp.

– 1997. 'Interview with Dennis Erlich.' Los Angeles, Calif., 30 March: 18pp.

- 1997. 'Interview with Monica Pignotti,' 6 April: 31pp.
- 1997. 'Interview with Karl Ernesto [pseudonym],' 8 June: 18pp.
- 1997a. 'Interview with Pat [pseudonym],' 12 March: 35pp.
- 1997b. 'Interview with Pat [pseudonym],' 12 March: 16pp.
- 1997. 'Interview with Stephanie [pseudonym],' June 6: 14pp.
- 1998. 'Interview with Jesse Prince.' 29 July: 51pp.

Kent, Stephen A., and Deana Hall. 1997. 'Brainwashing and Re-indoctrination Programs in the Children of God/The Family.' Paper presented at the Association for the Sociology of Religion. August: Revised version available at <http://www.excognet.com/>

Kintzinger, Axel [Interviewer]. 1997. '"Wer Aufmuckt, wird isoliert."' *Focus* (July): 51–2.

Koff, Stephen. 1989. 'Scientology Faces New Charges of Harassment.' *The Newkirk Herald Journal* (July 6): 5–7. Reprinted from *The St Petersburg Times* (22 December 1988): 1A, 6A–7A.

Kominsky, Morris. 1970. *The Hoaxers: Plain Liars, Fancy Liars, and Damned Liars.* Boston: Branden Press.

La Mattery, Auty. 1998. 'The Rotten Apple Camp AKA Retraining Center – Location Matsumoto, Japan – Time Frame 2 Years.' Posting on <excognet> (3 July): 5pp.

Maria. 1990a. 'JETT/Teen Discipleship Revolution.' Maria #136, DO 2658 (October). In World Services, *Daily Bread* 10 (January 1992): 612–22.

- 1990b. 'Who's Responsible for Our JETTs & Teens?' Maria #137, DO 2659 (October). In World Services, *Daily Bread* 10 (January 1992): 622–9.

- 1990c. 'Revolutionary Kids!' Maria #138, DO 2660 (October). In World Services, *Daily Bread* 10 (January 1992): 630–42.

- 1991. 'The Discipleship Training Revolution.' Maria #142, DO 2677 (February). In World Services, *Daily Bread* 10 (January 1992): 730–43.

Mayo, David. 1994. 'Affidavit.' (14 October): 4pp. Downloaded from the World Wide Web, 28 September 1997, at: <http://www.sky.net/~sloth/sci/mayo.html>

Mayo, Julie. 1996. 'Statement.' (16 April): 16pp. Downloaded from the World Wide Web, 28 September 1997, at: <http://www.freezone.org/Reports/e_jmayo.htm>

McNeil, Julie [Julia]. 1998a. 'Human Rights – To Auty and julie – My Opinion.' <excognet.com> (10 July): 6pp.

McNeil, Julie [Julia]. 1998b. 'What has the COG/FOL/Family Done @ [Yo]ur Complaints?' <excognet.com> (30 July): 4pp.

Melton, J. Gordon. 1994. 'Sexuality and Maturation of The Family.' In *Sex, Slander, and Salvation: Investigating The Family / Children of God*, edited by James R.

Lewis and J. Gordon Melton, 71–95, 273–7. Stanford, Calif.: Center for Academic Publication.

Miller, Russell. 1987. *Bare-Faced Messiah. The True Story of L. Ron Hubbard*. London: Michael Joseph.

Millikan David. 1994. 'The Children of God, Family of Love, The Family.' In *Sex, Slander, and Salvation: Investigating The Family/Children of God*, edited by James R. Lewis and J. Gordon Melton, 181–261, 286–88. Stanford, Calif.: Center for Academic Publication.

Nefertiti [pseudonym]. 1997. 'The Church of Scientology or the Guru's Gulags. Story of An Escape.' <http://www.cnbc.cmu.edu/~dst/Lerma/english.html> (May).

Pignotti, Monica. 1989. 'My Nine Lives in Scientology.' World Wide Web: 36pp. www.cs.cmu.edu/~dst/Library/Shef/pignotti/

Priebe, Amalia B. 1995. 'Statement about Lonnie Davis.' Certified Before Edward K. Kaye, Barrister and Solicitor, Chilliwack, B.C. (8 December): 6pp.

Reichelt, Peter. 1997. *Helnwein und Scientology*. Mannheim: Verlag Brockmann und Reichelt GMBH.

Rosenblum, Anne. N.d. [pre-1980]. 'Declaration of Anne Rosenblum.' Foreword by Dennis Erlich. *The Informer* 10 (March 1992). <http://wpxx02.toxiuni.wuerzburg.de/~krasel/CoS/aff_ar.htm>

Royal Courts of Justice. 1984. Decision in 'B & G Wards,' High Court, London. Judge J. Latey. (23 July): 53pp.

SB. 1998a. 'By Req: My Story of Leaving the Sea Org (warning, long).' Article segment 1 of 3. <alt.religion.scientology> *Deja News* (6 August): 2pp.

– 1998b. 'Project Forces of the Sea Org Explained .' <alt.religion.scientology> (8 August): 2pp.

– 1998c. 'By Req: My Story of Leaving the Sea Org (warning, long).' Article segment 2 of 3. <alt.religion.scientology> *Deja News* (6 August): 2pp.

– 1998d. 'Project Forces of the Sea Org Explained.' <alt.religion.scientology> *Deja News* (7 August): 3pp.

– 1998e. 'Delurk: Another Scientologist Decides to Pitch in His.' <alt.religion.scientology> *Deja News* (7 August): 2pp.

– 1998f. 'By Req: My Story of Leaving the Sea Org (warning, long).' Article segment 1 of 2. <alt.religion.scientology> *Deja News* (8 August): 3pp.

– 1998g. 'RPF Book Review Request.' <alt.religion.scientology> *Deja News* (10 August): 3pp.

– 1998h. 'Project Forces of the Sea Org Explained (was "My Story").' Article segment 1 of 2. <alt.religion.scientology> *Deja News* (26 August): 3pp.

– 1998i. 'Project Forces of the Sea Org Explained (Story was My).' Article segment 2 of 2. <alt.religion.scientology> *Deja News* (26 August): 3pp.

Scheflin, Alan. W., and Edward M. Opton, Jr. 1978. *The Mind Manipulators*. New York: Paddington.

Schernekau/Elleby, Susanne. n.d. [1990]. 'RPF MAA.' (1? October): 1p.

Sea Organization. 1977. 'What's Happening on the EPF/RPF.' Newsletter. (17 March): 5pp.

Shelor, George-Wayne. 1984. 'Ex-Members Denounce Sect Rehab Program.' *Clearwater Sun* (August 28): 1B, 2B.

Shepherd, Gary, and Lawrence Lilliston. 1994. 'Field Observations of Young People's Experience and Role in The Family.' In *Sex, Slander, and Salvation: Investigating The Family / Children of God*, edited by James R. Lewis and J. Gordon Melton, 57–70. Stanford, Calif.: Center for Academic Publication.

Superior Court of the State of California for the County of Los Angeles. 1984. *Church of Scientology of California, Plaintiff, v. Gerald Armstrong, Defendant.* Mary Sue Hubbard, Intervenor. No. C 420153. Reporters' transcript of proceedings. 10 May. Vol. 9: 1389–1563.

Tabayoyon, Andre. 1994. 'Declaration of Andre Tabayoyon.' In *Church of Scientology International v. Steven Fishman and Uwe Geertz*. United States District Court, Central District of California. Case No. CV 91 6426 HLH (Tx), (4 April): 64pp. (Attachments Plus)

Timnick, Lois. 1991. '8 Arrested on Child Slavery Indictment.' *Los Angeles Times*, 9 February, B1, B6.

Tongi, Stephan. 1998. 'Scientology Shows Its True Face in "Happy Valley" California.' *Mannheimer Morgen* (28 July); translated by Joe Cisar at <http://cisar.org/trnmenu.htm>

United Nations. 1996a. *The Committee on Economic, Social and Cultural Rights*. Geneva: United Nations.

– 1996b. *The International Bill of Human Rights*. Geneva: United Nations.

Van Zandt, David. 1991. *Living in the Children of God*. Princeton, N.J.: Princeton University Press.

Ward, Right Honourable Lord Justice Alan. 1995. 'W 42 1992 in the High Court of Justice. Family Division. Principal Registry, in the Matter of ST (A Minor) and in the Matter of the Supreme Court Act 1991.' (19 October): 295pp.

Welkos, Robert W., and Joel Sappell. 1990. 'Defectors Recount Lives of Hard Work, Punishment.' *Los Angeles Times* (26 June): [24–5].

Whitfield, Hana. 1989. 'Affidavit.' (8 August): 11pp. <alt.religion.scientology>

Whitfield, Hana (Eltringham). 1994. 'Revised Declaration of Hana Whitfield Re Motion for Costs.' United States District Court, Central District of California. No.Cv 91-6426 HLH (Tx). (4 April): 44pp; Posting by Tilman Hausherr on <alt.religion.scientology> (12 April 1997).

WMNF. 1996. 'Radio Activity.' Interview with Jeff Jacobsen, Dennis Erlich, Jeff

Lee, and Brian Anderson. (7 March): 14pp; <http://www.lermanet.com/cos/exhibit.html>

World Services. 1993. 'Our Response to Allegations of Mind Control and Brainwashing.' (March): 32pp.

Young, Stacy Brooks. 1994. 'Declaration of Stacy Brooks Young.' In *Church of Scientology International v. Steven Fishman and Uwe Geertz*. United States District Court, Central District of California, Case No. CV 91 6426 HLH (Tx), (4 April): 82pp. (Plus Attachments)

Young, Robert Vaughn. 1995. 'Reich des Bosen.' *Der Spiegel* (25 September): 105ff.

Zablocki, Benjamin. 1997. 'The Blacklisting of a Concept: The Strange History of the Brainwashing Conjecture in the Sociology of Religion.' *Nova Religio* 1 no. 1 (October): 96–121.

– 1998. 'Exit Cost Analysis: A New Approach to the Scientific Study of Brainwashing.' *Nova Religio* 1 no. 2 (April): 216–49.

9. Raising Lazarus: A Methodological Critique of Stephen Kent's Revival of the Brainwashing Model

Lorne L. Dawson

In recent years two sociologists of some note have published articles and presented papers to academic societies running counter to the dominant current of thought in the sociology of new religious movements. To the surprise of many, Stephen Kent (e.g., 1991, 1994, 1997a, 1997b; Kent and Hall 1997) and Benjamin Zablocki (1996, 1997, 1998) are seeking to reconceptualize and re-establish 'brainwashing' as a legitimate social scientific concept, reversing the results of twenty years of academic and legal struggle between sociologists of religion (and others) and the anticult movement (e.g., Anthony 1990; Anthony and Robbins 1992, 1994, 1995; Barker 1984; Beckford 1985; Bromley and Richardson 1983; Bromley and Robbins 1993; Coleman 1984; Richardson 1991, 1993; Robbins 1984; Robbins and Anthony 1979, 1982; Robbins and Bromley 1993; Young and Griffiths 1992; for a summary of the essential issues under debate and the results of research see Dawson 1998, chap. 5). Some efforts have been made to address the views of Zablocki by David Bromley (1998b, 1999), but to date no formal rebuttal has been offered to the work of Kent, outside of oral responses to his conference presentations. Yet his views are disturbing to those who disagree with his opinions, both in and outside of the academic community, because his efforts are designed to encourage and facilitate the introduction of new legal sanctions and restrictions on minority religions in North America and elsewhere (i.e., in Europe, most especially Germany). In fact, in this regard Kent's activism clearly exceeds that of Zablocki, who has been careful to restrict his analyses to conceptual concerns and aspects of the politics of knowledge in academia. This chapter offers a critique of the arguments advanced by Kent in his chapter in this book (2001), as well as in a recent conference paper presented to the Society for the Scientific Study of Religion (Kent 1997a). Kent's chapter in this book relies heavily on arguments developed at greater length and with greater frankness in the revised version of this conference paper, which was circulated among scholars of religion and made available to me by Kent in the fall of 1998. Both essays suffer from methodological flaws so grievous as to call into question the validity and reliability of Kent's conclusions, especially as the foundation for sound legal or legislative action (with regard to conflicts with new religious movements at either the individual or collective levels). In fact the methodological inadequacies detected are indicative of a prejudice inappropriate to the practice of the social sciences (given the consensus on maintaining at least the regulative ideal of objectivity and value-neutrality).

In this limited context, little attempt will be made to question directly the veracity of the evidence reported by Kent, derived largely from media reports, court documents, religious texts, and organizational memoranda, and interviews with ex-members done by Kent. My comments will be restricted to Kent's criticisms of the Church of Scientology, though the methodological critique developed can be readily extended in principle to his criticisms of The Family. The specific factual claims Kent makes may or may not be true. I do not have access to the materials he uses in order to make my own assessment. But in some respects it is not relevant whether or not the facts are true. My argument is that, by the established methodological standards of social scientific study, there is no way of determining clearly if the evidence Kent presents is reliable or warrants making generalizations about the activities of new religious movements. Given the existing scholarship on both the substantive and methodological issues at stake, there is considerable reason for treating his conclusions with great caution, if not outright scepticism.

Kent's efforts suffer from at least three serious methodological failings, which I will address in sequence. First, he builds his argument around an idiosyncratic definition of brainwashing which he derives from a skewed discussion of the existence and nature of this phenomenon in cults as debated in the sociology and psychology of religion, as well as from court cases involving new religions. Second, his arguments rely heavily on the testimony of a small sample of apostates (i.e., individuals who have left Scientology and now bear a grudge against it; see Bromley 1998a). Third, certain kinds of evidence for his case are presented in a manner that displays either his ignorance of other well-known perspectives that would ameliorate his conclusions, or his systematic choice to ignore relevant but inconvenient information (as indicated, for example, in his treatment of Scientological 'success stories').[1] Before explaining the problem in each instance, let me briefly review Kent's critique of the practices of the Church of Scientology.[2]

Kent's Critique of Scientology

Kent argues that the Church of Scientology is guilty of violating the fundamental human rights of many of its members by subjecting them to 'brainwashing' when they participate in a specific sub-program or institution of the religion called the Rehabilitation Project Force (RPF), which was established in 1974. He acknowledges that the concept of brainwashing no longer has any scientific validity as a description of the processes of recruitment and conversion used by new religious movements. He seems to concede, that is, that there is little reliable evidence or logical need to use the concept of brainwashing to account for how people first join a new religion. He is not seeking, then, to specifically reinvoke many of the issues raised in the first extended round of debate between proponents and opponents of the notion of coercive persuasion in cults. Rather, like Zablocki, he is trying to justify the continued use of the term in a new context: to explain why, in some cases, people seemingly find it hard to leave a new religion, even when, supposedly, it is abusive. Brainwashing, we are told, is being used premeditatedly by the Church of Scientology to 'break the will' of recalcitrant or dissident members and to strip them of 'the individuality' of their minds through intensive indoctrination in the ideology of the group (Kent 1997a: 1–3).[3] To this end, Kent's critique of the Church of Scientology in his conference paper traces accounts of the RPF in the courts and media, provides an ideational history of the RPF, and seeks to delineate many aspects of the creation, nature, and operation of the RPF. The account provided is consistently negative and critical, dwelling, as his chapter in this book does, on 'the framework of forcible confinement, physical and social maltreatment, intensive reindoctrinating, and forced confessions' that Kent claims 'were (and are) central to the program's operation' (1997a: 11).

The RPF is one of several programs designed specifically for the Sea Org (elite inner core) of the Church of Scientology. Others Kent mentions are the Deck Project Force, the Pursers Project Force, the Stewards Project Force, and the Estates Project Force (1997a: 9). These programs were intended to provide members of the Sea Org, with integrated training in their duties on board ship and with the teachings and practices of Scientology, while also instilling the discipline demanded by both pursuits. As the title of the RPF makes clear, its purpose was to enforce the rules and regulations of the church and to curb inappropriate behaviour. It was in effect a form of punishment directed at the rehabilitation of church members who were not interested in leaving the Sea Org but, in some significant way, were judged to be unwilling to meet the demands of the church. It was a measure of last resort, similar in its purpose, I would argue, to forms of discipline used in the military, Catholic religious orders, and other kinds of religious communities around the world and throughout human history. Kent asserts, however, that the RPF became in effect a form of unlawful imprisonment and abuse, and that it was used by Hubbard and others for 'personal retaliation' (1997a: 10), to stifle internal dissent, and to compel an abnormal measure of conformity to the dictates of the church leadership. This was accomplished, we are assured, by subjecting the 'inmates'[4] of the RPF to a systematic program of brainwashing.

As noted, at present I have no means at my disposal to specifically assess the veracity of this depiction. The many abuses Kent discusses may or may not have happened, may or may not be exaggerated. But whatever ultimately may be the case, the evidence he has provided so far does not warrant the use of the term 'brainwashing' (or such synonymous terms as 'mind control').

Kent's Inadequate Reconceptualization of Brainwashing

Kent's whole argument hinges on the acceptance of the following statement presented in his brief summary of the brainwashing debate in his conference paper (1997a, 2):

> The social scientific attacks [on the anticult use of the brainwashing argument] concluded that the brainwashing term was valid only if the group in question used incarceration and physical maltreatment against members (see Anthony 1990: 304) in situations of uninformed consent (Young and Griffith 1992: 93). This threefold requirement was a minimalist one, since a brainwashing program also would have to include an intense indoctrination program coupled with personal confessions of past 'sins.' Since neither the term's supporters or detractors provided concrete evi-

dence that even these minimalist activities uniformly occurred in most groups' conversion activities, sociologists and others concluded that 'brainwashing' was not an appropriate term for describing how and why people join new or controversial religions.

On first reading, this statement seems more than fair, even generous, for someone wishing to argue that brainwashing does in fact occur in the Church of Scientology. Having read the entire essay, however, it becomes apparent that Kent has framed matters in this way in order to better make his case, since he thinks he can demonstrate concretely that the RPF does, rather uniquely, meet these minimalist criteria. Participants were, he asserts, physically confined against their will and maltreated, deceived about the nature of the RPF, forced to make personal confessions, and subjected to extensive indoctrination. In other words, he thinks he can use the views of his opponents to surprisingly and ironically support his contrary position, and in this instance he really only needs to establish that deception and physical constraint were involved. But a moment's reflection reveals that this statement inaccurately represents the social scientific assessment of the concept of brainwashing. Rather it represents a statement of the 'legal status' of the concept of brainwashing as it has emerged, rather unsystematically, from numerous court cases fought in the United States with regard to various different aspects of cult activities. The two sources Kent cites to authorize his claims clearly reveal this, as the discussions of Anthony (1990) and Young and Griffith (1992) are specifically focused on legal issues and not on the full range of scholarship associated with the brainwashing debate (e.g., see Richardson 1993, or Dawson 1998; chap. 5).

The actual social scientific record, shaped by dozens of different kinds of studies over a twenty-year period, demonstrates that there is little concrete evidence to support any of the many different kinds of accusations levelled against new religions by the anticult movement and others under the rubric of brainwashing or mind control. Rather, these studies have consistently discovered contrary evidence (e.g., psychological studies of members and ex-members of new religious movements have largely concluded that involvement entails either no discernable or significant negative side-effects or may even be therapeutic; see the summary analyses of Rochford et al. 1989, and Richardson 1995). In both the legal and social scientific debates about brainwashing in the 'cults,' the lack of evidence that members of new religions have ever been physically held against their will became crucial for two reasons.

In the legal context, the American courts were looking for some means of differentiating clearly between the strong forms of persuasion accepted in other contexts in society, like the military, Catholic seminaries, and fundamentalist Christian schools, and the kinds used by cults. They recognized the dangers of condemning new religions practices that were equally present and tolerated in other institutions. In the end, as Young and Griffiths specify (1992: 98–9), the courts concluded: 'Coercive persuasion ... fails as a theoretical construct for linking potentially questionable acts by unconventional religious movements directly to identifiable harm. Either the issue is narrower, such as physical constraint or preying on the susceptible, or the acts in question do not differ significantly from those by established churches that are never seriously accused of coercive persuasion.' This conclusion applies equally well to charges of brainwashing in association with processes of conversion, training, or exiting.

In the social scientific context, it seemed for a time that the only situation in which brainwashing could safely be said to have occurred was that of prisoners of war and other political captives, all of whom were physically compelled to participate in programs of indoctrination. Even in these instances, however, there is considerable doubt in the social scientific community that the experience warrants being called brainwashing. As far back as 1956, for example, psychiatrists Lawrence Hinkle and Harold Wolff of Cornell University undertook a definite study of brainwashing, with the support of the government and full access to the secret files of the CIA as well as some former Communist interrogators and their prisoners. Their report, which was overlooked for many years, refutes the effectiveness of all efforts to brainwash anyone – especially through inducing altered states of consciousness, the modus operandi that anticultists say new religions favour (e.g., Hassan 1988; Singer 1995). Where thought reform techniques do seem to have produced results, Hinkle and Wolff argue, we are merely witnessing behavioural compliance brought on by threats and the experience of physical abuse (see Anthony and Robbins 1994: 460–1).

Kent's summary of these matters incorrectly suggests that proof of the existence of physical coercion can be used, legally and social scientifically, as evidence of the probable occurrence of brainwashing. This approach not only deceptively minimizes the true complexity of the debate over brainwashing, it seeks to conflate two separate things. To make practical legal sense of the claims made in court, judges and jurors focused on the presence or absence of physical coercion as a way of arriving at decisions independently, really in lieu of, determining whether brainwashing had or had not happened. They did not really use physical coercion as a minimal criterion of brainwashing, on its own or in conjunction with other criteria.

Likewise, contrary to Kent's statement, social scientists have never done so. The social scientists engaged in this debate were interested solely in determining if it was reasonable to even entertain that new religious movements may have brainwashed their converts. They came to the conclusion that such a charge would have to be supported first and minimally by proof of physical coercion, thinking of the test case of actual prisoners. Of course, they also realized that no scholarly study had found evidence of the use of physical coercion in any of the new religious movements investigated. In other words, contrary to Kent's claim, they were by no means implying that the mere presence of physical constraint, let alone physical maltreatment (or deception, which is another matter), was a sign of probable brainwashing. The research record shows that physical coercion in itself may or may not be evidence that brainwashing is happening. To date most researchers have been unable to delineate what else might have to be present to make a reliable determination that something like brainwashing is happening.

The other criteria Kent invokes, like 'personal confessions,' are subject to the same limitations of application identified by the courts with regard to physical coercion. Consequently, and contrary to the implication of Kent's statement, they have never played a defining role in any academic investigation of whether cults engage in coercive persuasion.

In methodological terms, the criteria Kent specifies may be *necessary* features of religious brainwashing, but they are not *sufficient* to identify if it is the case in any particular situation. But I stress 'may be necessary,' because we have good reason to doubt, as will become apparent, that Kent has even established this much.

Interestingly, Kent's discussion of the brainwashing debate diverts attention from any consideration of a key feature of this process. As the word 'brainwashing' clearly indicates, we are talking about something more than ordinary coercion or indoctrination, no matter how intense. Brainwashing is thought to effect a significant and permanent change in the self-conception of the person brainwashed, so that the continued use of surveillance and coercion is not necessary. Such is the understanding conveyed by Kent's formal definition of brainwashing on the first page of his conference paper: 'This study argues that brainwashing [is] the systematic, scientific [,] and coercive elimination of the individuality of the mind of another (Scheflin and Opton 1978, 40)' (Kent 1997a). The trouble is, short of subjecting specific individuals to an extensive psychiatric investigation, supported with good information about intimate aspects of the person's nature and thoughts prior to, during, and after a supposed experience of brainwashing, how could we know that such a change had occurred? Especially, as by definition, we cannot rely on the statements made by the subjects under study themselves, for these statements may be the product of the very brainwashing we are seeking to detect. But this raises methodological problems to which I will return below, in response to other claims made by Kent. Here, I would just note that while Kent says much to convince us of the deplorable conditions experienced by some people in the RPF, he makes no specific effort to argue or document that those who participated in Scientology's RPF did have the individuality of their minds eliminated. He simply omits this key component of his own definition, while relying almost exclusively on the reports of ex-participants of the RPF who apparently managed not to have their own sense of self washed from their brains.

Curiously, even with the evidence presented by the sources that Kent cites, the apostates' testimony about the use of physical constraint and coercion is not always convincing. This is not always apparent, however, from the attenuated presentation of this evidence in Kent's chapter in this book. We are told, for instance, that Julie Mayo 'snuck out of a guarded Scientology compound when a gate was momentarily open' (Kent 2001 [p. 6 of a single-spaced copy I have]). The more detailed report of this 'escape' provided in Kent's earlier conference paper states: she 'waited one morning until the guard opened the gate to allow someone to walk across the street for breakfast, and slipped out to the road, unnoticed, before it closed' (1997a: 15). This 'escape' sounds remarkably easy, especially if we are to believe Kent's repeated assertion that the RPF was in the habit of truly locking people away and subjecting them to quite torturous conditions. Who knows what really happened? But her account suggests a possible dramatization of more mundane circumstances. Much the same seems true of the escape account offered by Pat (1997a: 15; 2001 [p. 6 of my single-spaced copy]). Likewise, in the conference paper we have the admission that 'some people allowed themselves to be talked back into the program' after supposedly escaping. Of course, Kent, citing the testimony of one of these people (i.e., Robert Vaughn Young), characteristically interprets this turn of events as evidence of 'the power of the organization.' In other words, he interprets these reversals as implicit evidence that people were brainwashed. Just as plausibly, however, one might suggest that this indicates that the program was not really as bad as these apostates later chose to say. Either way, the fact that people were talked back into the program undercuts the assumption that people would only be in the RPF because they were physically compelled to be.

Kent's Suspect Reliance on Apostate Accounts

It soon became apparent to social scientists involved in the debate over brainwashing that the literature of the anticult movement is distorted by sampling bias (Barker 1984: 128–31). The brainwashing scenario as applied to new religious movements relies heavily on the testimony of individuals who have undergone deprogramming or 'exit-counselling.' The later is the non-coercive equivalent of the former. These people are under great pressure to account for their aberrant behaviour (joining a cult) and to direct blame away from themselves, their families, and the community. This may be necessary to make peace with their families and regain entry into other community groups (e.g., when returning to school or a job), or simply to resolve the cognitive dissonance they are experiencing from the contrast of their present and past behaviour. The brainwashing scenario, to which they are 'programmed,' provides a non-stigmatizing way to absolve everyone, most importantly themselves, of responsibility and actually secure the sympathy of others for themselves (see Bromley 1988; Wilson 1990: 19). Not surprisingly, several academic studies have revealed a marked and consistent discrepancy between the post-involvement attitudes of converts who leave these groups voluntarily and those who are deprogrammed. Only the latter show a strong statistical correlation with negative views of their cult experience (e.g., Galanter 1989; Lewis 1986; Lewis and Bromley 1987; Solomon 1981; Wright 1984). Most individuals who leave a new religion do so voluntarily, and these people continue to express some very positive feelings about their involvement. Wright found that 67 per cent of voluntary defectors said they were 'wiser for the experience' of membership, and only 9 per cent invoked the brainwashing explanation for joining in the first place (Wright and Ebaugh 1993: 127; see Levine 1984: 188 as well). From their study of the

Unification Church, Marc Galanter and his associates report 'a striking contrast' between the attitudes of voluntary defectors, on the one hand, and those who were deprogrammed on the other:

> The first group had mixed feelings about their experience but expressed a relatively benign view of both their own involvement and the ongoing participation of their remaining compatriots. Most (62%) still felt strongly that they 'cared for the ten members they knew best,' and the large majority (89%) believed that they 'got some positive things' out of membership. On the other hand, those who were deprogrammed had a much more negative attitude toward the sect and ... eight out of ten deprogrammed ex-members had participated in attempts to coerce other members to leave, whereas none of those who left voluntarily had done so. (Galanter 1989: 116)

In fact, Wright (1984) and Jacobs (1989) found that half to three-quarters of those who voluntarily deconvert from one new religious movement eventually join another similar group.

This discussion raises a related and more complicated problem, that of accounts in general (Beckford 1978; Dawson 1994; Turner 1978; Wallis and Bruce 1983; Zablocki 1996). The debate over brainwashing is largely dependent on the 'accounts' provided by members or ex-members of the new religions in question. The problem is, to what extent can we trust peoples' descriptions of their actions, especially past actions and, even more so, controversial actions? Everyday life, history, the social sciences, and the law all demonstrate that there is much potential for inaccuracy and deception (self-deception and otherwise). Studies of the accounts of deviants (e.g., murders and child molesters) and of natural scientists – two seeming extremes – reveal similar interpretive problems (see Dawson 1994). But religious accounts have proven to be particularly problematic since converts to a new religion often view the occasion to provide accounts as an opportunity to witness or proselytize for their faith. Moreover, some scholars have argued that the single best indicator that a religious conversion has occurred is evidence of the rhetorical phenomenon of biographic reconstruction (Snow and Machalek 1984; Staples and Mauss 1987). Religions normatively expect converts to reinterpret their pasts in ways commensurate with their new identities. Converts to all religions, new and old, are strongly inclined to exaggerate the sinfulness or distress of their pre-conversion lives hand-in-hand with the rewards

of their post-conversion lives. The obverse surely holds true for apostates, especially those who have been deprogrammed. In her research
on the Unification Church, Barker (1984: 170–1) found that respondents often change their interpretations of experiences at some later
point. Many who have left the church 'admitted that they had believed
at the time that they were having a religious experience, but had subsequently come to the conclusion that it had been their imagination or
the result of some mundane trigger. Conversely, those who had since
become part of a religious community were more likely to say that they
had dismissed the experience at the time, but now realized that God
had been talking to them.' So at the very least, we must be very cautious in accepting conversion accounts at face value, far more cautious
than the anticultists have even thought to be, but also more cautious
than most other scholars studying new religions have been. All of this
applies even more so to the contested testimony of apostates, like those
Kent relies on to characterize the RPF. In the words of the eminent sociologist of religion Bryan Wilson (1990: 19): 'Augustine, as a source on
the Donatists, was scarcely concerned to present a full, objective, and
detached view of that sect, any more than was Irenaeus of the Gnostics,
or the inquisitors of Montaillou of the local Albigensians. The sociologist of contemporary sectarianism need rely neither on fragments nor
on biased witnesses. Indeed, with good reason, sociologists generally
treat the evidence of a sect's theological opponents, of the aggrieved
relatives of sectarians, and of the disaffected and apostate with some
circumspection' (1990, 19).

Richardson, Balch, and Melton (1993) and Carter (1998) strongly rec-
ommend that researchers follow the accepted practice of triangulation
(Denzin 1978) in studying any aspect of new religions. Researchers
should seek, that is, to utilize 'a number of data sources simultaneously ... data should be gathered from members and ex-members,
from apologists *and* detractors, from leaders *and* followers within the
group, from parents *and* from sons and daughters who are members,
and so on' (Richardson, Balch, and Melton 1993: 217). The inevitable
clash of claims will have to be weighed against each other and against
the hopefully more neutral and exacting observations of the researcher.
To locate the truth we must triangulate our position from several different sources of information.

Kent shows little circumspection in his use of apostate accounts, and
he makes no effort at triangulation at all. His primary source of information in his conference paper are his interviews with six ex-members

of the Church of Scientology 'who had been on RPFs in different parts of the world' (Kent 1997a: 5). To this he adds the statements of fourteen more people, which he derives from court documents, affidavits, and correspondence. He supplements this further with the views of nine more people, drawn from another of his interviews and from other correspondence and anonymous news-group postings. These nine are people 'who ... claim to have seen inmates on the program' (1997: 5). In his chapter in this book, Kent says similarly that he is relying on material drawn from various books by ex-members, court documents, and interviews with eight ex-Scientologists. As the quotations he cites in his paper and in the chapter indicate, all of these sources are hostile to the Church of Scientology. No one from the church, from either its leadership or membership, is interviewed or quoted. In fact, Kent indicates that he did not even seek such interviews.

In his conference paper, then, we are presented with some of the views of twenty-nine individuals in all, and there are many potential problems. These are all people who have either actively sought to express or agreed to express their criticisms of the RPF. But we do not know how to assess this sampling of opinion, since we are never supplied with an accurate figure for how many people have ever been in the RPF in the first place. How typical are these criticisms? What of the many other people who have participated in the RPF? What are their views? We know little or nothing of the background of the twenty-nine people he does cite, their motives, present religious commitments, their mental state, and so on. How reliable are they as witnesses? How could we gauge the truthfulness of their testimony? How could Kent gauge their reliability, since he only met six of them? We are given passages of testimony and accounts out of context. Having more information or fuller access to the sources may lead to different interpretations of the meaning, significance, and reliability of the statements quoted. As every participant in a legal proceeding knows, affidavits do not always provide the whole truth, nor are they free from exaggeration and other errors. All of these same concerns and questions apply with equal force to Kent's chapter in this book.

Most disingenuously, Kent offers the following circular and surprisingly lame excuses for his reliance on this small and skewed sample. First, in the chapter herein he simply says in parentheses (2001 [p. 2 of my single-spaced copy]):

(I decided not to attempt to interview current Scientologists or Family members because I feared that they likely would suffer unacceptable consequences if they were to reveal aspects about these camps and programs that their respective groups want to keep concealed.)

In his conference paper Kent is a little more forthcoming:

... former members who went through the RPF are difficult to find and, once found, often are reluctant to speak with a researcher. The difficulty of finding former RPF inmates stems partly from the fact that the program's design is to feed repentant (and some would say emotionally broken) Sea Org members back into the organization. Consequently, many potential informants remain in Scientology under threat of being either ex-communicated or sent back into RPF itself for talking negatively about their time in it. Moreover, as RPF participants they spend countless (in some cases, hundreds) of hours confessing to alleged sins and crimes, and they fear that the organization would use these confessions against them if they were to talk. Indeed RPFers who complete their programs must write or sign a statement before they leave which praises the RPF and extols its virtues. For all of these reasons, I did not attempt to interview active Scientologists who had been RPF inmates. (1997a: 5)

Expanding Kent's sample to increase its reliability may well be difficult, and perhaps for the reasons he specifies. But we cannot know this in advance, as Kent assumes we can, for the characteristics of the RPF he mentions to justify his skewed sample are the very things he is supposedly trying to establish with this study in the first place. In this passage, he is seeking to use his own insufficiently substantiated and suspect suppositions about the RPF to justify the exclusion of other sources of information. He does this because he has already decided that no statements made by Scientologists about their own religion are reliable because they are bound to disagree with the accounts provided by his existing sample. At a later point (1997: 13), Kent invokes this same bit of indefensible circular reasoning to dismiss the official pronouncements of the church on the RPF as mere propaganda. Under these circumstances, how could any disconfirming information ever be found that would be acceptable to Kent? His views are arbitrarily insulated from any possibility of falsification – other than the unlikely event of members of his own sample changing their minds.

To be perfectly clear about the methodologically bogus nature of this strategy, let us switch the focus and consider, for example, the Catholic

Church. The Catholic Church has been the subject of vociferous criticism by hundreds, if not thousands of people, for centuries. Yet it would be hard to imagine that any credible historian or social scientist would think to investigate the church by seeking only the views of its critics, while dismissing all of the pronouncements of the church out of hand. What is the difference? The Catholic Church, by virtue of its size and longevity, has a greater measure of legitimacy in our society than the Church of Scientology. It is not, in other words, in the vulnerable position of being a minority.

Kent's Misrepresentation of Information

Information can always be packaged in ways that serve one's argument. But when social scientists present information in a manner that disregards contrary views that are well known in the field, they are inviting criticism. As already indicated, such is the case with much that Kent has said about brainwashing. In the case of his specific criticisms of the RPF, this kind of error of omission comes most flagrantly to the fore in his brief discussion of the so-called success stories that Kent says all inmates of the RPF must write before being allowed to leave the program (1997a: 24; 2001 [p.11–12 of my single-spaced copy]). In his conference paper, Kent points out that these success stories are in line with the general policy of the Church of Scientology to publicize 'win' stories, or positive testimonials about the value of Scientological training. These stories are used for public relations and to attract new members. He implies that there is something unusual and manipulative in this practice. Yet every sociologist of religion knows that such testimonials have been used for these same purposes by sects and denominations within the Christian church for centuries. In fact they were common to the primitive church itself under the oppression of the Roman Empire. The Jehovah's Witnesses, to cite one well-known contemporary example, keep a record of the conversion testimonials of all their members (see Beckford 1978), and one need only consult the testimonials regularly recorded at Holiness Movement camp meetings in Canada and the United States in the nineteenth and early twentieth centuries for another relatively recent historical example (e.g., see Greenshields 1993). Further, Kent states that the success stories 'may have provided some protection in the future if former RPFers became critical of their incarceration in the program.' This, of course, is speculation, as he does not document that these stories are used in this manner. Perhaps that is why this criticism is not repeated in his chapter in this book. But even if these success stories are used in this way, it would again not be unusual for a religion to 'protect' itself from what it deems to be false claims by citing evidence of how an ex-member clearly once felt otherwise about the group. As with almost every aspect of Kent's critique, the issues under debate are susceptible to different interpretations depending on the context in which they are presented. This is not to say that Kent's views are necessarily incorrect, but to reiterate that matters at hand are much more ambiguous and subject to interpretation than he is willing to acknowledge.

This failure to deal fairly with the material is demonstrated most clearly by Kent's last criticism of the success stories in the more extensive critique provided in his conference paper. There he admits that the RPF success stories are 'far less extensive in content or design than the final confessions that Chinese and Western victims of thought reform programs had to write for their "re-educators" in the late 1940s and early 1950s (see Lifton 1961: 266–73, 473–84).' But, he argues, the success stories, like the latter confessions, appear 'to follow an outline or formula,' which he then tries to illustrate (1997a: 24–5). In other words, he is implying that these success stories are both forced and insincere, like the Chinese thought reform confessions. Much the same is implied in his discussion of success stories in the chapter in this book. But once again, sociologists of religion recognize that it is far from uncommon for conversion stories and other religious testimonials to follow a normative template, or formula, provided by the religious group (see Beckford 1978; Turner 1978; Greenshields 1993; Stromberg 1993; Dawson 1994). Ironically, a good example of this situation is provided in an article on coercive persuasion by John Young and Ezra Griffith (1992), which Kent cites in his conference paper in implicit support of his views. The passage is worth quoting at length:

> There are services and ceremonies among black churches that have elements similar to those of rituals among the less conventional religious movements. For example, Griffith, Young, and Smith (1984) have described the conventional week night service in a typical black church within the Baptist umbrella. The service included an extended period of testimony during which individuals presented the most important problems that they were struggling with at the time. By repeated attendance at these services newcomers learned how to frame the solutions to these

problems in a context culturally set out by the traditions and values of the group.

The individuals discussing their testimony and proposing solutions were dramatically encouraged by means of clapping and singing coming from others sitting in the service. Under this influence, each individual was regularly expected to progress to what the group called 'Holy Spirit possession,' a trance-like state characterized by rhythmic speech and dancing as well as speaking in tongues. It was usual for the service to continue until most present had testified, and it concluded with all present holding hands, praying, singing, and once again becoming 'possessed.' By these means the group members reaffirmed their commitment to one another and to the group's values. (1992: 91–2)

Numerous similar accounts could be provided from the literature, and Young and Griffiths go on to provide another illustration drawn from the Spiritual Baptists of the Caribbean. So the formula-like character of the success stories proves little in itself, as Young and Griffith demonstrate with their examples, because a measure of psychological homogenization is common to many religious groups and situations. Thus, as the American courts eventually recognized, to accept the charge of brainwashing against an unconventional religion, was to open a Pandora's box for the potential persecution of other religions.

Concluding Remarks

Kent says that he cannot understand why, with his analysis in hand, social scientists should continue to entertain the worry that other religions could become subject to persecution if the model of brainwashing were revived for some new religious movements (2001: [p. 12 of my single-spaced copy]). Yet the first time the brainwashing model was promoted as an explanation of 'cult activity' it did quickly spawn attempts by deprogrammers to 'rescue' people from such other groups as the Pentecostalists or various Catholic sects. Only two paragraphs later in his chapter, Kent himself draws specific parallels between the brainwashing he says is happening in The Family and Scientology and that associated with the Soviet purges of the 1940s, the Chinese Communists of the 1950s, and the North Koreans during the Korean war (2001: [p. 13 of my single-spaced copy]). In doing so Kent may be referring primarily to the alleged common presence of physical coercion in these cases. There is little reason to be confident, however, that either the public or the media, which provides the public with most of their information about new religious movements – will either appreciate or honour the delimited basis of this comparison, even if it could be established credibly that some new religions do engage in physical coercion of some of their members (e.g., see Pfeifer 1992).

For the reasons outlined above, and in light of many other criticisms that could not be developed here because of space limitations,[5] I can only say that Kent's attempt to revive the brainwashing model is unwarranted. To make his case, and then use it to justify the imposition of serious legal sanctions against the Church of Scientology in Germany, or anywhere else (see Kent 1997a: 28), Kent will have to set his prejudices (i.e., literally pre-judgments) aside in favour of making a more cogent and careful argument with the reliable evidence at hand, and with that yet to be discovered. Minimally, as a social scientist he cannot methodologically justify giving voice and credence to only the opinions of the opponents of the Church of Scientology. More regard must be given to the results of scholarly research into new religious movements.

Notes

1 A fourth line of criticism could be discussed as well: in the critique of Scientology developed in his conference paper, Kent relies heavily on a selective and too literalistic reading of documents of a suspect nature and questionable relevance – documents that were presumably, but not necessarily, written by L. Ron Hubbard. But most of this material is not used in his chapter in this book, so I will not develop this line of criticism here. One brief illustration of the kind of thing I have in mind is provided in note 5.

2 Stephen Kent and I were both employed as expert witnesses in a recent civil suit involving the Church of Scientology in Edmonton, Alberta, Canada. Much of this critique was prepared at the request of the Church of Scientology, to help prepare a defence against Dr Kent's testimony at this trial. It appears, however, that no court case will be proceeding. In preparing these materials I carefully stipulated to the Church of Scientology that I would make a strictly academic assessment of Dr Kent's views, and I secured permission to use whatever I submitted to them in my own academic publications.

3 The references are to a 3 December 1997 second and revised draft of the original paper presented to the Society for the Scientific Study of Religion, at

San Diego, California, on 7 November 1997. Page references are to the single-spaced manuscript copy in my possession, which lacks any pagination other than that provided in the Table of Contents, to what seemingly was a double-spaced original. The Table of Contents reveals that the original of the copy I am working with was over 61 pages in length, typed double-spaced. I have numbered the pages of my single-spaced copy, starting with the first page of text (i.e., the second actual page), and all references are to these page numbers.

4 Kent's prejudicial treatment of the subject is reflected in his consistent use of such terminology throughout his conference paper. The language employed in the chapter in this book is much more guarded.

5 When the RPF was created in 1974, for example, Russell Miller, a well-known critic of Scientology, argued (1987: 318–23) that there is strong evidence that Hubbard acted rather impulsively and was emotionally and mentally unbalanced. He seemed to be experiencing some kind of nervous breakdown. As Miller presents matters, the creation of the RPF is but one of a number of 'bizarre' behaviours that 'indicated that he was losing his facility to distinguish ... between fact and fiction' (323). The Church of Scientology may well wish to dispute this account, but Miller is one of Kent's prime sources for information about the origins of the RPF (see Kent 1997a: 11; 2001: [p. 4 of my single-spaced copy]). It is curious, then, that Kent never mentions anything about the mental condition of Hubbard when the RPF was founded. Of course, to do so would undermine the impression he works so hard to create – that the RPF is the product of a carefully planned program of true thought reform.

References

Anthony, Dick. 1990. 'Religious Movements and Brainwashing Litigation: Evaluating Key Testimony.' In *In Gods We Trust. New Patterns of Religious Pluralism in America*. 2d ed. Edited by T. Robbins and B. Anthony, 295–344. New Brunswick, N.J.: Transaction Books.

Anthony, Dick, and Thomas Robbins. 1992. 'Law, Social Science and the "Brainwashing" Exception to the First Amendment.' *Behavioural Sciences and the Law* 10 (1): 5–27.

– 1994. 'Brainwashing and Totalitarian Influence.' In *Encyclopedia of Human Behavior*, vol. 1, 457–71. San Diego, Calif.: Academic Press.

– 1995. 'Negligence, Coercion and the Protection of Religious Belief.' *Journal of Church and State* 37 (3): 509–36.

Barker, Eileen. 1984. *The Making of a Moonie: Choice or Brainwashing?* Oxford: Basil Blackwell.

Beckford, James. 1978. 'Accounting for Conversion.' *British Journal of Sociology* 29 (2): 249–62.

– 1985. *Cult Controversies. The Societal Response to the New Religious Movements.* London: Tavistock.

Bromley, David G., and James T. Richardson, eds. 1983. *The Brainwashing/ Deprogramming Controversy: Sociological, Psychological, Legal and Historical Perspectives.* Lewiston, N.Y.: Edwin Mellen Press.

– 1988. 'Deprogramming as a Mode of Exit from New Religious Movements: The Case of the Unification Church.' In *Falling from the Faith: Causes and Consequences of Religious Apostasy,* edited by D.G. Bromley, 185–204. Newbury Park, Calif.: Sage.

– 1998a. 'The Social Construction of Contested Exit Roles: Defectors, Whistle-blowers, and Apostates.' In *The Politics of Apostasy: The Role of Apostates in the Transformation of Religious Movements,* 19–48, edited by D.G. Bromley. Westport, Conn.: Praeger.

– 1998b. 'Listing (In Black and White) Some Observations on (Sociological) Thought Reform.' *Nova Religio* 1 (2): 250–65.

– 1999. 'A Tale of Two Theories: Brainwashing and Conversion as Competing Political Narratives.' In *Misunderstanding Cults.* Toronto: University of Toronto Press.

Bromley, David G., and Thomas Robbins. 1993. 'The Role of Government in Regulating New and Nonconventional Religions.' In *The Role of Government in Monitoring and Regulating Religion in Public Life,* edited by J. Wood and D. Davis, 205–41. Waco, Tex.: Dawson Institute for Church-State Studies, Baylor University.

Carter, Lewis F. 1998. 'Carriers of Tales: On Assessing Credibility of Apostate and Other Outsider Accounts of Religious Practices.' In *The Politics of Apostasy,* edited by D.G. Bromley, 221–37. Westport, Conn.: Praeger.

Coleman, John. 1984. 'New Religions and the Myth of Mind Control.' *American Journal of Orthopsychiatry* 54 (2): 322–5.

Dawson, Lorne L. 1994. 'Accounting for Accounts: How Should Sociologists Treat Conversion Stories?' *International Journal of Comparative Religion and Philosophy* 1 (1, 2): 46–66.

– 1998. *Comprehending Cults: The Sociology of New Religious Movements.* Toronto and New York: Oxford University Press.

Denzin, Norman. 1978. *The Research Act: A Theoretical Introduction to Sociological Methods.* 2d ed. New York: McGraw Hill.

Galanter, Marc. 1989. *Cults: Faith, Healing and Coercion.* New York: Oxford University Press.

Greenshields, Malcolm. 1993. 'Testimonies from a Camp Meeting: Holiness Movement Meetings, Stittsville, Ontario, May 1907.' *North American Religion* 2: 218–31.

Hassan, Steven. 1988. *Combatting Cult Mind-Control.* Rochester, Vt.: Park Street Press.

Hinkle, Lawrence E., and Harold E. Wolf. 1956. 'Communist Interrogation and the Indoctrination of "Enemies of the States."' *American Medical Association Archives of Neurological Psychology* 76: 117–27.

Jacobs, Janet L. 1989. *Divine Disenchantment: Deconverting from New Religions.* Bloomington, Ind.: Indiana University Press.

Kent, Stephen A. 1991. 'International Social Control by the Church of Scientology.' Paper presented to the Society for the Scientific Study of Religion, San Diego, Calif.

– 1994. 'Misattribution and Social Control in the Children of God.' *Journal of Religion and Health* 33 (1): 29–43.

– 1997a. 'Brainwashing in Scientology's Rehabilitation Project Force.' Paper presented to the Society for the Scientific Study of Religion, San Diego, Calif.

– 1997b. 'Scientology – Is This a Religion?' Presentation at the 27th Deutscher Evangelischer Kirchentag, 20 June.

– 2001. 'Brainwashing Programs in The Family and Scientology.' In *Misunderstanding Cults*, edited by B. Zablocki and T. Robbins. Toronto: University of Toronto Press.

Kent, Stephen A., and Deana Hall. 1997. 'Brainwashing and Re-Indoctrination Programs in the Children of God/The Family.' Paper presented to the Association for the Sociology of Religion, Toronto.

Levine, Saul. 1984. *Radical Departures: Desperate Detours to Growing Up.* New York: Harcourt Brace Jovanovich.

Lewis, James R. 1986. 'Reconstructing the Cult Experience: Post-Involvement Attitudes as a Function of Mode of Exit and Post-Involvement Socialization.' *Sociological Analysis* 47 (2): 151–9.

Lewis, James R., and Bromley, David G. 1987. 'The Cult Withdrawal Syndrome: A Case of Misattribution of Cause?' *Journal for the Scientific Study of Religion* 26 (4): 508–22.

Pfeifer, Jeffrey E. 1992. 'The Psychological Framing of Cults: Schematic Representations and Cult Evaluations.' *Journal of Applied Social Psychology* 22 (7): 531–44.

Richardson, James T. 1991. 'Cult/Brainwashing Cases and Freedom of Religion.' *Journal of Church and State* 33 (1): 55–74.

– 1993. 'A Social Psychological Critique of "Brainwashing" Claims About Recruitment to New Religions.' In *Religion and The Social Order*. Vol. 3, pt. B. *The Handbook on Cults and Sects in America*, edited by D.G. Bromley and J.K. Hadden, 75–97. Greenwich, Conn.: JAI Press.

– 1995. 'Clinical and Personality Assessment of Participants in New Religions.' *The International Journal for the Psychology of Religion* 5 (3): 145–70.

Richardson, James T., Robert Balch, and J. Gordon Melton. 1993. 'Problems of Research and Data in the Study of New Religions.' In *Religion and the Social Order*, Vol. 3, pt. B. *The Handbook on Cults and Sects in America*, edited by D.G. Bromley and J.K. Hadden, 213–29. Greenwich, Conn.: JAI Press.

Robbins, Thomas. 1984. 'Constructing Cultist "Mind Control".' *Sociological Analysis* 43 (3): 241–56.

Robbins, Thomas, and Dick Anthony. 1979. 'Cults, Brainwashing, and Counter-Subversion.' *The Annals of the American Academy of Political and Social Science* 446 (Nov.): 78–90.

– 1982. 'Deprogramming, Brainwashing and the Medicalization of Deviant Religious Groups.' *Social Problems* 29 (3): 283–97.

Robbins, Thomas, and David Bromley. 1993. 'State Regulation of Marginal Religious Movements.' *Syzygy: Journal of Alternative Religion and Culture* 2 (3–4): 225–42.

Rochford, E., et al. 1989. 'New Religions, Mental Health, and Social Control.' In *Research in the Social Scientific Study of Religion*. Vol. 1, edited by M. Lynn and D. Moberg, 57–82. Greenwich, Conn.: JAI Press.

Scheflin, Alan W. and Edward M. Opton, Jr. 1978. *The Mind Manipulators*. New York: Paddington.

Singer, Margaret T. 1995. *Cults in Our Midst. The Hidden Menace in Our Everyday Lives*. San Francisco, Calif.: Jossey-Bass.

Snow, David, and Richard Machalek. 1984. 'The Sociology of Conversion.' In *Annual Review of Sociology*, edited by Ralph H. Turner and James F. Short, 167–190. Palo Alto, Calif.: Annual Reviews.

Solomon, Trudy 1981. 'Integrating the "Moonie" Experience: A Survey of Ex-members of the Unification Church.' In *In Gods We Trust: New Patterns of Religious Pluralism in America*, edited by T. Robbins and D. Anthony, 275–95. New Brunswick, N.J.: Transaction Publications.

Staples, Clifford L., and Armand Mauss. 1987. 'Conversion or Commitment? A Reassessment of the Snow and Machalek Approach to the Study of Conversion.' *Journal for the Scientific Study of Religion* 26 (2): 133–47.

Stromberg, Peter G. 1993. *Language and Self-Transformation: A Study of the Christian Conversion Narrative*. Cambridge: Cambridge University Press.

Turner, Bryan. 1978. 'Recollection and Membership: Converts' Talk and the Ratiocination of Commonality.' *Sociology* 12: 316–24.

Wallis, Roy, and Steve Bruce. 1983. 'Accounting for Action: Defending the Common Sense Heresy.' *Sociology* 17 (1): 97–111.

Wilson, Bryan R. 1990. *The Social Dimensions of Sectarianism.* Oxford: Clarendon Press.

Wright Stuart A. 1984. 'Post-Involvement Attitudes of Voluntary Defectors from Controversial New Religious Movements.' *Journal for the Scientific Study of Religion* 23 (2): 172–82.

Wright, Stuart A., and Helen Rose Ebaugh. 1993. 'Leaving New Religions.' In *Religion and the Social Order.* Vol. 3, pt. B. *The Handbook on Cults and Sects in America,* edited by D.G. Bromley and J.K. Hadden. Greenwich, Conn.: JAI Press.

Young, John L., and Ezra E.H. Griffiths. 1992. 'A Critical Evaluation of Coercive Persuasion as Used in the Assessment of Cults.' *Behavioral Sciences and the Law* 10: 89–101.

Zablocki, Benjamin. 1996. 'Reliability and Validity of Apostate Accounts in the Study of Religious Communities.' Paper presented to the Association for the Sociology of Religion, New York.

– 1997. 'The Blacklisting of a Concept: The Strange History of the Brainwashing Conjecture in the Sociology of Religion.' *Nova Religio* 1 (1): 96–121.

– 1998. 'Exit Cost Analysis: A New Approach to the Scientific Study of Brainwashing.' *Nova Religio* 1 (2): 216–49.

10. Compelling Evidence: A Rejoinder to Lorne Dawson's Chapter

Stephen A. Kent

At stake in this debate with Lorne Dawson about 'brainwashing' is a body of social scientific literature that has rejected the applicability of the term in relation to groups often called new religions. My research on brainwashing programs that both Scientology and the Children of God/The Family imposed upon hundreds of their respective members challenges this body of literature, but only in a limited way. I specifically demonstrate that Scientology's Rehabilitation Project Force (RPF) program and The Family's Victor program were efforts that fit the classic definition of brainwashing. Both programs utilized forcible confinement, physical maltreatment, and social degradations, in combination with intense ideological study, forced confessions, and obligatory personal 'success' stories. The groups in question combined these techniques in the attempt to retain members. (Almost all of the existing social scientific literature refuting brainwashing examines its inapplicability as a concept to explain groups *acquiring* members [i.e., converts], but the efforts of Benjamin Zablocki, myself, and others is to see the brainwashing model enter social scientific discourse for a specific set of circumstances directed towards membership *retention*.) While persons who escaped or otherwise departed from the RPF indicate that Scientology's brainwashing efforts do not always succeed, even in the short run, I hypothesize that these programs had a profound impact upon most persons who went through them. This hypothesis, of course, should become the subject of research, but (specifically regarding Scientology) the isolated and highly controlled environment in which the RPF (for example) operates makes normal scientific research

next to impossible. I also suggest that at least four other groups –
Synanon, the Ecclesia Athletic Ass[ociatio]n, Colonia Dignitad, and
People's Temple at Jonestown – appear to have implemented brain-
washing programs as a retention strategy.

Dawson has accepted the established body of dismissive sociological
literature, even though it has neglected to address the harsh and
demanding dimensions of the RPF as first described in publicly available material in 1980 (Burden 1980). Subsequently, RPF information
has appeared in at least two court decisions (one American, the other
British), sworn affidavits, newspaper and magazine articles, radio (and
most recently television) accounts, Internet postings, and books by and
about Scientology. (With the exception of the recent television shows
[A&E 1998; ABC News 1998], I provide the citations for this material in
the original article). Part of the challenge that my study presents, therefore, is that it causes readers to wonder why prominent social scientists
such as Dawson have ignored such a large and diverse body of material in their conclusion that the term brainwashing should be rejected.
Readers also may wonder why some social scientists resist considering
the possibility that brainwashing exists as a member-retention strategy
in specific instances.

Dawson's reaction to my study's challenge attempts to undermine
the accuracy of the article's methodology (along with the methodology
that underlies my more extensive RPF analysis, which is available on
the World Wide Web [Kent 1997]). Indeed, he shows remarkable fervour in that attempt, having been retained by the Church of Scientology as an expert witness in an Edmonton, Alberta, case in which I
already was scheduled to testify. Even though the civil case in question
had nothing to do with the RPF, Dawson wrote much of his critique 'at
the request of the Church of Scientology, to help prepare a defence
against Dr Kent's testimony at this trial' (Dawson 1999: n2). The trial,
however, was supposed to have been about Scientology's alleged
efforts to use the law in an attempt to harass, if not destroy, its opponents (what used to be called Scientology's 'fair game' practice) – a
practice that critics insist still occurs and which may explain why some
of my informants demand anonymity. The RPF connection to this trial
remains a mystery.

Mention of my informants, however, highlights another challenge
that my article raises. I take seriously the accounts of former members;
Dawson adopts the position shared by some sociologists of religion
that the accounts of former members (whom Dawson calls 'apostates')

are highly suspect. He speaks about the presumed effects that exit counselling and deprogramming have upon members of controversial religions, and then raises the general question about the reliability of accounts of any kind that either former members or current members offer about a particular faith. The accounts by former members are, in Dawson's words, 'contested testimony.'

How Does Dawson Build His Methodological Critique?

Most remarkably, Dawson begins his critique of my methodology by exempting himself from examining any of my documents – Scientology's own printed material about the RPF – the court decisions, the affidavits, the testimonies, and so on. These documents are vital for evaluating my triangulation efforts (to which I will return shortly), but Dawson claims, '[t]he specific factual claims [that] Kent makes may or may not be true. I do not have access to the materials he uses in order to make my own assessment.' Now, one wonders why he did not ask Scientology for the key documents, but I suspect that had he done so, then he would have received the same response that I did a year or so ago – no documents. Even though the RPF material has nothing to do with Scientology's alleged upper level secret beliefs, the organization classifies the RPF materials as confidential documents with restricted access.

Far easier for Dawson would have been for him to do an Internet search on the Rehabilitation Project Force. After all, Dawson himself has published an article (written with two others) on using the World Wide Web to research new religious movements and the anticult movement (Cottee, Yateman, and Dawson 1996). If he had followed his own advice, then he would have found hundreds of Web pages devoted to the RPF. (The AltaVista search engine alone found 307.) Among these pages are many of the key documents that I used: the crucial Flag Order 3434 RB; the American court decision about Lawrence Wollersheim; the British court case that mentions the RPF; and testimonies or affidavits from Vicki Aznaran, Tonya Burden, Dennis Erlich, David Mayo, Monica Pignotti, Anne Rosenblum, Andre Tabayoyon, Hanna Whitfield, Robert Vaughn Young, and Stacy Young. Additionally, important material about the Rehabilitation Project Force's Rehabilitation Project Force (the quite severe RPF's RPF) appears in a widely circulated book published by Scientology (Hubbard 1976). The only external source that I cited and that Dawson also used was Russell Miller's biography (1987) of Scientology's founder, L. Ron Hubbard, and even that source had at least eleven mentions of the RPF. In sum, I cannot accept Dawson's statement, '[a]t present, I have no means at my disposal to specifically assess the veracity of [Kent's RPF] depiction.' The easiest means of assessment at his disposal was only a few mouse clicks away.

Because Dawson failed to assess the accuracy of my description of several RPF programs ('[t]he specific factual claims Kent makes may or may not be true'), he has no basis for then making analogies between the RPF and other institutions. If he does not know how the RPF works, then he cannot say to what its operation is similar. So, for example, he likens forms of RPF discipline to 'the military, Catholic religious orders, and other kinds of religious communities around the world and throughout human history' (cf. Singer with Lalich 1995: 98–101). He makes this claim, however, based merely on the RPF's title. Likewise, he dismisses my conclusion that the obligatory RPF success stories represent (in his words) 'something unusual and manipulative,' and then provides examples (once again) of conversion testimonials from several religious traditions. Dawson seems not to appreciate that the RPF testimonials are obligatory – required by policy – for persons who wish to 'graduate' from the program (Boards of Directors of the Churches of Scientology 1980: 7). Unless people give the testimonials, they can remain in the RPF indefinitely.

On this issue of the obligatory success stories, Dawson quoted me as saying that they '"may have provided some protection [to Scientology] in the future if former RPFers became critical of their incarceration in the program"' (Dawson 1999: 14, quoting Kent 1997: 60). He summarily dismissed this statement as 'speculation.' This precise scenario, however, played itself out on American television at the end of 1998. In *ABC News*'s hour-long television show on Scientology (which the program *20/20* aired on 20 December 1998), Scientology provided the newscast with copies of Vaughn and Stacy Young's signed RPF success stories, since now these former members were indicating that the RPF was abusive. Vaughn Young insisted, '[t]hey want it in your own handwriting. So that when your handwriting's done [*sic*], they say, "See we have it in his handwriting. He confessed to this. He did this."' Investigative reporter Tom Jarriel then queried Scientology spokesperson Mike Rinder about the signed documents, saying, 'Vaughn Young says he was forced to sign a statement he did not believe in, and it was a prerequisite to get out of what he wanted to get away from.' Rinder responded dismissively: 'Well, you know, what do you want to believe? Do you want to believe what Vaughn Young wrote at the time and signed, or do you want to believe him now saying, ["]well, I didn't mean to write that"'? (*ABC News* 1998: 9). In essence, the Scientology spokesperson used the signed success story in an attempt to discredit the accuser, neatly side-stepping the fundamental question about the coercive conditions under which Young first wrote and signed it.

The final, but absolutely crucial, point to make about Dawson's decision not to examine any of my documents is that he exempted himself from seeing the extensive, and varied, forms of triangulation that I used. This self-imposed exemption is most peculiar, since Dawson himself lists the broad range of my sources. I obtained data from nine different types of sources. First, information provided by former members came from court decisions, legal affidavits (many sworn under oath), in-person and telephone interviews, Internet postings, books about Scientology, magazine accounts, and newspaper accounts. Second, the position of Scientology towards its RPF program came from the organization's publications and internal documents. Third, in the chapter that appears earlier in this book, I also utilized information from one current Scientologist – a source that Dawson missed and one to which I will return in a moment. I had first-hand accounts from twenty-two people who had been on the RPF and/or the RPF's RPF, with an additional ten accounts of people who saw the program in action. Consequently, I had information about the RPF from thirty-two people. (Ironically, Dawson calls this sample 'small and skewed,' but he was the second author on an article about a Buddhist group in Halifax that used information from interviews with only fifteen members [Eldershaw and Dawson 1995: 7].) Most of my RPF sources date from the 1980s and 1990s. In material collected or presented by judges, lawyers, reporters, a professional writer, former-members-turned-authors, and myself, there appear remarkably consistent accounts about RPFs in three countries (possibly seven programs in the United States, one in the United Kingdom, and one in Denmark). These reports describe Scientology's first RPF program in 1974, and then identify others that operated (at least in one case) into the 1990s. In sum, the multiple forms of triangulation that I used – multiple data collection methods, varied sources, different investigators, accounts over time; and accounts across space (see Fielding and Fielding 1986: 25; Maxwell 1996: 75–6) qualify my RPF research as multiply triangulated studies.

If Dawson had read the chapter published in this book carefully, he would not have erred by claiming, '[n]o one from the church, from either its leadership or membership, is interviewed or quoted.' As my chapter clearly indicated: '[r]ecently an active Scientologist posted some of his RPF experiences on the <alt.religion.scientology> newsgroup,' and then cited nine of his postings. In the body of the text where I discussed examples of 'physical maltreatment,' it stated very clearly: '[a] current Scientologist and former RPFer in the Los Angeles Scientology facility wrote about inmates having to clean a narrow, roach-infested tunnel beneath the food preparation area that was criss-crossed with hot pipes and smelled so badly that in one instance he passed out (SB 1998b: 2).' His actual descriptions of this narrow, odorous tunnel area were dramatic, but Dawson did not see them since he failed to check my sources.

This Internet informant was a second-generation Scientologist 'in good standing' who decided to post on <alt.religion.scientology> partly because he was bothered by his organization's efforts to limit the free speech of members on the Internet. (He specifically reacted to Scientology's dissemination to its members of an Internet censoring software program that prevents computers from reading numerous Web sites, newsgroups, subject discussions, and postings by perceived opponents.) In addition, previous postings on <alt.religion.scientology> by another Scientologist had 'really inspired' him. He concluded his first posting by inviting newsgroup members to 'feel free to ask me what you will,' and promised that 'I will answer to the best of my ability and honestly' (2). All indications from his subsequent postings are that he attempted to keep his promise, as demonstrated by the range and content of the facts and issues that he discussed (including his time on the RPF and the RPF's RPF).

Other Scientologists have to be able to speak freely if they are going to be useful aides to researchers. They also must know that they will not suffer retaliation from the organization. (For his part, SB realized that his participation on the newsgroup was 'pretty much taboo' [SB 1998a, 1]. Actually, it violated at least six different policies about handling 'entheta' or negative information about Scientology [Chester 1996].) Along these lines, note 2 of my earlier chapter in this book contained several examples from Scientology's policies that directly curtail the free speech of its followers, at the same time that the organization labels such free speech actions as 'suppressive acts.' More dramatic, however, is the 'Non-Disclosure Bond and Release' that 'a religious volunteer at the Church of Scientology' must sign, and which attempts to prevent any current or former Scientologist from ever discussing a program like the RPF. Parts of the four-page, eight-section document state:

> 3. Except as required by law, I further agree that while I am performing my duties as a religious worker or as a staff member of any Church, Mission, or affiliated organization of the Scientology religion, and at all times thereafter, any 'confidential information' that I possess or come to possess will remain confidential and will not be revealed, disclosed, implied, or told by me, directly or indirectly, to anyone other than those individuals who are authorized to receive such information. I further acknowledge and agree that the term 'confidential information' includes all information of any Church, Mission or affiliated organization of the Scientology religion, their staff members, volunteers and parishioners that is not publicly available and generally known to others concerning internal organization, personnel, functions or past, present or future activities.
>
> 4. My intention in signing this agreement is to protect the Church from the disclosure of information which may tend to harm, damage, injure, or otherwise adversely affect the Church or any of its activities, functions, or personnel.
>
> 5. I further agree that for each breach of this promise of non-disclosure that is caused by me, either directly or indirectly, I will pay to the Church of Scientology _____ [fill in which Church] One Million Dollars ($1,000,000). (Department of Special Affairs [1991]: 1, 2)

With Scientologists having to live under the weight of such severe restrictions on their communications, it is impossible to expect either ordinary members or leaders to be acceptable research participants. Indeed, serious ethical questions about endangering research subjects – all related to the likelihood of Scientology retaliation – would arise from researchers even attempting to get Scientologists to speak candidly under these circumstances. Dawson may be able to cite academics who hold out the laudable ideal of researchers speaking to leaders and followers within the groups that they research, but this ideal collapses in the presence of Scientology's repressive and restrictive non-disclosure bond against its own upper-level members. The most that researchers on Scientology can hope to do is obtain information from those rare members who operate outside of the organization's direct controls, as did the Scientologist on the Internet whose postings I cited.

Two additional aspects of Dawson's critique demand comment.

First, he was critical of my identification of forcible confinement and physical coercion as minimum requirements that social scientists had agreed must be present before a program might be identified as brainwashing. Although he claimed that 'this statement inaccurately represents the social scientific assessment of the concept of brainwashing,' Dawson elsewhere had concluded very differently. Specifically, he wrote, 'as the original studies of thought control suggest, the evidence is weak for assuming that the full and involuntary transformation of identity signified by "brainwashing" can occur in the absence of physical restraint and abuse' (Dawson 1998: 116). Dawson and I agree, therefore, when identifying the importance of forcible confinement and physical maltreatment as key (but by themselves inadequate) aspects of a brainwashing definition.

The final set of significant disagreements with Dawson concerns the importance of former members' testimonies. Dawson attempts to discredit my informants through his long discussion about the impact on the credibility of witnesses who had either been 'deprogrammed' or exit-counselled. The fatal flaw in this reasoning, however, is that none of my informants had been through either experience. Dawson assumes that these informants must have gained their negative evaluations of Scientology with the assistance of 'agents' of the so-called anti-cult movement, which is what some sociological literature would have predicted. This type of stereotypical prediction, with its resulting label placed on these informants as 'apostates,' allowed Dawson to think he knows how they left Scientology and why they provided information about the RPF. Indeed, it is troubling that some social scientists, who should be well aware of the potential damage caused to people who receive a deviant 'master status' (like 'apostate'), continue to refine and apply this label at the expense (at least in Dawson's case) of evaluating the content of their claims (see Becker 1963: 33–4; Schur 1971: 30, 52, 69–70). Judging the motives behind actions is very difficult, so researchers cannot always determine why these people have either spoken out publicly or conveyed information privately. Ultimately, however, their motives matter far less than the consistent content of their information. In the case of these RPF accounts, the high degree of triangulation leads me to conclude that the informants are providing accurate accounts. First, people's accounts are consistent with much of Scientology's written policies and documents. Second, research subjects provide similar, first-hand accounts of the same RPF programs. Third, different types of researchers working in different periods of time obtain similar RPF information. Finally, some of the people provide information despite risk to themselves.

Concluding Remarks: How to Understand Dawson's Critique

It seems curious that a respected, well-published, and highly successful academic like Lorne Dawson would contest the propriety of my methods regarding a Scientology institution – the RPF – about which he knows little. The only way his entry into this debate makes sense is to view it within the context of a struggle for interpretive control within a particular body of social scientific literature, with Dawson attempting to defend his previously published positions. The RPF material makes a compelling case for the existence of a brainwashing program, and this program (along with several others) will require social scientists to adjust their positions on brainwashing as an applicable concept for some aspects of specific controversial religions. I include myself among a network of social scientists (see Mullins with Mullins 1973: 21–2) attempting 'theory proliferation,' in which an understanding of brainwashing as a means of retaining members 'expands the range of application of ideas about social phenomena beyond the original domain' of existing brainwashing research (Wagner and Berger 1985: 708). Dawson and others, however, see the efforts of this network as 'theory competition' (708) in which its members' understanding of brainwashing seeks to replace existing literature.

Moreover, the brainwashing debate has become intertwined with other contentious issues among scholars of alternative religions. These issues include the utility of former members' accounts, the possible implications for groups that now operate (or in the immediate past have operated) abusive re-education programs for their members, triangulation when studying high-demand groups, and even the professional reputations of some of the researchers themselves (see Kent and Krebs 1998a; 1998b; 1999; Lewis 1999; Melton 1999; Shupe 1999). Rather than reading Dawson's critique as a careful analysis of my work (which it clearly is not), scholars will find it to be an excellent example of what happens when a social scientist seeks to defend existing theories, models, or concepts against both new information and its resultant theoretical implications.

References

A&E. 1998. 'Inside Scientology.' *Investigative Reports* (14 December).

ABC *News*. 1998. 'The Church of Scientology.' *20/20 Sunday* (*ABC* Transcript #1881): 16pp.

Becker, Howard. 1963. *Outsiders: Studies in the Sociology of Deviance*. New York: The Free Press of Glencoe.

Boards of Directors of the Churches of Scientology. 1980. 'RPF Graduation Requirements Checklist.' Flag Order 3434-RC-56 (Written by Tech Comps Pjt I/C and Snr C/S Int for Int Pgms Chief CMO Int; Approved by D/CO CMO Int and CO CMO Int). (17 March): 13pp.

Burden, Tonya. 1980. 'Affidavit.' Signed in Las Vegas, Nevada (25 January): 1–12pp. See also <ftp://ftp.lightlink.com/pub/archive/homer/cd7.memo>

Chester, Ron. 1996. [subject title deleted in original for security reasons]. <alt.religion.scientology> (20 September): 4pp.

Cottee, Tim, Nicky Yateman, and Lorne Dawson. 1996. 'NRMs, the ACM, and the WWW: A Guide for Beginners.' In *Cults in Context: Readings in the Study of New Religious Movements*, 459–68. Toronto: Canadian Scholars' Press.

Dawson, Lorne L. 1998. *Comprehending Cults: The Sociology of New Religious Movements*. Toronto: Oxford University Press.

– 1999. 'Raising Lazarus: A Methodological Critique of Stephen Kent's Revival of the Brainwashing Model.' Chap. 9 in *Misunderstanding Cults*, Edited by Benjamin Zablocki and Thomas Robbins. Toronto: University of Toronto Press.

Department of Special Affairs. [1991]. 'Non-Disclosure Bond and Release.' [N.p.]: 4pp.

Eldershaw, Lynn, and Lorne L. Dawson. 1995. 'Refugees in the Dharma: The Buddhist Church of Halifax as a Revitalization Movement.' *North American Religion*. Waterloo, Ont.: Wilfrid Laurier University Press.

Fielding, Nigel G., and Jane L. Fielding. 1986. *Linking Data: Qualitative Research Methods*. Vol. 4. Beverly Hills: Sage.

Hubbard, L. Ron. 1976. *Modern Management Technology Defined*. Copenhagen: New Era Publications.

Kent, Stephen A. 1997. 'Brainwashing in Scientology's Rehabilitation Project Force,' Revised version of a presentation at the Society for the Scientific Study of Religion, San Diego, Calif. (7 November); see also <http://www.lermanet.com/cos/brainwashing.html> and <http://www.innenet.net/joecisar/rpf1000.htm>

Kent, Stephen A., and Theresa Krebs. 1998a. 'Academic Compromise in the

Social Scientific Study of Alternative Religions.' *Nova Religio* 2 (1): (October): 44–54.

– 1998b. 'When Scholars Know Sin: Alternative Religions and Their Academic Supporters.' *Skeptic* 6 (3): 36–44.

– 1999. 'Clarifying Contentious Issues: A Rejoinder to Melton, Shupe, and Lewis.' *Skeptic* 7 (1) [forthcoming].

Lewis, James R. 1999. 'Let the Scholar Who Is Without Sin Cast the First Stone.' *Skeptic* 7 (1) [forthcoming].

Maxwell, Joseph A. 1996. *Qualitative Research Design: An Interactive Approach.* Applied Social Research Methods Series. London: Sage.

Melton, J. Gordon. 1999. 'Mea Culpa. Mea Culpa.' *Skeptic* 7 (1) [forthcoming].

Miller, Russell. 1987. *Bare-Faced Messiah: The True Story of L. Ron Hubbard.* London: Michael Joseph.

Mullins, Nicholas C., with Carolyn J. Mullins. 1973. *Theories and Theory Groups in Contemporary American Sociology.* New York: Harper & Row.

SB. 1998a. 'Delurk: Another Scientologist Decides to Pitch in his .02.' <alt.religion.scientology> (2 August): 2pp.

– 1998b. 'Project Forces of the Sea Org Explained (Was My Story).' Article Segment 1 of 2. <alt.religion.scientology> downloaded from *Deja News* (26 August): 3pp.

Schur, Edwin M. 1971. *Labeling Deviant Behavior: Its Sociological Implications.* New York: Harper & Row.

Shupe, Anson. 1999. [Letter to the editor] *Skeptic* 7 (1) [forthcoming].

Singer, Margaret Thaler, with Janja Lalich. 1995. *Cults in Our Midst.* San Francisco: Jossey-Bass.

Wagner, David G., and Joseph Berger. 1985. 'Do Sociological Theories Grow?' *American Journal of Sociology* 90 (4): 697–728.

Part Three

HOW CONCERNED SHOULD SOCIETY BE?

11. Child-Rearing Issues in Totalist Groups

Amy Siskind

Cults as Total Institutions

There has been much social scientific misunderstanding of child rearing in those groups commonly referred to as cults, new religious movements, high-demand movements, or totalistic groups. Many social scientists have largely ignored the presence of children in new religious movements, treating these groups as simple voluntary aggregations of consenting adults. Others have recognized the presence of children in these groups but have argued that groups that oppose or retreat from mainstream society are often unfairly persecuted merely because they deviate from the unwritten norms of child rearing in our society. This argument maintains that such persecution violates members' freedom of religious expression. While these concerns have some validity, they fail to address the fact that some groups have been known to violate with impunity the human rights of young dependent children, while hiding behind the pious assertion that they are simply helping these young people to become saved or to attain self-realization. Misconceptions about the role of children in cults can be harmful in situations in which social scientists are attempting to help society understand the dynamics of childhood socialization within high-control groups. While each group differs in belief system and practice and no group should be prejudicially stigmatized because of the misdeeds of others, there are structural similarities which can be helpful in advancing the social scientific understanding of the vulnerabilities of children in cults.

The structural similarities I am referring to are the consequences of the social organization of total institutions as characterized by Goffman (1961) and Lifton (1961), as well as of the existence in many groups of charismatic leaders, many of whom exercise unchecked and unbalanced power over adult members and their dependent children. The characteristics of total institutions are as follows:

1 All aspects of life are conducted in the same place and under the same single authority.
2 Each phase of the member's daily activity is carried out in the immediate company of a large batch of others.
3 All phases of the day's activities are tightly scheduled, with one activity leading at a prearranged time into the next, the whole sequence of activities being imposed from above by a system of explicit formal rulings, and a body of officials.
4 The various enforced activities are brought together into a single rational plan purportedly designed to fulfill the official aims of the institution. (Goffman 1961: 6)

While total institutions exert a powerful impact on adults who come to reside within them for various reasons, their impact on children is even more dramatic. Children who are raised in such environments have not had the experience of living in 'the outside world,' and adapt much more readily than adults do to the totalistic environment and its demands. The relative ease with which children accommodate to these environments has its mirror image in the difficulties they face when they choose or are forced to leave the confines of these institutions and begin to live in mainstream society. Unlike most adults, they may never have encountered a society in which their lives are not extremely circumscribed and preordained. They also face the challenge of entering a culture that may stigmatize them as cultists if they choose to be open about their backgrounds.

In groups that function as total institutions, both the form and the function of the family are often quite different from the multiple forms that families take in mainstream society. The five groups discussed here – the Fourth Wall, Oneida, the Children of God, the Bruderhof, and the Hare Krishna[1] – are similar their institutional totalism and their communitarian withdrawal from the larger society. The founding leaders of all groups were charismatic men who functioned as father surrogates to members, not only emotionally but in terms of power over members and their families.

However, they were not necessarily similar in other ways. Approval of these leaders was necessary, in some of these groups, in order to have children. In some of them, marriage partners were chosen or suggested by the leadership, or, in cases in which members chose their own mates, approval of the leadership was required before a marriage could take place. Once children were born, parents in all five groups were expected to follow the community's precepts regarding child rearing. In all five cases mothers were required to leave their children in community-run daycare or individual child care so they could continue to work. Such basic decisions as whether parents choose to stay at home with their children or to put them in daycare were not in the hands of the parents. This control over key decisions by the leaders resulted in situations in which parents acted as 'middle management' towards their children (Lan-gone and Eisenberg 1993: 328). In some cases the parents themselves were the primary agents of socialization; in other cases the primary caregivers were not the parents, but designated members of the communities.

In scholarly discussion about totalistic groups, radical modification of the parental role has often been noted. Parents are not the sole, nor even the predominant, arbiters of their children's lives within these groups. They have given up a portion of their parental authority to the leaders of their communities, just as they have given up part of their own powers of self-determination. It cannot be assumed that parents will play roles that are similar to the roles they often play in protecting the interests and welfare of their children in mainstream society.[2] However, the opposite side of the coin is that totalist groups are good at unmasking abuses of young children that otherwise might have gone unnoticed behind the wall of privacy that protects harm-inflicting parents in alcoholic or other types of abusing families in the larger society. So I hope it will be clear that I am not attempting any blanket condemnation of cult child rearing as always inferior to mainstream child rearing. My goal is only to aid in the creation of situation-specific guidelines for the apprehension of abuse when it occurs in cultic situations, to complement the very different sort of guidelines that have proven useful for the apprehension of child abuse in the larger society.

Due to the controversial nature of any allegations of child abuse or neglect, it is important to mention the personal experiences I bring to this chapter. I was a first a child and later a member of the Fourth Wall, for twenty-two years. After leaving the community, I attended graduate school and received a PhD in sociology at the New School. In the course of my dissertation research, I did extensive interviewing and research on the origins, development, and later the dissolution of the Fourth Wall. In doing this research, I had certain unique and important resources at my disposal through my contacts with ex-members who had left the community after occupying leadership positions. I was also able to use scripts for the theatre productions written by the leadership, court transcripts, and the writings of the founders themselves.

In this chapter I discuss child rearing in five charismatic communal organizations. However, I certainly do not wish to claim that these five groups are in any way a representative sample of the full population of such communal groups. Nor do they necessarily share any characteristics other than a totalistic social structure. Some are urban and others rural. One was founded in the nineteenth century, one in the early twentieth century, one in the 1950s, and two in the 1960s. Some attracted primarily high-income members while others recruited primarily from those with low incomes. Three are hostile to the nuclear family, one is neutral to it, and one idealizes it as the basis of true communal life. Finally, the groups differ in ideology, one following the religious teachings of a Hindu guru and one the psycho-political teachings of a psychoanalytic pioneer. The other three are Christian but represent three distinct branches of Christianity: the evangelical, the Perfectionist, and the Anabaptist, respectively. These ideological differences among groups suggest that it is not shared ideological traits but shared structural characteristics that account for the observed similarity in certain child-rearing challenges. I wish to show that these characteristics very often result in a specific type of internal structure, regardless of specific belief systems. Although the groups discussed below differ greatly in the content of their beliefs, all of them believe in their ability to use charisma and totalism to 'save' people from their 'corrupt' former lives.

The Specific Vulnerabilities of Cult Children

The five groups this chapter examines are similar to each other in that each one isolated itself from the larger culture in an attempt to purify its members and/or to create a better society. In this sense they can be viewed as 'total institutions.' Each group practised 'mortification of the self' (Goffman, 1961) and discouraged close relationships with outsiders (except for the purpose of proselytizing). In addition to these similarities, each group took a stand against the institution of the self-sufficient autocephalous nuclear family as it was found in the larger society.

These characteristics had very specific impacts on children who were raised within the confines of the five communities. Condoned instances of what the secular society currently would consider sexual abuse were complained of in quite similar forms in four of the groups (except the Bruderhof). Systematic physical abuse in the form of severe and traumatic corporal punishment is not reported to have taken place in Oneida or the Fourth Wall, but was complained of by numerous ex-members of the Children of God, the Bruderhof, and the Hare Krishna. Severe mental and emotional abuse was reported by ex-members in all five of the groups.

It is not clear whether the rate of child abuse and neglect in these five communities is higher or lower than the rate within the general population. This chapter is not concerned with such comparisons. Our concern here will rather be to identify the distinctive types of neglect and abuse that occurred within these communities and to discuss as well the particular psychological milieux of these groups and their effects on children.

Burke Rochford (1998, 2) argues that while child abuse is present within any community in the United States, specific forms of it are likely to be found in religious groups and denominations, particularly those that follow the Judeo-Christian tradition, which preaches using the 'rod' to discipline children. To this statement I would also add that child abuse is also likely to be found in groups in which there are powerful charismatic leaders who control the labour and economic resources of members. While corporal punishment may be more predominant in communities that adhere to religious canonical teachings, mandatory work away from children is required of most parents in totalistic groups. The consequence of this requirement is that children are put in daycare that secular society may consider substandard because group leaders are not able or do not wish to spend the money that adequate or high-quality daycare requires. Or, in the case of the Hare Krishna and the Fourth Wall, children have been sent away to boarding schools at much younger ages than is customary for mainstream children in the United States.

Perhaps the most important factor that distinguishes child rearing in totalistic groups from mainstream child rearing is the fact that parents have ceded substantial parental authority to the community's leaders. From the moment they are born, the way children are treated is largely dictated by the beliefs and norms of the community. Parents are not parents in the same sense that mainstream parents are. The parents do not decide where they or their children will live, what they will eat, when they should go to sleep, or when and where they will go to school. In some of the cases discussed in this chapter, parents have input into some of these decisions, but overall they are much less likely to exercise power over a large part of their own lives, let alone those of their children.

Little empirical work has been done on the long-term effects of such child-rearing practices. One notable exception is the work of Martin Katchen (1997), which shows evidence of an alarmingly high rate of dissociative disorders among children raised in totalistic cults. This is an area that needs a great deal of further research.

All five of these communities were founded by charismatic male leaders who remained the most powerful individuals in these groups until they died or became too infirm to continue. Saul Newton, John Humphrey Noyes, David Berg, Eberhard Arnold, and Swami Prabhupada were all viewed as the 'fathers' of their communities. Hierarchies within the groups were established by the leaders, along with their inner circles of closest advisers and proteges. While the hierarchical structures differed according to the size and living arrangements of the communities, they all had the same pyramid-like structure.

Children who are raised in totalistic groups are at risk for specific types of psychological problems. Three of the groups discussed in this chapter were theologically or ideologically opposed to the monogamous nuclear family structure. The fact that members of these groups live similar alternative lifestyles also raises the possibility that the children living within these communities will share certain characteristics. One of the most common problems faced by these children is the lack of time either parent is available to them. Due to the financial pressures of most communal situations, parents are expected to dedicate most of their time either to earning money or to serving the purposes of the group directly. This structural characteristic can lead to physical and emotional neglect of children, as well as the problems associated with neglect. Infants, toddlers, and older children who are separated from their caretakers often experience a painful and crippling sense of loss (Bowlby 1969).

If scholars tend to be puzzled and confused about child rearing and child abuse in cults, it is difficult to blame them. It is not only that cults are so secretive and good at hiding their behavior that causes this confusion, it is also that the attitudes of cults towards their children are genuinely complex and ambiguous. Zablocki (1998) demonstrates this in his typology of childhood cult roles in which he identifies the *hallmark*, the *hooligan*, and the *hostage* as three very different and contradictory aspects of the image of children in totalist ideological groups. Many cults are extremely proud of their 'good' children, seeing them as hallmarks of ideological success – our product, proof that we must be on the right track. On the other hand, these same groups are often made extremely uncomfortable by their hooligans – children who do not conform to cult norms. Often cults find it difficult to tolerate the physical presence of these so-called hooligans; therefore, children who are eager for their parents to leave the cult may deliberately act out in order to force a crisis that may lead to expulsion and freedom. But counteracting that impulse to some degree is the parallel sense that children are the hostages that prevent their parents from leaving even if they want to. Leaving the group, especially if one parent is more likely to leave than the other (as frequently happens), may well mean never seeing one's children again. With all these agendas going on simultaneously, it is difficult for an outside ethnographer to make sense of the picture.

Some things are clear, however. In all five of the groups discussed in this chapter, children were separated from their parents early and for longer periods of time (on average) than children of parents with similar backgrounds and of similar socioeconomic status who were not in totalistic groups. In some cases children resided in the same living quarters with their parents; in others they were placed in separate 'children's quarters' or in boarding schools. Additionally, parents were not in control of their children's situations in the sense that the leaders of their respective groups exercised control over living and childcare arrangements. This includes choice of child care personnel, rate and method of compensation (if any), and choice of schools. This high degree of control by leaders can lead to the alienation of children from one or both parents. The results of this alienation are quite serious: psychosocial and developmental regression, extremes of anxiety, and the later surfacing of repressed feelings from childhood, of anger, loneliness, resentment, and abandonment (Clawer and Rivlin 1991). The specifics of these arrangements follow.

The Five Groups Examined

The Fourth Wall

Charismatic Founders
The Sullivan Institute for Research in Psychoanalysis was founded by
Jane Pearce and Saul Newton in 1957 and was disbanded in 1992. Jane
Pearce was a psychiatrist who had studied with Harry Stack Sullivan,
a well-known U.S. innovator in the treatment of schizophrenic adolescents. Saul Newton was an ex-member of the U.S. Communist Party
who had fought in the Spanish Civil War and worked at the William
Alanson White Institute, where Pearce studied and Sullivan taught.
Newton was a charismatic who impressed many people with his cryp-
tic but forceful pronouncements. Pearce was remote and intellectual,
and provided the theoretical bedrock for their new community.

History of the Group
Initially founded as a psychoanalytic institute, the Sullivan Institute
for Research in Psychoanalysis was a social group and later a residential community, developed as a result of the ideology and the charisma
of the leaders. From 1957 to approximately 1970 it was a relatively
small community of psychotherapists and their patients. After 1970 the
inception of a new training program for young therapists without educational credentials resulted in the expansion of the group to between
350 and 500 members. From 1970 to 1992 the group metamorphosed
into a theatre company (The Four Wall Repertory Company) and
began to engage in outreach through theatrical productions and films,
whose object was to educate the general public concerning the group's
psychological and political beliefs. While it began as a relatively loose-
knit affiliation of patients and therapists, the community evolved into
a highly structured and authoritarian organization with strict guidelines dictating most aspects of personal and social life. In 1992 a combinations of factors, including the death of Saul Newton and several
lawsuits brought by ex-members, resulted in the dissolution of the
group.

General Ideology
The Sullivan Institute/Fourth Wall had a communal ideology in the
sense that it abjured the nuclear family, viewed interpersonal relationships outside the family as the important determinant of mental health

and happiness, and believed that group living was the optimal choice for adults and children. The belief system was also political in that it connected the mid-century U.S. family to the form of democratic capitalism that exists in this country. The ideal situation for the founders of the group would have been a socialist world in which the autonomous nuclear family had been replaced by communal living and child rearing.

Child-Rearing Ideology

Pearce and Newton, founders of the Sullivan Institute, viewed childhood as the crucial period in the socialization process; if children could be raised by adults who were not envious and did not try to squelch their creativity and enjoyment of life, then a better world would be possible because these children would not in turn oppress their children.

Based on their critique of the contemporary (1950s) American mainstream family of their time, Fourth Wall founders also believed that an alternative form of family structure was needed in order to produce the 'perfect' individual. The community was their attempt to create this alternative family. Those who joined were expected to commit themselves to the communal structure and to reject their mainstream beliefs regarding family and community. This often involved cutting off contact with parents and other relatives, as well as ending marriages that had existed prior to joining the group. Later, when members began to have children, childbearing and child rearing were strictly controlled on the basis of the belief that children must be raised in a radically different way than the founders and adult members had been raised themselves.

Child-Rearing Practice

Due to the Fourth Wallers' belief that most psychopathology stemmed from childhood encounters with hostile or neglectful parents, the leadership attempted to define and control the role parents within the community played in their children's lives. The major features of these policies:

1 No member could become a parent without approval from the leadership.
2 Prospective parents had to obtain approval for their choice of partners.

3 Parents were not allowed to live together (with the exception of the four leaders of the community).
4 Children were sent to boarding schools at age seven and under (until 1978).
5 Therapists supervised all decisions affecting children.
6 Children were removed from the custody of mothers who were thought to be envious or incompetent.
7 All children were required to have full-time (and more) caregivers in order to limit the amount of time children spent with parents (after 1978).

Members lived in same-sex group apartments, and children usually resided with their mothers. One of the primary goals of the community was to provide members with an alternate family. After a brief period in therapy, patient-members were directed to break off contact with their families of origin. The mainstream (white) nuclear family of 1950s America was the 'straw man' against which the leaders and therapists of the Fourth Wall built their critique and their blueprint for an alternative to 'traditional' family life.

In the group's early years, childbearing was limited to therapists and favored patients because it was held that only the most mature individuals should have children. In later years, more patient-members were allowed to have children, but the leadership exercised strict control over their choice of partners and their living situations.

Children born within the group were raised according to the dictates of the leadership, which were passed down via supervision to the therapists and patients. Children were raised by full-time caregivers, who received directives not only from their parents but from the leadership and therapists as well. Many were sent to outside boarding schools; others lived within the community, but spent little time with their parents.

Evidence of Abuse
The Fourth Wall did not allow parents to become 'overly' involved with their children These limitations on the amount of time parents could spend with children were often harmful to the parent-child relationship. As discussed above, parents who were members of this group did not have the same control over their children's lives as most parents in the larger society. Some mothers, after giving birth, were told that they were unfit parents, and that for the 'good of their chil-

dren' they should relinquish custody to another woman in the group. Mothers and fathers were often simply 'partners' in the 'project' of raising a child; they did not have strong affective ties. Children did not, for the most part, live with their fathers. Or they might spend part of their time at one house and part at another in order to split their time between parents.

The attitudes towards sexuality within the Fourth Wall extended to children in the sense that children were free to experiment sexually, either alone or with each other. Some interesting circumstances arose in the context of the community belief that children, if given enough free-dom, would grow up without the neurotic repression of their parents. On one occasion it was reported that two little girls decided to play 'baby' with their babysitter and wanted him to wear a diaper. In accor-dance with the group belief that children should be allowed as much freedom as possible, the babysitter allowed himself to be undressed and diapered by these (approximately) six-year-old girls (Siskind 1999).

When children within the community reached puberty, they were expected to experiment with sex. In the building where the four lead-ers lived, a 'playroom' that could be locked from the inside was set aside in the basement for the children to use as they pleased. While sex between children and adults was not openly advocated, one of the babysitters for the leadership was asked to 'initiate' one of their teen-age boys into sexual activity. Saul Newton, the charismatic leader of the community and one of its founders, began to approach his daugh-ter for sex before he was diagnosed with Alzheimer's disease and moved out of the house. Newton also routinely solicited sexual favours from the household help (who were members and therefore found it more difficult to refuse him), including some of his patients. One of the other male leaders was rumoured to have had sexual con-tact with girls as young as seven.

It was difficult for parents within the Fourth Wall to take action to protect their children from unwelcome attention. They did not always know who was caring for the children, and even when they did, ques-tioning the leadership came at a price. One mother was told that her child preferred to live at the home of the leadership because she (the mother) was a 'psychopath,' and the girl was given her own sleeping area at the leaders' home.

Corporal punishment was generally frowned upon, except in certain exceptional situations. However, psychological punishment was used frequently to enforce the decision of the leadership regarding children's behaviour. In one instance, a child who had been coming to Saul Newton's home on a regular basis to play with his son was barred from the household because he seemed to be afraid of Newton. The child was told it was mean to treat Saul in this manner, and he was later kept away from other children as well. This social ostracism was extremely painful to the child, and may have contributed to his later psychological difficulties.

Social Visibility

The Fourth Wall was known to many people who lived on the upper west side of Manhattan, or who came into contact with members in the Hamptons, in academia, or in certain parts of the arts community in New York City. While members generally did not allow outsiders to examine its living arrangements, individuals who were favourably disposed to the ideology of the group, or who were personal friends of members, were at times invited to group apartments and parties. When it became absolutely necessary to do so, in the cases of 'green card' marriages or adoption case studies, 'show apartments' were set up that, on some occasions, existed for years.

Oneida

Charismatic Founders

John Humphrey Noyes, who attended Yale divinity school, was inspired by the revivalist movement (the second Great Awakening) that swept through New England and New York in the period between 1820 and 1860. At Yale, after transferring from Andover, which he reportedly found too conservative, Noyes began to question established religious beliefs. He was not alone; this was a time of religious foment. Noyes believed that the Second Coming of Christ had taken place in AD 70, at the time Jerusalem was destroyed; therefore, the world was already in a potential state of perfection which only required the awareness of His followers. Unfortunately, Christians had strayed from the true path after the days of the primitive church (DeMaria 1978: 12).

The Oneida Community was a nineteenth-century Christian group that was founded by Noyes in approximately 1843 and lasted until 1881. It was only one of many new Christian sects that were formed during the 'Second Great Awakening' – a period of religious and social experimentation which began in the 1840s and ended in the 1880s.

Oneida spent a great deal of time and money publicizing its theology, as well as its views on marriage and family. While these views eventually resulted in prosecution for Noyes, for almost thirty years the community lived in relative prosperity and harmony with its neighbours. While it appears to historical researchers that there was little discrepancy between the behaviour within the group and the 'face' presented to outsiders, this is impossible to determine and may very well be due to the relative difficulty of obtaining source material regarding 'disgruntled ex-members' over one hundred years later.

According to Noyes's perfectionist theology, for those who had become free of sin, the laws that applied to ordinary people did not apply to them because these converts had incorporated the *spirit* of Scripture. Laws were only necessary for those who were still in a state of sin. Noyes even went so far as to declare that he did not feel bound to obey the Constitution of the United States, or any other secular laws. All men and women were believed to have the ability to 'inspire' those less perfect than themselves and to receive inspiration from those who were more 'perfect.' Salvation functioned like a chain, beginning with God and those who are directly inspired by Him, through his disciples to their followers, and so on down to the lowliest sinner. This concept was applied rigorously in the community that Noyes was to form: each member had a hierarchical ranking denoting his or her spiritual ascendancy. It was necessary for community members to allow themselves to be influenced by those who were closer to Christ.

Noyes's teachings held that among those who had accepted the Lord and been cleansed of sin, simple marriage could be replaced by its heavenly form: complex marriage. All men in Oneida were considered to be married to all women. In practice, this type of marriage did not entail the cohabitation and exclusive sexual or property relations that was the norm in mainstream society. Noyes considered 'exclusive love,' including monogamous marriage, to be 'a tyrannical institution that prevented the individual from loving his or her neighbor' (Carden 1969). He believed that 'The heart should be free to love all the true and worthy.'

Child-Rearing Ideology

Procreation was discouraged in the earlier years of the Oneida Community for primarily economic reasons. By the late 1860s, Noyes decided to embark on an experiment in scientific breeding, which he referred to as 'stirpiculture.' His ideas were based primarily on his interpretation of Darwin and a study of the Bible, wherein he determined that the Jewish people had practised 'scientific breeding.' He made a chart of the marriages mentioned in the Bible and concluded that many of the early Jews had married within their own families. Noyes limited the number of children per couple, and only those who were considered to be spiritually advanced were permitted to become parents.

Child-Rearing Practice

Based on these precepts, Noyes initiated a program of stirpiculture in 1869. A committee was set up, overseen by Noyes, which accepted applications from couples who wanted to have children. The selection procedure was initially based on Noyes's (Lamarckian) belief that the more spiritually advanced individuals would transmit this advancement to their children. Later, when his son Theodore took over the management of the committee, more interest was taken in the physical condition of the applicants. Some couples were also asked by the committee to have children without having initiated the process. Both women and men agreed to abide by Noyes's decisions as to whether or not they were fit to have children, and with whom.

Most women had only one child, some had two, and a very few had three. Noyes believed very strongly in the superiority of his family line, and acted on this belief by siring ten children. His son Theodore fathered three, and the rest of the men in the community (who fathered children) had between one and two children apiece.

After children were born, they stayed with their mothers until they were weaned. They were then moved to the Children's Wing, a part of the communal living quarters set aside for children. The Children's House, as it was called, had house parents and teachers assigned to it. In keeping with the community's belief that exclusive attachments were ungodly, children were not encouraged to form 'overly close' relationships with their parents. If 'unhealthy attachments' seemed to be developing, the parents were restricted in the amount of time they could spend with their children. In his autobiography of his years spent as a child in Oneida, Pierrepont Noyes mentions that he felt his mother experienced more suffering from this attenuation of their relationship than he did.

Evidence of Abuse

Oneida's practices of group marriage and the initiation of young girls into sexual activity by older men were illegal, and eventually resulted in the dissolution of the community when Father Noyes was forced to leave the country.

Oneida had the most stable situation of all the five groups with regard to its child-rearing practices. The numbers of children in the community were small relative to the Children of God, and all children went to live in the Children's House after they were weaned. Their contact with their parents was limited, but in spite of this parents were able to 'check in' on their children because they all lived in one location. The community was committed to secular as well as religious education for all its members, including the children. Many of the children went on to university education when they were of age (Kanter 1972).

Given the small number of accounts on this topic it is difficult to draw conclusions about the experience of children in Oneida. Pierrepont Noyes, one of John Humphrey Noyes's children, wrote an autobiography in which he discusses his upbringing in the community. He reports that the Children's House was a comfortable, nurturing place, and that he had a happy and productive childhood within the community. From our perspective (late twentieth-century) it is possible to raise some questions about the impact of institutional child rearing on children, and similar questions have been raised by parents and scholars in the kibbutz movement and possibly others as well. Additionally the practice of the older Noyes initiating young 'women' (some as young as ten) into sexual activity is certainly questionable from the point of view, not only of legality, but also of optimal sexual/ mental health for these young girls.

Social Visibility
It is interesting to note that when Oneida disbanded in 1881 the precipitating incident was a public scandal arising over sexual conduct. It had been traditional for Noyes to initiate the young girls in the community into sexual activity. When he became too old to perform this duty on a regular basis, he designated certain other men as 'first husbands.' Two of these men, William Hinds and James Towner, disputed Noyes's right to choose who would introduce young women to sexual experience. A group of members joined them, and a dissenting faction, called the Townerites, was formed within the community. This dissension, combined with threats of prosecution by outside clergymen, triggered the breakup of the community (Carden 1969). In effect, without the active leadership of Noyes, Oneida could not continue to exist.

The Children of God

Charismatic Founders

David Berg, known later as Moses David, or "Mo," was raised and ordained in a southern Protestant family. David both formed and articulated (with the help of others) the formal ideology of the Children of God (COG) movement, and he did so in the form of writings, known as 'Mo Letters,' which were usually published and circulated to members. He claimed to have received a series of prophecies directly from God in 1952, identifying him as the Prophet of the End-Time. While the Family views the Bible as literal and infallible, they also include the Mo Letters as equally valid sources for the determination of God's will. Some later statements suggest that the Mo Letters may have even overridden biblical rules (Van Zandt 1991).

History of the Group

The Children of God was founded by Moses David (then David Berg) in the late 1960s (Bromley, 1994). Although it was originally founded in southern California, the group grew rapidly and eventually shifted its base to Europe, with members in South America, the Caribbean, Australia, and the Philippines at various points in its history. The group's structure has changed several times, as has its policies and practices. In the late 1970s, COG changed its name to The Family of Love (usually referred to as The Family) due to the notoriety it received for the practice of 'flirty fishing,' the name they gave to the practice of sending Family women to nightclubs and bars to proselytize through sexual encounters. In the late 1980s, members began to move back to the United States (Bromley 1994). This community has been a source of bitter controversy between the leadership and ex-members, and between scholars of new religious movements as well.[3] One of the predominant sources of this controversy was a series of accusations of child abuse and neglect both by ex-members and the children of members. In the early 1990s these accusations led to raids on COG homes and the removal of children by local officials (Richardson 1999). The combination of publicity and litigation has resulted in a retaliatory campaign by the group to convince the public that they do not engage in child abuse or other deviant practices.

General Ideology

In order to be saved from the coming damnation a person has only to accept Jesus into his/her heart. Once a person is saved, good works will determine what position he or she will have in the future kingdom. David also had a strong critique of Western society and social relations; he espoused a form of Christian socialism. The United States was viewed as the most degenerate example of the capitalist system, but he denounced the 'godless communism' of the communist states of that period as well. Nor was he looking back to a 'golden era' of Christianity; he had a vision for the future (Van Zandt 1991). The Children of God's job was to proselytize. While members often needed to rely on secular society for financial support, they were not allowed to establish long-term contractual relations. Members were not supposed to hold 'system' jobs unless absolutely necessary. They were to commit themselves completely to God's work, to live communally as did the early apostles, and to 'forsake all' personal possessions.

Berg preached that the System was soon to be replaced by a new social order. Jesus would return prior to the millennium on earth, but after the Great Tribulation – a period of economic collapse, war, and other catastrophic events. David also had an elaborately worked out sequence of events that he predicted would take place before and after the second coming of Christ. The members of the Children of God would be saved, but would continue to help God proselytize among those who were still not saved (Van Zandt 1991). This eschatology led to the Children of God's policies regarding communal living, marriage, and child rearing.

Child-Rearing Ideology
Initially there were large communal settlements in different parts of the United States. Within these settlements single members were expected to remain celibate until they chose partners; married members were expected to be monogamous and to share a bed. Many members did not choose their mates; they were paired off by leadership in some cases, and in others men asked to marry specific women and were granted permission without the consent of the woman herself. Children of God policy regarding the marital relationship was patriarchal – wives were expected to submit to the will of their husbands.

In 1973–4 the policy regarding marriage and sexuality changed drastically when 'Mo' instituted the practices of 'sexual sharing' and flirty fishing. Sexual sharing referred to the notion that monogamy was selfish and that 'partiality toward your own wife or husband or children strikes at the very foundation of communal living' (249: 9,12) (Williams

1998). Flirty fishing was predominantly a method of recruitment. The flirty fishers were always female members who were encouraged to initiate sexual liaisons with male outsiders. During and after sex, the women would 'witness' to the men and attempt to 'save' them by asking them to repeat a short prayer asking Jesus into their hearts. The flirty fishing policy resulted in a number of 'Jesus Babies,' the term used by the Children of God with reference to babies fathered by 'fish.'

With regard to children and sexuality in the Children of God, the first public comments to be made on this topic appeared in a Mo Letter entitled 'My Childhood Sex! – Doing What Comes Naturally.' In this letter, 'Mo' described one of his own childhood experiences – his mother chastising him for masturbating – and expressed his hope that members would allow their children's sexuality to develop naturally. He also described the pleasurable experience of having his Mexican babysitter manipulate his penis in order to get him to sleep (Melton 1994). In a pamphlet 'Sex Questions & Answers' and in *The Story of Davidito* (Family of Love 1982) David again discussed childhood sexuality. He reiterated his belief that childhood sexuality should be allowed, including the observation by children of adults having sex. He argued that this should be limited to certain cases (Melton 1994).

Child-Rearing Practice
COG prohibited birth control and encouraged marriage, practices which over time have resulted in a relatively high ratio of children per adult member. Mothers were expected to return to work after childbearing although their workload was one-half that of male members. They were sometimes sent to live away from their children. While their mothers were working, children were cared for by designated members of each community. Facilities in these community daycare centres varied greatly depending on the size of the group home and the importance of the members living there (Williams 1998). Older children were often sent to different homes from their parents, or were sent away with one parent but rarely saw the other. It was not considered important to keep the nuclear family unit together, because it was the larger group that was the 'true' family.

According to Williams (2000):

> Children were educated in many different ways but mostly at home in the commune. 'If a mother or father was capable, it was the parent. If there were other people in the home capable – it was the 'brother or sister.' Few

times did we have a certified teacher. Often we used family school supplies, which were very good up to a certain grade level (about 12 years).
However, witnessing came first, and children traveled extensively, so
education was sporadic. Some kids went to public or private schools,
depending on where they lived.

Difficulties with the socialization of teenagers into the community
arose and were dealt with through the inception of Victor Camps (Hall
and Kent 1998). These were programs designed to discipline and train
recalcitrant youth. Teenagers who were considered troubled were sent
there by house parents or other leaders, where they lived in conditions
that some of them later described as ones of neglect, deprivation, and
sometimes physical abuse.

Evidence of Abuse
The Children of God was the most radical of our five groups on the
subject of childhood sexuality. As discussed above, 'Mo' encouraged
children to be curious and to experiment with their bodies. Whether or
not he meant this to result in adult/child sexual contact, several
reports state that this did take place (Kent 1998). One woman reported
that she was put on the sexual 'sharing schedule' in the group home
she was living in at the age of twelve, meaning that she was expected
to have sex with adults who lived in this home. She had moved away
from her parents because she was having difficulties with them.
Whether they knew about this practice or not is immaterial; they had
effectively relinquished control over their own lives as well as hers.
    The Children of God developed 'Victor Camps' for its teen members
aimed at ensuring their socialization into the community. They were
known as Victor Camps because their purpose was to help young people gain victory over evil inclinations. These camps involved physical
and socio-emotional punishment. Their purpose was to heighten commitment to the organization's leadership. Preteens and teenagers with
'problems' were sent to the camps in an effort to reintegrate them into
the movement (Hall and Kent 1998; see also Millikan 1994; Ward 1995).
According to Kent's (1992a) interview with Merry Berg – a granddaughter of David Berg, who was sent to one of these camps – teenagers were ordered to keep silent and were in the presence of adult
guards most of the time. They were assigned manual labour for long
hours. Other sources (Kent 1998) reported beatings with wooden paddles that ranged from painful to severely debilitating.

Scholars disagree sharply on the question of whether abuse of children took place in the Children of God. Researchers like James Richardson (1999) and Susan Palmer, who were invited by the Children of God to observe their child rearing and educational practices, state that no child abuse was occurring during the times of their visits. Lilliston and Shepherd (1994) gave psychological tests to thirty-two children in two of the group's homes in California, and conclude that no child abuse took place within the group at any time in its thirty-five-year history. Both of these teams had extremely limited experience with members, and disregarded ex-members' statements that they were abused as children during the time their families belonged to the Children of God (see Kent interviews with Cheryl, 'Emily,' and 'Lorna,' 1995–6).

I am not saying that the Children of God deliberately set out to harm its children. David Berg advocated corporal punishment in his writings, but he also advocated restraint. However, some of the children raised in the Children of God later claimed that they were abused by parents or other adults, who, for personal and situational reasons, did not exercise restraint. The Children of God leadership may not have expected older men to demand sex from younger women, but this practice is reported to have taken place on numerous occasions in many different locations. Similarly, they may not have expected adults to engage in sexual activity with very young children, but the Davidito book (Family of Love 1982) combined with the cult's teachings about free childhood sexuality provided an atmosphere in which such activities could go on undetected and unchecked.

Social Visibility
Those scholars and other individuals who have been asked to visit Children of God homes in the 1990s cannot document the group's past. They can certainly document its present in the few homes they have been able to visit.

The Children of God have also changed their practices with regard to sexuality and procreation a great deal since their formation in the late 1960s. According to recent reports, they now conform to a more traditional family structure, educate children more systematically than previously, and prohibit adult-child and child-child sexual activity.

In the case of the Children of God it is quite possible that a dynamic similar to the one that took place within the Fourth Wall is under way. The negative publicity and custody cases by former members may have pushed the leaders to modify practices that lead to negative attention. This is also a survival mechanism: if the charges against the group are false, then it is the outside world that is at fault.

The existence of 'media homes' in the Children of God was discussed in Miriam Williams's book, *Heaven's Harlots* (1998). A media home is a group dwelling that is organized for the purpose of showcasing a group's lifestyle to the media. Given the fact that the researchers mentioned above were invited by The Family into these particular homes and that interviewees were selected by the group, it is necessary to be extremely cautious about making any generalizations as to the existence or nonexistence of sexual abuse within this group. On the other hand, many ex-member accounts are also unverifiable. Unfortunately, this leaves researchers in the position of being unable to obtain any scientifically verifiable data.

The Bruderhof

Charismatic Founders
The Bruderhof was founded by Eberhard Arnold in Germany in 1920. Arnold was a Christian theological scholar from a wealthy German-American family. He was active as a Christian youth group leader during the post First World War period of the German Youth Movement. He was inspired by the antinomian spiritual awakening he experienced at the heart of the Youth Movement. He attempted to reconcile this movement's love of nature, personal freedom, and equality for men and women with his nostalgia for the lost fervor of the original (first century AD) Christian church. This effort led him to reach into the German Youth Movement for followers who were willing to attempt to live as the first Christians lived, in evangelical communes practising complete elimination of private property (Zablocki 1980). Arnold died suddenly in 1935. After a twenty-year period of collective leadership, one of his sons, Heini Arnold, assumed overall leadership of the commune. After Heini's death in 1982, the leadership role was assumed by his son, Christoph Arnold, who currently serves as leader of the group (Oved 1996).

History of the Group
Now celebrating the eightieth anniversary of its founding, the Bruderhof is one of the oldest surviving 'new religious movements.' Its opposition to Nazism resulted in persecution and eventual exile from Germany dur-

ing the Hitler period. During the Second World War, the Bruderhof was settled in England and Paraguay. After the war ended, communal branches of the movement were also established, at various times, in Uruguay, Germany, the United States, and Nigeria. However, a major schism, known as 'the great crisis' in the early 1960s radically reduced the membership of the Bruderhof and led to consolidation into fewer communes (or 'hofs' as the Bruderhof calls them). Currently, the Bruderhof is a prosperous and actively evangelical Christian movement in which well over 2,000 people live in eight closely linked hofs in the United States and England, still practising complete community of property.

General Ideology
As is the case with many new religious movements, the ideology of the Bruderhof is an amalgam of traditions drawn from many sources and forged into a coherent (if not always workable) vision by the religious imagination of its founder and his inner circle of group leaders. The Bruderhof has had a stormy on-again, off-again relationship with the Hutterians, an older, more established Anabaptist communal movement with which the Bruderhof shares many aspects of structural similarity. During its early destitute years, the Bruderhof was heavily dependent upon the Hutterians for economic survival. Several times in its eighty-year history, the Bruderhof has formally become a part of the larger Hutterian Church, but these marriages have always ended in stormy, recriminatory divorces. However, large chunks of Hutterian Anabaptism remain at the core of Bruderhof ideology, where, they interact uneasily with equally important chunks of nature-loving experiential Christian revivalism drawn from the German Youth Movement and Eberhard Arnold's somewhat romanticized vision of first-century Christianity seen through the highly emotional prism of early twentieth-century German Pietism (Rubin 2000).

Child-Rearing Ideology
Unlike the other groups examined in this chapter, the Bruderhof glorifies the nuclear family and sees it as the fundamental building block of its solidarity. But the Bruderhof sees the strength of the nuclear family as paradoxically dependent upon its uncompromising subordination to the larger community, which forbids divorce and birth control absolutely. The ideology requires all married members to pledge that, if one's spouse ever leaves or is kicked out, the remaining member will stay with the Bruderhof rather than follow the spouse (Zablocki 1980).

Bruderhof parents are clearly middle managers whose authority and whose physical custody of dependent children can and often has been pre-empted by the group's leadership, for short or long periods of time. Following basic Anabaptist teaching, children are not considered members of the Bruderhof even as little Christians-in-training. Rather, they are wards of the community who will only become Christians and Bruderhof members if they can somehow be brought to a state of spiritual receptivity that allows the Holy Spirit to enter them as rational adults (or older adolescents) who can make their own independent decision to choose this way of life.

Bruderhof attitudes towards child rearing have been shaped in part by the free-spirited notions of the German Youth Movement, but even more by the strict and somber doctrine of *Gelassenheit*, as borrowed from Hutterian Anabaptism. The *Gelassenheit* doctrine teaches that the humble and uncompromising submission of the individual to the wisdom of the collectivity is fundamental to true Christianity in a fallen world (Rubin 2000). This doctrine, as applied to children, teaches that the spirits of children must be broken for Christianity to take root. It is not that the Bruderhof believes that children are evil but rather that they are weak and wayward and prone to evil influences, especially in the sexually corrupt modern world in which we live. The harshest measures of psychological and (at least in times past) physical punishment are therefore justified towards the end of salvation. And, because evil spiritual influences are highly contagious in a close-knit communal group, the ideology has taught the necessity of strictly isolating from their peers (sometimes to the point of solitary confinement) any children infected with a 'bad spirit,' and for as long as necessary, just as a physically ill child whose illness is contagious would be isolated.

Child-Rearing Practice
Since birth control is strictly forbidden, families with eight to ten children are far from uncommon (Oved 1996). And since Bruderhof members own no private property, not even the clothes on their backs, it is difficult for these large families to consider leaving even if both spouses are equally unhappy. After the age of six weeks, children spend much of their time, not with their families but with their peer cohort group, at first in the 'Baby House' and later in the Bruderhof-run schools. Adolescents, however, go to public high school followed by a two- or four-year college or vocational school for specialized training (Zablocki 1980).

The Bruderhof tries to keep its children as sexually innocent as possible prior to marriage. Dating is strictly forbidden and courtship (for older adolescents) requires prior approval of the Bruderhof leaders and is heavily chaperoned and controlled. Only other Bruderhof children are available for courtship. At least in the past (and possibly in the present as well) even the most innocuous of early childhood sexual curiosity or sexual exploration is considered toxic by the Bruderhof, and the child or children involved may be severely punished and would at the very least be strictly isolated from his or her peers until the evil impulse is expunged.

Evidence of Abuse

Many children who grew up in the Bruderhof have complained of experiencing traumatic physical and psychological abuse that has left them permanently scarred (Holmes 1997). There is no evidence that sexual abuse of children has ever been officially condoned or tolerated by the Bruderhof when it was discovered. But a number of people who grew up in the Bruderhof have reported being sexually abused by unscrupulous or twisted teachers or other authority figures. Such sexual abuse, according to these witnesses, sometimes remained undetected for long periods of time because the emphasis that the Bruderhof places on childhood innocence sometimes prevented the children from realizing that what was happening to them was sexual. Furthermore, the attitude of meek and uncompromising obedience to authority that the Bruderhof attempts to teach its young people can easily lead them to believe that anything a teacher or an adult in authority does must be right even if it feels wrong.

Parents who have left the Bruderhof have reported that though they came to realize their children were being traumatized by community child-rearing practices, they felt helpless to intervene on their behalf. One mother reported the following:

> We were not considered dedicated enough and our children were found lacking and not participating fully in the life. They were not on the same spiritual level as others ... Whenever the [leaders] discussed our children with us, we felt they were talking down to us. Gradually, we developed an inferiority complex about our children and about our spirituality ... Else had seen how we beat Franklin [on the direct orders of the leadership] when he was sent home [from school] with a note. She became very scared and buried the notes [that she was sent home with] in the garden

or in a secret place. [My husband] and I did not know what to do about this, but one thing was certain: we had to stop beating our boys to make them toe the line. It was not helping. Else became so scared that she started to have stomach ulcers, and she was not even in first grade! Augusto [her older brother] already had developed stomach ulcers and was being treated for them. (Pleil 1994: 274)

This family could not of course continue to live in the Bruderhof while defying its orders as to how to raise their children, so the family eventually left, experiencing great financial hardship for many years. Other families were either unable or unwilling to leave, and some of their adult children have reported childhoods of unremitting physical and psychological abuse. Because of the totalism of the Bruderhof environment, some of these adult children cannot bring themselves to believe, even as adults living outside the community, that the abuse was not somehow due to their own shortcomings and misbehaviour.

Social Visibility
The Bruderhof is very proud of its children, and holds them up to public scrutiny as proof of the superiority of its way of life. Naturally, the other side of this coin is that children who do not turn out so well are a major embarrassment to the Bruderhof and have sometimes been sent away and allowed no contact with parents or other relatives remaining in the community. The Bruderhof, to its credit, has acknowledged its own sinful imperfection and has apologized for isolated instances of severe abuse when these have been publicized. However, the Bruderhof has never been able to recognize the structural aspects of its way of life that make it possible that such abuse will continue to occur. In recent years, severe criticism from ex-members has led the Bruderhof to be more closed and protective of its privacy than ever before. External surveillance of Bruderhof child rearing may thus become more difficult.

The Hare Krishna

Charismatic Founders
The Krishna Consciousness Movement was founded in New York in 1966 by a 70-year-old Indian expatriate, A.C. Bhaktivedanta, who was believed to be the direct link to the deity Krishna. He had apparently relinquished a successful business career in India to come to the East

Village in New York City in 1965 to establish an American version of an old Indian religious discipline (Johnson 1974). After founding the International Society of Krishna Consciousness (ISKON) in 1966, Bhaktivedanta took about half the members from New York and moved to San Francisco to proselytize among the members of the counterculture in Haight Ashbury. He died in 1977, after leading the group for twelve years, and the eleven commissioners he had appointed were charged with leading the organization and expanding it to other parts of the world (www.religioustolerance.org/hare.htm/).

History of the Group
A.C. Bhaktivedanta founded ISKON in 1966. The organization flourished in San Francisco in 1967 and 1968, and by 1974 had grown to fifty-four temples throughout the world (Johnson 1974). ISKCON and Hinduism both trace their beginnings to the Vedas and to the *Bhagavad Gita*. Whereas mainstream Hinduism regards Krishna to be the eighth incarnation of Vishnu (the Preserver and one of the Hindu trinity of deities), ISKCON regards Krishna to be the supreme Lord over all deities, including Vishnu. They are therefore a monotheistic faith group, one that stresses bhakti, the way of devotion (www.religioustolerance.org/hare.htm/).

ISKCON is structured into two sectors: an order of monks and priests who live at a temple, and congregation members, who live outside. Male monks shave their heads, except for a central patch called a sikha. They receive a Sanskrit name (one of the many names of God), plus the suffix 'dasa,' which means 'servant of ...' and saffron-coloured robes, dhotis, to signify celibacy. Married monks wear white dhotis. Female residents of a temple wear traditional saris and do not shave their heads. All monks vow to abandon cigarettes, alcohol, and other drugs, reject gambling, and follow a nonviolent vegetarian diet. They also make a commitment to chant the names of God a prescribed number of times each day. They rise before sunrise and chant and pray at intervals during the day. Celibacy is preferred and is mandatory for single devotees; sexual activity for married couples is only for the purpose of procreation.

General Ideology
The belief system of ISKON was based on a translation of the *Bhagavad Gita* by Bhakitivedanta. Bhakitivedanta had attempted to reduce the sacred texts to simple directives that would apply to the lives of the people he was interested in recruiting. He taught that the present age

was undergoing a decisive transformation, characterized by unprecedented confusion and turmoil. Devotees claimed that the world was near the end of the materialistic age of Kali-Yuga, the last cycle of a four-cycle millennium. If the populace could be persuaded to transform its consciousness, then a new age of peace, love, and unity would come about (Johnson, 1974). The new consciousness could be attained through renouncing the material world and embracing the practices of chanting, self-surrender, and ascetic denial.

Child-Rearing Ideology
Marriage and children were not prestigious in ISKON. Householder life was defined by ISKON's elite as a symbol of spiritual weakness (Rochford 1998). Because Prabhupada saw the public school system in America as indoctrinating 'children in sense gratification and mental speculation,' he referred to the schools as 'slaughterhouses' (Goswami 1984). Children were of special importance to the leadership of ISKON because they would demonstrate the superiority of the beliefs and practices of the movement. Therefore the education of children took on a special significance as well (Rochford 1998).

Child-Rearing Practice
Children were sent to *gurukulas* (the Hindi word or school), whose primary purpose was to train students in spiritual life. Prabhupada believed children could not learn self-control in their parents' homes, so they were removed from their families as young as four and five. 'Householders' were a politically marginal group and were powerless to assert their parental authority over the lives of their children (Rochford 1998). Therefore the children were sent to school at the age deemed ideal by the leadership.

ISKON's first formal gurukula was established in Dallas, Texas, in 1971. 'The Dallas gurukula remained the only school of its type within the movement, until 1976, when it was forced to close by state authorities (Rochford 1998). Between 1975 and 1978, eleven schools opened in North America and other schools were founded in Europe, Australia, and South Africa. In 1980 and 1981 regional schools opened in Lake Huntington, N.Y. and in central California (Dasa, M., 1998).

Evidence of Abuse
One important exception to the norm of accusation and denial with regard to child abuse and/or neglect in totalistic groups is E. Burke

Rochford's (1998) discussion of abuse in the Hare Krishna gurukulas (schools) between 1971 and 1986. Rochford interviewed ex-students, teachers, and parents and was able to get corroboration from all these groups with regard to both the abuse that occurred and its structural causes. The abuse that was documented within the Hare Krishna movement took place in boarding schools in which members were required to enroll their children. In some schools staff administered severe physical punishment, and in others students were sexually abused. Rochford was asked by the leadership of Hare Krishna to write an article discussing the problem of child abuse. The article was published by the official journal of the Hare Krishna, and has been part of an ongoing campaign on their part to make reparations to those who were abused and to ensure that no further abuse is allowed to occur (ISKCON Communications 1999).

Rochford administered a Second Generation Survey (n=87) to a non-random sample of Hare Krishna youth in North America in 1992–3. He also interviewed seventy first-generation parents in four Hare Krishna communities in the United States (Rochford 1999). Due to his status as an outside observer, and his relationship with the Hare Krishna leadership, Rochford's credibility with regard to this study is extremely high. Unfortunately, groups that are willing to police themselves in this manner are quite rare. What would have happened if the Hare Krishna leadership were not receptive to the accusations of child abuse that have surfaced in the past ten years?

Social Visibility
The Hare Krishna, as they are popularly called, have been quite visible since their inception in Haight Ashbury in 1966. They have always attracted attention to themselves and proselytized in various aggressive modes. There have been extended battles over the presence of large numbers of orange-robed pamphleteers in airports around the world, and in the United States there has been an official government ruling that the organization cannot accost passengers in airports. ISKON argued that airports are public spaces, and that discourse in those spaces cannot be regulated by the state. The government, however, ruled that airports are private spaces, and therefore not subject to First Amendment claims.

Another example of the visibility of ISKON members is the parades they hold in some locations, where groups of members walk and drive through the streets in elaborately decorated vehicles or carrying brightly colored banners. While they are highly visible, these behaviours do not always lead to increased social contact with outsiders. While they are probably able to interest some individuals on approach, a large number of people who have come into contact with members find them frightening and 'weird,' because of their appearance and behaviour.

Conclusions

The issue of child abuse has become a touchstone for our concern about the rapid social changes that have been taking place in contemporary American society, especially as they bear on family life. This issue serves to problematize the constantly shifting boundary between public and private behaviour and our beliefs regarding freedom and individuality. The women's and gay rights movements have also touched upon these boundaries, and in the process have caused continuing controversy over which behaviours are acceptable in public and in private. The same is true for the children's rights movement, which includes the increased public concern with child labour, child abuse, and child neglect.

This chapter has not argued that cult leaders set out deliberately and maliciously to abuse children. Nor would I argue that child abuse is inevitable in all cults. But I think a clear pattern has emerged from our discussion regarding the absence of both external and internal checks and balances to limit such abuse when it does take place. The absence of these checks and balances makes cult children more vulnerable than children within the larger society, which does have these checks and balances (however imperfectly they are sometimes implemented). This is the key to understanding the distinctive challenge of preventing child abuse in totalist groups.

With regard to external checks which would militate against child abuse or neglect, members of these groups are not in regular or extended contact with people outside their own closed communities. The outside world has very little means of detecting whether or not any abusive behaviour or neglect is occurring. Many of the children in these groups attend schools within their own communities, and physical or psychological problems which would often be detected by school authorities in the 'outside world' go unacknowledged or even undetected by community teachers and administrators. The same may be true for the medical community, which has often served as an external sanction against child abuse and neglect. Many children in these communities only see doctors who are part of the community as well. These doctors might not be inclined to report incidents or abuse.

Children who attend public schools are regularly in contact with people who are not in their families, and who are not involved in the same social or residential groups. Teachers and other staff in the schools provide an alternate value system, and in some cases a safety valve whereby children who seem to be in distress or in need can possibly be helped. Health care professionals, in a different way, also serve as such an external check on abusive practices in non-cultic nuclear families. In the case of children who are being raised in total institutions there is very little contact with the outside world. Such children have often been taught not to confide in outsiders, and this increases the chance that any difficulties they are having will not be addressed.

Unfortunately, internal checks are also weakened or non-existent in such groups. It is not that the adults in these groups are intrinsically more abusive of children than adults in the larger society. It is rather that, without limits, child abuse, when it does occur, is in danger of increasing. Those in positions of leadership are the least likely to be confronted if they are engaging in abusive activity. This is seen most dramatically in the runaway sexual predation that has occurred in some of these groups.

In the case of the Oneida Community, John Humphrey Noyes clearly had access to more women than did the other men in the community. He fathered more children because his genetic material was thought to be of a higher quality than that of other males. He also reserved the right to initiate the young girls in the community into sexual activity.

In the Fourth Wall, Saul Newton played a similar role. He fathered more children with more women than any other male in the community, and demanded sexual favours from large numbers of young community members. None of them, however, were known to be under the legal age of consent. This was not true of Ralph Klein, the second most powerful male leader, who was known to have an interest in young girls and reportedly had sex with at least one daughter of a member of the group. Child sexual abuse was not institutionalized in the Fourth Wall in the manner in which this was true of Oneida and the Children of God.

In the Children of God, as mentioned above, David Berg made it explicit in the 'Mo Letters' that childhood sexuality was viewed as healthy. By sexuality, Berg was referring not only to the expression of erotic feelings by children, but also to sexual stimulation of children by adults and 'sexual sharing' between children and adults. Young girls and boys of eleven and twelve years of age were moved out of homes with their parents, moved into group homes in other locations, and put on the 'sharing' calendars of the houses they lived in; in other words, they were assigned to specific adults as sexual partners. Berg himself was also known to have been sexually involved with large number of women, including one of his daughters.

All five groups had in common a sectarian communal approach to living which involved a denial of 'selfish' needs or desires in favour of some higher purpose (God, enlightenment, social revolution). The members of the Fourth Wall and the Oneida were largely from higher socioeconomic levels – middle to upper income – while the membership of the Children of God, the Bruderhof, and the Hare Krishna consisted more of people from middle to low-income backgrounds.

While the belief systems of the five groups differ greatly, there are also striking similarities between them in both beliefs and practices. While Van Zandt (1991) wrote about the difference between formal and practical ideology, arguing that the practical ideology was often quite distant from formal statements or writings, nevertheless the ideology or theology of any particular group affects its practices.

Leaders who articulate these beliefs often urge their followers to break with societal and legal norms. This is a point that outsiders often neglect to take into consideration when dealing with leaders and members. Deceiving outsiders is certainly justifiable as well because the ends justify the means. In the case of the Fourth Wall activities such as 'gray market' adoptions, sham marriages for insurance or immigration purposes, and disregard for child safety seat regulations are just a few examples of behaviours that were sanctioned within the group because the leadership was thought to simply know better than the government.

The child-rearing practices of these five groups were always adaptable to outside pressure. For example, up to the time that the *Bollinger v Bollinger* case was decided in 1978, most members of the Fourth Wall were encouraged to send their children to boarding schools. After a judge ruled in the father's favour because the mother, who was a member of the community, spent so little time with her son, children were no longer sent to boarding schools. Instead they had full-time child care, and the amount of time parents could spend with their children was limited by the therapists.[4]

All five groups viewed the world outside their confines as corrupt and dangerous. They attempted to shield their children from this world, but in the process subjected them to conditions that some of these children later identified as harmful. The leaders and members of all five of these groups did not feel themselves to be bound in any way by the norms – either formal or informal – of their host societies. This finding raises important questions: What are the dangers of creating a closed world for oneself and one's children? Is it safer to keep our children away from those aspects of life that we deem to be harmful, or to expose them to other beliefs and practices, and teach them our beliefs at the same time? As social scientists, we can only look at the outcomes of the choices that parents make. They clearly make sacrifices in either case, and have dangers to be confronted as well.

The combination of the power of a charismatic leader with a belief system that puts both his actions and the actions of all group members above the jurisdiction of the law, results in a situation which can put children at risk. In all five of these communities, practices occurred which fit definitions of child abuse.[5] Interestingly enough, differences in social class and education between members of these groups made little to no difference in the degree to which they were able to subsume their own cultural backgrounds to the edicts of their leaders. These class and cultural differences affected the types of groups they joined, but not the degree of authoritarian control that they accepted.

Although three of the five groups discussed here take positions against the nuclear family, deeming it selfish and possessive and essentially unable to provide the kind of love and support necessary to raise an 'evolved' individual, it is not this position per se that puts children at risk for abuse and neglect. Rather, it was the patriarchal and hierarchical manner in which these groups were structured that put children at risk. It was the parents' willingness to subsume their children's interests to the 'greater good' that led them to follow the directives of their leadership even when these directives ran counter to their own perceptions and beliefs regarding their children's well-being. While totalistic groups are certainly not the only organizational structures that can and do harm children, they are among those that have and continue to do so. While the structure of the post-modern family may leave much to be desired in terms of addressing all children's needs, it is also subject to constant re-evaluation and change based on the actions of individuals. It may be this more fluid structure that enables parents to respond to children's needs in a more immediate and individualized manner.

This chapter has been an attempt to lay a groundwork for further study of children in totalistic groups. The structure of these groups results in environments for children that differ in several ways from those who meet comparable socioeconomic and cultural criteria, but are not members of totalistic groups. Child abuse and neglect have never been topics that we have studied for purely academic reasons. Gathering data regarding such groups – especially data dealing with child rearing and potential abuse and neglect – is a difficult and conflict-laden proposition. Any group that believes it is being observed, either from the outside or from the inside, is likely to change or hide any practices it believes might dispose outsiders to interfere with its lifestyle. Both the Fourth Wall and the Children of God did exactly that, and it is not possible to determine from the data I now have whether or not the Oneida also changed their practices as a result of outside scrutiny.

I would encourage scholars who have not been involved with totalistic groups to examine child-rearing practices in these groups with neither an antagonistic nor a defensive set of preconceptions. Both sets of assumptions lead to conclusions which are unreliable. While it may be true that our society is more likely to assume the worst regarding unconventional groups, this does not rule out the possibility that harmful practices may exist in certain groups. Additionally it is possible that the very act of studying a group will provide an impetus to eliminate practices that the general public would consider damaging. Not only would further research be useful for academic reasons, but it might also prove valuable to those who are charged with helping children who live in totalist groups.

Notes

1 Most cults have more than one name by which they are generally known, and the groups discussed in this chapter are no exception. For the sake of clarity, I have chosen just one of these names for each group. The name chosen has generally been the one by which the group is most widely known, not necessarily the name preferred by the group itself. The Fourth Wall is also known as the Sullivan Institute. The Children of God officially changed its name to The Family in 1978, and that is the name it uses at the present

time. The Bruderhof has been known by many names in its 80-year history, including the Society of Brothers, the Eastern Hutterians, and the Arnold-leut. The Hare Krishna is officially known as the International Society For Krishna Consciousness, or ISKCON.

2 I am aware that 'mainstream' society is composed of myriad subcultures, all of whom may have different norms with regard to parental responsibility. Nevertheless I believe there are grounds for making the distinction between parenting within and outside of a totalistic environment.

3 See the ex-member website at www.excognet.com and the CounterCOG website at countercog.officehiway.com.

4 It was believed that if the amount of time parents spent with their children was limited, the children would be overly damaged by their parents.

5 But no implication is intended that this abuse was more frequent or more severe than in non-religious communities or in secular cities or towns. It may or may not have been. I have no data on that subject.

References

Barker, Eileen. 1989. 'New Religious Movements: A Practical Introduction.' London: Her Majesty's Stationery Office.

Bowlby, John. 1969. *Attachment and Loss.* New York: Basic Books.

Bromley, David. 1994. 'The Family: History, Organization, and Ideology.' In *Sex, Slander, and Salvation: Investigating The Family / Children of God*, edited by James R. Lewis and J. Gordon Melton, 41–6. Stanford, Calif.: Center for Academic Publications.

Carden, Maren Lockwood. 1969. *Oneida: Utopian Community to Modern Corporation.* Baltimore: Johns Hopkins University Press.

Clawer, Stanley S., and Brynne Rivlin. 1991. *Children Held Hostage: Dealing with Programmed and Brainwashed Children.* Chicago: American Bar Association.

Cohen, Michael, and Bray, Michael. 1987. 'Manipulation of Transference in Psychotherapy as a Means of Creating a Psychotherapeutic Cult.' Paper presented at the Conference on Law and Society, Washington, D.C., 12 June.

Conason, Joe, and McGarrahan, Ellen. 1986. 'Escape from Utopia: One Woman's Fight Against an Upper West Therapy Cult. *The Village Voice* (New York) 22 April, 19–21.

Dasa, M. 1998. Gurukula Alumni Database.

DeMaria, Richard. 1978. Communal Love at Oneida: 'A Perfectionist Vision of Authority, Property, and Sexual Order.' New York and Toronto: The Edwin Mellen Press.

Family of Love, The. 1982. *The Story of Davidito*. Zurich, Switzerland.

Goffman, Erving. 1961. *Asylums: Essays on the Social Situation of Mental Patients and Other Inmates*. New York: Anchor Books.

Goswami, J. 1984. *Srila Prabhupada on Guru-Kula*. Los Angeles: Bhaktivedanta Book Trust.

Hall, Deana, and Stephen A. Kent. 1998. 'Brainwashing and Re-Indoctrination Programs in the Children of God/The Family.' Unpublished.

Handbook of the Oneida Community. [1732]. Oneida, N.Y.: Office of the Oneida Circular.

Holmes, Miriam. 1997. *Cast Out in the World*. San Francisco: Carrier Pigeon.

ISKON Communications. 1999. 'Krishna Pledge One Million Dollars to Child Protection.' Potomac, Md.

Johnson, Gregory. 1974. 'The Hare Krishna in San Francisco.' In *The New Religious Consciousness*, edited by Charles Y. Glock and Robert Bellah, 31–51. Berkeley: University of California Press.

Katchen, Martin. 1997. 'The Rate of Dissociativity and Dissociative Disorders in Former Members of High Demand Religious Movements.' PhD diss., University of Sydney, Sydney, Australia.

Kanter, Rosabeth Moss. 1972. *Commitment and Community: Communes and Utopias in Sociological Perspective*. Cambridge, Mass.: Harvard University Press.

Kent, Stephen A. 1994. 'Lustful Prophet: A Psychosexual Historical Study of the Children of God's Leader, David Berg,' *Cultic Studies Journal* 11: 135–88.

Kent, Stephen A. 1992a. 'Interview with Merry Berg' (11 December): 84 pp.

– 1992b. 'Interview with Merry Berg' (14 December): 20 pp.

– 1995. 'Interview with Emily' (14 December): 43 pp.

– 1996. 'Kent, Interview with Cheryl' (9 February): 204 pp.

1996. 'Kent, Interview with Lorna [Pseudonym]' (16 January): 42 pp.

– 1997. 'Kent, Interview with Stephanie [Pseudonym] (16 June): 14 pp.

Kent, S., and D. Hall. 1998. 'Brainwashing and Re-indoctrination Programs in the Children of God / The Family.' Unpublished.

Langone, Michael D., and Gary Eisenberg. 1993. 'Children and Cults.' In *Recovery From Cults: Help for Victims of Psychological and Spiritual Abuse*, edited by Michael D. Langone, 327–42. New York and London: W.W. Norton.

Lifton, Robert. 1961. *Thought Reform and the Psychology of Totalism*. Chapel Hill: University of North Carolina Press.

Lilleston, L., and G. Shepherd. 'Psychological Assessment of Children in The Family.' In *Sex, Slander, and Salvation: Investigating The Family / Children of God*, edited by J.R. Lewis and J.G. Melton. Stanford, Calif.: Center for Academic Publication.

Male Continence. [1872]. Oneida, N.Y.: Office of the Oneida Circular.

Mandelker, Ira. 1984. *Religion, Society, and Utopia in Nineteenth-Century America.* Amherst: University of Massachusetts Press.

Melton, J. Gordon. 1994. 'Sexuality and the Maturation of The Family. In *Sex, Slander, and Salvation: Investigating The Family / Children of God,* edited by James R. Lewis and J. Gordon Melton, 71–95. Stanford, Calif.: Center for Academic Publications.

Millikan, David. 1994. 'The Children of God, Family of Love, The Family. In *Sex, Slander, and Salvation: Investigating The Family / Children of God,* edited by James R. Lewis and J. Gordon Melton, 181–261. Stanford, Calif.: Center for Academic Publications.

New York Law Journal. 5/4/76. *Bollinger v Bollinger,* 6–7.

Noyes, John Humphrey. 1875. *Essay on Scientific Propagation.* Oneida, N.Y.: Oneida Community.

– 1876. *Mutual Criticism.* Oneida, NY: Office of the American Socialist.

Noyes, Pierrepont. 1937. *My Father's House: An Oneida Boyhood.* Farrar & Rinehart. New York.

Oved, Yaacov. 1996. *The Witness of the Brothers.* New Brunswick, NJ: Transaction.

Parrington, Vernon Louis. 1927. *Main Currents in American Thought.* Vol. 2. *The Romantic Revolution in America, 1800–1860.* New York: Harcourt Brace Jovanovich. 1927 Reprint. Norman, Okla. and London: University of Oklahoma Press, 1987.

Pearce, Jane and Newton, Saul. Nd. 'Establishment Psychiatry – and a Radical Alternative.' Unpublished.

Pearce, Jane and Newton, Saul. 1963. *Conditions of Human Growth.* New York: Citadel Press.

Pleil, Nadine. 1994. 'Free from Bondage: After Forty Years in Bruderhof Communities on Three Continents. San Francisco: Carrier Pigeon.

Richardson, James T. 1999. 'Social Control of New Religions: From "Brainwashing" Claims to Child Sex Abuse Accusations.' In *Children in New Religions,* edited by Susan J. Palmer and Charlotte E. Hardman, 172–86. Piscataway, N.J.: Rutgers University Press.

Robertson, Constance Noyes. 1970. *Oneida Community: An Autobiography, 1851–1876.* New York: Syracuse University Press.

Rochford, Jr., and E. Burke. 1998. 'Child Abuse in the Hare Krishna Movement: 1971–1986.' *ISKCON Communications Journal* 6: 43–69.

– 1999. 'Education and Collective Identity: Public Schooling of Hare Krishna Youths.' In *Children in New Religions,* edited by Susan J. Palmer and Charlotte E. Hardman. Piscataway, N.J.: Rutgers University Press.

Rubin, Julius. 2000. *The Other Side of Joy: Religious Melancholy Among the Bruder-hof*. New York: Oxford University Press.

Sandeen, E.R. 1971. 'John Humphrey Noyes as the New Adam.' *Church History* 40: 82–90.

Siskind, Amy. 1988. 'The Sullivanian Self: Psychotherapy as Social Control.' Unpublished ms.

– 1999. 'Interview with MB.' 3 March 1999. 25 pp.

Van Zandt, David. 1991. *Living in the Children of God*. Princeton, N.J.: Princeton University Press.

Ward, The Right Honorable Lord Just. Alan. 1995. 'W 42 1992 in the High Court of Justice. Family Division. Principal Registry in the Matter of ST (a Minor) and in the Matter of the Supreme Court Act 1991.' (19 October): 295 pp.

Williams, Marion. 1998. *Heaven's Harlots: My Fifteen Years as a Sacred Prostitute in the Children of God Cult*. New York: William Morrow.

– 2000. Personal communication.

Zablocki, Benjamin. 1980. *The Joyful Community*. Chicago: University of Chicago Press.

– 1998. 'Hallmarks, Hooligans, and Hostages: Three Aspects of Children in Cults.' Paper presented at the annual meeting of the American Family Foundation, Philadelphia.

12. Contested Narratives: A Case Study of the Conflict between a New Religious Movement and Its Critics

Julius H. Rubin

'The battle has been about free speech, and free speech is about disagreement. And so we disagree.' Salman Rushdie regarding Ayatollah Ruhollah Khomeini's 1989 religious edict charging blasphemy and authorizing Rushdie's death for *The Satanic Verses*.

(Lyall 1998)

This essay examines the strange and troubling story of how one new religious group, in my opinion, has attempted to suppress freedom of speech for apostates and for social scientists who have published critical analyses or, raised troubling questions, and made serious charges about the institutional practice and individual conduct of members of this religious group. We will consider the masterful public relation efforts where this sect has manipulated the media to produce puff pieces that have supported their protected and idealized image. We will detail the strategies employed to attack and quiet the voices of apostates and academic critics, branding them as the demonic 'enemies of the faith.' This story reveals an irony: to protect their religious brotherhood the sect appears to me to have engaged in unbrotherly actions as they oppose their critics and the organized resistance of apostates.

The group in question, the Bruderhof, is a high-demand Christian community of goods. Within their church-community, they struggle to create and maintain the absolute unity of their brotherhood. The faithful surrender in radical discipleship to the mandate of the Holy Spirit, as mediated to them by their leadership. The Bruderhof cleaves to a single belief system, a dogmatic orthodoxy. The leadership prevents their rank-and-file brothers and sisters from enjoying unrestricted access to newspapers, radio, television, popular culture, and the Internet. Within the sect, they do not tolerate open debate, but instead demand unquestioning conformity to community standards of belief and practice.

Within their religious community, Bruderhof true believers may indeed choose to abdicate liberty of conscience and free speech. However, they have attempted to impose their narrow orthodoxy and understanding of the 'truth about the Bruderhof' upon the outside world. In an open, democratic society founded upon the constitutional principles of freedom of speech, citizens enjoy a broad spectrum of protected speech. In the academy, I believe that a sociologist of religion has the right to pursue theoretical and empirical investigations of the discipline even when this inquiry takes the researcher into areas of controversy and conflict between orthodoxy and apostates.

Learned Hand articulated the underlying constitutional principle that forms the foundation of academic freedom in the academy and freedom of speech – the open marketplace of ideas in the public sphere. He writes that 'the interest, which [the First Amendment] guards, and which gives it its importance, presupposed that there are no orthodoxies – religious, political, economic, or scientific – which are immune from debate and dispute.'[1] The actions of a religious group that seek to impose orthodoxy and abridge freedom of speech and academic freedom are a threat to the fundamental tenets of liberal democracy.

The Bruderhof Communities

The Bruderhof (also known in past times as the Society of Brothers or Hutterian Brethren) is a Christian intentional community founded in the 1920s in Germany by Eberhard Arnold. It is now entering its fourth generation, with eight settlements or 'hofs,' and approximately 2,200 members in America and England. They support themselves by manufacturing quality children's toys under the trade name Community Playthings, and products for disabled people through Rifton Enterprises.

Visitors to the Bruderhof encounter a peculiar combination of a medieval village community and late twentieth-century technological sophistication that includes ultramodern telecommunications, Japanese manufacturing techniques, a community-owned Gulfstream jet, and extensive computerization. Hof life appears idyllic. Violent crime, illicit drug abuse, or economic and material concerns are largely absent from their lives. Premarital sexual activity is prohibited, and single-parent families are largely unknown in the community. Divorce is not permitted. Thus, Bruderhof families are not disrupted by family patterns that characterize the wider society.

The ethical mandate of the Sermon on the Mount serves as the biblical foundation for Bruderhof settlements. Believers, surrendered into radical discipleship to Jesus, strive to overcome their sinful alienation from God through conversion and adult baptism. They emulate the apostolic church by devoting themselves to the fulfilment of the Sermon on the Mount and espousing the principles of pacifism and non-resistance to evil. The brotherhood holds all things in common, rejecting the divisiveness caused by private property and the pursuit of worldly privilege and power. The faithful are bound together in unanimity of thought and belief and espouse an ethic of brotherly love.

In strict conformity to the teachings of Jesus, the community enforces purity of conduct, thought, and intentionality in the hearts and minds of true believers. The Church community keeps close watch to ensure that members hold to their religious ethos, motivated by the leadings of the Holy Spirit. They practice the brotherly watch to purify themselves from sin. Their ethos strictly regulates all forms of conduct, belief, appearance, dress, and demeanour, with particular emphasis upon the repression of premarital or extramarital sexual expression. Brothers and sisters are prohibited from gossip or idle chatter. Should differences or conflicts arise between members, they must go directly to the person or persons in question and strive to bring a peaceful and loving resolution of these differences or 'unpeace.' Church discipline requires public confession and repentance of sin, and exclusion of the errant sinner into the world. Only by fostering absolute unity, the Bruderhof maintains, can it collectively form a vessel to capture the Holy Spirit in childlike joy, humility, and surrender to Jesus.

The first Bruderhof community at Sannerz, Germany, in 1921, began as a charismatic group devoted to Eberhard Arnold. This countercultural commune attracted educated, middle-class youth from the student movement and German Christian Movement, who rejected the rationalized orders of modern society. The early members of the Bruderhof embraced an ethic of universal brotherhood, assured of the millennial advent of the Redeemer's Kingdom in their lifetime. The Bruderhof relocated in 1927 to Fulda, Germany, to the Rhön community.

In the period 1928–32, Arnold struggled to develop financial, organizational, and doctrinal stability for his charismatic church. He found the solution to the 'routinization of charisma' by adopting the religious orders and administrative blueprint of North American Hutterite communities. Arnold travelled to America, received ordination as a Hutterite minister, and affiliated his community with this Anabaptist conventicle.

Bruderhof members steadfastly refused to cooperate with the Nazis, to surrender their sons for compulsory military service, or to utter the oath of allegiance to the Nazi race-based salvation state. One year before Arnold's untimely death in 1935, they founded the Alm Bruderhof in neutral Liechtenstein and secreted draft-age men out of Germany. The Gestapo and SS closed the Rhön community in 1937, seizing the property and deporting the members. The Alm community relocated in England in 1939–41, until the British forced the relocation of German nationals. The Bruderhof could not find asylum in North America, but was permitted to migrate to the underdeveloped Chaco region of Paraguay. The Primavera, Paraguay, and El Arado, Uruguay, hofs served as the centre of Bruderhof communitarianism until their closing in 1961. After the Second World War, new hofs were started in Germany and in England.

Heinrich (Heini) Arnold, Eberhard's middle child, championed the conservative counter-trend, and continually attempted to redirect the movement to revitalize his father's theological vision. The critical turning point in the Bruderhof movement came in 1954 with the founding of the Woodcrest Hof in Rifton, New York. As Servant of the Word at Woodcrest, Heini allied with enthusiastic American converts.

Heini dissolved the Primavera and European brotherhoods, liquidated the community assets, and excluded several hundred baptized members during what is known as the Great Crisis of 1959–61. Hundreds of people were uprooted; many saw their lives shattered as they were rejected from the new brotherhood lists and made to forge new lives after decades of faithful service to the pioneering communities in Paraguay, Germany, and England.

The Great Crisis became the watershed that transformed the Bruderhof. Heini revitalized the movement in separation from the world as an introversionist sect, emphasizing evangelical pietist conversion models and extreme emotional fervour and devotionalism.

The Bruderhof and Hutterites have shared the Anabaptist vision of a community of goods, pacifism, and separatism in a church community to recreate the Kingdom of Christ in dynamic tension with the carnal kingdom of the world. They are organized as inclusive church-communities, where the exercise of administrative and religious power is concentrated in the hands of church leaders who interpret the Holy Spirit and the Word of God.

The Bruderhof members have passed down control of their movement to Eberhard Arnold's son and grandson in what is in effect a hereditary succession of office. This traditionalism is legitimated as emanating from the will of God, whose divine order has also created a hierarchy of patriarchal relations between husband and wife, parent and child, and leader and follower. Authority patterns are believed to have originated with God; leaders serve as His instrument, providing spiritual and temporal rulership over the congregation. They also believe that God decreed an organic social order where men exercise authority over women, and parents over children.

The promises of salvation are inextricably tied to the surrender to God's will and the believer's submission to divinely legitimated hierarchical authority. In this manner, the Bruderhof instill habits of unquestioning obedience to the authority of the Witness Brothers and the Servant of the Word. Church discipline derives from the book of Matthew, enjoining brothers, motivated by love, to engage in fraternal correction and admonishment of the offending member, urging the offender to seek repentance, reform, and return to good standing within the community. However, those persons whose ideas or individual consciences endanger doctrinal orthodoxy; those who stand against the leadership and threaten unity; those who cannot or will not repent and reform from sinful thoughts and conduct, must be punished with increasingly severe forms of church discipline.

The threat of exclusion proves a powerful and dreaded method of social control in the Bruderhof. A brotherhood member's baptismal vow to the community takes precedence over any natural ties of blood to spouse, children, or kin. Exclusion invariably disrupts families as those who remain must shun the offending brother, or watch helplessly as their loved one is forced to depart the community. The trauma of ostracism, exclusion, family disruption, and shame is shared by the family, falling most heavily upon children. Paradoxically, the Bruderhof stresses joyful surrender and abiding love, yet imposes the most severe penalties of civic-religious 'death,' mental suffering, and unbrotherly rejection of the unrepentant sinner.

The members of the Bruderhof are, by their own account, 'authoritarian with respect to Christ,' requiring the undivided loyalty of their members (Mow 1989). The concentration of spiritual and political power into an elite leadership group of servants, ever-obsessed with unity, has resulted in the continued and systematic abuse of church discipline as a political device to expel members, who, because of individual conscience, question or oppose community policy. Such persons stand charged with sins of pride, selfishness, and egoism, and are said to be motivated by 'the wrong spirit,' or to have lukewarm zeal. Many Bruderhof apostates recount childhoods marked by family disruptions when one or both parents were excluded. Children suffered beatings, administered by parents, as ordered by leaders, with the purpose of using physical discipline to 'win the children to the life' (Pliel 1994). Others tell of times in childhood when adults conducted interrogations, known as 'clearances,' to garner confessions of sexual sin and impurity. Young women confront the issues of powerlessness and gender inequality in spiritual and temporal roles, and severe limits are placed upon their aspirations and participation in the community. Women especially bear the burdens of *Gelassenheit* – resignation and self-renunciation to the will of God, as enforced by the patriarchy.

Many journalists, visitors, and guests have extolled the virtues of this Christian community by writing uncritical accounts of the Bruderhof. In the past five years, more than fifty articles in local and national publications such as *Sojourners, Christian Century,* and the *New York Times* have presented an apologetic, uncritical, idealized, and sentimentalized portrait of the community (Clines, 1995; Holiday, 1984; Nash 1994). Local newspapers in American communities adjacent to Bruderhof settlements print a seemingly endless series of human interest stories that, for example, portray blond children weaving garlands of flowers in celebration of nature and the coming of spring. Sombre, bearded men in plain shirts, suspenders, and trousers march in a 'peace witness' against nuclear war or the death penalty. Women with heads covered in polka-dot kerchiefs and attired in long, modest dresses go about their daily routine with heads bowed in humility. High-minded men and women unite in Christian community as seekers of God's Kingdom. I term these one-sided accounts of the Bruderhof, telling the 'Bruderhof story,' as a public relations exercise that presents the community in an unreflective and uncritical light. The community has attempted to preserve the Bruderhof story as the only credible and legitimate presentation of Bruderhof history and social reality by suppressing and discrediting the voices of apostates and academic critics.

Who Controls the Interpretation of Bruderhof History?

I began my research for a book about the Bruderhof in the spring of 1991, when they were called the Eastern Brotherhoods of the Hutterian Church and were still affiliated with the Hutterites and Anabaptism. Hutterites have actively cooperated with social scientists who have conducted community mental health surveys. Hutterites have developed a folk psychiatry to diagnose and treat the spiritual affliction, *Anfechtung*, where believers suffer religious melancholy (Eaton and Weil 1955; Kaplan and Plaut 1956; Hostetler, 1974). The Hutterite confession of faith enjoins them from using the state or courts of law. I assumed that the Eastern Brotherhoods would, like their Western co-religionists, allow me to study their group, freely acknowledge the propensity of the faithful to suffer religious despondency, and view the use of lawsuits as anathema to their faith commitment. I was mistaken on all counts.

The Bruderhof has steadfastly opposed my research and refused to assist me. In the beginning, I informed the Bruderhof and ex-members of my belief that the spiritual crises of Bruderhof young men and women were related to the central tenets of their theology, practice, church discipline, and communal life. The Bruderhof disagreed and found this critical perspective unacceptable. They did, however, grant permission to the Israeli scholar, Yaacov Oved, to write an authorized history, *Witness of the Brothers*. Oved's book was, in my opinion, a celebratory and uncritical account that reflected considerable editorial and scholarly control exercised by the Bruderhof.[2] The issues that divided my research from Oved's scholarship in were control and academic autonomy. The Bruderhof opposed all scholarship in which they did not control the questions asked, the evidence made available for investigation, the interpretative framework employed, and the conclusions drawn.

Who 'owns' Bruderhof history? Who has the right or the power to articulate the 'authentic,' 'true,' and 'objective' interpretation of the Bruderhof movement – their doctrine, communal organization, and church practice? Who controls the collective memory about the Bruderhof? Who can speak with authority about their 'invented traditions' – Bruderhof rituals, ceremonials, and commemorations?[3]

From the founding of the first American Bruderhof, Woodcrest in Rifton, New York, in 1954 until 1989, the Bruderhof religious leadership controlled their collective memory and the interpretation of their tradition. Through their publishing company, the Bruderhof has printed their canonical writings and two histories of the sect. A monthly magazine, *The Plough*, advanced the 'Bruderhof story.' Employing skilful public relations with the national media, the Bruderhof has garnered endorsements by renowned theologians and religious leaders such as Thomas Merton, John Yoder, Henri Nouwen, and Mother Teresa; and sociologists John A. Hostetler and Pitriam Sorokin. Sympathetic politicians and church leaders extol their community. These efforts have fostered a climate of opinion that casts the Bruderhof as quaint, 'Amish-like' folk who embrace religious brotherhood and community.

Each year the Bruderhof welcomes a diverse ensemble of guests: religious seekers, people from the margin, curious neighbours, reporters, and persons from a broad spectrum of religious beliefs and spiritual politics, from the Left to the Right. Many guests are predisposed to see and experience a confirmation of the Bruderhof story. The Bruderhof appears to them as a remedy to the social problems of modern societies. I marvel at how the Bruderhof has served as a Rorschach test, an ink-blot for individuals and groups who are troubled by frustrations, malaise, and insecurities, and use the Bruderhof as a screen to project their deepest spiritual aspirations. Reporters and guests are taken on limited tours of the community where they experience the joyous aspects of group solidary – communal dining, working, and singing. (They do not attend brotherhood meetings and do not see the exercise of church discipline. Guests are not prevented from having free access to books, news media, and information.) Their first impressions after a staged, carefully scripted, and supervised visit, invariably confirm the 'Bruderhof story.'

Mainstream Americans typically live individuated lives, pursuing careers in a competitive, capitalist market economy. Our postindustrial mass society has demonstrated a genius for commodifying all aspects of material and symbolic production (including religious and secular holidays) under the ethos of consumerism. We pursue festive retailing in malls – our secular cathedrals. Here we shop for what the mass media packages as lifestyles – claims to prestige and happiness – ideas, 'value and belief systems.' Participation in institutional religion is compartmentalized and limited to major holidays and sabbath worship. 'Spirituality' has become a privatized, individual exercise in the consumption of commodified avenues to the transcendental, to healing, and to self-realization, largely cut free from ecclesiastical and theological moorings.

The Bruderhof story, alternatively, speaks to the highest ideals of Christian religious vocation, and appears, at first glance, as an antidote to the crisis of modernity. In place of subjectivism, individualism, and relativism of belief, the Bruderhof calls for an absolute commitment to ultimate values. In place of consumerism, the Bruderhof demands a simplified life of all things in common, an end of private wants and property. In place of violence, competition, and coercion, the Bruderhof promotes the ethic of brotherhood and love espoused in the Sermon on the Mount.

In 1989, Ramon Sender began publication of *KIT* (Keep In Touch) a monthly newsletter of the memories and accounts of Bruderhof apostates – persons expelled from or who had left the community. For the first time, the Bruderhof faced an organized opposition to their collective memory and public image. Sender, an excluded novice who had to leave his wife and young daughter in Woodcrest in 1957, discovered by happenstance that his daughter had recently died. The community had for decades denied him the right to visit, telephone, or correspond with his daughter. He learned of her death a month after the funeral. Sender wished to learn more about the daughter he had been prevented from knowing, and to write a book to commemorate her life. He explains: 'When the Bruderhof leadership turned down my request to interview Bruderhof members, I began to search for ex-members ... By the end of the month, I had talked to more than thirty and personally visited four. By the end of the second month, I had spoken to over sixty. They all asked about the others I had contacted and wanted their news and addresses.'[4]

Soon, the ex-members began corresponding with one-another in a round-robin letter which Sender and a small editorial group instituted as a monthly newsletter. He explains: 'The *KIT* newsletter started as a modest two-sheet page sent to thirty or so names, but within four months it expanded to ten-thousand word issues mailed every month to over one hundred addresses. As the volume of incoming mail grew, four Bruderhof graduates and survivors formed the newsletter staff.

By 1990, the newsletter grew to 20,000 words per issue and was mailed to over 450 addresses. Most of the copy consisted of letters received from ex-Bruderhofers scattered all over the world.'[5]

KIT now operates under the umbrella of the tax-exempt Peregrine Foundation (founded in 1992), which hosts an Internet web site and sponsors annual reunions. In 1993, *KIT* added a summer reunion in England for European ex-members. *KIT* also publishes book-length memoirs of apostates under the imprimatur of the Carrier Pigeon Press. Since 1992, the press has published Roger Allain's *The Community That Failed* and Elizabeth Bohlken-Zumpe's *Torches Extinguished: Memories of a Communal Bruderhof Childhood in Paraguay, Europe and the USA*, Belinda Manley's *Through Streets Broad and Narrow*, Nadine Moonje Pleil's *Free From Bondage*, and Miriam Arnold Holmes's *Cast Out in the World*.

The letters printed in *KIT* express their outrage at the official Bruderhof apologetic where KITfolk, as bearers of a contested collective memory, reveal the traumatic events of the Great Crisis and more recent Bruderhof history. Many define themselves as survivors, 'graduates,' and exiles who are compelled to remember and inform an indifferent world that the truths about the Bruderhof must now be told. These truths have to do with abuse of church discipline resulting in the disruption of families, and refusal by the Bruderhof to permit family reunions and visitation by former members.

The newsletter *KIT* and the Bruderhof have waged a war over contested collective memory. For example, the Plough publishes *Torches Rekindled* as an apologetic defense of Bruderhof doctrine and history, while *KIT* publishes the counter-claim, *Torches Extinguished*. This battle has continued over the Internet with competing Bruderhof and *KIT* homepages on the World Wide Web,[6] alt.support.bruderhof and websites created by other Bruderhof apostates.

KIT public relations effectively used Internet, print, and electronic media to challenge Bruderhof orthodoxy. By 1992, *KIT* sent 'media packets' containing reprints of articles about the Bruderhof to reporters and news outlets that were writing about the Bruderhof. *KIT* had become an institutionalized opposition to the commune, contesting many of their claims to be a loving brotherhood of disciples of Jesus. Bruderhof religious leadership considered *KIT* and those who possessed the demonic 'KIT Spirit' to be avowed enemies of the faith, determined to destroy the Bruderhof and all those who surrendered their lives to Jesus.

The Attack upon the 'Enemies of the Faith'

During the 1990s, after its schism with the Western Hutterite Church, the Bruderhof evolved into a series of secular business enterprises and a charitable tax-exempt organization known as the Bruderhof Communities. They secured trademark protection for their name, instituted a legal affairs office, and named corporate presidents and vice-presidents of their manufacturing, aircraft leasing, and business ventures. For the first time in Bruderhof history, these corporate officers, with the knowledge and consent of the religious leadership, could use the courts and legal strategies to defend themselves against KIT and all perceived enemies of the faith.

The Bruderhof instituted new policies in the 1990s that appear to contradict its history of pacifism and its Anabaptist belief that Christians must not use the courts or police to defend themselves. In the past, the Bruderhof advocated that they must place their unconditional trust in Jesus. Although they might suffer injustice and even martyrdom at the hands of their enemies, they must bear witness to their profound faith commitment.

In 1990–91, Johann Christoph Arnold, the head religious leader, secured a permit to carry a concealed weapon in New York, and allegedly purchased two handguns. (The Bruderhof maintains that Arnold has since disposed of any guns.) Bruderhof corporate presidents aggressively pursued their right to legal self-defence. The leadership called the Connecticut police to arrest an ex-member for trespassing when he attended a Bruderhof open house in 1995. The commune initiated criminal charges for fraud and extortion in 1996 against a disturbed ex-member who threatened to write a book about the community unless he was granted the right to visit his family, living inside the commune.

By late 1995, Bruderhof corporate and religious leaders believed that KIT had acquired the customer mailing lists and subscriber lists to Bruderhof enterprises and constituted a dire threat to the economic survival of the commune. At this time, KIT public relations and criticism of the Bruderhof had broken through to regional and national media markets. In response to what the Bruderhof perceived as ominous threat to their existence, it began what seems to me to be a campaign of harassment and litigation against KIT and other Bruderhof critics.

In October 1995 the Boston ABC Network televised a report critical of the Bruderhof in their 'Chronicle' news program. The Chronicle report investigated charges that Bruderhof elder Johann Christoph Arnold had secured a concealed weapons permit and purchased two handguns in 1991, as well as allegations that the Bruderhof practised forms of church discipline that refused to allow apostates contact with family members inside the commune.

Following the Chronicle broadcast, two Bruderhof corporate presidents requested a meeting with me which took place on 25 October, 1995 at Yale University. During our two-hour conversation, the leaders again emphasized that I did not have their permission to study the community or write a book about the Bruderhof. The message was clear: stop speaking with the media and do not proceed with your scholarship.

In the spring of 1995, a small group of *KIT* activists formed a membership organization, 'Children of the Bruderhof, International' (COBI). They initiated a toll-free telephone number intended to assist persons inside and outside the Bruderhof who wanted information or assistance. COBI's helpline appeared in the New York Yellow Pages, nestled between Bruderhof and Hutterian Church telephone numbers. The COBI officers claim that the community responded with more than 2,000 harassing telephone calls. The billing records reveal that these calls originated either from Bruderhof community telephones or from public telephones near their hofs. Somebody printed fluorescent bumper stickers with the COBI help number. These were distributed at several airports, giving the mistaken impression that this number was a free telephone sex line: 'SWEET TALK – Joella and Karen are waiting FOR YOUR CALL – 24 Hours – 7 Days.'[7] Bruderhof spokesperson Joseph Keiderling attributed the phone calls to Bruderhof adolescents acting outside the control of the leadership (Schweitzer 1995). Bruderhof officials deny responsibility for the SWEET TALK advertisements.

In September 1995, the Bruderhof filed a civil lawsuit in federal district court in Albany, New York, charging COBI with trademark infringement over the use of the names *Bruderhof* and *Hutterian* in their Yellow Pages helpline advertisement. The Bruderhof sought $50,000 in damages and hoped to compel COBI to change their name and refrain from using the Bruderhof trademark. The Bruderhof reached an out-of-court settlement with COBI in the summer of 1996. The settlement protected the Bruderhof trademark, ended COBI and the help telephone line, and dismissed any Bruderhof claim to monetary damages.

In March 1996, the Bruderhof sponsored in Philadelphia the first of a series of planned regional debates regarding the death penalty in America. The Bruderhof leadership met in New York City on 13 September 1995 with attorney Leonard Weinglass and Ben Chaney, brother of the slain civil rights leader James Chaney, to form an ad hoc coalition under the umbrella agency, the National Commission of Capital Punishment (NCCP). The NCCP advisory committee included notables such as Sr Helen Prejean, of *Dead Man Walking* fame, actor Edward Asner, former Attorney General Ramsey Clark, and numerous organizations that promote social justice for the poor and advocate for minority rights. The NCCP's mission was to revisit the question of capital punishment, twenty years after the Supreme Court allowed states to resume executions. The Commission hoped to educate the public and foster a national conversation and debate that would lead to legislative efforts to end what the Bruderhof considered to be 'the ultimate revenge.' The Bruderhof formed a tax-exempt Bruderhof Foundation to solicit contributions for their Death Row Inmate Legal Defense Fund. The community formed a youth folk band, 'Just-US' (pronounced 'justice'), and produced a first album, *Within the Justice System*. Most important for the Bruderhof, they scheduled the first of a series of regional hearings under the auspices of the NCCP in Philadelphia on 25–7 March 1996, centred in part upon the controversial case of Mumia Abu-Jamal, who was convicted in 1982 of the murder of a Philadelphia police officer, Daniel Faulkner, and has spent more than a decade on death row, appealing the conviction and awaiting execution. He has written his memoirs and become a national *cause célèbre*.

Ramon Sender contacted Philadelphia media and the Fraternal Order of Police (FOP) before the hearings, providing them with the *KIT* public relations packet. Sender argued that the Bruderhof, as an authoritarian group, does not respect the individual rights of its members, does not value democratic process, and they should not mediate the public debate over the controversial issue of capital punishment. The Bruderhof had scheduled the first hearings in Philadelphia City Hall, which gave the appearance of official political endorsement of their stand in the Jamal case. The FOP, under the leadership of Richard Costello, held a news conference on the morning of 25 March, airing the videotape of the Chronicle report and calling the Bruderhof a 'cult.' Local newspapers, television stations, and a late-night radio show recounted KIT allegations. News accounts with interviews of Bruderhof leaders counterpoised by questions raised by Sender and other KITfolk, and by sociologists Benjamin Zablocki and Julius Rubin, made the Bruderhof religious controversy, not capital punishment, the centre of public debate. Although the Bruderhof mobilized political and religious groups to defend them, the remaining regional death penalty hearings were cancelled and the NCCP disappeared from the website.

On 27 March 1997, CBS News magazine *48 Hours* televised a report critical of the Bruderhof, broadcasting this piece together with a sensational breaking story about the Heaven's Gate religious suicide. As background to this news story, the Walek Group, a Manhattan public relations firm, then contracted by the Bruderhof, had contacted CBS in October 1996, urging *48 Hours* to film a short piece on the beauty of Advent and Christmas at the Bruderhof. I received a telephone call from the executive producer, who had just returned to her offices in Manhattan following a visit to the Woodcrest Bruderhof outside of Albany, New York. The news crew taped a Christmas musical program with Cardinal John O'Connor in attendance as the Bruderhof's 350 voices united in four-part harmony to celebrate Advent. She told me that she found the performance transporting, moved to tears by their simplicity, unity, and joyous religious brotherhood.

The producer demanded to know how I had the audacity to criticize this group or to associate their spirituality with depressive illness. 'Why are you their enemy? Why do you oppose their commitment to Jesus?' she demanded. 'You know nothing about this group and yet you persist in attacking them!' This harangue continued for thirty minutes until she had vented her anger. She said that the Bruderhof had supplied her with my name and telephone number, characterizing me as an 'enemy.' The Bruderhof leadership had urged CBS to contact me and KITfolk, apparently, believing that the national media might effectively discredit my work. I urged CBS staff to investigate a variety of news sources, both critical and supportive of the Bruderhof, when they researched their story.

In the ensuing four months, CBS had interviewed scores of KITfolk, Benjamin Zablocki, and me, and had reached a more balanced, albeit critical story on the Bruderhof/KIT controversy. The Bruderhof strategy of using the media to discredit their enemies had failed, bringing unfavourable national notice to the Bruderhof. The Bruderhof mobilized to defend itself. It contested the facts of the news account and protested the association with a 'cult,' calling upon famous and influential friends to denounce the story, CBS, and Dan Rather, who narrated the program.

On 7 April the 'Refuse and Resist' website, allied with the Bruder-hof's campaign to free Mumia Abu-Jamal and end capital punishment, posted a broadside urging supporters to protest against CBS, listing the address and telephone numbers of the producer. James M. Wall, executive editor of *The Christian Century*, wrote a lead editorial in the 21–8 May issue, characterizing the program as a 'distorted and shame-ful display of an antireligious bias for which Dan Rather, the show's producers, and CBS should apologize profusely to the Bruderhof com-munity' (Wall 1997). Former Attorney General Ramsey Clark, now a prominent New York Attorney and Bruderhof associate in the NCCP, sent Dan Rather a scathing letter on 11 June 1997 (also posted on the Bruderhof website), demanding an apology and stating: 'The program was a great disservice to truth, an assault on the right of everyone to freely exercise a chosen religion, and an insult to the common sense of the American people.'

According to the Wall, Clark, and others, when CBS broadcast a story that raised probing questions about Bruderhof church discipline and treatment of former members, or asked if the commune had become 'cultlike' in ways that resembled Heaven's Gate, then CBS was guilty of dishonesty, anti-religious bias, and abusing the public trust. Apparently the Bruderhof and their friends believed that only an uncritical puff piece that restated 'the Bruderhof story' constituted the responsible exercise of freedom of speech in a democratic society.

CBS did not retract the show or apologize to the Bruderhof. On 15 June, 1997, the Bruderhof brought legal action in the Manhattan Supreme Court, seeking discovery and disclosure of reporter's notes, unedited videotapes, and materials from the many persons and sources used in this story. According to CBS sources, the Bruderhof attempted to discover evidence of slander and defamation from the reporter's sources and interviews as a method of gathering evidence to prepare a defamation lawsuit against CBS, the KITfolk, and social scientists interviewed for the story. On 5 August 1997, the case was dismissed.

During the dispute with CBS, the Bruderhof launched a many-sided attack upon their perceived enemies. On 24 March 1997, the Bruderhof served Ramon Sender, editor of *KIT*, with a suit for copyright infringe-ment in federal District Court after he reprinted a letter sent by Chris-tian Domer, a Bruderhof corporate president, on 23 January 1997, to Michael Waldner, a Hutterite living in South Dakota. The Hutterites, as is their practice, faxed Domer's letter to scores of separate colonies.

Eventually, a fax reached the *KIT* newsletter. *KIT* publishes opinion and news about the Bruderhof/Hutterite schism as an integral part of KIT's public service as a tax-exempt organization.

In late July 1997, the Bruderhof filed a $15.5 million defamation lawsuit against Ramon Sender, Blair Purcell, myself, and the Peregrine Foundation, sponsor of the *KIT* newsletter. Sender and Purcell were sued for writing allegedly defamatory statements in *KIT*. I was charged with defamation for remarks that I made during an interview with a Philadelphia radio station in March 1996, where I questioned their sponsorship of death penalty hearings and raised questions about their participation in the Social Security System. (The suit was dismissed in November 1997, and the Bruderhof dropped their appeal on 20 December 1997 and withdrew the copyright infringement lawsuit against Ramon Sender.)

The Bruderhof strategies in dealing with KIT and academic critics first attempted to quiet them by private persuasion or manipulating the media to discredit them. When these efforts failed, the Bruderhof mobilized the Internet and influential friends to bring pressure upon the media to retract critical stories and apologize. When these efforts proved unsuccessful, the Bruderhof began a series of lawsuits intended to punish their critics and to prevent the publication of my book.

'You Do Not Have Permission to Study Us'[8]

In February 1997, Oxford University accepted the second revision of my manuscript, *The Other Side of Joy: Religious Melancholy among the Bruderhof* (OSJ), and issued a contract for the publication of this book. By early June the work had entered the production process. Oxford University Press advertised the work in their fall catalogue and secured a copyright and ISBN with the Library of Congress. Amazon.com, the Internet bookseller, listed the title as a forthcoming work in their database. The anticipated November 1997 publication of my book became public knowledge. (The book was taken out of production in late June after I informed my editor of the lawsuit brought against CBS. The manuscript has been vetted by an intellectual property attorney and is currently being revised before returning to production and manuscript preparation at Oxford University Press.) The Bruderhof devised what appears to me to have been a concerted strategy to prevent the publication of my book. The defamation complaint filed against me constituted a SLAPP suit (Strategic Lawsuit Against Public Participation). I cannot help but wonder if this was intended to intimidate me, to prevent me from speaking and writing about the Bruderhof, and to frighten my publisher.

There has been a social trend towards costly and burdensome lawsuits to be filed by corporations against individuals and groups who speak out about public issues concerning real-estate development, the environment, and consumer issues, as well as new religious movements. In what has frequently become an abuse of the courts, corporations and religious groups have used their economic power to sue their critics, thereby transforming public debates about political and social issues into narrowly defined 'private' disputes over libel, slander, and defamation. In this manner, the debate is removed from the public sphere. Now private citizens and grass-roots community organizations, without access to wealth and political influence, must defend themselves in expensive lawsuits, ever confronted with the threat that the court will award monetary damages. Even if the lawsuit is dropped or dismissed, the defendants frequently are 'devastated, drop their political involvement, and swear never again to take part in American political life' (Pring and Canan 1996). As George W. Pring and Penelope Canan argue: 'Normally thought of as the protectors of constitutional and political rights, courts are being used, in SLAPPS, to transform public political disputes into private judicial disputes, to the unfair advantage of one side and the disadvantage of the other.'[9]

In early August 1997, a Bruderhof spokesperson called my Oxford editor, informing her of the defamation lawsuit against me and the Bruderhof concern that I may have accused the community of committing criminal acts. Thus began a round of telephone calls and letters from the Bruderhof that continued into 1998, urging my editor to reconsider the publication of OSJ. The Bruderhof also sent me copies of these letters so that I would be aware of their tactics. In December, 1997 a Bruderhof corporate president asked me to pressure Oxford to meet with its representatives. In 1998, the editor had Oxford legal counsel instruct the Bruderhof to stop these 'harassing' communications. The Bruderhof has repeatedly requested a meeting with Oxford to discuss these matters, assuring the editor that once the facts were known about my work and the truth was presented about the Bruderhof, Oxford would reconsider this book.

Strange, unsigned reviews of the yet-to-be published book appeared on Amazon.com on 1 November, when OSJ was originally scheduled to appear.

One review read:

A Reader from Albany, N.Y. , 11/01/97, rating=1:
'I would rather read the *Readers Digest* than this book.'

Professor Julius Rubin should be ashamed about this book. To me it is garbage because he writes about something he does not know anything about. To top it all off this comes under the name of Scholar ship [*sic*]. I pity all those students who study under him at St Joseph's College in Hartford. I have read the manuscript and it was a complete waste of my time. They are being greatly deceived. Julius Rubin should give them all a refund for the tuition they have paid. A book to be ignored.

In late November, the Society for Promoting Christian Knowledge, (SPCK), a respected British publisher, mission society, and charity with a 300-year history as a patron of the Queen in association with the Church of England, published my essay about the Bruderhof in an edited book, *Harmful Religion*. This book was sold only in the U.K. and Europe, as SPCK did not have a North American distributor.

Harmful Religion presented the proceedings of a 1995 academic conference at King's College, London, that involved Pentecostal, healing, and deliverance ministries in Britain, the abuse of religious authority in new religious movements, and allied topics. Although I had not attended the conference, the academic editors, Lawrence Osborn of Cambridge University and Andrew Walker of King's College, commissioned my essay on the Bruderhof. The book was advertised in the *KIT* newsletter in November and entered the SPCK bookshops in the U.K. in early December. (SPCK would sell the work directly to American customers by special order.) Several weeks later, on 18 December 1997, I received an e-mail from Lawrence Osborn. He wrote that his co-editor 'just had a visit from a nice man from the Bruderhof. He tells us that they have been advised to sue us over your paper, but, of course, they are too nice to want to do anything like that.'

One month later, in frantic efforts to prevent a libel suit, SPCK had removed *Harmful Religion* from their shops and distributors and sold the entire first-printing run to the English Bruderhof communities. These actions allowed the publisher to recoup production costs, avoid a lawsuit, and make the disingenuous statement that the book was temporarily out of stock with no certain date set for the second-edition printing. Through these strategies, the Bruderhof successfully suppressed my writings and the publication of a critical essay about their sect. Threats of litigation and the tactic of buying out the print run allowed the sect to use its economic power to stifle academic freedom or freedom of the press when the writing was critical of its community.

Martin Wroe, a correspondent for *The Observer* in London broke the story on 22 March 1998, in 'A Cult Best Seller ... And Why You Can't Read It.' He quoted one of the authors, who stated that SPCK 'decided the book was not worth going to court over ... It looks as though it will come back on the shelves without that chapter.' Osborn and Walker wrote a 'statement of clarification' to the Bruderhof. A spokesperson for the English Bruderhof informed a senior official of Oxford University that SPCK had taken the book out of print because it contained my essay. (Oxford University Press is a division of the University.) This university official informed top officials at the press, who then contacted my editor in Oxford's New York office. The American Bruderhof spokesperson had sent her this information, adding to the pressure to drop the publication of OSJ.

On 29 December 1997, a Bruderhof leader again wrote to my editor at Oxford informing her that my essay in *Harmful Religion* was filled with false, inaccurate, and misleading statements. He listed three pages of objectionable material. The letter further stated that when the Bruderhof appealed to SPCK, they quickly realized their mistake in printing my words. The Bruderhof did concede my First Amendment right to publish, but urged Oxford, in the interest of fairness and accuracy, to meet with them and publish a balanced work. Two weeks later, on 13 January 1998, Oxford received a follow-up letter from the Bruderhof with the SPCK statement of clarification, written by Osborn and Walker. They lauded the Bruderhof as an inspiring example of Christian witness to pacifism and religious community, embodying the highest ideals of faith and ethical practice. They explained that there is nothing inherently or intentionally abusive or wrong with the Bruderhof and that it is not a cult. They apologized for any negative inferences that might be drawn from my essay. Appended to this letter was a statement by a clinical psychologist who stated that case studies taken from Bruderhof history have no relevance to the contemporary community. The Bruderhof letter concluded with another appeal to meet with Oxford and with an offer to provide additional letters from distinguished journalists, academics, editors, and Catholic theologians.

Oxford received several letters from these friends of the Bruderhof who discredited my writing after having read excerpts from my chapter in *Harmful Religion*. Each correspondent lauded the idealism of the Bruderhof communities and denounced my critical essay as erroneous, mean-spirited, and flawed social science.

During the spring of 1998, the Bruderhof sent my editor copies of critical reviews of my first Oxford book, *Religious Melancholy and Protestant Experience in America* as further evidence of my problematic scholarship. The Bruderhof also contacted and shared their concerns with the general editor of Oxford's *Religion in America Series*, a distinguished professor at a major American research university. In December 1998, after sixteen months, Oxford University Press had not yet agreed to meet with Bruderhof representatives. Joseph Keiderling, Bruderhof's corporate president, requested that the *KIT* newsletter publish his five letters to Oxford (for the January 1999 issue). These letters were also posted on alt.support Bruderhof. It appears that Keiderling went public with this correspondence in an attempt to exert additional pressure upon Oxford.

My personal impression of all this is that the Bruderhof had formulated a concerted strategy of pressure to stifle my voice, first by suppressing the SPCK essay, and then by using this small victory as leverage in an attempt to pressure Oxford to reconsider the manuscript. They then commissioned letters from prominent friends who would discredit my work and impugn my scholarly reputation.

The Bruderhof attacked another critic and threatened legal sanctions to suppress public criticism. In June 1997, Bill Peters, the husband of a Bruderhof apostate, created alt.support.Bruderhof, an Internet newsgroup. The newsgroup provides a free and uncensored forum that hosts threaded discussions to air complaints and ventilate anger about the commune. On 16 June, Bruderhof attorneys sent Peters a letter charging him with trademark infringement for using the term *Bruderhof*, demanded that he remove the newsgroup from the Web, and threatened legal action should he fail to comply by a two-week deadline. (Newsgroups, once initiated, take on a life of their own and cannot be removed. Bruderhof threats could not change this curious fact of the Internet.)

News of this controversy and the threat against Peters spread on the Net. Frank Copeland, a critic of Scientology living in Australia, took up the conflict between the Bruderhof and its critics. Copeland posted a web page with the story of the newsgroup conflict, information about

KIT, and the story of *Harmful Religion*. He posted a web page with my out-of-print chapter, which browsers could download.

Chris Stamper of 'The Netly News' broke this story on 7 July, 1997 in 'The Great Bruderhof Newsgroup Fight.' He interviewed me for this story and I offered my opinion that 'They want to use legal remedies to stop criticism ... They don't want to see any critical statements made by anyone.'[10]

In July 1998, Elizabeth Bohlken-Zumpe, the granddaughter of the Bruderhof's founder and author of the critical history *Torches Extinguished*, presented a paper in Amsterdam at CENSUR, the Center for the Study on New Religions. Before the session began, she was confronted by her brother Ben. She reports that he threatened to 'expose me as a liar and traitor' (Bohlken-Zumpe 1998). Shaken by this intimidation and reduced to tears, Bohlken-Zumpe did not want to deliver her paper in an atmosphere of intimidation. Yaacov Oved, author of *Witness of the Brothers*, an authorized history of the Bruderhof, reassured her: 'We are academic here, this is a University, and we invited you. We did not invite Ben ... Just calm yourself and I will do the rest!'[11] Her paper was delivered without interference by her brother and sister-in-law.

Conclusion

During an extended conversation in 1995 with two corporate officers who are part of the sect's core leadership, they repeatedly told me, 'You are not listening.' This phrase, according to many ex-members, is a code-word meaning that I disagreed with their account of the facts, their interpretation of events, and the motives attributed to the actions of others. Inside the Bruderhof, when a leader tells a common brother 'You are not listening,' the brother must hurriedly change his belief, attitude, demeanour, and behaviour to comply. Inside the commune, leaders have the authority to interpret social reality and the power to make their interpretations stick. However, the enforcement of a single belief system and total unanimity of thought, belief, and practice does not apply in mainstream society. The Bruderhof continually chafes at their loss of control over the interpretation of their movement by *KIT* and academics, and the freedom of public and academic discourse that openly questions orthodox accounts. *KIT* publications, the Internet, academic conferences, and university presses can contest the once-unchallenged public relations promulgated by 'the Bruderhof story.'

The contested narrative of the Bruderhof and its critics is neither new nor unique. American religious innovation in the past two centuries has fostered the emergence of a seemingly unending diversity of sects and utopian experiments from the Second Great Awakening in the first decades of the nineteenth century until the counterculture of the 1960s. New religious movements, formed in response to ethical prophets who have proclaimed that they serve as the instrument of divine will or as the emissary of a transcendental other, have institutionalized their charismatic messages, actively proselytized, gathered new converts, and issued challenges to the wider society. Not infrequently, public controversy, contested narratives, and litigation result. The Shakers and Mother Ann Lee, the Mormons and Joseph Smith, the Oneida Perfectionists and John Humphrey Noyes, and Christian Science and Mary Baker Eddy are four groups from a list that could include many other lesser-known sects. Each exemplifies the common theme of contested narratives, public controversy, and conflict between true believers and critical outsiders (Foster 1984; Weisbrod 1980).

The case of Christian Science proves instructive. In 1907–8, *McClure's Magazine*, known as a leader of muckraking journalism, accused the Mormon leadership of again embracing polygamy, and published a critical biography of Mary Baker Eddy and a history of Christian Science. Written by Georgine Milmine, with considerable editorial assistance and co-authorship by Willa Cather, this exposé largely discredited Eddy as the absolute head of the church. Harold S. Wilson writes: 'A parallel between authoritarian religious institutions and the trusts was quickly drawn in *McClure's* articles exposing the Mormons and the Christian Scientists ... Mrs Eddy was touted as the 'priestess,' the 'old queen,' and the 'absolute ruler' of the church' (Wilson 1970).

The magazine series was reprinted as a book in 1909, although this work quickly disappeared and remained unavailable for sixty-two years, until the publication of the second edition in 1971. Christian Scientists purchased all copies and kept the book on permanent loan from public libraries.[11] Here, a new religious movement devised strategies to silence the critical reporting of muckraking journalists.

Using similar tactics ninety years later, the Bruderhof has responded to critical accounts of their sect by demonizing these enemies of faith. From the sect's increasingly extremist position, it seems to me that they feel attacked by forces of evil, and are struggling for the very survival of their religion. Melvyn L. Fein argues in *Hardball without an Umpire: The Sociology of Morality* that religious sectarians, in defence of orthodoxy, can become extremist. Here morality is 'systematically immoral. It is an unregulated contest in which skulls get cracked open ...' (Fein 1997). Groups defend orthodoxy by recourse to legal and extralegal measures, violence, and intimidation of their enemies who are portrayed as increasingly dehumanized monsters deserving of destruction. Conflicting groups are divided into a 'good-guy/bad-guy' dichotomy. Fein explains: 'The good guys must prevail. Whatever it takes to win, they must not shrink from the effort ... As the only ones fit to make a decision, they must grind the bad guys into the dust. Were they to abdicate this duty, the depravity of the black hats would generate waves of pollution that might engulf society.'[12]

The good-guy/bad-guy syndrome of polarization and extremism can also apply to apostates who aggressively criticize and attack their former religions, seeking to discredit them as a 'cult.' Jeffrey Kaplan argues in *Radical Religion in America*, 'that the anti-cult movement and watchdog groups form as a dialectical opposition to the religious group; a highly motivated cadre of opponents dedicated to the task of 'exposing' the alleged dangers of the movement. The jury associated with court of public opinion may be a religious denomination, but it may as easily be the general public or the agencies of local, state, or federal government. Often, not content with merely publicizing the iniquities of the movement, these watchdog groups may organize to harass, intimidate, or even outlaw the target group' (Kaplan 1997). The Bruderhof, self-proclaimed as the good guy, denounces its critics as the demonic enemies of faith and adopt a complex legal, public relations, and extra-legal strategy to quiet those who disagree with them. The courts become the tool to punish those who disagree by costly litigation and SLAPP suits intended to intimidate critics. Alternatively, *KIT* apostates, self-proclaimed as the good guy, denounce the Bruderhof as a 'destructive cult' and attempt to discredit them in the court of public opinion. In the escalating conflict of dialectical opposition, the exercise of free speech and academic freedom is held hostage.

Notes

1 *Learned Hand, 'International Brotherhood of Electrical Workers,' Local 501 v NLRB, 181 F.2nd 34* (2 Cir. 1950), 40. Quoted from Frederick Schauer, 'The First Amendment as Ideology,' in *Freeing the First Amendment, Critical Perspectives on Freedom of Expression*, edited by David S. Allen and Robert

Jensen (New York: New York University Press, 1995), 10–28.

2 Yaacov Oved, *Witness of the Brothers* (New Brunswick, N.J.: Transaction Books, 1996).

3 See Maurice Halbwachs, *On Collective Memory,* for the discussion of the social and cultural dynamic of group collective memory and collective representations. See also Eric Hobsbawm, *The Invention of Tradition.*

4 Ramon Sender Barayon, 'The Evolution of the Peregrine Foundation,' http://www. Perefound.org/phist.html

5 Ibid., 'The Peregrine Foundation Information Sheet.'

6 The KIT Internet address is http://www.perefound.org/
The Bruderhof address is http://www.Bruderhof.com/

7 *KIT,* vol. 7, No. 7 (July 1995).

8 Quotation is from an interview with two Bruderhof spokespersons, at Yale University, 24 October 1995.

9 *KIT,* vol. 7, no. 7 (July 1995).

10 Chris Stamper, 'The Great Bruderhof Newsgroup Fight,' *The Netly News,* 7 July, 1997. (Http:www.cgi.pathfinder.com/netly/article/0,2334,12554,00. html)

11 Ibid., 15.

12 See Steward Hudson, preface to *The Life of Mary Baker G. Eddy,* 2d ed. 1971, xv. I am indebted to Cynthia A. Read, executive editor at Oxford University Press, for bringing this example to my attention.

13 Ibid., 152.

References

Allain, Roger. 1192. *The Community That Failed.* San Francisco: Carrier Pigeon Press.

Bohlken-Zumpe, Elizabeth. 1998. 'Report of Censur.' *KIT* (August): 15.

Clines, Francis X. 1995. 'Thou Shalt Not Traffic in Demon Gossip.' *New York Times,* 2 March, 1995.

Eaton, Joseph W., and Robert J. Weil. 1955. *Culture and Mental Disorders: A Comparative Study of Hutterites and Other Populations.* Glencoe: Free Press.

Eaton, Joseph W., Robert J. Weil, and Bert Kaplan. 1951. 'The Hutterite Mental Health Study.' *Mennonite Quarterly Review* 25 (Jan/Oct): 47.

Fein, Melvyn L. 1997. *Hardball without an Umpire: The Sociology of Morality.* London: Praeger.

Foster, Lawrence. 1984. *Religion and Sexuality: The Shakers, the Mormons and the Oneida Community.* Urbana: University of Illinois Press.

Halbwachs, Maurice. 1992. *On Collective Memory.* Edited, translated, with an introduction by Lewis A. Coser. Chicago: University of Chicago Press.

Hobsbawm, Eric. 1983. *The Invention of Tradition.* Cambridge: Cambridge University Press.

Holiday, Joyce. 1984. 'The Stuff of Life, A Visit to the Bruderhof.' *Sojourners* (May).

Holmes, Miriam Arnold. 1997. *Cast Out in the World.* San Francisco: Carrier Pigeon Press.

Hostetler, John A. 1974. *Hutterite Society.* Baltimore: Johns Hopkins University Press.

Johnson, Paul E., and Sean Wilentz. 1994. *The Kingdom of Matthias.* New York: Oxford University Press.

Kaplan, Jeffrey. 1997. *Radical Religion in America, Millennial Movements from the Far Right to the Children of Noah.* Syracuse: Syracuse University Press.

Lyall, Sarah. 1998. 'Rushdie, Free of Threat, Revels in Spontaneity.' *New York Times* 26 September, A7.

Manley, Belinda. 1995. *Through Streets Broad and Narrow.* San Francisco: Carrier Pigeon Press.

Milmine, Georgine. 1971. *The Life of Mary Baker G. Eddy and the History of Christian Science.* 2d ed., with a preface by Stewart Hudson, ed. Grand Rapids, Mich.: Baker Book House.

Mow, Merrill. 1989. *Torches Rekindled, The Bruderhof's Struggle for Renewal.* Ulster Park, N.Y.: Plough Publishing House.

Nash, Connie. 1994. 'Bruderhof Women, A Testimony of Love.' *History Today.*

Plaut, Thomas F.A., and Bert Kaplan. 1956. *Personality in a Communal Society. An Analysis of the Mental Health of Hutterites.* Lawrence Kansas: University of Kansas.

Pleil, Nadine Moonje. 1994. 'Free from Bondage, After Forty Years in Bruderhof Communities on Three Continents. In *Women from Utopia,* edited by Gertrude Enders Huntington. San Francisco: Carrier Pigeon Press.

Pring, George W., and Penelope Canan. 1996. *SLAPPS: Getting Sued for Speaking Out.* Philadelphia: Temple University Press.

Rubin, Julius H. 1994. *Religious Melancholy and Protestant Experience in America.* Religion in America, edited by Harry Stout. New York: Oxford University Press.

– 1997. 'The Other Side of Joy, Harmful Religion in an Anabaptist Community.' In *Harmful Religion, An Exploration of Religious Abuse,* edited by Lawrence Osborn and Andrew Walker, 81–98. London: SPCK.

Schauer, Frederick. 1995. 'The First Amendment as Ideology.' In *Freeing the*

First Amendment, Critical Perspectives on Freedom of Speech, edited by David S. Allen and Robert Jensen, 10–28. New York: New York University Press.

Schweitzer, Blaise. 1995. 'For Hutterians, There's a Storm Before the Calm.' *Kingston Daily Freeman*, 27 July.

Stamper, Chris. 1997. 'The Great Bruderhof Newsgroup Fight.' *The Netly News*, 7 July.

Walker, Andrew, and Lawrence Osborn, eds. 1997. *Harmful Religion: An Exploration of Religious Abuse*. London: SPCK.

Wall, James M. 1997. 'Cults and Communities.' *The Christian Century* (May): 21–8.

Weisbrod, Carol. 1980. *The Boundaries of Utopia*. New York: Pantheon.

Wilson, Harold S. 1970. *McClure's Magazine and the Muckrakers*. Princeton: Princeton University Press.

Wroe, Martin. 1998. 'A Cult Bestseller ... and why you can't read it.' *The Observer*, 22 March, 4.

Zablocki, Benjamin. 1971. *The Joyful Community*. Baltimore: Penguin.

13. The Roots of Religious Violence in America

Jeffrey Kaplan

For, behold, the day cometh, that shall burn as an oven; and all the proud, yea, and all that do wickedly, shall be stubble: and the day that cometh shall burn them up, saith the LORD of hosts, that it shall leave them neither root nor branch.

Malachi 4:1

In the waning days of the twentieth century, religious violence had all but lost its shock value. In 1978, the mass suicides at Jonestown shocked the nation. By 1997, however, the mass suicide of the Heaven's Gate group stirred little more than a brief spasm of news coverage and a week's worth of material for the nation's stand-up comedians. Only a few short years ago, the fires of Waco begat the bombing of the Oklahoma City Federal Center, and created a minor cottage industry of pundits and experts who sought to make sense of (or make a buck from) religiously inspired violence. The connection between the two events, however, was noted only in passing as attention was focused on a more tangible 'enemy within'; the faction of the American Patriot movement that has been popularly reified as the militia movement. With the turn of the millennium, it seems, Americans have come to accept apocalyptic sects and religious violence as the expected norm rather than the dreaded exception.

The federal government, ever behind the curve on emerging trends, has struggled gamely to catch up in the wake of Waco. Where the Justice Department, the FBI, and the hapless Bureau of Alcohol, Tobacco and Firearms (ATF) were perplexed by the beliefs and behaviour of the

Branch Davidians, the post-Waco era has seen the creation of a group of concerned scholars, including Michael Barkun and Nancy Ammerman, who are tasked with bringing federal security agencies up to speed on the subject of doomsday cults and religious violence (Ammerman 1995; Wessinger 2000).

Yet, objectively speaking, how pervasive is the phenomenon of religious violence in contemporary America? This essay will attempt to posit an answer to this question by placing the current situation in the broader context of American religious history. It is hoped that through such a historicist approach, the very real incidents of violence involving contemporary new religious movements will appear to the reader to be less exotic, less the product of a society placed on the defensive and forced to act against an inexplicable and threatening 'other,' than as a symptom of a process that, in a very real sense, we have seen before.

In this regard, I would offer once again the challenge of Jonathan Z. Smith to the academy in the wake of the Jonestown tragedy: 'How then, shall we begin to think about Jonestown as students of religion, as members of the academy? ... A basic strategy ... is to remove from Jonestown the aspect of the unique, of its being utterly exotic. We must be able to declare that Jonestown on 18 November 1978 was an instance of something known, something we have seen before ... We must reduce Jonestown to the category of the known and the knowable. (Smith 1982: 111–12).

In the last several years, a number of excellent works have appeared which have responded well to this challenge. For example, Mary McCormick Maaga's fine book on the people of the People's Temple has gone a long way towards removing from Jonestown the aspect of the unknown and unknowable (Maaga 1998), while a number of books and articles have furthered our understanding of various incidences of violence which in recent years have involved new religious movements throughout the world. It is hoped that this brief historical survey, involving only the religious history of the United States, will contribute somewhat to the process placing the subject of religious violence and the NRMs well within the category of 'the known and the knowable,' for truly this is something we have seen before.

Indeed, it would be a fair statement to say that religious violence was a feature of the American project from its late fifteenth-century inception. An alternative reading of history, however, would suggest that religiously inspired violence was more the exception than the norm in the United States – a state of affairs for which the framers of the American Constitution, in their wisdom, are in good measure responsible. The First Amendment's Establishment Clause ('Congress shall make no law respecting an establishment of religion, or prohibiting the free exercise thereof') reflected the founders' determination to avoid the bloody wars of religion which had ravaged Europe. Yet religious violence has taken place in the United States, and these outbreaks may be classified according to distinct patterns which may be deemed (1) expansionary violence, (2) millenarian and antinomian violence, (3) violence attendant on questions of sexuality and moral crusades, (4) youth rebellion violence, and (5) self-destructive or suicidal violence. Of these, new religious movements have figured in all but the first category. Before a consideration of these categories, however, it should at this point be noted that this taxonomy is adopted primarily as an analytical convenience. There is in fact considerable overlap between the categories. For example, the Covenant, Sword, and Arm of the Lord, which is considered here as a millenarian/antinomian appeal, had, through the polygamous practices of its leader, important elements of sexuality/moral crusades. Similarly, the Branch Davidians, considered under the heading of sexuality/moral crusades, had powerful millenarian and antinomian currents at the core of their theological appeal. While assignment to a particular category must in the last analysis be somewhat arbitrary, the governing logic is to isolate that element which was most important in catalyzing or justifying religious violence. With this proviso then, we can proceed to expansionary violence.

Expansionary Violence

Expansionary violence came first. This form of religious violence is that which can arise from the contact of two civilizations, and often results from the resistance of native populations to religious conversion and social marginalization. Thus, it might fairly be argued that religious violence came to American shores in the vanguard of European settlement, in that Christianization was a stated objective of the colonization of the New World. This was particularly true in the Spanish territories, where conversion and conquest were deemed two sides of the same coin and where the King of Spain acted under an extraordinary papal grant of authority. Significantly, however, the first unambiguous act of religious violence to take place on these shores occurred in 1565 in a clash which reflected Old World religious and dynastic controversies rather than intolerance toward Native-American religious beliefs. In that year, Spanish forces slaughtered a group of French Huguenots who had sought to settle in the New World (Ahlstrom 1972: 40). Be this as it may, from the colonial era through the various Indian Wars of the nineteenth century, religiously sanctioned violence against Native Americans was all too frequent.

A distinction must be made, however, between religiously sanctioned violence and religiously motivated violence. In general, there has been a tendency for religious authorities to sanction, often after the fact, violence directed at Native-American groups attendant to the 'civilizing project' in North America. Similarly, religious terminology was often used in colonial descriptions of the large-scale killing of settlers by Indians, as occurred for example at Jamestown in 1622 and again in 1644. A classic example of this mind-set may be seen in the wake of the 1622 massacre. Faced with the irrefutable evidence of the failure of the colonists' conversion project, Edward Waterhouse was moved to opine: 'Because our hands which before were tied with gentleness and faire visage are now set at liberty ... the way of conquering them is much more easie than of civilizing them of faire meanes (Waterhouse 1622: 22, 24; Miller 1996: 122).

Yet if one excludes the Spanish conquest, the case for religious violence against Native Americans is less clear. The French presence in what would become the United States was fleeting, and British, Scandinavian, and other Protestant colonists held religion as an important – but subsidiary – factor in their dealings with Native-American populations. Moreover, American history records innumerable cases of missionaries and Christian leaders whose denunciation of the treatment of Native Americans come down to us today. Examples abound, such as the anti-slavery campaign of Antonio Montesinos, the learned writings of Roger Williams, the passionate sermons of Jonathan Edwards, who spent his most productive years at a mission church, or the remarkable career of John Eliot, who began his career as a missionary only to find that he rather preferred the company of Indians to Europeans, and so spent much of his later life among them.

Millenarian and Antinomian Violence

Millenarian violence is predicated on the assumption of imminent apocalypse. Antinomian violence may be part of a millennial excitement, but is most often associated with a particular religious leader who decides, upon the basis of some private revelation, to supersede the Divine Law (i.e., the Ten Commandments) with a new, 'higher' code of conduct. Millenarian hopes have from the earliest days of colonization been attached to the New World, which was perceived by many to be, in the words of Gov. John Winthrop (d. 1649), God's 'city on the hill,' established for the express purpose of being raised up as the New Jerusalem of the Last Days (Ahlstrom 1972: 147).

Given the fact of such powerful millenarian currents, it is perhaps remarkable that most millennial excitements which arose in the United States have been untainted by violence. Rather, the pattern of the nineteenth-century Millerites has been by far the norm. Here, William Miller, on the basis of his reading of the Bible, prophesied in 1835 that the Second Coming of Christ would occur in March 1843. The Millerite movement soon gained thousands of adherents, who, as the appointed time approached, sold their belongings and withdrew from society to await the Great Event. Disappointed, alternative dates were proposed, but when the last of these, 22 October 1844, passed without event, the movement peacefully disbanded, only to be reconstituted under the charismatic leadership of Ellen White as the Seventh Day Adventists (Boyer 1992: 81–5; Festinger, et al. 1956: 12–23; O'Leary 1994: 93–133; St Claire 1992: 93–133).

While peaceful withdrawal from society is more the norm in U.S. religious history, there have been instances of violence or potential violence arising from American millennial excitements. These conflicts have come in two typical forms: confrontations with state authority and self-destructive or suicidal violence. Of the latter, the cases of Jonestown, Waco, and Heaven's Gate may be posited as typical, and these will be considered briefly below. Here, we will consider as examples of anti-state millennial violence (or potentially violent situations) the contemporary cases of the pro-life rescue and Christian Identity movements.

Religious violence involving Christian millennial movements such as Christian Identity tends to follow a consistent general pattern. First, in the eyes of the millenarians, there is often a distinctly different perception of time from that of the dominant culture. History in this conception is seen as coming to a violent denouement, with a future terrestrial paradise promised to the faithful if they can but persevere in the present time of testing. This may account for the suicidal audacity of a tiny handful of believers challenging the overwhelming power of the state. Moreover, that edenic 'new heaven and new earth' (Rev. 21:1) paradise will often be posited to resemble the 'Golden Age' past, which the faithful believed was lost through human sinfulness or to the malign conspiracy of a satanic 'other' (i.e., the Jews, the Illuminati, the forces of anti-Christ, ad infinitum), which has eventuated in a monstrous theft of culture that in the present day has deprived the faithful of both the memory of their glorious past and the covenantal promise of future bliss. In this sense, the imagined past and longed-for future blend into a single stream of time, with the present a fulcrum at which past and future converge. Finally, and of greatest importance, is the role of inerrant text, which is seen as the key to interpreting world events in light of the End Times scenario. When millennialist groups are stirred from their preferred mode of withdrawal to the greatest possible extent from the culture they see as beyond redemption and awaiting the chastisement of an angry God, it is invariably because the 'signs of the times' are such that action is imperative (Kaplan 1997a: 164–77). Both the Christian Identity community and the pro-life 'rescue movement' illustrate different facets of this form of millenarian violence.

Christian Identity evolved from nineteenth-century British-Israelism, an eccentric form of biblical interpretation which posited the British people as the descendants of the biblical Israelites (Barkun, 1994; Dobratz and Shanks-Meile 1997; Flynn and Gerhardt, 1990; Kaplan, 1995: 50–6; Kaplan, 1997: 1–10, 47–68). Transplanted to the United States, British-Israelism by the 1940s had combined with anti-Semitic currents drawn from the *Protocols of the Elders of Zion* and the 'International Jew' series run in Henry Ford's company newspaper, the *Dearborn Independent*, to create the virulently anti-Semitic and racist doctrines of Christian Identity.

Identity's most distinctive theological motif is the 'two seeds doctrine,' which posits the Jewish people as the demonic offspring of Eve and the serpent in the Garden of Eden (Gen. 3:1, 3:4). The non-white races in this interpretation are seen as the 'beasts of the field' (2:19–20), over whom Adam as the first white man was given dominion (1:28–30). Identity Christians see the Book of Revelation's dread Tribulation period as imminent, but these believers have no hope of supernatural rescue via the rapture (1 Thess. 4:17). Thus the Identity community's predilection for stockpiling arms and supplies in rural redoubts as they await the End. And from this biblical worldview comes the acceptance of the Zionist Occupation Government (ZOG) discourse which holds that the Jews have succeeded in establishing control, not only over the

American government but over the world system itself (Rev. 2:9, Rev. 3:9, John 8:44). See also Kaplan (2000 b).

Despite the often violent rhetoric emanating from Christian Identity quarters, the movement has rarely initiated violence. This may be attributed to the faithful's awareness of their own tiny numbers (between 10,000 and 50,000 worldwide) and to disagreements over the interpretation of world events within the apocalyptic scenario of the Bible. Yet throughout the 1980s, there were confrontations between state authorities and Identity communities which took place at several Identity compounds, most notably at the Covenant, Sword and Arm of the Lord (CSA) in rural Missouri in 1985. Because CSA was atypical in that it initiated violence, and because of the strongly antinomian currents within CSA stemming from the leadership of James Ellison, we will concentrate on the evolution of that group.

The Covenant, Sword and Arm of the Lord was founded in 1976 under the leadership of James Ellison in a rural redoubt that hugged the Missouri border with Arkansas and which the biblically minded founders dubbed Zarephath-Horeb (Flynn and Gerhardt 1990: 256–61; Kaplan 2000 a; 1995: 57–9; Noble, 1998; author interview with Kerry Noble, 22 May 1998; various CSA publications and documents). Interestingly, the communal group that evolved into the CSA originated as a charismatic Christian community with no overt racial or anti-Semitic overtones. Rather, membership was composed of disaffected refugees from the Children of God and followers of the controversial evangelist William Branham, as well as an ever-changing number of other religious seekers who drifted into and out of the Zarephath-Horeb orbit (Noble 1998: 25–78). It was not until James Ellison's fortuitous discovery of a cassette sermon by longtime Missouri Identity preacher Dan Gayman that the Covenant, Sword and Arm of the Lord as an Identity End-Time enclave came into being (Kaplan 1993; Noble 1998: 85–6; interview with Dan Gayman, 30 October 1996). With this conversion to Identity beliefs, a process that took more than six months of argument and prayer, CSA emerged as a kind of final refuge for the Christian Identity faithful in the times of the oncoming apocalypse. Until the onset of the dark days of the Tribulation, however, the CSA came to fill the role of elite armourer and training ground for the most militant members of the American radical right. This powerful sense of mission is made clear in a statement published in the premier issue of the *CSA Journal* in 1982: 'In the early days of 1981, we received a prophesy from the Lord saying that as He established our name locally, so He would establish our name across the United States, to be a Beacon of Light unto Him and His people, that others could see what a Christian is to be. Two weeks later, we were on the NBC Nightly News.' This would not be the last evening news appearance for the CSA, although that publicity would not be as welcome as this NBC report.

Throughout the 1970s and early 1980s, James Ellison was a charismatic, if highly divisive, figure in the American radical right-wing scene. He attended and addressed numerous movement gatherings including the Aryan Nations' annual meeting in Idaho and the Christian Patriots Defense League Freedom Festivals in upstate Illinois. As a result of these appearances and of the CSA's publications, a small but steady stream of seekers made their way to the CSA property on the Missouri-Arkansas border, often living in trailers or sharing quarters until such time as a more permanent solution to the housing problem could be found. To the frustration of the founders, who saw the CSA as the 'city on a hill' which would serve as a beacon for the white remnant community during the 'soon-coming' horrors of the Last Days, many of those attracted to the CSA's various seminars and training sessions, as well as to the community itself, were motivated by the violent message preached in the CSA's publications rather than the religious faith that fired the original residents of the Zarephath-Horeb community. (interview with Kerry Noble, 22 May 1998). In this sense, the violence which followed was as much a response to the demands of the faithful as it was a result of the will of the leadership.

By 1981 sufficient interest in the doings of the CSA had been expressed that the group felt constrained to publish a fifteen-point statement of beliefs. These, with what would prove to be a deeply ironic 'Declaration of Non-Surrender,' were duly published in a 1982 edition of the *CSA Journal*. Based on Ellison's interpretation of the Bible, these included:

1 statements of belief in the Bible as the 'inspired (although not necessarily perfect) Word of God';
2 belief in the oneness of God;
3 faith that Jesus Christ is the Son of God;
4 faith that 'the white race is the Israel race of God and is the superior race on this earth';
5 belief in the 'Born Again' experience including the Pentecostal gifts of healing and speaking in tongues;

6 belief that God is actively saving a remnant of the (white) nations or in Identity parlance, the nations or tribes of biblical Israel;

7 faith that God is about to visit a wrathful judgment on the earth in these, the Last Days;

8 faith that 'the commonly-called Jews of today are not God's chosen people, but are in fact an anti-Christ race, whose purpose is to destroy God's people and Christianity, through its Talmudic teachings, forced inter-racial mixings, and perversions';

9 belief that miscegenation is a sin and (again) in the dominion of the white race;

10 belief in the Declaration of Independence and the Constitution as divinely inspired documents which 'have become a farce today because of evil forces in our government';

11 belief in a dispensational reading of history in which all things would in the fullness of time be gathered unto Christ;

12 belief in the reality of the devil and his demons as spiritual beings who are nonetheless under the dominion of God;

13 belief that 'the Scandinavian-Germanic-Teutonic-British-American people [are] the Lost Sheep of the House of Israel which Jesus was sent for';

14 belief in the God given right of self-defense against the enemies of God and that the time is almost come for the people of God to take possession of the earth; and

15 belief that it is 'mandatory to come out of the confusion of Babylon and its political, religious, worldly, city, sinful systems, and not to touch these unclean things.'

All of this is standard Identity fare. What distinguished the CSA from even so histrionically racialist and militant an Identity community as the Aryan Nations, however, was the lack of a cautious elder statesman such as Richard Butler to curb the enthusiasm of firebrands such as Ellison. Thus, CSA's rhetoric became increasingly revolutionary in the early 1980s, and their side business of gunsmithing for the movement boomed. Such was the bravado of the times that the CSA would boldly state in their 'Declaration of Non-Surrender' that they would 'refuse any treaty, pact or declaration of surrender' with the hated 'Babylon' government of the United States.

The population at Zarephath-Horeb/CSA reached almost 200 at its peak (Miller 1985: A12). By the time the community turned to serious revolutionary violence in the early 1980s, however, the resident population was about a quarter of that number. Moreover, the fifty to sixty people that remained at CSA were almost all newcomers, interested in the violent racialist message rather than what the leadership felt was the vital biblical foundation of the group's beliefs. In 1982, a mass exodus occurred in which almost two-thirds of the community parted ways with the group over the question of polygamy (Noble 1998: 122). When over the virtually unanimous objections of the church elders, James Ellison insisted on taking a second wife, the original Zarephath-Horeb community fragmented, opening the way for the violent radicalism which was to follow (Noble, 1998: 122; interview with Kerry Noble, 22 May 1998). In fact, the polygamy question was disastrous for all concerned. Ellison's first wife went along with it only under extreme duress, and Kerry Noble's wife agreed to it as well, although Noble in the end did not take a second wife. In the case of both women, it was a tragic situation that caused great hurt. Noble today expresses great shame for the entire episode. Both of Ellison's wives divorced him when he turned state's evidence in the Fort Smith Sedition Trial of 1987.

Even before the polygamy controversy, however, all was not well at the CSA. Disaffected adherents began to filter out of Zarephath-Horeb with lurid stories of sexual improprieties and fraudulent dealings with members' property and finances. Ellison in particular was charged with interpreting scripture to suit his whims and with forming a cult of personality, and the group in general was charged with such un-Christian activities as shoplifting in local stores. The latter charge was particularly telling in that it indicated the dire state of the group's finances as well as the CSA's convenient code of morality (interview with Kerry Noble, 22 May 1998). The charges were in fact quite true, and they were taken seriously by the Identity community. Shoplifting, theft, armed robbery, and various scams perpetrated on the 'Beast system' and the right-wing faithful alike became the CSA's stock in trade. Meanwhile, Ellison's constant battles with rival leaders and his polygamous lifestyle had already clouded the CSA with an aura of considerable suspicion.

John Harrell of the Christian Patriots Defense League took particular exception to Ellison's pretensions. As a result, CSA defectors found in Harrell a champion to publicize their grievances to the movement. The controversy peaked in 1982 with a series of open letters between Harrell and the CSA which featured some nasty charges and counter-charges. In an open letter on 19 October 1982, Harrell offered a concise summary of the image of the CSA that was becoming pervasive in movement circles: 'You are rapidly gaining the reputation of being the Jim Jones of the patriotic effort, plus there are charges that you are dealing in illegal foodstamps, merchandise, and weaponry; holding in psychological fear some of your group who wish to leave the CSA base; making physical threats against those who you feel have wronged you, including the threatening of Federal Agents – if these accusations are so, unless you can quickly 'turn around' you are indeed leading a suicide squad, as was also mentioned in our July 7 letter.' Some among the CSA faithful took Ellison's violent rhetoric more seriously than the leader himself. A few, most notably Richard Wayne Snell, would become notorious in their own right for crimes up to and including murder (a crime for which Snell would be executed on the very day of the Oklahoma City bombing, 19 April 1995 (Hamm 1997; Kaplan 1997a; Noble 1998; Snell 1986).

The CSA's course of revolutionary violence took place between 1982 and 1984. As with everything at CSA, the violence was incremental, and it resulted from the group's increasing impatience with the Lord to fulfill the group's prophesies of imminent apocalypse. The group in both it's Zarephath-Horeb and CSA incarnations maintained a charismatic Christian focus that depended on personal prophecy – a Word of Power inspired by God – for direction. Prophecy was practiced in church services, and was open to both men and women. Indeed, in the patriarchal world of CSA, prophecy became a principle access to power for women. How prophecies were analysed, accepted, or rejected by the group is a fascinating study in itself, but here it will suffice to say that in Kerry Noble's view, no collusion was ever a part of the prophetic component of CSA spirituality, but, at the same time, prophecy tended to reinforce the group's beliefs. Thus, prophecy supported Ellison's desire for polygamy, the group's turn to violence, and, ultimately, its surrender to the vastly superior force of federal agents that surrounded the compound (Noble 1998; interview with Kerry Noble, 22 May 1998).

The ingredients for violence were there from the beginning. The group, living in isolation and under the authority of a charismatic and highly eccentric leader who was convinced of his role as a prophet of God in the Last Days, and had amassed a considerable stockpile of illegal automatic weapons. Further, the group was blessed by the presence of no less than two experts in armaments and explosives, and soon the group boasted of a remarkable stockpile of weaponry. The CSA thus emerged in the early 1980s as the elite training ground of the radical right, and their *CSA Survival Manual* remains the standard work on irregular warfare to emerge from the American radical right.

Thus armed, petty shoplifting and various forms of fraud soon evolved into more serious crime. One such, an armed robbery of a pawn shop in Texarkana, Arkansas, resulted in the murder of the pawnshop owner by Richard Wayne Snell, who felt the man looked Jewish and thus needed to die. This incident spelled the beginning of the end for CSA. Kerry Noble, the second in command at CSA, notes that Ellison and others at CSA were not pleased that Snell had killed William Stumpp, the pawnshop owner, fearing that it would bring down more heat on the group than they needed. But Snell's defence – that the man was a Jew – allowed everyone to overlook the indiscretion. Not one to be easily discouraged by criticism, Snell followed this fiasco with another pointless killing. Snell, who insisted, against the advice of all, on riding around in a van loaded with illegal arms, later shot and killed a Black state trooper during a routine traffic stop with Snell at the wheel (Flynn and Gerhardt 1990: 260–1; Kaplan 1997a: 59–61; interview with Kerry Noble, 22 May 1998). Nor was this all. Other actions included an attempted arson of a gay church in Springfield, Missouri, and the bombing of a Jewish community centre in Bloomington, Indiana, both in 1983 (Noble 1998: 133).

Fortunately, CSA's more grandiose schemes were not carried out. One such, the bombing of a gay church during services, was aborted when the putative bomber, Kerry Noble, sat in the church with the bomb and then decided, for both instrumental and emotional reasons, that he simply couldn't do it. Noble recalls that he thought of the carnage the bomb would cause, and weighed that against the certainty that the killings would not, as the group hoped, ignite a white revolution in America (Noble 1998: 146–7). A hit list of assassination victims was drawn up, but not acted upon. And the most ambitious plot of all – the blowing up of the Oklahoma City Federal Center – was ultimately deemed too dangerous, and this too was forgotten (134–5).

While all this was going on, the drumbeat of criticism of Ellison and the CSA from movement circles had, if anything, increased in intensity. As Ellison and the CSA leadership struggled to defend themselves from the swirl of charges and counter-charges, more serious problems loomed on the horizon. By 1984, the federal government began a series of prosecutions of the CSA membership which would culminate in the seizure of the property itself. Ellison, Noble, and the CSA hard core, in keeping with the 'Declaration of Non-Surrender,' vowed to defend the compound to the death, if need be. Given the large cache of armaments and supplies at their disposal, the threat was not taken lightly by the government, and in April of 1985 the compound was besieged with a force of some 300 FBI agents.

After an initial show of bravado, Ellison meekly surrendered without a shot being fired. Some residents were allowed to remain on the property after the arrests of the leadership, but the faithful soon dwindled to less than thirty. With the news that Ellison had betrayed the movement and would testify for the government at the Fort Smith, Arkansas, sedition trial, the once powerful Covenant, Sword and Arm of the Lord flickered and died (Coates 1987: 123–56; Finch 1983: Flynn and Gerhardt 1990: 256–61).

Today, Ellison resides at the Elohim City Identity enclave and Kerry Noble has left the movement and renounced his racist beliefs (interview with Kerry Noble, 22 May 1998).

The pro-life rescue movement presents a remarkable case study of a contemporary American Christian millenarian movement that evolved over the course of two decades from a rigorous pacifism to the point when a small minority of the faithful would lose hope that a fallen nation could be redeemed and would therefore take up arms in defence of the unborn (Alcorn 1990; Blanchard 1994; Blanchard and Prewitt 1993; Bray 1994; Foreman 1992; Ginsburg 1989; Risen and Thomas 1998; Scheidler 1985; Terry 1988; 1990). The rescue movement, defined here as pro-lifers who practise 'interposition' (in rescue parlance 'those who interpose their bodies between the killer and his victim, i.e., the abortionist and the unborn child), emerged slowly from the religious opposition to the 1973 *Roe v Wade* Supreme Court decision legalizing abortion (Trewhella and Sedlack, n.d.). The first halting attempts at interposition were undertaken by individuals such as Joan Andrews in the early 1980s, and took the form of such minor vandalism as unplugging suction machines. The punishment meted out to Andrews and others for these early forays were sufficiently draconian to inspire her and others to attempt to destroy machines or damage patient files, correctly assuming that the sentences would be no worse for the greater level of destruction (Andrews and O'Keefe 1989).

The example of these early, largely Catholic rescuers was taken to heart, and in 1986–7 Operation Rescue was formed under the leadership of Randall Terry. Operation Rescue marked both the emergence of a large, organized rescue movement and the shift in the movement from a primarily Roman Catholic to a primarily evangelical and fundamentalist Protestant constituency. Operation Rescue's tactical approach involved large-scale demonstrations aimed at shutting down abortion clinics in selected cities for limited periods of time. Thus, in such cities and towns as Buffalo, Fargo, Los Angeles, and Pittsburgh, and especially at the so-called 'Siege of Atlanta' during the 1988 Democratic Convention, Operation Rescue mobilized rescuers throughout the country. The operation, however, consciously modelled its actions on the non-violent civil disobedience of the 1960s-era civil rights movement and insisted that anyone seeking to take part in their actions sign a pledge to eschew violence in any form (Kaplan 1996; Lawler 1992; Terry 1988).

The experience of the Atlanta jails split the movement, and after 1988 new rescue groups appeared, some of whom were less committed to non-violence than Operation Rescue. The Lambs of Christ, for example, a primarily Catholic Rescue group, is led by a charismatic priest named Norman Weslin, who, like his second-in-command Ron Maxson, is from a military background. The Lambs added an element of increased militancy to the rescue movement, while the Milwaukee-based Missionaries to the Pre-Born, led by two former Operation Rescue stalwarts, Pastors Joseph Foreman and Matt Trewella, added direct confrontations with abortionists, destruction of property, and a form of spiritual warfare they called imprecatory prayer, that is, calling upon God to either show the abortionist the error of his ways or strike him dead (Kaplan 1996).

Meanwhile, in the late 1980s and early 1990s, individuals such as John Brockhoeft, Marjorie Reed, Michael Bray, and Shelly Shannon began to take more resolute action by firebombing clinics. They were scrupulous in their determination that the destruction of buildings would be accomplished with absolutely no loss of life. Moreover, all of them explained their actions by reference to biblical text and a passionate belief that abortion was symptomatic of the fact that these were indeed the Last Days and that God's Judgment on a fallen world was rapidly approaching. It was this belief that at last broke the twenty-year commitment to non-violence on the part of a minority of the rescue movement. Thus, when Michael Griffin, at best a peripheral figure in the tightly knit rescue community, shot and killed Dr David Gunn in Pensacola, Florida, in 1993, the final barrier to lethal violence was broken. In short order, Shelley Shannon wounded Dr George Tiller in Milwaukee and Paul Hill shot and killed another Pensacola doctor, John

Britton, and his volunteer bodyguard (Kaplan 1996; Risen and Thomas 1998). In 1998 another abortion doctor, Bernard Slepian, was shot and killed in upstate New York. The killing remains unsolved, but does demonstrate the continued viability of lethal force within the most radical sectors of the rescue movement.

The core group of rescuers who opted for force – Shannon, Brock-hoeft, Bray, Reed, and others around the country – created an organizational symbol in the early 1990s called the Army of God (AOG). The AOG produced a manual which contained the experiences of the group as they tried to learn the art of domestic terrorism from scratch. *The AOG Manual* offered both the optimum recipes for bombs and fervent expressions of religious faith (AOG, 3d ed., n.d.). Today, in the writings and journals of the pro-force wing of the rescue movement (i.e., *Prayer + Action News* and *Life Advocate*), an apocalyptic analysis of American culture and an explicit endorsement of the use of force are ubiquitous. The *Prayer + Action News* in particular has taken the lead in the current convergence of the pro-force wing of rescue with the far right's fears of one world government and what they see as the subversion of the republic spearheaded by the United Nations. No better symbol of this convergence may be posited than the serialized pro-life version of the *Turner Diaries*, 'Rescue Platoon,' by David Macabee, which appeared in *Prayer + Action News* in 1997–8. Further evidence may be found in the same journal: for example, the tongue-in-cheek Black Helicopter Award given to those pro-lifers whose actions are such that they serve as 'black helicopter bait' to shield others in the movement (*Prayer + Action News* 308 1997: 58). Meanwhile, in the wake of the killing of Dr Bernard Slepian, a bizarre website operated by Neal Horzey, founder and probably sole member of the Creator's Rights Party, came to public prominence with press revelations of the site's 'Nuremberg Files,' which lists the descriptions and whereabouts of abortion doctors with a strong suggestion that these doctors should themselves be terminated. Horzey, however, is seen as an extreme figure even in the most extreme reaches of the rescue movement. Long before the creation of the Nuremberg Files, Horzey's website scandalized the movement by posting violently obscene pornographic pictures depicting gay sado-masochistic sex, bestiality, and other acts as documentary evidence of the fallen state of American culture. After the mainstream press became aware of the Nuremberg Files in 1998, the site was pulled from the Net by its Web hosting service, and after several abortive attempts at resuscitation, the Nuremberg Files disappeared, re-emerging only fitfully between 1999 and 2001. Undaunted, Horzey offers the full contents of the website on CD-ROMs to all who ask, as his lawsuit against the original provider, MindSpring Enterprises, wends its way through the courts (State of Georgia, Civil Action No 99-A-9543-4).

Sexuality and Moral Crusades

The next form of religious violence – occasioned by sensitivities about sexuality or in the course of moral crusades – pervades the history of religious violence in America. Two primary examples will be posited here; the paradigmatic 'Mormon Wars' of the nineteenth century, which constitute the bloodiest episodes of religious violence in American history, and Waco, where reports of David Koresh's antinomian sexual practices served as an effective 'after the fact' public justification for the botched raid.

Accusations of sexual misdeeds – in particular, homosexuality, orgiastic revels, incest, and pedophilia – have always been the common coin of religious polemic. The early Christians, for example, faced just such accusations, and the medieval church employed virtually identical charges against heretical sects. Nor have these charges lost their power to mobilize public outrage against minority religions. One need only recall the anti-Catholic agitation of the 1920s, which was fed by the publication of the salacious tome, *The Awful Disclosures of Maria Monk*; the book is still in print, albeit with the front cover adorned with the picture of a young nun wearing a head covering and nothing else, which would have been a bit much even by Roaring Twenties standards (Anon. 1969; Bellah and Greenspahn 1987).

It may seem odd to contemporary readers to apply this polemic to the Church of Jesus Christ of Latter-Day Saints (Mormons), given the conservative image of the church and the Mormons' remarkable success in terms of church growth and financial power. But in the nineteenth century, the Mormon practice of polygamy, or the taking of 'spiritual wives,' aroused an unprecedented wave of persecution, beginning as scattered cases of vigilantism and culminating in an armed confrontation with the state itself (Quinn 1993). That the Church of Latter-Day Saints survived this period with its core theology intact to become arguably the most successful new religious movement of modern times is a remarkable feat in itself.

Almost from the beginning, when Joseph Smith was shown the Golden Plates which would become the Book of Mormon in 1827, the

Mormons have had external teachings which were disseminated to the public via their missionary outreach, and a core of esoteric teachings held only for trusted believers. Polygamy was the most incendiary of these internal doctrines, and reports of these teachings, often wildly exaggerated, were, from the early days of the community, revealed by Mormon dissidents and apostates. It was the local indignation over these reports that had much to do with the forced exodus of the Mormon faithful from their upstate New York origin ever westward, with important stops in Missouri and Illinois on their way to their ultimate sanctuary in Utah in the middle years of the nineteenth century.

The so-called Mormon Wars were actually a series of vigilante skirmishes and confrontations with state and federal authorities. There began in 1838 with Joseph Smith's promise to strike back at the tormentors of his community. This eventually resulted in the murder of the prophet in Nuavoo, Illinois, in 1844, and culminated in the bloody 'Mountain Meadows Massacre' in Utah in 1857.

Nuavoo was seen by the Mormon faithful as a self-governing refuge, immune to the kind of persecution that had harried them from Missouri (1833 and 1839) and Ohio (1838). The Illinois legislature had in 1840 injudiciously given the town a charter that allowed the Mormons under Joseph Smith and John Cook Bennett to produce its own courts and legally raise a militia in times of crisis. The crisis was not long in coming, as the Mormon community immediately found itself embroiled in conflicts with local residents and the citizens of surrounding townships. At issue were a number of legal and political disputes, with reports of Mormon polygamy provided the rallying cry. Following an intense series of legal skirmishes between the Nuavoo courts and those of its neighbours – including the arrest of Joseph and Hyrum Smith, which was countermanded by a writ from the Nuavoo Court – Smith in 1844 made a fatal miscalculation by ordering the destruction of a critical local newspaper, the *Nuavoo Expositor*, and later jailing its editor. The state responded by sending in the Carthage Greys, the local militia, to which Smith responded by raising the Nuavoo Legion. Full-scale hostilities were in the end averted, but the Smith brothers and several others were incarcerated in nearby Carthage. On 27 June 1844, a mob of local citizens and off-duty Carthage militia members broke into the jail and lynched the prisoners (Porter 1994; Quinn 1991; Schindler 1996: 1)

What followed these events was a year of low-intensity violence between the Mormons and their neighbours, which escalated to house burnings and shootings before the Mormons, under the leadership of Brigham Young, began the trek west in February 1846. By May, 16,000 Mormons had departed, leaving only a few thousand Mormon residents of Nuavoo. Then, on 12 September 1846, a force of some 600 descended on Nuavoo, and after a battle lasting only an hour, forced the town to surrender, ending the Mormon experiment in Illinois (Schindler 1996).

The Mormon community regrouped in Utah in 1850, but they had hardly left the polygamy controversy behind. The issue came to a head in 1852 when Brigham Young for the first time publicly proclaimed Joseph Smith's doctrine of polygamy, known to Mormons as the 'Order of Jacob.' The federal government reacted mildly at first by rejecting repeated applications for Utah statehood. However, in 1857 President James Buchanan deposed Young as the governor of the Utah territory and replaced him with a non-Mormon. What followed was a bloody confrontation which culminated in September of that year with the massacre of a group of settlers headed towards California by a Mormon force under the leadership of John Doyle Lee, and a band of Paiute Indians. Of the 137 settlers, only the youngest children survived what came to be known as the 'Mountain Meadows Massacre.' The federal reaction was not long in coming, and in the face of federal troops, overt Mormon control of the Utah territory was ended. The Supreme Court officially decided against polygamy in 1879 and a series of congressional actions in 1882 and 1884 added teeth to the decree. In response, a new revelation in 1890 by Mormon President Wilford Woodruff ended the practice of polygamy by mainstream Mormons, and, as a result, Utah became a state in 1896 (Ahlstrom 1972: 501–9). Today, the official position of the Church of Latter-Day Saints is that the practice of Mormon polygamy survives only among the so-called fundamentalists (dissident sects) in rural areas of the American West. In fact, the practice of Mormon polygamy was never as effectively ended as many in the mainstream LDS community have claimed. Today, polygamy continues, albeit in a semi-clandestine manner, throughout Utah. The state authorities intervene only in cases of incest, underage marriage, or domestic violence (Brooke 1998: Quinn 1991).

The 1993 confrontation between the federal government and the inhabitants of the Branch Davidian compound in Waco, Texas, stands as the single most divisive topic among the already deeply factionalized students of American new religious movements. The event continues to stir impassioned debate in these circles today. Already, the events of Waco and its aftermath have generated a mini-library of texts, anthologies, journal articles, and op-ed pieces offered by scholars seeking to influence public and scholarly debate on the Waco tragedy.

Given this intensely polarized situation, it is important to set out several points at the outset of this brief consideration of Waco as an instance of American religious violence arising from concerns surrounding sexuality and moral crusades. First, unlike the history of the LDS church, sexuality was not the reason for the federal actions against David Koresh. Rather, Koresh's antinomian sexual teachings were offered only after the stand-off had settled into a protracted war of nerves, and served as a partial justification for the federal decision to end the siege forcefully; to, in the unfortunate phraseology of Attorney General Janet Reno, 'save children.' The unusual level of public support for Reno and the federal government in this action, however, demonstrates in part the effectiveness of such appeals to moral order. Second, while the case for the LDS church as the initiators of violence is at best ambiguous – at least before the Mountain Meadows Massacre – there can be no question of the Branch Davidians initiating violence with anyone. By all accounts they lived peacefully with their neighbours, and even very real questions of child abuse, which had been referred to the local department of social services, were handled amicably. Quite simply, there appears to be no justification whatever for the violent denouement to the Branch Davidian stand-off.

This said, however, the resonance of the claims of federal authorities that their actions were taken at the deepest levels in defence of moral order are deserving of some consideration in this category. These charges tend to fall into two separate but closely interrelated categories: David Koresh claimed all adult female members of his 'cult' as his exclusive sexual property; he engaged in the physical abuse of children and the sexual abuse of young girls.

The first charge, that Koresh created of his female followers a kind of harem which alienated wives from husbands and destroyed nuclear families is most easily dealt with. In general, considerable evidence exists that these charges were true. Koresh did indeed gradually convince his flock that, on the basis of his biblical hermeneutics, he was divinely meant to sire a new race of the 'House of David' as outlined in his theology of the New Light. This mission of course required the cooperation of an ever-expanding circle of 'spiritual wives' who had shown themselves worthy of being 'sown with the Light' (Bromley and Silver 1995: 58–61).

Salacious stuff indeed, and in suitably popularized form the press had a field-day with the information as it was filtered through government, defector, and anticult movement sources (Lewis 1995; Richardson 1995; Schupe and Hadden 1995; Wright 1995). And yet the America of the last two decades of the twentieth century is a very different place than the America of Joseph Smith and Brigham Young. The taking of any number of spiritual wives in contemporary America is generally considered to be a private matter, so long as those involved are adults past the age of consent, and so long as no effort is made to regularize the relationship through registration with the appropriate legal and government agencies. This Koresh and the Branch Davidians never did, and so the government neither had, nor did it claim, any brief to intervene in these matters at Mt Karmel.

On the other hand – and here, it would seem, is the key point to be made – the widespread publicity accorded these charges did much to fix in the public mind the image of the Branch Davidians as 'brain washed cultists' who lived under the complete domination of a mad and debauched prophet. Such people, it was widely thought, could hardly be capable of reaching an independent decision to surrender, making the ultimate assault on the compound and the deaths of the Branch Davidians at best unavoidable, at worst a form of divine punishment, on a modern-day Sodom and Gommorah (Gen. 19:24).

The questions of child abuse and the sexual abuse of minors are not so lightly dismissed. Here, the government does have a responsibility to intervene if credible evidence comes to light that activities are taking place which supersede any claims of First Amendment protection. Of course, such claims were put forward by the government only after the stand-off had begun, effectively negating the claim that the raid or its violent conclusion were in any way intended to 'protect children.' That said, however, serious questions remain regarding the treatment of children in the Branch Davidian compound – questions for which definitive answers are yet to emerge.

There does seem to be some credibility to charges regarding the physical abuse of children. Corporal punishment does not seem to have been unusual among the Branch Davidians (as among Americans in general), but whether these charges rose to the level of abuse is uncertain. The charges were investigated by the local social services department, and despite the belief of some investigators that action was warranted, none was taken (Ellison and Bartkowski 1995). More serious were charges that David Koresh had sexual relations with underage girls, and here the charges do appear, based on a reading of the sources on all sides of the conflict, to have some foundation in fact. Nothing justifies this sexual abuse of minors. Although the charges were made only after the fact of the raid, however, it is safe to say that the charges themselves constituted in the public mind the most convincing evidence of all that federal action was warranted, and that the tragedy that followed was completely the fault of David Koresh, whose demonization in the public mind was now complete.

Youth Rebellion Violence

In recent years, skinheads on the Right and the many tribes of young anarchists on the Left have become synonymous with youth violence. However, despite the presence of Christian Identity and Odinist skinheads, the violence engaged in by these groups tends to be spontaneous, and participants rarely attribute their actions to religious motivations (Hamm 1984; Heider 1994). Therefore, this section will concentrate on the youth Satanist subculture, from which significant acts of violence have emanated in recent years.

The era of modern Satanism began on Walpurgisnacht, 30 April 1966, by proclamation of Anton Szandor LaVey, who on that night officially founded the Church of Satan. The year 1966 thus became year 1 of the Satanic Era (Aquino 1993; Barton 1992). Since that night, the Satanic subculture has grown remarkably, developing a number of branches representing many shades of belief.

It is important to state that neither LaVey's Church of Satan, nor any of the other 'Satanic churches' (i.e., the Temple of Set, the Werewolf Order et al.), have been implicated in acts of violence (although the Werewolf Order has on occasion appeared to advocate violence). At the same time, the cumulative impact of LaVey's *The Satanic Bible* and other Church of Satan literature to 'do as thou wilt,' when combined with the powerful strain of social Darwinism which implied that the 'superior man' has the right to gratify his whims at the expense of the weak, has an undeniable appeal to a population of adolescents – especially adolescent males – whose search for a meaningful identity found an important focus in the works of the Church of Satan and the words of Anton LaVey (LaVey 1969). It was from this population that most acts of violence which may be linked to Satanism have come.

To be sure, very few self-styled youth Satanists have been involved in violence. Most content themselves with a copy of *The Satanic Bible* or a collection of CDs from bands associated with the Satanic subculture. For these young people, it is enough to dream of power, of revenge on those who have slighted them, and, most of all, of sexual gratification. Much the same can be said of the European youth Satanism scene, save that the black clothing and sallow complexions have become a uniform for alienated young people. A few, however, have gone considerably further.

Three points should be noted as a preface to what follows. First, there is no body of statistics upon which to base a reliable estimate of the level of violence associated with youth Satanism. Moreover, police reports often confuse youth Satanism with such manifestations of youth culture activity as the gothic scene or role-playing games. Second, interviews with youth Satanists indicate that many began their involvement either with material from the Satanic churches, which they soon found too tame, or through involvement with the 'black metal' music scene. Third, thanks to the transnational appeal of the music scene and the ubiquitous presence of the Internet, the youth Satanism subculture today knows no borders. For this reason, the considerable violence of youth Satanists in Scandinavia has had a significant impact on American youth.

The violence which does emerge from the youth Satanist subculture tends to take stereotypical forms. By far the most common is violence against property. Graffiti with satanic symbols such as '666' and pentagrams have been used to deface gravestones, churches, or public buildings. These may be accompanied by animal bones or signs of a 'ritual' having taken place (Peterson 1988; III).

The apex of violence to property involves the burning of churches. Despite the epidemic of church-burning in the American South in the late 1990s, few of these cases have been traced to youth Satanists. In Norway, however, Varg Vikernes of the one-man 'black metal' band Burzum, was responsible for burning Fantoft church near Bergen in 1992. What followed was a rash of forty-five to sixty arsons or attempted arsons in Norway, and a number of copycat instances in Sweden and Germany (Moynihan and Søderlind 1998).

More serious is the sacrifice or mutilation of animals. Evidence of animal sacrifice stemming from rituals associated with the practice of Santeria or Candomblé, two Afro-Caribbean religions in which animal sacrifice plays a central role, is often mistakenly attributed to youth

Satanists. Rituals involving the killing or maiming of animals in the youth Satanist subculture, by contrast, tends to be relatively opportunistic, demonstrating little advance planning and leaving clear signs that the intent was to torture rather than simply dispatch the sacrificial animal (Balch and Gilliam 1991; Hermonen, 2000; Hicks 1991; Johnston 1991).

Serious violence against persons is quite rare in the youth Satanist subculture, but some high-profile cases have emerged. Here it is important to differentiate between two forms of this sort of Satanist violence: self-inflicted violence and violence against others. In the former, the media have carried a number of reports of suicides by young people said to have been influenced by heavy metal music with Satanic themes since the 1980s. Drugs are invariably a part of the mix, and several of these cases have ended in civil litigation. The most recent case involved an unsuccessful civil suit against Judas Priest by the parents of a boy who killed himself after listening to one of the group's records (Johnston 1991: 15–16; Moynihan and Søderlind 1998: 267–332).

The most serious instances of youth Satanist violence are not so easily dismissed. Charges of rape have been substantiated as committed by youth Satanists on both sides of the Atlantic when women changed their mind about participating in self-styled orgiastic black masses (Introvigne forthcoming). More serious still are cases of murder attributed to youth Satanists. Here we will exclude from the discussion self-described Satanist serial killers like Richard Ramirez, the Night Stalker (Carlo 1996), who were adults when committing their crimes. Youth Satanist killings tend to fall into two general scenarios: opportunistic killings of perceived enemies, defectors, or simply innocent bystanders, and killings performed in a ritual context. The former is by far the most common.

The most commonly cited case of a youth Satanist killing is that of Sean Sellers, currently on death row in Oklahoma for the murder of a convenience store clerk in the course of a robbery. Sellers subsequently became a born-again Christian and attributed his crime to Satanism (Johnston 1991: 17–21). A number of similar cases could be posited. Michael Hayward, Joel Brock, Jason Brumwell, and Daniel Paul Rabago in Eugene, Oregon, also robbed and murdered a convenience store clerk. Ricky Casso in Northport, New York, killed a classmate for allegedly refusing to declare allegiance to Satan (St. Clair 1987).

Running the gamut of youth Satanist crime was a group of teenage

Satanists calling themselves the Lords of Chaos, in Fort Myers, Florida, who imitated the Norwegian black metal subculture by burning a church before graduating to murder and an attempted robbery, which was conceived as a way to finance a plan to murder black visitors to Disney World. What links all of these cases is that Satanism was a factor in the killings, but was invariably less important than other motives. The Fort Myers case and the killing of homosexuals in Scandinavia represented the first public manifestation of a convergence of youth Satanism and racist politics that is a feature of a small segment of the Satanic subculture (Moynihan and Søderlind 1998).

Murder in a ritual context is extremely rare. Only one underground Satanist organization, the British-based Order of the Nine Angles, condones human sacrifice, although there is no evidence that the leaders of the group, Anton Long and Christos Beest, have themselves committed murder (Kaplan 1998, 2000; interview with Christos Beest, 20 June 1996). Moreover Ken Lanning, an FBI agent who authored a report on the charges of Satanic killings, discounts such activities due to the lack of forensic confirmation (Lanning, n.d.; interview with Kenneth Lanning, 2 August 1991). Despite widespread popular fears of Satanic cults practising human sacrifice, there is no reliable evidence of the practice. Yet in the idiosyncratic world of youth Satanism, it is possible that one or more such cases may have occurred in the past, or may occur in the future.

Suicidal or Self-Destructive Violence

Since the mass suicides in Jonestown, Guyana, in 1978, the image of 'brainwashed cultists' going to their deaths at the whim of a mad cult leader has become ingrained in the public consciousness. This image was reinforced by the conflagration at Waco (which was not a suicide, but the distinction is most often lost in the public debate), and it was much reinforced by the March 1997 mass suicides of the Heaven's Gate group and of members of the Solar Temple (Mayer 1999). So common has this perception become that in recent confrontations between federal agents and isolated Christian Patriot enclaves such as the Justice Freemen, the question of possible mass suicides was raised in both press and official quarters, and this may have effected the tactics of both sides.

Certainly this forum allows too little space for an in-depth exploration of the complex issues surrounding the phenomenon of mass suicide, but in the context of an exploration of religious violence, a few preliminary, and somewhat speculative, comments might be made. First, in line with the findings of Thomas Robbins and Dick Anthony, the popular image of groups going unquestioningly to their deaths at the behest of a charismatic leader is as unlikely as is the counter-scenario posited occasionally by scholars sympathetic to a particular group (or unsympathetic to government agencies and/or anticult groups), namely, that if only the group had been left entirely to its own devices all would have been well. More to the point, as argued by Robbins and Anthony, there are a complex of push/pull forces at play, which they call exogenous and endogenous factors (Robbins 1989: 32–7; Robbins and Anthony 1995: 237). Within the interplay of these variables and the influence of charismatic leadership, the ultimate choice to opt for suicide may be said to take root. Yet if this were all there were to say on the subject, we could close this examination with the comforting finding that the suicide of a religious group is simply a matter of rational choice, and that it is really not connected to the phenomenon of religious violence at all.

Yet it would seem that there is something more at work here. The taking of one's own life seems unlikely to be amenable to simple rational choice analysis. Violence or the perception of violence, for example, was never far from People's Temple. Beatings did occur and corporal punishment of children did occasionally rise to – and exceed – the level of what any reasonable observer would term child abuse (Chidester 1988; Mills 1989; Moore 1985, 2000; Reiterman and Jacobs 1982). Moreover, in Guyana Jones's contacts with the Soviet embassy, contacts which resulted in the visit of a Soviet cultural attaché to Jonestown, would surely have drawn the attention of the American embassy in Georgetown, and much of the later rhetoric of Jim Jones as recorded in his nightly harangues centred on the fear that the CIA, using defector testimony and an ongoing child custody case as a pretext, would soon descend on the group. Indeed, during the suicides themselves, there is considerable evidence that not all of the group met their deaths willingly. Finally, after the suicides, there were several mysterious, violent deaths of former People's Temple, members in San Francisco. In the case of People's Temple it would seem, religious violence was a factor in the ultimate tragedy.

In Waco, violence was undeniably a factor in the deaths of the Branch Davidians. These circumstances have been considered elsewhere in this article, so suffice to say here only that, as with the People's Temple tragedy, the sense of a group besieged by a hostile world does appear to play a considerable role in the decision of a group to opt for fealty to their beliefs and to their leader, regardless of the cost.

Yet if this is so, how can we consider the Heaven's Gate suicides in the context of religious violence? Here a small group of flying saucer millenarians who made a reasonably good living with computers and whose lives aroused little curiosity among neighbours or authorities chose to take their own lives. While definitive scholarly analysis is yet to appear, failed prophecy, world weariness, and impatience, coupled with cultic speculation about the import of the Hale-Bopp comet, seems to have had more to do with the suicides than violence, real or imagined. Parenthetically, much of the speculation surrounding Hale-Bopp seems to have circulated through the *Art Bell Show*, a syndicated radio call-in program in which flying saucer aficionados, conspiracy theorists, and deviant science enthusiasts of every description exchange information and ideas on everything from alien abductions to the predations of the dreaded chupacabra (goat sucker). The Heaven's Gate group seems to have either gotten the idea, or support for the idea, that the comet was in fact a precursor of an alien spaceship – an event that the Heaven's Gate group had been awaiting for decades. Art Bell has helpfully consolidated all of these speculations from a number of shows and archived them as a document, *Art Bell-Hale-Bopp Companion*, dated 28 March 1997, which is available as an HTML file from the Art Bell website (Balch 1982).

The better-studied cases of the Solar Temple suicides hold more interest for students of religious violence. Here, outside pressures *à la* Jonestown and Waco were present in the form of investigations into the group's financial dealings and increasing conflict with defectors. Indeed, a fascinating example of how groups within the milieu of cults/new religious movements are acutely aware of each other's doings may be seen in a cassette tape recording from 1994, in the possession of Swiss investigators in which Solar Temple leaders Luc Jourette and Joseph Di Mambro can be heard complaining that Waco had beaten them to the punch, and that their own deaths should have occurred 'six months before them [the Branch Davidians]' to have achieved maximum effect (Mayer 1999). What seems clear about the Solar Temple deaths is that, while they share in some respects aspects of the Heaven's Gate group's flying saucer millenarianism, the suicides within the Solar Temple were the products of protracted and meticulous planning, while there is evidence that mentions of suicide made over the years by Marshall Applewhite fell on deaf ears and were quickly forgotten (Bearack 1997). Moreover, as with the People's Temple, the sense of persecution from all quarters seems to have been intense within the Solar Temple leadership, and, like the Jonestown tragedy, it seems likely that not all of the deaths of Solar Temple members were voluntary. Once again, the Solar Temple would fall well into a study of religious violence.

As stated above, however, this section is intended to merely introduce some of the issues involved in the study of mass suicide as an instance of religious violence. The subject is hardly new; scholars have for many years pondered the phenomenon from the days of ancient Israel to the present (Girard 1972; Rappoport 1984; 1988). While a number of scholars from a variety of disciplines have in recent years provided much insight into the issues surrounding the subject of mass or revolutionary suicide, the fact remains that, as this brief discussion suggests, our understanding of the phenomenon remains at best incomplete.

Conclusion

If there is one primary conclusion to be drawn from this brief historical sketch of religious violence in America, it is this: while America from its foundation to the present day remains a deeply religious nation, instances of unambiguous religious violence have in fact been few and rather far between. Even in it's earliest day, the Puritan settlements of colonial Massachusetts were, by the standards of their day, more tolerant than is generally credited (Miller 1956: 144–5). Religious dissidents in early Massachusetts had, as Nathaniel Ward pointed out at the time, every liberty to go elsewhere. Failing that, they could remain at perfect peace and in a state of legal if not political equality, if they simply kept their views to themselves. Failing that, they were exiled. If they returned, they were exiled again. Most got the message, at least the second time around. Those that did not, however, were dealt with by a range of penalties which included flogging, the amputation of the ears, or in the cases of certain witches and Quakers, execution. Harsh by the standards of the present day perhaps, but in eighteenth-century terms, the policy was hardly the harshest to be found in Christendom (Hoffer 1997). In the era of American independence, the protections afforded religious practice, combined with the decision to eschew a state-church model, has allowed the nation to develop along a path that managed to avoid the destructive forms of religious violence that wracked, first Europe and later the developing world. If the American project often fell far short of religious amity – indeed, bigotry and exclusion based on religion have been all too common – these conflicts only rarely eventuated in the loss of life.

Yet religious violence has occurred, and continues to sporadically recur, in the United States. And no greater flashpoint for religious violence in the contemporary United States may be posited than in the world of new religious movements, defined to embrace not only the so-called cults, but the religious appeals of the far right, and of such deviant Christian movements as the pro-life rescue movement. Here, in recent years violence has all too often involved state actors whose actions both reflected and deepened the public perception of adherents of these movements as 'brainwashed' and incapable of rational thought, and of their leaders as manipulative, dangerous, and, in the last analysis, violent and ultimately suicidal. From this mind-set came Waco, and, before that event a rash of potentially deadly confrontations between state authorities and new religious movements.

In these cases, it must be borne in mind that the state retains the overwhelming preponderance of power, and it is thus to the state that the primary responsibility to exercise restraint must fall. Historically, oppositional religious movements in America have sought the path of withdrawal rather than confrontation. Even the most militantly oppositional religious communities know all too well that, despite the protections afforded by the First Amendment, in the last analysis they survive on sufferance. Should the suspicions of their neighbours turn violent – as the Mormons learned to their cost – the Constitution has not always been enough to assuage popular passions. Worse, should the state itself engage the religious movement, as in the cases of the Covenant, the Sword and Arm of the Lord, and the Branch Davidians, the movement's faith in the divine protection or the ultimate rightness of their cause has done little to redress the resulting asymmetry of power.

As the cases in this essay suggest, the incidences of religious violence involving new religious movements have been in part somewhat reactive in character. This was certainly true at Waco, but in a wider sense this has been true of even such stigmatized movements as those emanating from Christian Identity or the pro-life rescue movement. In the former case, the rare outbreaks of actual as opposed to rhetorical violence have come from confrontations with state authority over matters held by the faithful to be matters of religious principle – licences and building codes have been a frequent flashpoint – or through the actions of 'lone wolves' acting out of the leaderless resistance conception of revolutionary activism (Kaplan 1997c). For the rescue movement, recourse to lethal violence was undertaken only after more than twenty years of considerable brutalization, which was met primarily by non-violent resistance (Kaplan 1996).

Conversely, none of this absolves the religious movements themselves from the obligations of all American citizens to follow the law. When the requirements of the law and the dictates of conscience conflict, however, recourse must in the last analysis be made to the courts rather than to the gun. Just as the Jehovah's Witnesses found the Supreme Court willing to grant their right to withdraw from the American civil religion of the day (and just as Native Americans found the courts unwilling to grant their claim to practise rites centred on the ceremonial consumption of peyote), it is to the courts that the conflicting claims of the religious right must be addressed. The path of violent confrontation has proven futile on two counts. First, and perhaps in the last analysis, most important, it simply doesn't work. From the Ghost Dance to the Branch Davidians, God has simply not been moved to intervene to redress the imbalance of forces facing oppositional religious movements. Second, and more subtly, violence serves to reinforce in the public mind the already widespread public perception that the adherents of 'religious cults' represent a danger to the nation and to its citizens. It is ultimately this perception that both motivates and justifies the use of force against religious communities.

Oppositional religious communities must accept that the state does have legitimate interests in questions ranging from the safety of children to the maintenance of public order, and that they will pursue these interests with whatever degree of force the state deems necessary to accomplish its ends. Neither 'PR' offensives nor made-to-order academic studies commissioned by the religious movements will change that fact. Lacking this sense of mutual legitimization, violent confrontation is virtually inevitable.

Fortunately, as the events in Montana surrounding the Freemen demonstrate, violence need not characterize even the most serious confrontations between state authorities and religious appeals of even the most anti-government hue. Save for those instances – also rare but certainly present – of violence initiated by NRMs, which, it goes without saying, require a proportionate state response – it is possible that we are entering an era when confrontations between the state and new religious movements may become as rare as are instances of religious violence between individuals.

Postscript: Breaking the Cycle of Violence

From the remove of Helsinki, Finland, in the year 2000, *Radical Religion in America*, my first published book, seemed a rather distant island left behind in the remote (and, thankfully, only distantly remembered) past. Certainly over the last several years I have not had occasion to significantly change the core ideas which the book suggested. That radical movements of wildly diverse theological and ideological hues interact, and react, in a kind of netherworld of oppositional ideas as their adherents seek the key to unlock perhaps unanswerable secrets, has not changed (although the Internet and the advent of the Fox Network has allowed for the mainstreaming of these once-forbidden thoughts). Borrowing from Colin Campbell, I suggested that this cultic milieu remains a permanent aspect of the modern world. And so it does.

More controversial, however, was my suggestion that the various watchdog groups, ranging from the anticult movement (in those pre-'Fall of CAN' days a more fearsome beast than it is today) to the Jewish and left-wing political guardians of the nation's moral and political well-being, were themselves a significant factor in the radicalization of dissident religio-political movements, and were thus themselves in part responsible for the catalyzation of violence. Over the years, I attempted to refine these ideas, most notably (and most controversially) in a history of the radicalization of the pro-life rescue movement, 'Absolute Rescue.' This article in turn occasioned a fascinating debate with Thomas Robbins in the pages of *Nova Religio* (Kaplan 1997b; Robbins 1997), which gave birth to the term Interpretive Approach for the methodology that Bron Taylor, Mattias Gardell, Heléne Lööw (Gardell 1998; Lööw 1995; Taylor 1995) and myself, among others, sought to employ as a descriptive device to allow the reader to, if only partially, and if only for a moment, glimpse the world through the eyes of adherents of apocalyptic and millenarian movements.

Among the findings this methodology brought home to us, with crystal clarity, was this: for those who would dare to identify themselves as a part of the righteous remnant of God's people, cast adrift in a world bereft of goodness, of justice, or even of a moment's respite from corruption and overweening evil, the world is a terrible and threatening place. The Devil's snares lay everywhere, and his minions wait only for the opportunity to destroy the faithful remnant of God's people. A paranoid vision, yes, but real paranoids have real enemies (Kaplan, 2000). In the late 1980s and early 1990s, while conducting the research for *Radical Religion*, the enemies of these real paranoids left little to the imagination. The movements withdrew to the furthest fringes of the culture – both psychologically, and, in the case of the rise of rural compounds and individual survivalism, physically as well.

The watchdogs watched, and reported, and raised copious funds in the process, to carry on the good work. The paranoids grew more paranoid and more genuinely perplexed at the changes taking place at the heart of the dominant culture. And eventually, for a variety of reasons and in a variety of ways, the government acted. As James Gibson so presciently pointed out in *Warrior Dreams* (Gibson 1994), both sides now had starring roles in a movie which they themselves had written and in which the fate of the nation (or for the millenarians of the far right, the fate of all creation) hung in the balance. Tragically, neither side in the confrontations that followed had taken the trouble to read the other's script, and the blood flowed, culminating in 1993 with the tragedy of Waco.

Since Waco, many changes on both sides have taken place. Some positive, some positively ominous. But perhaps the most remarkable of these changes was reflected in late 1999, when, at the height of the apprehension by federal and state authorities, the news media, and ordinary citizens, the millennium would bring the paranoid's madness into the streets of mainstream America. The spectre of millenarian terrorism was now posited as the contemporary equivalent of the 'Enemy Within' of international communism in the early 1950s. It was then that the FBI released a report titled *Project Megiddo* (FBI 1999). While one could point to various errors and inaccuracies in the portrayal of various movements in *Project Megiddo*, the overall tone, at least in the public version of the document, was one of remarkable moderation. But perhaps the most important passage with reference to the occurrence of millenarian violence was this:

The violent tendencies of dangerous cults can be classified into two general categories: defensive violence and offensive violence. Defensive violence is utilized by cults to defend a compound or enclave that was created specifically to eliminate most contact with the dominant culture. The 1993 clash in Waco, Texas, at the Branch Davidian complex is an illustration of such defensive violence. History has shown that groups that seek to withdraw from the dominant culture seldom act on their beliefs that the endtime has come unless provoked (FBI 1999: 28–9).

Although *Radical Religion in America* was cited for this finding, the FBI's increasing recognition that much of the violence of the 1980s and 1990s (although by no means all!) was indeed reactive – and thus avoidable – appears to reflect the interaction of scholarship and law enforcement that took place after the Waco tragedy (Rosenfeld 1997). If this is the case, America in the early years of the twenty-first century may be a safer place in which to dwell for all of its citizens.

References

Ahlstrom, Sydney E. 1972. *A Religious History of the American People*. New Haven: Yale University Press.

Alcorn, Randy. 1990. *Is Rescuing Right: Breaking the Law to Save the Unborn*. Downers Grove, Ill.: InterVarsity Press.

Ammerman, Nancy T. 1995. 'Waco, Federal Law Enforcement and Scholars of Religion.' In *Armageddon in Waco*, edited by Stuart Wright. Chicago: University of Chicago Press.

Andrews, Joan, with John Cavanaugh O'Keefe. 1989. *I Will Never Forget You*. San Francisco: Ignatius Press.

Anon. 1969. *The Awful Disclosures of Maria Monk*. London: Canova Press.

Aquino, Michael A. 1993. *The Church of Satan*. 3d ed. San Francisco: Michael A. Aquino.

Army of God. N.d. *Army of God Manual*. 3d ed.

Balch, Robert W. 1982. 'Bo and Peep: A Case Study of the Origins of Messianic Leadership.' In *Millennialism and Charisma*, edited by Roy Wallis. Belfast: Queen's University.

Balch, Robert W., and Margaret Gilliam. 1991. 'Devil Worship in Western Montana: A Case Study in Rumor Construction.' In *The Satanism Scare*. Edited by Joel Best and David Bromley. New York: Aldine De Gruyter.

Barkun, Michael. 1994. *Religion and the Racist Right*. Chapel Hill: University of North Carolina Press.

Barton, Blanch. 1992. *The Secret Life of a Satanist*. Los Angeles, Calif.: Feral House.

Bearak, Barry. 1997. 'Eyes on the Glory: Pied Pipers of Heaven's Gate.' *New York Times* 28 April.

Bellah, Robert N., and Frederick E. Greenspahn. 1987. *Uncivil Religion: Interreligious Hostility in America*. New York: Crossroad.

Blanchard Dallas A. 1994. *The Anti-Abortion Movement and the Rise of the Religious Right*. New York: Twayne Publishers.

Blanchard Dallas A., and Terry J. Prewitt. 1993. *Violence and Abortion: The Gideon Project*. Gainesville, Fla.: Florida State University Press.

Boyer, Paul. 1992. *When Time Shall Be No More*. Cambridge: Harvard University Press.

Bray, Michael. 1994. *A Time to Kill*. Portland, Ore.: AFL.

Bromley, David G., and Edward D. Silver. 1995. 'The Davidian Tradition.' In *Armageddon at Waco*, edited by Stuart A. Wright. Chicago: University of Chicago Press.

Brooke, James. 1998. 'Utah Struggles With a Revival of Polygamy.' *New York Times*. 23 August.

Carlo, Phillip. 1996. *The Night Stalker*. New York: Pinnacle Books.

Chidester, David. 1988. *Salvation and Suicide: An Interpretation of Jim Jones, the Peoples Temple, and Jonestown*. Bloomington, Ind.: Indiana University Press.

Coates, James. 1987. *Armed and Dangerous*. New York: Hill & Wang.

Dobratz, Betty A., and Stephanie L. Shanks-Meile. 1997. *White Power, White Pride*. New York: Twayne Publishers.

Ellison, Christopher G., and John P. Bartkowski. 1995. 'Babies Were Being Beaten.' In *Armageddon at Waco*, edited by Stuart A. Wright. Chicago: University of Chicago Press.

Federal Bureau of Investigation. 1999. *Project Megiddo*.<www.fbi.gov>

Festinger, Leon, Henry W. Reicken, and Stanley Schacter. 1956. *When Prophesy Fails*. New York: Harper Torchbooks.

Finch, Phillip. 1983. *God, Guts and Guns: A Close Look at the Radical Right*. New York: Seaview/Putnam.

Flynn, Kevin, and Gary Gerhardt. 1990. *The Silent Brotherhood*. New York: Signet.

Foreman, Joseph. 1992. *Shattering the Darkness: The Crisis of the Cross in the Church Today*. Montreat, N.C.: Cooling Spring Press.

Gardell, Mattias 1998. *Rasrisk*. Stockholm and Uppsala: Federativs and Swedish Science Press.

Gibson, James William. 1994. *Warrior Dreams: Violence and Manhood in Post-Vietnam America*. New York: Harper Collins.

Ginsburg, Faye. 1989. *Contested Lives*. Berkeley: University of California Press.

Girard, René. 1972. *Violence and the Sacred*. Translated by Patrick Gregory. Baltimore: Johns Hopkins University Press.

Hamm, Mark S. 1984. *American Skinheads*. Westport, Conn.: Praeger.

— 1997. *Apocalypse in Oklahoma*. Boston: Northeastern University Press.

Heider, Ulrike. 1994. *Anarchism: Left, Right and Green*. San Francisco, Calif.: City Lights.

Hermonen, Merja. 2000. 'Aspects Of Youth Satanism In Finland.' In *Beyond the Mainstream: The Emergence of Religious Pluralism in Finland, Estonia and Russia*, edited by Jeffrey Kaplan. Helsinki: Suomalaisen Kirjallisuuden Seura.

Hicks, Robert D. 1991. *In Pursuit of Satan: The Police and the Occult*. Buffalo, N.Y.: Prometheus Books.

Hoffer, Peter Charles. 1997. *The Salem Witchcraft Trials: A Legal History*. Lawrence, Kans.: University Press of Kansas.

Introvigne, Massimo. Forthcoming 'The Gothic Milieu.' In *The Cultic Milieu Reconsidered*. Edited by Jeffrey Kaplan and Heléne Lööw. Stockholm: CEIFO.

Johnston, Jerry. 1991. *The Edge of Evil: The Rise of Satanism in North America*. Buffalo, N.Y.: Prometheus Books.

Kaplan, Jeffrey. 1993. 'The Context of American Millenarian Revolutionary Theology: The Case of the "Identity Christian" Church of Israel.' *Journal of Terrorism and Political Violence* 5:1 (spring).

— 1995. 'Right-Wing Violence in North America.' In *Terror From the Right*, edited by Tore Bjørgo. London: Frank Cass.

— 1996. 'Absolute Rescue: Absolutism, Defensive Action and the Resort to Force.' In *Millennialism and Violence*, edited by Michael Barkun. London and Portland, Ore.: Frank Cass.

— 1997a. *Radical Religion in America*. Syracuse: Syracuse University Press.

— 1997b. 'Interpreting the Interpretive Approach: A Friendly Reply to Tom Robbins.' *Nova Religio* 1:1 (October).

— 1997c. 'Leaderless Resistance.' *Terrorism and Political Violence* 9: 3 (fall).

— 1998. 'Religiosity and the Radical Right: Toward the Creation of a New Ethnic Identity.' In *Nation and Race: The Developing Euro-American Racist Subculture*, edited by Jeffrey Kaplan and Tore Bjørgo. Evanston: Northeastern University Press.

— 2000. 'Real Paranoids Have Real Enemies: The Genesis of the ZOG Discourse.' In *Millennial Beliefs, Persecution and Violence*, edited by Catherine Wessinger. Syracuse: Syracuse University Press.

— 2000 a. *Encyclopedia of White Power: A Sourcebook on the Radical Right*. Walnut Creek, Calif.: AltMira.

— 2000 b. 'Religious Violence.' In *Encyclopedia of Violence in the United States*. New York: Charles Scribner's Sons.

Lanning, Kenneth V. N.d. 'Satanic, Occult, Ritualistic Cirme: A Law Enforcement Perspective.' Unpublished report.

LaVey, Anton Szandor. 1969. *The Satanic Bible*. New York: Avon.

Lawler, Phillip F. 1992. *Operation Rescue: A Challenge to the Nation's Conscience*. Huntington, Ind.: Our Sunday Visitor.

Lewis, James R. 1995. 'Self-Fulfilling Stereotypes, the Anti-Cult Movement and the Waco Confrontation.' In *Armageddon at Waco*, edited by Stuart A. Wright. Chicago: University of Chicago Press.

Lööw, Heléne. 1995. 'Racist Violence and Criminal Behaviour in Sweden: Myths and Reality.' *Terrorism and Political Violence* 7:1 (spring).

Mayer, Jean-François. 1999. 'The Order of the Solar Temple: Myth and Reality.' *Nova Religio* (April).

McCormick Maaga, Mary. 1998. *Hearing the Voices of Jonestown*. Syracuse: Syracuse University Press.

Miller, Perry. 1956. *Errand into the Wilderness*. Cambridge: Harvard University Press.

Miller, Tom. 1985. 'Five More Neo-Nazis Arrested in Ozarks.' *Kansas City Times*, (1 June).

Mills, Jeannie. 1989. *Six Years with God*. New York: A and W.

Moore, Rebecca. 1985. *A Sympathetic History of Jonestown: The Moore Family Involvement in Peoples Temple*. Lewiston NY: Edwin Mellen Press. ·

– 2000. '"American as Cherry Pie: People's Temple and Violence in America."' In *Millennial Beliefs, Persecution, and Violence*, edited by Catherine Wessinger. Syracuse: Syracuse University Press.

Moynihan, Michael, and Didrik Søderlind. 1998. *Lords of Chaos*. Venice, Calif.: Feral House.

Noble, Kerry. 1998. *Tabernacle of Hate*. Prescott, Ont.: Voyageur Publishing.

O'Leary, Stephen D. 1994. *Arguing the Apocalypse*. New York: Oxford University Press.

Peterson, Alan H., ed. 1988. *The American Focus on Satanic Crime*. Vol. 1. Millburn, N.J.: American Focus Publishing.

Porter, Larry C. 1994. 'Going as a Lamb to the Slaughter.' *Deseret News Archive* (2 July).

Quinn, D. Michael, ed. 1991. *The New Mormon History: Revisionist Essays on the Past*. Salt lake City: Signature books.

– 1993. 'Plural Marriage and Mormon Fundamentalism.' In *Fundamentalisms and Society*, edited by Martin E. Marty and R. Scott Appleby. Chicago: University of Chicago Press.

Rapoport, David C. 1984. 'Fear and Trembling: Terrorism in Three Religious Traditions.' *American Political Science Review* 78 (September).

– 1988. 'Messianic Sanctions for Terror.' *Comparative Politics* 20 (January).

Reiterman, Tim, with John Jacobs. 1982. *Raven*. New York: Dutton.

Richardson, James T. 1995. 'Manufacturing Consent about Koresh.' In *Armageddon at Waco*, edited by Stuart A. Wright. Chicago: University of Chicago Press.

Risen, James, and Judy L. Thomas. 1998. *Wrath of Angels*. New York: Basic Books.

Robbins, Thomas. 1989. 'Reconsidering Jonestown.' *Religious Studies Review* 15:1 (January).

Robbins, Thomas. 1997. 'Religious Movements and Violence: A Friendly Critique of the Interpretive Approach.' *Nova Religio* 1:1 (October).

Robbins, Thomas, and Dick Anthony. 1995. 'Sects and Violence.' In *Armageddon at Waco*, edited by Stuart A. Wright. Chicago: University of Chicago Press.

Robbins, Thomas, and Susan J. Palmer. 1997. *Millennium, Messiahs and Mayhem*. New York: Routledge.

Rosenfeld, Jean. 1997. 'The Importance of the Analysis of Religion in Avoiding Violent Outcomes: The Justus Freeman Crisis.' *Nova Religio* 1:1 (October).

Scheidler, Joseph M. 1985. *Closed: 99 Ways to Stop Abortion*. Westchester, Ill.: Crossway Books.

St. Clair, David. 1987. *Say You Love Satan*. New York: Dell.

St. Claire, Michael J. 1992. *Millenarian Movements in Historical Context*. New York: Garland.

Schindler, Harold. 1996. 'Come, Come, Ye Saints – A Reprise.' *Salt Lake City Tribune*, 16 June.

Schupe, Anson, and Jeffrey K. Hadden. 1995. 'Cops, News Copy and Public Opinion.' In *Armageddon at Waco*, edited by Stuart A. Wright. Chicago: University of Chicago Press.

Smith, Jonathan Z. 1982. 'The Devil in Mr. Jones.' In *Imagining Religion*, edited by Jonathan Z. Smith. Chicago: University of Chicago Press.

Snell, Richard Wayne. 1986. *The Shadow of Death! (Is There Life After Death?)*. Self-Published.

Taylor, Bron. 1995. *Ecological Resistance Movements: the Global Emergence of Radical and Popular Environmentalism*. Albany, N.Y.: SUNY.

Terry, Randall A. 1988. *Operation Rescue*. Springdale, Pa.: Whitaker House.

– 1990. *Accessory to Murder: The Enemies, Allies and Accomplices to the Death of Our Culture*. Brentwood, Tenn.: Wolgemuth & Hyatt.

Trewhella, Matt, and Wayne Sedlak. N.d. 'The Historic Christian Doctrine of Interposition.' Milwaukee, Wis.: Missionaries to the Preborn.

Waterhouse, Edward. 1622. *A Declaration of the State of the Colony and Affaires in Virginia*. London.

Wessinger, Catherine. 2000. 'The Interacting Dynamics of Millennial Beliefs,

Persecution, and Violence.' In *Millennial Beliefs, Persecution and Violence*, edited by Catherine Wessinger. Syracuse: Syracuse University Press.

Wright, Stuart A. 1995. 'Dissecting Moral Panic and Official Reaction to the Branch Davidians.' In *Armageddon at Waco*, edited by Stuart A. Wright. Chicago: University of Chicago Press.

Appendix:
Further Reading and
Web Browsing

This is not a list of suggested readings. In compiling this list, we have made no attempt to select only the 'best' books and web sites, nor have we attempted to exclude some of the worst. Instead, our concern has been to provide a wide range of points of view about this controversial subject. In order to be as fair as possible, we want to make sure that the reader has the opportunity to gain access to the points of view of the specific cults themselves as well as to those of their ex-members, insofar as we have been able to find such references. The six religious groups on which we have provided specific information do not necessarily have anything in common with one another beyond the fact that they are all extensively discussed in one or more of the chapters of this book.

Print Media

Note: There are two English language journals devoted solely to articles about cults and new religious movements. One is called *Nova Religio*, published by Seven Bridges Press, 135 Fifth Avenue, New York, 10010–7101. The other is *Cultic Studies Journal*, published by the American Family Foundation, P.O. Box 2265, Bonita Springs, Fla. 34133.

General Books about Cults

Bainbridge, W.S. 1997. *The Sociology of Religious Movements*. New York: Routledge.

Barker, E. 1989. *New Religious Movements: A Practical Introduction*. London: Her Majesty's Stationery Office.

Dawson, L.L. 1998. *Comprehending Cults: The Sociology of New Religious Movements*. New York: Oxford University Press.

Galanter, M. 1999. *Cults: Faith, Healing, and Coercion*. New York: Oxford University Press.

Guthrie, S. 1988. *A Japanese New Religion*. Ann Arbor: Center for Japanese Studies, University of Michigan.

Hall, J., et al. 2000. *Apocalypse Observed: Religious Movements and Violence in North America, Europe, and Japan*. New York: Routledge.

Hassan, S. 1988. *Combatting Cult Mind Control*. Rochester, Vt.: Park Street Press.

Hexham, I., and K. Poewe. 1997. *New Religions as Global Cultures: Making the Human Sacred*. Boulder, Colo.: Westview.

Kahaner, L. 1988. *Cults That Kill: Probing the Underworld of Occult Crime*. New York: Warner.

Langone, M.D. 1993. *Recovery from Cults: Help for Victims of Psychological and Spiritual Abuse*. New York: Norton.

Lawson, E. 1985. *Religions of Africa*. New York: Routledge.

Melton, J.G. 1986. *Encyclopedic Handbook of Cults in America*. New York: Garland.

Miller, T. 1995. *America's Alternative Religions*. Albany: State University of New York Press.

Robbins, T. 1988. *Cults, Converts, and Charisma: The Sociology of New Religious Movements*. Beverly Hills: Sage.

Shupe, A.D.J., and D.G. Bromley. 1980. *The New Vigilantes: Deprogrammers, Anti-Cultists, and the New Religions*. Beverly Hills: Sage.

Singer, M.T. 1995. *Cults in Our Midst*. San Francisco: Jossey-Bass.

Towler, R., ed. 1995. *New Religions and the New Europe*. Aarhus, Denmark: Aarhus University Press.

Wessinger, Catherine. 2000. *How the Millennium Comes Violently: From Jonestown to Heaven's Gate*. New York: Seven Bridges.

Zablocki, B.D. 1980. *Alienation and Charisma: A Study of Contemporary American Communes*. New York: Free Press.

Specific Books about Scientology

Church of Scientology. 1998. *Scientology: Theology & Practice of a Contemporary Religion*. Los Angeles: Bridge Publications.

Cooper, P. 1971. *The Scandal of Scientology*. New York: Tower Publications.

Wallis, R. 1977. *The Road to Total Freedom: A Sociological Analysis of Scientology*. New York: Columbia University Press.

The Church of Scientology also publishes a magazine which is available by writing: Freedom Editor, 6331 Hollywood Blvd., Suite 1200, Los Angeles, CA 90028–6329

Specific Books about COG / The Family
Chancellor, J., and W. Bainbridge. 2000. *Life in the Family: An Oral History of the Children of God*. Syracuse: Syracuse University Press.
Van Zandt, D.E. 1991. *Living in the Children of God*. Princeton, Princeton: University Press.
Williams, M. 1998. *Heaven's Harlots: My Fifteen Years as a Sacred Prostitute in the Children of God Cult*. New York: William Morrow.

Specific Books and articles about ISKCON
Palmer, S.J. 1994. *Moon Sisters, Krishna Mothers, Rajneesh Lovers: Women's Roles in New Religions*. Syracuse: Syracuse University Press.
Rochford, E.B.J. 1985. *Hare Krishna in America*. New Brunswick, N.J. Rutgers University Press.
Rochford, E.B.J. 1998. 'Child Abuse in the Hare Krishna Movement: 1971–1986.' *ISKCON Communication Journal* 6: 43–69.
ISKCON publishes a journal called ISKCON Communications Journal, available at 10310 Oaklyn Drive, Potomic, MD 20854. 63 Divinity Road, and a newsletter called the Hare Krishna Report, Oxford OX4 1LH, U.K.

Specific Books about the Bruderhof
Rubin, J. 2000, *The Other Side of Joy: Religious Melancholy among the Bruderhof*. New York: Oxford.
Zablocki, B.D. 1971. *The Joyful Community*. Chicago: University of Chicago Press.
The Torches books: This isn't a trilogy but three separate books all beginning with the word 'Torches.' The first two are official Bruderhof publications and the third was written by an ex-member opposed to the official Bruderhof perspective.

In addition, both the Bruderhof and an organization made up of ex-Bruderhof members maintain active publishing companies. The Bruderhof's is called Plough Publishing House (Farmington, PA 15437; 800–521–8011). It publishes *The Plough*, a magazine available by subscription, as well as a number of books. The ex-members' press is Carrier Pigeon Press (Peregrine Foundation, PO Box 460141, San Francisco, CA 94146–0141). It also has published a number of books and it publishes the monthly newsletter *KIT* (Keep in Touch), also available by subscription from the same address.

Specific Books about the Unification Church

Barker, E. 1984. *The Making of a Moonie: Choice or Brainwashing.* Oxford: Basil Blackwell.

Hong, N. 1998. *In the Shadow of the Moons: My Life in the Reverend Sun Myung Moon's Family.* Boston: Little, Brown.

Moon, S.M. 1980. *Outline of The Principle: Level 4.* New York: Holy Spirit Association for the Unification of World Christianity.

Specific Books about Aum Shinrikyō

Lifton, R. 1999. *Destroying the World to Save It: Aum Shinrikyō, Apocalyptic Violence, and the New Global Terrorism.* New York: Henry Holt.

Reader, I. 2000. Religions Violence in Contemporary Japan: The Case of Aum Shinrikyō. Honolulu: University of Hawaii Press.

Electronic Media

Websites with a General 'Defense of Religious Liberty' Perspective

www.religionwatch.com
www.cesnur.org
www.acs.ucalgary.ca/~nurelweb
http://religiousmovements.lib.virginia.edu

Websites with a general secular 'Anti-Cult' Perspective

www.csj.org
www.trancenet.org
www.rickross.com

Websites with a general religious 'Counter-Cult' Perspective

www.gospelcom.net/apologeticsindex
www.watchman.org

There is one website about which a note of caution is needed to avoid possible confusion. There was an anti-cult organization known as The Cult Awareness Network (CAN). In 1996 this organization was forced into bankruptcy and its assets (including its name) were bought by a member of the Church of Scientology. The official website using this name now promotes a very different message from that of the old Cult Awareness Network. With that warning, here is the site address: www.cultawarenessnetwork.org

Websites Specifically Concerned with Scientology

www.scientology.org (the official site of the organization)
www.freedommag.org (the site's official magazine)
www.factnet.org (the perspective of some ex-members)

Websites Specifically Concerned with COG / The Family

www.thefamily.org (the official site of the organization)
www.excult.org (the perspective of some ex-members)

Websites Specifically Concerned with ISKCON

www.iskcon.com (the official site of the organization)

Websites Specifically Concerned with The Bruderhof

www.Bruderhof.com (the official site of the organization)
www.perefound.org (the perspective of some ex-members)

Websites Specifically Concerned with Unification Church

www.unification.org (the official site of the organization)
www.xmoonies.com (the perspective of some ex-members)

Websites Specifically Concerned with Aum Shinrikyō

www.aum-shinrikyo.com/english

Contributors

Benjamin Beit-Hallahmi received a PhD in clinical psychology from Michigan State University in 1970, and since then has held clinical, research, and teaching positions in academic institutions in the United States, Europe, and Israel. He is currently professor of psychology at the University of Haifa. Among his best-known publications are *Despair and Deliverance* (1992), *The Psychology of Religious Behaviour, Belief, and Experience* (1997), and the *Illustrated Encyclopedia of Active New Religions* (1998).

Thomas Robbins is an independent scholar in the sociology of religion (PhD University of North Carolina). He is the author of *Cults, Converts, and Charisma* (1988) and has co-edited five collections of original papers, including *In Gods We Trust* (Transaction 1981, 1990) and *Millennium, Messiahs and Mayhem* (Routledge 1997). He has published numerous articles, essays, and reviews for journals in social science and religious studies. He resides in Rochester, Minnesota.

Susan J. Palmer is a professor of Religious Studies at Dawson College in Quebec and an adjunct professor at Concordia University. She has written or edited six books on new religions, notably *Moon Sisters, Krishna Mothers, Rajneesh Sisters* (Syracuse University Press) and *Millennium, Messiahs, and Mayhem* (edited with Tom Robbins, Routledge). She is currently researching apocalyptic new religious movements in Quebec, and their ties to the sovereignty movement and to Old France, supported by SSHRC. She is also involved in a membership survey of

Falun Gong with Professor David Owenby at the Université de Mont-réal.

Janja Lalich specializes in the study of charismatic relationships, ideology, and social control, and issues of gender and sexuality. She received her PhD from the Fielding Institute in Santa Barbara, California, and currently teaches in the Department of Sociology at California State University, Chico. Her works include *'Crazy' Therapies*; *Cults in Our Midst*; *Captive Hearts, Captive Minds*; and *Women Under the Influence: A Study of Women's Lives in Totalist Groups*. Her forthcoming book, *Bounded Choice: True Believers and Charismatic Commitment* (University of California Press), is based on a comparative study of Heaven's Gate, the group that committed collective suicide in 1997, and the Democratic Workers Party.

Benjamin D. Zablocki is a professor of sociology at Rutgers University. He received his PhD from Johns Hopkins University and has taught at the University of California – Berkeley, California Institute of Technology, and Columbia University. He has published two books on cults, *The Joyful Community* (University of Chicago Press 1971) and *Alienation and Charisma* (The Free Press 1980). He has been studying religious movements for thirty-six years, with sponsorship from the National Institutes of Health and the National Science Foundation. Currently he is working on a twenty-five-year longitudinal study of religious belief and ideology.

Dick Anthony, a research and forensic psychologist, received his PhD from the Graduate Theological Union in Berkeley, California. He has served as an expert in many legal cases involving allegations of coercive organizational influence. While at the University of North Carolina Medical School, and later at the Center for the Study of New Religions at the Graduate Theological Union, his research on NRMs was funded by government agencies and philanthropic foundations. He has published many professional articles and co-edited several books on this topic.

David Bromley received his PhD from Duke University and currently is Professor of Sociology at Virginia Commonwealth University. He is former president of the Association for the Sociology of Religion and past editor of the Journal for the Scientific Study of Religion. He is currently completing two books, *Toward Reflexive Ethnography* (Elsevier/ JAI) and *Dramatic Denouements* (Cambridge University Press).

Stephen A. Kent is a professor in the Department of Sociology, University of Alberta. He received his BA in sociology from the University of Maryland (College Park) in 1973; an MA in the History of Religions from American University in 1978, and an MA (in 1980) and PhD in Religious Studies from McMaster University (Hamilton, Ontario) in 1984. From 1984 to 1986 he held an Izaac Walton Killam Postdoctoral Fellowship in the Department of Sociology. He has published articles in *Philosophy East and West, Journal of Religious History, British Journal of Sociology, Sociological Inquiry, Sociological Analysis, Canadian Journal of Sociology, Quaker History, Comparative Social Research, Journal of Religion and Health, Marburg Journal of Religion*, and *Religion*. His current research concentrates on nontraditional and alternative religions.

Lorne L. Dawson (PhD) is Associate Professor of Sociology and Chair of the Department of Religious Studies at the University of Waterloo (Canada). His most recent book is *Comprehending Cults: The Sociology of New Religious Movements* (Oxford University Press 1998). He has published many essays on issues of theory and method in the study of religion and the study of new religious movements.

Amy Siskind received her PhD in sociology from the New School for Social Research in 1995. She has written extensively about the Sullivan Institute/Fourth Wall community, a group she had belonged to for twenty-two years. Recently she has written about the effects of totalistic groups on children and the conditions within these groups that can result in child abuse and neglect. Her writing experience includes several journal articles, applied research reports, and a book in progress (Praeger/Greenwood Publishers). Dr. Siskind has taught sociology at New York University, Hunter College, and SUNY/Purchase. Her current professional activities include conducting an evaluation research project for a National Science Foundation grant to the New York Hall of Science in Flushing, New York. She lives in Brooklyn, New York, with her husband and daughter.

Julius H. Rubin is a Professor of Sociology at Saint Joseph College, West Hartford, Connecticut, where he has taught since receiving a PhD in Sociology from the New School for Social Research in 1979. He is the author of two books, *Religious Melancholy and Protestant Experience in America* (1994) and *The Other Side of Joy: Religious Melancholy among the Bruderhof* (2000).

Jeffrey Kaplan is the author of *Encyclopedia of White Power: A Sourcebook on the Radical Racist Right* (AltaMira Press 2000); *Radical Religion in America: Millenarian Movements from the Far Right to the Children of Noah* (Syracuse University Press 1997); *The Emergence of an Euro-American Radical Right* [Co-authored with Leonard Weinberg] (Rutgers University Press 1998); *Beyond The Mainstream: The Emergence Of Religious Pluralism In Finland, Estonia And Russia* (Suomalaisen Kirjallisuuden Seura 2000); and is co-editing with Bron Taylor the *Encyclopedia of Religion and Nature* (Cassell/Continuum, forthcoming 2002). He has published a number of articles on millenarian movements, which have appeared in *Terrorism and Political Violence, Syzygy, Christian Century,* and *Nova Religio*. He is currently teaching at the University of Alaska, Anchorage, and is working with the Stockholm International Forum on Conscience and Humanity.